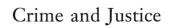

Crime and Justice

Crime and Justice
A Review of Research
Edited by Michael Tonry

VOLUME 38

The University of Chicago Press, Chicago and London

The University of Chicago Press, Chicago 60637
The University of Chicago Press, Ltd., London

© 2009 by The University of Chicago
All rights reserved.
Printed in the United States of America

ISSN: 0192-3234

ISBN: 978-0-226-80876-5

LCN: 80-642217

The paper used in this publication meets the minimum requirements of American National Standard for Information Sciences—Permanence of Paper for Printed Library Materials, ANSI Z39.48-1984. ∞

Contents

Preface

The original idea for *Crime and Justice*, initially conceived and titled as an "annual review of research," came from within the National Institute of Justice (NIJ). The precipitant was a report by the National Academy of Sciences on the work of NIJ's predecessor during the Law Enforcement Assistance Administration era, the National Institute of Law Enforcement and Criminal Justice (NILECJ). The report, largely critical, acknowledged that NILECJ had sponsored some good research, amid much that was substandard, but observed that even the good work was neither well known nor widely accessible. Paul Cascarano, NIJ's deputy director, following examples in other federal government departments, proposed that NIJ establish an annual review of research in order better to disseminate the best of NIJ's work and, to avoid charges of parochialism, of scholarly research on crime and criminal justice more broadly. Blair Ewing, NIJ's director, went along. A planning meeting was convened in Reston, Virginia, in the fall of 1977. A multidisciplinary editorial board was appointed. It included such distinguished scholars as Alfred Blumstein, Daniel Glaser, Ted Robert Gurr, Sheldon Messinger, Lloyd Ohlin, Albert J. Reiss Jr., Nigel Walker, James Q. Wilson, and Franklin E. Zimring. It also included prominent practitioners (Solicitor General Wade McCree, former New York Police Department Commissioner Patrick Murphy, and federal appellate judge Patricia Wald). Norval Morris and I were asked to serve as editors. The rest, if not exactly history, flowed from that beginning.

Crime and Justice received continuous funding from the federal government for 25 years, through four presidencies (Carter, Reagan, Bush I, and Clinton) and the early days of a fifth. From the beginning, there was a hands-off understanding that the series was editorially independent of the U.S. Department of Justice. Suggestions would be respectfully, and usually gratefully, received from NIJ and elsewhere in government, but decisions about topics, writers, and publication were solely for the editors to make. Only once or twice in a quarter century did officials make heavy-handed efforts to influence publication decisions; these were quietly but firmly resisted, and in the longer term no harm was done.

Each of the five administrations placed its own stamp on NIJ and its sister agencies in the Department of Justice. Partly these differences reflected the personalities and interests of agency directors and senior civil servants. They also reflected differences between administrations in their views about the roles of research and rationality in criminal justice policy making. The Carter and Clinton administrations were broadly supportive of scientific values, attempted to launch and operate strategic programs of research, accepted that research should be free from political influence, and appointed competent people. The Reagan administration was not so very different. There were more attempts at political intrusion into NIJ's research program, and there was more political infighting about NIJ inside the Department of Justice. But long-time director James K. (Chips) Stewart, usually supported by Attorney General Edwin Meese, resisted those pressures and maintained NIJ's functional autonomy. The two Bush administrations were disasters from these perspectives, exemplified by a request during Bush I for research proposals on occult crime, the forced retirement during Bush II of career civil servant Laurence Greenfeld as director of the Bureau of Justice Statistics (which also had operated under a hands-off policy) because he refused to bowdlerize statistical reports to achieve political objectives, and the appointments during both Bush administrations of NIJ directors with neither relevant experience nor—in the event—discernible competence as heads of a research agency. The Bush II administration's first NIJ director decided *Crime and Justice* was too "academic" and ended support.

These musings are provoked by the inauguration of a new president who expresses commitments to humane values, scientific integrity, and policy rationality. Whether that will translate into larger and more socially useful and constructive roles for federally funded research on crime and the criminal justice system is too early to tell.

When *Crime and Justice* began all those years ago, its primary purpose was to commission and publish state-of-the-art review essays on topical subjects. The disciplinary ambit was broad, ranging from medieval history through philosophy to neuropsychology, but with an emphasis on research in the social sciences. To assure breadth, topics were approved by the editorial board. To maintain quality, essays were commissioned and paid for, half again more were commissioned than could be published, paid referees were consulted, and writers were asked to make substantial alterations to respond to editors' and referees' suggestions.

Much of that description remains the same. Most of the essays published continue to be review essays. It appeared for a while that meta-analyses and Campbell Collaboration–style systematic reviews might make *Crime and Justice* obsolete, but they are so numerous and variable in quality that they too need intelligent integration and distillation. An editorial board still approves topics, more essays are commissioned than can be published, paid referees play major roles, and major revisions are the norm. Remarkably, one member of the original editorial board—Franklin E. Zimring—continues as a member a third of a century later.

Whether *Crime and Justice* can reasonably be said to have achieved its goals is for others to decide. There are some objective indicators that the series has not been completely unsuccessful. The 2005 *Journal Citation Reports* of the ISI Web of Knowledge, for example, ranked the series first among the 27 leading criminology and penology journals for "impact" (frequency of citation per article published; *Criminology* was second) and second for "immediacy" (a law review was first). Such indices, however, are inevitably incomplete and idiosyncratic, so it is never clear exactly what their rankings mean.

This volume contains essays on a mixture of distinctly topical subjects (terrorism, death penalty abolition, racial disparities, whether imprisonment reduces reoffending) with more timeless ones (mandatory penalties, bullying in school, victims' roles in the justice system). I hope they prove useful and instructive.

Michael Tonry
Deer Isle, Maine, August 2009

Roger Hood and Carolyn Hoyle

Abolishing the Death Penalty Worldwide: The Impact of a "New Dynamic"

ABSTRACT

The number of countries to abolish capital punishment has increased remarkably since the end of 1988. A "new dynamic" has emerged that recognizes capital punishment as a denial of the universal human rights to
life and to freedom from tortuous, cruel, and inhuman punishment, and
international human rights treaties and institutions that embody the abolition of capital punishment as a universal goal have developed. We pay attention to the political forces important in generating the new dynamic:
the emergence of countries from totalitarian and colonial repression, the
development of democratic constitutions, and the emergence of European
political institutions wedded to the spread of human rights. Where abolition has not been formally achieved in law, we discuss the extent to which
capital punishment has been bridled and by what means. Finally, we examine the prospects for further reduction and final abolition in those countries that hang on to the death penalty. More and more of these countries
are accepting that capital punishment must be used sparingly, judiciously,
and with every safeguard necessary to protect the accused from abuse and
wrongful conviction. From there, it is not a long step to the final elimination of the death penalty worldwide.

I. Introduction and a Road Map

On January 1, 2008, Uzbekistan became the ninety-second country to
have abolished the death penalty for all criminal offenses, whether
committed in wartime or peacetime or under civil or military criminal
codes. In addition, 10 other nations had already abolished it for all

Roger Hood is professor emeritus of criminology at the University of Oxford and
emeritus fellow of All Souls College. Carolyn Hoyle is reader in criminology at the
University of Oxford and fellow of Green College. Parts of this essay are drawn from
Hood and Hoyle (2008).

1

ordinary crimes against the person committed in peacetime, making the 102 abolitionist nations the majority among the 196 nations in the world.[1] Only 49 of the 94 countries that retained the death penalty in their criminal laws had judicially executed anyone within the previous 10 years, and of the 45 that had not done so, 33 were regarded by Amnesty International as truly "abolitionist in practice," for they apparently had no intention of resuming executions.

Nineteen years earlier, at the end of 1988, twice as many countries (101) both retained the death penalty and had carried out executions within the previous decade, and only 35 had abolished it for all crimes. Uzbekistan was then a part of the Soviet Union, with a wide range of capital offenses and an unknown but no doubt active program of executions. Even as an independent nation, Uzbekistan carried out executions until 2003, with at least 35 people executed between 1999 and 2003.

The purpose of this essay is to chart the characteristics of this remarkable decline in the resort to capital punishment, the routes and processes through which it has been achieved, and the factors and forces that have been most influential in bringing it about. Unlike some studies that focus on individual cultural, demographic, and political differences between abolitionist and retentionist countries (see Greenberg and West 2008), this essay will concentrate on the overarching influence of the spread of international human rights norms, which do not permit cultural relativism or national sovereignty to define what should be regarded as universal rights—here, the right to life and/or the right to be free from cruel, inhuman, and degrading treatment or punishment.

---

[1] Such is the pace of change that while this manuscript was in press, there were further developments during the latter part of 2008 and early in 2009. Argentina, which had been abolitionist for ordinary crimes, abolished the death penalty for military and other crimes against the state, thus becoming abolitionist for all crimes, as did the Cook Islands earlier in 2008 (see n. 5). In April 2009 Burundi abolished the death penalty completely (see nn. 14 and 58), as did Togo, which had been abolitionist de facto, in June 2009 (see nn. 4 and 47). On the other hand, Liberia reintroduced the possibility of capital punishment for crimes in which death occurs during the commission of an armed robbery, terrorism, or hijacking. However, this was a patent violation of Liberia's international obligations, since the country ratified the second protocol to the International Covenant on Civil and Political Rights in 2005. Amnesty International has recently reclassified Liberia as "abolitionist in practice." Thus as of June 2009, there are 95 countries that are completely abolitionist and eight that are abolitionist for ordinary crimes, for a total of 103 abolitionist nations. Among those that retain the death penalty in law, Amnesty International now regards 35 to be abolitionist in practice (see n. 55). We know of only 48 countries that as of January 2009 have executed any person within the past 10 years.

Section II sets the scene by briefly describing the progress of abolition throughout the world since the mid-nineteenth century. It shows how each country followed its own unique trajectory to abolition, motivated by its particular cultural and political notions of crime control and punishment, albeit for the most part influenced by a developing international climate that saw abolition as the appropriate goal for civilized countries. In describing these paths, it demonstrates the obsolescence of Marc Ancel's model, which considered abolition to be the product of a lengthy process that had clearly demarcated steps (1962*b*, p. 3).

Section III provides the evidence for the claim that there has been a new dynamic at work since the end of the 1980s, by describing the dramatic increase in the rate of abolition from 1989 to 2008 and the processes through which it was achieved. Section IV discusses the ideological basis of the new dynamic, namely, the rejection of utilitarian justifications for capital punishment in favor of the view that it inevitably involves a denial that captives of the state have a universal human right to life and/or to be free from tortuous, cruel, and inhuman punishment.

Section V considers the importance of the development of international covenants, treaties, and legal institutions under the auspices of the United Nations and regional political institutions that embody a commitment to abolish and never reintroduce the death penalty. It also discusses the difficulties of interpreting the scope of capital punishment raised by article 6, section 2, of the International Covenant on Civil and Political Rights, which allows signatories to retain the death penalty pending abolition only for the "most serious" crimes.

Section VI describes the political muscle employed by the Council of Europe and the European Union in bringing about a "death penalty free" continent and their subsequent role in promoting worldwide abolition. Reflecting on certain U.S. Supreme Court judgments, it also suggests that international views on capital punishment are gaining a foothold in North America. Section VII shows how the new dynamic described in this essay has had an impact on many retentionist countries through restricting the number and types of crimes and people subject to the death penalty and, more generally, by providing safeguards to protect the accused from wrongful conviction and the convicted from wrongful execution.

Finally, Section VIII considers the prospects for abolition in the next few decades in those jurisdictions that have so far remained resistant to the human rights dynamic (i.e., Muslim countries, non-Muslim Asia, the Commonwealth, and the United States). It shows that although 54 countries voted in December 2007 against a UN resolution calling for a worldwide moratorium that would lead to the abolition of capital punishment, many of them appear to be moving toward a minimal use of capital punishment, where the threat that the penalty could be imposed is allowed to remain as a symbol of the state's power. Experience has shown that in most countries, once capital punishment has reached this stage, it is just a matter of time before it is discarded.

II.   Previous Patterns of Abolition

In 1966, the year that the International Covenant on Civil and Political Rights was approved by the UN General Assembly (it went into effect 10 years later), there were only 26 abolitionist countries, several of them very small.[2] At that time it was common to say, following the analysis of the distinguished French jurist Marc Ancel, that the abolition of capital punishment had usually been the outcome of a very long process, starting with the elimination of executions for common crimes that did not involve the intention to cause serious physical harm, until only murder was left as a capital crime, plus serious crimes against the state—notably treason—and serious crimes of indiscipline under military law, particularly during wartime (Ancel 1962a, 1962b). There had then followed a suspension of executions for a considerable period of time (known as "de facto abolition" when suspension had lasted at least 10 years) until abolition for murder and any other "common crimes" that may have remained subject to capital punishment was achieved, leaving only capital punishment for exceptional crimes against the state and under military law to be finally abolished some considerable time later.

This, in fact, was too tidy a story, for many countries followed their own idiosyncratic paths. For example, Venezuela got rid of capital punishment in 1863 in one swoop, as did Ecuador in 1906 and Uruguay in 1907. Some American states were forerunners in the abolitionist movement—a point often forgotten in discussions of American attitudes toward capital punishment today. In 1846 Michigan became the

---

[2] There were also nine abolitionist states in the United States, two in Australia, and 24 in Mexico.

first jurisdiction in modern times to abolish capital punishment for murder. Rhode Island followed suit in 1852 (except in the case of murder of a prison guard by a convict serving a life sentence), and 1 year later Wisconsin became the third abolitionist state. Great Britain, France, and Germany, along with other European nations, all reduced the number of crimes subject to the death penalty from a large number at the end of the eighteenth century to only murder and crimes against the state and in the military by the mid-nineteenth century. Some moved quite swiftly to abolish it for murder, such as the Netherlands in 1870 and Norway in 1905. Others hung on to it for murder and state crimes but did not enforce it for many years. For example, the Australian state of New South Wales abolished capital punishment in 1955, 15 years after its last execution in 1940. Others, like Great Britain and France, had no period of de facto abolitionism. The last execution in England was in 1964, and capital punishment for murder was abolished in 1965; in Italy and Austria following the Second World War, the death penalty was abolished for murder in the same year that the last execution took place (1947 and 1950, respectively); and it was abolished for murder in Finland in 1949, just 4 years after the last execution.

Yet unlike the South American countries mentioned above, no European country (with the exception of West Germany in 1949) abolished the death penalty altogether before 1966. The Netherlands, for example, abolished capital punishment for murder as long ago as 1870 but not for all crimes until 1982; the United Kingdom abolished it for murder in 1965 but finally abolished it for all crimes only in 1998. Italy abolished it for peacetime crimes in 1947 but not until 1994 for military offenses in time of war. Complete abolition of the death penalty was not achieved in Portugal until it was embodied in article 24, section 2, of the new 1976 constitution, 2 years after the fall of the fascist regime in the Carnation Revolution of 1974.

Thus, the idea that those countries that led the abolitionist movement all passed through the same "prescriptive" route outlined by Ancel needs to be consigned to the dustbin of history. The truth is that each country, while influenced by a developing international climate that saw abolition as a civilized goal in penal reform, nevertheless chose its own path influenced by its own cultural and political interpretation of the need for capital punishment as an arm of its crime-control policy.

III.   Evidence of a New Dynamic

A new dynamic was brewing in the years following the Second World War that was to erupt around the end of the 1980s. The number of countries to abolish capital punishment increased steadily between 1966 and 1988 from 26 to 52, 35 of which abolished it completely. But several of these countries (as already indicated) were not new converts to abolition, having already abolished the death penalty for "ordinary" crimes well before 1966 (Austria, Denmark, Finland, the Netherlands, Norway, Portugal, and Sweden). Indeed, the only large states to abolish the death penalty completely "in one go" during this period were France in 1981 and former East Germany in 1987. Spain, Argentina, Brazil, El Salvador, and Fiji abolished it only for ordinary crimes. By and large, the other countries that swelled the list of abolitionist nations between 1966 and the end of 1988 (at which time only 35 UN member states, or 19 percent, had completely abolished the death penalty) were small, often newly emerged states.[3]

But then the rate of change increased dramatically. Over the 11 years from 1989 through 1999, 40 countries abolished capital punishment, 39 of them for all crimes in all circumstances. And although the pace of change then dipped somewhat between the end of 2000 and September 2008, a further 17 countries abolished capital punishment completely, and two others abolished it for all ordinary crimes. The tally on September 30, 2008, was 92 completely abolitionist countries (46 percent of the total) and 10 nations that were abolitionist for ordinary crimes. As figure 1 shows, there are now many more abolitionist nations than there are actively retentionist nations (those that executed someone within the past 10 years), whereas 20 years ago there were many more actively retentionist than abolitionist jurisdictions.

Although this increase in abolitionist nations since 1988 reflected to some extent the breakup of several states and the emergence of newly independent nations from them, most notably in Africa and the former Soviet Union, the change was nevertheless remarkable in a number of ways that suggest that the "surge" in the movement toward worldwide abolition had been the result of a different dynamic from that evident in the earlier phase of the abolitionist movement, one fueled by dif-

---

[3] These small and/or newly emerged independent states were Cape Verde, Haiti, the Vatican (Holy See), Liechtenstein, Luxembourg, Kiribati, the Marshall Islands, Micronesia, Nicaragua, Tuvalu, and Vanuatu. The Solomon Islands, which abolished the death penalty for all crimes in 1978, had already abolished it for ordinary crimes in 1966.

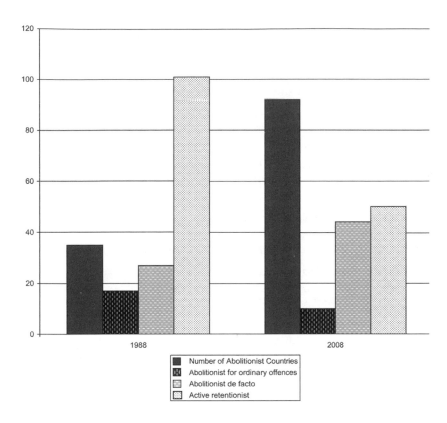

FIG. 1.—A comparison of abolitionist and retentionist countries (from 1998 to September 2008).

ferent forces and ideas. The new dynamic has seen countries marching from retention to abolition in an unprecedentedly short period of time as they have come to embrace the view that capital punishment is not simply a weapon to be chosen by a state in response to its perceived and actual problems of crime but a punishment that fundamentally involves—and cannot be administered without—a denial of the universal human right to be free from tortuous, cruel, and inhuman punishment.

As a result, the abolitionist movement has now spread far beyond its cradle in Europe, where only Belarus now retains capital punishment, and South America, where only three small countries—Belize, Suriname, and Guyana—hang on to it (although none has carried out an execution for at least 10 years). It has spread over almost all the former Soviet empire. In the African region, 14 countries are now completely abolitionist and another 21 are abolitionist de facto, whereas 20 years ago only Seychelles (for ordinary crimes in 1979) and Cape Verde (completely in 1981) had abolished capital punishment.[4] Although most countries in the Middle East and in North and East Africa, where Islam is the dominant religion, retain the death penalty, several of them— Tunisia, Algeria, Morocco, and Comoros—have not carried out any judicial executions for over 10 years, nor have executions occurred frequently in most of the Gulf states. Several secular states with large Muslim majorities have joined the abolitionist movement: Azerbaijan, Bosnia-Herzegovina, Kyrgyzstan, Senegal, Turkey, Turkmenistan, and Uzbekistan.

While only four Asian states (Nepal, Bhutan, Cambodia, and the Philippines) have so far completely abolished the death penalty, the populations of Hong Kong and Macau, which are special administrative regions of the People's Republic of China, both live without the threat of the death penalty being imposed (save for cases of rendition for offenses committed on the Chinese mainland). Six others are now abolitionist de facto, including, most recently, South Korea (Brunei Darussalam, Laos, Maldives, Myanmar, South Korea, and Sri Lanka). Among the islands of the Pacific, 11 have abolished the death penalty and a further three are abolitionist de facto, all of them recognized as truly abolitionist in practice by Amnesty International.[5] In several other Asian countries, most notably India and Thailand, executions are now rarely carried out, and Taiwan, where executions have ceased, is now officially on the road to abolition (Taiwan Ministry of Justice 2007).

Ninety percent (92) of the 102 abolitionist countries have now completely abolished the death penalty, in peacetime and in wartime, under civil as well as military law. This is a much higher proportion than at the end of 1988, when only two-thirds of abolitionist countries had

---

[4] Angola, Burundi, Cape Verde, Côte d'Ivoire, Djibouti, Guinea-Bissau, Liberia, Mauritius, Mozambique, Namibia, Rwanda, São Tomé and Príncipe, Senegal, Seychelles, and South Africa have all abolished the death penalty completely. There have been no executions for at least 10 years in Benin, Burkina Faso, Cameroon, Central African Republic, Comoros, Congo (Brazzaville), Eritrea, Gabon, Gambia, Ghana, Kenya, Lesotho, Madagascar, Malawi, Mali, Mauritania, Niger, Swaziland, Tanzania, Togo, and Zambia.

[5] Kiribati, the Marshall Islands, Micronesia, Palau, Samoa, the Solomon Islands, Timor-Leste, Tuvalu, and Vanuatu have abolished the death penalty completely, and the Cook Islands and Fiji are abolitionist for ordinary crimes. There have been no executions for at least 10 years in Nauru, Papua New Guinea, and Tonga.

abolished it for all crimes. As mentioned above, the European nations that abolished capital punishment before the mid-1960s, with the exception only of Germany in 1949, first abolished the death penalty for ordinary crimes long before doing so for all crimes. In contrast, 49 (84 percent) of the 58 countries that joined the "completely abolitionist" list after the beginning of 1989 were entirely new converts to abolition during this period, not having already abolished it for ordinary crimes before 1989.[6] Of these 49 countries, only eight first abolished the death penalty for ordinary crimes (after 1989) before proceeding to abolish it for all crimes; in two of them there was only a 2-year gap between "ordinary" and "complete" abolition, and in another two there was a short gap between constitutional and legislative abolition.[7] Furthermore, only three countries abolished capital punishment solely for ordinary crimes during this period without going on to abolish it for all crimes: Chile, Kazakhstan, and Latvia (see app. table A1).

Thus, a total of 52 countries have been entirely new converts to abolition (49 of them completely and three for ordinary crimes) since the beginning of 1989, and 94 percent of them (49 of 52) have moved from retention of the death penalty for murder and sometimes other ordinary crimes to complete abolition since the beginning of 1989. Furthermore, abolition was swiftly achieved once the process to get rid of it had begun. Only a minority—20 (38 percent) of the 52 countries that first abolished the death penalty after January 1, 1989 (including the three that abolished it for ordinary crimes only)—had been through a 10-year abolitionist de facto stage.[8] The majority moved much faster to remove capital punishment by law. For example, Turkmenistan abolished capital punishment in 1999, just 2 years after the last execution; South Africa in 1995, just 4 years after; Latvia in 1999,

[6] The nine countries that had abolished capital punishment for ordinary crimes before 1989 but did not abolish it completely until after then were Canada, Cyprus, Italy, Malta, New Zealand, Seychelles, Spain, Switzerland, and the United Kingdom.

[7] The eight countries that first abolished capital punishment for ordinary crimes after 1989 and then proceeded to complete abolition before 2008 were Albania (2002/2007, respectively), Bosnia (1997/2001), Greece (1993/2004), Nepal (1990/1997), Serbia-Montenegro (2000/2002), and Turkey (2002/2004). Abolition in Bolivia in 1995 was endorsed by the 1997 constitution, and abolition in South Africa by the interim constitutional court in 1995 was endorsed by legislation in 1997. In these two instances, abolition could also be regarded as having been achieved "in one go."

[8] Ten of them had been abolitionist de facto for over 30 years: Andorra (47 years), Belgium (46), Bhutan (40), Côte d'Ivoire (40), Ireland (36), Mexico (68), Paraguay (64), Samoa (42), Senegal (37), and Slovenia (32). Ten had been abolitionist de facto for 11–22 years: Armenia (12), Chile (16), Cyprus (21), Djibouti (18), Greece (22), Montenegro (13), Nepal (11), São Tomé and Príncipe (15), Serbia (13), and Turkey (18).

3 years after; Cambodia in 1989, 2 years after; both the Czech and Slovak Republics in 1990, only 1 year after; and Romania in 1989, immediately after the downfall and summary trial and execution of its president and his wife. The latest example, already mentioned, is Uzbekistan.[9] Thus, the old pattern of a long, drawn-out process leading to abolition was not observed in well over half of those countries that have embraced abolition in the past 20 years under the influence of the new dynamic (see table A1).

In at least 22 of the 49 countries that had by the beginning of 2008 completely abolished the death penalty, having been new converts to abolition since the beginning of 1989, abolition was embodied in a new constitution, usually related to the article specifying the right to life and/or the right to freedom from cruel and inhuman punishment or treatment.[10] For example, article 6 of the Constitution of Namibia

[9] The full list of the remaining 30 countries (i.e., excluding the new states of Palau and Timor-Leste) is given here, with the number of years between the last execution and abolition in parentheses: Albania (5), Angola (probably 2), Azerbaijan (5), Bosnia (6), Bulgaria (7), Cambodia (2), Croatia (4), Czech Republic (2), Estonia (7), Georgia (3), Guinea-Bissau (7), Hungary (2), Kazakhstan (4), Kyrgyzstan (9), Latvia (3), Lithuania (3), Macedonia, former Yugoslavia (4), Mauritius (8), Moldova (9), Mozambique (4), Namibia (2), the Philippines (6), Poland (9), Romania (less than 1), Rwanda (9), Slovakia (2), South Africa (4), Turkmenistan (2), Ukraine (2), and Uzbekistan (2–3).

[10] The countries that abolished capital punishment in a new constitution (dates of abolition in parentheses) included Andorra (1990), Angola (1992), Belgium (1996), Bosnia-Herzegovina (Dayton Agreement, 1998), Cambodia (1989), Côte d'Ivoire (2000), Croatia (1991), Guinea-Bissau (1993), Kyrgyzstan (2007), Macedonia (1991), Mozambique (1990), Namibia (1990), Paraguay (1992), Romania (1989), São Tomé and Príncipe (1990), Seychelles (1993), Slovenia (1989), and Timor-Leste (1999). Sometimes constitutional reform preceded the legislation abolishing capital punishment in the criminal code, as in South Africa and recently in Kyrgyzstan. On other occasions, the death penalty was first suspended by governmental action, as in Romania, where the provisional government following the overthrow of President Ceausescu issued a decree in January 1990 that replaced the death penalty with life imprisonment. This was given legality by the new constitution in November 1991. In Slovenia, where the last execution occurred in 1959, abolition of the death penalty was embodied in a constitutional amendment in 1989, and a year later a decree declared that the Yugoslavian federal code's provisions did not apply in Slovenia. One year later, the death penalty was forbidden by the new constitution of 1991. Sometimes—as in Poland, where the death penalty was abolished in the 1997 penal code—the change was reflected in a new constitution. Article 38 of Poland's 1997 constitution stated, "The Republic of Poland shall ensure the legal protection of the life of every human being." Also, in the Czech and Slovak Republics, abolition by the former government of Czechoslovakia in July 1990 was followed by embodiment of abolition in article 6 of the Czech and Slovak Federal Republic's Charter of Fundamental Rights and Freedoms, part of the new constitution of 1991, and then was applied to both Czech and Slovak Republics when they became independent in 1992. Moldova abolished the death penalty by legislation in 1995, and 5 years later the Constitutional Court agreed on amendments to the constitution to bring it into line with the legislation. Similarly, in Georgia, a constitutional reform in 2006 cleared up any ambiguity as to whether the death penalty had been completely abolished by the legislation of 1997.

states, "The right to life shall be respected and protected. No law may prescribe death as a competent sentence. No court shall have the power to impose a sentence of death upon any person. No executions shall take place in Namibia." More directly, the Constitution of Romania, article 22, section 3, states simply, "The death penalty is prohibited"; the Mozambique Constitution, article 70, section 2, states, "In the Republic of Mozambique there shall be no death penalty"; and article 18 of the Belgian Constitution states, "The death penalty is abolished and cannot be brought back into force." In six other countries (Albania, Hungary, Lithuania, Nepal, South Africa, and Ukraine), constitutional courts had interpreted the provisions of the constitutions as barring the imposition of the death penalty. For example, in South Africa, article 11 of the constitution states, "Everyone has the right to life"; in the Ukraine, articles 27 and 28 state, "Every person has the inalienable right to life" and "No one shall be subjected to torture, cruel, inhuman or degrading treatment or punishment that violates his or her dignity." With those countries that first abolished capital punishment by legislation and later introduced it into their constitutions taken into account, over half of the countries that have joined the abolitionist movement and have abolished capital punishment completely since the beginning of 1989 have also ensured through their own constitutions that the death penalty cannot be reintroduced. Furthermore, Ireland, which abolished the death penalty completely in 1990, added a constitutional amendment in 2001, agreed to by a 62 percent majority of voters in a plebiscite, that stated, "The Oireachtas [Parliament] shall not enact any law providing for the imposition of the death penalty" (art. 15, sec. 5, cl. 2).

The processes and speed with which abolition was achieved under this new dynamic are illustrated in the following examples. In the Balkan area, Albania, a country in some turmoil after becoming independent in 1991, nevertheless moved quite rapidly toward abolishing the death penalty as it prepared for membership of the Council of Europe. The last execution took place in 1995, and a year later the president of the parliament declared a moratorium on executions. In December 1999, the Albanian Constitutional Court ruled that the death penalty was incompatible with the new 1998 constitution, and in September 2000 it was removed from the criminal code.[11] In 1988 the last exe-

---

[11] See Peshkopia and Imami (2008) for an in-depth study of the stages of abolition in Albania.

cution took place in Poland, followed by a moratorium and the elimination of the death penalty for the offense of organizing and directing
a major economic crime. In 1996 a new penal code without capital
punishment passed through the legislature and went into effect in
1998. In its response to the Sixth UN Survey on Capital Punishment
in 1999, Poland stated that the motivation for abolition was a combination of "political will, official inquiry, and the influence of United
Nations policy," and in an explanatory report on the penal code, the
legislature stated that "the death penalty cannot be reconciled with the
principle of human dignity and contemporary values, and it also does
not deter [people] from committing a crime" (see Gliszczynska, Sekowska, and Wieruszewski 2006, p. 21).

In Lithuania there had already been public consultations on the
question of capital punishment when the Constitutional Court ruled
in December 1998, only 3 years after the last execution had been carried out, that the provisions in the criminal code relating to the death
penalty were unconstitutional. And later that month, the parliament
abolished capital punishment by amendment to the criminal code. As
Dobryninas put it, "The attitude towards the death penalty in Lithuanian society became a test of the maturity of its democratic outlook"
and of citizens' willingness to rid themselves "of its former totalitarian
and inhumane system" (2004, p. 234). Ukraine agreed to place an immediate moratorium on executions and to ratify Protocol 6 to the European Convention for the Protection of Human Rights and Fundamental Freedoms within 3 years from the date of its accession to the
Council of Europe in November 1995. But executions continued on a
considerable scale—a total of 180 from the beginning of 1996 until the
moratorium was eventually put into effect in March 1997. The then
minister of justice, Serhiy Holovatiy, a committed abolitionist, accused
the president of Ukraine of failing in political leadership by not signing
the decree to implement the moratorium, but it is also true to say that
there was very strong public and press opposition to abolition (Holovatiy 1999, pp. 145–47). However, in December 1999 the Supreme
Court of Ukraine ruled that all provisions of the criminal code relating
to the death penalty were incompatible with articles 27 and 28 of the
Ukrainian Constitution (Council of Europe 1999, pp. 124–25; Holovatiy 1999; OSCE 1999, pp. 23–24). Finally, in February 2000 the
Ukrainian Supreme Council (the parliament) removed provisions on

the death penalty from the criminal code, the code of criminal procedure, and the penitentiary code.

The change in policy and practice in Turkmenistan (where 89 percent of the people are Muslim) was also remarkable. Although no official figures were published, it was thought that well over 100 people were executed each year in 1994, 1995, and 1996—one of the highest ratios in the world in relation to population. The new criminal code adopted in 1997 provided the death penalty for as many as 17 offenses; yet on January 1, 1999, the president announced a moratorium on executions, and by December of that year he had abolished the death penalty completely by presidential decree. In Kyrgyzstan, the process began with a bill introduced in 1997 to abolish capital punishment for economic crimes as well as for several other offenses, a process that ended by retaining it solely for three crimes—murder, rape of a female minor, and genocide. In 1998 the last execution was carried out, the president having established a moratorium on executions in December of that year, and it was expected that a new criminal code would be introduced in 2001 that would totally remove the death penalty. This did not happen, but in 2002 the president issued a policy decree stating that "one of the objectives for Kyrgyzstan in the field of human rights is the gradual reduction of the application of the death penalty and its eventual abolition." The Ministry of Justice and the Constitutional Council of Kyrgyzstan then developed draft laws and amendments to the constitution that envisaged abolition of the death penalty and accession to the Second Optional Protocol of the International Covenant on Civil and Political Rights; as a result, after some prevarication in parliament, President Kurmanbek Bakiyev signed a new constitution in November 2006 in which provisions for the death penalty were removed. The final stage, the abolition of capital punishment in the Kyrgyz criminal code, was approved by the president in June 2007.

With very few exceptions, once capital punishment has been abolished, it has not been reintroduced. Although a very small number of abolitionist countries reported to the UN Seventh Quinquennial Survey on Capital Punishment in 2003–4 that there had been some proposals to reintroduce capital punishment emanating from "individuals, members of Parliament or minority political parties" (United Nations 2005, p. 5), none had made any impact. Real setbacks have been rare and in all but one instance have not led to a resumption of executions. Only four of the nations that have abolished capital punishment since

1961 have reintroduced it: Nepal in 1985, the Philippines in 1987, Gambia in 1991, and Papua New Guinea in 1995. It was soon abolished again in Nepal for murder in 1990 and for all offenses in 1997. Only one of the other three—the Philippines—resumed executions (seven between 1999 and 2000), but then, after a moratorium on executions, it again abolished the death penalty completely in June 2006 by overwhelming majorities of both the Senate and House of Representatives with the full support of the president. In the United States, New York State reinstated the death penalty in 1995 after 30 years without it, and Kansas, which had not enacted a new law providing for the death penalty in accordance with the *Gregg* decision in 1976, reinstated the death penalty in 1994, 29 years after the last execution had been carried out.[12] But yet again, no executions have followed. Indeed, the death sentence was found unconstitutional by the supreme courts of both states. It appears unlikely that it will be reinstated in New York.[13] And while the U.S. Supreme Court upheld the constitutionality of the Kansas statute by a majority of 5–4 in 2006, no executions have as yet taken place.

Furthermore, following the publication of the report of a commission to study the administration of capital punishment, New Jersey abolished the death penalty in 2007 with the full approval of its governor, having carried out no executions since the enactment of the New Jersey death penalty statute 24 years earlier (New Jersey Death Penalty Study Commission 2007). The Massachusetts legislature in 2005 threw out a bill to reintroduce the death penalty that had been based on recommendations from a commission established by Governor Romney to create a supposedly fault-free system for its administration (Governor's Council on Capital Punishment 2005). In February 2007, Governor O'Malley urged Maryland lawmakers to repeal the state's death penalty, saying that the punishment is "inherently unjust, does not serve as a deterrent to murder and saps resources that could be better spent on law enforcement" (Wagner and Wiggins 2007). He too

---

[12] In 1972 the U.S. Supreme Court found in Furman v. Georgia that the death penalty as then administered was unconstitutional. All but two of the 38 states affected by this decision enacted new laws that restricted the scope of capital punishment, and these statutes were found to be constitutional by the Court in 1976 in Gregg v. Georgia and companion cases.

[13] In October 2004, the New York Court of Appeals ruled that the death sentence was unconstitutional under state law; subsequently, in April 2005, the Codes Committee of the New York Assembly voted 11–7 against considering legislation to reinstate the death penalty.

established a commission to assess whether the state's death penalty procedures meet basic standards of fairness and avoid bias and error (see Maryland Governor's Office of Crime Control and Prevention, http://www.goccp.maryland.gov/capital-punishment/index.php). The Maryland Commission on Capital Punishment voted on November 12, 2008, to recommend the abolition of the death penalty in the state. In a 13–7 vote, the commission cited the possibility that an innocent person could be mistakenly executed and argued that capital punishment does not deter crime and is affected by racial and jurisdictional disparities (White 2008). These and other commissions established in other retentionist states with a similar agenda—for example, in Illinois (see Sec. IV)—suggest that public inquiries into the systemic faults inherent in the administration of capital punishment in America could provide the necessary legitimacy to move forward to abolition.

It is not merely that a great many more countries have abolished capital punishment: among those that have retained it in law, a greater proportion have not carried out an execution for at least 10 years. At the end of 1988, 27 of the 128 retentionist countries (21 percent) were abolitionist de facto, whereas by mid-2008, 45 of the 95 retentionist countries (47 percent) had not carried out an execution for at least 10 years.[14] Indeed, the number of countries that imposed at least one death sentence in a year was as high as 79 as recently as 1995. But by 2007, in line with the increase in the number of abolitionist countries, it had fallen to 51 (54 percent of the 94 countries with capital punishment on their statute books). Similarly, the number of countries that actually carried out an execution fell from 41 in 1995 to only 24 in 2007. Furthermore, only 13 countries carried out an execution in every one of the 5 years from 2002 through 2006: Bangladesh, China, Iran,

[14] Some abolitionist de facto countries have announced from time to time that they intend to resume executions, but they have not done so: Sri Lanka is a case in point. It is also true that, after 1994, 10 countries that appeared to be abolitionist de facto resumed executions after at least 10 years of abstention—although none on a regular basis—and returned to the retentionist camp (Bahamas, Bahrain, Burundi, Chad, Comoros, Guatemala, Guinea, St. Kitts and Nevis, Trinidad and Tobago, and Qatar). And in some American states, executions have taken place after very long periods of abeyance. For example, as the new millennium got under way, both Tennessee and New Mexico resumed executions after 40 and 41 years, respectively; in 2005 Connecticut executed a person just 4 days short of 45 years after the last execution; and in 2007 South Dakota carried out its first execution in 60 years when Elija Page, age 25 years, "volunteered," having decided not to pursue any further appeals. Of even greater significance were the two federal executions in June 2001, the first in 38 years, of Timothy McVeigh and Juan Raoul Garza.

Japan, Jordan, North Korea, Pakistan, Saudi Arabia, Singapore, Somalia, the United States, Vietnam, and Yemen. And only seven of these countries are known to have executed at least 100 people during the whole of this period, averaging 20 or more people a year: China (by far the largest number), Iran, Pakistan, Saudi Arabia, the United States, Vietnam, and Yemen.[15] When the 5-year periods of 1996–2000 and 2002–6 are compared, there appear to have been very substantial falls in the number of executions in several countries—for example, Nigeria (from 56 to 1) and Belarus (from 130 to 12; see table 3.2 in Hood [2002, p. 92]). In Singapore (which had executed 242 people in 1994–98, or 13.85 for every million people, the world's highest annual number of people per capita), the number fell from 28 in 2002 to only five in 2006 and two in 2007.[16] In Egypt, there were 29 reported executions in 1999, 49 in 2002, none in 2005, only four in 2006, and "at least one" in 2007 (Amnesty International 2008). Forty-one executions were carried out in Taiwan in 1999 and 2000, but only three in 2005 and none in 2006 or 2007. Ninety-eight people were executed in the United States in 1999, but the number fell to 66 in 2001 and to 53 in 2006. Indeed, over the 5 years from 2002 through 2006, only 20 of the 38 U.S. states with the death penalty carried out an execution, and only 14 of them did so in 2006. Thus, 24 of the 38 states with the death penalty on their statute books did not execute anybody, and when the 12 wholly abolitionist states plus the District of Columbia are added to them, 37 of the 51 U.S. state jurisdictions had no executions in 2006.[17] Very few countries have in the past few years increased the number of people executed—Iran, Iraq, Pakistan, and Saudi Arabia being notable exceptions.

[15] If one were to count the Democratic Republic of the Congo, the number of countries would rise to eight; but this might be misleading because all of the 125 executions there during this 5-year period took place in only 1 year.

[16] We are grateful to David T. Johnson of the University of Hawaii for providing these figures, based on reports from Amnesty International. They should be regarded as estimates, as official data are rarely published.

[17] There were only 42 executions in 2007 in 11 states, 62 percent of which took place in Texas, but a moratorium was put into place after the last execution on September 25 as the Supreme Court considered the constitutionality of lethal injection. On April 16, 2008, the Court upheld the constitutionality of lethal injection as a mode of execution, and since then executions have resumed. By the end of 2008, 23 executions had been carried out in nine states, 49 percent of them in Texas.

IV. Generating the New Dynamic: The
     Ideological Dimension

As already indicated, foremost among the factors that have promoted this new wave of abolition has been the political movement to transform consideration of capital punishment from an issue to be decided solely or mainly as an aspect of national criminal justice policy to one with the status of a fundamental violation of human rights: not only the right to life but the right to be free from excessive, repressive, and tortuous punishments—including the risk that an innocent or undeserving person may be executed (Zimring 2003, pp. 16–42; Bae 2007).

This movement gained force as more and more countries emerged from totalitarian and colonial repression to embrace values that seek, in the name of democracy and freedom, to protect citizens from the power of the state and the tyranny of the opinions of the masses. This new dynamic has embraced the view that capital punishment should be regarded neither as a weapon of national criminal justice policy to be enforced according to a government's assessment of its value as a crime-control measure nor as an issue to be judged in terms of local cultural or sociopolitical values (see Zimring 2003, pp. 16–41; Neumayer 2008, pp. 263–65).

The human rights approach to abolition rejects the most persistent of the justifications for capital punishment, namely, retribution and the necessity to denounce and expiate crimes that shock the sensibilities of citizens by their brutality. It also rejects the utilitarian justification that nothing less severe can act as a sufficient general deterrent to those who contemplate committing capital crimes. This is because most abolitionists believe not only that the social science evidence does not support the claim that capital punishment is necessary in order to deter murder but that even if it did have some marginal deterrent effect, this could be achieved only by high rates of execution, mandatorily and speedily enforced. This, they assert, would inevitably lead to the probability of a higher proportion of innocent or wrongfully convicted persons being executed as well as to the unjust execution of people who, because of the mitigating circumstances in which their crimes were committed, do not deserve to die. They also argue that it is precisely when there are strong reactions to serious crimes that the use of the death penalty as an instrument of crime control is most dangerous. Pressure on the police and prosecutors to bring offenders to justice, especially those suspected of committing outrages, may lead to short-

cuts, breaches of procedural protections, and simple myopia in investigations once a suspect is identified, making it more likely that there
will be miscarriages of justice.

These problems appear to be endemic to the systematic use of the
death penalty and not simply a reflection of human error or faults in
the administration of criminal justice in a particular country. For many
abolitionists, even the smallest possibility that an innocent person
could be executed is an unacceptable breach of the right to life. Thus,
in a speech delivered in 2001, the then European Union commissioner
for external relations, Chris Patten, spoke of "the inhumane, unnecessary and irreversible character of capital punishment, no matter how
cruel the crime committed by the offender. . . . That stance is rooted
in our belief in the inherent dignity of all human beings and the in-
violability of the human person. . . . It is impossible to reduce the risk
to zero of applying the penalty in error" (2001, p. 2). Similarly, the
Illinois commission set up by Governor Ryan concluded in 2002: "The
Commission was unanimous in the belief that no system, given human
nature and frailties, could ever be devised or constructed that would
work perfectly and guarantee absolutely that no innocent person is ever
again sentenced to death" (Illinois Commission on Capital Punishment
2002, p. 39).

But although the possibility of error is an important lever in the
argument of the human rights case against capital punishment, those
committed to the cause contend that even if the system could be made
"foolproof," it would still be indefensible. In particular, abolitionists
who have embraced the view that all citizens have a right to life argue
that the issue cannot be left to public opinion, not only because such
opinion may not be fully informed as to the consequences of employing
capital punishment but because the appeal to human rights centers on
the protection of all citizens, including those in captivity, from cruel
and inhumane punishment, whatever crimes they may have committed.[18] Furthermore, most abolitionists also contend that the means
could never justify the ends: for them, the control of serious crime is
more appropriately and better achieved through tackling the factors
that contribute to it rather than relying on the inhumane punishment
of putting people to death.

---

[18] Indeed, it has been shown that even "death-qualified" jurors in the United States
are often misinformed about the law governing capital punishment (see Hood and Hoyle
2008, pp. 241–42).

V. Generating the New Dynamic: The International Legal Framework

The ideals outlined above have been spread through the development of international covenants, treaties, and legal institutions under the auspices of the United Nations and regional political institutions. In the long process, lasting from the Universal Declaration of Human Rights in 1948 (which made no mention of capital punishment in relation to article 3's injunction that "every human being has an inherent right to life") until 1966, when the International Covenant on Civil and Political Rights (ICCPR) was adopted by the UN General Assembly (it did not go into force until 10 years later), the question of capital punishment in relation to the right to life was keenly debated. What emerged was a compromise allowing for "limited retention," for, as mentioned above, only a minority of states at that time had embraced the abolitionist position. Article 6, section 1, the draft of which had been agreed on in 1957, stated: "Every human being has the inherent right to life. This shall be protected by law. No one shall be arbitrarily deprived of his life." And article 6, section 2, stated: "In countries that have not abolished the death penalty, sentence of death may be imposed only for the most serious crimes in accordance with the law in force at the time of the commission of the crime." In the circumstances pertaining in 1957, it was hardly surprising that it was not possible to define more precisely those offenses for which capital punishment could be retained. Certainly some countries would have preferred a clear and very narrow enumeration of the crimes for which it would remain permissible to impose the death penalty instead of having to rely on the concept of "most serious" (Schabas 2004a, p. 46; see also Rodley 2004, pp. 128–29). This is probably because they recognized that "most serious" could be interpreted differently according to national culture, tradition, and political complexion—the very antithesis of the notion of an attempt to create a universal declaration and definition of human rights. In fact, the term "most serious crimes" in article 6, section 2, was nothing more than a "marker" for the policy of moving toward abolition through restriction. Far from indicating that those countries that had not abolished the death penalty could proceed under the protection of article 6, section 2, as several countries have subsequently argued, the chairman of the working party on the drafting of article 6 stated: "It was interesting to note that the expression: 'in countries which have not abolished the death penalty' was intended to show the direction in which the drafters of the Covenant hoped that the situation would develop" (Schabas 2002, pp. 68), as was the addition of article 6, section 6—namely, that "nothing in this article shall be invoked to delay or prevent the abolition of capital punishment by any State party to the present Covenant." The very notion of "progressive restriction" made it clear that the degree of "seriousness" that would justify the death penalty would need to be evaluated and re-evaluated always in a narrowing of definition until abolition was eventually achieved. It was in 1971 (Resolution 28/57) and again in 1977 (Resolution 32/61) that this message, this aspiration, was reinforced by the UN General Assembly, which stated that the main objective of the United Nations, "in accordance with Article 3 of the Universal Declaration of Human Rights and Article 6 of the ICCPR" is to "progressively restrict the number of offenses for which capital punishment might be imposed, with a view to its eventual abolition."

Covenants, in the form of protocols to human rights treaties banning the use of the death penalty, appeared first in Europe in 1982 when Protocol 2 to the European Convention for the Protection of Human Rights and Fundamental Freedoms (ECHR) was adopted by the Parliamentary Assembly of the Council of Europe. Article 1 of the protocol provided for the abolition of the death penalty in peacetime, although article 2 allowed a state to make provision in its law for the death penalty in time of war or of imminent threat of war. The protocol opened for signature in 1983. Six years later, in 1989, the UN General Assembly adopted the Second Optional Protocol to the ICCPR, article 1 of which stated that "no one within the jurisdiction of a State Party . . . shall be executed." While not specifically stated, the implication appears to be that once capital punishment is abolished, it should not be reinstated. Although article 2, like the Sixth Protocol to the ECHR, allows a reservation to be made that provides for the application of the death penalty in time of war pursuant to a conviction for a most serious crime of a military nature committed during wartime, the reservation can be made only at the time of ratification or accession. According to William Schabas, "only a handful [of such reservations] have been formulated" (2004a, p. 42). In 1990, the General Assembly of the Organization of American States adopted the Protocol to the American Convention on Human Rights to Abolish the Death Penalty. Article 1 calls on states to abstain from the use of the death penalty but does not impose an obligation on them to erase it from their statute books. Thus de facto abolitionist countries may also ratify the protocol. In addition, any country that has abolished the death penalty and ratified the American Convention on Human Rights is forbidden by article 4, section 3, of the convention from reintroducing it, even if they have not ratified the protocol.

Of particular significance, given the limitation of all these prior protocols to offenses committed in peacetime, was the adoption in Vilnius, Lithuania, on May 3, 2002, of Protocol 13 to the ECHR, in order to send "a strong political signal." "Convinced that everyone's right to life is a basic value in a democratic society and that the abolition of the death penalty is essential for the protection of this right and for the full recognition of the inherent dignity of all human beings," the member states resolved "to take the final step to abolish the death penalty in all circumstances, including acts committed in time of war or the imminent threat of war." Protocol 13 came into force on July 1, 2003.

By the beginning of 2008, a total of 77 abolitionist countries had undertaken a commitment, through their ratification of one or another of these treaties or conventions, not to reintroduce the death penalty, and a further four had signed but not yet ratified one of these treaties. This leaves 21 of the 102 abolitionist countries that have yet to commit themselves in this way not to reintroduce capital punishment.[19] In other parts of the world, regional human rights movements are seeking to follow this example. Thus, in November 1999, the African Commission on Human and People's Rights, meeting in Kigali, Rwanda, urged states "to envisage a moratorium on the death penalty," and the Asian Human Rights Charter adopted in 1998 (under art. 3, sec. 7, "Right to Life") declares that "all states must abolish the death penalty."[20]

Further momentum was added to the abolitionist cause when an

[19] Some of them have only recently become abolitionist, such as Rwanda and Kyrgyzstan; others (with only three exceptions—Angola, Cambodia, and Israel) are very small states, many of which have been abolitionist since gaining independence. It seems very unlikely that any of these small abolitionist countries will in the future revert to capital punishment. The following countries have, since December 31, 2008, ratified Protocol 2 to the ICCPR: Argentina, Chile, Honduras, Nicaragua, Rwanda, and Uzbekistan. This means there are now 80 countries that have ratified one or another of these treaties.

[20] On the other hand, the Arab Charter on Human Rights—a revised version of which was adopted by the League of Arab States in 2004—allows the imposition of the death penalty and executions of minors if allowed under national laws. The charter makes no mention of "cruel, inhuman or degrading punishment," although it does prohibit torture.

agreement reached at the United Nations did not give the power to impose the death penalty to international criminal tribunals set up to try cases of genocide and crimes against humanity in former Yugoslavia in 1993 and Rwanda in 1994, and later in Sierra Leone and Lebanon. Similarly, the Statute of the International Criminal Court, adopted by the Rome Conference in July 1998, did not provide the death penalty for any of the exceptionally grave offenses, encompassing genocide and other crimes against humanity, covered by the statute.[21] It could now be argued that if these, the most serious of all crimes, were not punishable by the death penalty, why should lesser offenses be so punished?

VI.   Generating the New Dynamic: The Political Muscle

This human rights approach to the issue of capital punishment would have lacked political force had it not been taken up and insisted on by two postwar political entities: first by the Council of Europe and a little later by the powerful European Union, both of which became determined to spread the goal from a "death penalty free continent" to a "death penalty free world" (Yorke 2006, pp. 23–24). Foremost was the desire to fashion a new politics free from the symbols of a repressive past. In a series of resolutions beginning in 1994 and reaffirmed in 1999 in Resolution 1187, *Europe: A Death Penalty–Free Continent*, the Parliamentary Assembly called on all the parliaments in the world that had not yet abolished the death penalty to do so promptly, following the example of the majority of Council of Europe member states (Wohlwend 1999, pp. 55–67; app. 2, pp. 171–84). In accordance with this, in 1994 the Assembly made it a precondition that any country that wished to become a member of the Council of Europe should agree to implement an immediate moratorium on executions and then sign and ratify, within a set number of years, the Sixth Protocol to the ECHR. Four years later, in 1998, a year after the Amsterdam Treaty of the European Union had included a "Declaration on the Abolition of the Death Penalty," the European Union followed suit, making abolition a precondition for membership. This policy had an enormous impact on the former Soviet bloc of countries in Eastern Europe as

---

[21] UN Doc. A/CONF.183/9 (July 17, 1998), art. 77. The Rome Statute of the International Criminal Court (ICC) entered into force on July 1, 2002. The ICC has its seat in The Hague. By June 1, 2008, 106 countries had ratified or acceded to the Rome Statute of the ICC. On May 6, 2002, the United States announced that it was withdrawing from the treaty.

well as on several states of the former Soviet Union, including the Russian Federation itself, all of which hoped to gain the political and economic benefits associated with membership of the Council of Europe or, at a later date, of the European Union. Every one of these countries has abolished the death penalty, with the exception of Russia (which has signed but not yet ratified the Sixth Optional Protocol to the ECHR and has enforced a moratorium on executions since 1996), Tajikistan, and Belarus. Since it is now seeking membership of the Council of Europe, Belarus will have to comply in due course by instituting a moratorium, as a prelude to abolition within 3 years of acceding, if it is to be successful.

Yet, important as the formal requirement of abolition for membership of these European bodies has been, it should be noted that the movement toward abolition in Eastern Europe had started well before 1994, beginning with the German Democratic Republic (East Germany) in 1987. Capital punishment was eliminated when independence was obtained from communist rule in Slovenia in 1989, in the Czech and Slovak Republics in 1990, in Romania after the fall of Ceausescu at the end of 1989, and in Hungary in 1990. Even in Lithuania, where abolition took somewhat longer to achieve, it was not simply that parliamentarians in 1998 chose "national interests in strategically important international policy" (meaning the possibility of enjoying the benefits of joining the Council of Europe and the European Union) over their constituents' preference for capital punishment. Rather, they embraced a principled opposition to the death penalty as a violation of fundamental human rights (Dobryninas 2004, p. 234). They did so at a time when the numbers of murders were rising, from 224 in 1990 to 442 in 1996, and when public support for abolition had fallen from 27 to 19 percent. Parliamentarians prepared the electorate for this change through the dissemination of findings from public opinion polls that showed that support for the death penalty was, on the whole, contingent: the majority of both the general public and members of the legal and political elite regarded retention as only a temporary measure until the security situation could be improved. They also made clear that the death penalty could be abolished if offenders were securely imprisoned and that the death penalty contradicted Lithuanian aspirations to enter the European Union. In Albania, one of the last Eastern European countries to abolish the death penalty, it was declared unconstitutional in 2000 by the Albanian Constitutional Court, following a moratorium imposed in 1995, despite a lack of enthusiasm for abolition among the general public (Peshkopia and Imami 2008).[22]

Both the Council of Europe and the European Union have declared that "the death penalty has no legitimate place in the penal systems of modern civilized societies, and its application may well be compared with torture and be seen as inhuman and degrading punishment" (Parliamentary Assembly of the Council of Europe, Resolution 1044, October 4, 1994). The language is uncompromising. The Europeans will not accept the argument that capital punishment can be defended on relativistic grounds of religion or culture or as a matter that sovereign powers ought to be left to decide simply for themselves. Thus, in 1998, the European Union embarked on a diplomatic offensive through the adoption of *Guidelines to EU Policy towards Third Countries on the Death Penalty*. This document stated that the objectives of the European Union are to "work towards universal abolition of the death penalty [in those countries that still retained it] as a strongly held policy view agreed by all EU member states." The guidelines also stressed that "abolition of the death penalty contributes to the enhancement of human dignity and the progressive development of human rights" (Council of the European Union, http://www.eurunion.org/legislat/ DeathPenalty/Guidelines.htm; Council of Europe 2007; see also Girling 2005, pp. 112–28). Meeting in Nice in December 2000, the European Council, in conjunction with the European Parliament and Commission, welcomed the draft Charter of Fundamental Rights, article 2, section 2, of which states that "no one shall be condemned to the death penalty or executed."[23]

Some European scholars have suggested that, notwithstanding article 6 of the ICCPR, the time has come to recognize that article 7, which states categorically that "no one shall be subject to torture or cruel, inhuman or degrading punishment," should be interpreted to ban capital punishment (Nowak 2000, p. 44). Indeed, in the Grand Chamber judgment of May 12, 2005, in *Öçalan v. Turkey*, the European

---

[22] Similarly, capital punishment was abolished in Ukraine when, in 1999, the Supreme Court ruled that it was incompatible with articles 27 and 28 of the Ukrainian Constitution (guaranteeing the inalienable right to life and the right not to be subjected to torture or cruel, inhuman, or degrading treatment or punishment that violates one's dignity), despite very strong public and press opposition to abolition (Holovatiy 1999, pp. 145–47).

[23] The EU Memorandum on the Death Penalty, dated February 25, 2000, states, "Offenders are human beings who committed a crime but who also enjoy an inherent and inalienable dignity, the very same dignity claimed by rationalist philosophy, all relevant religions and by law, the death penalty being a denial of human dignity."

Court of Human Rights noted that capital punishment in peacetime had come to be regarded as an unacceptable form of punishment that was no longer permissible under article 2 of the ECHR, which guarantees the right to life, thus endorsing the view that capital punishment amounts to a form of inhuman treatment that can "no longer be seen as having any legitimate place in a democratic society."[24]

Capital punishment has therefore become stigmatized internationally by the abolitionist countries, so much so that they have felt justified in having nothing to do with the policy or practices of countries that retain the death penalty. Abolitionist countries have put political pressure on these retentionist countries by refusing to cooperate with them whenever they request extradition of an offender wanted for trial on a capital charge in their country unless guarantees are forthcoming that the death penalty will not be imposed. In this regard, the judgment of the European Court of Human Rights in 1989 in the case of *Soering v. United Kingdom and Germany* was of cardinal significance. The court prohibited the extradition of Soering from the United Kingdom to the state of Virginia, where he had been charged with a capital offense, on the grounds that in facing the death penalty he would suffer from an inevitably long period on death row (known as "the death row phenomenon"), which would amount to "inhuman or degrading treatment or punishment" contrary to article 3 of the ECHR, especially in light of the fact that the United Kingdom itself had abolished capital punishment for murder.[25] Since then, this has developed into a firm policy concerned not just with the possibility of suffering on death row but with any possibility that the person for whom extradition has been requested could be sentenced to death. Article 19, section 2, of the Charter of Fundamental Rights, adopted by the European Union in Nice in December 2000, states categorically: "No one may be removed, expelled or extradited to a State where there is a serious risk that he or she would be subjected to the death penalty, torture or other inhuman or degrading treatment or punishment" (also see Amnesty International 2001). And in July 2002, the Committee of Ministers of

---

[24] Öcalan v. Turkey (application no. 46221/99), ECHR judgment, March 12, 2003, p. 125. The Grand Chamber held on May 12, 2005, that the imposition of the death sentence on the applicant following an unfair trial by a court whose independence and impartiality were open to doubt amounted to inhuman treatment in violation of article 3 of the ECHR; UN Doc. E/CN.4/2006/83, p. 7.

[25] Soering v. United Kingdom, Federal Republic of Germany intervening, 161 Eur. Ct. H.R. (Ser. A) 34 (1989).

the Council of Europe adopted *Guidelines on Human Rights and the Fight against Terrorism*, which provides that extradition of a person to a country where the person risks being sentenced to death may not be granted unless the guarantees mentioned above are given by relevant authorities in the requesting state.[26] The UN Sub-Commission on the Promotion and Protection of Human Rights has urged all states to endorse this policy, and it has also been affirmed by the UN Commission on Human Rights.[27]

A striking illustration of how views of supreme courts and international human rights bodies have changed as the new human rights dynamic has evolved is the decision in 2001 of the Canadian Supreme Court in the case of *United States v. Burns* (1 S.C.R. 283, 2001 SCC 7; see Schabas 1994, 2001). Ten years earlier, the majority of the Court had ruled that it was not unconstitutional for the Canadian government to extradite a person accused of capital murder to the state of Pennsylvania, which had not entered an assurance that the death penalty would not be imposed. In reaching its judgment in *Kindler v. Canada (Minister of Justice)* in 1991, the majority of the Court stated: "Extraditing an individual accused of the worst form of murder to face capital prosecution does not shock the conscience of the Canadian people, nor is it in violation of international standards. . . . In determining what is fundamentally just, the global context must be considered. Although there is a growing trend towards the abolition of capital punishment, the vast majority of the nations in the world retain the death penalty. There is no international norm" ([1991] 2 SCR 77).[28]

---

[26] Guideline XIII, para. 2. A similar provision was included in the Amending Protocol to the 1977 European Convention on the Suppression of Terrorism, which opened for signature on May 15, 2003. A note of caution is necessary. In the wake of the terrorist attacks of September 11, 2001, the European Union and the United States drew up a new Agreement on Extradition. Jon Yorke (2006) has pointed out that article 13 appears to allow extradition where, for procedural reasons, the state cannot guarantee that the death penalty will not be imposed, as long as it guarantees that it will not be carried out by execution. It is unclear whether this means that the person could remain on death row indefinitely, which would be contrary to the ECHR.

[27] UN Doc. E/CN.4/Sub.2/2003/6, para. 3(a); Commission on Human Rights Resolution 2004/67. In response to the UN secretary general's Seventh Quinquennial Survey in 2004, all but one (Cambodia) of the 33 abolitionist countries that replied stated that they had adopted a policy to refuse to extradite a person charged with a capital offense to a requesting state that had not abolished capital punishment unless that state would give assurances that he or she would not be sentenced to death or executed (United Nations 2005, para. 11).

[28] The minority (two justices) held that the death penalty did constitute cruel and unusual punishment and that extradition to a state with the death penalty would therefore be a breach of the Canadian Charter (see Schabas 1993).

Furthermore, when the case came before the UN Human Rights Committee in 1993, it decided by a majority of 13–5 that there had been no breach of ICCPR article 6 (protecting the right to life) or article 7 (protecting against cruel and unusual punishment) by the Canadian government.[29] And yet in February 2001, the Canadian Supreme Court in *Burns* decided that his unconditional extradition to the state of Washington for the crime of murder, without assurance that the death penalty would not be imposed, would violate section 7 of the Canadian Charter of Rights and Freedom (which protects the right to life, liberty, and security of the person and the right not to be deprived thereof except in accordance with "the principles of fundamental justice"). There is no doubt that the Court was influenced by the controversy that surrounds the use of the death penalty in the United States, particularly as regards the danger of wrongful conviction. But it further made the following telling observation:

> While the evidence does not establish an international law norm against the death penalty, or against extradition to face the death penalty, it does show significant movement towards acceptance internationally of a principle of fundamental justice Canada has adopted internally, namely the abolition of capital punishment. . . . It also shows that the rule requiring that assurances be obtained prior to extradition in death penalty cases not only accords with Canada's principled advocacy on the international level, but also is consistent with the practice of other countries with which Canada generally invites comparison, apart from retentionist jurisdictions in the United States.[30] ([2001] 1 SCR 7 283)

---

[29] Kindler v. Canada, communication no. 470/1991, views adopted July 30, 1993 (see Schabas 1994, pp. 916–17). However, the Human Rights Committee did hold Canada's extradition of Charles Ng to California to face execution by lethal gas to be a breach of the convention.

[30] Once the State of Washington, which had sought the extradition, had given these assurances, the prisoner and his associate were surrendered to face trial in the United States. Significantly, at the international level, the UN Human Rights Committee, in conformity with the *Burns* decision in Canada, also reversed the views it had held in 1993 in Kindler v. Canada when it held in August 2003 in Judge v. Canada that abolitionist countries had an obligation not to expose a person to the real risks of its application, as this would constitute a violation of the defendant's right to life under article 6 of the ICCPR (Judge v. Canada, communication no. 829/1998, views adopted August 5, 2003, UN Doc. A58/40, vol. 1, pp. 85–87). The committee also reversed itself on the grounds that "since that time [1993] there has been a broadening international consensus in favour of abolition of the death penalty, and in states which have retained the death penalty, a broadening consensus not to carry it out" (UN Doc. CCPR/L/78/D/829/1998, 2003, para. 10.3).

In South Africa, too, the Constitutional Court made it plain that the authorities had acted wrongly in deporting to the United States illegal immigrants suspected of bombing the U.S. Embassy in Dar es Salaam in 1998, without first obtaining an assurance from the U.S. government that the suspects would not be executed if convicted of a capital offense.[31]

This policy has proved to be effective. The UN Seventh Quinquennial Survey on Capital Punishment found that the governments of Morocco, Trinidad and Tobago, and the Philippines had all agreed to guarantee that persons of whom they had sought extradition would not be sentenced to death. Also, China, which wishes to bring serious economic violators to justice, has signed extradition treaties with Spain, France, and Australia in which it has agreed not to execute criminals who are repatriated to China. Furthermore, a major reason why the death penalty was abolished in Rwanda in June 2007 was that European countries, as well as the International Criminal Tribunal for Rwanda (sitting in Tanzania), would not extradite "masterminds" of the genocide to Rwanda for fear that they would be sentenced to death and executed. And as far as the United States is concerned, the guarantees that it has been willing to give to Mexico as regards nonimposition of death sentences on "drug lords" has led to a considerable increase in the number recently extradited from that country.[32]

In addition to this "blocking" strategy, the European Union has mounted a diplomatic offensive, including human rights dialogues with China, Vietnam, and other countries in which the question of the death penalty has figured high on the agenda.[33] It has regularly sent diplomatic démarches to American states to plead for reprieves where prisoners are known to be close to execution and has on several occasions

---

[31] See Mohamed v. President of the Republic of South Africa and Others (2001) 3 SA 893. The extradition or deportation of a Tanzanian national to the United States by South Africa to stand trial on federal capital charges was judged to be an infringement of the rights embodied in the South African constitution to life, to dignity, and not to be subjected to cruel, inhuman, or degrading punishment. In due course, this defendant was convicted of a capital offense, but the jury in New York did not impose the death penalty.

[32] Mexico had denied extradition to any country that retained the death penalty. But after guarantees were given, the number of drug lords extradited increased from 41 in 2005 to 63 in 2006.

[33] In addition, delegations have visited Belarus, Botswana, Guinea, Japan, Lebanon, Malaysia, the Palestine Authority, the Philippines, Russia, South Korea, Sri Lanka, Taiwan, Uzbekistan, and Vietnam. See Delegation of the European Commission to the USA, "Hot Topics: EU Policy and Action on the Death Penalty," European Union, http://www.eurunion.org/legislat/DeathPenalty/deathpenhome.htm.

provided an amicus curiae ("friend of the court") brief to the U.S. Supreme Court when the Court has considered death penalty cases that raise constitutional issues, most notably those relating to juveniles and the mentally retarded (Yorke 2007, pp. 29–30).[34] The Parliamentary Assembly of the Council of Europe has repeatedly threatened the United States and Japan with withdrawal of their observer status unless they both make "significant progress" on abolishing executions. Although this has so far not been put into effect, it has been one of the factors that has made American diplomats aware of how greatly the reputation of their country for civilized values has suffered from its retention of capital punishment.[35] The politicization of the issue was emphasized when the European Union stated that abolition of capital punishment was "an essential element in relations between the European Union and third countries and one that should be taken into account, in concluding agreements with third countries" (*Death Penalty in the World*, resolution adopted by the European Parliament, July 5, 2001, para. 10).

With the support of other abolitionist nations, the European countries have, since the early 1990s, attempted to bring resolutions calling for a worldwide moratorium on all executions with a view to later abolition before international forums: at UN Crime Congresses (United Nations 1990, p. 277), at the Commission on Human Rights (now the Human Rights Council), and at the General Assembly, beginning in 1994.[36] They met with fierce opposition in 1994 from over 70 reten-

---

[34] Furthermore, the European Union has supported projects in other countries, especially by providing training for lawyers, parliamentarians, and opinion makers in states that still retain the death penalty, as well as by promoting research on capital punishment in China and in Trinidad and Tobago.

[35] The Parliamentary Assembly of the Council of Europe passed Resolution 1253 on June 25, 2001, to remove the observer status of both these countries by January 1, 2003. In October 2003, the Parliamentary Assembly found these countries "in violation of their fundamental obligation to respect human rights due to their continued application of the death penalty." They were given until the end of 2006 to comply but have not done so (Parliamentary Assembly minutes, final ed., October 10, 2003). The European Parliament also passed resolutions applauding developments or discussions relating to the possible abolition of the death penalty in other countries, such as South Korea and Taiwan, as well as in Japan (Resolution P5_TA [2002] 0332). For American views on their country's standing as regards capital punishment, see Rohatyn (2001), Koh (2002, p. 1105), and Warren (2004).

[36] See General Assembly, Draft Resolution A/C.3/49/L.32, December 29, 1994. In 1997, a resolution was adopted (27 countries voted in favor, 11 voted against, and 14 abstained from voting). In October 1999, a draft resolution (A/C.3/54/L.8) was introduced by Finland at the fifty-fourth session of the UN General Assembly, on behalf of the European Union, with 73 cosponsors. Also in 1999, the UN Sub-Commission on the Promotion and Protection of Human Rights (previously the Sub-Commission on Pre-

tionist nations, on the grounds that capital punishment was "not a human rights issue" but a matter of policy that states had a right to choose without interference from the United Nations or other states.[37] However, pressure from the European nations paid off, for in November 2007 a resolution put before the Third Committee of the General Assembly was passed by a 99–52 vote, with 33 countries abstaining, and the resolution was endorsed by the General Assembly in December 2007 in a 104–54 vote, with 29 abstentions.[38] The fact that only 54 countries (including China and the United States) eventually voted against a worldwide moratorium (and that only 46 voted against it in 2008) suggests that the hard opposition is weakening. At the UN Commission on Human Rights in 2005, 66 countries had dissociated themselves from the moratorium resolution on the grounds that there was, in their view, no international consensus that capital punishment should be abolished. Thus, it is clear that the number of countries that refuse to accept that capital punishment is a violation of a universal human right and should therefore be subject to a ban under international law has declined substantially.

There is not space here to do justice to the work of nongovernmental bodies in bringing about the changes described above, but mention must be made of the outstanding efforts of Amnesty International,

---

vention of Discrimination and Protection of Minorities) called on retentionist states to apply a moratorium on executions throughout 2000 in order to mark the millennium and to commute the sentences of those under sentence of death on December 31, 1999 (Resolution, UN Doc. E/CN.4/SUB.2/RES/1999/4, August 24, 1999).

[37] Singapore argued that the resolution went "some way towards dictating a particular set of values from countries which have abolished capital punishment on those which have not" (statement by Singapore proposing no action to Draft Resolution A/C.3/49/L.32). Seventy-one states voted in favor of this amendment, 65 voted against it, and 21 abstained from voting. Many of those states that had originally sponsored the resolution for a moratorium were unwilling to accept the Singaporean amendment because it failed to uphold the universal principles of human rights and made no mention of international law. As a result, 74 countries abstained, and the resolution was lost. See also similar statements by representatives of Libya, Algeria, Thailand, and the United States at the Fifty-seventh Session of the UN Commission on Human Rights on April 25, 2001 (United Nations, "Commission of Human Rights Adopts Ten Resolutions, Measures on the Death Penalty," Impunity, and Other Issues Concerning the Promotion and Protection of Human Rights," news release, April 25, 2001). For a more detailed account of these proceedings, see Hood and Hoyle (2008, pp. 32–34).

[38] After this essay had been completed, a similar resolution was approved by the UN General Assembly in December 2008 by a 106–46 vote, with 34 abstentions (six countries were absent). It was too late to change the analysis in this essay, but it should be noted that two countries that voted against the motion for a moratorium in 2007 voted in favor of it in 2008 (Ethiopia and Somalia), and six abstained (Bahrain, Jordan, Mauritania, and Oman—all Muslim-majority states—plus Papua New Guinea and Suriname).

which now has supporters and subscribers in over 150 countries and territories, enabling it to publish authoritative reports on the status of capital punishment worldwide. But it is not alone. Also working actively for abolition by maintaining a flow of valuable information on international trends are Hands Off Cain, founded in Brussels in 1993 but now operating from Rome; the French-led organization International Federation for Human Rights (FIDH); Ensemble Contre la Peine de Mort (Together Against the Death Penalty), which campaigns for moratoria across the world and on behalf of particular individuals facing execution and has organized three international congresses; the American-based Human Rights Watch; and the World Coalition Against the Death Penalty, which was founded to bring together nongovernmental organizations, bar associations, unions, local governments, and other concerned bodies in a campaign for the universal abolition of the death penalty.[39] The latter organization represents over 38 human rights organizations and has declared October 10 as the annual World Day Against the Death Penalty, on which events, rallies, and demonstrations are held in many countries.[40] On this day in 2006, activists and organizations across the Asia-Pacific region joined to launch the Anti–Death Penalty Asia Network (ADPAN).

VII.   Constraining the Scope and Application of the Death Penalty Pending Abolition

Even those countries that have resisted the call for complete abolition have been affected by the new dynamic described above. It has had an impact through restricting the number and types of crimes for which the penalty is death, in restricting the categories of persons who may be put to death, in making the application of the death penalty discretionary rather than mandatory, and more generally in providing safeguards to protect the accused from wrongful conviction and the convicted from wrongful execution.

In 1984, the UN Economic and Social Council issued, for the first time, *Safeguards Guaranteeing Protection of the Rights of Those Facing the*

---

[39] Ensemble Contre la Peine de Mort organized international conferences in Strasbourg in 2001, Montreal in 2004, and Paris in 2007.

[40] On November 30 each year, there is now a Cities for Life event organized by the Rome-based Community of San Edigio. This event is marked by the illumination of public buildings or spaces around the world to symbolize the value of life. In 2007, buildings were illuminated in 752 cities, including 33 capital cities.

Death Penalty in order to strengthen and enlarge the provisions already included in the ICCPR. The first of these safeguards defined somewhat more precisely the scope of what could be regarded as the "most serious crimes" for which the death penalty could be imposed under article 6, section 2, of the ICCPR pending complete abolition (see Sec. V), by adding the words "it being understood that their scope should not go beyond intentional crimes with lethal or other extremely grave consequences." While it is true that the words "other extremely grave consequences" have been open to a variety of interpretations, the UN Human Rights Committee laid it down in 1982 that the "death penalty should be a quite exceptional measure," and international bodies have set about identifying crimes that should not fall within its compass.[41] Thus, article 4, section 4, of the American Convention on Human Rights stipulates that "in no case shall capital punishment be inflicted for political offenses or related common crimes." The Commission on Human Rights, in its Resolutions 1991/61 and 2004/67, urged all states that still maintain the death penalty to ensure that it is not imposed for nonviolent financial crimes or for nonviolent religious practices or expressions of conscience. In a series of judgments (Schabas 2004*a*, pp. 48–50), the UN Human Rights Committee has extended this list to include offenses such as "evading military service several times," abetting suicide, drug-related offenses, apostasy, committing a third homosexual act, "illicit sex," "vague categories of offence relating to internal and external security," "a person whose life endangers or corrupts society," and aggravated robbery in which the use of firearms did not produce death or wounding of any person.[42] And at its fifty-eighth session in 2002, the Commission on Human Rights added to this list "sexual relations between consenting adults" (UN Doc. E/CN.4/2002/L.104, para. 4c). With respect to Vietnam, it noted that capital punishment could in that country be imposed for "opposition to order and national security violations," both of which "are excessively vague and inconsistent with Article 6(2) of the Covenant" (UN Doc. A/57/40, vol. 1, 2002, 82/7, p. 68; UN Doc. A/54/40, para. 128).

[41] See UN Human Rights Committee, "CCPR General Comment No. 6: The Right to Life (Article 6)," 16th sess., April 30, 1982 (reproduced in app. 5 in Schabas [2002, p. 402]).

[42] UN Doc. E/CN.4/2002/L.104, para. 4c, "Promotion and Protection of Human Rights." UN Commission on Human Rights Resolution 2005/59, para. f, declared "that the death penalty is not [to be] imposed for non-violent acts such as financial crimes, religious practice or expression of conscience and sexual relations between consenting adults nor as a mandatory sentence."

These attempts to define more clearly what does not constitute a "serious crime" for the purpose of capital punishment—more specifically, for which offenses it is a disproportionate penalty, whatever other justifications for capital punishment may be employed—has had an impact in countries that have retained capital punishment. For example, Belarus, while not ceasing executions (three were recorded in February 2008), greatly reduced the number of capital crimes in its new criminal code of 1999 and recently announced that the death penalty can now be imposed only "when it is dictated by special aggravating circumstances as well as an exceptional danger posed by the offender."[43] In 2001, the Human Rights Committee, on receiving a report from the Democratic People's Republic of Korea (North Korea), welcomed the reduction of capital offenses from 33 to five, as well as the readiness, confirmed by the delegation, to review further the issue of capital punishment with a view to its abolition (United Nations 2005). Vietnam also signaled its intentions by reducing the number of capital crimes from 44 to 29—still, of course, a very high number. China too has indicated that it will reduce the number of offenses for which capital punishment can be inflicted (see Sec. VIII).

As regards the use of capital punishment for nonhomicidal crimes, the evidence suggests that the law's bark is generally worse than its bite. As far as we have been able to ascertain, only 15 countries carried out at least one execution for an offense other than homicide during the 5 years from 2002 to 2006.[44] And only eight of the 31 countries in which trading in illicit drugs is a capital offense did so (Hood and Hoyle 2008, p. 151).[45] Thus, executions for crimes other than murder are now rare events.[46]

Pressure has been building through the influence of the UN secretary general's 5-yearly reports on the status of capital punishment and the implementation of safeguards for those facing the death penalty,

[43] There are 14 fewer offenses in the 1999 code than in that of 1960. Article 59, section 1, states: "The Criminal Code provides that the death penalty may be imposed for severe crimes connected with the deliberate deprivation of life with aggravating circumstances" (July 9, 1999; amended on July 17, 2006). See OSCE (2008).

[44] These countries were China, Egypt, Indonesia, Iran, North Korea, Kuwait, Malaysia, Pakistan, Saudi Arabia, Singapore, Sudan, Syria, Thailand, Uzbekistan, and Vietnam.

[45] These countries were China, Indonesia, Iran, Kuwait, Saudi Arabia, Singapore, Thailand, and Vietnam. In Singapore, about three-quarters of those executed had committed drug offenses.

[46] However, there have been continuing reports of executions for morals offenses, such as adultery between married persons in Iran, sometimes by stoning. See, e.g., Fathi (2007).

as well as from the UN special rapporteur on extrajudicial, summary, and arbitrary executions, to restrict capital punishment where it still exists to the gravest cases of intentional and culpable murder (United Nations 2007, para. 65). In this respect, the recent majority decision of the U.S. Supreme Court in *Kennedy v. Louisiana* (docket no. 07-343, decided June 25, 2008), which held that the Eighth Amendment "bars Louisiana from imposing the death penalty for the rape of a child where the crime did not result, and was not intended to result, in the victim's death," is fully in line with this restricted interpretation of article 6, section 2, of the ICCPR.

This trend is also evident in the jurisprudence on whether the death penalty can be mandatorily imposed on conviction of a capital offense or whether the sentence must always be at the discretion of the judge and, if so, what restrictions should be placed on that discretion if it is not to become arbitrary and discriminatory. Of the 94 countries that retained the death penalty on their statute books in mid-2008 (49 of which we classify as actively retentionist and 45 as abolitionist de facto), two-thirds have no mandatory death sentences for any crime. In the one-third of countries that do have a mandatory death penalty, it is now usually appointed only for a restricted class of capital murder.[47] And although 12 countries make the possession of illicit drugs over a certain weight a mandatory capital offense, it is now by no means always enforced.[48]

It has come to be widely recognized, as it was during the 1970s in the United States, that mandatory sentences are both too broad in their

[47] The countries with a mandatory death penalty are Bahrain, Barbados (see n. 51), Brunei Darussalam (abolitionist de facto [ADF]), China (for two articles of the criminal code), Comoros (for offenses against the state, treason, and espionage), Egypt, Ghana (ADF), Guatemala (for rape of a child), Guinea, Guyana, India (for violation of the Arms Act, the Prevention of Atrocities Act, and the Narcotic Drugs and Psychotropic Substances Act), Iran, Jordan, Kenya (ADF), Kuwait (for drug offenses), Lebanon (for treason and collaboration with the enemy), Malaysia, Morocco (ADF), Nigeria, Pakistan, Qatar, Saudi Arabia (for drug importers, smugglers, and recidivist distributors), Singapore, Taiwan (in the military code, certain offenses by military personnel in time of war, and for "causing major disturbance of the financial order or counterfeiting"), Tanzania (ADF), Thailand, Togo (ADF), Trinidad and Tobago, the United Arab Emirates, Yemen, Zambia, and Zimbabwe. Similarly, the death penalty in Guinea is mandatory not just for murder but for a "wide range of offences" (Amnesty International 2006, p. 129).

[48] Some countries have devised an attenuated form of mandatory death sentence for murder by invoking the principle of "exceptional circumstances." In Africa, several countries—Botswana, Lesotho, Swaziland, and Zimbabwe—have imported Roman-Dutch common law, with its concept of "extenuating circumstances," sufficient proof of which gives the court the discretion to reduce a capital to a noncapital offense and impose a sentence other than death. A similar provision exists also in Belize.

impact, as they mandate death in cases in which it is not warranted, and too rigid, as they preclude an individualized consideration of the facts of the case at sentencing.[49] UN bodies have made it abundantly and repeatedly clear that the death penalty "should under no circumstances be mandatory" (United Nations 2000). Both the UN Human Rights Committee and the Inter-American Commission on Human Rights have also held that the mandatory death penalty is a violation of the right to life. These decisions have included cases emanating from the Bahamas, Barbados, Jamaica, the Philippines, and Trinidad and Tobago, as well as from Grenada and St. Vincent and the Grenadines.[50] Similarly, under its appellate jurisdiction for some former British colonies, the Judicial Committee of the Privy Council has struck down mandatory death sentences in the Commonwealth Caribbean, even in cases where the mandatory penalty was restricted to a class of capital murders and where there was review of the mandatorily imposed penalty by a "mercy committee."[51] The reason for this was very well sum-

[49] As the Indian Supreme Court put it in the case of Mithu v. The State of Punjab (1983), a mandatory death sentence would reduce the sentencing process to a "farce." Since *Mithu*, a mandatory death penalty has been introduced under a section of the Narcotic Drugs and Psychotropic Substances Act 1985 and the Prevention of Atrocities Act 1989. However, no case has come before the Indian Supreme Court to test its constitutionality.

[50] Kennedy v. Trinidad and Tobago (March 28, 2002), UN Doc. CCPR/C/74/D/845/1998; Thompson v. St Vincent and the Grenadines (2000), UN Doc. CCPR/C/70/D906/1998; Baptiste v. Grenada, CR 38/00 (2000), para. 59. Also see Chan v. Guyana, UN Doc. CCPR/C/85/D/913/2000, views adopted October 31, 2005; Hilaire v. Trinidad and Tobago, Inter-American Commission Report 66/99 (1999). In Hilaire, Constantine and Benjamin and Others v. Trinidad and Tobago (June 21, 2002, Ser. C No. 94 [2002]), the Inter-American Court of Human Rights held that the mandatory death penalty in Trinidad and Tobago was contrary to the provisions of article 4, section 2, of the American Convention on Human Rights. It did so again in Boyce et al. v. Barbados (November 20, 2007, Ser. C No. 16). See also Carpo v. The Philippines (no. 1077/2002, views adopted March 28, 2003), where the Human Rights Committee held that the mandatory imposition of the death penalty (prior to abolition in 2006) for the broadly defined offense of murder by article 48 of the Revised Penal Code of the Philippines violated article 6 of the ICCPR.

[51] Spence and Hughes v. The Queen, Criminal Appeal No. 20 of 1998, East Caribbean Court of Appeal, Judgment (April 2, 2001). See Lehrfreund (2001); The Queen v. Peter Hughes (2002) UKPC 12, para. 30; Berthill Fox v. The Queen (2002) 2 AC 284; Patrick Reyes v. The Queen (2002) UKPC 11, para. 43; Lambert Watson v. The Queen (2005) 1AC 400; Forrester Bowe Jr. and Trono Davis v. The Queen (2006) UKPC 10, para. 42; Bernard Coard and Others v. The Attorney General of Grenada (2007) UKPC 7. The exception was in relation to Barbados and Trinidad and Tobago, where it was held that the mandatory death penalty was protected by a "savings clause" in their constitutions. On May 4, 2009, the attorney general of Barbados announced that legislation would be introduced to abolish the mandatory death penalty and replace it with a discretionary death penalty ("Barbados Government Abolishing Mandatory Death Sentence," *Caribbean360.com*, May 4, 2009, http://www.caribbean360.com/News/Caribbean/Stories/2009/05/04/NEWS0000007321.html). On this see Hood and Hoyle (2008, pp. 104–10, 281–83).

marized by UN Special Rapporteur Philip Alston in January 2007:

> The proper application of human rights law—especially of its pro
> visions that "[n]o one shall be arbitrarily deprived of his life" and
> that "[n]o one shall be subjected to . . . cruel, inhuman or degrad-
> ing . . . punishment"—requires weighing factors that will not be
> taken into account in the process of determining whether a defen-
> dant is guilty of committing a "most serious crime". As a result,
> these factors can only be taken into account in the context of indi-
> vidualized sentencing by the judiciary in death penalty cases. . . .
> The conclusion, in theory as well as in practice, was that respect
> for human rights can be reliably ensured in death penalty cases
> only if the judiciary engages in case-specific, individualized sen-
> tencing that accounts for all of the relevant factors. . . . It is clear,
> therefore, that in death penalty cases, individualized sentencing by
> the judiciary is required to prevent cruel, inhuman or degrading
> punishment and the arbitrary deprivation of life. (United Nations
> 2007, para. 55)

The same arguments against the mandatory death penalty have been
successfully employed in Uganda and Malawi, both former British colonies in Africa. In 2005, the Constitutional Court of Uganda, in the
case of Susan Kigula and 416 others, brought by all the prisoners on
death row at the time, held the mandatory death penalty to be unconstitutional. Two years later, in April 2007, the Malawi High Court came
to the same conclusion in the case of Francis Kafantayeni—the state
having remained neutral on the issue. As a result, the mandatory death
sentences of all 30 prisoners on death row were vacated, and the defendants were remitted for sentencing.[52] It is difficult to see on what
grounds similar arguments will not win the day when the mandatory
death penalty is contested in Kenya (in a case already listed to be
heard), Nigeria, and Tanzania.

In addition, great progress has been made in excluding altogether
from the threat of the death penalty those who were juveniles—defined
as under the age of 18 years—at the time the capital crime was committed. There is now an international consensus that capital punishment should not be inflicted on pregnant women and new mothers,

---

[52] Susan Kigula and 416 Others v. The Attorney General of Uganda, Constitutional
Petition No. 6 of 2003 [2005], Constitutional Court of Uganda. This decision was upheld
by the Supreme Court of Uganda in Attorney General v. Susan Kigula and 417 Others,
Constitutional Appeal No. 3 of 2006 [2009], UGSC 6, January 21, 2009. Kafantayeni v.
Attorney General, Constitutional Case No. 12 of 2005, High Court of Malawi, April 27,
2007.

nor should it be used where the defendant is mentally retarded (the now discredited term still used in the United States and in the UN *Safeguards*). In all countries, the clearly insane are excused because they simply cannot be convicted, although the mentally ill still pose a problem because of the failure to diagnose severe mental illness in many countries that do not have an adequate number of professional psychiatrists prepared to work in the forensic field. Furthermore, there are disputes about how mentally ill the person must be to be disqualified from execution, to what extent the mentally ill can be treated and then executed, and how much emphasis death penalty statutes should place on protecting the public from people deemed to be "dangerous" because of their mental illnesses.

International human rights conventions mandate that criminal sanctions can be imposed only against an individual who has been subject to due process of law that guarantees a presumption of innocence, a fair opportunity to answer the charges brought against him or her before a duly constituted court, and the assistance of a well-qualified defense counsel. In the context of capital punishment, because execution is irrevocable, due process protections become even more significant. For this reason, the UN Economic and Social Council in 1989 called for special protection for those facing charges for which the death penalty is provided, by allowing time and facilities for the preparation of their defense, including the adequate assistance of counsel at every stage of the proceedings, above and beyond the protection afforded in noncapital cases. The fourth UN safeguard for the protection of the rights of those facing the death penalty is aimed at avoiding any danger that an innocent person could be sentenced to death by providing that "capital punishment may be imposed only when the guilt of the person charged is based on clear and convincing evidence leaving no room for an alternative explanation of the facts." The fifth safeguard, which mentions the "final judgment," makes it clear that the question of the safety of the conviction must be questioned throughout the process, right up to appeal and clemency proceedings (which should be automatic), and that capital punishment may be carried out pursuant to final judgment rendered by a competent court only after a legal process that employs all possible safeguards to ensure a fair trial, at least ones equal to those contained in article 14 of the ICCPR, including the right to adequate legal assistance at all stages of the proceedings for anyone suspected of or charged with a crime for which capital punishment may be imposed. There is not space here to discuss the extent to which these safeguards are honored in practice, but undoubtedly their very existence has provided a normative basis greatly restricting the use of capital punishment.[53]

VIII. The Resisters: Can They Be Converted?

At several stages of the abolition movement, commentators expressed their belief that all the countries likely to abolish the death penalty had already done so, only to be proved within a short period of time to have been far too pessimistic.[54] So to what extent is resistance to abolition likely to be overcome within, say, the next few decades?

Taken together, the developments discussed above suggest that many, probably the majority, of countries that retain capital punishment are not wedded to or reliant on executions to enforce the criminal law. Many of them appear to be moving toward a minimal use of capital punishment, where the threat that the penalty could be imposed is allowed to remain as a symbol of the state's power. Experience shows that in most countries, once capital punishment has reached this stage, it is just a matter of time before it is discarded.

Thus, the remaining retentionist countries should not be regarded as a solid "rump" of states all committed to the death penalty. There is, as will be shown, considerable diversity among them as regards their willingness to accept the goal of abolition as a universal human rights norm.

Some indication of the likelihood that states will move to embrace abolition may be gained by examining the characteristics and policies of the 61 retentionist countries: 48 are still, at the time of writing (August 2008), actively retentionist, and 13 may be regarded as "suspended retentionist" (some of them being "thwarted executioners")—those not accepted by Amnesty International to be abolitionist in practice, even though for various reasons they have not executed anyone for at least 10 years.[55] A striking fact (that can be seen in app. table

---

[53] For a lengthy review of these safeguards and evidence of the extent to which they are abided by, see Hood and Hoyle (2008, chaps. 5–7).

[54] Radzinowicz wrote of a "plateau" having been reached (1999, p. 293).

[55] One of the 49 actively retentionist countries in table A2, as of December 2007, became suspended retentionist in June 2008, 10 years after its last execution—St. Kitts and Nevis—but it resumed executions in December 2008. There are now, as of June 2009, 35 countries that are regarded by Amnesty International as truly abolitionist in

A2) is that countries with a majority Muslim population account for over half (26, or 53 percent) of the 49 actively retentionist countries (as of December 2007), and only two Muslim-majority countries are suspended retentionist. The next highest group comprises non-Muslim states that are members of the Commonwealth (mostly the former British colonies in Asia, Africa, and the Caribbean), seven (11 percent) of which were actively retentionist and 10 that were suspended retentionist (eight of them in the Anglophone Caribbean), together accounting for 28 percent of the 61 retentionist countries. Seven non-Muslim and non-Commonwealth countries in Asia and five in Africa are actively retentionist, none being suspended retentionist. There are now only three actively retentionist countries in the Americas and one in Europe and no suspended retentionists. One way to try to gauge the attitude toward abolition of these states is to examine the pattern of votes at the UN General Assembly in December 2007 on the European-led resolution calling for a moratorium on all executions, pending abolition, when 54 countries voted against the resolution and 29 abstained (see n. 38 for details of the vote taken in December 2008).

Although the representative of Mexico, speaking on behalf of 87 delegations, stressed that "the resolution was not intended to interfere and impose views but to promote and strengthen the growing trend towards the elimination of capital punishment," it was clear from the record of the debates that the opponents, as on previous occasions when moratorium resolutions had been brought forward at the Commission on Human Rights and at the General Assembly, would not accept this.[56] First, they argued that the resolution was no more than an attempt by abolitionist countries, several of them former colonial powers, to override their sovereign right to fashion their criminal justice system according to their own judgments of the needs and culture of their country (Parsons 2007). Second, they argued that the matter was not one of human rights but of criminal justice policy shaped by and responding to the wishes of the majority of the population. Third, they argued that it was not in fact prohibited under international law. For example, Singapore stressed that it "had a sovereign right to choose its own political, criminal and judicial systems" and that "capital

---

practice, having indicated that they do not intend to resume executing those sentenced to death.

[56] See UN General Assembly (2007). For an account of these earlier resolutions, see Hood and Hoyle (2008, pp. 32–33).

punishment was a criminal rather than a human rights issue." The delegate from Egypt stated that the resolution was "in contradiction to religious, practical and legal norms that were agreed upon. . . . No side was more right than the other. . . . Each side would continue to choose its own path to maintain social order, security and peace."[57] The representative of China "reiterated that in today's world the issue was a matter of judicial process to decide on the use of or a moratorium on the death penalty, and not a matter of human rights. It was each country's right, on the basis of cultural background and other factors, to decide when to use that punishment. Each state should be able to exercise that right without interference. The issue should be resolved through dialogue."

However, 14 of the 61 actively retentionist and suspended retentionist countries did not vote against the European-led resolution: 11 of them abstained (Belarus, Cameroon, Cuba, the Democratic Republic of the Congo, Equatorial Guinea, Guinea, Lebanon, Lesotho, Sierra Leone, the United Arab Emirates, and Vietnam), and three voted for the resolution (Burundi, Guatemala, and Tajikistan), all of them states in which abolition is already firmly on the political agenda.[58] Eleven of these 14 countries were actively retentionist. Thus, a sizable proportion of the 48 currently actively retentionist nations clearly indicated that they were not hostile to the aims of the resolution.[59]

Of the 54 countries that voted against the resolution, only 36 were actively retentionist at that time, and nine were suspended retentionist. Eight were classed by Amnesty International as abolitionist in practice, and one (the Solomon Islands) was abolitionist for all crimes.[60] It seems

---

[57] Nevertheless, Egypt "recognised the responsibility of States, in the case of serious crimes, to execute the death penalty in a system based on due process of law."

[58] In Burundi, where there have been no executions since 2001, a new criminal code that has no provisions for the death penalty is under consideration by Parliament (Gorchs-Chacou and Sculier 2008, pp. 10–11); in Guatemala, the president announced in 2005 that he would seek legislation to abolish the death penalty; and in Tajikistan, the president imposed a moratorium on executions in 2004 without a time limit. President Rahmonov stated that "the right to life is of supreme value and no one should deprive anyone else of this right" (Khamidov 2006, p. 33). Note that Bahrain, Jordan, and Oman abstained when the resolution came before the General Assembly in 2008 (see n. 38).

[59] Two such countries are not members of the UN and therefore did not have a vote: the Palestinian Authority and Taiwan (a country already moving toward abolition).

[60] The eight abolitionist in practice countries that voted against the resolution were Brunei Darussalam, Grenada, Maldives, Mauritania, Myanmar, Papua New Guinea, Suriname, and Tonga. The 14 abolitionist in practice countries that abstained from the vote were Central African Republic, Eritrea, Gambia, Ghana, Kenya, Laos, Malawi, Morocco, Niger, South Korea, Swaziland, Tanzania, Togo, and Zambia. Tunisia was absent. Thus, only 10 of the 33 countries at that time regarded by Amnesty International as abolitionist

likely that countries that were abolitionist in practice yet voted against the resolution or abstained did so because they accepted the argument that the matter should be left to nations to decide for themselves (rather than because they completely rejected the case for abolition) and because they felt that the time was not yet right for them to be able to achieve de jure abolition.

As regards the 36 actively retentionist states that opposed the resolution, 21 (58 percent) had majority Muslim populations; seven were non-Muslim member states of the Commonwealth (two in Asia, two in Africa, and three in the Caribbean); two others were from non-Muslim Africa (Ethiopia and Zimbabwe); five were from non-Muslim Asia (China, Japan, North Korea, Mongolia, and Thailand); and one was from the Americas (the United States).[61] And of the nine suspended retentionist countries that voted against the resolution, one was a Muslim state (Comoros), but the other eight were countries in the Anglophone Caribbean—all, in reality, "thwarted" executioners.

From this analysis it can be seen that resistance to the movement for worldwide abolition is strongest in the Muslim world, in non-Muslim Asia, in the countries of the former British Commonwealth (now the Commonwealth), and in the United States. It seems likely that somewhat different considerations will affect whether—and, if so, at what pace—members of these groups of countries might move toward abolition. Here there is space to give only a broad indication of the prospects.[62]

As regards the largest group—the countries with majority Muslim populations—the prospects for abolition will depend on whether political stability can be achieved and whether governments remain politically and legally dominated by fundamentalist interpretations of Islam or whether they move toward secular democratic government, which allows for a more modern, "scientific," and less authoritarian

---

in practice (and usually added to the list of abolitionist nations) actually voted for the resolution: Algeria, Benin, Burkina Faso, Congo (Brazzaville), Gabon, Madagascar, Mali, Nauru, the Russian Federation, and Sri Lanka.

[61] The 21 countries with majority Muslim populations were Afghanistan, Bahrain, Bangladesh, Chad, Egypt, Indonesia, Iran, Iraq, Jordan, Kuwait, Libya, Malaysia, Nigeria (which is 50 percent Muslim but is listed here because the death penalty is most strongly supported in the Muslim-majority northern states of Nigeria), Oman, Pakistan, Qatar, Saudi Arabia, Somalia, Sudan, Syria, and Yemen. Four of these countries are members of the Commonwealth: Bangladesh, Malaysia, Nigeria, and Pakistan.

[62] For a detailed account of the prospects of abolition in the various regions of the world, see Hood and Hoyle (2008, chaps. 2–3).

interpretation of Islam.[63] As already mentioned (see Sec. III), several countries with large Muslim-majority populations have already abandoned capital punishment. In addition, neither Comoros nor Tajikistan now carries out executions, and the latter voted for the moratorium resolution. Ten other Muslim countries are classified as abolitionist in practice, most notably Algeria (the only Arab nation to vote for the moratorium at the United Nations; see Oldfield 2007, p. 4), Brunei Darussalam, Burkina Faso (which is 50 percent Muslim), Gambia, Maldives, Mali, Mauritania, Morocco, Niger, and Tunisia. Morocco and Tunisia are already on the road to abolition (Oldfield 2007, p. 4), and yet others appear willing to consider moving in this direction—for example, Lebanon, Jordan, and the United Arab Emirates, which abstained on the moratorium resolution, and perhaps Bangladesh, whose representative at the UN General Assembly recognized that "the resolution just adopted was representative of the growing trend against the death penalty. His country believed, however, that the time was not right for its total abolition" (UN General Assembly 2007). Yet others, notably Egypt and Nigeria's northern states, have in recent years shown greater restraint in sanctioning executions (see Sec. III), and indeed there have been recent moves to introduce a bill into the Nigerian Federal Assembly to abolish capital punishment under federal law (Usigbe 2008). Only a handful of the countries listed above in this actively retentionist group of Muslim countries make regular and large-scale use of capital punishment as a crime-control measure: Iran, Saudi Arabia, Pakistan, Iraq, and Yemen. Of these, the election of a new democratic government in Pakistan may herald a change, as witnessed by the recently reported recommendation of the prime minister that mass clemency be given to 7,000 prisoners sentenced to death, and it is possible that if security can be established in Iraq and Afghanistan, their governments may in time be persuaded to abandon capital pun-

---

[63] See the excellent article by the human rights lawyer M. Cherif Bassouini (2004). Bassouini argues that there is nothing in the Qur'an or the Sunna that requires the death penalty, save perhaps for the crime of brigandage when a death occurs. For all other crimes it is optional, not mandatory. There is much debate among the different schools of jurisprudence as to whether the Qur'an and the Sunna are to be interpreted literally or on the basis of the intent and purpose of the text, or both. Bassouini's view is that the interpretation of the Qur'an has been dominated by traditionalists and fundamentalists, who are in the main intransigent and literal, whereas the few secular reformists and "forward thinking traditionalists" would emphasize the need to interpret scripture in the light of scientific knowledge and the Islamic emphasis on mercy, in order to create a just and humane society.

ishment.[64] Overall, therefore, the prospects for a steady movement toward abolition in the Muslim world are not nearly as bleak as some may imagine.

As far as the countries of the non-Muslim-majority Commonwealth are concerned, resistance to abolition is most evident in Singapore and the island states of the Anglophone Caribbean, all but two of which (the exceptions being the still actively retentionist Bahamas and Trinidad and Tobago) may be classified as thwarted executioners.[65] They have been thwarted by the activities of dedicated human rights lawyers who have challenged the constitutionality of the death penalty, particularly the mandatory death penalty, and many aspects of the procedures leading to conviction, sentencing, and beyond. Many successful appeals have been made to international tribunals, especially to the Judicial Committee of the Privy Council (the highest court of appeal for these countries) and most notably in the case of *Pratt and Morgan v. the Attorney General for Jamaica* (4 All ER 769 [PC] [1993]) in 1993, in which it was laid down that it would amount to inhuman and degrading treatment and punishment to execute a person who had been under sentence of death for longer than 5 years—a period within which it has not proved possible, in most instances, to complete all the processes of appeal available to prisoners—as well as several other cases that have challenged the constitutionality of a mandatory death penalty and review procedures (for further details, see Hood and Hoyle [2008, pp. 103–11]).

By contrast, in Asia and Africa, Commonwealth countries that retain capital punishment and wish to continue to execute offenders are now in the minority. And when one examines the incidence of executions, it becomes clear that only four of the seven actively retentionist non-Muslim Commonwealth countries (Botswana, India, Singapore, and Uganda) carried out any executions from 2003 to 2007, and only one of them (Singapore) conducted an execution in every one of these 5 years. Furthermore, in all these countries the rate of executions has been falling—most notably in Singapore, where the number of people

---

[64] This recommendation was made to mark the fifty-fifth birthday of the late Benazir Bhutto, who had been assassinated on her return to Pakistan to contest a general election. The clemency was welcomed by Pakistan's Human Rights Commission (Qaiser Felix, "Stop Executions to Honour Bhutto, Pakistani PM Says," *AsiaNews.it*, June 26, 2008, http://www.asianews.it/index.php? = en&art = 12608).

[65] The most recent execution in the Bahamas took place in 2000. The most recent executions in Trinidad and Tobago happened in 1999, when 10 men were hanged, nine of them on the same occasion.

put to death fell from a reported 76 in 1994 to 19 in 2004 and to only two in 2007. Therefore, it appears evident that most retentionist Commonwealth countries maintain the power to apply the death sentence for local political reasons and that in doing so they believe that it is necessary to reject the view that the issue is one that should be decided by reference to international customary human rights norms.

In November 2007, an important statement, *Realising People's Potential*, directed to the Commonwealth Heads of Government Meeting in Kampala, was issued by the Kampala Civil Society, for the purposes of "*reaffirming* and *underscoring* the importance of the Commonwealth's stated commitment to internationally-agreed human rights, including the right to life" (Kampala Civil Society 2008, p. 15). It called on member states to "*respect* the *Moratorium on the Death Penalty* voted by the UN General Assembly's Third Committee and proactively work towards the total abolition of the death penalty" (p. 31). Closing the conference of the Commonwealth Human Rights Forum, held in Kampala in the same month, the Commonwealth deputy secretary-general, Florence Mugasha (speaking on behalf of Secretary-General Don McKinnon), "emphasised the Commonwealth's commitment and mandate to support and promote human rights within its 53 member states" ("Delegates Call for Increased Promotion of Human Rights," November 21, 2007, http://www.thecommonwealth.org/news/172778/ 211107delegatesathumanrights.htm). As one of the barriers to abolition appears to be the perception that other (mainly European) countries are seeking to impose their worldview on countries that retain capital punishment in law, it may be that leadership on the abolition of capital punishment generated from within the Commonwealth, perhaps by those governments that have adopted new postcolonial constitutions that embody the right to life and freedom from cruel and degrading punishments, such as South Africa, might be more successful.

In many Commonwealth countries in Africa and Asia that do not, or only very rarely, carry out judicial executions, political leadership strongly backed by human rights organizations will be required to bring about de jure abolition. In the Anglophone countries of the Caribbean, in which constitutions have been under review, the removal of the "handed-down" savings clauses from the colonial era, which protected the law as it was at the time that these countries gained their independence, would make it easier both for politicians to abolish capital punishment through legislation and for the courts (including the

Caribbean Court of Justice) to interpret the law in light of the provisions guaranteeing the right to life and freedom from inhuman and degrading or cruel and unusual punishments, which are already embodied in the constitutions of these countries.[66] It was notable that at the UN General Assembly in December 2007, the representative of Antigua and Barbuda, speaking on behalf of 13 Caribbean Community (CARICOM) countries, "reiterated that Caribbean States were committed to the promotion and protection of all human rights, in line with international law" and that "states must provide an environment conducive for protecting human rights" (UN General Assembly 2007). The issue now is for these countries to face the fact that experience has shown that the death penalty cannot be applied without the violation not only of the right to life but of the right to freedom from cruel, inhuman, or degrading treatment or punishment.

In Asia, the two countries with the largest populations on earth both retain capital punishment, but with entirely different effects. In India, it is, in principle, to be imposed in only the "rarest of rare" cases. And although there is a good deal of evidence that this standard is not always strictly interpreted (Amnesty International 2008), the fact of the matter is that the executive branch of government has used its power to delay executions through the clemency process so that very few people have been executed—and then only sporadically. The last execution took place in 2004, the first since 1997. The death penalty is retained, but purely for symbolic purposes: a few executions now and then cannot be regarded as a tool of criminal justice in such a populous country. It appears that India could easily abolish capital punishment without any serious internal political consequences.

By contrast, China has until very recently pursued a vigorous policy of using capital punishment in its "strike-hard" campaigns (Hood and Hoyle 2008, pp. 98–102; also, Trevaskes 2007) against a wide variety of crimes—68 of them—including economic and sexual crimes as well as various offenses against the state. However, the past few years have witnessed a distinct change in the discourse, evidenced by the willingness of the Chinese authorities to discuss the death penalty in human rights seminars and dialogues with European countries, the gradual

[66] On the nature and problems that have arisen from these savings clauses, see Fitzgerald (2001, pp. 113–26), cited in Hood and Hoyle (2008, p. 104). See the excellent discussion along these lines in Burnham (2005); see also the forceful article by the Honorable Justice Desiree Bernard (2008).

opening up of the subject to research, and the signing, although not yet the ratification, of the ICCPR. While Chinese political leaders still strongly defend capital punishment as an essential tool to fight crime and preserve social order in a country of 1.3 billion that is undergoing wrenching economic and social changes, it appears that they are becoming increasingly uncomfortable that it is applied too readily and, apparently, in an arbitrary way. Cases of innocent persons being sentenced to death have been uncovered and widely discussed. Reform of the death penalty would be in step with President Hu Jintao's commitment to "build a harmonious society."[67] As Zhao Bingzhi of Beijing Normal University, has put it, "In a word, with the development of economy and society, and the better conditions of public security, the Chinese People show a more reasonable attitude towards the death penalty. They claim more eagerly that the judicial authority [should] apply the death penalty correctly" (2007, p. 163).

Indeed, Zhao claims that the former policy of "severe striking" had not reduced crime but had reduced "the standards of the death penalty." In line with the "Decision on the Construction of a Socialist Harmonious Society" in 2006 by the Sixteenth Central Committee of the Chinese Communist Party, criminal policy aims to "combine punishment with leniency" (Zhao 2007; see also Trevaskes 2008). Now that China has signed the ICCPR (1998) and is preparing to ratify it, Zhao and other scholars are pressing for China to make provisions in its domestic law so that it comes into line with international human rights standards, especially as regards greatly improving pretrial and trial procedures and limiting the scope of capital punishment, pending complete abolition, as required by article 6, section 2. Abolition of the death penalty for all economic crimes is now being openly discussed, and a book of essays entitled *The Road of the Abolition of the Death Penalty in China*, as a signifier of the final goal, was published in Beijing by Chinese People's Public Security University Press in 2004 (Zhao 2004).

In order to ensure more uniformity in the imposition of the ultimate sanction and to reserve its infliction for only the most serious crimes, the Supreme People's Court decided in 2004 that, in the future, it would review all death penalty cases itself (thus returning the legal

---

[67] David Lague, "China Acts to Reduce High Rate of Executions," Amnesty International Death Penalty Information Blog, November 2, 2006, http://deathpenaltyinformation .blogspot.com/2006_11_01_archive.html.

position to where it had been before 1983, when the power was de-
volved to the provincial high courts). The new review system came
into effect on January 1, 2007, with an order that execution should be
reserved for "an extremely small number of serious offenders" and that
the death penalty should not be imposed in certain cases of crimes of
passion, crimes associated with family disputes, and economic crimes
(*BBC News* 2007). Chief Justice Xiao Yang, president of the Supreme
People's Court, stated that as few executions as possible should be
carried out and as cautiously as possible, in order to avoid wrongful
executions. One cannot judge objectively how this policy is affecting
the number of death sentences imposed and executions carried out
because such data are still classified as a national secret. But already by
June 2007 it was claimed that the number of executions ordered by
two courts in Beijing had been reduced by 10 percent (Yardley 2007),
and by August 2007 the authorities were claiming that the number of
death sentences upheld by the Supreme People's Court had already
been reduced by some 20 percent.

The most definitive recent statement on China's position on the
death penalty was made (as a right of reply) at the UN Human Rights
Council, at the fourth session in March 2007. La Yifan stated that
"China was a country with a rule of law, where the death penalty only
applied to the worst crimes, and this was in agreement with the
ICCPR. The death penalty's scope of application was to be reviewed
shortly, and it was expected that this scope would be reduced, with the
final aim of abolishment" (Human Rights Council 2007, p. 9). No one
can tell how quickly and by what steps China will move toward abolition, but it cannot be denied that the process has begun.

As far as the other actively retentionist countries in Asia are concerned, Taiwan appears to be well on the road toward abolition. It may
be too that political change in Thailand, where there have been no
executions since the new constitution of 2007, will lead this predominantly Buddhist country toward abolition. Vietnam, like China, has
entered into dialogues with the European Union on the scope of capital punishment, and it is indicative of a more open mind on the issue,
despite the secrecy that surrounds data on executions, that Vietnam
chose to abstain from the UN vote on the moratorium resolution in
December 2007. The Japanese government continues to protest that
capital punishment is a matter for its own sovereignty and that it is an
issue of criminal justice, not human rights. Nevertheless, abolition is

being openly debated, and the Japan Federation of Bar Associations, along with an anti–death penalty organization known as Forum 90, has brought many human rights abuses associated with the secretive administration of capital punishment to the attention of the Japanese public and parliament. The fact that the relatively small annual number of executions varies according to the willingness of different ministers of justice to sign execution orders shows how contentious a subject capital punishment has become in Japan (see, generally, Johnson [2006, p. 263]). In our judgment, Japan will change its policy before many years have passed. North Korea may well be affected by South Korea's new status as an abolitionist de facto nation that is moving clearly in the direction of de jure abolition.[68] In Malaysia, too, there are signs of change. In 2006 the Malaysian Bar Association called for the abolition of the death penalty, and the Malaysian cabinet minister in charge of law was reported as saying: "I welcome the proposal. For me, a life is a life. No one has the right to take someone else's life, even if that person has taken another life."[69]

As mentioned already, Belarus is the only European country to retain the death penalty and to carry out executions. The fact that it abstained on the moratorium resolution at the United Nations and has aspirations to join the Council of Europe indicates that it will probably not be long before capital punishment, already much restricted, is abandoned altogether (Vasilevich and Sarkisova 2006).

In the Americas, two of the last three actively retentionist countries are moving toward abolition. There have been no executions in Cuba since 2003, and Cuba abstained from voting on the recent moratorium resolution at the United Nations. Both the president and secretary of state for human rights of Guatemala, where no executions have taken place since 2000, have spoken out strongly in favor of abolition. Furthermore, the Constitutional Court declared in 2000 that in matters of human rights, international law prevails over national legislation, and in 2004 the Supreme Court proposed a new penal code without capital punishment. Such proposals have yet to find favor with the

---

[68] On October 3, 2008, the *Korea Times* reported that a provincial court (the Gwangju High Court) had filed a petition with the Constitutional Court on behalf of a person convicted of homicide, challenging the constitutionality of the current law legalizing capital punishment. See Si-soo (2008).

[69] "Justice Minister Backs Abolition of Death Penalty," *AsiaNews.it*, March 21, 2006, http://www.asianews.it/index.php?l = en&art = 5693&size = A.

Guatemala Congress, but it remains highly probable that capital punishment will be abolished in the not too distant future.

The United States has not embraced the aspiration, embodied in article 6 of the ICCPR and in UN resolutions, to abolish the death penalty in due course. The persistence of capital punishment in the United States, a country that proudly champions democratic values, human rights, and political freedom, has become, in our opinion, one of the greatest obstacles to the acceptance by other retentionist countries that capital punishment inherently and inevitably violates human rights. So what prospects are there that the United States will abandon capital punishment?

The government of the United States made its position clear in 2005 in its response to the UN Seventh Quinquennial Survey on capital punishment and the implementation of the safeguards for those facing the death penalty: "When administered in accordance with all the aforementioned safeguards, the death penalty does not violate international law. Capital punishment is not prohibited by customary international law or by any treaty provisions under which the United States is currently obligated. . . . We believe that in democratic societies the criminal justice system—including the punishment prescribed for the most serious and aggravated crimes—should reflect the will of the people freely expressed and appropriately implemented through their elected representatives" (United Nations 2005, para. 17).

Similarly, an article by two senior lawyers from the U.S. Department of Justice (Margaret Griffey and Laurence Rothenberg), written for the Organization for Security and Co-operation in Europe (OSCE) publication *The Death Penalty in the OSCE Area, 2006*, brushed aside criticisms relating to "alleged racial disparities," conviction of the innocent, inadequate representation, and the "death row phenomenon." It concluded: "Despite criticism of its justness and accuracy, public support for the death penalty in the United States remains high. Proponents and supporters cite its retributive and deterrent values as both morally required and practically necessary to ensure a safe society. Its application is subject to constitutional constraints and has been tested many times in court, leading to a complex jurisprudence that serves to protect defendants' rights while also enforcing the desire of the American public for just criminal punishment" (OSCE 2006, p. 44).

The negative attitude of the U.S. government toward international human rights treaties that have sought to limit the use of capital punishment and the hesitant approach of the Supreme Court toward claims based on international human rights norms have been major barriers to change. For example, in its report to the UN Committee Against Torture, the U.S. government claimed that it was not obliged to report on the use of the death penalty because the United States had made a condition of its ratification the proposition that the United States was bound only to article 16 of the UN Convention Against Torture, to the extent that the definition of "cruel, inhuman or degrading treatment or punishment" matches the "cruel and unusual punishment" prohibited by the U.S. Constitution as interpreted by the U.S. Supreme Court. The United States also registered an "understanding" that the convention did not "restrict or prohibit the United States from applying the death penalty consistent [with the Constitution], including any constitutional period of confinement prior to the imposition of the death penalty" ("United States' Response to the Questions Asked by the Committee Against Torture," Geneva, May 8, 2006). Given the extraordinarily long periods of time that inmates in the United States spend on death row before execution—an average of 12 years and sometimes more than 20 years—when compared with the limit of 5 years set by the Judicial Committee of the Privy Council (see above in this section), the failure of the U.S. Supreme Court to deal decisively with this issue is another example of its distance from developing international norms.[70] The importance of this issue was underlined when, in September 2008, Jack Alderman, a model inmate who had been convicted of the murder of his wife—of which he had maintained his innocence—was executed by the State of Georgia, having been denied clemency, after 33 years on death row.[71]

It should also be noted that although the United States signed the American Convention on Human Rights in 1977, it has never ratified and acceded to it and is therefore not subject to the jurisdiction of the Inter-American Court of Human Rights. Nevertheless, as Richard Wilson has pointed out (2003, pp. 154–55), under the American Declaration on the Rights and Duties of Man, the Inter-American Com-

[70] See Hood and Hoyle (2008, pp. 180–83). It should be noted that Justice Breyer, in the cases of Elledge v. Florida in 1998 and Knight v. Florida and Moore v. Nebraska in 1999, all of them involving "astonishing delays," stated that "the claim that time has rendered the execution inhuman is a particularly strong one."

[71] By comparison, his codefendant, who had admitted being party to the murder but who pleaded guilty and gave evidence against Alderman, was paroled after 12 years of imprisonment by the Georgia Parole Board, which later denied Alderman clemency.

mission on Human Rights can hear individual complaints against the United States. Yet the American government has categorically refused to accept that the findings and recommendations of the commission have any legal force. For example, in 2001, it refused to comply with a call from the commission to commute the death sentence imposed on Juan Raul Garza under federal law, on the grounds that he had been denied a fair trial. Garza was executed on June 19, 2001.

Furthermore, the U.S. Supreme Court has not halted the executions of several foreign citizens who had not been informed of their right to consular assistance, despite the fact that the United States had ratified the Vienna Convention on Consular Rights in 1969 and in defiance of an order by the International Court of Justice (ICJ) that a stay of execution be granted. Angel Breard, a citizen of Paraguay, was executed by the State of Virginia in 1998 despite a strongly worded appeal to the governor by Madeleine Albright, the U.S. secretary of state, which emphasized that the execution of Breard in the face of the order from the ICJ "could be seen as a denial by the United States of the significance of international law and the Court's processes in international relations." Similarly, in 1999, Walter LaGrand, a German citizen, was executed by the State of Arizona in defiance of an order from the ICJ not to do so pending a final decision by the ICJ. The latest instance concerned Jose Ernesto Medellin, who was executed by the State of Texas on August 5, 2008. Medellin was one of 51 Mexicans whom the ICJ found—in *Avena and Other Mexican Nationals (Mexico v. USA)*— had not been informed of their right to have their consulate informed of their detention (2004 ICJ 128, March 31, 2004, International Court of Justice, General List No. 128). In 2004, the ICJ had ruled that the United States was obliged to reconsider the sentences of these Mexican nationals and to take into account this violation of their rights. In February 2005, President George W. Bush directed state courts to hear the cases of all Mexicans nationals—57 of them—under sentence of death to decide whether "actual prejudice" had occurred. In Medellin's case, Texas declined to accept the authority of the ICJ and challenged the right of the U.S. president to deliver an executive order to the state. The Supreme Court, by a majority on two occasions, held that without an act of Congress giving the federal government power to enforce orders of the ICJ, the president did not have the power to intervene, and the Court refused to order a stay of execution on the grounds that the possibility that legislation would be passed by either

Congress or the Texas legislature to provide a remedy for the treaty violation in this case was "too remote" to justify delaying the execution.[72] These cases have undoubtedly harmed America's reputation in the international sphere as regards its commitment to its treaty obligations, especially when seen in the light of the fact that, in March 2005, the United States withdrew from the Optional Protocol to the Vienna Convention so that, in the future, it would no longer be subject to adjudications under the treaty by the ICJ. Furthermore, it has emphasized the autonomy of the individual states as regards their policy on capital punishment.

Abolitionists therefore deemed it to be of great significance when the majority of the Supreme Court, in *Atkins v. Virginia* (536 U.S. 304 [2002]), cited worldwide condemnation of the execution of mentally retarded (to use the American phrase) defendants, as laid down in the UN *Safeguards*, among its reasons for deciding that such executions would now be declared "cruel and unusual punishment." In 2005, a 5–4 majority of the Court again referred to international opinion and practice in *Roper v. Simmons* (543 U.S. 551 [2005]) as providing "respected and significant confirmation of the Court's determination that the [death] penalty is disproportionate punishment for offenders under 18" at the time of the commission of the crime. In both of these cases, the Court had received amici curiae briefs from the European Union and other organizations representing the international community, as well as from former U.S. diplomats, in support of the petitioners (see Sec. VI).

To what extent the Supreme Court will build on these judgments as capital punishment comes under more and more critical scrutiny in the United States remains to be seen. It will depend on where the balance will tip between those like Justices Breyer and Ginsburg, who believe that international norms are relevant to U.S. law in assessing "evolving standards of decency," and those who side with Chief Justice Roberts and Justice Scalia, who believe that international norms are not at all relevant.[73] In the meantime, international criticism has continued un-

---

[72] On the *Medellin* case, see "Medellin Executed as Court Refuses Delay," Supreme Court of the United States Blog, August 5, 2008, http://www.scotusblog.com/wp/final-filings-in-medellin. More generally on the *Breard*, *LaGrand*, and *Avena* cases, see Hood and Hoyle (2008, pp. 233–35).

[73] See the reports of the testimony of Justice Alito before the Senate Judiciary Committee on his nomination. He declared, "I don't think it appropriate or useful to look at foreign law in interpreting the provisions of the Constitution. I think the framers would be stunned by the idea that the Bill of Rights is to be interpreted by taking a poll of

abated. Thus in July 2006, when considering the report by the United States under article 40 of the ICCPR, the UN Human Rights Committee included in its observations a statement calling for a moratorium to be placed on capital sentences, "bearing in mind the desirability of abolishing the death penalty." It criticized the United States for expanding the scope of capital punishment and urged a review of federal and state legislation so as to restrict the number of crimes carrying the death penalty. It also expressed concern that studies had shown that "the death penalty may be imposed disproportionately on ethnic minorities as well as on low income groups, a problem which does not appear to be fully acknowledged" (UN Human Rights Committee, 87th sess., July 10–28, 2006, CCPR/c/USA/co/3/Rev.1, para. 29, p. 9).

Those who continue to support the death penalty in the United States obviously hope that the reforms emanating from the various state commissions set up to examine the administration of capital punishment will tighten the system sufficiently, so that citizens will come once again to believe that only the most egregious and clearly guilty criminals are executed—especially if DNA evidence becomes statutorily available to inmates to help at least some of them establish their innocence. Yet given the evidence of the low incidence of the death penalty's use in all but a handful of southern states—where, as Carol and Jordan Steiker put it, "the legal process that follows the return of a death sentence is far more likely to be nasty, brutish and short" (Steiker and Steiker 2006, p. 1915)—the concerns about the possibility of error, the impossibility of extinguishing all possibility of arbitrariness and discrimination, the excessive and costly delays in the administration of capital punishment, and the cruelty inherent in the death row phenomenon, it seems more likely that more states will follow the example of New Jersey in 2007 and abolish it altogether. It then might wither away, leaving a few outliers and maybe in the end only Texas as an executing state.[74]

---

countries of the world." This statement was quoted and strongly criticized by F. G. Rohatyn (2006), former U.S. ambassador to France.

[74] Note that 14 of the 35 states that retained the death penalty on June 6, 2009, had executed no more than six people since 1976—at most, one person every 4 or 5 years, and in most of these states there had been much longer periods between executions—and two had executed no one. Since 1976, 81 percent of all executions have been carried out in just nine states: Texas, Virginia, Oklahoma, Missouri, North Carolina, South Carolina, Georgia, Alabama, and Florida, and 38 percent have been carried out in Texas alone (see Death Penalty Information Center, "Executions in the United States, 1608–1976, by State," http://deathpenaltyinfo.org/executions-united-states-1608-1976-state). The re-

As Franklin Zimring has opined, "The endgame in the effort to purge the United States of the death penalty has already been launched" (2003, p. 205; see also Sunby 2006). It may not be many years before the Supreme Court is able to find that the majority of states do not enforce the death penalty and, as in other nations with which the United States shares common values, "the emerging standards of decency that mark the progress of a nation" no longer tolerate the use of such an inhuman and degrading punishment in the United States (see *Weems v. United States*, 217 U.S. 349, 378 [1910]; *Trop v. Dulles*, 356 U.S. 86, 101 [1958]).

However, it should be recognized that the same considerations have, so far, not been applied to the common alternative to capital punishment in the United States, namely, imprisonment for life without the prospect of parole (LWOP), a penalty that was held to be constitutional by the U.S. Supreme Court in *Schick v. Reed* (419 U.S. 256, 267 [1974]). In all death penalty states, LWOP is now available as a discretionary sentence to the judge or jury considering whether or not to impose a death sentence, and in some of these states, such as Kansas, every defendant who is eligible for the death penalty but is not executed must be given LWOP (*Harvard Law Review* 2006). Furthermore, in six states, all life sentences are imposed without the possibility of parole, and seven states have more than 1,000 prisoners serving LWOP sentences. Given the small proportion of death-eligible defendants who are sentenced to death in America, the substitution of LWOP for all or even the majority of death-eligible prisoners would mean that not only the few who would have been sentenced to death but also a much larger number who would not have been because of strong mitigating circumstances would all be treated equally harshly.[75]

While some abolitionists have shied away from recommending LWOP as a replacement for capital punishment, considering it to be just as offensive to human dignity, others have seen it as a political

---

port of the California Commission on the Fair Administration of Justice (2008) described the death penalty system as "dysfunctional." It is also remarkable to foreign observers that it put forward recommendations that it hoped "would enable California to achieve the national average of a twelve year delay between pronouncement of sentence and the completion of all judicial review of the sentence" (p. 5). Contrast this with the judgment of the Judicial Committee of the Privy Council that a period longer than 5 years would be inhuman and degrading punishment.

[75] For an excellent discussion of the issues involved, see Appleton and Bent (2007); for a much fuller treatment of our views on this issue, see Hood and Hoyle (2008, chap. 11).

necessity if the public is to accept the abolition of capital punishment. However, all the evidence suggests that to replace the death penalty with a mandatory sentence of LWOP is unnecessary, is liable to punish too severely people who formerly would not have been sentenced to death and executed, and is arbitrary in its infliction of the same punishment on persons whose crimes and punishments should be individually assessed. A sentence that forecloses any future decision as to the character and dangerousness of the person punished and therefore extinguishes all hope is as inhumane as the death penalty, especially when it is mandatorily applied. It is clear to many campaigners for the abolition of capital punishment that to replace it with lifetime imprisonment without any possibility of release is to replace one human rights abuse—the lack of respect for the dignity of the individual through the application of an inhumane, repressive, and tortuous punishment—with another.

IX. Conclusion

The recognition of the death penalty as a human rights issue, combined with the development of international human rights law and the political weight that has been given to the campaign led by European institutions to get rid of capital punishment completely, is the main explanation for the surge in abolition over the past quarter of a century. This does not mean, of course, that all countries have followed the same route (as shown in the examples already given), and, certainly, there are no instances in which it was initially achieved by popular consensus or the demand of the masses, although a consensus might emerge postabolition, as was the case in Ireland (Schabas 2004b, p. 444). Abolition after the late 1980s came about everywhere through political and/or judicial leaders, sometimes aided by local pressure groups, who accepted the ideological premises of the international human rights movement.

This essay has shown that, with very few exceptions, those countries that still retain capital punishment have come to accept a good deal of the human rights case against the death penalty—namely, that it may be inflicted in only the very worst of cases and only then subject to the highest standard of safeguards to avoid wrongful conviction. It is not a large step from there to accept that, in practice, no system can ensure this, that human rights are inevitably in danger of being breached when capital punishment is enforced, and that the right to life is better protected if states declare the execution of prisoners to be no longer acceptable.

APPENDIX

TABLE A1

Countries and Territories That Abolished Capital Punishment between January 1, 1989, and January 1, 2008

Country	Year of Abolition		Abolitionist De Facto*
	All Offenses	Ordinary Offenses	
Cambodia	1989	. . .	No
New Zealand	1989	1961	Yes
Romania	1989	. . .	No
Slovenia	1989	. . .	Yes
Andorra	1990	. . .	Yes
Croatia	1990	. . .	No
Czech Republic	1990	. . .	No
Hungary	1990	. . .	No
Ireland	1990	. . .	Yes
Mozambique	1990	. . .	No
Namibia	1990	. . .	No
São Tomé and Príncipe	1990	. . .	Yes
Slovakia	1990	. . .	No
Macedonia (former Yugoslavia)	1991	. . .	No
Angola	1992	. . .	No
Paraguay	1992	. . .	Yes
Switzerland	1992	1942	No
Guinea-Bissau	1993	. . .	No
Seychelles	1993	1979	No
Italy	1994	1947	No
Palau	1994	. . .	No
Djibouti	1995	. . .	Yes
Mauritius	1995	. . .	No
Moldova	1995	. . .	No
Spain	1995	1978	No
Belgium	1996	. . .	Yes
Bolivia	1997	1995	Yes
Georgia	1997	. . .	No
Nepal	1997	1990	Yes
Poland	1997	. . .	No
South Africa	1997	1995	No
Azerbaijan	1998	. . .	No
Bulgaria	1998	. . .	No
Canada	1998	1976	Yes
Estonia	1998	. . .	No
Lithuania	1998	. . .	No
United Kingdom	1998	1965	No
Timor-Leste	1999	. . .	No

TABLE A1 (*Continued*)

Country	Year of Abolition All Offenses	Ordinary Offenses	Abolitionist De Facto*
Latvia	. . .	1999	No
Turkmenistan	1999	. . .	No
Ukraine	1999	. . .	No
Côte d'Ivoire	2000	. . .	Yes
Malta	2000	1971	Yes
Bosnia-Herzegovina	2001	1997	No
Chile	. . .	2001	Yes
Cyprus	2002	1983	Yes
Serbia-Montenegro†	2002	2001	Yes
Armenia	2003	. . .	Yes
Greece	2004	1993	Yes
Turkey	2004	2002	Yes
Bhutan	2004	. . .	Yes
Samoa	2004	. . .	Yes
Senegal	2004	. . .	Yes
Liberia	2005	. . .	Yes
Mexico	2005	. . .	Yes
Philippines	2006	. . .	No
Albania	2007	2000	No
Rwanda	2007	. . .	No
Kazakhstan	. . .	2007	No
Kyrgyzstan	2007	. . .	No
Uzbekistan	2008	. . .	No

SOURCE.—Amnesty International documents.

NOTE.—This table lists a total of 61 countries—58 that have abolished capital punishment for all crimes and three that have done so for ordinary crimes only. Of the 58 countries, nine had already abolished the death penalty for ordinary offenses before 1989: Canada, Cyprus, Italy, Malta, New Zealand, Seychelles, Spain, Switzerland, and the United Kingdom. For an update, see n. 1.

* Last execution at least 10 years prior to first abolition.

† Montenegro became independent in 2006.

TABLE A2

Votes of 49 Actively Retentionist and 12 Suspended Retentionist Countries on the UN Resolution for a Worldwide Moratorium on Executions, Leading to Abolition of the Death Penalty (December 2007)

Decision	Muslim Majority	Non-Muslim-Majority Commonwealth	Non-Muslim Majority and Non-Commonwealth				Total
			Asia	Africa	Americas	Europe	
Against	Afghanistan, Bahrain, Bangladesh,* Chad, Egypt, Indonesia, Iran, Iraq, Jordan, Kuwait, Libya, Malaysia,* Nigeria (north),* Oman, Pakistan, Qatar, Saudi Arabia, Somalia, Sudan, Syria, Yemen, Comoros*†	Antigua and Barbuda,† Bahamas,† Barbados,† Belize,† Botswana, Dominica,† Guyana,† India,† Jamaica,† Singapore, St. Kitts and Nevis, St. Lucia,† St. Vincent and the Grenadines,† Trinidad and Tobago, Uganda	China, Japan, North Korea, Mongolia, Thailand	Ethiopia, Zimbabwe	United States	. . .	45
Abstained	Guinea, Lebanon, Sierra Leone,* United Arab Emirates	Cameroon,† Lesotho†	Vietnam	Democratic Republic of the Congo, Equatorial Guinea	Cuba	Belarus	11
In favor	Tajikistan†	. . .	. . .	Burundi	Guatemala	. . .	3
No vote	Palestine Authority	. . .	Taiwan	. . .	. . .	. . .	2
Total	28	17	7	5	3	1	61

* Commonwealth countries.
† Countries that had had no executions for 10 years and had been classified as suspended retentionist.

REFERENCES

Amnesty International. 2001. *United States of America: No Return to Execution; The US Death Penalty as a Barrier to Extradition*. Index no. AMR 51/171/ 2001. London: Amnesty International Publications.

————. 2006. *Amnesty International Report, 2006: The State of the World's Human Rights*. London: Amnesty International Publications.

————. 2008. *Lethal Lottery: The Death Penalty in India; A Study of Supreme Court Judgments in Death Penalty Cases, 1950–2006*. Index no. ASA 20/006/ 2008. London: Amnesty International Publications.

Ancel, Marc. 1962a. *Capital Punishment*. UN Doc. ST/SOA/SD/9. New York: United Nations.

————. 1962b. *The Death Penalty in European Countries*. Strasbourg: Council of Europe.

Appleton, Catherine, and Grøver Bent. 2007. "The Pros and Cons of Life without Parole." *British Journal of Criminology* 47:597–615.

Bae, Sangmin. 2007. *When the State No Longer Kills: International Human Rights Norms and Abolition of Capital Punishment*. Albany: SUNY Press.

Bassouini, M. Cherif. 2004. "Death as a Penalty in the Shari'a." In *Capital Punishment: Strategies for Abolition*, edited by Peter Hodgkinson and William Schabas. Cambridge: Cambridge University Press.

BBC News. 2007. "China to Reduce Death Penalty Use." September 14. http:// news.bbc.co.uk/2/hi/asia-pacific/6994673.stm.

Bernard, Desiree. 2008. "Human Rights and the Caribbean Commonwealth." *Commonwealth Lawyer* 17(1):27–32.

Burnham, Margaret A. 2005. "Indigenous Constitutionalism and the Death Penalty: The Case of the Commonwealth Caribbean." *International Journal of Constitutional Law* 3(4):582–616.

California Commission on the Fair Administration of Justice. 2008. "Report and Recommendations on the Administration of the Death Penalty in California." Report, June 30.

Council of Europe. 1999. "Compliance with Member States Commitments." Unpublished Report no. AS/Inf. 2. Strasbourg: Council of Europe.

————. 2007. *Death Is Not Justice: The Council of Europe and the Death Penalty*. Strasbourg: Council of Europe.

Dobryninas, Alexandras. 2004. "The Experience of Lithuania's Journey to Abolition." In *Capital Punishment: Strategies for Abolition*, edited by Peter Hodgkinson and William A. Schabas. Cambridge: Cambridge University Press.

Fathi, Nazila. 2007. "Executions Are Under Way in Iran for Adultery and Other Violations." *New York Times*, July 11. http://www.nytimes.com/2007/ 07/11/world/middleeast/11iran.html.

Fitzgerald, Edward. 2001. "Savings Clauses and the Colonial Death Penalty Regime." In *Commonwealth Caribbean Human Rights Seminar*. London: Simons, Muirhead & Burton.

Girling, Evi. 2005. "European Identity and the Mission against the Death Penalty in the United States." In *The Cultural Lives of Capital Punishment:*

Comparative Perspectives, edited by A. Sarat and C. Boulanger. Stanford, CA: Stanford University Press.

Gliszczyńska, Aleksandra, Katarzyna Sekowska, and Roman Wieruszewski. 2006. "The Abolition of the Death Penalty in Poland." In *The Death Penalty in the OSCE Area: OSCE Background Paper, 2006*. Warsaw: Office for Democratic Institutions and Human Rights (ODIHR).

Gorchs-Chacou, Franck, and Caroline Sculier. 2008. *The Death Penalty in the Great Lakes Region of Africa*. Montrouge, France: World Coalition Against the Death Penalty. http://www.worldcoalition.org/modules/wfdownloads/singlefile.php?cid=29&lid=128.

Governor's Council on Capital Punishment. 2005. "Report of the Governor's Council on Capital Punishment: Introduction." *Indiana Law Journal* 80:1–27.

Greenberg, David E., and Valerie West. 2008. "Siting the Death Penalty Internationally." *Law and Social Inquiry* 33(2):295–343.

Harvard Law Review. 2006. "A Matter of Life and Death: The Effect of Life-without-Parole Statutes on Capital Punishment." 119:1838–45.

Holovatiy, Serhiy. 1999. "Abolishing the Death Penalty in Ukraine: Difficulties Real or Imagined?" In *The Death Penalty: Abolition in Europe*. Strasbourg: Council of Europe.

Hood, Roger. 2002. *The Death Penalty: A Worldwide Perspective*. 3rd ed. Oxford: Oxford University Press.

Hood, Roger, and Carolyn Hoyle. 2008. *The Death Penalty: A Worldwide Perspective*. 4th ed. Oxford: Oxford University Press.

Human Rights Council. 2007. "Human Rights Council Opens Fourth Session." News release, March 12. United Nations, Geneva.

Illinois Commission on Capital Punishment. 2002. "Report of the Governor's Commission on Capital Punishment." Report submitted to Governor George H. Ryan, State of Illinois, April.

Johnson, David T. 2006. "When the State Kills in Secret: Capital Punishment in Japan." *Punishment and Society* 8:252–85.

Kampala Civil Society. 2008. *Realising People's Potential: The Kampala Civil Society Statement to the 2007 Commonwealth Heads of Government Meeting, November 2007*. London: Commonwealth Foundation.

Khamidov, Khalifaboro. 2006. "International Experience and Legal Regulation of the Application of the Death Penalty in Tajikistan." In *The Death Penalty in the OSCE Area: OSCE Background Paper, 2006*. Warsaw: ODIHR.

Koh, Harold H. 2002. "Paying 'Decent Respect' to World Opinion on the Death Penalty." *UC Davis Law Review* 35:1085–1113.

Lehrfreund, Saul. 2001. "International Legal Trends and the 'Mandatory' Death Penalty in the Commonwealth Caribbean." *Oxford University Commonwealth Law Journal* 1:171–94.

Neumayer, Eric. 2008. "Death Penalty: The Political Foundations of the Global Trend towards Abolition." *Human Rights Review* 9:241–68.

New Jersey Death Penalty Study Commission. 2007. "New Jersey Death Penalty Study Commission Report." Final report submitted to the State of New Jersey, January 2.

Nowak, Manfred. 2000. "Is the Death Penalty an Inhuman Punishment?" In *The Jurisprudence of Human Rights Law: A Comparative Interpretive Approach*, edited by T. S. Orlin, A. Rosas, and M. Scheinin. Turku, Finland: Abo Akademi University Institute of Human Rights.

Oldfield, Jackson. 2007. *The Death Penalty in the Arab World, 2007: ACHRS Second Annual Report.* Amman, Jordan: Amman Center for Human Rights Studies.

OSCE (Organization for Security and Co-operation in Europe). 1999. *The Death Penalty in the OSCE Area: A Survey, January 1998–June 1999.* Review Conference, September 1999, Background Paper 1999/1. Warsaw: ODIHR.

———. 2006. *The Death Penalty in the OSCE Area: Background Paper, 2006.* Warsaw: ODIHR.

———. 2008. *The Death Penalty in the OSCE Area: Background Paper, 2008.* Warsaw: ODIHR.

Parsons, Claudia. 2007. "EU under Fire during U.N. Death Penalty Debate." Reuters, November 14. http://www.reuters.com/article/worldNews/idUSN1423839620071114.

Patten, Chris. 2001. "First World Congress Against the Death Penalty: Intervention at the Council of Europe, on behalf of Chris Patten, delivered by Angel Viñas, Director for Multilateral Relations and Human Rights at DG Relex, European Commission." Speech to the First World Congress Against the Death Penalty, European Commission, Strasbourg, June 21. http://www.eurunion.org/eu/index.php?option=com_content&task=view&id=1783.

Peshkopia, Ridvan, and Arben Imami. 2008. "Between Elite Compliance and State Socialisation: The Abolition of the Death Penalty in Eastern Europe." *International Journal of Human Rights* 12(3):353–72.

Radzinowicz, Leon. 1999. *Adventures in Criminology.* London: Routledge.

Rodley, Nigel. 2004. "The United Nation's Work in the Field of the Death Penalty." In *Death Penalty: Beyond Abolition.* Strasbourg: Council of Europe.

Rohatyn, Felix G. 2001. "America's Deadly Image." *Washington Post*, February 20.

———. 2006. "Dead to the World." *New York Times*, January 26.

Schabas, William A. 1993. "Note on *Kindler v. Canada (Minister of Justice)*." *American Journal of International Law* 87:128–33.

———. 1994. "Soering's Legacy: The Human Rights Committee and the Judicial Committee of the Privy Council Take a Walk Down Death Row." *International and Comparative Law Quarterly* 43:913–23.

———. 2001. "From *Kindler* to *Burns*: International Law Is Nourishing the Constitutional Living Tree." Paper presented at the Conference on Capital Punishment and International Human Rights Law, Galway, Ireland, September 20.

———. 2002. *The Abolition of the Death Penalty in International Law.* 3rd ed. Cambridge: Cambridge University Press.

———. 2004a. "International Law and the Death Penalty: Reflecting or Promoting Change?" In *Capital Punishment: Strategies for Abolition*, edited by

Peter Hodgkinson and William Schabas. Cambridge: Cambridge University Press.

———. 2004*b*. "International Law, Politics, Diplomacy and the Abolition of the Death Penalty." *William and Mary Bill of Rights Journal* 13:417–44.

Si-soo, Park. 2008. "Constitutionality of Death Penalty to Be Reviewed." *Korea Times*, October 3. http://www.koreatimes.co.kr/www/news/nation/2008/10/117_32131.html.

Steiker, Carol S., and Jordan Steiker. 2006. "A Tale of Two Nations: Incidence of Executions in 'Executing' versus 'Symbolic' States in the United States." *Texas Law Review* 84:1869–1927.

Sunby, Scott E. 2006. "The Death Penalty's Future: Charting the Crosscurrents of Declining Death Sentences and the McVeigh Factor." *Texas Law Review* 84:1929–72.

Taiwan Ministry of Justice. 2007. "Taiwan's Policy of Gradual Abrogation of Capital Punishment and State of Implementation." Taipei, October 22.

Trevaskes, Susan. 2007. "Severe and Swift Justice in China." *British Journal of Criminology* 47(1):23–41.

———. 2008. "The Death Penalty in China Today: Kill Fewer, Kill Cautiously." *Asian Survey* 48(3):393–413.

United Nations. 1990. *Report of the Eighth United Nations Congress on the Prevention of Crime and the Treatment of Offenders: Havana, 27 August–7 September 1990.* UN Doc. A/Conf. 144/28, October 5. New York: United Nations.

———. 2000. *Interim Report of the Special Rapporteur on Extrajudicial, Summary or Arbitrary Executions.* UN Doc. A/55/288. Report to UN General Assembly, 55th sess., August 23.

———. 2005. *Capital Punishment and Implementation of the Safeguards Guaranteeing Protection of the Rights of Those Facing the Death Penalty: Report of the Secretary-General* (also known as the UN Seventh Quinquennial Survey on Capital Punishment). UN Doc. E/2005/3. New York: United Nations Economic and Social Council.

———. 2007. *Civil and Political Rights, Including the Questions of Disappearances and Summary Executions: Report of the Special Rapporteur on Extrajudicial, Summary or Arbitrary Executions, Philip Alston.* UN Doc. A/HRC/4/20. Report to UN Human Rights Council, 4th sess., January 29.

UN General Assembly. 2007. "General Assembly Adopts Landmark Text Calling for Moratorium on Death Penalty." UN Doc. GA/10678. News release, December 18. United Nations, New York. http://www.un.org/News/Press/docs/2007/ga10678.doc.htm.

Usigbe, Leon. 2008. "Nigeria: Reps Seek End to Death Penalty." *Vanguard* (Lagos), June 1. http://allafrica.com/stories/200806020004.html.

Vasilevich, Gregory A., and Elissa A. Sarkisova. 2006. "Prospects for the Abolition of the Death Penalty in the Republic of Belarus." In *The Death Penalty in the OSCE Area: Background Paper, 2006.* Warsaw: ODIHR.

Wagner, John, and Ovetta Wiggins. 2007. "O'Malley Seeks End to Md. Executions: Death Penalty Repeal Splits Assembly." *Washington Post*, February 22.

Warren, Mark. 2004. "Death, Dissent and Diplomacy: The U.S. Death Penalty as an Obstacle to Foreign Relations." *William and Mary Bill of Rights Journal* 13:309–37.

White, B. 2008. "Commission Votes to Abolish Death Penalty in Md." Associated Press, November 13.

Wilson, Richard J. 2003. "The Influence of International Law and Practice on the Death Penalty in the United States." In *America's Experiment with Capital Punishment*, edited by James R. Acker, Robert M. Bohm, and Charles S. Lanier. 2nd ed. Durham, NC: Carolina Academic Press.

Wohlwend, Renate. 1999. "The Efforts of the Parliamentary Assembly of the Council of Europe." In *The Death Penalty: Abolition in Europe*. Strasbourg: Council of Europe.

Yardley, Jim. 2007. "With New Law, China Reports Drop in Executions." *New York Times*, June 9.

Yorke, Jon. 2006. "The Evolving European Union Strategy against the Death Penalty: From Internal Renunciation to Global Ideology—Part 1." *Amicus Journal* 16:23–28.

———. 2007. "The Evolving European Union Strategy against the Death Penalty: From Internal Renunciation to a Global Ideology—Part 2." *Amicus Journal* 17:26–33.

Zhao Bingzhi. 2004. *The Road of the Abolition of the Death Penalty in China: Regarding the Abolition of the Non-violent Crime at the Present Stage*. Series of Criminal Jurisprudence, vol. 44. Beijing: Chinese People's Public Security University Press.

———. 2007. "Existing State and Prospect of Death Penalty Reform in China at Present Time." Working paper presented at "Moving the Debate Forward: China's Use of the Death Penalty," Launch Seminar of the China-EU Project. College for Criminal Law Science of Beijing Normal University and Great Britain–China Centre, Beijing, June 20–21.

Zimring, Franklin E. 2003. *The Contradictions of American Capital Punishment*. New York: Oxford University Press.

Michael Tonry

The Mostly Unintended Effects of Mandatory Penalties: Two Centuries of Consistent Findings

ABSTRACT

Policy and knowledge concerning mandatory minimum sentences have long marched in different directions in the United States. There is no credible evidence that the enactment or implementation of such sentences has significant deterrent effects, but there is massive evidence, which has accumulated for two centuries, that mandatory minimums foster circumvention by judges, juries, and prosecutors; reduce accountability and transparency; produce injustices in many cases; and result in wide unwarranted disparities in the handling of similar cases. No country besides the United States has adopted many mandatory penalty laws, and none has adopted laws as severe as those in the United States. If policy makers took account of research evidence (and informed practitioners' views), existing laws would be repealed and no new ones would be enacted.

The greatest gap between knowledge and policy in American sentencing concerns mandatory penalties. Experienced practitioners, policy analysts, and researchers have long agreed that mandatory penalties in all their forms—from 1-year add-ons for gun use in violent crimes in the 1950s and 1960s, through 10-, 20-, and 30-year federal minimums for drug offenses in the 1980s, to three-strikes laws in the 1990s—are a bad idea. That is why the U.S. Congress in 1970, at the urging of Texas Congressman George H. Bush, repealed most of

Michael Tonry is professor of law and public policy, University of Minnesota Law School, and senior fellow, Netherlands Institute for the Study of Crime and Law Enforcement. He is grateful to Andrew Ashworth, Anthony E. Doob, Arie Freiberg, Kevin Reitz, Julian Roberts, and Dirk van zyl Smit for helpful comments on an earlier draft.

the mandatory minimum sentence provisions then contained in federal law (U.S. Sentencing Commission 1991). It is why nearly every authoritative nonpartisan law reform organization that has considered the subject, including the American Law Institute in the *Model Penal Code* (1962), the American Bar Association in each edition of its *Criminal Justice Standards* (e.g., 1968, standard 2.3; 1994, standard 18–3.21[*b*]), the Federal Courts Study Committee (1990), and the U.S. Sentencing Commission (1991) have opposed enactment, and favored repeal, of mandatory penalties. In 2007, the American Law Institute approved a partial second edition of the *Model Penal Code* that repudiated mandatory penalties. In 2004, an American Bar Association commission headed by conservative Justice Anthony Kennedy of the U.S. Supreme Court called upon states, territories, and the federal government to repeal mandatory minimum sentence statutes (Kennedy 2004). The recommendations were overwhelmingly approved by the ABA House of Delegates.

Mandatory sentencing laws for felonies take a number of forms. Typical laws specify minimum prison sentences for designated violent and drug crimes (e.g., minimum 5 years' imprisonment for selling 10 grams of crack cocaine). Others require that incremental penalties be imposed on convicted offenders meeting specified criteria (e.g., anyone convicted of an offense involving a firearm must receive 2 years' imprisonment in addition to that imposed for the offense). Sometimes they specify minimum sentences to be imposed on people convicted of a particular offense who have prior felony convictions. Three-strikes laws, for example, are mandatory sentencing laws. Typically they provide that anyone convicted of a designated (usually violent or drug) crime, who has previously twice been convicted of similar crimes, be sentenced to a prison sentence of 25 years or more.

Several other kinds of "mandatory" sentencing laws are not addressed in this essay. I do not discuss mandatory sentences for misdemeanors; a common example is laws that mandate short jail terms for some drunk-driving offenses. I do not discuss laws that use the word "mandatory" but do not mean it. "Mandatory life" sentences for murder are legally required in England and in some Australian states. The terminology, however, is misleading. In most cases, the judge also indicates how long the offender should be held before release on parole. Utterance of the words "mandatory life imprisonment" is obligatory; a life spent behind bars is not. Finally, I do not discuss mandatory confinement under civil law authority. This primarily affects people being held for immigration law violations pending hearings or deportation.

Policy makers promoting mandatory penalties usually offer three justifications. Mandatory penalties are said to assure evenhandedness: every offender who does the crime will do the time. They are said to be transparent: mandatory penalty laws assure everyone, offenders, practitioners, and the general public alike, that justice will be done and be seen to be done. They are said to prevent crime: the certainty of punishment will deter would-be offenders. The insuperable difficulty with all these claims is that centuries of evidence show them to be untrue.[1]

There is a fourth justification, but it is one that has no place in a society that takes human rights seriously. Enactment of mandatory penalties is sometimes justified in expressive terms, irrespective of their effects. Their enactment is said to acknowledge public anxiety and assuage victims' anger.[2] They are a sign that policy makers are listening, and care, and are prepared to take action. This assumes, however, that offenders' interests in being treated justly and fairly do not warrant consideration. People may sometimes feel that way, but that cannot be a legitimate basis for making policy in a free society. In no other setting would the claim be allowed that harm may properly be done to individuals solely because doing so might give pleasure to other people.

Objections to mandatory penalties are well documented and of long standing. They are not mandatory, whatever the law may say, and they are not transparent. When mandatory penalty laws require imposition of sentences that practitioners believe are too severe, three things happen. Sometimes prosecutors sidestep the laws by not bringing charges subject to them or by agreeing to dismiss them in plea negotiations. Sometimes sentences are imposed that everyone involved believes are unjustly severe. Sometimes judges and prosecutors disingenuously evade their application. Because these things happen, mandatory pen-

---

[1] Another possible argument for mandatory penalties is that they encourage defendants to plead guilty (Boerner 1995). This is a non sequitur. Were there no mandatories, defendants now affected by them would remain subject to all the pressures that face every criminal defendant. They would simply no longer face out-of-the-ordinary—and therefore unfair—pressures resulting from the rigidity and excessive severity of many mandatory minimum sentence laws. In any case, as studies discussed in Secs. I–III demonstrate, prosecutors are often complicit in circumvention of mandatory penalties.

[2] A substantial public opinion literature shows that support for mandatory minimums is typically high when people are asked about them in the abstract but falls to low levels when people are asked about particular cases (Roberts 2003).

alties produce wide disparities between cases that are comparable in every way except how they were handled. And because practitioners often feel they must devise ways to circumvent their application, critical decisions are not made in court openly, transparently, and accountably. Laws ostensibly meant to produce consistent penalties on center stage produce inconsistent ones behind the scenes.

Nor does the evidence show that mandatory penalties provide effective deterrents to crime. From the accounts of pockets being picked at the hangings of pickpockets in eighteenth-century England (Teeters and Hedblom 1967; Hay et al. 1975) to the systematic empirical evaluations of the past 30 years, similar conclusions emerge. Mandatory penalty laws have not been credibly shown to have measurable deterrent effects for any save minor crimes such as speeding or illegal parking or for short-term effects that quickly waste away.[3]

Two separate claims are sometimes conflated. One is that mandatory penalty laws prevent crimes by means of their putative certainty of application. Relatively little research has been done on that question. When probabilities of suspicion, arrest, prosecution, and conviction are compounded and the time required to dispose of cases is taken into account, certainty is an unrealistic aim in any case. The second claim, sometimes referred to as the marginal deterrence hypothesis, is that increases to previously applicable penalties will prevent crimes by raising their prospective punitive cost. A few studies by economists have found marginal deterrent effects (e.g., Shepherd 2002; Levitt and Miles 2007),[4] but they have been refuted by other economists.[5] Most other social scientists conclude that the hypothesis cannot be confirmed (e.g., Doob and Webster

---

[3] Laurence Ross (1982) showed that apparent effects even of drunk-driving crackdowns soon waste away. Lawrence Sherman (1990) demonstrated the wasting effect of police crackdowns and proposed that police harness that effect by repeatedly shifting their geographical focus after brief periods of "residual deterrence" can be expected to end.

[4] Economists generally assume that increased penalties will reduce crime rates and attempt in their research to determine by how much. Ronald Coase, the Nobel Prize–winning pioneer of the law-and-economics movement, observed: "Punishment, for example, can be regarded as the price of crime. *An economist will not debate whether increased punishment will reduce crime*; he will merely try to answer the question, by how much?" (1978, p. 210; emphasis added). Other social scientists attempt to determine *whether* punishment increases affect behavior. This disciplinary difference may be why economists generally conclude that increased punishments deter and other social scientists generally conclude that the hypothesis cannot be confirmed.

[5] John Donohue (2006, p. 4), observing that "[Nobel Prize winner Gary] Becker suggests that price theory can fill in where empirical evidence is lacking: capital punishment is akin to a rise in the price of murder and hence might be expected to lessen the number of murders," rhetorically asks whether many economists' vigorous defense of traditional economic models in relation to crime is in effect a defense of price theory itself.

2003; Webster, Doob, and Zimring 2006; Tonry 2008) or that occasional findings of deterrent effects in studies of particular policies in particular places have no generalizable policy implications (e.g., Cook 1980; Nagin 1998; Pratt et al. 2006, p. 379). The clear weight of the evidence is that the marginal deterrence hypothesis cannot be confirmed. In any case, the hypothesis has only limited relevance to understanding the effects of mandatory penalties and provides no basis for making policy decisions. Even in theory, it is germane only to the period immediately after enactment of a new or harsher law.

No one who has lived in the United States, however, can be unaware that conservative politicians for 3 decades consistently promoted passage of more and harsher mandatory sentence laws. Moderate and liberal politicians, most famously former President Bill Clinton, from the mid-1980s onward more often than not followed suit. Between the mid-1970s and the mid-1980s, every American state but one enacted at least one new mandatory penalty law (Shane-DuBow, Brown, and Olsen 1985). Most adopted many such laws for violent, sexual, and drug offenses and for "career criminals." The U.S. Congress repeatedly, between 1984 and 1996, enacted new mandatory sentencing laws and increased penalties under existing ones (Austin et al. 1994). The first "three strikes and you're out" law was enacted by referendum in Washington State in 1993 and was followed most famously in California in 1994 but also by more than 23 other states and the federal government (Dickey and Hollenhorst 1999; Chen 2008, table 1).

The pace of new enactments has slowed. Except in Alaska in 2006, no new three-strikes laws were enacted in American states after 1996 (Chen 2008, table 1). In some states, the scope of mandatory penalty laws has been narrowed, though only slightly, and in a few states judges were given new discretion to impose some other sentence in narrowly defined categories of cases (Butterfield 2003; Steinhauer 2009). As these words were written in March 2009, New York's governor and legislature were reported to have agreed on repeal of most of the Rockefeller Drug Laws (Peters 2009). In 2007, the U.S. Sentencing Commission changed its guidelines to narrow the ramifications of mandatory penalties for drug crimes.[6] Taken as a whole, and with the

---

[6] It is a long story. The initial commissioners in the 1980s set sentences for many offenses not subject to mandatory penalties longer than they needed to be on the logic that if the mandatory penalty statutes had applied, those offenses would have been covered as the commission prescribed.

exception of repeal of the New York laws, if that happens, as Adam Liptak (2007, p. A21) noted of the U.S. Sentencing Commission changes, these changes only nibble at the edges: "The sentencing commission's striking move . . . will have only a minor impact. Unless Congress acts, many thousands of defendants will continue to face vastly different sentences for selling different types of the same thing." No major laws have been repealed, no major laws have been enacted retroactively to shorten the sentences of the hundreds of thousands of prisoners serving time under mandatory minimum laws, and most new laws narrowing their scope have been restrictively drafted to cover only minor offenses and offenders.

The decent thing to do would be to repeal all existing mandatory penalties and to enact no new ones. If that is politically impracticable, there are ways to avoid or ameliorate the foreseeable dysfunctional effects of mandatory penalties. First, make penalties presumptive rather than mandatory. Second, add "sunset provisions" providing that the laws lapse and become presumptive after 3–5 years, and include such provisions in any new mandatory minimum sentencing laws. Third, limit lengthy prison terms—whether or not subject to mandatory penalties— to serious crimes such as grievous assaults causing serious injury, aggravated rape, murder, and flagrant financial crimes. Fourth, authorize correctional officials to reconsider release dates of all offenders receiving prison sentences exceeding a designated length (say 5 or 10 years).

This essay summarizes research on the implementation, operation, and deterrent effects of mandatory sentencing laws. Sections I, II, and III are chronological and survey knowledge concerning the implementation of mandatory penalties since the eighteenth century.[7] I discuss the handful of most ambitious studies in some detail—some might think belaboredly—to show that centuries-old knowledge continues well founded in our world. Section I examines research before 1970. Section II examines the major empirical evaluations of mandatory penalties in the 1970s and 1980s, including the 1978 evaluation of New York's "Rockefeller Drug Laws." Section III discusses the U.S. Sentencing Commission's 1991 study of federal mandatory minimum sentence laws and the small body of research that has accumulated since then. Section IV summarizes the small literature on mandatory minimums in other countries, primarily Australia, England and Wales, and

---

[7] Sections I and II draw heavily on an earlier essay that summarized research on mandatory penalties through the early 1990s (Tonry 1996, chap. 5).

South Africa. Although the mandatory penalties are much less harsh in those countries and the research is less extensive, the findings are indistinguishable from those in the United States. Section V examines research on deterrent effects. Section VI tries to make sense of these findings and to outline their policy implications.

I. Mandatory Penalties before 1970

The foreseeable problems in implementing mandatory penalties have been well known for 200 years. A U.S. House of Representatives report, explaining why the Congress in 1970 repealed almost all federal mandatory penalties for drug offenses, accurately summarized what was then known: "The severity of existing penalties, involving in many instances minimum mandatory sentences, has led in many instances to reluctance on the part of prosecutors to prosecute some violations, where the penalties seem to be out of line with the seriousness of the offenses. In addition, severe penalties, which do not take into account individual circumstances, and which treat casual violators as severely as they treat hardened criminals, tend to make conviction . . . more difficult to obtain" (quoted in U.S. Sentencing Commission 1991, pp. 6–7).

The least subtle way to avoid imposition of harsh penalties is to nullify them. "Nullification," a term in common usage for more than two centuries, encapsulates the process by which judges and juries refuse to enforce laws or apply penalties that they consider unjust. Oliver Wendell Holmes Jr. described the jury's capacity to nullify harsh laws as among its principal virtues (Holmes 1889). Harvard Law School Dean Roscoe Pound claimed that "jury lawlessness is the great corrective of law in its actual administration" (1910, p. 18). John Baldwin and Michael McConville, in a review of jury research, observed: "The refusal of juries to convict in cases of criminal libel, the 'pious perjury' they welcomed in order to avoid conviction on a capital offense, the indulgence shown toward 'mercy killings' and the nullification of the Prohibition laws during the 1920s are simply the most famous examples of this exercise of discretion" (1980, p. 272). The leading criminal law casebook in use in American law schools for 30 years, Jerome Michael and Herbert Wechsler's *Criminal Law and Its Administration* (1940), gave lengthy and respectful consideration to nullification.

A. The Death Penalty in Eighteenth-Century England

The death penalty debate in eighteenth- and nineteenth-century England is strikingly similar to contemporary American debates about mandatory penalties. In July 1991, in the face of claims that newly proposed mandatory penalty laws would overburden the courts and have little practical effect, one congressman told the *New York Times*: "Congressmen and Senators are afraid to vote no" on crime and punishment bills, "even if they don't think it will accomplish anything." A Senate aide suggested that "it's tough to vote against tough sentences for criminals" (Ifill 1991, p. A6). At the end of the eighteenth century, Edmund Burke declared "that he could obtain the consent of the House of Commons to any Bill imposing the punishment of death" (Select Committee on Capital Punishment 1930, paras. 10, 11). Samuel Romilly, England's most celebrated nineteenth-century death penalty opponent, repeatedly called for repeal of capital punishment laws because they were applied erratically and unfairly and because the erratic application inevitably undermined whatever deterrent effects they might possibly have had (Romilly 1820).

During the reigns of the four Kings George, between 1714 and 1830, the British Parliament created 156 new capital offenses. By 1819, British law recognized 220 capital offenses, most of them property crimes. During the same period, however, the number of executions steadily declined. Douglas Hay (1975), in a famous essay "Property, Authority, and the Criminal Law," explained the anomaly. The propertied classes in the early years of the Industrial Revolution, he argued, attempted to protect their financial interests through promotion and passage of laws that emphasized the importance of private property (by making numerous property crimes punishable by death). At the same time, the same people, often serving as magistrates and judges, operated a legal system that provided exemplary punishments and, by making frequent merciful exceptions and observing procedural rules that made death sentences difficult to obtain, protected the system's legitimacy in the eyes of the general public.

Judges and juries went to extreme lengths to avoid imposing death sentences. Juries often refused to convict. A variant, with twentieth-century echoes, was to convict of a lesser offense. According to a 1930 report of the British Select Committee on Capital Punishment, describing eighteenth-century practices,

In vast numbers of cases, the sentence of death was not passed, or if passed was not carried into effect. For one thing, juries in increasing numbers refused to convict. A jury would assess the amount taken from a shop at 4s. [shillings] 10d. [pence] so as to avoid the capital penalty which fell on a theft of 5s. In the case of a dwelling, where the theft of 40s. was a capital offense, even when a woman confessed that she had stolen £5, the jury notwithstanding found that the amount was only 39s. And when later, in 1827, the legislature raised the capital indictment to £5, the juries at the same time raised their verdicts to £4 19s. (Select Committee on Capital Punishment 1930, para. 17)

As more capital offenses were created, the courts adopted increasingly narrow interpretations of procedural, pleading, and evidentiary rules. Seemingly well-founded prosecutions would fall because a name or a date was incorrect or a defendant was wrongly described as a "farmer" rather than as a "yeoman" (Radzinowicz 1948–68, vol. 1, pp. 25–28, 89–91, 97–103; Hay 1980, pp. 32–34).

Even among those sentenced to death, the proportion executed declined steadily. According to the Select Committee on Capital Punishment, "The Prerogative of the crown [pardon] was increasingly exercised. Down to 1756 about two-thirds of those condemned were actually brought to the scaffold; from 1756 to 1772 the proportion sank to one-half. Between 1802 and 1808 it was no more than one-eighth" (1930, para. 21). Most of those pardoned received substituted punishments of a term of imprisonment or transportation (Stephen 1883, vol. 1, chap. 13).

B. Mandatory Penalties in the 1950s

The American Bar Foundation's Survey of the Administration of Criminal Justice in the United States in the 1950s confirmed the lessons from eighteenth-century England. Frank Remington, director of the 18-year project, noted: "Legislative prescription of a high mandatory sentence for certain offenders is likely to result in a reduction in charges at the prosecution stage, or if this is not done, by a refusal of the judge to convict at the adjudication stage. The issue . . . thus is not solely whether certain offenders should be dealt with severely, but also how the criminal justice system will accommodate to the legislative charge" (1969, p. xvii).

The survey's findings are exemplified by three processes the reports described. First, Donald Newman described how Michigan judges dealt with a lengthy mandatory minimum for drug sales:

Mandatory minimums are almost universally disliked by trial judges. . . . The clearest illustration of routine reductions is provided by reduction of sale of narcotics to possession or addiction. . . . Judges . . . actively participated in the charge reduction process to the extent of refusing to accept guilty pleas to sale and liberally assigning counsel to work out reduced charges. . . . To demonstrate its infrequent application, from the effective date of the revised law (May 8, 1952) to the date of tabulation four years later (June 30, 1956), only twelve sale-of-narcotics convictions were recorded in Detroit out of 476 defendants originally charged with sale. The remainder (except a handful acquitted altogether) pleaded guilty to reduced charges. (Newman 1966, p. 179)

Second, Newman described efforts to avoid 15-year mandatory maximum sentences for breaking-and-entering and armed robbery:

In Michigan conviction of armed robbery or breaking and entering in the nighttime (fifteen-year maximum compared to five years for daytime breaking) is rare. The pattern of downgrading is such that it becomes virtually routine, and the bargaining session becomes a ritual. The real issue in such negotiations is not whether the charge will be reduced but how far, that is, to what lesser offense. . . . [A]rmed robbery is so often downgraded that the Michigan parole board tends to treat a conviction for unarmed robbery as prima facie proof that the defendant had a weapon. And the frequency of altering nighttime burglary to breaking and entering in the daytime led one prosecutor to remark: "You'd think all our burglaries occur at high noon." (1966, p. 182)

Third, Robert O. Dawson described "very strong" judicial resistance to a 20-year mandatory minimum for sale of narcotics: "All of the judges of Recorder's Court, in registering their dislike for the provision, cited the hypothetical case of a young man having no criminal record being given a twenty-year minimum sentence for selling a single marijuana cigarette. Charge reductions to possession or use are routine. Indeed, in some cases, judges have refused to accept guilty pleas to sale of narcotics, but have continued the case and appointed counsel with instructions to negotiate a charge reduction" (1969, p. 201).

These findings from the American Bar Foundation Survey differ in detail from those of eighteenth-century England, but only in detail. When the U.S. Congress repealed most mandatory penalties for drug offenses in 1970, it was merely acknowledging enforcement problems that had long been recognized.

II. Mandatory Penalties in the 1970s and 1980s

Between 1975 and 1996, mandatory minimums were America's most frequently enacted sentencing law changes. By 1983, 49 of the 50 states (Wisconsin was the holdout) had adopted mandatory sentencing laws for offenses other than murder or drunk driving (Shanc-DuBow, Brown, and Olsen 1985, table 30). By 1994, every state had adopted mandatory penalties; most had several (Austin et al. 1994). Most mandatory penalties apply to drug offenses, murder or aggravated rape, felonies involving firearms, or felonies committed by people who have previous felony convictions. Between 1985 and mid-1991, the U.S. Congress enacted at least 20 new mandatory penalty provisions; by 1991, more than 60 federal statutes subjected more than 100 crimes to mandatory penalties (U.S. Sentencing Commission 1991, pp. 8–10). More followed, including the federal three-strikes law, in the next few years. Few if any new mandatory penalty laws were enacted after 1996.[8]

The experience in most states in the late 1980s and early 1990s was similar. In Florida, for example, seven new mandatory sentencing laws were enacted between 1988 and 1990 (Austin 1991, p. 4). In Arizona, mandatory sentencing laws were so common that 57 percent of felony offenders in fiscal year 1990 were potentially subject to mandatory sentencing provisions, although in the vast majority of cases defendants were allowed to plead guilty to offenses not subject to minimums (Knapp 1991, p. 10).

The empirical evidence for this period comes primarily from four major studies. One is an evaluation of the "Rockefeller Drug Laws" (Joint Committee on New York Drug Law Evaluation 1978). One concerns the Michigan law requiring imposition of a 2-year mandatory prison sentence on persons convicted of possession of a gun during commission of a felony (Loftin and McDowall 1981; Loftin, Heumann, and McDowall 1983). Two concern a Massachusetts law requiring a 1-year prison sentence for persons convicted of carrying a firearm unlawfully (Beha 1977; Rossman et al. 1979). These studies differ from those in the 1950s in that they examined court processes but also used quantitative data to look for effects on overall system operations, especially guilty plea and trial rates, and overall sentencing patterns.

---

[8] I have not checked the statutes of every U.S. jurisdiction. The National Conference of State Legislatures publishes annual reports entitled "State Crime Legislation in [e.g.] 2006"; these describe minor changes in state mandatory penalty laws since the mid-1990s but no major new ones (http://www.ncsl.org).

TABLE 1

Drug Felony Processing in New York State

	1972	1973*	1974	1975	1976 (January–June)
Arrests	19,269	15,594	17,670	15,941	8,166
Indictments:					
N	7,528	5,969	5,791	4,283	2,073
Percent of arrests	39.1	38.3	32.8	26.9	25.4
Indictments disposed	6,911	5,580	3,939	3,989	2,173
Convictions:					
N	6,033	4,739	3,085	3,147	1,724
Percent of dispositions	87.3	84.9	78.3	78.9	79.3
Prison and jail sentences:					
N	2,039	1,555	1,074	1,369	945
Percent of convictions	33.8	32.8	34.8	43.5	54.8
Percent of arrests	10.6	10.0	6.1	8.6	11.6

SOURCE.—Joint Committee (1978), tables 19, 24, 27, 29.

* The drug law went into effect on September 1, 1973.

A. The Rockefeller Drug Laws in New York

The most exhaustive evaluation concerned the "Rockefeller Drug Laws" (Joint Committee on New York Drug Law Evaluation 1978). They took effect on September 1, 1973. They mandated lengthy prison sentences for narcotics offenses and included statutory limits on plea bargaining. The key findings were these: drug felony arrests, indictment rates, and conviction rates all declined; for those who were convicted, however, the likelihood of being imprisoned and the average length of prison term increased; the two preceding patterns canceled each other out, and the likelihood that a person arrested for a drug felony was imprisoned was about the same after the law took effect as before—around 11 percent; the proportion of drug felony dispositions resulting from trials tripled between 1973 and 1976, and the average time for processing of a single case doubled.

Table 1 shows case processing patterns for drug felony cases in New York during the period 1972–76. The percentage of drug felony arrests resulting in indictments declined steadily from 39.1 percent in 1972, before the law took effect, to 25.4 percent in the first half of 1976. Similarly, the likelihood of conviction, given indictment, declined from 87.3 percent in 1972 to 79.3 percent in the first half of 1976.

Practitioners made vigorous efforts to avoid application of the mandatory sentences in cases in which they viewed those sentences as being too harsh; the remaining cases were dealt with as the law dictated (Blumstein et al. 1983, pp. 188–89). Thus, the percentage of drug felonies in New York City disposed of by means of a trial rather than a guilty plea rose from 6 percent in 1972 to 17 percent in the first 6 months of 1976. Many fewer defendants pled guilty, and the trial rate tripled. It took between 10 and 15 times as much court time to dispose of a case by trial as by plea, and the average case processing time for disposed cases increased from 172 days in the last 4 months of 1973 to 351 days in the first 6 months of 1976. Backlogs rose commensurately (Joint Committee on New York Drug Law Evaluation 1978).[9]

Sentencing severity increased substantially for defendants who were convicted. Only 3 percent of sentenced drug felons between 1972 and 1974 under prior law received minimum sentences longer than 3 years. Under the new law, 22 percent did. The likelihood that a person convicted of a drug felony in New York State received a prison sentence grew from 33.8 percent in 1972 to 54.8 percent in the first 6 months of 1976 (Joint Committee on New York Drug Law Evaluation 1978, pp. 99–103).

B. Massachusetts's Bartley-Fox Amendment

Massachusetts's Bartley-Fox Amendment required imposition of a 1-year mandatory minimum prison sentence, without suspension, furlough, or parole, for anyone convicted of unlawful carrying of an unlicensed firearm. An offender need not have committed any other crime.

Two major evaluations were conducted (Beha 1977; Rossman et al. 1979). Some background on the Boston courts may make the following discussion of their findings more intelligible. The Boston Municipal Court is both a trial court and a preliminary hearing court. If a defendant is dissatisfied with his or her conviction or sentence, an appeal may be made to the Suffolk County Superior Court for a new trial.

James Beha's (1977) analysis was based primarily on comparisons of police and court records for the 6-month periods before and after the law's effective date. David Rossman and his colleagues (1979) dealt with official records from 1974, 1975, and 1976 supplemented by interviews with police, lawyers, and court personnel.

---

[9] However, anticipating a finding from later studies, later analyses by Feeley and Kamin (1996) showed that, within a few years, a new "going-rate" equilibrium was established and trial rates and case processing times returned to former levels.

The primary findings were these:

1. Police altered their behavior in ways aimed at limiting the law's reach. They became more selective about whom to frisk; the absolute number of reports of gun incidents taking place out of doors decreased, which meant a concomitant decrease in arrests, and the number of weapons seized without arrest increased by 120 percent from 1974 to 1976 (Carlson [1982, p. 6], relying on Rossman et al. [1979]).
2. The number of persons "absconding" increased substantially between the period before the law took effect and the period after (both studies).
3. Outcomes favorable to defendants, including both dismissals and acquittals, increased significantly between the before and after periods (both studies).
4. Of persons convicted of firearms carrying charges in Boston Municipal Court, appeal rates increased radically (Beha 1977, table 2). In 1974, 21 percent of municipal court convictions were appealed to the Superior Court. The appeal rate in 1976 was 94 percent (Rossman et al. 1979).
5. The percentage of defendants who entirely avoided a conviction rose from 53.5 percent in 1974 to 80 percent in 1976 (Carlson [1982, p. 10], relying on Rossman et al. [1979]).
6. Of that residuum of offenders who were finally convicted, the probability of receiving an incarcerative sentence increased from 23 percent to 100 percent (Carlson [1982, p. 8], relying on Rossman et al. [1979]).

C. The Michigan Felony Firearms Statute

The Michigan Felony Firearms Statute created a new offense of possessing a firearm while engaging in a felony and specified a 2-year mandatory prison sentence that could not be suspended or shortened by release on parole and that had to be served consecutively to a sentence imposed for the underlying felony. The law took effect on January 1, 1977. The Wayne County prosecutor banned charge bargaining in firearms cases and took measures to enforce the ban, suggesting that the likelihood of circumvention should have been less than was experienced in New York and Massachusetts.

Heumann and Loftin (1979) observed a strong tendency in Wayne

County toward early dismissal of charges other than on the merits. They interpreted this as evidence of efforts to avoid applying the mandatory penalties. They focused on three offenses: armed robbery, "other assaults," and felonious assault. "Felonious assaults" tend to arise from "disputes among acquaintances or relatives and are less predatory than armed robbery." "Other assaults" is an intermediate category.

Case processing patterns for felonious assault, the low-severity offense, did not change after the mandatory penalty provision took effect. There was some increase in early dismissal of armed robbery charges and a substantial increase in dismissals of "other assaults." These findings are consistent with the hypothesis that efforts were made to avoid application of the mandatory penalty to defendants for whom lawyers and judges believed it inappropriately severe.

The probabilities of conviction differed after implementation depending on the offense. Consistent with the Massachusetts findings that mandatory sentences reduce the probability of convictions, conviction probabilities declined for "other assaults" and armed robbery (Loftin, Heumann, and McDowall 1983, p. 295).

The effects of the Felony Firearm Statute on sentencing severity were assessed in two ways. Using quantitative methods, Loftin, Heumann, and McDowall (1983) concluded that the statute did not generally increase the probability that prison sentences would be imposed, but for those receiving prison sentences, it increased the expected lengths of sentences for some offenses (pp. 297–98). Using simpler tabular analyses, they concluded that, overall, the percentage of defendants vulnerable to the firearms law who were incarcerated did not change markedly (Heumann and Loftin 1979).

As table 2 indicates, the probability of a prison sentence, given filing of the charge, increased slightly for felonious assault and other assault and decreased slightly for armed robbery. The probability of incarceration given conviction also did not change markedly for felonious assault or armed robbery. It did change for other assault, increasing from 57 percent of convictions prior to implementation of the firearm law to 82 percent afterward. This resulted in part from the substantial shift toward early dismissal of other assault charges, reducing the residuum of cases to be sentenced from 65 percent of cases to 50 percent.

Finally, trial rates remained roughly comparable before and after implementation, except for the least serious category of offenses, fe-

TABLE 2

Disposition of Original Charges in Wayne County, Michigan, by
Offense Type and Time Period

	N	Dismissed at/before Pretrial (%)	Dismissed or Acquitted after Pretrial (%)	Convicted/ No Prison (%)	Some Prison (%)	Total (%)
Felonious assault:						
Before*	145	24	31	31	14	100
After[†]	39	26	26	31	18	101
Other assault:						
Before	240	12	24	28	37	101
After	53	26	24	9	41	100
Armed robbery:						
Before	471	13	19	4	64	100
After	136	22	17	2	60	101

SOURCE.—Cohen and Tonry (1983), tables 7–10; adapted from Heumann and Loftin (1979), table 3.

NOTE.—The totals do not always sum to 100 percent because of rounding.

* Offense committed before January 1, 1977, and case disposed between July 1, 1976, and June 30, 1977.

[†] Offense committed and case disposed between January 1, 1977, and June 30, 1977.

lonious assaults, for which the percentage of cases resolved at trial increased from 16 percent of cases to 41 percent (Heumann and Loftin 1979, table 4). This is explained by Heumann and Loftin in terms of an innovative adaptive response, the "waiver trial." By agreement or by expectation, the judge would convict the defendant of a misdemeanor rather than the charged felony (the firearms law applied only to felonies) or would simply, with the prosecutor's acquiescence, acquit the defendant on the firearms charge. Either approach eliminated the threat of a mandatory sentence. A third mechanism for nullifying the mandatory sentencing law was to decrease the sentence that otherwise would have been imposed by 2 years and then add the 2 years back on the basis of the firearms law (Heumann and Loftin 1979, pp. 416–24).

D. The New York, Massachusetts, and Michigan Studies

The Massachusetts, Michigan, and New York laws are especially good illustrations of the operation of mandatory sentencing laws. For differing reasons, vigorous and highly publicized efforts were made to make them effective. The New York law was the first piece of high-visibility law-and-order legislation enacted in the 1970s in the United

States; it attracted enormous attention both because it happened in New York and because its proponent, Governor Nelson Rockefeller, long known as a liberal Republican, used it in part to attempt to establish more conservative credentials.[10] Amid enormous publicity and massive media attention, the legislature authorized and funded 31 new courts, including creation of additional judges, construction of new courtrooms, and provision of support personnel and resources, and expressly forbade some kinds of plea bargaining to assure the mandatory sentences were imposed. In Massachusetts, while the statute did not address plea bargaining, it expressly forbade "diversion in the form of continuance without a finding or filing of cases," both devices used in the Boston Municipal Court for disposition of cases other than on the merits.[11] In Michigan, the Wayne County prosecutor established and enforced a ban on plea bargaining. He also launched a major publicity campaign, promising on billboards and bumper stickers that "One with a Gun Gets You Two."

Nothing in these findings would surprise the authors of the American Bar Foundation Surveys or observers of eighteenth-century English courts.

III. Mandatory Minimums since 1990

The evaluators of the Rockefeller Drug Laws and the Michigan Felony Firearms law investigated deterrent effects of mandatory penalties, but most research before 1990 paid primary attention to sentencing patterns and case processing. Since 1990, only two major published studies looked primarily at those subjects. Most studies, discussed in Section V, investigated deterrent (and sometimes incapacitative) effects.

A. U.S. Sentencing Commission Report

The U.S. Sentencing Commission report, *Mandatory Minimum Penalties in the Federal Criminal Justice System*, demonstrates that mandatory minimum sentencing laws shift discretion from judges to prosecutors, result in higher trial rates and lengthened case processing times, fail to acknowledge salient differences between cases, and often punish

---

[10] It seems to have worked. President Gerald Ford, himself initially an unelected successor to Vice President Spiro Agnew, later appointed Rockefeller as his vice president.

[11] Filing is a practice in which cases are left open with no expectation that they will ever be closed; continuance without finding leaves the case open in anticipation of eventual dismissal if the defendant avoids further trouble.

minor offenders more harshly than anyone involved believes is warranted. Heavy majorities of judges, defense counsel, and probation officers disliked mandatory penalties; prosecutors were about evenly divided. Judges and lawyers often circumvented mandatory sentence laws.[12]

The commission analyzed three data sets describing federal sentencing and two sources of data concerning the opinions of judges, assistant U.S. attorneys, and others. The three data sets were FPSSIS, U.S. Sentencing Commission monitoring data for fiscal year 1990, and a 12.5 percent random sample of defendants sentenced in fiscal year 1990. Data for the random sample were augmented by examining computerized and paper case files to identify cases (there were 1,165 defendants) that met statutory criteria for receipt of a mandatory minimum drug or weapon sentence.

The sources of data on practitioners' views were structured interviews of 234 practitioners in 12 sites (48 judges, 72 assistant U.S. attorneys, 48 defense attorneys, and 66 probation officers) and a May 1991 mail survey of 2,998 practitioners (the same groups as were interviewed; 1,261 had responded by the time the report was written).

1. *Sentencing Analyses.*   The sentencing data revealed a number of not unexpected patterns. First, prosecutors often did not file charges that carried mandatory minimums when the evidence would have supported such charges. Prosecutors failed to file charges for mandatory weapons enhancements against 45 percent of drug defendants for whom they would have been appropriate. Prosecutors failed to seek mandatory sentencing enhancements for prior felony convictions in 63 percent of cases in which they could have done so. Only in 74 percent of cases were defendants charged with the offense carrying the highest applicable mandatory minimum.

Second, prosecutors used mandatory provisions tactically to induce guilty pleas. Among defendants fully charged with applicable mandatory sentence charges and convicted at trial, 96 percent received the full mandatory minimum sentence. Of those pleading guilty, by contrast, 27 percent pled to charges bearing no mandatory minimum or a lower one. Of all defendants who pled guilty (whether or not initially charged with applicable mandatory-bearing charges), 32 percent had no mandatory minimum at conviction; 53 percent were sentenced be-

[12] The U.S. General Accounting Office (1993) reached similar conclusions.

low the minimum the evidence would have justified. Among defendants against whom mandatory weapons enhancements were filed, the weapons charges were later dismissed in 26 percent of cases.

Third, mandatory penalties increased trial rates and thereby increased work loads and case processing times. Nearly 30 percent of those convicted of offenses bearing mandatory minimums were convicted at trial, a rate two-and-one-half times the overall trial rate for federal criminal defendants.

Fourth, judges were often willing to work around, and under, the mandatory penalties. Forty percent of defendants whose cases the commission believed warranted mandatory minimums received shorter sentences than applicable statutes specified. Mandatory minimum defendants received downward departures 22 percent of the time. The commission observed that "the increased departure rate may reflect a greater tendency to exercise prosecutorial or judicial discretion as the severity of the penalties increases" (U.S. Sentencing Commission 1991, p. 53). To like effect, "the prosecutors' reasons for reducing or dismissing mandatory charges . . . may be attributable to . . . satisfaction with the punishment received [after the reduction or dismissal]" (U.S. Sentencing Commission 1991, p. 58).[13]

Other studies confirmed the commission's principal findings.[14] A series of analyses of plea bargaining under the federal guidelines conducted by Stephen Schulhofer showed that prosecutors and defense counsel, in nearly a third of cases examined, manipulated the guidelines, often with tacit judicial approval, to achieve sentence reductions (Schulhofer and Nagel 1989; Nagel and Schulhofer 1992). This finding is not on its face surprising; plea negotiation is common everywhere in the United States, and sentence reductions are what defendants want (Schulhofer 1997).

Schulhofer's conclusion that sentences in a third of cases were reduced by prosecutorial manipulation was probably an underestimate. The manipulations were in violation of commission (and often De-

---

[13] Judicial and prosecutorial avoidance of mandatory penalties is probably much greater in 2009 than it was at the time of the commission's 1991 study; analyses by Bowman and Heise (2001, 2002) showed that overall circumvention of guidelines increased steadily during the 1990s and average sentence lengths decreased.

[14] In the text I mention studies only of federal mandatory minimums. There is a large general literature on how and why prosecutors, often in consort with judges and defense lawyers, circumvent sentencing laws and guidelines. There are studies on three-strikes in California (e.g., Harris and Jesilow 2000) and federal (e.g., Johnson, Ulmer, and Kramer 2008) and state (e.g., Ulmer, Kurlychek, and Kramer 2008) guidelines.

partment of Justice) policies and sometimes involved judicial acquiescence.[15] Neither assistant U.S. attorneys nor judges have an interest in publicly acknowledging their willful evasion of sentencing guidelines and mandatory penalties. A Federal Judicial Center survey of all federal district court judges and probation officers in 1996 showed that 73.2 percent of judges and 93.2 percent of probation officers "strongly" or "somewhat agree" that "plea bargains are a source of hidden unwarranted disparity in the guidelines system" (Johnson and Gilbert 1997, table 7).[16]

2. *Opinion Surveys.*   No category of federal court practitioners, including prosecutors, much liked mandatory minimum sentencing laws (U.S. Sentencing Commission 1991, chap. 6). In 1-hour structured interviews, 38 of 48 federal district court judges offered unfavorable comments. Among 48 defense counsel, only one had anything positive to say, and he also had negative comments. Probation officers were also overwhelmingly hostile. The most common complaints for all three groups were that the mandatory penalties were too harsh, resulted in too many trials, and eliminated judicial discretion. Only among prosecutors was sentiment more favorable; even among them, however, 34 of 61 were wholly (23) or partly (11) negative.

The mail survey showed that 62 percent of judges, 52 percent of private counsel, and 89 percent of federal defenders wanted mandatory penalties for drug crimes eliminated. A 1993 Gallup Poll survey of judges who were members of the American Bar Association found that 82 percent of state judges and 94 percent of federal judges disapproved of mandatory minimums (*ABA Journal* 1994). A 1994 Federal Judicial Center survey reported that 72 percent of circuit court judges and 86 percent of district court judges moderately or strongly supported changes in "current sentencing rules to increase the discretion of the judge" (Federal Judicial Center 1994). Although the 1996 Federal Judicial Center survey did not ask what respondents thought about mandatory penalties, 78.7 percent of district court judges "strongly" or

---

[15] The tension between local prosecutors wanting to do justice in individual cases and political officials in the Department of Justice in Washington wanting to enforce standardized policies continues (e.g., Stith 2008).

[16] A U.S. General Accounting Office study covering 1999–2001 found that, even among cases in which mandatory minimums were not circumvented by prosecutors, judges sentenced below the minimum in 52 percent of cases (U.S. General Accounting Office 2003, p. 14).

"somewhat agreed" that their influence on the federal guidelines should be reduced (Johnson and Gilbert 1997, table 10).

B. Oregon's Measure 11

Oregon's Measure 11, adopted by voters in a referendum in 1994, required imposition of mandatory minimum prison sentences from 70 to 300 months on anyone (including children as young as 15) convicted of any of 16 designated crimes. The law's coverage was later extended to five additional crimes. A person who knew nothing about how courts operate might expect that anyone who committed those 21 crimes would receive the mandated sentences.

RAND Corporation evaluators understood how courts operate (Merritt, Fain, and Turner 2006). They supposed that judges and lawyers would alter previous ways of doing business, especially in filing charges and negotiating plea bargains, to achieve results that seemed to them sensible and just. To find out whether they were right, they interviewed a considerable number of practitioners, analyzed data on sentences for offenses subject to Measure 11 and lesser related offenses for periods before and after Measure 11 took effect, and conducted another round of interviews to test their readings of the statistical analyses.

On the basis of the research summarized in Section II, they expected that, compared with sentencing patterns before Measure 11, relatively fewer people would be convicted of Measure 11 offenses and more of non–Measure 11 offenses, those convicted of Measure 11 offenses would receive harsher sentences, and jury trial rates would rise for a while and then return to prior levels. The rationales were that practitioners would divert some cases that would once have been Measure 11 offenses into less serious offense categories, that the remaining Measure 11 cases would be of greater average seriousness than before the law changed, and that the threat of harsher sentences would for a while cause more defendants to take their chances on a trial rather than plead guilty (but new going rates would in due course be established and guilty plea rates would return to normal).

The research confirmed the hypotheses and in addition showed that sentences for non–Measure 11 offenses also became harsher, that the mandatory minimums increased prosecutors' power, and that the changed sentencing patterns resulted primarily from changes in charging (fewer Measure 11 crimes, more lesser crimes) and plea bargaining (fewer pleas to initially charged offenses, more to lesser included offenses).

The only other major related evaluation was carried out in New Jersey by Candace McCoy and Patrick McManimon (2004), who examined sentencing patterns and case processing in New Jersey after enactment of a "truth-in-sentencing" law requiring people convicted of designated offenses to serve 85 percent of the announced sentence. This was not a mandatory minimum sentence law, but similar hypotheses apply: that power would be shifted to prosecutors, that charging and bargaining patterns would change to shelter some defendants from the new law, that sentences would be harsher for those not sheltered, and that new plea negotiation "going rates" would be established. Each of the hypotheses was substantiated.

Nothing found in any of these studies contradicts findings from earlier periods.

IV. Mandatory Penalties in Other Countries

No Western country besides the United States has adopted a large number of broad-based mandatory penalties. The small literature concerns Australia, Canada, England and Wales, and South Africa. No ambitious evaluations comparable to those discussed in Sections I–III have been undertaken. There have been efforts, however, to take stock of their effects. The most recent and comprehensive is a report by the Sentencing Advisory Council of the Australian State of Victoria. Its conclusions are in line with every other major analysis: "Ultimately, current research in this area indicates that there is a very low likelihood that a mandatory sentencing regime will deliver on its [deterrent] aims. . . . There is, in any case, ample evidence that mandatory sentencing can and will be circumvented by lawyers, judges, and juries both by accepted measures (such as plea bargaining) and by less visible means. The outcome of this avoidance is to jeopardize seriously another aim of mandatory sentencing; that is, to ensure that proportionate and consistent sentences are imposed" (Sentencing Advisory Council 2008, p. 21).

A. England and Wales

By American standards, some other countries' mandatory penalty laws are not mandatory at all. Three mandatory sentence laws were enacted in England and Wales as part of the Crime (Sentences) Act 1997. The first provided for an automatic life sentence (though affected offenders remained eligible for parole release) for a second serious violent or sexual offense unless there were "exceptional" circumstances. The other two specified a minimum 7-year sentence for third-time trafficking in class A drugs and a minimum 3-year sentence for third-time domestic burglary. These laws, however, provided that judges could impose a lesser sentence if they concluded that imposition of the mandatory sentence would be unjust "in all the circumstances." Andrew Ashworth (2001), the preeminent British sentencing scholar, has argued that that provision emasculated the law. The Court of Appeal, in an opinion by Lord Chief Justice Wolfe, in a case involving mandatory life sentences for second serious violent or sexual crimes, ruled that a finding that the offender "was not felt to present a significant risk to the public" would satisfy the "exceptional circumstances" test (Jones and Newburn 2006, p. 787). Cavadino and Dignan observed that the decision would "presumably allow sentencers to avoid passing life sentences in many—perhaps most—of these 'two-strikes'" cases (2002, p. 106). The mandatory life sentence for a second violent or sexual offense was repealed as part of the Criminal Justice Act 2003.[17]

B. South Africa

The South African laws were enacted in 1997 at a time of rapidly rising crime rates, with a 2-year sunset clause and ostensibly as an interim measure. They provided for mandatory minimums for certain serious offenses and minimum 10-, 20-, and 30-year sentences for first, second, and third rapes, respectively, and for specific types of murder. Similar to the English law, the initial proposed law provided that courts could impose less severe sentences if there were "circumstances" that would justify them. Before the departure criterion was enacted, it was redefined to require a finding of "substantial and compelling circumstances."[18] The mandatory penalties remained in effect in mid-2009 after a series of 2-year extensions.

Constitutional challenges were raised. In *S. v. Malgas*, 2 SA 1222 (2001), the South African Supreme Court of Appeal, not unlike the

---

[17] The story of the enactment and experience with the English laws is told most fully by Jones and Newburn (2006). Convictions for murder trigger an automatic (but parolable) life sentence.

[18] Van zyl Smit (2000) tells the tale in considerable detail.

English Court of Appeal before it, broadened the departure test: "'Substantial and compelling circumstances' may arise from a number of factors considered together—taken one by one, these factors need not be exceptional. If the sentencing court considers all the circumstances and is satisfied that the prescribed sentence would be unjust, as it would be 'disproportionate to the crime, the criminal, and the needs of society,' the court may impose a shorter sentence" (pp. 1234–35).

In the aftermath of *Malgas*, South Africa is repeating an old American story. Stephan Terblanche (2003) has argued that minimum sentence legislation has worsened disparities and inconsistencies in South African sentencing. Evaluations have shown that judges depart from the mandatory minimums in a majority of cases (O'Donovan and Redpath 2006). There is evidence that circumvention of the law is widespread (Roth 2008, pp. 169–70) and that sentences for those not benefitting from departures became harsher after the 1997 law was enacted (Sloth-Nielsen and Ehlers 2005).

The most comprehensive examination of the effects of South Africa's mandatory penalties concluded that, because of *Malgas*, the laws did not substantially increase constraints on judicial discretion. The study documented increased inconsistency in sentencing and increases in court costs and delays (O'Donovan and Redpath 2006, pp. 81–84).

C. Australia

Three-strikes laws in Western Australia and the Northern Territory attracted considerable attention in Australia even though, by American, English, and South African standards, they were mild (Hogg 1999; Law Council of Australia 2001). The Northern Territory, which traditionally has much the highest imprisonment rates in Australia, enacted a mandatory penalty law in 1997 for a broad range of low-level offenses, including theft, receiving stolen property, criminal damage, and unlawful use of a vehicle. First-time adult offenders faced a mandatory minimum 14-day prison sentence, second-timers a minimum 90 days, and third-timers a minimum of a year. A 28-day detention term was mandated for 15- and 16-year-olds convicted of a second or subsequent offense. In 1999, sexual and violent offenses were made subject to mandatory penalties. As in the English and South African laws, an "exceptional circumstances" provision in all these laws allowed judges to avoid imposing the minimum sentences on adults when they made appropriate findings (Brown 2001). Johnson and Zdenkowski (2000), in an assessment of the effects, concluded that discretion had been shifted from judges to prosecutors and that more case dispositions moved out of the spotlight and into the shadows as defense lawyers negotiated charge dismissals and agreements to permit informal dispositions (e.g., restitution). The mandatories for property offenses were repealed in 2001. The mandatories for violent and sexual offenses remained in effect in 2007 (Warner 2007).

Western Australia had two such laws. The first, enacted in 1992, was precipitated by a rash of automobile thefts by juveniles that produced police chases and 16 related traffic deaths in 18 months. It mandated indeterminate (parolable) detention in addition to at least 18 months' imprisonment. Only two juveniles were sentenced to indeterminate detention under the law. An evaluation by the Western Australian Crime Research Centre concluded that the law's enactment had no effect on rates of automobile theft (Broadhurst and Loh 1993). The law was repealed in 1994 (Brown 2001; Warner 2007).

A 1996 three-strikes law subjected people convicted for the third and subsequent times of household burglary to a 12-month minimum sentence to confinement. An Australian judge observed that such adult offenders already typically received 18- to 36-month sentences, making the mandatory penalty "less than the term of an imprisonment that an adult might have expected before the law was changed" and therefore largely symbolic (Yeats 1997, p. 375). The burglary three-strikes law remained in effect in 2007. Kate Warner observed: "The heat seems to have gone out of the debate, perhaps because in practice it has little effect on adults and the courts have circumvented mandatory detention for juveniles by imposing Conditional Release Orders" (2007, p. 337).

Neil Morgan's evaluation concluded that "there is compelling evidence from WA that neither the 1992 nor the 1996 laws achieved a deterrent effect. . . . There was a leap in residential burglaries immediately after the introduction of the new [1996] laws at precisely the time when the greatest reduction would have been expected" (2000, p. 172).

D. Canada

Canada is a federal country in which the criminal code and its sentencing laws are federal but prosecutions are handled in provincial courts. There have been three major sets of mandatory penalties.[19] A

---

[19] Crutcher (2001) provides a detailed account of the history of mandatory penalties in Canada.

minimum sentence of 7 years was mandated for importation of narcotics, but this was declared unconstitutional by the Canadian Supreme Court because it was "grossly disproportionate to what the offender deserves" (*R v. Smith*, 34 C.C.C. 3d 97 [1987], at p. 139). New mandatories for drug importation were not enacted. A 1996 law mandated minimum 4-year prison sentences for offenders committing any of 10 violent crimes with a firearm. Cheryl Webster and Anthony Doob, after analyzing data on Canadian prison populations, concluded: "While the mandatory minimum sentences for violent crimes did in fact increase the sentences that *some* offenders received, it is likely that the 'new' sanction would not significantly differ from one that would have been handed down under the prior legislation for most offenders. . . . It is probable they would already have been dealt with in a harsh manner by Canadian judges" (2007, p. 317; emphasis in original). Legislation introduced in 2006 (Bill C-10, 39th Parliament, 1st session) requires a 5-year mandatory minimum for gang-related gun crimes or gun use in relation to designated serious crimes and a longer minimum for second convictions. It applies only to handguns and involves only marginally more severe punishments than the 1996 legislation. It took effect a few months before the time of writing. Doob and Webster (2009) describe it, like its 1996 predecessor, as a primarily symbolic tough-on-crime initiative of a conservative government.

None of the laws in Canada, England, South Africa, and Australia are as severe as the harsher American laws and few are as rigid. To a considerable extent these countries have recognized the foreseeable nullification problems that face all rigid or severe sentencing laws by creating "exceptional circumstance" authority for judges to depart openly and accountably. The South Africans, however, have replicated the pattern of stark and unjust disparities that result when some like-situated offenders benefit from low-visibility circumvention of severe laws and others go to prison for many years.

V. Deterrent Effects

One claim often made for mandatory minimum sentence laws is that their enactment and enforcement deter would-be offenders and thereby reduce crime rates and spare victims' suffering. This claim, if true, makes a powerful case. Unfortunately, the accumulated evidence shows that it is not true.

There are three kinds of sources of relevant evidence. First, governments in many countries have asked advisory committees or national commissions to survey knowledge of the deterrent effects of criminal penalties in general. Second, a sizable number of comprehensive reviews of the literature on deterrence have been published. Third, evaluations have been conducted of the deterrent effects of newly enacted mandatory penalty laws.

A. National Advisory Bodies

No one doubts that society is safer having some criminal penalties rather than none at all, but that choice is not in issue. On the real-world question of whether increases in penalties significantly reduce the incidence of serious crimes, the consensus conclusion of governmental advisory bodies in many countries is possibly, a little, at most, but probably not.

After the most exhaustive examination of the question ever undertaken, the National Academy of Sciences Panel on Research on Deterrent and Incapacitative Effects concluded: "In summary . . . we cannot yet assert that the evidence warrants an affirmative conclusion regarding deterrence" (Blumstein, Cohen, and Nagin 1978, p. 7). Daniel Nagin of Carnegie Mellon University, a principal draftsman of the report, was less qualified in his assessment: "The evidence is woefully inadequate for providing a good estimate of the magnitude of whatever effect may exist. . . . Policymakers in the criminal justice system are done a disservice if they are left with the impression that the empirical evidence . . . strongly supports the deterrence hypothesis" (1978, pp. 135–36).

The National Academy of Sciences Panel on Understanding and Controlling Violence reached a similar conclusion in 1993. After documenting that the average prison sentence per violent crime tripled between 1975 and 1989, the panel asked, "What effect has increasing the prison population had on violent crime?" and answered, "Apparently very little" (Reiss and Roth 1993, p. 6). That answer took account of both deterrent and incapacitative effects.

Similar bodies in other Western countries have reached similar conclusions. British Prime Minister Margaret Thatcher's government created a Home Office advisory committee on criminal penalties. The resulting white paper, which led to an overhaul of English sentencing laws in 1991, expressed skepticism about the deterrent effects of penalties: "Deterrence is a principle with much immediate appeal. . . . But much crime is committed on impulse, given the opportunity presented by an open window or unlocked door, and it is committed by offenders who live from moment to moment; their crimes are as impulsive as the rest of their feckless, sad, or pathetic lives. It is unrealistic to construct sentencing arrangements on the assumption that most offenders will weigh up the possibilities in advance and base their conduct on rational calculation" (Home Office 1990, p. 6).

The same conclusions were earlier reached by the Canadian Sentencing Commission: "Evidence does not support the notion that variations in sanctions (within a range that reasonably could be contemplated) affect the deterrent value of sentences. In other words, deterrence cannot be used with empirical justification, to guide the imposition of sentences" (1987, p. xxvii). The Committee on Justice of the Canadian Parliament, chaired by a member of the then-governing Conservative Party, a few years later observed: "If locking up those who violate the law contributed to safer societies, then the United States should be the safest country in the world. In fact, the United States affords a glaring example of the limited impact that criminal justice responses have on crime. . . . [The] evidence from the US is that costly repressive measures alone fail to deter crime. The Committee unanimously agrees that crime prevention is the best policy choice" (Canada 1993, p. 2).

Negative findings concerning the deterrent effects of penalties are not unique to English-speaking countries. The Finnish government made a conscious policy decision in the mid-1970s to reduce the prison population from what was widely seen as unacceptably high levels, and it succeeded. The incarceration rate per 100,000 population fell by 60 percent between 1970 and 1992. The policy decision was based in large part on an examination of evidence on deterrence. A report issued by the Finnish Ministry of Justice's National Research Institute of Legal Policy explained: "Can our long prison sentences be defended on the basis of a cost/benefit assessment of their general preventative effect? The answer of the criminological expertise was no" (Törnudd 1993).

Alfred Blumstein, chairman of the National Academy of Sciences panels on deterrence and incapacitation (Blumstein, Cohen, and Nagin 1978), sentencing research (Blumstein et al. 1983), and criminal careers (Blumstein et al. 1986) and long America's leading authority on crime-control research, explained why, on empirical grounds, three-strikes laws (and by implication all mandatory penalties) are misconceived:

"However hard it is for rational folks to conceive of it, there are some people who simply do not respond to whatever threat is presented to them. The problem is that any serious three-strikes candidate probably falls into that category. For people who see no attractive options in the legitimate economy, and who are doubtful that they will live another ten years in any event, the threat of an extended prison stay is likely to be far less threatening than it would be to a well-employed person with a family" (Blumstein 1994, p. 415).

The government committees and commissions agree that insufficient evidence exists for basing detailed sanctioning policies on the deterrence hypothesis. The American National Academy of Sciences panel reports concur.

B. Surveys of the Literature

The critical question is whether marginal changes in sanctions have measurable deterrent effects. The heavy majority of broad-based reviews reach similar conclusions that no credible evidence demonstrates that increasing penalties reliably achieves marginal deterrent effects. A few reviews by economists, relying solely on work by economists, come out the other way. They have been convincingly refuted. The surveys by noneconomists discuss social science work generally, including that of economists.

Philip Cook, one of a handful of senior economists who have specialized on crime topics, surveyed the literature in 1980. He concluded that existing studies showed that "there exist feasible actions on the part of the criminal justice system that may be effective in deterring [certain] crimes . . . [but the studies] do *not* demonstrate that all types of crimes are potentially deterrable, and certainly they provide little help in predicting the effects of any specific governmental action" (1980, p. 215; emphasis in original).

Daniel Nagin, in 1998, revisiting the work of the 1978 National Academy of Sciences panel 20 years later, observed that he "was convinced that a number of studies have credibly demonstrated marginal deterrent effects," but he concluded that it was "difficult to generalize from the findings of a specific study because knowledge about the factors that affect the efficacy of policy is so limited" (1998, p. 4). He highlighted four major factors: the relation between short- and long-term effects, the relation between risk perceptions and sanctions policies, the methods of implementation, and the extent of implementation.

Andrew von Hirsch and his colleagues (1999), in a survey of the literature commissioned by the Home Office of England and Wales, concluded that "there is as yet no firm evidence regarding the extent to which raising the severity of punishment would enhance deterrence of crime" (p. 52). Anthony Doob and Cheryl Webster, in 2003, in yet another major review of the literature, noted some inconclusive or weak evidence of marginal deterrence, but they concluded: "There is no plausible body of evidence that supports policies based on this premise [that increased penalties reduce crime]. On the contrary, standard social scientific norms governing the acceptance of the null hypothesis justify the present (always rebuttable) conclusion that sentence severity does not affect levels of crime" (2003, p. 146).[20] A meta-analysis by Travis Pratt and his colleagues (2006) produced a main finding on deterrence, one "noted by previous narrative reviews of the deterrence literature," that "the effects of severity estimates and deterrence/sanctions composites, even when statistically significant, are too weak to be of substantive significance (consistently below $-.1$)" (p. 379).

Three literature surveys by economists, summarizing work principally by themselves and other economists, conclude that increases in punishment achieve marginal deterrent effects. The insularity of work by economists creates a serious problem: although other social scientists regularly explain data problems and unwarranted assumptions that bedevil many economic analyses of punishment, economists seldom acknowledge the criticisms, the problems, or the existence of deterrence research by noneconomists.[21] Donald Lewis describes "a substantial body of evidence which is largely consistent with the existence of a deterrent effect from longer sentences" (1986, p. 60). Steve Levitt, relying principally on data from two of his own analyses, describes them as evidence "for a deterrent effect of increases in expected punishment" (2002, p. 445). Levitt and George Miles (2007) conclude:

---

[20] I reached the same conclusion in a 2008 *Crime and Justice* essay (Tonry 2008).

[21] In a classic instance, Joanna Shepherd, e.g., author of several economic studies finding a deterrent effect of capital punishment, in 2004 testified before the U.S. Congress that there was a "strong consensus among economists that capital punishment deters crime" and that "the studies are unanimous" (2004, pp. 10–11), without mentioning the equally strong consensus among noneconomists (with agreement of many economists [Donohue and Wolfers 2005; Donohue 2006] that capital punishment cannot be shown to deter homicide).

"The new empirical evidence [produced exclusively by economists] generally supports the deterrence model. . . . Evidence of the crime-reducing effects of the scale of policing and incarceration is consistent across different methodological approaches" (p. 456). Much of their discussion focuses on whether capital punishment, recent increases in the scale of imprisonment, and changes in use of police manpower have reduced crime rates; the marginal deterrence hypothesis receives little attention except concerning a study by Kessler and Levitt (1999) of the effects of a change in California law.[22]

C. Evaluations and Impact Assessments

Two literatures are germane. Evaluations of mandatory minimum laws in the 1970s and 1980s focused on effects on sentencing outcomes and court processes. These generally conclude that deterrent effects cannot be shown to be associated with passage and implementation of mandatory penalty laws. A second literature, all focused on California in the 1990s, examines the effects on crime rates of changes in California sentencing laws. Most of it concerns the three-strikes law. None of the major California studies focused primarily on implementation and case processing or was as ambitious as the federal mandatory minimum study or the New York drug law evaluation. The divide in California between some economists and other social scientists is stunning. Work by non-economists and some economists concludes that no crime-preventive effects can be shown. Work by other economists concludes that the new laws have had substantial deterrent effects.

1. *Mandatory Minimum Evaluations.*   No individual evaluation has demonstrated crime reduction effects attributable to enactment or implementation of a mandatory minimum sentence law. One analysis combined data from four studies that had not found deterrent effects and concluded that a small deterrent effect could be shown. For reasons given below, the finding is not credible.

The evaluators of the Rockefeller Drug Laws expended most of their efforts trying to identify effects on drug use or drug-related crime. They found none (Joint Committee on New York Drug Law Evaluation 1978).

---

[22] Kessler and Levitt (1999) sought to identify deterrent effects from passage in 1982 of a California referendum that increased penalties for certain crimes. They examined crime data at 2-year intervals and thereby missed a downward trend that began in 1980 and continued after passage of the referendum. This made the post-1982 decline as likely to be the extension of a preexisting trend as a deterrent effect (Webster, Doob, and Zimring 2006).

A number of studies were made of the crime-preventive effects of the Massachusetts law requiring a 1-year minimum sentence for people convicted of possession of an unregistered firearm. The studies concluded that it had either no deterrent effect on the use of firearms in violent crimes (Beha 1977; Rossman et al. 1979; Carlson 1982) or a small short-term effect that quickly disappeared (Pierce and Bowers 1981).

Studies in other states reached similar results. An evaluation of the mandatory sentencing law for firearms offenses in Detroit, Michigan, concluded that "the mandatory sentencing law did not have a preventive effect on crime" (Loftin, Heumann, and McDowall 1983). Assessments of the deterrent effects of mandatory penalty laws in Tampa, Jacksonville, and Miami, Florida, "concluded that the results did not support a preventive effect model" (Loftin and McDowall 1984, p. 259). The results of evaluations of the crime-preventive effects of mandatory penalty laws in operation in Pittsburgh and Philadelphia, Pennsylvania, "do not strongly challenge the conclusion that the statutes have no preventive effect" (McDowall, Loftin, and Wiersema 1992, p. 382).

One analysis based on evaluation data concluded that mandatory penalties had deterrent effects. McDowall, Loftin, and Wiersema (1992), the team of researchers who conducted the Michigan, Florida, and Pennsylvania deterrence analyses mentioned in the preceding paragraph, combined the data from all six sites in three states and concluded that mandatory penalties for gun crimes reduced gun homicides but not assaults or robberies involving guns. This is counterintuitive. Homicides by definition are lethal assaults, and the ratios of assaults and robberies that involve guns and result in deaths should be relatively stable, assuming there have been no substantial changes in the lethality of available weapons. If the proportions of assaults and robberies involving guns decline, gun homicides should decline commensurately, and vice versa. If a deterrent effect can be shown for relatively small numbers of homicides, it should be much easier to demonstrate for vastly larger numbers of assaults and robberies.

2. *California Studies.*   The gap between politics and knowledge concerning the effects of California's three-strikes law has been enormous. Most credible empirical assessments of the law's effects on crime rates and patterns have concluded that none can be shown. From the law's initial passage in 1994 during the administration of Republican Governor Pete Wilson, California politicians have claimed to believe its

passage and implementation were major causes of California's substantial crime-rate decline during the 1990s.

a. California Government Views.   Although it took a dozen years, some agencies of California government eventually expressed views consistent with those of (most) researchers. It was a long time coming. In 1999, California Secretary of State Bill Jones claimed: "After five years, we now have strong statistical data to show the law is working as intended. California's murder and robbery rates are down by 50% [and] the overall crime rate in California has declined 38%. . . . It is clear that the implementation of the Three Strikes and You're Out Law has made a considerable positive impact on the incidence of crime and California" (Secretary of State 1999, pp. 1, 3).

Governor Wilson, in vetoing legislation creating a commission to study the law's effects, said its aim was to "disprove the obvious positive impact of the Three Strikes law. . . . There are many mysteries in life, but the efficiency of 'Three Strikes' . . . is not one of them" (quoted in California District Attorneys Association 2004, p. 32). Wilson's successor, Democrat Grey Davis, vetoing a similar bill calling for a study commission, observed that "the savings associated with the law, in terms of lives not destroyed, injuries not sustained, and property not stolen . . . is ultimately incalculable, but very serious" (quoted in California District Attorneys Association 2004, p. 32).

By 2004, when the accumulation of studies suggesting otherwise had become huge, even the California District Attorneys Association expressed more cautious views: the "dramatic drop in California's crime rate might be properly attributable to several substantial factors. It is counter-intuitive, however, to think that incarcerating violent recidivist felons for longer periods (whether under the two- or three-strikes provisions of this law) was not one of them" (2004, p. 21).

In 2005, the Legislative Analyst's Office, after presenting an analysis showing that the declines in overall and violent crime rates in the four counties in which the law was most often applied and the four in which it was least often applied were indistinguishable, concluded: "For now, it remains an open question as to how much safer California's citizens are as a result of Three Strikes" (p. 33).

b. California Impact Assessments.   Many three-strikes laws are not, strictly speaking, mandatory minimum sentence laws. Under California's, for example, both prosecutors and judges can "strike" the prior convictions that trigger the law's mandatory minimum sentences; if

TABLE 3

California Three Strikes: Effects on Reduced Crime Rates

Authors	Method	Deterrent Effect
Schiraldi and Ambrosio (1997)	Yes/no three-strike state comparisons	None
Stolzenberg and D'Alessio (1997)	Time series: 10 largest California cities	None
Males and Macallair (1999)	California age group comparisons	None
	California county comparisons	None
Chen (2000, 2008)	Time series: 50 states	None
	Time series: California	Not significant
Austin et al. (2000)	California county comparisons	None
	Yes/no three-strike state comparisons	None
Caulkins (2001)	National econometric model	None
Marvell and Moody (2001)	Time series: 50 states	None: increased murder rates
Moody, Marvell, and Kaminski (2003)	Time series: 50 states	None: increased murder rates
Zimring et al. (2001)	California county comparisons	None
	California age group comparisons	None
Shepherd (2002)	California econometric model	Yes
Ehlers et al. (2004)	California county comparisons	None
	Yes/no three-strike state comparisons	None
Kovandzic et al. (2004)	Model: U.S. cities	None: increased murder rates
Justice Policy Institute (2004)	Yes/no three-strike state comparisons	None
Tonry (2004)	Time series: 10 most populous states	None
Legislative Analyst's Office, California (2005)	California county comparisons	None

they do so, the law and its penalties do not apply. I discuss the literature briefly. It is well known and with only rare exceptions reaches the same conclusion—that the law's passage and implementation had no demonstrable effects on crime rates (or, perversely, increased homicide rates).

Table 3 summarizes the findings of 15 empirical efforts to assess the crime-preventive effects of California's three-strikes law. They involve four principal research designs: econometric time-series designs (e.g., Chen 2000, 2008; Caulkins 2001; Marvell and Moody 2001; Shepherd 2002); noneconometric time-series comparisons of California crime-rate trends with those of other states (e.g., Schiraldi and Ambrosio

1997; Austin et al. 2000; Ehlers et al. 2004; Tonry 2004); time-series comparisons within California of crime-rate trends in counties in which three-strikes charges were filed often and seldom (e.g., Males and Macallair 1999; Zimring, Hawkins, and Kamin 2001; Ehlers et al. 2004; Legislative Analyst's Office 2005); and comparisons within California of crime-rate trends for people of different ages (e.g., Males and Macallair 1999; Zimring, Hawkins, and Kamin 2001).

Only two of the studies shown in table 3 conclude that the three-strikes law reduced California crime rates (Chen 2000; Shepherd 2002). Three studies (Marvell and Moody 2001; Kovandzic, Sloan, and Vieraitis 2002; Moody, Marvell, and Kaminski 2003) concluded that enactment of three-strikes laws produced *increases* in homicide rates. Chen's findings were weak, and her conclusions were hedged.[23] Joanna Shepherd (2002) produced the only assessment finding significant effects: "During the first two years after the legislation's enactment, approximately eight murders, 3,952 aggravated assaults, 10,672 robberies, and 384,488 burglaries were deterred in California by the two- and three-strikes legislation" (p. 174).

Shepherd's findings on this subject correspond to findings of herself and other economists on the deterrent effects of capital punishment (e.g., Dezhbakhsh, Rubin, and Shepherd 2003) and enactment of "shall issue" laws that authorize private citizens to carry concealed firearms in public (e.g., Lott and Mustard 1997; Lott [1998] 2000). In all three cases, the economic analyses reach conclusions about strong deterrent effects that are different from almost all studies by noneconomists. In the latter two cases, other economists have demonstrated why the findings are not credible (capital punishment: e.g., Donohue and Wolfers 2005; Donohue 2006; concealed weapons: Ayres and Donohue 2003*a*, 2003*b*). Problems recurringly identified are the reliance solely on official data analyzed at county or state levels, lack of awareness of case processing differences at local levels, and poorly specified models. It is common for other economists, when reanalyzing data in published works, to show that minor changes in assumptions in economic models produce enormous changes in results (often changing the sign; e.g., showing that the change appears to have increased rather than de-

---

[23] "The approach taken in California has not been dramatically more effective at controlling crime than other states' efforts. . . . [California's law] is not considerably more effective at crime reduction than alternative methods that are narrower in scope" (Chen 2008, pp. 362, 365). Doob and Webster (2003) have demonstrated fundamental problems with her analysis.

creased crimes rates). The fundamental problem, however, is that econ-omists assume what other social scientists investigate—that increased penalties reduce crime rates. Shepherd, for example, observes that her "model predicts that offenses covered by two- and three-strikes legis-lation will be deterred" (2002, p. 173). That economists' models are often devised to confirm their assumptions ("predictions") may be why they so often do and why others can pick the models apart. In the case of California's three-strikes law, however, Shepherd is an outlier; other economists' analyses concur with the no-deterrent-effect conclusions of noneconomists (Marvell and Moody 2001; Kovandzic, Sloan, and Vieraitis 2002; Moody, Marvell, and Kaminski 2003).

No matter which body of evidence is consulted—the general liter-ature on the deterrent effects of criminal sanctions, work more nar-rowly focused on the marginal deterrence hypothesis, or the evaluation literature on mandatory penalties—the conclusion is the same. There is little basis for believing that mandatory penalties have any significant effects on rates of serious crime.

VI.   Undoing the Harm

The policy and human rights implications of this two-century-old body of knowledge are clear. Mandatory penalties are a bad idea. They often result in injustice to individual offenders. They undermine the legiti-macy of the courts and the prosecution system by fostering circum-ventions that are willful and subterranean. They undermine achieve-ment of equality before the law when they cause comparably culpable offenders to be treated radically differently when one benefits from practitioners' circumventions and another receives a mandated penalty that everyone immediately involved considers too severe. And the clear weight of the evidence is, and for nearly 40 years has been, that there is insufficient credible evidence to conclude that mandatory penalties have significant deterrent effects.

Supporters of mandatory penalties in anxious times are concerned with political and symbolic goals. Put positively, elected officials want to reassure the public generally that their fears have been noted and that the causes of their fears have been acted on. Officials who support mandatory penalties often do not much care about problems of imple-mentation, foreseeable patterns of circumvention, or the certainty of excessively and unjustly severe penalties for some offenders. Their interests are different. Put negatively, officials want to curry public favor and electoral support by pandering, by making promises that the law can at best imperfectly and incompletely deliver.

The most famous and most far-reaching mandatory sentencing law, California's three-strikes law, resulted from politicians' competing attempts to use punishment policies to pursue purely political goals. It was enacted not because thoughtful policy makers really believed that people who stole pizza slices in schoolyards or handfuls of compact discs from Wal-Mart deserved decades-long prison sentences but because Republican Governor Pete Wilson and California Assembly Leader Willie Brown played a game of chicken from which, in the end, neither backed down. Democratic legislators agreed among themselves to pass any proposal Governor Wilson offered, in hopes "that he would back down from an unqualified 'get tough' stand or be politically neutralized if he persisted." Wilson did not blink. Nor did the Democrats. The law was passed as proposed because both sides were "unwilling to concede the ground on 'getting tough' to the other side in the political campaign to come." As a result California adopted the most far-reaching and rigid three-strikes law in the country (Zimring, Hawkins, and Kamin 2001, p. 6).

However their motives are portrayed, for many legislators, their primary purpose has been achieved when their vote is cast. They have been seen to be tough on crime. Calls for enactment of mandatory penalties, or introductions of bills, or castings of votes are symbolic statements. Instrumental arguments about effectiveness or normative arguments about injustice to offenders fall on deaf ears.

The dilemma is that the public officials who enact mandatory sentencing laws support them for symbolic and political reasons while the public officials who administer mandatory sentencing laws oppose them for instrumental and normative reasons. The instrumental arguments against mandatory penalties are clear. First, they increase public expense by increasing trial rates and case processing times. Second, in every published evaluation, judges and prosecutors were shown to have devised ways to circumvent application of the mandatory penalties.

The normative arguments against mandatory penalties are also straightforward. First, simple justice: because of their inflexibility, such laws sometimes result in imposition of penalties in individual cases that everyone involved believes to be unjustly severe. Second, perhaps more importantly, mandatory penalties encourage hypocrisy on the part of prosecutors and judges.

The hypocrisies that mandatory penalties engender are what most troubles prosecutors and judges. Plea bargaining may be a necessary evil, an essential lubricant without which the machinery of justice would break down, but it is typically routinized. Armed robbery is pled down to robbery, aggravated assault to assault, theft 1 to theft 2. Prosecutors, defense counsel, judges, probation officers—all who are involved—know what is happening, understand why, and acknowledge the legitimacy of the reasons.

Legislators, whatever their purposes for supporting mandatory sentencing laws, once the vote is cast, move on to other issues. For judges, prosecutors, and defense counsel, it is another story. They must live with their own consciences and with their shared views of the bounds of fair treatment of offenders. They must also keep the courts functioning. That they sometimes devise ways to avoid application of laws they believe to be undeservedly harsh should come as no surprise.

Ironically, most mandatory penalty provisions enacted during the 1980s and 1990s concerned drug crimes, behaviors that both practitioners and researchers believe to be uniquely insensitive to the deterrent effects of sanctions. Despite risks of arrest, imprisonment, injury, and death, drug trafficking offers economic and other rewards to disadvantaged people that appear to far outweigh any available in the legitimate economy. Market niches created by the arrest of dealers are as a result often filled within hours, as many studies of drug marketing by ethnographers have shown, (e.g., Johnson et al. 1990; Padilla 1992; Fagan 1993). As a result, according to Alfred Blumstein, there is no evidence that harsh drug law enforcement policies have been at all successful: "Of course, that result is not at all surprising. Anyone who is removed from the street is likely to be replaced by someone drawn from the inevitable queue of replacement dealers ready to join the industry. It may take some time for recruitment and training but experience shows that replacement is easy and rapid" (1994, p. 400).

Both police officials and conservative scholars agree. James Q. Wilson (1990, p. 534) has observed that "significant reductions in drug abuse will come only from reducing demand for those drugs . . . the marginal product of further investment in supply reduction [law enforcement] is likely to be small." He reports: "I know of no serious law-enforcement official who disagrees with this conclusion. Typically, police officials tell interviewers that they are fighting a losing war or, at best, a holding action" (p. 534). Similarly, U.S. Senator Daniel Patrick Moynihan of New York, a sometime supporter of the drug wars, has acknowledged: "'Drug busts are probably necessary symbolic acts, but nothing more" (1997, p. 208).

In a sensible world of rational policy making, no mandatory penalty laws would be enacted. Those that exist would be repealed. That would be the simplest way to address the problems revealed by the literature and canvassed in this essay. That is not the world we live in. There are other ways the problems could be addressed or at least diminished.

A. Make Mandatory Penalties Presumptive

Much of what legislators hope to accomplish with mandatory sentencing laws could be achieved by making such laws presumptive. In a few states—Minnesota is an example—judges are given authority to disregard most mandatory penalties and impose some other sentence if reasons are given. Prosecutors who wish to can appeal the adequacy of the reasons given. Converting all mandatory penalties to presumptive penalties would sacrifice few of the values sought to be achieved by such laws but would avoid many of the undesirable side effects.

Prosecutors and judges both have powerful voices in sentencing. Disregard of the presumption would usually require that both agree that the penalty would be too severe in a particular case or that the political climate has altered and public sensibilities no longer demand especially harsh penalties. The final word, however, should be the judge's. Prosecutors too often are motivated by the notoriety of a case, their personal ideology, or their political self-interest to insist on severity when a more detached view would suggest otherwise.

By enacting a mandatory (presumptive) penalty law, the legislature would be expressing its policy judgment that, say, people who commit robberies with firearms deserve at least a 3-year minimum prison term. Most prosecutors and judges would accept that such policy decisions are the legislature's to make and that that one is not patently unreasonable. The law's facial legitimacy would cause many prosecutors and judges to deal with it in good faith. The law's presumptive character, however, would let judges take account of mitigating circumstances (the defendant was an underage, bullied, unarmed participant who remained in the car) without resort to subterfuge.

If official circumvention of mandatory penalties in cases where they seem unduly harsh is foreseeable, and it is, conversion to mandatory (presumptive) penalties is likely to result in no less systematic enforcement but to lessen hypocritical efforts at avoidance.

B. Enact "Sunset" Clauses

Our understandings of the politics and empirical experience of mandatory penalties could be married by including sunset clauses in all future mandatory penalty laws and adding them to existing ones. Sunset clauses provide for automatic repeal of a statute at a fixed time unless a new vote is taken to extend its life. This proposal, first made, to my knowledge, by Alfred Blumstein of Carnegie Mellon University at a "presidential crime summit" in 1991, would both acknowledge felt political imperatives and limit the damage mandatory penalties do.

Any honest politician will concede two points—that it is often difficult to resist political pressures to vote for tough penalties and that it is always difficult to vote to make penalties more "lenient." Blumstein's proposal addresses both propositions. If a charged political climate or campaign or a series of notorious crimes makes it difficult to resist "tough-on-crime" proposals, such laws will continue to be enacted. Statute books are cluttered with provisions passed on the passions of moments. Often, however, passions subside with time, and competing values and calmer consideration make the wisdom of such laws less clear.

Sunset clauses would assure that laws passed in the passion of a moment do not endure for decades, long after many people think them good policies—as the Rockefeller Drug Laws and the federal crack/powder 100-to-1 laws have done for more than 35 and 20 years, respectively. Few people support either of those laws on the merits. Proposals to repeal them have been being made for decades, but risk-averse elected officials have been unwilling to vote for repeal. With sunset clauses in place, legislators unwilling to take responsibility for voting for repeal of a punitive law may feel able more comfortably acceding to its lapse.

C. Narrow Mandatory Penalties' Scope

If the bases for passing sentencing laws were concerns for justice and institutional effectiveness, most mandatory penalties would be repealed and few others would be enacted to take their places. That is unlikely. Horrible, senseless crimes do occur, public fears and anxieties are heightened, and elected officials want to respond. There being in practice little that officials can do about crime, the attractions of mandatory penalties as a rhetorical demonstration of concern are great. A *New York Times* article about mandatory proposals offered by U.S. Senator Alfonse D'Amato of New York, for example, reports: "Mr. D'Amato conceded that his two successful amendments, which Justice Department officials say would have little practical effect on prosecution of crimes, might not solve the problem. 'But,' he said, 'it does bring about a sense that we are serious'" (Ifill 1991, p. A6).

The most extreme versions of nullification and circumvention involve laws that mandate severe penalties for minor crimes. In eighteenth-century England, juries often refused to convict of capital offenses those who were charged with property crimes. In Michigan in the fifties, judges refused to impose mandatory minimum 20-year sentences for drug sales. Modern federal prosecutors and judges often work to avoid imposition of lengthy minimum sentences on minor offenders.

One way, therefore, to bring the symbolic goals of legislators and the instrumental and normative concerns of criminal justice practitioners into better balance would be to confine the scope of mandatory penalties to patently serious crimes such as homicide and aggravated rape and to maintain an empirically realistic balance between the gravity of crimes and the severity of punishments.

D. *Authorize Correctional Reconsideration of Lengthy Sentences*

Little public harm would accrue, and considerable private benefit obtain, if correctional or parole authorities were authorized periodically to reconsider lengthy sentences (say 5 or 10 years) and to release prisoners. Increasing numbers of prisoners are now being held under 10-, 20-, and 30-year mandatory minimum terms or under sentences of life without the possibility of parole. In many states, the steady accumulation of such prisoners promises sizable long-term increases in prison populations and budgets. Many such long-term prisoners continue to be held long after they present any threat to anyone and long after any clamor for their continuing incarceration has subsided. Under the laws of most states, such prisoners can be released only by pardon or commutation. In our era, these powers are seldom exercised. Giving correctional authorities power to reconsider the need or desirability of long sentences would allow eventual release of people receiving unusually long sentences without requiring extraordinary political decisions such as gubernatorial pardons or commutations.

The argument for administrative reconsideration of lengthy mandatory sentences parallels the argument for sunset clauses in mandatory penalty statutes—some decisions present such difficult political problems for elected officials that it is better to eliminate the need to make them. Almost despite the desirability of repealing a mandatory penalty or releasing old and harmless people from prison, feelings of political vulnerability prevent decisions that on their merits ought to be made. Permitting corrections or parole officials to decide when a prisoner under lengthy sentence has served long enough would remove those decisions from the public eye.

Mandatory penalties is not a subject on which research has counted for much in the United States for the past 30 years. Policy debates neither waited for nor paid much attention to research results. We now know what we are ever likely to know, and what our predecessors knew, about mandatory penalties. They do little good and much harm. If New York does repeal its Rockefeller Drug Laws and if that proves a harbinger of change generally, the time may be coming when policy and knowledge will point in the same direction. There will be little need for mandatory penalties, and academics will have no need to propose "reforms" premised on the inability of elected officials to make sensible decisions. If that does not happen, proposals such as those offered here provide mechanisms for reconciling the perceived symbolic and rhetorical needs of elected officials with the legal system's needs for integrity in process and justice in punishment.

REFERENCES

ABA Journal. 1994. "The Verdict Is In: Throw Out Mandatory Sentences: Introduction." 79:78.
American Bar Association. 1968. *Sentencing Alternatives and Procedures.* Chicago: American Bar Association.
———. 1994. *American Bar Association Standards for Criminal Justice: Sentencing Alternatives and Procedures.* 3rd ed. Washington, DC: American Bar Association.
American Law Institute. 1962. *Model Penal Code (Proposed Official Draft).* Philadelphia: American Law Institute.
———. 2007. *Model Penal Code: Sentencing (Tentative Draft No. 1).* Philadelphia: American Law Institute.
Ashworth, Andrew. 2001. "The Decline of English Sentencing and Other Sto-

ries." In *Sentencing and Sanctions in Western Countries*, edited by Michael Tonry and Richard Frase. Oxford: Oxford University Press.

Austin, James. 1991. *The Consequences of Escalating the Use of Imprisonment: The Case Study of Florida*. San Francisco: National Council on Crime and Delinquency.

Austin, James, John Clark, Patricia Hardyman, and D. Alan Henry. 2000. "Three Strikes and You're Out: The Implementation and Impact of Strike Laws." Final Report submitted to the U.S. Department of Justice, U.S. National Institute of Justice.

Austin, James, Charles Jones, John Kramer, and Phil Renninger. 1994. *National Assessment of Structured Sentencing*. Washington, DC: U.S. Department of Justice, Bureau of Justice Assistance.

Ayres, Ian, and John J. Donohue. 2003*a*. "The Latest Misfires in Support of the 'More Guns, Less Crime' Hypothesis." *Stanford Law Review* 55:1371–98.

———. 2003*b*. "Shooting Down the 'More Guns, Less Crime' Hypothesis." *Stanford Law Review* 55:1193–1312.

Baldwin, John, and Michael McConville. 1980. "Criminal Juries." In *Crime and Justice: An Annual Review of Research*, vol. 2, edited by Norval Morris and Michael Tonry. Chicago: University of Chicago Press.

Beha, James A., II. 1977. "'And Nobody Can Get You Out': The Impact of a Mandatory Prison Sentence for the Illegal Carrying of a Firearm on the Use of Firearms and on the Administration of Criminal Justice in Boston." *Boston University Law Review* 57:96–146 (pt.1), 57:289–333 (pt. 2).

Blumstein, Alfred. 1994. "Prisons." In *Crime*, edited by James Q. Wilson and Joan Petersilia. San Francisco: Institute for Contemporary Studies.

Blumstein, Alfred, Jacqueline Cohen, Susan Martin, and Michael Tonry, eds. 1983. *Research on Sentencing: The Search for Reform*. Washington, DC: National Academy Press.

Blumstein, Alfred, Jacqueline Cohen, and Daniel Nagin, eds. 1978. *Deterrence and Incapacitation: Estimating the Effects of Criminal Sanctions on Crime Rates*. Washington, DC: National Academy of Sciences.

Blumstein, Alfred, Jacqueline Cohen, Jeffrey Roth, and Christy Visher, eds. 1986. *Criminal Careers and Career Criminals*. Washington, DC: National Academy Press.

Boerner, David. 1995. "Sentencing Guidelines and Prosecutorial Discretion." *Judicature* 78(4):196–200.

Bowman, Frank O., III, and Michael Heise. 2001. "Quiet Rebellion? Exploring Nearly a Decade of Declining Federal Drug Sentences." *Iowa Law Review* 86(4):1043–1136.

———. 2002. "Quiet Rebellion II: An Empirical Analysis of Declining Federal Drug Sentences Including Data from the District Level." *Iowa Law Review* 87(2):477–561.

Broadhurst, Roderic, and Nini Loh. 1993. "The Phantom of Deterrence: The Crime (Serious and Repeat Offenders) Sentencing Act." *Australian and New Zealand Journal of Criminology* 26(3):251–71.

Brown, David. 2001. "Mandatory Sentencing: A Criminological Perspective." *Australian Journal of Human Rights* 7(2):31–51.

Butterfield, Fox. 2003. "With Cash Tight, States Reassess Long Jail Terms." *New York Times* (November 10), p. A1.

California District Attorneys Association. 2004. *Prosecutors' Perspectives on California's Three Strikes Law: A 10-Year Retrospective.* Sacramento: California District Attorneys Association.

Canada, Standing Committee on Justice and the Solicitor General. 1993. "Crime Prevention in Canada: Toward a National Strategy." Thirty-fourth Canadian Parliament, 1991–93, 3rd session.

Canadian Sentencing Commission. 1987. *Sentencing Reform: A Canadian Approach.* Ottawa: Canadian Government Publishing Centre.

Carlson, Kenneth. 1982. *Mandatory Sentencing: The Experience of Two States.* National Institute of Justice, U.S. Department of Justice. Washington, DC: U.S. Government Printing Office.

Caulkins, Jonathan P. 2001. "How Large Should the Strike Zone Be in 'Three Strikes and You're Out' Sentencing Laws?" *Journal of Quantitative Criminology* 17(3):227–48.

Cavadino, Michael, and James Dignan. 2002. *The Penal System: An Introduction.* 3rd ed. London: Sage

Chen, Elsa Y. 2000. "'Three Strikes and You're Out' and 'Truth in Sentencing': Lessons in Policy Implementation and Impacts." PhD dissertation, Department of Political Science, University of California, Los Angeles.

———. 2008. "Impacts of 'Three Strikes and You're Out' on Crime Trends in California and throughout the United States." *Journal of Contemporary Criminal Justice* 24:345–70.

Coase, Ronald. 1978. "Economics and Contiguous Disciplines." *Journal of Legal Studies* 7(June): 210–11.

Cohen, Jacqueline, and Michael Tonry. 1983. "Sentencing Reforms and Their Impacts." In *Research on Sentencing: The Search for Reform*, vol. 2, edited by Alfred Blumstein, Jacqueline Cohen, Susan Martin, and Michael Tonry. Washington, DC: National Academy Press.

Cook, Philip J. 1980. "Research in Criminal Deterrence: Laying the Groundwork for the Second Decade." In *Crime and Justice: An Annual Review of Research*, vol. 2, edited by Norval Morris and Michael Tonry. Chicago: University of Chicago Press.

Crutcher, Nicole. 2001. "Mandatory Minimum Penalties of Imprisonment: An Historical Analysis." *Criminal Law Quarterly* 44(3):279–309.

Dawson, Robert O. 1969. *Sentencing.* Boston: Little, Brown.

Dezhbakhsh, Hashem, Paul H. Rubin, and Joanna M. Shepherd. 2003. "Does Capital Punishment Have a Deterrent Effect? New Evidence from Post-moratorium Panel Data." *American Law and Economics Review* 5(2):344–76.

Dickey, Walter, and Pamela Hollenhorst. 1999. "Three Strikes Laws: Five Years Later." *Corrections Management Quarterly* 3(3):1–18.

Donohue, John J. 2006. "The Death Penalty: No Evidence for Deterrence." *Economists' Voice* 3(5):1–6.

Donohue, John J., and Justin Wolfers. 2005. "Uses and Abuses of Empirical Evidence in the Death Penalty Debate." *Stanford Law Review* 58:791–846.

Doob, Anthony, and Cheryl Webster. 2003. "Sentence Severity and Crime: Accepting the Null Hypothesis." In *Crime and Justice: A Review of Research*, vol. 30, edited by Michael Tonry. Chicago: University of Chicago Press.

———. 2009. "Under Siege? Assessing the Future for Canada's Stable Rate of Imprisonment." In *International and Comparative Criminal Justice and Urban Governance: Convergence and Divergence in Global, National and Local Settings*, edited by Adam Crawford. Cambridge: Cambridge University Press.

Ehlers, Scott, Vincent Schiraldi, and Jason Ziedenberg. 2004. *Still Striking Out: Ten Years of California's Three Strikes*. San Francisco: Justice Policy Institute.

Fagan, Jeffrey. 1993. "The Political Economy of Drug Dealing among Urban Gangs." In *Drugs and the Community*, edited by Robert C. Davis, Arthur J. Lurigio, and Dennis P. Rosenbaum. Springfield, IL: Thomas.

Federal Courts Study Committee. 1990. *Report*. Washington, DC: Administrative Office of the U.S. Courts.

Federal Judicial Center. 1994. *The Consequences of Mandatory Minimum Prison Terms: A Summary of Recent Findings*. Washington, DC: Federal Judicial Center.

Feeley, Malcolm, and Sam Kamin. 1996. "The Effect of 'Three Strikes and You're Out' on the Courts: Looking Back to See the Future." In *Three Strikes and You're Out, Vengeance and Public Policy*, edited by David Shichor and Dale Sechrest. Thousand Oaks, CA: Sage.

Harris, John C., and Paul Jesilow. 2000. "It's Not the Old Ball Game: Three Strikes and the Courtroom Work Group." *Justice Quarterly* 17(1):185–203.

Hay, Douglas. 1975. "Property, Authority, and the Criminal Law." In *Albion's Fatal Tree: Crime and Society in Eighteenth Century England*, edited by Douglas Hay, Peter Linebaugh, and E. P. Thompson. New York: Pantheon.

———. 1980. "Crime and Justice in Eighteenth and Nineteenth Century England." In *Crime and Justice: An Annual Review of Research*, vol. 2, edited by Norval Morris and Michael Tonry. Chicago: University of Chicago Press.

Hay, Douglas, Peter Linebaugh, John G. Rule, E. Thompson, and Cal Winslow. 1975. *Albion's Fatal Tree: Crime and Society in Eighteenth-Century England*. New York: Pantheon.

Heumann, Milton, and Colin Loftin. 1979. "Mandatory Sentencing and the Abolition of Plea Bargaining: The Michigan Felony Firearms Statute." *Law and Society Review* 13:393–430.

Hogg, Russell. 1999. "Mandatory Sentencing Laws and the Symbolic Politics of Law and Order." *University of New South Wales Law Journal* 22(1):263–79.

Holmes, Oliver Wendell. 1889. "Law in Science and Science in Law." *Harvard Law Review* 12:443–63.

Home Office. 1990. *Crime, Justice, and Protecting the Public*. London: Home Office.

Ifill, Gwen. 1991. "Senate's Rule for Its Anti-crime Bill: The Tougher the Provision, the Better." *New York Times* (July 8, national ed.), p. A6.

Johnson, Brian, Jeffrey T. Ulmer, and John Kramer. 2008. "The Social Context of Guidelines Circumvention: The Case of Federal District Courts." *Criminology* 46(3):737–83.

Johnson, Bruce D., Terry Williams, Kojo A. Dei, and Harry Sanabria. 1990. "Drug Abuse in the Inner City: Impact on Hard-Drug Users and the Community." In *Drugs and Crime*, edited by Michael Tonry and James Q. Wilson. Vol. 13 of *Crime and Justice: A Review of Research*, edited by Michael Tonry and Norval Morris. Chicago: University of Chicago Press.

Johnson, Dianne, and George Zdenkowski. 2000. *Mandatory Injustice: Compulsory Imprisonment in the Northern Territory*. Sydney: Centre for Independent Journalism.

Johnson, Molly Treadway, and Scott A. Gilbert. 1997. "The U.S. Sentencing Guidelines: Results of the Federal Judicial Center's 1996 Survey." Report to the Committee on Criminal Law of the Judicial Conference of the United States, Federal Judicial Center, Washington, DC

Joint Committee on New York Drug Law Evaluation. 1978. *The Nation's Toughest Drug Law: Evaluating the New York Experience*. Project of the Association of the Bar of the City of New York and the Drug Abuse Council, Inc. Washington, DC: U.S. Government Printing Office.

Jones, Trevor, and Tim Newburn. 2006. "Three Strikes and You're Out: Exploring Symbol and Substance in American and British Crime Control Policies." *British Journal of Criminology* 46(5):781–802.

Justice Policy Institute. 2004. "Three Strikes and You're Out: An Examination of the Impact of Three Strikes Laws 10 Years after Their Enactment." San Francisco: Justice Policy Institute.

Kennedy, Anthony, chairman. 2004. *American Bar Association Justice Kennedy Commission Report with Recommendations to the ABA House of Delegates, August 2004*. Chicago: American Bar Association.

Kessler, Daniel, and Steven Levitt. 1999. "Using Sentence Enhancements to Distinguish between Deterrence and Incapacitation." *Journal of Law and Economics* 42:343–63.

Knapp, Kay A. 1991. "Arizona: Unprincipled Sentencing, Mandatory Minimums, and Prison Crowding." *Overcrowded Times* 2(5):10–12.

Kovandzic, Tomislav, John Sloan, and Lynne Vieraitis. 2002. "Unintended Consequences of Politically Popular Sentencing Policy: The Homicide Promoting Effects of 'Three Strikes' in U.S. Cities (1980–1999)." *Criminology and Public Policy* 1(3):399–424.

———. 2004. "Striking Out as Crime Reduction Policy: The Impact of 'Three Strikes Laws' on Crime Rates in U.S. Cities." *Justice Quarterly* 21(2):207–45.

Law Council of Australia. 2001. *The Mandatory Sentencing Debate*. Canberra: Law Council of Australia.

Legislative Analyst's Office, California Legislature. 2005. *A Primer: Three Strikes: The Impact after More than a Decade*. Sacramento: Legislative Analyst's Office.

Levitt, Steven D. 2002. "Deterrence." In *Crime: Public Policies for Crime Control*, edited by James Q. Wilson and Joan Petersilia. Oakland, CA: Institute for Contemporary Studies Press.

Levitt, Steven D., and Thomas J. Miles. 2007. "Empirical Study of Criminal Punishment." In *Handbook of Law and Economics*, vol. 1, edited by A. Mitchell Polinsky and Steven Shavell. Amsterdam: Elsevier.

Lewis, Donald E. 1986. "The General Deterrent Effect of Longer Sentences." *British Journal of Criminology* 26(1):47–62.

Liptak, Adam. 2007. "Whittling Away, but Leaving a Gap." *New York Times* (November 17), p. A21.

Loftin, Colin, Milton Heumann, and David McDowall. 1983. "Mandatory Sentencing and Firearms Violence: Evaluating an Alternative to Gun Control." *Law and Society Review* 17:287–318.

Loftin, Colin, and David McDowall. 1981. "'One with a Gun Gets You Two': Mandatory Sentencing and Firearms Violence in Detroit." *Annals of the American Academy of Political and Social Science* 455(1):150–67.

———. 1984. "The Deterrent Effects of the Florida Felony Firearm Law." *Journal of Criminal Law and Criminology* 75:250–59.

Lott, John R., Jr. [1998] 2000. *More Guns, Less Crime: Understanding Crime and Gun Control Laws*. 2nd ed. Chicago: University of Chicago Press.

Lott, John R., Jr., and David B. Mustard. 1997. "Crime, Deterrence, and Right-to-Carry Concealed Handguns." *Journal of Legal Studies* 26(1):1–68.

Males, Mike, and Dan Macallair. 1999. "Striking Out: The Failure of California's Three Strikes and You're Out Law." *Stanford Law and Policy Review* 11(1):65–81.

Marvell, Thomas B., and Carlisle E. Moody. 2001. "The Lethal Effects of Three Strikes Laws." *Journal of Legal Studies* 30(1):89–106.

McCoy, Candace, and Patrick McManimon. 2004. "New Jersey's 'No Early Release Act': Its Impact on Prosecution, Sentencing, Corrections, and Victim Satisfaction." Final report (unpublished), National Institute of Justice, Washington, DC (obtainable from the National Criminal Justice Reference Service).

McDowall, David, Colin Loftin, and Brian Wiersema. 1992. "A Comparative Study of the Preventive Effects of Mandatory Sentencing Laws for Gun Crimes." *Journal of Criminal Law and Criminology* 83:378–94.

Merritt, Nancy, Terry Fain, and Susan Turner. 2006. "Oregon's Get Tough Sentencing Reform: A Lesson in Justice System Adaptation." *Criminology and Public Policy* 5(1):5–36.

Michael, Jerome, and Herbert Wechsler. 1940. *Criminal Law and Its Administration*. Brooklyn, NY: Foundation.

Moody, Carlisle E., Thomas B. Marvell, and Robert J. Kaminski. 2003. "Unintended Consequences: Three-Strikes Laws and the Murders of Police Officers." Cambridge, MA: National Bureau of Economic Research.

Morgan, Neil. 2000. "Mandatory Sentences in Australia: Where Have We Been and Where Are We Going?" *University of New South Wales Law Journal* 24(3):164–83.

Moynihan, Daniel Patrick. 1997. *Miles to Go: A Personal History of Social Policy*. Cambridge, MA: Harvard University Press.

Nagel, Ilene H., and Stephen J. Schulhofer. 1992. "A Tale of Three Cities: An

Empirical Study of Charging and Bargaining Practices under the Federal Sentencing Guidelines." *Southern California Law Review* 66:501 66.

Nagin, Daniel S. 1978. "General Deterrence: A Review of the Empirical Evidence." In *Deterrence and Incapacitation*, edited by Alfred Blumstein, Jacqueline Cohen, and Daniel Nagin. Washington, DC: National Academy Press.

———. 1998. "Criminal Deterrence Research at the Outset of the Twenty-first Century." In *Crime and Justice: A Review of Research*, vol. 23, edited by Michael Tonry. Chicago: University of Chicago Press.

Newman, Donald. 1966. *Conviction*. Boston: Little, Brown.

O'Donovan, Michael, and Jean Redpath. 2006. *The Impact of Mandatory Sentencing in South Africa*. Capetown: Open Society Foundation.

Padilla, Felix. 1992. *The Gang as an American Enterprise*. New Brunswick, NJ: Rutgers University Press.

Peters, Jeremy W. 2009. "Albany Reaches Deal to Repeal '70s Drug Laws." *New York Times* (March 26), p. A1.

Pierce, Glen L., and William J. Bowers. 1981. "The Bartley-Fox Gun Law's Short-Term Impact on Crime in Boston." *Annals of the American Academy of Political and Social Science* 455(1):120–32.

Pound, Roscoe. 1910. "Law in Books and Law in Action." *American Law Review* 44:12–36.

Pratt, Travis C., Francis T. Cullen, Kristie R. Blevins, Leah H. Daigle, and Tamara D. Madensen. 2006. "The Empirical Status of Deterrence Theory: A Meta-analysis." In *Taking Stock: The Status of Criminological Theory*, edited by Francis T. Cullen, John Paul Wright, and Kristie R. Blevins. New Brunswick, NJ: Transaction.

Radzinowicz, Leon. 1948–68. *A History of English Criminal Law and Its Administration from 1750*. 4 vols. London: Stevens.

Reiss, Albert J., Jr., and Jeffrey Roth, eds. 1993. *Understanding and Preventing Violence*. Washington, DC: National Academy Press.

Remington, Frank. 1969. "Introduction." In *Sentencing*, by Robert Dawson. Boston: Little, Brown.

Roberts, Julian. 2003. "Public Opinion and Mandatory Sentencing: A Review of International Findings." *Criminal Justice and Behavior* 30(4):483–508.

Romilly, Sir Samuel. 1820. "Sir Samuel Romilly's Speeches." In *Criminal Law and Its Administration*, edited by Jerome Michael and Herbert Wechsler. Chicago: Foundation.

Ross, H. Laurence. 1982. *Deterring the Drinking Driver: Legal Policy and Social Control*. Lexington, MA: Lexington.

Rossman, David, Paul Froyd, Glen Pierce, John McDevitt, and William Bowers. 1979. *The Impact of the Mandatory Gun Law in Massachusetts*. Report to the National Institute of Law Enforcement and Criminal Justice. Washington, DC: U.S. Government Printing Office.

Roth, Sandra. 2008. "South African Mandatory Minimum Sentencing: Reform Required." *Minnesota Journal of International Law* 17:155–82

Schiraldi, Vincent, and Tara-Jen Ambrosio. 1997 "Striking Out: The Crime

Control Impact of 'Three-Strikes' Laws." San Francisco: Justice Policy Institute.

Schulhofer, Stephen J. 1997. "Plea Negotiations under the Federal Sentencing Guidelines: Guideline Circumvention and Its Dynamics in the Post-Mistretta Period." *Northwestern University Law Review* 91:1284–1316.

Schulhofer, Stephen J., and Ilene H. Nagel. 1989. "Negotiated Pleas under the Federal Sentencing Guidelines: The First Fifteen Months." *American Criminal Law Review* 27(2):231–88.

Secretary of State, State of California. 1999. *Three Strikes and You're Out: Five Years Later*. Sacramento: California Secretary of State.

Select Committee on Capital Punishment. 1930. *Report*. London: H. M. Stationery Office.

Sentencing Advisory Council. 2008. *Sentencing Matters: Mandatory Sentencing*. Melbourne: Sentencing Advisory Council.

Shane-DuBow, Sandra, Alice P. Brown, and Erik Olsen. 1985. *Sentencing Reform in the United States: History, Content, and Effect*. Washington, DC: U.S. Government Printing Office.

Shepherd, Joanna M. 2002. "Fear of the First Strike: The Full Deterrent Effect of California's Two- and Three-Strike Legislation." *Journal of Legal Studies* 31(1):159–201.

———. 2004. "Testimony Printed in Terrorist Penalties Enhancement Act of 2003: Hearing on H.R. 2934 before the Subcommittee on Crime, Terrorism, and Homeland Security of the House Committee on the Judiciary, 108th Congress," pp. 10–11. http://judiciary.house.gov/media/pdfs/printers/108th/93224.pdf.

Sherman, Lawrence W. 1990. "Police Crackdowns: Initial and Residual Deterrence." In *Crime and Justice: A Review of Research*, vol. 12, edited by Michael Tonry and Norval Morris. Chicago: University of Chicago Press.

Sloth-Nielsen, Julia, and Louise Ehlers. 2005. "Assessing the Impact: Mandatory and Minimum Sentences in South Africa." *South African Crime Quarterly* 14(December):15–22.

Steinhauer, Jennifer. 2009. "To Cut Costs, States Relax Prison Policies." *New York Times* (March 24), p. A1.

Stephen, James Fitzjames. 1977. *A History of the Criminal Law of England*. New York: Franklin. (Originally published 1883. London: Macmillan).

Stith, Kate. 2008. "The Arc of the Pendulum: Judges, Prosecutors, and the Exercise of Discretion." *Yale Law Journal* 117:1420–97.

Stolzenberg, Lisa, and Stewart J. D'Alessio. 1997. "'Three Strikes and You're Out': The Impact of California's New Mandatory Sentencing Law on Serious Crime Rates." *Crime and Delinquency* 43(4):457–69.

Teeters, Negley K., with Jack H. Hedblom. 1967. *Hang by the Neck: The Legal Use of Scaffold and Noose, Gibbet, Stake, and Firing Squad from Colonial Times to the Present*. Springfield, IL: Thomas.

Terblanche, Stephan. 2003. "Mandatory and Minimum Sentences: Considering S. 51 of the Criminal Law Amendment Act of 1997." *Acta Juridica*, pp. 194–220.

Tonry, Michael. 1996. *Sentencing Matters*. New York: Oxford University Press.

———. 2004. *Thinking about Crime: Sense and Sensibility in American Penal Policy*. New York: Oxford University Press.

———. 2008. "Learning from the Limitations of Deterrence Research." In *Crime and Justice: A Review of Research*, vol. 37, edited by Michael Tonry. Chicago: University of Chicago Press.

Törnudd, Patrik. 1993. *Fifteen Years of Declining Prisoner Rates*. Research Communication no. 8. Helsinki: National Research Institute of Legal Policy.

Ulmer, Jeffery T., Megan C. Kurlychek, and John H. Kramer. 2008. "Prosecutorial Discretion and the Imposition of Mandatory Minimum Sentences." *Journal of Research in Crime and Delinquency* 44(4):427–58.

U.S. General Accounting Office. 1993. *Federal Drug Offenses: Departures from Sentencing Guidelines and Mandatory Minimum Sentences, Fiscal Years 1999–2001*. Washington, DC: U.S. General Accounting Office.

———. 2003. *Mandatory Minimum Sentences: Are They Being Imposed and Who Is Receiving Them?* Washington, DC: U.S. General Accounting Office.

U.S. Sentencing Commission. 1991. *Special Report to the Congress: Mandatory Minimum Penalties in the Federal Criminal Justice System*. Washington, DC: U.S. Sentencing Commission.

van zyl Smit, Dirk. 2000. "Mandatory Sentences: A Conundrum for the New South Africa?" *Punishment and Society* 2:197–212.

von Hirsch, Andrew, Anthony E. Bottoms, Elizabeth Burney, and Per-Olof H. Wikström. 1999. *Criminal Deterrence and Sentence Severity: An Analysis of Recent Research*. Oxford: Hart.

Warner, Kate. 2007. "Mandatory Sentencing and the Role of the Academic." *Criminal Law Forum* 18(3–4):321–47.

Webster, Cheryl Marie, and Anthony N. Doob. 2007. "Punitive Trends and Stable Imprisonment Rates in Canada." In *Crime, Punishment, and Politics in Comparative Perspective*, edited by Michael Tonry. Vol. 36 of *Crime and Justice: A Review of Research*, edited by Michael Tonry. Chicago: University of Chicago Press.

Webster, Cheryl Marie, Anthony N. Doob, and Franklin E. Zimring. 2006. "Proposition 8 and Crime Rates in California: The Case for the Disappearing Deterrent." *Criminology and Public Policy* 5:417–48.

Wilson, James Q. 1990. "Drugs and Crime." In *Drugs and Crime*, edited by Michael Tonry and James Q. Wilson. Vol. 13 of *Crime and Justice: A Review of Research*, edited by Michael Tonry and Norval Morris. Chicago: University of Chicago Press.

Yeats, Mary Ann. 1997. "'Three Strikes' and Restorative Justice: Dealing with Young Repeat Burglars in Australia." *Criminal Law Bulletin* 8:369–85.

Zimring, Franklin E., Gordon Hawkins, and Sam Kamin. 2001. *Punishment and Democracy: Three Strikes and You're Out in California*. New York: Oxford University Press.

*Daniel S. Nagin, Francis T. Cullen,
and Cheryl Lero Jonson*

Imprisonment and Reoffending

ABSTRACT

Imprisonment is the most severe punishment in democratic societies except for capital punishment, which is used only in the United States.
Crime prevention is its primary rationale. Imprisonment may affect reoffending in various ways. It may be reduced by some combination of rehabilitation and what criminologists call specific deterrence. Sound arguments can be made, however, for a criminogenic effect (e.g., due to
antisocial prison experiences or to stigma endured upon release). Remarkably little is known about the effects of imprisonment on reoffending. The
existing research is limited in size, in quality, in its insights into why a
prison term might be criminogenic or preventative, and in its capacity to
explain why imprisonment might have differential effects depending on offenders' personal and social characteristics. Compared with noncustodial
sanctions, incarceration appears to have a null or mildly criminogenic effect on future criminal behavior. This conclusion is not sufficiently firm to
guide policy generally, though it casts doubt on claims that imprisonment
has strong specific deterrent effects. The evidence does provide a basis for
outlining components of an agenda for substantive and policy relevant
research.

Imprisonment is intended to prevent crime by incapacitation and deterrence. Incapacitation refers to crime prevention resulting from the
physical isolation of offenders. Deterrence refers to a behavioral response. Criminologists have long drawn a distinction between general

Daniel S. Nagin is Teresa and H. John Heinz III University Professor of Public Policy
and Statistics, Heinz College, Carnegie Mellon University; Francis T. Cullen is Distinguished Research Professor of Criminal Justice, School of Criminal Justice, University
of Cincinnati; and Cheryl Lero Jonson is Criminal Justice PhD candidate, School of
Criminal Justice, University of Cincinnati. We thank Michael Tonry and anonymous
reviewers for helpful commentary. Support for this review was in part provided by the
National Science Foundation (SES-0647576).

deterrence, the response to the threat of punishment in the population at large, and the response to punishment of the punished, called specific or special deterrence. This essay addresses the latter, the effect of imprisonment on reoffending. We use this more generic label because the experience of imprisonment may affect reoffending by mechanisms other than deterrence. For example, a preventive effect may arise from involvement in rehabilitation programs or a criminogenic effect may result from such mechanisms as stigma or association with fellow inmates.

Despite a growing literature on the effect of imprisonment on reoffending and previous attempts to assess this research (Gendreau, Goggin, and Cullen 1999; Villettaz, Killias, and Zoder 2006), rigorous scientific knowledge is in short supply. Given that in the United States alone over 2.3 million offenders reside in correctional institutions, this is a remarkable omission. Much work remains to be done. As part of this undertaking, this essay attempts to systematize the existing literature, to furnish a provisional statement of prisons' likely effect on individual offenders, and to identify issues for future research. We expand upon Gendreau, Goggin, and Cullen (1999) and Villettaz, Killias, and Zoder (2006) by examining a larger body of research than those analyses did, by discussing the methodological challenges to inferring imprisonment effects from nonexperimental data in detail, and by laying out an agenda for future research. Our concern is in assessing how imprisonment affects individuals' reoffending and not on how macro-level variations in imprisonment affect crime rates.

Although research on the effect of custodial sanctions on reoffending is international—with some of the best work coming from Europe and Australia—the evidence is reviewed from an American-centric perspective. This is because the scale of imprisonment in the United States dwarfs that of other democratic societies absolutely and per capita. Still, other nations incarcerate tens of thousands of offenders and must struggle with the wisdom of expanding their institutional capacity. Regardless of location, sound scientific knowledge about the effects of imprisonment is integral to an informed policy discussion of crime control.

In the early 1970s, the United States had experienced relative stability in imprisonment for at least half a century, with rates of incarceration hovering around 100 state and federal inmates per 100,000 population (Blumstein and Cohen 1973; Greenfeld and Langan 1987).

The use of prison as a mechanism of social control seemed to be on the decline. The prison population, which had risen to 220,149 in 1961, dipped over the next decade to under 200,000 (Greenfeld and Langan 1987). Scholars wrote about the inevitability of "decarceration" (Scull 1977) and the "end of imprisonment" (Sommer 1976). Talk of abolishing prisons was not seen as far-fetched (Mitford 1973). Menninger's *The Crime of Punishment* (1968) earned wide popular acclaim, suggesting a growing consensus that mean-spirited penal policies should be regarded as a relic of less civilized days (see also Toby 1964).

In Massachusetts, Jerome Miller, head of the state's Department of Youth Services, boldly emptied the state's juvenile reformatories in the early seventies. When youth crime failed to spike upward, the "Massachusetts experiment" in deinstitutionalization was heralded as showing that incarceration did not reduce lawbreaking (Miller 1991). At about this same time, observers of corrections learned of the Stanford Prison Experiment (Haney, Banks, and Zimbardo 1973). Psychologically normal students were randomly assigned roles as guards or inmates. The newly minted guards quickly began to abuse and otherwise mistreat the unlucky students assigned to be prisoners. This reinforced the view of many that prisons were inherently coercive and inhumane (Zimbardo 2007). During the prisoner insurgency in 1971 at Attica Correctional Facility, 29 inmates and 10 correctional officers were killed in retaking the institution. The word "Attica" came to symbolize not vicious inmates rioting uncontrollably but the willingness of the state to abuse its power by wantonly shooting down inmates whose protests had merit (Cullen and Gilbert 1982). When bank robber Al Pacino chanted "Attica, Attica" in the film *Dog Day Afternoon*, audiences cheered; they were not on the side of the police surrounding the bank.

Yet shortly thereafter, a sea change transformed penal policy in the United States. Over the next 4 decades, the incarceration rate for state and federal inmates rose more than fivefold from 96 per 100,000 in 1970 to 501 at year-end 2006 (Greenfeld and Langan 1987; Sabol, Couture, and Harrison 2007). Counting those housed in jails, the nation's total incarceration rate surpassed 750 per 100,000 (Liptak 2008). In absolute terms, the number of state and federal prison inmates jumped from below 200,000 in 1970 to over 1.5 million in 2008. When those held in local jails and other secure facilities are added, the daily count exceeds 2.3 million (Sabol, Couture, and Harrison 2007). This inexorable expansion was not confined to a few states but reflects a trend that, with some variation, occurred across all states and regions (Zimring and Hawkins 1991).

The 4-decade-long rise in prison populations in the United States is unique. Some advanced Western nations, such as Great Britain and the Netherlands, increased their prison populations (Garland 2001; Tonry 2004; Downes 2007; Tonry and Bijleveld 2007). But others, such as the Scandinavian nations and, most notably, Canada just to the north of the United States, displayed substantial stability in their imprisonment rates over 30 years (Lappi-Seppälä 2007; Webster and Doob 2007). And even among those Western countries that expanded prison use, the scale of imprisonment is simply not comparable. England and Wales, for example, imprisoned around 80,000 in 2006 and had an incarceration rate of 142 per 100,000 (Newburn 2007). These figures make England and Wales "the highest incarcerator in Western Europe" (Newburn 2007, p. 435). For Western nations generally, the incarceration rate falls between 50 and 150—figures dwarfed by America's rate of 751 (Tonry 2004; Liptak 2008; Warren 2008). When all the comparative statistics are lined up, it is clear that the United States' "crime control policies" have become "much harsher than in earlier American times or in other places" (Tonry 2004, p. 23).

A lengthy roster of works seeks to document and dissect the sustained increase in incarceration in the United States (see, e.g., Zimring and Hawkins 1991; Clear 1994; Beckett 1997; Currie 1998; Blumstein and Beck 1999, 2005; Garland 2001; Wacquant 2001; Whitman 2003; Tonry 2004; Gottschalk 2006; Harcourt 2006; Lynch 2007; Raphael and Stoll 2007; Simon 2007; Useem and Piehl 2008). Diverse factors have been proposed: increased rates of crime; harsh, mandatory sentencing policies; a "war on drugs" that brought into the justice system many noncriminal drug users and low-risk offenders; the politicization of crime in which "get tough" promises enjoyed wide public support; efforts to contain and repress minority group members; the reallocation of resources to the criminal justice system from the mental health system, where large numbers of patients once housed in state facilities are now substantially deinstitutionalized; the emergence of a "culture of control" that welcomed efforts to protect citizens, especially those of the middle class; and a changed "sensibility" about crime and punishment that encourages harsh justice. As Tonry (2004) notes, these accounts are of differential merit; none is a complete explanation. At best, they should be viewed as "risk factors" whose cumulative effect has been to sustain a 4-decade growth in prison populations (Tonry 2007).

Regardless of one's views on the rightness of the policies that have given rise to increased imprisonment, the United States now incarcerates a disturbingly large proportion of its residents. A recent report by Pew Charitable Trusts calculates that one in every 99.1 adults is in custody (Warren 2008). The differential impact of imprisonment on minorities is particularly disquieting. For African American men ages 20–34, one in nine is incarcerated (Warren 2008). It is estimated that one-third of all black males will spend time in a state or federal prison during their lives (Bonczar 2003). Concerns have been voiced about the negative effect on inner-city communities of removing into custody such a substantial segment of the male population for repeated and often lengthy periods (Clear 2007). More critically, Wacquant (2001, p. 95) proposes that the "ghetto and prison" are now so interconnected that they exist in a "deadly symbiosis."

Imprisonment is costly, exacts an economic and psychological toll on family members of the incarcerated, particularly children, and raises issues of social justice due to its differential impact on minority members and communities. Thus, beyond being an instrument for meting out just deserts, prison's justification must rest heavily on its demonstrated capacity to protect the social order. Understanding the effects of incarceration on reoffending is thus a key consideration in formulating correctional policy.

As noted at the outset of this essay, criminologists have long drawn a distinction between general deterrence and specific deterrence. The theory of general deterrence is clear and particularly well articulated in economic theory (Becker 1968; Cook 1980). It is the empirics that remain unclear. What is the magnitude of the effect? How does it vary across sanction types, crimes, and people? These are not trifling uncertainties. They are fundamental to the efficacy of crime control by the threat of formal sanctions (Nagin 1998; Doob and Webster 2003; Tonry 2007). By contrast, the very logic of special deterrence is murky. More than 30 years ago, Zimring and Hawkins (1973, p. 225) observed: "To talk of 'the impact of punishment on potential offenders' and the 'impact of punishment on the offender' as 'two kinds of deterrence' is rather like saying that a storm warning and the storm are two different kinds of disturbance. The use of the expression 'impact of punishment' twice in one sentence to denote two quite separate and distinct processes generates a confusion of categories and obscures an important distinction." We agree.

The studies that are the focus of this essay examine how placing an offender in prison affects the person's future criminal involvement or "reoffending." We use the concept of reoffending to refer to all criminal acts committed by a person following a legal sanction, in this case imprisonment. Reoffending subsumes the concept of "recidivism," which is defined as the commission of at least one criminal act after the completion of a sentence. When computed for a given group of offenders, recidivism is typically expressed as a percentage—for example, as the percentage of a prison release cohort who commit one or more criminal acts within a designated period following their release. Reoffending is conceptually broader than recidivism because it also subsumes measures such as the rate of offending—number of crimes committed over a specified time interval. The measurement of reoffending and recidivism poses many technical challenges that are beyond the scope of this essay.[1] One involves the specification of the time window over which the reoffending measure will be calibrated (e.g., 3 years). Perhaps the most controversial is the specification of what event should properly constitute a return to crime—the self-reported criminality of the offender, arrest, conviction, or reimprisonment. Most of the studies reviewed here employ measures of rearrest or reconviction. These are "official" measures because they depend on an offender's detection by the state.

An initial reason to be skeptical of specific deterrence, as an empirical matter, is that reoffending among prison inmates is high, with rates of official recidivism often reaching 60 percent within 3 years (Langan and Levin 2002). But using these data is potentially misleading. Rates of official recidivism among those receiving community-based sanctions—especially felony offenders who might have been sent to prison—are also high (Petersilia 2002). The litmus test for assessing the impact of imprisonment on reoffending is to compare the experiences of offenders in prison with those of similar offenders given a noncustodial sanction.

Estimating the effect of imprisonment on the subsequent criminal career development of those actually imprisoned is complicated by

[1] See Maltz (1984) for a full discussion of the measurement and calibration of recidivism.

many factors. One is that a priori, even the sign of the effect of the prison experience on subsequent criminality is indeterminate. Sound arguments can be made that the experience of imprisonment either increases or decreases criminality. Further, the effect may be contingent on prior experience with imprisonment, stage of criminal career development, and age. Imprisonment is selectively imposed. Persons who are sentenced to prison have committed more serious crimes and have more extensive prior records of offending, on average, than their counterparts who receive noncustodial sanctions. These differences must be carefully accounted for to isolate statistically the effect of imprisonment on subsequent criminal behavior.

The challenges to making this inference are discussed at length in Section II. Particular emphasis is given to accounting for age. This is important because involvement in crime is highly age dependent, and recidivism, by definition, is time dependent and thereby age dependent. Consequently, even small differences in the ages of those imprisoned relative to the ages of the nonimprisoned may significantly contaminate estimates of the effect of imprisonment on reoffending.

Most studies of the impact of imprisonment on subsequent criminality find no effect or a criminogenic effect. Only a few studies find evidence of a preventive effect. We conclude, however, that existing research is not nearly sufficient for making firm evidence-based conclusions for either science or public policy. The limitations of the evidence stem from a combination of factors. As a matter of public policy, there is a fundamental difference between concluding that imprisonment reduces or has no effect on reoffending and concluding that it exacerbates reoffending. The evidence on neither side of this dichotomy is sufficiently strong to distinguish convincingly between them. In many nonexperimental studies, insufficient control for the relationship between age and reoffending rates may be seriously biasing estimates of the effect of custodial compared to noncustodial sanctions. Many of the studies involve juveniles or compare very short periods of confinement with noncustodial sanctions, or both. Both attributes limit the relevance of a study's conclusions about the effects of imprisonment on reoffending in contemporary society. In medical parlance, it is important to understand the "dose-response" relationship between the experience of imprisonment and subsequent criminality. We lack even a crude estimate of this relationship. We have little evidence on the mechanisms that underlie any effect imprisonment may have on reoffending.

This essay is organized as follows: Section I examines competing perspectives on the effects of imprisonment. Sociologically inspired criminology portrays imprisonment as a social experience that is criminogenic due to in-prison and postprison experiences. Conversely, economic analysts see imprisonment as a cost that, because it exacts a higher price than alternative sanctions, deters reoffending more than noncustodial sanctions. Section II discusses the statistical issues that must be addressed to estimate imprisonment effects on reoffending with nonexperimental data. In Section III, the evidence on the effect of custodial sanctions on reoffending is reviewed. We distinguish two broad categories of studies: those examining the effects of custodial compared with noncustodial sanction and those examining the effects of length of confinement. Section IV addresses policy and theoretical implications of our analysis.

I. Perspectives on Imprisonment

In the 1820s and 1830s, the United States embarked on a bold experiment in institutionalization. The belief was widespread that prisons— optimistically called "penitentiaries"—would transform the lawbreaking into the law abiding (Rothman 1971). This reformist spirit is embodied in the current use of the term "correctional institutions" to refer to prisons. Since their invention, however, these facilities have had their critics, claiming that words such as "penitentiary" and "correctional institution" are more euphemism than reality—or, in the language of Rothman (1980), more claims to "conscience" than admissions of the "convenience" that actually prevails. Amidst this critical scrutiny has been the long-standing worry that imprisonment not only does not reform but, rather, exacerbates inmates' criminality.

Rothman (1971, p. 214) observed that in 1850s America, commentators, "convinced that confinement was inherently unnatural, and therefore injurious, . . . wanted to return convicts, with appropriate precautions and supervision, to the community as quickly as possible. The sooner the criminal reentered society, the more likely he would become law-abiding; the longer he remained secluded, the more incorrigible he would grow." Similar comments are found in every era. To highlight but one other example, we can point to "Stanley," the subject of Shaw's (1930) life history, *The Jack-Roller: A Delinquent Boy's Own Story*. At the end of his stay in a House of Corrections—referred to by Shaw as a "House of Corruption"—Stanley took stock of what he had learned and of what awaited him:

> I tried to think of my future but more crimes and jail bars stared me in the face at every angle. There was no hope but in crime. All my friends were criminals and besides I was a criminal and nobody would trust me—only look down on me and shun me. Somehow I was different from anybody but criminals and I always felt drawn to crime. Circumstance had turned me back into jail every time before when I tried to make good. But now I had lost my ambition and didn't care for anything but crime. Was I not completely alone in the world except for my buddies in crime and did I not always feel pulled to them and to the adventures and luxuries that crime offered? I was educated in crime. (Shaw 1930, pp. 162–63)

Critics thus tend to see prisons as sources of inhumanity and, in turn, of crime. By contrast, others see experience with the correctional system as just that—correctional. The prison experience demarcates moral boundaries and teaches those within its walls the lesson that crime does not pay. Austere institutional conditions may convince inmates that imprisonment is an experience not to be repeated. Further, educational and treatment programs within the prison may provide the inmates with skills that can be used in legal labor markets or reduce the propensities such as drug addiction that were the cause for their incarceration.

It is possible that these two global views—prisons as criminogenic and prisons as a preventative deterrent—are both correct. Thus, imprisonment might have differential effects, pushing some offenders toward and others away from crime. The effect might be conditioned by characteristics of the offender (e.g., low risk or high risk), of the institution (e.g., harsh or therapeutic), or of the sanction (e.g., length). And the effect is comparative, assessed in relation to what a noncustodial sanction, if applied instead of custody, might have entailed. Current research is not sufficiently developed to address issues of this specificity.

In this section, we elaborate on these two global perspectives. This discussion is relevant because it illuminates the conduits through which incarceration might increase or decrease criminal involvement. These are factors that potentially specify the impact of imprisonment and thus should be of concern in future research.

A. Prisons as a Specific Deterrent

According to the economic model of crime, imprisonment is a key cost to offending (Becker 1968). Imprisonment exacts a variable price; it is more costly to the extent that the sentence assigned is longer rather than shorter or to the extent that the conditions of confinement are harsher rather than nicer. Prisons deter because they influence the expected utility of future criminal pursuits. Further if a custodial sanction is perceived to be more costly than a noncustodial sanction, the imprisonment sanction will exert a greater deterrent effect.[2]

Why, then, did we earlier indicate that the logic of specific deterrence is murky? From an economic perspective, the experience of imprisonment is only relevant to future offending decisions if it influences perceptions of the costs and benefits of future offending. The precise effects on perceptions or expectations of being in prison, however, are not straightforward and likely hinge on a number of contingencies. Thus, if the experience of imprisonment is sufficiently distasteful, some of the punished may indeed conclude that it is an experience not to be repeated. The structure of the law itself may cause previously convicted individuals to revise upward their estimates of the likelihood or severity of punishment for future lawbreaking. The criminal law commonly prescribes more severe penalties for recidivists. For example, sentencing guidelines routinely dictate more severe sentences for individuals with prior convictions. Prosecutors may also be more likely to prosecute individuals with criminal histories. These offenders might expect that an arrest would bring, with much greater certainty, a harsher prison sentence and hence be more susceptible to specific deterrence.

Other offenders, however, may respond differently to the experience of imprisonment. They may conclude that prisons were not as unpleasant as anticipated; if so, they may revise downward their expected utility loss from a future experience of imprisonment and thus be more likely to reoffend. Further, evidence from behavioral economics points to additional mechanisms by which the experience of punishment may decrease rather than increase expectations about sanction costs. For

---

[2] Research on the differential effect of prison conditions is sparse and conflicting (Katz, Levitt, and Shustorovich 2003; Chen and Shapiro 2007); accordingly, we do not consider this aspect of specific deterrence in this essay.

example, research on substance abuse and driving under the influence finds a positive effect (i.e., offending becomes more likely) of experience with punishment on subsequent offending (Paternoster and Piquero 1995; Piquero and Paternoster 1998). Pogarsky and Piquero (2003) propose the idea of a "resetting" effect to explain this positive association. The resetting effect is an application of the concept of the "gambler's fallacy" (Gilovich 1983; Clotfelter and Cook 1993). Just as folk meteorology holds that "lightning never strikes twice in the same place," the gambler's fallacy holds that bad or good things do not run in quick succession. Consequently, the experience of punishment may lead to a decrease, not an increase, in the punished individuals' estimate of the certainty of being punished which, in turn, may encourage them to offend more frequently.

Beyond altering expectations, the experience of punishment may affect the likelihood of future crime by increasing or decreasing the attractiveness of crime itself or by expanding or contracting alternatives to crime. While imprisoned, the individual may benefit from educational or vocational training that increases postrelease noncriminal income-earning opportunities (MacKenzie 2002). Other types of rehabilitation are designed to increase the capacity for self-restraint when challenged by situations, like a confrontation, that might provoke a criminal act such as violence (Cullen 2002). There also are many reasons, however, for theorizing that the experience of punishment might increase an individual's future proclivity for crime beyond its impact on perceptions of the amount, cost, and likelihood of future punishment, a subject that we now turn to.

B. Prisons as Criminogenic

Deterrence theorists conceptualize prison as a price that is calculated when making the choice to commit a crime. For those who portray prisons as criminogenic, such thinking suffers from reductionism. For them, years behind bars cut off from the community is not simply a price tag that one weighs—as one would weigh prices when, say, buying a pair of shoes. Rather, imprisonment is a social experience that places offenders in a unique social domain—the "society of captives" (Sykes 1958)—and that qualitatively restructures their lives from ones of freedom to ones of substantial constraint. Although intended to prevent crime, this unique experience in social segregation is argued to have the unintended consequence of increasing exposure to crime-inducing influences and of decreasing exposure to prosocial influences. There are at least three perspectives, drawn from different scholarly traditions, which advance variants of this argument.

1. *Prisons as a Criminal Learning Environment.* Whether as a therapeutic community or as a tightly run disciplinary regime, prisons are intended to provide a social environment that induces conformity and offers prosocial lessons. Classic studies of the prison community, however, have revealed that institutions were potentially marked by an oppositional inmate subculture into which offenders were socialized (see, e.g., Clemmer 1940; Sykes 1958). One approach, called "deprivation theory," saw the criminogenic prison culture as an adaptation to what Sykes (1958) called the "pains of imprisonment." Inmate solidarity and specific "argot roles" within the subculture were ways of mitigating the deprivations of prison life. Another approach, called "importation theory," saw the prison culture as a continuation of the worldview that offenders learned on the street and thus "imported" or carried with them as they moved behind bars. The "convict code" was not a response to prison life but constituted it in the sense that inmates infuse the institutional culture with their preexisting views (Irwin and Cressey 1962). More recently, researchers have documented how the process of importation has included gang membership and values as well as a more violent street culture that places a premium on toughness (Jacobs 1977; Irwin 1980, 2005; Carroll 1988; Wacquant 2001).

The key insight is that regardless of the precise mechanism, prisons are marked by the presence of cultural values supportive of crime that can be transmitted through daily interactions. It is thus a social learning environment in which criminal orientations are potentially reinforced. Consistent with social learning theory (Akers 1998), it can be expected that a custodial sentence will intensify a commitment to a life in crime.

2. *Prisons as a Labeling Effect.* In the 1970s, labeling or societal reaction theory emerged as the dominant theory of crime and deviance (Cole 1975; see also Cullen and Cullen 1978). To a great extent, its popularity rested in what Hagan (1973) called the "sociology of the interesting"—that is, in advancing the ironic thesis that the state's efforts to stop crime have the unanticipated consequence of producing the very thing it was intended to suppress. This was often placed under the broader concept of the self-fulfilling prophecy.

Labeling theorists demarcated two broad ways in which labeling is criminogenic. First, publicly stigmatizing and treating a person as a "criminal" inculcated in the individual this stained identity. Offenders who internalized a criminal identity thus would subsequently act in a way consistent with this self-conception. Initial experimentation with offending (sometimes called "primary deviance") could be stabilized because labeled individuals would organize their life around their core identity (sometimes called "secondary deviance"; see Lemert 1951). Prisons were especially consequential because they provided a lengthy opportunity for a criminal identity to be reinforced, to be accepted, and to govern conduct.

Second, similar to important theorists of the time (e.g., Merton, Sutherland, Hirschi), labeling theorists agreed that socially induced strain, differential association, and weak social bonds fostered criminal involvement. However, they saw these criminogenic influences not as main effects but as intervening variables between labeling and crime (see also Braithwaite 1989). It was societal reaction, especially when it involved imprisonment, that was integral to denying opportunities (strain theory), to enforcing prolonged association with offenders (differential association theory), and to eroding ties to family and to the conventional order (social bond theory). Being in prison was criminogenic because of enforced association with other offenders and because the person was removed from the labor market and from family and social relationships. But reentry into the community, the necessary by-product of imprisonment, also was criminogenic because ex-inmates faced job discrimination, the daunting challenge of trying to reestablish frayed bonds to conventional institutions, and placement into neighborhoods where criminal associations were readily available (see also Petersilia 2003; Travis 2005). No wonder, labeling theorists pointed out, that inmate reoffending was high.

3. *Prisons as an Inappropriate Treatment.*   Mainly led by Canadian psychologists, other scholars have sought to develop principles of effective correctional intervention (Andrews and Bonta 2006; Gendreau, Smith, and French 2006). This approach starts by empirically demarcating predictors of recidivism (Gendreau, Little, and Goggin 1996) and then explores which treatments are capable of altering these factors (i.e., are "responsive" to these risk factors). Interventions that are consistent with the principles of effective treatment have been found to achieve meaningful reductions in recidivism. Notably, deterrence-oriented interventions (e.g., boot camps, scared straight programs) and

mere incarceration absent a treatment component are viewed, in this approach, as "inappropriate" interventions. These scholars cite evidence that such sanctions, including imprisonment, have little effect on recidivism or are criminogenic (Andrews et al. 1990; Gendreau, Goggin, and Cullen 1999; Andrews and Bonta 2006; Gendreau, Smith, and French 2006; Smith 2006; Smith, Gendreau, and Swartz 2009; see also MacKenzie 2006; Lipsey and Cullen 2007).

This approach is particularly concerned about offenders' risk level. High-risk offenders are preferred targets for intervention because there is much change that can take place—assuming that appropriate interventions are used. This is often called the "risk principle." By contrast, low-risk offenders should receive minimal intervention. The danger is that inappropriate treatments—including imprisonment—can have a criminogenic effect on low-risk offenders, transforming those with low chances of recidivating into those destined to offend again. There is some evidence to support such a differential effect of imprisonment on offenders by risk level (Smith 2006).

II. Estimating the Effect of Imprisonment on the Imprisoned

In this section, we discuss the primary methodological and substantive issues that will be emphasized in the following section's review of the empirical evidence. In the parlance of medical research on the effectiveness of drugs, our aim is to assess what is known about the dose-response relationship between imprisonment and reoffending. The review is divided between analyses of the impact on reoffending of receiving a custodial sentence or not and of the sentence length of those who are incarcerated.

We divide the literature in this fashion for two reasons. First and most importantly, for the reasons discussed in Section I, there are ample grounds for hypothesizing that the experience of imprisonment, independent of its length, may have an effect on the reoffending rate whether for the good or bad. The second reason is practical: the largest component of the literature assesses only the effects of confinement regardless of sentence length.

Although these two literatures examine conceptually distinct issues, most of the methodological issues we address apply to both. Thus, the discussion below does not distinguish between the two literatures unless otherwise noted. We use the term "treatment status" to distinguish individuals who were incarcerated or not or if incarcerated received different sentence lengths.

A. The Basic Inference Problem

Rates of recidivism of former prisoners are very high. The latest available analysis for the United States as a whole is based on 272,111 individuals released from the prisons of 15 states in 1993. Langan and Levin (2002) find that within 3 years 68 percent had been arrested, 46.9 percent had been convicted, and 25.4 percent had been reimprisoned. Three-year arrest recidivism rates were even higher for two groups that as matter of public policy might be candidates for nonincarcerative sanctions—property (73.8 percent) and drug (66.7 percent) offenders. Those findings are not anomalous. In an earlier analysis of data from the United States, Beck and Shipley (1989) found comparably high recidivism rates for a 1983 prison release cohort. Similarly high recidivism rates are also found in non-American data. For example, in a cohort of individuals convicted in Dutch courts in 1997, the 3-year recidivism rate as measured by reconviction exceeded 60 percent (Nieuwbeerta, Nagin, and Blokland, forthcoming). Among individuals discharged from prison in 1996 in England and Wales, the 2-year reconviction recidivism rate was 57 percent (Cullen and Minchin 2000).

The high recidivism rate of former prisoners clearly demonstrates that the prison experience is not so aversive as to make most individuals give up crime entirely. That said, high recidivism rates tell us little about whether on the margin the prison experience makes individuals more or less crime prone. Determination of the effect of imprisonment on recidivism requires a comparison with the counterfactual—what the rate would have been had the individual not been imprisoned. More subtly, seemingly small changes in the recidivism rate may be reflective of more substantial changes in the underlying rate of offending.

Analytically, recidivism rates and offending rates are "tied at the hip." Because offending does not occur with predetermined regularity, it is useful to think of the rate of offending as a long-term average about which there are random variations over time. Thus, over short periods, offending may be above or below this average. For some periods of time, no crimes may be committed, even though the individual's long-term average rate of offending remains greater than zero. From this

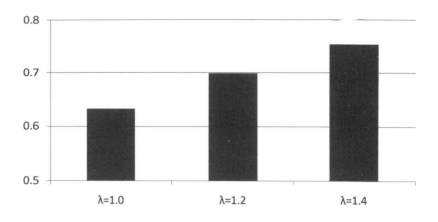

FIG. 1.—Three-year recidivism probabilities for different values of λ

perspective, recidivism is a forward-looking measure of offending risk for an individual with a record of prior offending. It is the probability that the individual will commit one or more offenses over a specified period of time.

Starting with the pioneering work of Avi-Itzhak and Shinnar (1973) on the incapacitation effect of imprisonment, it is commonly assumed that the random variations in offending over time can be modeled as a Poisson process. Avi-Itzhak and Shinnar used the now familiar notation of λ to denote the mean of this random process, namely, the mean rate of offending. Figure 1 reports recidivism probabilities for varying values of λ. Observe that for λ = 1.2 the recidivism probability is .7, which is about equal to the 3-year arrest recidivism rate reported by Langan and Levin (2002). Stated differently, under the assumption that arrests occur according to a Poisson process, if an individual's mean annual arrest rate is .4 (= 1.2/3) within 3 years, the probability of the person's having at least one arrest is .7. Also reported in figure 1 are recidivism probabilities for λ = 1.4 and λ = 1.0, which correspond to a fairly sizable 17 percent increase or decrease in rate of offending. Note, however, that the changes in recidivism probability are more modest: 10 percent or less in percentage terms—from .7 to .63 for the decline of λ to 1.0 and from .7 to .75 for the increase of λ to 1.4. The implication is that nontrivial effects of imprisonment on the mean rate of offending, whether up or down, will not necessarily be reflected in comparably large changes in recidivism probability. A

corollary point is that even though ex-prisoners have very high recidivism rates, the experience of imprisonment might still have resulted
in a sizable decline in their underlying rate of offending. This is yet
another important reason why high postprison recidivism rates are not
prima facie evidence of the ineffectiveness of the prison experience in
reducing criminality.

Recidivism rate is a muted indicator of the offending rate because
the classification of an individual as a recidivist requires only the detection of a single criminal event. As a result, the recidivism rates of
individuals with large differences in their underlying offending rate
may be very similar. For example, the 1-year recidivism probability is
nearly one for all values of λ in excess of 5. Stated differently, the 1-
year probability of reoffending one or more times is the same regardless whether the individual is offending at the rate of five crimes per
year or 100 crimes per year.

The distinction between recidivism rate and rate of offending also
has statistical implications for our review. Studies that use recidivism
rate as their primary outcome measure will have greater difficulty in
detecting differences across treatment status groups than studies that
compare reoffending rate across treatment status group. Thus, one issue that receives special attention is whether the outcome is a recidivism rate or a reoffending rate.

We return now to the observation that the effect of imprisonment
on reoffending rate is properly measured by the difference of two
quantities: the postrelease rate of offending of the imprisoned over a
specified period and their rate of offending over this same period had
they not been subject to a custodial sanction. We cannot know the
second quantity for the individuals who were actually imprisoned—it
is their counterfactual rate of offending. It must be inferred from the
behavior of others who were not imprisoned. The statistical gold standard for making this inference is a randomized experiment in which
individuals from a specified population are randomly assigned between
a custodial and a noncustodial sanction.

Few of the studies we review involve randomized experiments, but
we give special emphasis to experiments because several important design features of an experiment provide a valuable analytical perspective
for considering the much larger body of evidence based on analyses of
nonexperimental data—which we also refer to in this essay as "observational data." More than 4 decades ago, Cochran (1965) reflected on

the design of studies attempting to draw causal inferences from observational data. He framed his recommendations in the context of still earlier advice by Dorn (1953), who suggested that the design of an observational study be organized around the question, "How should the study be conducted if it were possible to do it by controlled experimentation?" Certain issues are common to an experiment and an observational study, and these shared issues are brought into focus by thinking about the simpler situation of an experiment. Three specific features of an experiment are important for our purposes here: inferences about treatment effects pertain to a specified population, treatment effects are measured relative to a specified alternative, and randomization.

B. Inferences Pertain to a Specific Population

Because randomization can occur only from a specified population, a key component of experimental design is specification of the population from which individuals will be randomly assigned between treatment and control. This design choice is of great importance because it establishes the boundary over which the results of the experiment apply. Findings about treatment effects apply only to the population from which subjects were drawn. Also important to keep in mind is that an experiment provides only an estimate of the average response to treatment. There may be large differences in the response to treatment across population members. For example, the U.S. Federal Food and Drug Administration's 2004 Blackbox warning that antidepressants may exacerbate suicidal tendencies in depressed adolescents is not inherently contradictory to the efficacy of these drugs for treating depression in the larger population. Similarly, there is no inherent contradiction between the conclusion that imprisonment exacerbates criminality within a population, on average, but for some groups within that population it reduces criminality. Because response to treatment may vary widely within the entire population, one important advantage of more narrowly defining the target population of the experiment is reduced heterogeneity in individual-level responses to treatment. The reduction in heterogeneity not only will make it easier to detect the average treatment effect but also will make the average response to treatment more representative of the response of all individuals within the sampled population. However, an important disadvantage of narrowly defining the population is that the experiment is not informative from a statistical perspective about the response to treatment in the larger unsampled population.

In experimental analyses consideration of the issue of the population from which the data are drawn is inescapable. In analyses of observational (or nonexperimental) data consideration of this issue often receives far less attention than it should. Inattention to the source of the data has many implications for the analysis and interpretation of the findings. Analysis of observational data requires that potential sources of bias somehow be "controlled for." The most frequently used method to accomplish this task is multivariate regression analysis. We discuss some important obstacles to success in accounting for sources of bias with regression as well as other methods in the discussion of randomization. Beyond the challenges of using regression to account for sources of bias, the results of a regression may be misinterpreted in ways that are relevant to the issues just discussed.

One common misinterpretation of regression is that limiting the analysis to one specific segment of a wider population of interest somehow biases the results. To be concrete, suppose that an analysis of the imprisonment effect on recidivism rate was limited to individuals with no prior record of imprisonment. Such a sample restriction does not bias the resulting estimate of the imprisonment effect. Rather, just as in an experiment, it limits the applicability of the estimate to only one specific segment of a larger population of interest—individuals receiving custodial sentences irrespective of their prior record.

Further, just as in experiments, in a regression-based analysis of observational data there is a trade-off between the costs of narrowness and the benefits of reduced individual heterogeneity. Consider again the example of a study that is limited to data on individuals with no prior record of imprisonment. Some analysts implicitly think of a regression coefficient as measuring the effect for all population members as opposed to the average effect across the population. The regression coefficient of the imprisonment or not variable does not measure the effect of imprisonment for all individuals sentenced to prison; it only measures the average of that effect. If the effect of imprisonment on recidivism depends upon prior experience with imprisonment, the advantage of restricting the sample to individuals with no prior experience with imprisonment is a reduction of that source of treatment effect heterogeneity within the population. The disadvantage is that the treatment effect estimate applies only to a narrower population.

We emphasize the narrowness-heterogeneity trade-off because the dose-response relationship between imprisonment and reoffending may vary across offender characteristics in ways that are important for science and public policy. The relationship may depend upon whether the individual has previously been imprisoned and on age. It may also depend on conviction offense. As we discuss in Section IV, variation across conviction offense in the effect of imprisonment has important policy implications. Thus, another issue that will be emphasized in the discussion is the characteristics of the population from which the data are drawn.

C. Specification of Treatment and Control Conditions

The design of an experiment requires a clear specification of what constitutes treatment under the experimental and control conditions. Thus, in an experimental study of the effect of custodial versus non-custodial sanctions on recidivism, it is necessary to specify the length and conditions of confinement for the custodial treatment as well as the length and conditions of the noncustodial sanction (control) treatment. The specification of the treatment and control conditions could greatly affect the outcome of the experiment. The response to spending 1 month in a well-managed jail is likely quite different than that to spending 1 year in a violence-ridden prison. The design of the non-custodial condition may have a similarly large impact on response. An interesting example is reported in Deschenes, Turner, and Petersilia (1995). This experimental study involved an attempt to randomly assign custodial and noncustodial sanctions in Minnesota. Implementation of treatment assignment proved difficult in part because the supervision requirements of the noncustodial sanction were deemed so onerous by some individuals that they refused placement into this condition and opted instead to remain in prison. Similarly, Wood and May (2003) report that for certain types of offenders, noncustodial sanctions are seen as overall being more costly than imprisonment. Ambiguity about the comparative harshness of custodial and noncustodial sanctions is likely to be largest in countries other than the United States, where sentences tend to be much shorter and prison conditions less onerous. Still another dimension of the sanction experience that may affect recidivism is whether the individual receives some sort of rehabilitative treatment in custody or in the community.

In an analysis of observational data, where the analyst does not design the experimental and control treatments, it is easier to neglect the issue of what the "imprisonment" and "nonimprisonment" conditions constitute. Imprisonment and nonimprisonment conditions not only may vary widely across studies but also may be very different across individuals within a study. Thus, the issue of what constitutes treatment and control also receives special attention in our review.

D. Randomization

The discussion below concerns the implications of the absence of randomization in observational studies of the effect of imprisonment. It addresses two distinct topics: the minimum set of characteristics that must be taken into account to obtain a credible estimate of the effect of imprisonment and the possible impact of unaccounted-for factors on the treatment effect estimate. These topics are discussed in turn, but before turning to them, we discuss the role of randomization in experiments.

Randomization's salient status in experimental design stems from its capacity to assure that subjects assigned to treatment and control groups systematically differ in only one way—their treatment status. More specifically, randomization ensures that in expectation there are no differences in any characteristic whether measured or not, or whether thought to be relevant or not, between treatment and control. In turn, this ensures that in expectation the difference in outcome between treatment and control measures the effect of treatment. Stated differently, in expectation the outcome for the controls provides the counterfactual for the treated—that is, what would have happened to them, on average, had they been in the control condition and vice versa. By contrast, in analyses of observational data, there is no such guarantee that the treated and control group differ only in their treatment status. As a result, other systematic differences may bias the treatment-effect estimate obtained from a simple comparison of outcomes for the treated and controls. For example, suppose the experience of imprisonment has no effect on recidivism. We would still likely observe higher reoffending among the imprisoned compared to the nonimprisoned because persons with more lengthy prior records are more likely to be imprisoned and are also more likely to return to crime.

The primary objective of most statistical methods for drawing causal inferences from observational data is to somehow take account of other variables that might bias the desired treatment-effect estimate. Thus, in observational studies, characteristics of individuals and their circumstances are generally taken into account to avoid bias. In contrast, in experimental studies blocking or stratifying by characteristics of study participants is not done to avoid bias; that is the job of randomization. Instead, it is done to reduce variance or to learn how treatment effects vary across selected characteristics of study participants (e.g., sex).

Suppose we had an observational data set that measured the postsanction offending of a sample of individuals who had received and not received a custodial sanction. Per the prior discussion of specification of treatment and control conditions, decisions would have to be made on how to account for differences in sentence length among the imprisoned perhaps by limiting the analysis to individuals receiving sentences within some specified interval, for example, less than 2 years. Similarly, design decisions would have to be made about whether to distinguish among different types of noncustodial sanctions. Having made these design decisions, the next crucial question that needs to be addressed is: what is a minimum set of characteristics of the individual that must be taken into account to assess the effect of imprisonment on subsequent offending? The answer to this question requires careful consideration of factors that might affect both the sentencing decision and the reoffending rate independent of the actual sentenced received. Any such variable may lead to bias in the treatment-effect estimate of imprisonment. Stated in such general terms, the list of potentially confounding variables is endless, so we reframe the question as: what variables do we know are strongly related to one or both outcomes, sentence and/or offending, based on prior research or on institutional realities? These variables should constitute the minimum necessary set of control variables. In our judgment, two case characteristic variables—prior record and conviction offense type—and three demographic variables—age, race, and sex—definitely should be included on this list.

The criminal statutes of all countries in Western Europe and North America prescribe criminal penalties according to the conviction offense type. More serious crimes are more likely to result in imprisonment and more lengthy sentences. According to the Langan and Levin (2002) analysis, recidivism rates also varied substantially by conviction offense type, a finding that is also borne out by other studies (Beck and Shipley 1989; Sabol et al. 2000; Sentencing Guidelines Commission 2005a, 2005b; Kentucky Department of Corrections n.d.).

Three-year arrest recidivism rates were highest for robbers (70.2 percent), burglars (74.0 percent), motor vehicle thieves (78.8 percent), and selling or possessing stolen property (77.4 percent) and lowest for homicide (40.7 percent), rape (48.0 percent), and other sexual assault (41.4 percent). One contributing factor to these differences across conviction offense type is likely age. The recidivism rates are lowest for conviction offense types that are more likely to result in lengthy sentences. Consequently, individuals convicted of these offences are likely on average to be older upon release. An extended discussion of the importance of controlling for age follows below.

Prior record of convictions is also generally relevant to the sentencing decision and is perhaps the best predictor of reoffending rate. An enormous literature shows that prior record—whether measured by arrest, conviction, or prior imprisonment—is a sturdy predictor of subsequent offending (Bureau of Justice Statistics 1988; Beck and Shipley 1989; Loeber and Le Blanc 1990; Nagin and Paternoster 1991; Gendreau, Little, and Goggin 1996; Langan and Levin 2002; Florida Department of Corrections 2003). The strength of this relationship is illustrated by the Langan and Levin (2002) analysis. They find that 3-year arrest recidivism rates increase from 40.6 percent for individuals with one prior arrest to 82.1 percent for individuals with 16 or more prior arrests. Data from the Cambridge Study of Delinquent Development (Farrington et al. 2006) also nicely illustrate this relationship with a general population sample rather than a prison sample. The study is based on a sample of about 400 males from a working-class neighborhood in London born around 1954. Conviction data are available from ages 10 to 50. Individuals with no convictions up to age 16 averaged 0.6 convictions from ages 17 to 50, whereas as those with one, two, or three convictions as juveniles, respectively, had an average of 3.8, 4.8, and 5.2 convictions over this age range.[3]

Turning now to the demographic variables, vast literatures document large differences in offending rates by age, sex, and race (Hindelang 1981; Bureau of Justice Statistics 1988; Blumstein 1995; Steffensmeier and Allan 1996; Hawkins et al. 2000; Sampson, Morenoff, and Raudenbush 2005; Haynie and Armstrong 2006; Fox and Zawitz 2007). There is also a smaller literature documenting differences in recidivism by demographic group (Beck and Shipley 1989; Gendreau, Little, and

---

[3] We thank David Farrington for making these data available to us.

Goggin 1996; Sabol et al. 2000; Florida Department of Corrections 2003; Cannon and Wilson 2005; Sentencing Guidelines Commission 2005a, 2005b; Kentucky Department of Corrections n.d.). The differences are smaller than for the offending rate in the general population, but demographic differences still persist. For example, the Florida Department of Corrections (2003) found that black males were 27.1 percent more likely to reoffend than their white male counterparts. This report also found that for males each 1-year increase in age lowered the probability of reoffending by 3.2 percent. Similarly, Sabol et al. (2000) found that males, blacks, and young offenders have higher rates of return to federal prisons than females, whites, and older offenders (16.2 percent vs. 11.6 percent, 24.4 vs. 13.4 percent, and 13.9 percent vs. 11.0 percent, respectively).

For our purposes here, we give special attention to the importance and manner in which age is accounted for in the analysis. Cochran (1965) used the adjective "disturbing" to label variables that might confound the treatment-effect estimate in observational data. The simplest and most direct way to statistically account for "disturbing" variables is by matching each treated unit with a control unit that is identical on all disturbing variables thought to be relevant. Although clean, rigorous, and straightforward, this approach quickly runs afoul of the "curse of dimensionality," namely, there are too many variables upon which it would be desirable to match to identify suitable matching controls. Other methods must be used to account for disturbing variables. Two of the most widely used are regression-based methods and propensity score matching. It is important, however, to recognize that the surest way of accounting for a variable that may somehow be biasing results is by exact matching. It is for this reason that we judge it important to match imprisoned and nonimprisoned individuals by age and thereafter to use other methods such as regression or propensity score matching to account for other potentially confounding variables. We give age this special status for control because offending rates are highly age dependent and because the postsanction outcome variable, offending rate or recidivism probability, necessarily must be measured over age. Therefore, we regarded it as very important in analyses of observational data to compare the postsanction offending rate of an imprisoned individual with that of one or more nonimprisoned individuals who are the same age.

Data from the Cambridge Study of Delinquent Development (Far-

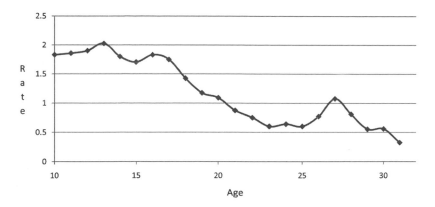

FIG. 2.—Three-year smoothed reoffending rate (Cambridge Study of Delinquent Development).

rington et al. 2006) illustrate the sensitivity of reoffending rate to age. The demonstration is based on the conviction counts of each study participant from age 10, the youngest age of criminal responsibility in England, to age 32. For individuals convicted at each age their average rate of offending was computed for the three subsequent years. For example, for all individuals convicted at age 16, their average conviction rate from ages 17 to 19 was computed. To smooth out year-to-year fluctuations in reoffending rate at each age, a smoothed reoffending rate was computed. At each age, it equals 50 percent of the reoffending average for that age plus 50 percent of the rate for the immediately prior age. The smoothed series is shown in figure 2. From the outset, the reoffending rate starts high, reflecting the high offending rate of a small group of early starters. It then makes a brief decline, which is followed by a new rise that peaks at age 17. Thereafter, the rate declines precipitously until age 23, whereupon it moves erratically.

Figure 3 shows a companion curve based on the conviction records of all individuals convicted in the Dutch courts in 1997. The Dutch data follow a different pattern. The smoothed reoffending rate rises erratically until about age 30, whereupon it declines rapidly.

Despite the differences between the Dutch and English data, both make clear that reoffending rates are very age dependent. Consequently, age must be very exactly controlled for to avoid age-related biases in postsanction comparisons of offending rates of individuals receiving different sanction types. Small imbalances in the age distri-

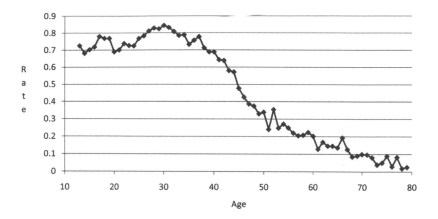

FIG. 3.—Three-year smoothed reoffending rate (Netherlands)

bution between comparison groups could contaminate the sanction effect difference with large age effects. For instance, in the Cambridge data the smoothed reoffending rate declines by an average of 18 percent per year between 17 and 23. Changes of this magnitude may well be larger than the effect, whether positive or negative, of the experience of imprisonment on the reoffending rate. Further, because the chances of incarceration increase with prior record and because a prior record takes time to accumulate and individuals necessarily age while incarcerated, there are likely to be age differences between the incarcerated and nonincarcerated convictees. For these reasons, we believe that exact matching on age is very important in studies of the effect of imprisonment on recidivism.[4]

E. Making Judgments about the Veracity of Findings

Suppose a study takes into account the minimum set of potentially confounding variables described above. How confident can one be of the resulting imprisonment effect estimate? There is, of course, no definitive answer to this question, but an econometric perspective provides a useful vantage point for considering an answer. In modeling

---

[4] One might think that a demonstration that the average age of treated and controls are the same is sufficient to rule out age as potential source of bias in the treatment effect estimate. This is not correct. If there is a nonlinear relationship between age and offending, as there clearly is, difference in higher order moments (e.g., variance) between the treated and the controls may still induce bias.

choice, in this case the judge's sentencing decision between a custodial versus noncustodial sanction, econometricians draw a strong distinction between information available to and used by the decision maker and information available to the statistical analyst (see Heckman 1990; Manski 1995). The decision makers are assumed to base their decision on a larger set of information than is available to the analyst. Failure to account for this disjuncture in the information set of the decision maker and analyst can lead to serious bias. For example, suppose sentencing decisions were influenced by whether the individual is a drug or alcohol addict, but that data on drug or alcohol addiction status are unavailable to the analyst. Because of the strong positive correlation of drug or alcohol addiction and crime (Anglin and Hser 1987; Anglin and Speckart 1988; Harrison and Gfroerer 1992; Fergusson, Lynskey, and Horwood 1996; Ge, Donnellan, and Wenk 2001; Gjeruldsen, Myrvang, and Opjordsmoen 2004; Dorsey, Zawitz, and Middleton 2007), the lack of statistical control for addiction will bias the treatment-effect estimate unless other controls used by the analyst somehow account for the absence of direct control for addiction.

From the econometric perspective, the question concerning our confidence in the imprisonment treatment-effect estimate is reframed more precisely as: how much information is left out of the minimal set of control variables that affect judges' sentencing decisions and also likely influence recidivism? The answer to this question depends in part upon the time and jurisdiction that are the source of the data under analysis. An individual's sentence in some jurisdictions is largely determined by the types of offenses for which the person is convicted and by his or her prior record. For data from jurisdictions such as these, whether in the United States or elsewhere, our minimal set is probably sufficient for making credible, albeit not conclusive, inferences about imprisonment effects.

For data from times and jurisdictions where judges have more sentencing discretion, research on clinical versus actuarial prediction of violence provides a useful perspective for judging the adequacy of our minimal set of controls. Clinical risk assessment refers to the unstructured judgments of trained mental health practitioners based on their theoretical orientation and clinical experience. Actuarial assessments are based on structured assessment instruments for collecting and analyzing data and ultimately making a prediction (Monahan 2006, 2008). Research has overwhelmingly demonstrated the superiority of actuarial methods (Grove and Meehl 1996; Swets, Dawes, and Monahan 2000; Ægisdóttir et al. 2006). This conclusion suggests that subtle characteristics of the individuals or their circumstances (e.g., demeanor) that may affect a judge's sentence decision and are unlikely to be recorded in the data are also unlikely to bias results because they are not very predictive of behavioral outcomes.

Thus, the adequacy of the minimal set of control variables in circumstances where judges have discretion would seem to turn on the overlap between the minimal set and the information in actuarial instruments. Monahan (2006, 2008) provides a valuable summary of the four categories of variables that are included in modern actuarial assessment instruments. One of Monahan's categories is labeled "what the individual 'is'" as measured by age, sex, race, and personality. A second category describes what the person "has" as measured by major mental disorders, personality disorders, and substance use disorders. The third category describes what the person "has done" as measured by prior crime and violence. The fourth category describes what has been "done to" the person as measured by pathological family environment and victimization.

Note that there are many important points of overlap between Monahan's list and our minimal list. Age, sex, race, conviction offense, and prior record are important components of what the individual "is" and "has done." There is also some degree of correspondence between what the person "has" and the offenses for which the person is convicted. For example, there are important points of similarity between criminal behavior and mental health diagnoses like conduct disorder and antisocial personality. However, this correspondence should not be overstated because criminal infractions and mental health diagnoses are not the same things. Depression and schizophrenia, for instance, have no symptoms that can be described as criminal behaviors. More generally, Monahan's list includes many items that might well appear in a presentence report or come up in a sentencing hearing. Thus, the ultimate judgment on whether the minimal list of controls achieves a threshold of credibility must necessarily be judged on a case-by-case basis. The determination should turn upon knowledge of the sentencing practices that generated the data underlying the study, such as how much discretion judges have, to what degrees sentencing is routinized by custom or bureaucratic procedure, and what information is available in presentence reports. Alas, in this review, we do not have the information to make such a determination for each of the studies that we consider.

III. Review of the Evidence

We separately review studies of the effect of custodial versus noncustodial sanctions and studies of the effect of sentence length on reoffending. The review of the evidence on custodial versus noncustodial sanctions is organized around four categories of studies based on their methodology: experimental and quasi-experimental studies, matching studies based on observational data, regression studies based on observational data, and a small group of studies using other methods.

The literature on the effects of imprisonment varies on many dimensions that are relevant to an assessment of its scientific quality and to its substantive interpretation. These include issues such as methodology used, vintage of the study, characteristics of the offender population, and type of custodial and noncustodial sanction examined. We organize our review along the dimension of the type of methodology used because the question being asked—what is the effect of imprisonment on reoffending?—is first and foremost a question that must be answered statistically. An assessment of the quality of the evidence, therefore, must focus on the rigor of statistical analysis. Because each class of methodology poses specific challenges to its application, we chose to use methodology as the primary organizing device for categorizing studies.

We also chose not to use meta-analysis as a device for summarizing the evidence. This decision was made due to a concern that, at this stage in the research, the synthesis of evidence through this statistical method would obscure important subtleties related to large differences in quality across studies, the types of sanction options being examined, and the characteristics of the offender population. Nonetheless, especially as studies on the impact of imprisonment on reoffending become more plentiful and of a higher quality, the application of meta-analysis to the extant body of evidence would be useful.

A prior review by Villettaz, Killias, and Zoder (2006) of the effects of incarceration on reoffending, which concluded that there was no systematic evidence for either a criminogenic or preventive effect, provided an invaluable starting point for identifying the studies included in this review. We are greatly indebted to these authors for their efforts in tracking down studies. The list of studies from Villettaz, Killias, and Zoder was supplemented by another review of the literature by Gendreau, Goggin, and Cullen (1999) and by our own efforts to identify relevant studies mostly of more recent vintage. (Gendreau, Goggin, and Cullen concluded that the evidence pointed to a criminogenic effect of the prison experience.) Although there are undoubtedly studies that we have not identified, we are confident that we have been successful in identifying all experimental studies and all studies based on observational data that account for our minimum list of control variables. We also expand on Villettaz, Killias, and Zoder (2006) by reviewing evidence on the relationship between time incarcerated and reoffending rate.

A. Experimental and Quasi-Experimental Studies

Only five studies randomly assigned custodial versus noncustodial sentences. To this group, we add one Netherlands-based quasi-experimental study that involved a royal pardon in celebration of the wedding of the Princess (now Queen) Beatrix. Prison sentences of 14 days or less were suspended for crimes committed prior to January 1, 1966. Persons sentenced to prison for 14 days or less for crimes committed after that date did not benefit from the pardon. The contrast between those benefiting and not benefiting from the royal pardon formed the basis for inferring the imprisonment effect.

Table 1 summarizes these five studies in terms of the characteristics of the population studied, the nature of the custodial and noncustodial sanctions that were randomized between treatment and control, and the outcome of the experiment. Three dimensions of outcome are summarized. The first is whether the outcome is measured by recidivism rate or offending rate. The former measure inherently has less statistical power for inferring a statistically significant treatment effect. The second is whether the point estimate of the treatment effect, the difference in outcome between the custodial and noncustodial groups, points to a lower or higher rate of recidivism/reoffending rate for the custodial group. The third is whether this difference is statistically significant at the .05 level or lower.

Consider first the outcomes of the studies. Among the experimental studies, all but Bergman (1976) measure outcomes using both offending and recidivism rates. The quasi-experimental study by Van der Werff (1979) is based on recidivism rates. All five studies report at least one point estimate suggesting a criminogenic effect of incarceration. While most are not statistically significant, three studies report at least one significant criminogenic point estimate. Three of five studies report at least one point estimate suggesting a preventive effect of a custodial sentence, but only in Barton and Butts (1990) is the preventive effect estimate statistically significant. We note, however, that this significant preventive effect may reflect an incapacitation rather than a behavioral response. Barton and Butts report data indicating that those assigned to secure confinement were actually incarcerated for nearly two-thirds of the 1-year follow-up period.

Taken as a whole, it is our judgment that the experimental studies point more toward a criminogenic rather than preventive effect of custodial sanctions. The evidence for this conclusion, however, is weak because it is based on only a small number of studies, and many of the point estimates are not statistically significant.

Several features of the populations used in these studies also limit their usefulness for understanding the effects of imprisonment on reoffending in the context of contemporary trends in the use of imprisonment. Two of the five studies involve juveniles, and all but one, Killias, Aebi, and Ribeaud (2000), use data that are more than 20 years old, with two based on data from more than 40 years ago. Among the four studies involving adults, only Bergman (1976) is based on populations that can be characterized as serious adult offenders. The subjects of the Killias, Aebi, and Ribeaud (2000) and the Van der Werff (1979) studies both involved populations of individuals who, if imprisoned, would have received sentences of 14 days or less. Thus, their offenses were unlikely to be very serious.

B. Matching Studies

Eleven studies are categorized as matching studies. Studies were designated as matching based if they relied principally upon either variable-by-variable matching or propensity score matching to account for potentially confounding variables.

In principle, variable-by-variable matching is the foolproof way of controlling for potentially confounding variables. In practice, the capacity to control for confounders via "by-variable" matching is limited by the tyranny of dimensionality. The availability of matches on multiple dimensions rapidly moves to the null set as more dimensions of matching are added. The tyranny of dimensionality is further exacer-

TABLE 1

Experimental and Quasi-Experimental Studies of Custodial versus Noncustodial Sanctions

Authors	Population Characteristics	Treatment Description		Outcome		
		Custodial	Noncustodial	Offending/ Recidivism Rate	Sign of Custodial Effect	Statistical Significance of Effect (5%)
Barton and Butts (1990)	Male juveniles from Wayne County, MI, Juvenile Court, serious violent offenders excluded (N = 511)	Training school (avg. = 12.8 months)	Intensive supervision (avg. = 5.6 months)	Both	Official records: 2 1+ Self-report: 5+	Official records: 2 of 2 − sig. 1 of 1+ sig. Self-report: 1 of 5+ sig.
Bergman (1976)	Mostly male second felony offenders, Oakland County, MI (N = 109)	Incarceration	Extensive probation	Recidivism	1+	1 of 1+ sig.
Killias, Aebi, and Ribeaud (2000)	Mostly male adults from Switzerland sentenced to prison terms of up to 14 days; only 22% convicted of a criminal code offense (N = 123)	Up to 14 days of jail	Community work: 8 hours = day in jail	Both	3+	0 of 3+ sig.

Study	Sample			Outcome		
Schneider (1986)	Mostly male juveniles in Boise, ID (N = 181)	8 days + 9 months probation	Restitution/community service + 9 months probation	Both	2+	0 of 2+ sig.
Van der Werff (1979; quasi-experimental)	Individuals with sentences of 14 days or less	14 days or less	Suspended sentence	Recidivism	Traffic offenders: No difference; Property offenders: 1−; Violent offenders: 1+	Property offenders: 0 of 1− sig.; Violent offenders: 1 of 1+ sig.

NOTE.—Avg. = average; + = criminogenic effect; − = preventive effect; sig. = significant.

bated for matches on continuous variables. Matching on continuous variables such as age or income necessarily requires converting the variable into range categories. More fine-grained ranges provide for better control but also make it more difficult to identify suitable matches.

Table 2 summarizes the variables that were matched in the studies based on by-variable matching. To varying degrees, these studies account for our minimum set of control variables—age, race, sex, prior record, and current offense. Kraus (1974) matches on the largest number of variables (seven) that, with the possible exception of race, covers all of the minimum set. Even more impressive is how fine grained the matching was. In most instances, for example, individuals were matched on age within a year of their birth. Savolainen et al. (2002) also had quite detailed matching criteria that, for example, distinguished among seven charge types and five felony severity levels. However, they did not match on race, and at older ages matching seemed to be quite coarse. Smith and Akers (1993) also matched over all dimensions of the minimum set except race, but their matching variable for prior record, probation violations, was crude compared to Savolainen et al. (2002) and Kraus (1974). Muiluvuori (2001) matches on all dimensions of the minimum set, but matching on age is only within 5 years, and prior record is measured only by number of prior imprisonments. Finally, Petersilia and Turner with Peterson (1986) directly match only on gender and conviction offense. The remaining variables are accounted for via a three-level summary score and regression.

The results of all matching-based studies are summarized in table 3. For those studies based on "by-variable" matching, the most consistent set of findings is reported in the Kraus study that, in our judgment, also did the best job of matching. For both first offender juveniles and recidivist juveniles, the results point overwhelmingly toward a criminogenic effect of custodial sanctions. A majority of the point estimates in the other "by-variable" matching studies also point to a criminogenic effect, but only in the Savolainen et al. (2002) study are they consistently statistically significant.

Three studies are based on propensity score matching. In this context, the propensity score is the conditional probability of receiving a custodial sanction rather than a noncustodial sanction given observed covariates (Rosenbaum and Rubin 1983). In the propensity score–based studies reviewed here, the propensity score was created by a logit re-

TABLE 2

"By-Variable" Matching Studies: Variables Matched Upon

Authors	Variables Matched from Minimum Set	Exact Matching or Age within 1 Year	Variables beyond Minimum	Comment
Kraus (1974)	All except possibly race*	Almost always yes	Age at first arrest	Generally succeeded in exact matching on key variables
Kraus (1978)	All except race	Yes	Number of current charges	Succeeded in matching
Kraus (1981)	All except possibly race*	No	None	Succeeded in exact matching on key variables
Muiluvuori (2001)	All†	No	None	Matching on age only within 5 years
Petersilia, Turner, with Peterson (1986)	Gender and conviction offense	No	Drug addiction, year of sentencing, county of conviction, three-level summary score	Prior record accounted for in a three-level summary score; age and race accounted for by regression
Savolainen et al. (2002)	All but race	No	Place of prosecution	
Scarpitti and Stephenson (1968)	All except current offense	All 16–17 years old	Socioeconomic status index (family income, education, and occupation of family breadwinner)	Matched on delinquency history index (age first known to court, number of delinquent offenses, types of prior offenses)
Smith and Akers (1993)	All except race	Not explicitly stated	None	Prior record was measured by probation violations not prior felonies and by sentencing cell

* Data are from the early 1960s, a time when Australia was almost entirely white except for Aboriginals. Not clear whether this racial minority was included in the study.

† Race was not explicitly matched upon, but the location of the study, Finland, is nearly all white.

TABLE 3

Matching Studies: Findings on Custodial Sanction Effect

Authors	Offending/ Recidivism Rate	Method of Matching	Treatment Description		Sign of Custodial Effect	Statistical Significance of Effect (5%)
			Custodial	Noncustodial		
Apel and Sweeten (2008)	Both	Propensity score	Incarcerated in an adult or juvenile facility (avg. = 4.1 months)	Convicted but not incarcerated	27+ 18−	3*/7† of 27+ sig. 1*/0† of 18− sig.
Kraus (1974)	Both	By variable	Detention	Probation	First offenders: 8+ 2− Recidivists: 19+ 2−	First offenders: 3 of 8+ sig. 1 of 2− sig. Recidivists: 19 of 19 + sig. 2 of 2− sig.
Kraus (1978)	Both	By variable	Remand in custody followed by probation	Remand at home followed by probation	5+ 2−	1 of 5+ sig. 0 of 2− sig.
Kraus (1981)	Both	By variable	Residential school for truants	Probation	3+ 2−	0 of 3+ sig. 2 of 2− sig.
Loughran et al. (2008)	Offending	Propensity score	Placement in custodial sanction (avg. = 11 months)	Probation	1+	0 of 1+ sig.

Study	Outcome	Matching	Harsher sanction	Less harsh sanction	Effect	Significance
Muiluvuori (2001)	Both	By variable	Prison (avg. = 7.8 months)	Community service (avg. = 3 months)	33+ 2−	No significance tests
Nieuwbeerta, Nagin, and Blokland (forthcoming)	Offending	Propensity score	Prison (less than 1 year)	Convicted but not imprisoned	11+ 1−	11 of 11+ sig. 0 of 1− sig.
Petersilia, Turner, with Peterson (1986)	Recidivism	By variable	Incarceration (avg. = 12.5 months)	Probation	12+	4 of 12+ sig.
Savolainen et al. (2002)	Both	By variable	Incarceration	Various types of supervision and counseling	10+ 8−	9 of 10+ sig. 2 of 8− sig.
Scarpitti and Stephenson (1968)	Recidivism	By variable (specifically three indices)	Residential group (avg. = 9 months) Reformatory school (avg. = 4 months)	Probation Nonresidential group center (avg. = 4 months)	3+ 1−	2 of 3+ sig. 0 of 1− sig.
Smith and Akers (1993)	Recidivism	By variable	Prison	Community control	9+ 3−	0 of 9+ sig. 0 of 3− sig.
Weisburd, Waring, with Chayet (2001)[a]	Both (offending rate is ordinal in nature)	Propensity score	Prison	Convicted but not imprisoned	10+ 5−	0 of 10+ sig. 0 of 5− sig.

NOTE.—Avg. = average; + = criminogenic effect; − = preventive effect; * = results for nearest neighbor matching; † = results for kernel matching; sig. = significant.

[a] Weisburd, Waring, and Chayet (1995) findings are included in this piece.

151

TABLE 4

Propensity Score–Based Matching Studies: Variables in Score

Authors	Variables from Minimum Set	Exact Matching or Age within 1 Year	Variables beyond Minimum
Apel and Sweeten (2008)	All	No	Many measures of family and educational background and miscellaneous risk factors such as substance abuse
Loughran et al. (2008)	All but current offense[a]	Not explicitly stated	Many measures of mental health, substance abuse, family, education, employment background, punishment costs, social capital, risk/need scores, involvement in the community, impulse control, gang membership, and social support
Nieuwbeerta, Nagin, and Blokland (forthcoming)	All	Yes	Married, children, early conviction, trajectory group, and very detailed measurement of prior record and current offense severity
Weisburd, Waring, with Chayet (2001)[b]	All	No	Geographic location, education, socioeconomic status, cooperation with prosecution, remorse for crime, and detailed measurement of current offense severity

[a] All participants were serious offenders, with most being guilty of felony offenses.
[b] Weisburd, Waring, and Chayet (1995) findings are included in this piece.

gression in which the dependent variable was receiving a custodial sanction or not and the regressors were the types of variables listed in table 4. Rosenbaum and Rubin (1983) demonstrate that if the propensity score is correctly specified, matching treated individuals with controls who have the same propensity score will balance all covariates included in the propensity score. This proof implies, for example, that if two individuals, one treated and one control, have the same propensity score, say a .2 chance of secure confinement, the covariates in the score will be of no further use in predicting which of these two individuals was actually incarcerated. Thus, by matching on a single metric, the propensity score, there will be no systematic tendency for the observed covariates determining that score to be different between the treated and the controls. A nontechnical survey of methods and results about propensity scores is given by Joffe and Rosenbaum (1999).

The principal advantage of propensity score matching compared to variable-by-variable matching is that it averts the curse of dimensionality because there is generally no practical limit to the number of covariates that can be included in the propensity score and thereby can be balanced between those receiving and not receiving secure confinement. Table 4 summarizes the variables included in the propensity score–based analyses. All include the minimum control set in the model plus many other variables.

The results of the propensity score–based analyses, which are reported in table 3, are mixed. Nieuwbeerta, Nagin, and Blokland (forthcoming) find consistent evidence of a statistically significant criminogenic effect of (first-time) incarceration in a Netherlands-based sample. In a study of white-collar criminals in the U.S. federal courts, Weisburd, Waring, and Chayet (1995) find no statistically significant evidence of an effect, but all point estimates point in a criminogenic direction. We note, per the discussion in Section II, that the lack of significance may be attributable to their relying solely upon a recidivism outcome measure. Finally, Apel and Sweeten (2008) report both positive and negative point estimates, with most nonsignificant.

Overall across both types of matching studies, the evidence points to a criminogenic effect of the experience of incarceration. Although the preponderance of criminogenic point estimates is not statistically significant, there is more evidence for statistically significant effects than in the experimental studies.

The type and vintage of the data used in the matching-based studies are quite varied. The most recent data are used in the Apel and Sweeten study, which is based on the 1997 National Longitudinal Study of Youth, and the oldest are used in the Kraus study, which is based on data from the early 1960s. Six studies examine incarceration effects in adulthood only (i.e., 18 years or older), one study's exclusive focus is juveniles (Kraus), and one study examines effects in juvenile and adult age periods (Apel and Sweeten). Also, as would be expected, the treatment conditions for custodial and noncustodial sanctions are less precisely defined than in the experimental studies. Variation in the length of incarceration was generally not reported, and in more than half of the studies noncustodial sanctions combined all possible noncustodial sanctions from probation to community service to fine.

C. Regression-Based Studies

Regression based studies form the largest body of evidence on the effect of custodial sanctions. The regression-based studies use various forms of multivariate regression analysis, such as logit regression or ordinary least squares regression, to account for potentially confounding variables. We identified 31 regression-based studies that included a dichotomous indicator variable distinguishing a custodial versus noncustodial sentence in the model. Table 5 summarizes the key features of these studies.

The studies examine a great variety of custodial and noncustodial sanction types. Some studies compare prison to different types of probation. Others combined prison with other forms of sanction (e.g., fines) or treatment (e.g., alcohol counseling) in making the comparison. Studies of juvenile populations focus on the effects of varying forms of institutional placement, such as shock incarceration or boot camps. The populations that are studied are also quite varied—there are studies of U.S. and non-U.S. populations, of juvenile and adult populations, and of different types of offenders such as drunk drivers or nonviolent offenders. The most commonly used outcome measure is recidivism.

In 22 studies, a majority of the custodial effect point estimates are positive, in seven a majority of the estimates are negative, and in two studies the estimates are equally split. Seventeen studies report at least one positive estimate that is statistically significant, and seven report at least one negative point estimate that is statistically significant. Thus, as in the matching studies, the predominant finding in the regression-based studies is an association suggesting a criminogenic effect of custodial sanctions. Although the variety of these studies makes it impossible to examine formally whether this pattern depends upon the type of custodial and noncustodial sanction examined or on the population studied, informally we could detect no such pattern.

Also reported in table 5 are the control variables utilized in these studies. Only 16 studies control for age, race, sex, prior record, and conviction offense type either by including the variable in the regression or limiting the analysis to specific types of people on one of these dimensions. A majority of the point estimates are positive in 13 of the studies. In the remaining three, a majority are negative. Twelve report at least one significant positive effect, and three report at least one significant negative effect. Thus, even for the subset of studies accounting for our minimum set of variables, the preponderance of the point estimates point to a criminogenic effect. Also summarized in the table are other variables controlled for beyond the minimum set. The addition of more variables does not seem to alter the conclusion that the imposition of custodial sanctions is generally associated with higher recidivism.

Our principal concern with the regression-based studies is the manner in which they account for age. Inclusion of age as a regressor is not equivalent to matching on age. Precise modeling of the underlying relationship between offending rate and age is imperative to avert bias. Otherwise small imbalances in the average age between those receiving and not receiving custodial sanctions could reflect model imperfections in accounting for age rather than the actual effect of custodial sanctions on recidivism. We return to this issue when we discuss the evidence on the relationship between time served in prison and reoffending. Even in the studies that control for the minimum set of control variables, to some degree, measures of prior record were often crude.

D. Other Studies

Below are brief descriptions of seven studies that do not neatly fit into the experimental, matching, or regression study categories. The studies are notable either because of the methodologies used or because of their findings—or both.

1. *Drago, Galbiati, and Vertova (2009).*   In May of 2006, Italy's Collective Clemency Bill resulted in the release of more than 20,000 inmates from Italian prisons. The release came with the condition that individuals convicted of another crime within 5 years of their release would have to serve the residual of the sentence that was suspended in addition to the sentence for the new crime. The residual sentence length varied between 1 and 36 months. This analysis examines whether the natural experiment created by the early release of these individuals had an effect on the reoffending rate. One key finding was that each month of residual sentence was associated with a 1.24 percent reduction in the propensity to recommit crime. The second key finding was that individuals who spent more time in prison for their clemency offense were less responsive to the incentive not to reoffend created by their having to serve out the residual sentence for that offense. This suggests that time served in prison reduces responsiveness to future punishment.

2. *Helland and Tabarrok (2007).*   This study examines whether Cal-

TABLE 5
Regression Studies: Findings on Custodial Sanction Effect

| Authors | Offending/Recidivism Rate | Controlled Directly for Age, Sex, Race, Prior Record, and Conviction Offense (Yes/No) | Other Control Variables | Treatment Description | | Sign of Custodial Effect | Statistical Significance of Effect (5%) |
				Custodial	Noncustodial		
Annan, Martin, and Forst (1986); Martin, Annan, and Forst (1993)	Recidivism	All but race	Blood alcohol content, counsel, judge with reputation for jail sentence	Jail (avg. = 2 days)	Fine	1+	0 of 1+ sig.
Bondeson (1994)	Recidivism	No	Risk score of 36 variables from six indices: (1) home and conditions of upbringing, (2) personal attributes and scholastic achievement, (3) maladjusted behavior and Child Welfare Board action, (4) abuse of alcohol and drugs, (5) occupational status, housing and accommodation, (6) sentences for earlier criminality[a]	Probation with institutional treatment	Conditional sentence Probation	2+	0 of 2+ sig.
Bonta, Wallace-Capretta, and Rooney (2000); same findings in Bonta, Wallace-Capretta, and Rooney (1999)	Recidivism	All but age, race, prior record, and current offense[b]	Controlled for risk through LSI-R score (includes criminal history, accommodation, emotional health, financial problems, attitudes/orientations, education/employment, companions, substance abuse, leisure/recreation, family relationships)[c]	Prison	Treated probation and EM combined	Low risk: 1− High risk: 1+	Low risk: No significance test High risk: No significance test
Brennan and Mednick (1994)	Recidivism	All but race[d]	Time in prison	Prison	Fines Probation	10+	1 of 10+ sig.

Study	Outcome	Race controlled	Other controls	Comparison groups	Reference	Effects	Significance
Clarke and Harrison (1992)	Recidivism	Yes	Time served	Regular parolee (avg. = 20 months), Max out parolee (avg. = 28 months), Paroled and terminated (avg. = 7 months), Split probation (up to 6 months)	Regular probation	17+ / 3−	15 of 17+ sig. / 0 of 3− sig.
De Jong (1997)	Recidivism	Yes	Days sentenced, positive drug tests, education, employment, marital status	Jail	No jail	2+	1 of 2+ sig.
De Young (1997)	Offending	Yes (race was controlled with an aggregate measure: % black in ZIP code)	Class of driver's license, prior crashes, ZIP code crash average, moving violation average, average travel time to work, % unemployed, % receiving public assistance, % renting residence, median family income	Treatment program, jail and license restriction / Treatment program and jail / Jail and license suspension / Jail only	Treatment program and license restriction / Treatment program	8+	4 of 8+ sig.[e]
Flowers, Carr, and Ruback (1991)	Offending	All but prior record	Place of conviction, risk score (including substance use, employment, address change, prior record, current offense), need scores (including substance use, health, mental ability, employment, education, and marital, emotional, financial, familial ability)	SAI graduates (boot camp) (avg. = 3 months, then probation) / Incarceration with no priors under 6 months / Incarceration with no priors 6–36 months / Incarceration with priors under 6 months / Incarceration with priors 6–36 months	Regular probation / Intensive probation supervision	8+ / 2−	6 of 8+ sig.[f] / 0 of 2− sig.[f]
Gordan and Glaser (1991)	Recidivism	Yes	Education, employment, drug problems	Probation + jail / Probation + jail + financial penalty	Probation only / Probation + financial penalty	5+ / 1−	5 of 5+ sig. / 0 of 1− sig.

TABLE 5 (Continued)

Authors	Offending/Re-cidivism Rate	Controlled Directly for Age, Sex, Race, Prior Record, and Conviction Offense (Yes/No)	Other Control Variables	Treatment Description		Sign of Custodial Effect	Statistical Signifi-cance of Effect (5%)
				Custodial	Noncustodial		
Gottfredson and Barton (1993)	Offending	All but sex, race, current offense[a]	Seriousness ranking for most serious alleged crime and place of residence	Youth facility	Noninstitutionalized (after facility closed)	Official: 8 − Self-report: 5 + 5 −	Official:[b] 4 of 8 − sig. Self-report:[b] 0 of 5 + sig. 1 of 5 − sig.
Gottfredson (1998)	Both	No	Multiple risk measures that include age, judge rating of arrest record, race, substance abuse, prior record, serious-ness of offense, type of offense, and sex, time served, time in community, selection for confinement (age, type of offense, seriousness, mitigating or ag-gravating factors, counsel and proba-tion recommendation, judge's impor-tance of rehabilitation or retribution)	Split sentence Youth facility Jail Prison (avg. = 44 months for people in jail or prison)	Probation	5 + 7 −	1 of 5 + sig. 1 of 7 − sig.
Jolin and Stipak (1992)	Recidivism	All but race and prior record	Risk assessment score, employment, marital status, substance abuse, time at risk	Work release	Intensive outpatient drug program (avg. = 7 months) ESP (EM and home confinement)	1 + 1 −	0 of 1 + sig. 0 of 1 − sig.
Jones and Ross (1997a)	Recidivism	Yes	14 client assessment items (including age at first conviction, attitude, fi-nances, associates, substance use, mari-tal status, prior record), follow-up pe-riod, county	Boot camp (IMPACT) (avg. = 3–4 months, then released on su-pervised probation)	EM/house arrest (avg. = 3 months, then released as high-risk case on regular probation)	5 −	5 of 5 − sig.

Study	Outcome	Controls	Covariates	Treatment	Comparison	Direction	Significance
Jones and Ross (1997b)	Recidivism	Yes	Education, employment, address change, county, follow-up period, marital status	Boot camp (IMPACT) (avg. = 3–4 months)	Probation	4+ / 1–	2 of 4+ sig. / 0 of 1– sig.
Jones (1991)	Recidivism	All but prior record and current offense[j]	Time at risk, drug abuse	Prison	Probation	1+	0 of 1– sig.
Lloyd, Mair, and Hough (1994)	Recidivism	All but race	None	Prison	Community service / Probation 4A/4B / Regular probation	3–	1 of 3– sig.
MacKenzie (1991)	Recidivism	All but race and current offense[k]	Intensity of supervision[l]	Shock incarceration (avg. = 3–4 months)	Probation	2+	0 of 2+ sig.
MacKenzie et al. (1995)	Recidivism	Yes	Intensity of supervision and time	Boot camp (separately for each state—GA, LA, SC, and TX)	Probation (separately for each state)	5+ / 14–	3 of 5+ sig. / 3 of 14– sig.
MacKenzie and Shaw (1993)	Recidivism	All but sex,[m] race, current offense[n]	. . .[o]	Shock incarceration	Probation	3+ / 2–	2 of 3+ sig. / 1 of 2– sig.
Nirel et al. (1997)	Recidivism	All but sex, race, and current offense[p]	Propensity score (PS) determined with stepwise regression with marital status, born in Israel, religion, sex, age, type of offense, sentencing agent, criminal history as covariates; however, the regression only led to the inclusion of marital status, type of offense, prior record, and sentencing agent in the PS	Prison (up to 6 months)	Service work	1+	1 of 1+ sig.[q]
Nunes et al. (2007)	Recidivism	All but race, prior record, and age	RRASOR score (age at release, prior sex offenses, victim gender, and victim-offender relationship)	Incarceration (avg. = 21.24 months)	Community sanction	2+	0 of 2+ sig.
Parisi (1981)	Recidivism	No, but all in risk score	Risk score (sex, race, age, marital status, education, prior record, current offense, and term of probation), time under supervision	Split sentence	Probation	5+ / 6–	0 of 5+ sig. / 0 of 6– sig.

159

TABLE 5 (Continued)

Authors	Offending/ Recidivism Rate	Controlled Directly for Age, Sex, Race, Prior Record, and Conviction Offense (Yes/No)	Other Control Variables	Treatment Description		Sign of Custodial Effect	Statistical Significance of Effect (5%)
				Custodial	Noncustodial		
Roeger (1994)	Recidivism	Yes	Marital status, education, employment	Parolees (after serving between 1 month and 2 years) Prisoners released sentence served	Probation Community service	4+	0 of 4+ sig.
Spohn and Holleran (2002)	Recidivism	Yes	Employment and predicted probability of imprisonment in 1993 (seriousness of offense, statutory classification of the offense, number of convictions, offender's prior criminal record, whether the offender was on probation at the time of arrest, whether a gun was used, type of disposition, pretrial status, race, age, gender, employment, type of attorney)	Prison	Probation	4+	4 of 4+ sig.
Tashima and Marelich (1989)	Offending	Yes[c]	Prior accidents, license class, ZIP code averages of single, separated, education, urban, carpool, own car, income	Jail only First offender program + jail	License suspension License restriction only First offender program + license restriction SB38 program + license restriction	14+ 2 −	12 of 14+ sig.[c] 0 of 2 − sig.[c]

Study	Outcome	Controls	Variables	More severe sanction	Less severe sanction	Sign	Significance
Taxman and Piquero (1998)	Recidivism	All but race	Numerous punishment (license restriction, fine, probation) and rehabilitative (abstinence, AA, alcohol education) measures	Jail	No jail	Full sample: 1+ First offenders only: 1−	Full sample: 0 of 1+ sig. First offenders only: 0 of 1− sig.
Ulmer (2001)	Recidivism	Yes	Education, marital status, drug treatment ordered, time since release/sentencing	Incarceration Work release	Probation House arrest	3+ 1−	0 of 3+ sig. 0 of 1− sig.
Van der Werff (1981)	Recidivism	All but race	None	Completely and partly unconditional custodial sanctions	Fines and all completely conditional custodial sentences	4+	3 of 4+ sig.
Weisburd, Waring, with Chayet (2001), separate analysis than presented in matched studies table	Recidivism	Yes	Marital status, home ownership, parenthood, community reputation, class position, education, substance abuse, education, informal sanctions (i.e., family suffering, loss of job, etc.)	Prison	Convicted but not imprisoned	1+	0 of 1+ sig.
Wheeler and Hissong (1988)	Recidivism	Yes	None	Jail	Fine Probation	2+	1 of 2+ sig.
Wiebush (1993)	Both	None[a]		Department of Youth Services placement	Intensive supervision unit (minimum = 6 months)	2+ 2−	0 of 2+ sig. 1 of 2− sig.
Wooldredge (1988)	Recidivism	Yes	GPA, county, parental marital status, learning disabilities, characterized as behavioral problems	1 month detention 1 year probation + 1 month detention 1 year probation + more than 1 month detention 2 years probation + 1 month detention 2 years probation + more than 1 month detention	Case dismissed 1 year probation 2 years probation	3+ 6−	1 of 3+ sig. 3 of 6− sig.

161

TABLE 5 (*Continued*)

Authors	Offending/Recidivism Rate	Controlled Directly for Age, Sex, Race, Prior Record, and Conviction Offense (Yes/No)	Other Control Variables	Treatment Description		Sign of Custodial Effect	Statistical Significance of Effect (5%)
				Custodial	Noncustodial		
Wright and Mays (1998)	Recidivism	Yes	None	Boot camp graduates Prisoners	Probationers	2+	1 of 2+ sig

NOTE.—Avg. = average; + = criminogenic effect; − = preventive effect; sig. = significant. EM = electronic monitoring.

[a] Risk score did not include race, age, current offense.

[b] Only included nonviolent, nonsexual offenders.

[c] Nonsignificant differences between groups on age, marital status, education, substance abuse, mental health, employment, finances, marital status.

[d] Race was not explicitly controlled but the location of the study, Denmark, is nearly all white. Only examined property offenders.

[e] Only report the first DUI offender results.

[f] Only report the 36-month follow-up.

[g] Only controlled for significant differences between groups (nonsignificant differences for sex, race, current offense).

[h] Only report longest follow-up, 2.5 years.

[i] Above variables were most related to recidivism; thus, there were other variables such as race that were not included in the risk score that did not predict recidivism.

[j] Most measures of prior record and current offense were not significantly related to rearrest, thus not included as controls.

[k] Nonsignificant differences on race, current crime type, and adult criminal history.

[l] Nonsignificant differences on education.

[m] Sex was not explicitly controlled; however, the number of women in the sample is small.

[n] Nonsignificant differences for race and type of current offense.

[o] Nonsignificant differences for education and age at first arrest.

[p] Sex, age, current offense are included in propensity score.

[q] Only report findings of regression analysis.

[r] Race is percent nonwhite in ZIP code and only report for first-time DUI offenders.

[s] Only report longest follow-up (2 years).

[t] Nonsignificant differences on age, race, sex, adjudicated complaints, offense history score, nature of current offense, prior probation, and risk score.

ifornia's "Three Strikes" law deters offending among individuals previously convicted of strike-eligible offenses. The future offending of individuals convicted of two strikable offenses was compared with that of individuals who had been convicted of only one strikable offense but who, in addition, had been tried for a second strikable offense but were ultimately convicted of a non-strike-eligible offense. The study demonstrates that these two groups of individuals were comparable on many characteristics such as age, race, and time in prison. Even so, it finds that arrest rates were about 20 percent lower for the group with convictions for two strikable offenses. The authors attribute this reduction to the greatly enhanced sentence that would have accompanied conviction on a third strikable offense.

3. *Bhati and Piquero (2008).* This analysis is based on the arrest histories of a very large sample of individuals released from U.S. prisons in 1994. The analysis uses an "information-theoretic" hazard model that projects a post-1994 offending trajectory based on the pre-1994 trajectory. This projected trend is then compared with the post-1994 actual offending to infer the imprisonment effect. Based on this contrast, it is concluded that the experience of imprisonment is associated with a very large reduction in future offending by a combination of deterrence and incapacitation.

4. *Wimer, Sampson, and Laub (2008).* This analysis is based on the data first assembled by Eleanor and Sheldon Glueck and subsequently updated by Robert Sampson and John Laub (Sampson and Laub 1993; Laub and Sampson 2003). The study is notable as much for the statistical methods used as for its results. It finds that periods of imprisonment are associated with subsequently higher rates of criminality as measured by arrest. However, when they apply methods recently developed by Robins and colleagues (Robins 1999; Hernán, Brumback, and Robins 2000; Robins, Hernán, and Brumback 2000) for causal inference with nonexperimental data, they find that the evidence of a seeming criminogenic effect of imprisonment is quite fragile.

5. *Manski and Nagin (1998).* This study, based on data from the Utah juvenile justice system, examines the effect on recidivism of placement in a secure residential facility. The study is based on a methodology that does not produce a point estimate of the effect of residential placement. Instead the methodology results in a bound on the residential placement treatment effect. The argument advanced for this approach is that point estimates based on observational data require

the use of models that make strong, often unverifiable, assumptions about treatment selection and outcomes. As a result, there are often strong disagreements about modeling assumptions. The bounding approach, it is argued, is based upon models that make fewer assumptions. The models and the attendant findings thus are less subject to dispute about the validity of underlying assumptions. The cost of the bounding approach is that the analysis does not provide a specific estimate of the treatment effect. For this application, the bounds do not definitely sign the treatment effect of secure confinement as either criminogenic or preventive. The analysis does suggest, however, that the likely sign of the effect depends upon the sentencing rule that is assumed to be used by juvenile court judges. If judges sentence juveniles to the treatment mode that will most likely reduce their recidivism, the evidence points toward a criminogenic effect of secure confinement. However, if judges employ a skimming model whereby they assign the highest rate offenders to secure confinement, the results point toward a preventive effect.

6. *Berube and Green (2007) and Green and Winik (2008).*   We combine these two studies because they both use the same methodological innovation. The validity of results based on nonexperimental data depends crucially on the adequacy of controls for potentially confounding variables like prior record. These two studies attempt to circumvent this vulnerability by taking advantage of a long-standing institutional feature of the U.S. federal court system—the random assignment of cases to judges. If there are differences in harshness across judges, such variation creates a natural experiment whereby otherwise comparable cases will be sentenced differently. Both studies report evidence of such variation in judicial harshness. Econometricians refer to variables that result in random assignment of treatment, in this case judge assignment, as instruments. Neither study finds statistically significant evidence that imprisonment affects recidivism. Point estimates of the treatment effect are equally divided between positive and negative values.

7. *Analysis.*   Although the analytical approaches used across these studies are quite different, a shared characteristic of each study is that each gives close attention to constructing a counterfactual. Drago, Galbiati, and Vertova's (2009) and Helland and Tabarrok's (2007) approaches to constructing the counterfactual are the least technical and most transparent. Drago, Galbiati, and Vertova take advantage of the

fact that the Collective Clemency Bill effectively randomly assigned a residual sentence length to prisoners given early release. Thus, comparisons of the recidivism rates across individuals with different residual sentence lengths provided the basis for estimating the "dose-response" curve between recidivism and sentence length. Helland and Tabarrok (2007) used the behavior of individuals with two convictions, one strikable but the other not strikable, to create the counterfactual for individuals with convictions for two strikable offenses. The other studies used more technically elaborate approaches to create the counterfactual. Berube and Green (2007) and Green and Winik (2008) exploit the random assignment of cases in the U.S. federal court system to construct an instrumental variable that provides the statistical basis for creating the counterfactual. Bhati and Piquero (2008) attempt to extrapolate the counterfactual from the individual's offending history prior to release in 1994. The approach used in Wimer, Sampson, and Laub (2008) to create a counterfactual cannot be described in a few sentences but involves inverse probability weighting based on time-dependent propensity scores. Finally, Manski and Nagin (1998) create bounds on the counterfactual over successively stronger assumptions about the treatment selection process.

What do we make of the substantive significance of these findings? We have concerns about the validity of Bhati and Piquero's (2008) approach to constructing the counterfactual. The validity of this approach rests upon the projection of the preincarceration offending trajectory providing a valid counterfactual of the postincarceration trajectory absent the experience of imprisonment. This counterfactual would seem to be biased toward showing a preventive effect because the prerelease offending trajectory necessarily requires criminal activity—otherwise the individual would not have been incarcerated. Thus, even if imprisonment had no effect on criminal behavior, a reduction in offending relative to the prerelease trajectory would be expected based solely upon regression to the mean. Also, as Bhati and Piquero recognize, their estimate includes an incapacitation effect. Although we admire the ingenuity of the Berube and Green (2007) and Green and Winik (2008) instrument, one important design feature of both studies is troubling: each retains in the estimation sample individuals who were acquitted or whose cases were otherwise dismissed post–random assignment to the judge. Thus, these individuals also contribute to the statistical construction of the counterfactual for imprisonment. In our judgment, these individuals should not have been included in the analysis. Further, due to the short follow-up period in the Green and Winik (2008) study, 3 years postassignment to a judge, a criminogenic effect of imprisonment may have been suppressed by an incapacitation effect. While we have no specific methodological criticism of the Manski and Nagin study (an admittedly biased assessment!), its focus on juveniles and its avowedly methodological emphasis makes its substantive findings of lesser interest for our purposes here. Likewise, we have no criticism of the methodology used in the Wimer, Sampson, and Laub study, but the fragility of findings forecloses substantive conclusions.

This leaves us with the Drago, Galbiati, and Vertova (2009) and Helland and Tabarrok (2007) studies. These two studies, we believe, have important substantive implications because they provide a perspective on why it might be that the experience of punishment may be both criminogenic and a deterrent. As discussed in Section I, there are many mechanisms by which the experience of punishment might be criminogenic. Similarly, there are many mechanisms by which the experience may have an ameliorative effect on criminality. Among the most compelling arguments for a preventive effect is one that involves expectations about punishment for future offending—namely, that future offending will be sanctioned even more harshly than prior offending. The Drago, Galbiati, and Vertova (2009) and Helland and Tabarrok (2007) findings are supportive of this expectations-based mechanism but in a specific sort of way. Most sanctioning systems punish repeat offenders more harshly, yet when Helland and Tabarrok replicated their analysis in states without three-strike laws, they found no differences in the recidivism of offenders with one and two strikable offenses by California standards. This suggests that expectations-based deterrence among repeat offenders requires a very tangible, "in your face" disincentive to reoffending that is hard to neglect. In the case of the Drago, Galbiati, and Vertova study, the disincentive was the residual sentence to be added to the penalty for any new offense. In the case of the California three-strikes sentencing regime, it was the threat of imprisonment for life for a third strike. Other evidence on the importance of tangible incentives to affect the behavior of active offenders is from an experiment conducted by Weisburd, Einat, and Kowalski (2008) that found that the imminent threat of incarceration was an effective incentive for getting convicted offenders to make payment on delinquent fines.

The second notable finding from the Drago, Galbiati, and Vertova study was that the deterrent effect of residual sentences diminished with length of incarceration for the offense that received clemency. This finding is consistent with the finding of much of the literature that points to a criminogenic effect of the experience of imprisonment. As emphasized in Section I, criminogenic and preventive effects are not mutually exclusive; they both can be operating in unison with the net effect either in a criminogenic or preventive direction depending on the summation of the combined criminogenic and preventive influences. The Drago, Galbiati, and Vertova findings suggest that the criminogenic influences may mount with time in prison.

E. Length of Imprisonment and Reoffending Rate

Most studies of the effect of custodial sanctions on reoffending do not examine the relationship between length of confinement and reoffending. Understanding this relationship is vital for both public policy and science. Custodial sanctions are very expensive. For adults the average cost of imprisonment is $30,000 per person-year or more, and for juveniles it can exceed $100,000 (Nagin et al. 2006). Thus, for public policy purposes, knowledge of the effect of length of confinement on reoffending rate is of manifest importance. It is also of scientific importance for testing many of the theories of a criminogenic effect of imprisonment that predict that a longer spell of incarceration will result in a higher reoffending rate.

In the parlance of medical research, the relationship between length of confinement and reoffending rate is an example of a dose-response function. We know of only two experimental studies of this dose-response relationship. They are summarized in table 6. The study conducted by Deschenes, Turner, and Petersilia (1995) compares incarceration to intensive community supervision (ICS). Because treatment assignment occurred after the eligible convictees had been incarcerated, assignment to ICS shortened the period in prison rather than averted the experience of imprisonment. For this reason, we describe Deschenes, Turner, and Petersilia as an investigation into how incarceration time dosage affects reoffending. After 2 years, treatment effect estimates of more lengthy confinement are about equally split between criminogenic and preventive effects. However, only one of 17 estimates is statistically significant. The second study was conducted by Berecochea and Jaman (1981). In this study, the custodial term of a random

TABLE 6
Experimental Studies of Time Served

Authors	Population Characteristics	Length Description		Outcome		
		Longer	Shorter	Offend-ing/Re-cidivism Rate	Sign of Length Effect	Statistical Significance of Effect (5%)
Berecochea and Jaman (1981)	All male Californian felon inmates who received a parole date between March and August 1970 set greater than 6 months from the time of the hearing	Custodial term not reduced by 6 months	Custodial term reduced by 6 months	Recidivism	1 year follow-up: 1− 2 year follow-up: 1−	1 year follow-up: 0 of 1− sig. 2 year follow-up: 0 of 1− sig.
Deschenes, Turner, and Petersilia (1995)	Offenders in Minnesota who had been recently convicted and committed to the state prison system for 27 months or less or offenders who had violated the terms of their probation and had been committed to the Commissioner of Corrections	Prison (avg. = 228 days)	Released on intensive community supervision (avg. = 124 days)	Both	10+ 7 −[a]	1 of 10+ sig. 0 of 7− sig.

NOTE.—Avg. = average; + = criminogenic effect; − = preventive effect; sig. = significant.
[a] Only report 24-month follow-up to ensure prison group has sufficient amount of time at risk.

sample of male felony inmates in California prisons was reduced by 6 months. Recidivism rates at 1 and 2 years were higher for these individuals compared to a control group that did not benefit from the reduction. The seeming preventive effect of experiencing a longer prison term, however, was not statistically significant.[5]

We identified 17 nonexperimental studies that report evidence on the dose-response relationship. Three were matching-based studies, and 14 were regression-based studies. The three matching-based studies are summarized in table 7. Two studies are more than 25 years old. Jaman, Dickover, and Bennett (1972) compare the recidivism of burglars who served 25 months or longer with those serving 24 months or less. This study controls for all the variables in our minimum set. By limiting the analysis to male burglars, gender and conviction offense are accounted for. By-variable matching was used to account for the remaining variables in the minimum set plus several others. Jaman, Dickover, and Bennett found that recidivism was higher for the longer-time-served group at 6, 12, and 24 months following release. However, the difference was only statistically significant at 24 months. Kraus (1981) studied juveniles. All the variables in the minimum set except possibly for race were accounted for. The dosage contrasts are summarized in table 7. For two age groups, longer confinement was associated with higher recidivism; for one age group, it was associated with lower recidivism. None of the differences were statistically significant. Loughran et al. (2008) is based on a contemporary longitudinal data set tracking serious juvenile offenders. It uses a propensity score matching–based methodology that balances on a very lengthy set of variables, including those in the minimum set. Their point estimate of the effect of custodial versus noncustodial placement is again in the criminogenic direction but falls short of significance. They find no evidence of length of confinement affecting reoffending rate either in a criminogenic or preventive direction.

Table 8 summarizes the 14 regression-based studies relating time served to reoffending. We note that the aim of most of these studies was some purpose other than studying the dose-response relationship. Time served was included only as a control variable usually among many others. The results of these studies are quite varied. In terms of

---

[5] Philip Cook of Duke University reports that in his own analyses of the results he finds that the preventive effects are statistically significant for a two-tailed test at the .10 level (personal communication).

TABLE 7
Matched Studies of Time Served

Authors	Offending/Recidivism Rate	Matched by Variable on Age, Sex, Race, Current Offense, and Prior Record (Yes/No)	Variables beyond Minimum Set	Comment on Matching	Length Description		Sign of Length Effect	Statistical Significance of Effect (5%)
					Longer	Shorter		
Jaman, Dickover, and Bennett (1972)	Recidivism	Yes[a]	Substance abuse, parole region of release, type of parole unit, base expectancy score (prior record, drug use, current offense, family criminality, employment, and living situation)	Found significant differences between groups on the following, which were also related to parole outcome: aliases, institutional academic rating, and home at final AA appearance	25 or more months prior to parole release	Less than 24 months prior to parole release	At 6-month follow-up: 1+ At 12-month follow-up: 1+ At 24-month follow-up: 1+	At 6-month follow-up: 0 of 1+ sig. At 12-month follow-up: 0 of 1− sig. At 24-month follow-up: 1 of 1+ sig.
Kraus (1981)	Recidivism	All except possibly race*	None	Succeeded in matching on key variables	For ages 9–12: 10–19 months For age 13: 9–16 months For ages 14–15: 8–20 months	For ages 9–12: up to 9 months For age 13: up to 8 months For ages 14–15: up to 7 months	For ages 9–12: 2+ For age 13: 2+ For ages 14–15: 1−	For ages 9–12: 0 of 2+ sig. For age 13: 0 of 2+ sig. For ages 14–15: 0 of 1− sig.

Loughran et al. (2008)	Offending	No; however, matched with propensity score	Mental health, substance abuse, family, education, employment background, punishment costs, social capital, risk/need scores, involvement in the community, impulse control, gang membership, and social support	All of the key variables except current offense were included in the propensity score[b]	6–10 months 10–13 months >13 months	0–6 months	1+ 2–	0 of 1+ sig.[c] 0 of 2– sig.[c]

NOTE.—+ = criminogenic effect; − = preventive effect; sig. = significant.
* Data are from the early 1960s, a time when Australia was almost entirely white except for Aboriginals. Not clear whether this racial minority was included in the study.
[a] Age not within 1 year and only report for burglary.
[b] All participants were serious offenders with most being guilty of felony offenses.
[c] Compared each time frame with 0–6 months.

TABLE 8
Regression Studies of Time Served

Authors	Offending/Recidivism Rate	Controlled Directly for Age, Sex, Race, Prior Record, and Conviction Offense (Yes/No)	Other Control Variables	Length Description		Sign of Length Effect	Statistical Significance of Effect (5%)
				Longer	Shorter		
Clarke and Harrison (1992)	Recidivism	Yes	Time served	Continuous variable of time served before release		4+ 1−	4 of 4+ sig. 0 of 1− sig.
De Jong (1997)	Recidivism	Yes	Days sentenced, urine positive for certain drugs, education, employment, marital status	Continuous variable of days sentenced		1+ 1−	0 of 1+ sig. 1 of 1− sig.
Deschenes, Owen, and Crow (2006)	Both	Yes	None	Continuous variables of sentence length and time served		6−	6 of 6− sig
Finn and Muirhead-Steves (2002)	Recidivism	Yes	Substance abuse, EM, education, total success score (prior record, drug use, current offense, employment, education), EM × crime type interactions	Continuous variable of time served in years		2−	0 of 2− sig.
Flowers, Carr, and Ruback (1991)	Offending	All but prior record	Place of conviction, risk score (including substance use, employment, address change, prior record, current offense), need scores (including substance use, health, mental ability, employment, education, and marital, emotional, financial, familial ability)	Incarceration with no priors 6–36 months Incarceration with priors 6–36 months	Incarceration with no priors under 6 months Incarceration with priors under 6–36 months	1+ 1−	0 of 1+ sig.' 0 of 1− sig.'

Study	Outcome	Controls	Variables	Measure	Direction	Significance
Gainey, Payne, and O'Toole (2000)	Recidivism	Yes	Days on EM, sentence length, marital status, employment, number of people in home, interaction of EM days × marital status, and interaction of jail days × priors, time at risk	Continuous variable of days in jail	1+ 1−	0 of 1+ sig. 0 of 1− sig.
Gottfredson (1998)	Offending	No	Risk measure that includes age, judge rating of arrest record, race, substance abuse, prior record, seriousness of offense, and type of offense, time served, time in community, selection for confinement (age, type of offense, seriousness, mitigating or aggravating factors, counsel/probation recommendation, judge's importance of rehabilitation or retribution)[b]	Continuous variable of months served in custodial sanction (youth facility, jail, or prison)	1+ 2−	0 of 1+ sig. 0 of 2− sig.
Harer (1994)	Both	All but current offense	Salient Factor Score, substance abuse, CJS supervision, prison misconduct, education, employment, type of release, living situation, ZIP population, poverty, unemployed	Continuous variable of prison term served in months	1+ 1−	0 of 1+ sig. 0 of 1− sig.
Holland, Pointon, and Ross (2007)	Recidivism	Yes	None	Continuous variable of time served in prison	0; the exponent was 0.00 with Exp(B) = 1.00	Not significant, no effect
Kim et al. (1993)	Recidivism	Yes	Employment, income, marital status, supervised release, number of sworn officers/1,000 population, probability of conviction for arrest for drugs, proportion of drug arrests to total arrests, population, average earnings	Continuous variable for number of days served in prior incarceration	1−	0 of 1− sig.

TABLE 8 (*Continued*)

Authors	Offending/Re-cidivism Rate	Controlled Directly for Age, Sex, Race, Prior Record, and Conviction Offense (Yes/No)	Other Control Variables	Length Description		Sign of Length Effect	Statistical Signifi-cance of Effect (5%)
				Longer	Shorter		
Maguire, Flana-gan, and Thornberry (1988)	Recidivism	Yes	Education, marital status, military ser-vice, employment, substance use, prison rule infraction rate	Continuous variable of number of years incarcerated		1 −	1 of 1 − sig.
Nunes et al. (2007)	Recidivism	All but race, prior rec-ord, and age	RRASOR score (age at release, prior sex offenses, victim gender, and victim-offender relationship)	Continuous variable of number of months incarcerated		2 instances of a 1.00 odds ratio	Not significant, no effect
Orsagh and Chen (1988)	Recidivism	Yes	Marital status, involved in prerelease rehabilitation program, unemployment rate in county of release, involved in work release program	Continuous variable of length of continuous incarceration up to the release date in natural logs		1 + 1 −	1 of 1 + sig.; 0 of 1 − sig.;
Petersilia, Turner, with Peterson (1986)[d]	Recidivism	All but current offense	Substance abuse, weapon use, injury to victim, relationship to victim, marital status education, living situation, county of conviction	Continuous variable of time served in months		12 −	5 of 12 − sig.
Wooldredge (1988)	Recidivism	Yes	GPA, county, parental marital status, learning disabilities, characterized as behavioral problems	More than 1 month detention	1 month detention	3 +	2 of 3 + sig.

NOTE.— + = criminogenic effect; − = preventive effect; sig. = significant. EM = electronic monitoring; DV = dependent variable.
[a] Only report 36-month follow-up.
[b] Above variables were most related to recidivism and included in the risk and selection score; however, there were other variables such as race and sex that were not included in the risk score and selection score because they did not significantly predict recidivism.
[c] Only reported logit analysis since DV is dichotomous.
[d] Unlike earlier in their study, they did not use matching when examining the impact of sentence length.

Time incarcerated

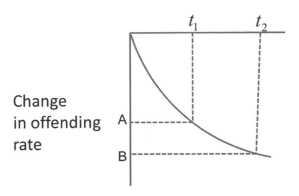

FIG. 4.—Dose-response relationship between time incarcerated and change in offending rate.

counts of point estimates, seven report equal numbers of positive and negative point estimates, five report a majority of negative estimates, and two report a majority of positive estimates. In half of the studies, none of the point estimates, whether positive or negative, are significant, four studies report at least one significant negative estimate, and three studies report at least one significant positive estimate.

What conclusions do we draw from these studies of the dose-response relationship between time served and reoffending? The one experimental study is suggestive of a preventive effect, but that effect may be attributable to incapacitation. Two of the matching studies point weakly to a criminogenic type dose-response relationship, but both are extremely dated. The Loughran et al. (2008) study suggests a possible criminogenic effect of placement but finds no linkage between time served and reoffending. We draw no conclusions from the results of the regression studies. Not only are results extremely varied, but more importantly all of the studies suffer from a fundamental analytical flaw. This flaw relates to the potential sensitivity of regression-based studies to specification errors in the model of the relationship of age and offending rate.

Figure 4 depicts a hypothetical dose-response relationship. It assumes a preventive effect, but the points we wish to make apply equally to a criminogenic dose-response relationship or to a curve that has

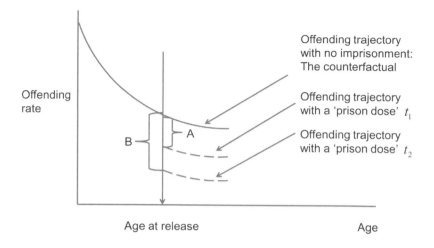

Age at release   Age

FIG. 5.—Rate of offending for different doses of "prison"

both criminogenic and preventive regions. The horizontal axis measures the dose—namely, time served in prison. The vertical axis measures the reduction in the offending rate. The curve measures the size of the reduction corresponding to each prison dosage. For a time served of t_1, the predicted reduction is A. For a longer time served t_2, the reduction B is even larger. These reductions are measured relative to an implicit counterfactual sentence of zero time served.

The change in offending rate is not observed or observable. It must be inferred from the actual offending rates of individuals who spent varying amounts of time in prison. Figure 5 depicts the inference problem. The vertical axis measures the offending rate, and the horizontal axis measures age. The vertical arrow in the graph denotes the age of release from prison. The curve to the right of the release age denotes the pretreatment age–offending rate relationship. It assumes a declining relationship, but a rising relationship could just as well have been assumed for the points we wish to make. To the right of the release arrow are the offending trajectories associated with prison dosages t_1 and t_2. Also, to the right of the release arrow is a solid trajectory denoting the counterfactual offending trajectory for a prison dosage of no time served. The t_1 dosage trajectory is A offending rate units below this counterfactual, and the t_2 dosage trajectory is B units below the counterfactual.

The objective of a statistical analysis is to infer these differences in offending rate from data on offending rates of individuals who spent varying amounts of time in prison. If the statistical analysis was conducted based on data from an experiment in which sentences of 0 and of t_1 and t_2 were randomized across subjects, then estimates of A and B could be obtained directly from the difference in postrelease offending between those receiving no prison sentence and those receiving sentences of t_1 and t_2, respectively. This straightforward approach works because, due to randomization, all potential confounders are balanced across treatment conditions. Most critical among these potential confounders is age. Because offending rate is changing with age, imbalances in age across dosage levels could seriously bias results. For example, if the average age of individuals receiving dosage t_1 was less than the average for the zero-dose individuals, the preventive effect, A, would be understated. Indeed, if the age imbalance were large enough, the effect estimate could be in the criminogenic direction.

Now consider the problem of using regression to uncover the dose-response relationship with nonexperimental data. In these data, individuals receiving prison sentences will have been released from prison at varying ages. Thus, the pre- and posttreatment offending histories of individuals will vary in length and by age. The pretreatment age-offending rate trajectory must somehow be statistically reconstructed from data in which there is no set pretreatment age. Similarly, the postrelease offending trajectories must be reconstructed for varying amounts of time served. This challenge has been the subject of much serious statistical work (see Imbens 2000; Lu et al. 2001; Zanutto, Lu, and Hornik 2005). Suffice it to say that solutions require far more than simply adding time and age to the list of regressors in a regression model.

IV. Implications for Policy and Future Research

A remarkable fact is that despite the widespread use of imprisonment across democratic nations and the enormous expansion of the prison system in the United States, rigorous investigations of the effect of incarceration on reoffending are in short supply. Among criminologists, there is no lack of commentary about prisons, with most scholars decrying their overuse generally and their disproportionate use with minority groups. But critical commentary is not equivalent to demarcating scientifically the comparative impact on future criminal involvement of custodial as opposed to noncustodial sanctions. A new generation of investigations is needed.

This is not to say that existing research does not allow for a provisional conclusion about the likely impact of incarceration. Thus, a key finding of our review is that the great majority of studies point to a null or criminogenic effect of the prison experience on subsequent offending. This reading of the evidence should, at least, caution against wild claims—at times found in "get tough" rhetoric voiced in recent decades—that prisons have special powers to scare offenders straight.

Still, it is equally important to note that several important exceptions to this overall pattern of results were found and are discussed below. Although in most studies the majority of point estimates imply criminogenic effects, estimated effects are not always statistically significant by conventional standards. More importantly, in many studies important variables like prior record or age are not adequately accounted for. Moreover, studies are often dated or involve juvenile populations. Thus, as imprisonment is used in contemporary democratic societies, the scientific jury is still out on its effect on reoffending. Even so, serious effort should be committed to studying the implications for public policy and social science of a possible criminogenic effect of imprisonment. In this section, we outline a conceptual framework and research agenda designed to explore these implications.

A. Imprisonment and Crime Rates

At the outset of this essay, a distinction was drawn between general and specific deterrence. We now reiterate that distinction with the observation that there is no inherent contradiction between the conclusions that the threat of punishment has a substantial deterrent effect in the population writ large, often called general deterrence, and the conclusion that the experience of punishment increases criminality. We do not assert that either of these conclusions is known with certainty, but we do assert that there is sufficient evidence for both and that they should be taken seriously. Accordingly, we need a theory and modeling structure that accounts for these contending effects of sanctions on crime rate.

Figure 6 is a schematic of such a modeling structure. We do not formalize the relationships depicted in the figure.[6] That must be left

---

[6] We thank Jonathan Caulkins for suggesting the basic form of this schematic.

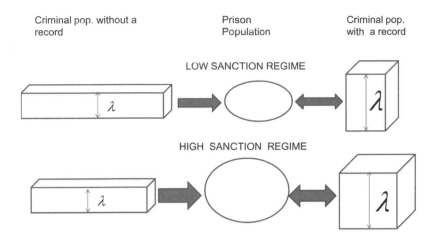

FIG. 6.—Crime and low versus high sanction regimes

for future research. Rather, the purpose of the figure is to provide a conceptual structure for commenting on the types of useful questions for policy and science that need to be addressed. The figure delineates three populations: the population of offenders without records of imprisonment, the population of offenders with imprisonment records, and the prison population. It compares the sizes and flow rates among these populations under regimes of low and high prison sanction severity. The prison population is designated by an ellipse, and its size is represented by the surface area of the ellipse. Offending populations are represented as three-dimensional rectangles. Their size is represented by the two-dimensional surface area of the rectangle.

Under a regime of high sanction severity, we anticipate that due to general deterrence the size of the offending population without criminal records will be smaller than that under a regime of low sanction severity. We also anticipate that the high sanction severity regime will result in a larger prison population that, in turn, results in a larger population of offenders with a criminal record.[7] The arrows connecting

---

[7] If the general deterrent effect is strong enough, a regime of high severity could actually reduce prison population. However, even the maximum elasticities of crime rates with respect to the imprisonment rate reported in Donohue (2007) are unlikely to be sufficient to result in falling prison populations. The model also anticipates that prisoners will eventually be released, which is the case for the vast majority of the prison population.

the populations represent flows between the populations. The arrow connecting the population of offenders without record to the prison population is one-headed to the right because exit from prison to the population without a record is impossible by definition. The arrow connecting the prison population to the population of criminals with a record is two-headed because individuals with a record can return to prison. The larger arrow sizes under the high severity regime reflect our expectation that flows out of the criminal population without a record into the prison population and eventually into the criminal populations with records will be higher than in the low severity regime.

The schematic depicts the population of offenders with and without records in three dimensions. The third dimension reflects their rate of offending, λ. Based on the findings of our review, the rate of offending for the population with a record is predicted to be higher than that of the offending population without a record.

Under which sentencing regime would crime rates be higher? This question has no definite answer. Compared to the high severity regime, the low severity regime would have more crime from the population of offenders without records due to the relatively larger size of this population. It would also have less crime averted by incapacitation because prison populations are smaller in the low severity regime. On the other hand, under the low severity regime, there would be comparatively less crime from the criminal population with records due to its smaller size. Reduction in the size of the population with records results in a proportionately larger number of crimes averted than reductions in the population without records because the former population offends at a higher rate than the latter population. Thus, the net difference in crime between the low and high regimes depends upon the size of the crime reduction from deterrence and incapacitation in the high versus low regime compared to the increase in crime from the criminogenic effect of prison in the high versus low regime.

B. A Research Program on the Effects of Imprisonment on Reoffending

Developing the empirical and analytic capacity to do this accounting of competing effects will require more research on general deterrence, incapacitation, and the effect of imprisonment on reoffending. Because general deterrence and incapacitation are not the focus of this essay, we refer readers to Nagin (1998), Doob and Webster (2003), and Donohue (2007) for extended discussions of important gaps in knowledge about these topics. Gaining a better fix on the effect of imprisonment on reoffending will require a research program that uses more policy-relevant data to ask more policy-relevant questions, measures the dose-response relationship between length of imprisonment and reoffending rate and between number of times imprisoned and reoffending rate, examines how the experience of punishment affects perceptions of sanction risk, tests the mechanisms by which the experience of imprisonment may be criminogenic, and unpacks the effect of different noncustodial sanctions. These components are discussed in turn.

1. *Using More Policy-Relevant Data to Ask More Policy-Relevant Questions.*   If the experience of imprisonment is criminogenic at least for some sizable segment of those imprisoned, the natural question from a public policy perspective is: what would be the impact on crime rates of incrementally cutting back on the use of the prison sanction? Part of the reason existing research falls well short of being useful for answering a question such as this is that most research is not relevant to predicting effects in the context of contemporary sanction policy. No matter how well done, studies of custodial sanctions on Australian youth based on data from the early 1960s or of the effect of a royal pardon for sentences of 2 weeks or less tell us little about the impact of consequential changes in contemporary sanctioning policy.

The challenge of laying out a policy-relevant research agenda is further complicated by large differences in the sanctioning policies and prison conditions across countries. We thus outline our recommendations for a workable, policy-relevant research program for one country with the hope that it will serve as a blueprint for other countries. We focus in particular on the United States not only because it has the highest imprisonment rate of all North American and Western European countries but also because the sources of the increase have been best documented.

Let us return to the question of how the crime rate would be affected by incrementally cutting back on the use of the prison sanction. The answer to this question requires a specification of the way in which the use of prison sanctions would be curtailed. We use the term "marginal" prisoners to label individuals whose terms of imprisonment would be affected by a specified change in sanction policy on the "margin."

How, then, might the marginal prisoner be conceived of in the United States? There is no easy answer to this question. One conception that has desirable social welfare virtues is to define the margin as those prisoners whose reoffending is most exacerbated by the experience of imprisonment (Manski and Nagin 1998). From a practical point of view this conception has two serious drawbacks. First, it begs the question because it provides no guidance on what type of individual that might be. Only the research itself can answer the question. Second, it is a conception whose answer might mightily offend the principles of equity and justice. Those most adversely affected might include individuals who have committed the most serious crimes or who have come from more privileged backgrounds. Sentencing such individuals to a noncustodial sanction or to shorter prison terms would be ethically offensive to many. Another vantage point that might provide a useful perspective for defining the marginal prisoner is recent history. In the United States, combined federal and state imprisonment rates have been rising more or less steadily for nearly 4 decades from a rate of about 100 per 100,000 population in the early 1970s to about 500 per 100,000 population at the present time. A reversal of selected policies that contributed to this massive increase is still another approach to defining the margin. This is the approach that we take here.

There are two basic mechanisms for reducing reliance on sanctions involving incarceration—one affects the extensive margin of use of imprisonment by reducing the fraction of the convicted who are incarcerated. The other affects the intensive margin by reducing the sentence length of those who are incarcerated. Still another relevant margin, at least in the American context, involves parole violators. In the United States, changes in the policies regarding conditions for parole revocation could also have a material impact on prison populations (Blumstein and Beck 2005).

Blumstein and Beck (1999) and Raphael and Stoll (2007) have closely scrutinized the primary sources of the increases in imprisonment since the 1980s. Since the mid-1980s, there has been a dramatic increase in the imprisonment of drug offenders whether measured on a per capita basis or as a percentage of the prison population. Escalation of the imprisonment of drug offenders has been particularly marked in the federal prison system; more than half of the federal prisoners were committed for drug offenses. There has been much criticism of the sanctioning policies that are the source of the dramatic increase in the incarceration of drug offenders. The criticisms focus on their disproportionate impacts on African Americans (Tonry 1995; Human Rights Watch 2008) and their ineffectiveness in curtailing illicit drug use (Rydell, Caulkins, and Everingham 1996; Caulkins et al. 1999). Thus, we recommend that priority attention be given to analyzing the effect of imprisonment on reoffending among drug offenders.

Blumstein and Beck (1999) also decompose the source of the increase in the imprisonment rate between the extensive margin, the probability of commitment given arrest, and the intensive margin, time served. The relative contribution of these two components varies by crime type. Aside from drugs, the only nonviolent crime that they examine is burglary. According to Blumstein and Beck, between 1980 and 1996 per capita rates of incarceration for burglary nearly doubled. The greatest part of that increase was attributable to increased time served. We thus recommend that priority attention be given to examining the relationship between time served and reoffending rate, for burglary in particular, because it is not a violent crime, and also other crimes even if they involve some element of violence. This brings us to the second element of the proposed research agenda.

2. *Measuring the Dose-Response Relationship between Length of Imprisonment and Reoffending Rate and between Number of Times Imprisoned and Reoffending Rate.*   As discussed in Section III, there is little convincing evidence on the dose-response relationship between time spent in confinement and reoffending rate. Because imprisonment is so costly, $30,000 per person-year or more, knowledge of this relationship has important implications not only for public safety but also for state, local, and federal budgets. Another dimension of the dose-response function is the relationship between offending rate and the number of prior spells of incarceration. Many of the theories of how the prison experience might affect reoffending, particularly those involving stigma, suggest that effects will decline with number of spells, yet to our knowledge no research has been conducted on this dimension of the dose-response function.

The primary statistical hurdle to estimating both of these dimensions of the dose-response relationship is that neither the length of incarceration nor the number of spells of incarceration is randomly assigned. Short of a randomized experiment, which is not likely feasible for the sorts of marginal populations that we recommend be studied, the analysis will have to be based on nonexperimental, observational data. What characteristics should these data have, and what methods should be used to analyze them to circumvent inference problems?

Concerning the characteristics of the data, we return to Monahan's

(2008) categories of variables in modern actuarial-based risk assessment instruments: what the person "is" as measured by age, sex, race, and personality; what the person "has" as measured by major mental, personality, or substance use disorders; what the person "has done" as measured by prior crime and violence; and what has been "done to" the person as measured by pathological family environment and victimization. It is important that the data have as many measurements on each of these dimensions as is practically possible. More complete measurements will set the stage for a more convincing set of statistical adjustments to account for the nonrandom assignment of sentences. In this regard, it is particularly important to have extensive measurements of what the individual has "done" as measured by prior record and characteristics of the conviction offense. Because these factors represent the primary determinants of sentence type and length, it is vital that they be measured on as many dimensions as possible. Also, for analyses of drug offenders, data on what the individual "has" as measured by the severity of their substance abuse are very important.

What methods should be used to analyze these data? Because it is unlikely that randomized experiments can be conducted in this setting, researchers should be on the lookout for natural experiments such as the random assignment of judges in the U.S. federal courts that Berube and Green (2007) and Green and Winik (2008) exploit or the variations in time served created by the Collective Clemency Act that are exploited by Drago, Galbiati, and Vertova (2009). Determinate sentencing grids, for example, may provide a quasi-experiment for constructing the dose-response relationship between sentence length and reoffending rate. The reoffending rates of individuals with sentencing scores that place them just above and below breakpoints on the sentencing grid could be compared. Finally, it is imperative that close attention be given to balancing on age and more generally to the statistical construction of the counterfactual. We recommend the use of methods such as those used in Loughran et al. (2008).

3. *Understanding How the Experience of Punishment Affects Perceptions of Sanction Risk.*   Balanced against the many studies finding evidence of a criminogenic effect of imprisonment are two important studies, Drago, Galbiati, and Vertova (2009) and Helland and Tabarrok (2007), that find convincing evidence of a deterrent effect. These studies are distinctive not only because of their findings but also because of their framing of the research question. In all other studies, the research

question is framed in terms of the effect of custodial versus noncustodial sanctions on reoffending. By contrast, the research question in Drago, Galbiati, and Vertova and in Helland and Tabarrok is framed in classic deterrence terms: does the threat of more punishment deter more crime?

Helland and Tabarrok examine whether the draconian consequences of a third strike in California deter reoffending, and Drago, Galbiati, and Vertova examine whether the threat of having to serve out the residual sentence on the clemency offense deters future offending. In both studies, the authors attempt to hold prior prison experience constant. In the Helland and Tabarrok study, the third-strike deterrent effect is estimated by comparing the behavior of individuals with two convictions, one strikable but the other not strikable, with individuals that have convictions for two strikable offenses. Thus, their analysis strategy holds constant the number of convictions and presumably also spells of imprisonment. By design, therefore, the analysis strategy provides no information on the effect of the prison experience itself on reoffending. By contrast, the Drago, Galbiati, and Vertova study is informative on whether the length of incarceration for the clemency offense affects recidivism. They find an interaction of the deterrent effect of the residual sentence and time served for the clemency offense: the longer the time served, the less deterrent effect. This finding aligns with our conclusion that the empirical evidence points to an overall criminogenic effect.

These studies were discussed under the heading "understanding how the experience of punishment affects perceptions of sanction risk" because, if indeed their results are a reflection of deterrence, prior contacts with the criminal justice system must have affected perceptions of future punishment. Nagin (1998, p. 1) commented that "knowledge about the relationship between sanction risk perceptions and policy is virtually nonexistent; such knowledge would be invaluable in designing effective crime-deterrent policies." He went on to recommend that research on the link between sanction policy and perceptions be a priority research topic. A decade later we re-endorse this recommendation.

The Drago, Galbiati, and Vertova and Helland and Tabarrok studies suggest that there is a link between policy and perception, at least in some circumstances. Both studies, however, focus on circumstances in which the threat of heightened punishment was likely and unusually tangible to a population whose prior offending had already demonstrated their lack of responsiveness to sanction threats. In the Helland and Tabarrok study, that tangibility was probably the draconian consequences of the third strike. Helland and Tabarrok concluded that the crime-reduction benefits of this draconian threat likely fell far short of the cost of a lifetime prison term. By contrast, Drago, Galbiati, and Vertova's study examines a policy that would be much more likely to pass a cost-benefit test. The saliency likely stemmed from the offender's certain knowledge of the residual sentence premium for future offending.

These are, of course, merely speculations for why the policy-to-perceptions link was closed in the Drago, Galbiati, and Vertova and Helland and Tabarrok studies. What is required is a systematic research program into questions previously elaborated upon in Nagin (1998). How do would-be offenders combine prior experience with the criminal justice system and new information on penalties? How long does it typically take for persons to become aware of new sanctioning regimes? How do they become aware of changes in penalties, and what information sources do they use in updating their impressions? How do novices form impressions of sanction risks? These questions speak to the broader issue of whether sanction risk impressions are easily manipulable.

4. *Analyzing the Mechanisms by Which the Experience of Imprisonment May Be Criminogenic.*   Relatively few studies seek to peer into the "black box" of imprisonment to understand why this experience might increase crime. One critical line of inquiry is to assess whether incarceration affects a person's perceptions of the costs of crime. Other potential mechanisms have been proposed. These include social learning, identity transformation, attenuated social bonds, and strains induced by being in prison and adapting to community reentry. This research enterprise also should consult the scholarship on the predictors of recidivism (e.g., Gendreau, Little, and Goggin 1996) to see if these are exacerbated by imprisonment. Finally, scholars may wish to pay particular attention to "dynamic" as opposed to "static" risk factors (Andrews and Bonta 2006). Dynamic risk factors are sources of reoffending that are mutable (e.g., antisocial attitudes). Static risk factors are "in the past" and thus cannot be altered (e.g., criminal history). Dynamic risk factors are salient because they can be targeted for change by interventions. Accordingly, they may be of particular rele-

vance in policy discussions on how best to minimize the criminogenic effect of imprisonment.

5. *Unpacking the Effect of Different Noncustodial Sanctions.* The effect of custodial sanctions on reoffending depends not only on the length and conditions of the custodial sanction but also on the type, term, and conditions of the noncustodial sanction that is the alternative. The variety of noncustodial sanctions available to policy makers is at least as varied as for custodial sanctions. Noncustodial sanctions include fines, community service, mandatory treatment, and probation of varying intensity. As demonstrated by the Deschenes, Turner, and Petersilia (1995) experiment in which some individuals randomized into intensive supervision probation opted instead to serve their prison term, a noncustodial sanction may be deemed more onerous than a custodial sanction (see also Wood and May 2003). Further, a noncustodial sanction can include the threat of incarceration for nonconformance with the conditions of the sentence. Thus, there is no inherent contradiction in the conclusion that a given custodial sanction is criminogenic compared with one type of noncustodial sanction (say a specific type of intensive supervision probation) but has a preventative effect compared to another type of noncustodial sanction (say a specified fine amount).

Accordingly, we offer two related recommendations. First, analyses of nonexperimental data should pay closer attention to specifying the type and conditions of the noncustodial sanction that is being compared to a custodial sanction. Second, data should be assembled that will allow the comparison of custodial sanctions to more specific types of noncustodial sanctions.

We close with the observation we made at the outset: it is remarkable that so many democratic societies, most especially the United States, incarcerate so many people without good estimates of the effects of this very expensive sanction on macro-level and individual-level crime rates. It is our hope that this essay in some small way will help to correct this regrettable state of affairs.

REFERENCES

Ægisdóttir, Stefanía, Michael J. White, Paul M. Spengler, Linda A. Anderson, Robert S. Cook, Cassandra N. Nichols, Georgios K. Lampropoulos, Genna

Cohen, and Jeffrey D. Rush. 2006. "The Meta-analysis of Clinical Judgment Project: Fifty-Six Years of Accumulated Research on Clinical versus Statistical Prediction." *Counseling Psychologist* 34(3):341–82.

Akers, Ronald L. 1998. *Social Learning and Social Structure: A General Theory of Crime and Deviance*. Boston: Northeastern University Press.

Andrews, D. A., and James Bonta. 2006. *The Psychology of Criminal Conduct*. 4th ed. Cincinnati: Anderson/LexisNexis.

Andrews, D. A., Ivan Zinger, Robert D. Hoge, James Bonta, Paul Gendreau, and Francis T. Cullen. 1990. "Does Correctional Treatment Work? A Clinically-Relevant and Psychologically-Informed Meta-analysis." *Criminology* 28(3):369–404.

Anglin, M. Douglas, and Yih-Ing Hser. 1987. "Addicted Women and Crime." *Criminology* 25(2):359–97.

Anglin, M. Douglas, and George Speckart. 1988. "Narcotics Use and Crime: A Multisample, Multimethod Analysis." *Criminology* 26(2):197–233.

Annan, Sampson O., Susan E. Martin, and Brian Forst. 1986. *Deterring the Drunk Driver: A Feasibility Study Technical Report*. Washington, DC: Police Foundation.

Apel, Robert, and Gary Sweeten. 2008. "Incarceration, Crime, and Employment." Unpublished manuscript. Albany, NY: State University at Albany.

Avi-Itzhak, Benjamin, and Reuel Shinnar. 1973. "Quantitative Models in Crime Control." *Journal of Criminal Justice* 1(3):185–217.

Barton, William H., and Jeffrey A. Butts. 1990. "Viable Options: Intensive Supervision Programs for Juvenile Delinquents." *Crime and Delinquency* 36(2):238–56.

Beck, Allen J., and Bernard E. Shipley. 1989. *Recidivism of Prisoners Released in 1983*. Washington, DC: Bureau of Justice Statistics, U.S. Department of Justice.

Becker, Gary S. 1968. "Crime and Punishment: An Economic Approach." *Journal of Political Economy* 76(2):169–217.

Beckett, Katherine. 1997. *Making Crime Pay: Law and Order in Contemporary American Politics*. New York: Oxford University Press.

Berecochea, John E., and Dorothy R. Jaman. 1981. *Time Served in Prison and Parole Outcome: An Experimental Study*. Sacramento: California Department of Corrections.

Bergman, Gerald R. 1976. "The Evaluation of an Experimental Program Designed to Reduce Recidivism among Second Felony Criminal Offenders." PhD dissertation, Wayne State University, Department of Measurement and Evaluation.

Berube, Danton, and Donald P. Green. 2007. "The Effects of Sentencing on Recidivism: Results from a Natural Experiment." Unpublished manuscript. New Haven, CT: Yale University.

Bhati, Avinash, and Alex R. Piquero. 2008. "Estimating the Impact of Incarceration on Subsequent Offending Trajectories: Deterrent, Criminogenic, or Null Effect?" *Journal of Criminal Law and Criminology* 98(1):207–54.

Blumstein, Alfred. 1995. "Youth Violence, Guns, and the Illicit-Drug Industry." *Journal of Criminal Law and Criminology* 86(1):10–36.

Blumstein, Alfred, and Allen J. Beck. 1999. "Population Growth in the U.S. Prisons, 1980–1996." In *Crime and Justice: A Review of Research*, vol. 26, edited by Michael Tonry and Joan Petersilia. Chicago: University of Chicago Press.

———. 2005. "Reentry as a Transient State between Liberty and Recommitment." In *Prisoner Reentry and Crime in America*, edited by Jeremy Travis and Christy Visher. Cambridge: Cambridge University Press.

Blumstein, Alfred, and Jacqueline Cohen. 1973. "A Theory of the Stability of Punishment." *Journal of Criminal Law and Criminology* 64(2):198–206.

Bonczar, Thomas P. 2003. *Prevalence of Imprisonment in the U.S. Population, 1974–2001*. Washington, DC: Bureau of Justice Statistics.

Bondeson, Ulla V. 1994. *Alternatives to Imprisonment: Intentions and Realities*. Boulder, CO: Westview.

Bonta, James, Suzanne Wallace-Capretta, and Jennifer Rooney. 1999. *Electronic Monitoring in Canada*. Ottawa: Solicitor General Canada.

———. 2000. "A Quasi-Experimental Evaluation of an Intensive Rehabilitation Supervision Program." *Criminal Justice and Behavior* 27(3):312–29.

Braithwaite, John. 1989. *Crime, Shame, and Reintegration*. Cambridge: Cambridge University Press.

Brennan, Patricia A., and Sarnoff A. Mednick. 1994. "Learning Theory Approach to the Deterrence of Criminal Recidivism." *Journal of Abnormal Psychology* 103(3):430–40.

Bureau of Justice Statistics. 1988. *Report for the Nation on Crime and Justice*. Washington, DC: U.S. Department of Justice.

Cannon, Michael D., and Brenda K. Wilson. 2005. *2001 Recidivism Study*. Pine Bluff: Arkansas Department of Correction.

Carroll, Leo. 1988. *Hacks, Blacks and Cons: Race Relations in a Maximum Security Prison*. Reissued ed. Prospect Heights, IL: Waveland.

Caulkins, Jonathan P., C. Peter Rydell, Susan S. Everingham, James Chiesa, and Shawn Bushway. 1999. *An Ounce of Prevention, a Pound of Uncertainty: The Cost-Effectiveness of School-Based Drug Prevention Programs*. Santa Monica, CA: RAND Corporation.

Chen, M. Keith, and Jesse M. Shapiro. 2007. "Do Harsher Prison Conditions Reduce Recidivism? A Discontinuity-Based Approach." *American Law and Economic Review* 9(1):1–29.

Clarke, Stevens H., and Anita L. Harrison. 1992. *Recidivism of Criminal Offenders Assigned to Community Correctional Programs or Released from Prison in North Carolina in 1989*. Chapel Hill: Institute of Government, University of North Carolina.

Clear, Todd R. 1994. *Harm in American Penology: Offenders, Victims, and Their Communities*. Albany: State University of New York Press.

———. 2007. *Imprisoning Communities: How Mass Incarceration Makes Disadvantaged Neighborhoods Worse*. New York: Oxford University Press.

Clemmer, Donald. 1940. *The Prison Community*. New York: Christopher.

Clotfelter, Charles T., and Philip J. Cook. 1993. "The 'Gambler's Fallacy' in Lottery Play." *Management Science* 39(12):1521–25.

Cochran, William G. 1965. "The Planning of Observational Studies of Human Populations" (with discussion). *Journal of the Royal Statistical Society, Series A* 128(2):134–55.

Cole, Stephen. 1975. "The Growth of Scientific Knowledge: Theories of Deviance as a Case Study." In *The Idea of Social Structure: Papers in Honor of Robert K. Merton*, edited by Lewis A. Coser. New York: Harcourt Brace Jovanovich.

Cook, Philip J. 1980. "Research in Criminal Deterrence: Laying the Groundwork for the Second Decade." In *Crime and Justice: An Annual Review of Research*, vol. 2, edited by Norval Morris and Michael Tonry. Chicago: University of Chicago Press.

Cullen, Christopher, and Martin Minchin. 2000. *The Prison Population in 1999: A Statistical Review*. Research Findings no. 118. London: Home Office Research, Development and Statistics Directorate.

Cullen, Francis T. 2002. "Rehabilitation and Treatment Programs." In *Crime: Public Policies for Crime Control*, edited by James Q. Wilson and Joan Petersilia. Oakland, CA: ICS Press.

Cullen, Francis T., and John B. Cullen. 1978. *Toward a Paradigm of Labeling Theory*. Lincoln: University of Nebraska Studies.

Cullen, Francis T., and Karen E. Gilbert. 1982. *Reaffirming Rehabilitation*. Cincinnati: Anderson.

Currie, Elliott. 1998. *Crime and Punishment in America*. New York: Metropolitan Books.

De Jong, Christina. 1997. "Survival Analysis and Specific Deterrence: Integrating Theoretical and Empirical Models of Recidivism." *Criminology* 35(4): 561–75.

Deschenes, Elizabeth Piper, Barbara Owen, and Jason Crow. 2006. *Recidivism among Female Prisoners: Secondary Analysis of the 1994 BJS Recidivism Data Set*. Washington, DC: National Institute of Justice.

Deschenes, Elizabeth Piper, Susan Turner, and Joan Petersilia. 1995. *Intensive Community Supervision in Minnesota: A Dual Experiment in Prison Diversion and Enhanced Supervised Release*. Santa Monica, CA: RAND Corporation.

De Young, David J. 1997. "An Evaluation of the Effectiveness of Alcohol Treatment, Driver License Actions and Jail Terms in Reducing Drunk Driving Recidivism in California." *Addiction* 92(8):989–97.

Donohue, John J. 2007. "Assessing the Relative Benefits of Incarceration: The Overall Change over the Previous Decades and the Benefits on the Margin." Unpublished manuscript. New Haven, CT: Yale University.

Doob, Anthony N., and Cheryl Marie Webster. 2003. "Sentence Severity and Crime: Accepting the Null Hypothesis." In *Crime and Justice: A Review of Research*, vol. 30, edited by Michael Tonry. Chicago: University of Chicago Press.

Dorn, Harold F. 1953. "Philosophy of Inferences from Retrospective Studies." *American Journal of Public Health* 43(6):677–83.

Dorsey, Tina L., Marianne W. Zawitz, and Priscilla Middleton. 2007. *Drugs and Crime Facts*. Washington, DC: Bureau of Justice Statistics, U.S. Department of Justice.

Downes, David. 2007. "Visions of Penal Control in the Netherlands." In *Crime, Punishment, and Politics in Comparative Perspective*. Vol. 36 of *Crime and Justice: A Review of Research*, edited by Michael Tonry. Chicago: University of Chicago Press.

Drago, Francesco, Roberto Galbiati, and Pietro Vertova. 2009. "The Deterrent Effects of Prison: Evidence from a Natural Experiment." *Journal of Political Economy* 117(2):257–78.

Farrington, David P., Jeremy W. Coid, Louise Harnett, Darrick Jolliffe, Nadine Soteriou, Richard Turner, and Donald J. West. 2006. *Criminal Careers Up to Age 50 and Life Success Up to Age 48: New Findings from the Cambridge Study in Delinquent Development*. Research Study no. 299. London: Home Office.

Fergusson, David M., Michael T. Lynskey, and L. John Horwood. 1996. "Alcohol Misuse and Juvenile Offending in Adolescence." *Addiction* 91(4): 483–94.

Finn, Mary A., and Suzanne Muirhead-Steves. 2002. "The Effectiveness of Electronic Monitoring with Violent Male Parolees." *Justice Quarterly* 19(2): 293–312.

Florida Department of Corrections. 2003. *Recidivism Report: Inmates Released from Florida Prisons July 1995 to June 2001*. Tallahassee: Florida Department of Corrections.

Flowers, Gerald T., Timothy S. Carr, and R. Barry Ruback. 1991. *Special Alternative Incarceration Evaluation*. Atlanta: Georgia Department of Corrections.

Fox, James Alan, and Marianne W. Zawitz. 2007. *Homicide Trends in the United States*. Washington, DC: Bureau of Justice Statistics, U.S. Department of Justice.

Gainey, Randy R., Brian K. Payne, and Mike O'Toole. 2000. "The Relationships between Time in Jail, Time on Electronic Monitoring, and Recidivism: An Event History Analysis of a Jail-Based Program." *Justice Quarterly* 17(4): 733–52.

Garland, David. 2001. *The Culture of Control: Crime and Social Order in Contemporary Society*. Chicago: University of Chicago Press.

Ge, Xiaojia, M. Brent Donnellan, and Ernst Wenk. 2001. "The Development of Persistent Criminal Offending in Males." *Criminal Justice and Behavior* 28(6):731–55.

Gendreau, Paul, Claire Goggin, and Francis T. Cullen. 1999. *The Effects of Prison Sentences on Recidivism*. Ottawa: Solicitor General Canada.

Gendreau, Paul, Tracy Little, and Claire Goggin. 1996. "A Meta-analysis of the Predictors of Adult Offender Recidivism: What Works!" *Criminology* 34(4):575–607.

Gendreau, Paul, Paula Smith, and Sheila A. French. 2006. "The Theory of Effective Correctional Intervention: Empirical Status and Future Directions." In *Taking Stock: The Status of Criminological Theory*. Advances in Criminological Theory, vol. 15, edited by Francis T. Cullen, John Paul Wright, and Kristie R. Blevins. New Brunswick, NJ: Transaction.

Gilovich, Tom. 1983. "Biased Evaluation and Persistence in Gambling." *Journal of Personality and Social Psychology* 44(6):1110–26.

Gjeruldsen, Susanne Rogne, Bjorn Myrvang, and Stein Opjordsmoen. 2004. "Criminality in Drug Addicts: A Follow-up Study over 25 Years." *European Addiction Research* 10(2):49–55.

Gordan, Margaret A., and Daniel Glaser. 1991. "The Use and Effects of Financial Penalties in Municipal Courts." *Criminology* 29(4):651–76.

Gottfredson, Denise C., and William H. Barton. 1993. "Deinstitutionalization of Juvenile Offenders." *Criminology* 31(4):591–611.

Gottfredson, Don M. 1998. *Choosing Punishments: Crime Control Effects of Sentences*. Sacramento, CA: Justice Policy Research Corporation.

Gottschalk, Marie. 2006. *The Prison and the Gallows: The Politics of Mass Incarceration in America*. New York: Cambridge University Press.

Green, Donald, and Daniel Winik. 2008. "The Effects of Incarceration and Probation on Recidivism among Drug Offenders: An Experimental Approach." Unpublished manuscript. New Haven, CT: Yale University.

Greenfeld, Lawrence A., and Patrick A. Langan. 1987. "Trends in Prison Populations." Paper prepared for the National Conference on Punishment for Criminal Offenses, Ann Arbor, MI, November.

Grove, William M., and Paul E. Meehl. 1996. "Comparative Efficiency of Informal (Subjective, Impressionistic) and Formal (Mechanical, Algorithmic) Prediction Procedures: The Clinical-Statistical Controversy." *Psychology, Public Policy, and Law* 2(2):293–323.

Hagan, John L. 1973. "Labeling and Deviance: A Case Study in the 'Sociology of the Interesting.'" *Social Problems* 20(4):447–58.

Haney, Craig, Curtis Banks, and Philip Zimbardo. 1973. "Interpersonal Dynamics in a Simulated Prison." *International Journal of Criminology and Penology* 1:69–97.

Harcourt, Bernard E. 2006. "From the Asylum to the Prison: Rethinking the Incarceration Revolution." *Texas Law Review* 84(7):1751–86.

Harer, Miles D. 1994. *Recidivism among Federal Prisoners Released in 1987*. Washington, DC: Federal Bureau of Prisons.

Harrison, Lana, and Joseph Gfroerer. 1992. "The Intersection of Drug Use and Criminal Behavior: Results from the National Household Survey on Drug Abuse." *Crime and Delinquency* 38(4):422–43.

Hawkins, Darnell F., John H. Laub, Janet L. Lauritsen, and Lynn Cothern. 2000. *Race, Ethnicity, and Serious and Violent Juvenile Offending*. Washington, DC: Office of Juvenile Justice and Delinquency Prevention, U.S. Department of Justice.

Haynie, Dana L., and David P. Armstrong. 2006. "Race- and Gender-Disaggregated Homicide Offending Rates: Differences and Similarities by Victim-Offender Relations across Cities." *Homicide Studies* 10(1):3–32.

Heckman, James J. 1990. "Varieties of Selection Bias." *American Economic Review* 80(2):313–18.

Helland, Eric, and Alexander Tabarrok. 2007. "Does Three Strikes Deter? A Nonparametric Estimation." *Journal of Human Resources* 42(2):309–30.

Hernán, Miguel Ángel, Babette Brumback, and James M. Robins. 2000. "Marginal Structural Models to Estimate the Causal Effects of Zidovudine on the Survival of HIV-Positive Men." *Epidemiology* 11(5):561–70.

Hindelang, Michael J. 1981. "Variations in Sex-Race-Age Incidence Rates of Offending." *American Sociological Review* 46(4):461–74.

Holland, Shasta, Kym Pointon, and Stuart Ross. 2007. *Who Returns to Prison? Patterns of Recidivism among Prisoners Released from Custody in Victoria in 2002–03*. Corrections Research Paper Series no. 1. Melbourne: Victoria Department of Justice.

Human Rights Watch. 2008. *Targeting Blacks: Drug Law Enforcement and Race in the United States*. New York: Human Rights Watch.

Imbens, Guido. 2000. "The Role of the Propensity Score in Estimating Dose-Response Functions." *Biometrika* 87(3):706–10.

Irwin, John. 1980. *Prisons in Turmoil*. Boston: Little, Brown.

———. 2005. *The Warehouse Prison: Disposal of the New Dangerous Class*. Los Angeles: Roxbury.

Irwin, John, and Donald R. Cressey. 1962. "Thieves, Convicts, and the Inmate Subculture." *Social Problems* 10(2):142–55.

Jacobs, James B. 1977. *Statesville: The Penitentiary in Mass Society*. Chicago: University of Chicago Press.

Jaman, Dorothy R., Robert M. Dickover, and Lawrence A. Bennett. 1972. "Parole Outcome as a Function of Time Served." *British Journal of Criminology* 12(1):5–34.

Joffe, Marshall M., and Paul R. Rosenbaum. 1999. "Propensity Scores." *American Journal of Epidemiology* 150(4):327–33.

Jolin, Annette, and Brian Stipak. 1992. "Drug Treatment and Electronically Monitored Home Confinement: An Evaluation of a Community-Based Sentencing Option." *Crime and Delinquency* 38(2):158–70.

Jones, Mark, and Darrell L. Ross. 1997a. "Electronic House Arrest and Boot Camp in North Carolina: Comparing Recidivism." *Criminal Justice Policy Review* 8(4):383–403.

———. 1997b. "Is Less Better? Boot Camp, Regular Probation and Rearrest in North Carolina." *American Journal of Criminal Justice* 21(2):147–61.

Jones, Peter R. 1991. "The Risk of Recidivism: Evaluating the Public-Safety Implications of a Community Corrections Program." *Journal of Criminal Justice* 19(1):49–66.

Katz, Lawrence, Steven D. Levitt, and Ellen Shustorovich. 2003. "Prison Conditions, Capital Punishment, and Deterrence." *American Law and Economics Review* 5(2):318–43.

Kentucky Department of Corrections. n.d. *Recidivism in Kentucky, 1999–2000, Executive Summary*. Frankfort: Kentucky Department of Corrections.

Killias, Martin, Marcelo Aebi, and Denis Ribeaud. 2000. "Does Community

Service Rehabilitate Better than Short-Term Imprisonment? Results of a Controlled Experiment." *Howard Journal* 39(1):40–57.

Kim, Il-Joong, Bruce L. Benson, David W. Rasmussen, and Thomas W. Zuehlke. 1993. "An Economic Analysis of Recidivism among Drug Offenders." *Southern Economic Journal* 60(1):169–83.

Kraus, J. 1974. "A Comparison of Corrective Effects of Probation and Detention on Male Juvenile Offenders." *British Journal of Criminology* 14(1):49–62.

———. 1978. "Remand in Custody as a Deterrent in Juvenile Jurisdiction." *British Journal of Criminology* 18(3):285–89.

———. 1981. "The Effects of Committal to a Special School for Truants." *International Journal of Offender Therapies and Comparative Criminology* 25(2): 130–38.

Langan, Patrick A., and David J. Levin. 2002. *Recidivism of Prisoners Released in 1994*. Washington, DC: Bureau of Justice Statistics, U.S. Department of Justice.

Lappi-Seppälä, Tapio. 2007. "Penal Policy in Scandinavia." In *Crime, Punishment, and Politics in Comparative Perspective*. Vol. 36 of *Crime and Justice: A Review of Research*, edited by Michael Tonry. Chicago: University of Chicago Press.

Laub, John H., and Robert J. Sampson. 2003. *Shared Beginnings, Divergent Lives: Delinquent Boys to Age 70*. Cambridge, MA: Harvard University Press.

Lemert, Edwin M. 1951. *Social Pathology*. New York: McGraw-Hill.

Lipsey, Mark W., and Francis T. Cullen. 2007. "The Effectiveness of Correctional Rehabilitation: A Review of Systematic Reviews." *Annual Review of Law and Social Science* 3:297–320.

Liptak, Adam. 2008. "American Exception: Inmate Count in U.S. Dwarfs Other Nations." *New York Times* (April 23). http://www.nytimes.com/2008/04/23/us/23prison.

Lloyd, Charles, George Mair, and Mike Hough. 1994. *Explaining Reconviction Rates: A Critical Analysis*. Research Study no. 136. London: Home Office.

Loeber, Rolf, and Marc Le Blanc. 1990. "Toward a Developmental Criminology." In *Crime and Justice: A Review of Research*, vol. 12, edited by Michael Tonry and Norval Morris. Chicago: University of Chicago Press.

Loughran, Thomas A., Edward P. Mulvey, Carol A. Schubert, Jeffrey Fagan, Sandra H. Losoya, and Alex R. Piquero. 2008. "Estimating a Dose-Response Relationship between Length of Stay and Recidivism in Serious Juvenile Offenders." Working paper. Pittsburgh: University of Pittsburgh Medical Center.

Lu, Bo, Elaine Zanutto, Robert Hornik, and Paul R. Rosenbaum. 2001. "Matching with Doses in an Observational Study of a Media Campaign against Drug Abuse." *Journal of the American Statistical Association* 96(456): 1245–53.

Lynch, Michael J. 2007. *Big Prisons, Big Dreams: Crime and the Failure of America's Penal System*. New Brunswick, NJ: Rutgers University Press.

MacKenzie, Doris Layton. 1991. "The Parole Performance of Offenders Released from Shock Incarceration (Boot Camp Prisons): A Survival Time Analysis." *Journal of Quantitative Criminology* 7(3):213–36.

———. 2002. "Reducing the Criminal Activities of Known Offenders and Delinquents: Crime Prevention in the Courts and Corrections." In *Evidence-Based Crime Prevention*, edited by Lawrence W. Sherman, David P. Farrington, Brandon C. Welsh, and Doris Layton MacKenzie. London: Routledge.

———. 2006. *What Works in Corrections: Reducing the Criminal Activities of Offenders and Delinquents*. New York: Cambridge University Press.

MacKenzie, Doris Layton, Robert Brame, David McDowall, and Claire Souryal. 1995. "Boot Camp Prisons and Recidivism in Eight States." *Criminology* 33(3):327–57.

MacKenzie, Doris Layton, and James W. Shaw. 1993. "The Impact of Shock Incarceration on Technical Violations and New Criminal Activities." *Justice Quarterly* 10(3):463–87.

Maguire, Kathleen E., Timothy J. Flanagan, and Terence P. Thornberry. 1988. "Prison Labor and Recidivism." *Journal of Quantitative Criminology* 4(1): 3–18.

Maltz, Michael. 1984. *Recidivism*. Orlando, FL: Academic Press.

Manski, Charles F. 1995. *Identification Problems in the Social Sciences*. Cambridge, MA: Harvard University Press.

Manski, Charles F., and Daniel S. Nagin. 1998. "Bounding Disagreements about Treatment Effects: A Case Study of Sentencing and Recidivism." *Sociological Methodology* 28:99–137.

Martin, Susan E., Sampson Annan, and Brian Forst. 1993. "The Special Deterrent Effects of a Jail Sanction on First-Time Drunk Drivers: A Quasi-Experimental Study." *Accident Analysis and Prevention* 25(5):561–68.

Menninger, Karl. 1968. *The Crime of Punishment*. New York: Penguin.

Miller, Jerome G. 1991. *Last One over the Wall: The Massachusetts Experiment in Closing Reform Schools*. Columbus: Ohio State University Press.

Mitford, Jessica. 1973. *Kind and Usual Punishment: The Prison Business*. New York: Vintage.

Monahan. John. 2006. "A Jurisprudence of Risk Assessment: Forecasting Harm among Prisoners, Predators, and Patients." *Virginia Law Review* 92(3): 391–435.

———. 2008. "Structured Violence Risk Assessment." In *Textbook on Violence Assessment and Management*, edited by Robert I. Simon and Kenneth Tardiff. Washington, DC: American Psychiatric Publishing.

Muiluvuori, Marja-Liisa. 2001. "Recidivism among People Sentenced to Community Service in Finland." *Journal of Scandinavian Studies in Criminology and Crime Prevention* 2(1):72–82.

Nagin, Daniel S. 1998. "Criminal Deterrence Research at the Outset of the Twenty-First Century." In *Crime and Justice: A Review of Research*, vol. 23, edited by Michael Tonry. Chicago: University of Chicago Press.

Nagin, Daniel S., and Raymond Paternoster. 1991. "The Preventive Effects of the Perceived Risk of Arrest: Testing an Expanded Conception of Deterrence." *Criminology* 29(2):561–86.

Nagin, Daniel S., Alex R. Piquero, Elizabeth S. Scott, and Laurence Steinberg. 2006. "Public Preferences for Rehabilitation versus Incarceration of Juvenile Offenders: Evidence from a Contingent Valuation Survey." *Criminology and Public Policy* 5(4): 627–52.

Newburn, Tim. 2007. "'Tough on Crime': Penal Policy in England and Wales." In *Crime, Punishment, and Politics in Comparative Perspective.* Vol. 36 of *Crime and Justice: A Review of Research*, edited by Michael Tonry. Chicago: University of Chicago Press.

Nieuwbeerta, Paul, Daniel S. Nagin, and Arjan A. Blokland. Forthcoming. "The Relationship between First Imprisonment and Criminal Career Development: A Matched Samples Comparison." *Journal of Quantitative Criminology.*

Nirel, Ronit, Simha F. Landau, Leslie Sebba, and Bilha Sagiv. 1997. "The Effectiveness of Service Work: An Analysis of Recidivism." *Journal of Quantitative Criminology* 13(1):73–92.

Nunes, Kevin L., Philip Firestone, Audrey F. Wexler, Tamara L. Jensen, and John M. Bradford. 2007. "Incarceration and Recidivism among Sexual Offenders." *Law and Human Behavior* 31(3):305–18.

Orsagh, Thomas, and Jong-Rong Chen. 1988. "The Effect of Time Served on Recidivism: An Interdisciplinary Theory." *Journal of Quantitative Criminology* 4(2):155–71.

Parisi, Nicolette. 1981. "'A Taste of the Bars?'" *Journal of Criminal Law and Criminology* 72(3):1109–23.

Paternoster, Raymond, and Alex R. Piquero. 1995. "Reconceptualizing Deterrence: An Empirical Test of Personal and Vicarious Experiences." *Journal of Research in Crime and Delinquency* 32(3):251–86.

Petersilia, Joan. 2002. "Community Corrections." In *Crime: Public Policy for Crime Control*, edited by James Q. Wilson and Joan Petersilia. Oakland, CA: ICS Press.

———. 2003. *When Prisoners Come Home: Parole and Prisoner Reentry.* New York: Oxford University Press.

Petersilia, Joan, Susan Turner, with Judith Peterson. 1986. *Prison versus Probation in California: Implications for Crime and Offender Recidivism.* Santa Monica, CA: RAND Corporation.

Piquero, Alex R., and Raymond Paternoster. 1998. "An Application of Stafford and Warr's Reconceptualization of Deterrence to Drinking and Driving." *Journal of Research in Crime and Delinquency* 35(1):3–39.

Pogarsky, Gregory, and Alex Piquero. 2003. "Can Punishment Encourage Offending? Investigating the 'Resetting' Effect." *Journal of Research in Crime and Delinquency* 40(1):95–120.

Raphael, Steven, and Michael Stoll. 2007. "Why Are So Many Americans in Prison?" Unpublished manuscript. Berkeley: University of California.

Robins, James M. 1999. "Association, Causation, and Marginal Structural Models." *Synthese* 121(1/2):151–79.

Robins, James M., Miguel Ángel Hernán, and Babette Brumback. 2000. "Marginal Structural Models and Causal Inference in Epidemiology." *Epidemiology* 11(5):550–60.

Roeger, Leigh S. 1994. "The Effectiveness of Criminal Justice Sanctions for Aboriginal Offenders." *Australian and New Zealand Journal of Criminology* 27(3):264–81.

Rosenbaum, Paul R., and Donald B. Rubin. 1983. "The Central Role of the Propensity Score in Observational Studies for Causal Effects." *Biometrika* 70(1):41–55.

Rothman, David J. 1971. *The Discovery of the Asylum: Social Order and Disorder in the New Republic*. Boston: Little, Brown.

———. 1980. *Conscience and Convenience: The Asylum and Its Alternatives in Progressive America*. Boston: Little, Brown.

Rydell, C. Peter, Jonathan P. Caulkins, and Susan S. Everingham. 1996. "Enforcement or Treatment? Modeling the Relative Efficacy of Alternatives for Controlling Cocaine." *Operations Research* 44(5):687–95.

Sabol, William J., William P. Adams, Barbara Parthasarathy, and Yan Yuan. 2000. *Offenders Returning to Federal Prison, 1986–97*. Washington, DC: Bureau of Justice Statistics, U.S. Department of Justice.

Sabol, William J., Heather Couture, and Paige M. Harrison. 2007. *Prisoners in 2006*. Washington, DC: Bureau of Justice Statistics, U.S. Department of Justice.

Sampson, Robert J., and John H. Laub. 1993. *Crime in the Making: Pathways and Turning Points through Life*. Cambridge, MA: Harvard University Press.

Sampson, Robert J., Jeffrey D. Morenoff, and Stephen Raudenbush. 2005. "Social Anatomy of Racial and Ethnic Disparities in Violence." *American Journal of Public Health* 95(2):224–32.

Savolainen, Jukka, Wayne Nehwadowich, Aïda Tejaratchi, and Bernice Linen-Reed. 2002. *Criminal Recidivism among Felony-Level ATI Program Participants in New York City*. New York: New York City Criminal Justice Agency.

Scarpitti, Frank R., and Richard M. Stephenson. 1968. "A Study of Probation Effectiveness." *Journal of Criminal Law, Criminology, and Police Science* 59(3): 361–69.

Schneider, Anne L. 1986. "Restitution and Recidivism Rates of Juvenile Offenders: Results from Four Experimental Studies." *Criminology* 24(3):533–52.

Scull, Andrew. 1977. *Decarceration: Community Treatment and the Deviant: A Radical View*. Englewood Cliffs, NJ: Prentice-Hall.

Sentencing Guidelines Commission. December 2005*a*. *Recidivism of Adult Felons 2004*. Olympia: State of Washington.

———. December 2005*b*. *Recidivism of Juvenile Offenders: Fiscal Year 2005*. Olympia: State of Washington.

Shaw, Clifford R. 1930. *The Jack-Roller: A Delinquent Boy's Own Story*. Chicago: University of Chicago Press.

Simon, Jonathan. 2007. *Governing through Crime: How the War on Crime Transformed American Democracy and Created a Culture of Fear*. New York: Oxford University Press.

Smith, Linda G., and Ronald L. Akers. 1993. "A Comparison of Recidivism of Florida's Community Control and Prison: A Five-Year Survival Analysis." *Journal of Research in Crime and Delinquency* 30(3):267–92.

Smith, Paula. 2006. "The Effects of Incarceration on Recidivism: A Longitudinal Examination of Program Participation and Institutional Adjustment in Federally Sentenced Adult Male Offenders." PhD dissertation, University of New Brunswick, Department of Psychology.

Smith, Paula, Paul Gendreau, and Kristin Swartz. 2009. "Validating the Principle of Effective Correctional Intervention: A Systematic Review of the Contributions of Meta-analysis in the Field of Corrections." *Victims and Offenders* 4(1), forthcoming.

Sommer, Robert. 1976. *The End of Imprisonment*. New York: Oxford University Press.

Spohn, Cassia, and David Holleran. 2002. "The Effect of Imprisonment on Recidivism Rates of Felony Offenders: A Focus on Drug Offenders." *Criminology* 40(2):329–57.

Steffensmeier, Darrell, and Emilie Allan. 1996. "Gender and Crime: Toward a Gendered Theory of Female Offending." In *Annual Review of Sociology*, vol. 22, edited by John H. Hagan and Karen S. Cook. Palo Alto, CA: Annual Reviews.

Swets, John A., Robyn Dawes, and John Monahan. 2000. "Psychological Science Can Improve Diagnostic Decisions." *Psychological Science in the Public Interest* 1(1):1–26.

Sykes, Gresham M. 1958. *Society of Captives: A Study of a Maximum Security Prison*. Princeton, NJ: Princeton University Press.

Tashima, Helen N., and William D. Marelich. 1989. *A Comparison of the Relative Effectiveness of Alternative Sanctions for DUI Offenders*. Sacramento: California Department of Motor Vehicles.

Taxman, Faye S., and Alex R. Piquero. 1998. "On Preventing Drunk Driving Recidivism: An Examination of Rehabilitation and Punishment Approaches." *Journal of Criminal Justice* 26(2):129–43.

Toby, Jackson. 1964. "Is Punishment Necessary?" *Journal of Criminal Law, Criminology, and Police Science* 55(3):332–37.

Tonry, Michael. 1995. *Sentencing Matters*. Oxford: Oxford University Press

———. 2004. *Thinking about Crime: Sense and Sensibility in American Penal Culture*. New York: Oxford University Press.

———. 2007. "Determinants of Penal Policies." In *Crime, Punishment, and Politics in Comparative Perspective*. Vol. 36 of *Crime and Justice: A Review of Research*, edited by Michael Tonry. Chicago: University of Chicago Press.

Tonry, Michael, and Catrien Bijleveld. 2007. "Crime, Criminal Justice, and Criminology in the Netherlands." In *Crime and Justice in the Netherlands*, edited by Michael Tonry and Catrien Bijleveld. Vol. 35 of *Crime and Justice: A Review of Research*, edited by Michael Tonry. Chicago: University of Chicago Press.

Travis, Jeremy. 2005. *But They All Come Back: Facing the Challenges of Prisoner Reentry*. Washington, DC: Urban Institute.

Ulmer, Jeffery T. 2001. "Intermediate Sanctions: A Comparative Analysis of the Probability and Severity of Recidivism." *Sociological Inquiry* 71(2):164–93.

U.S. Federal Food and Drug Administration. 2004. *Revisions to Product Labeling.* http://www.fda.gov/cder/drug/antidepressants/antidepressants_label_change _2007.pdf.

Useem, Bert, and Anne Morrison Piehl. 2008. *Prison State: The Challenge of Mass Incarceration.* New York: Cambridge University Press.

van der Werff, C. 1979. *Speciale Preventie.* Den Haag: WODC.

———. 1981. "Recidivism and Special Deterrence." *British Journal of Criminology* 21(2):136–47.

Villettaz, Patrice, Martin Killias, and Isabel Zoder. 2006. *The Effects of Custodial vs. Non-custodial Sentences on Re-offending: A Systematic Review of the State of Knowledge.* Philadelphia: Campbell Collaboration Crime and Justice Group.

Wacquant, Loïc. 2001. "Deadly Symbiosis: When Ghetto and Prison Meet and Mesh." *Punishment and Society* 3(1):95–133.

Warren, Jenifer. 2008. *One in 100: Behind Bars in America.* Washington, DC: Pew Charitable Trusts.

Webster, Cheryl M., and Anthony N. Doob. 2007. "Punitive Trends and Stable Imprisonment Rates in Canada." In *Crime, Punishment, and Politics in Comparative Perspective.* Vol. 36 of *Crime and Justice: A Review of Research*, edited by Michael Tonry. Chicago: University of Chicago Press.

Weisburd, David, Tomer Einat, and Matt Kowalski. 2008. "The Miracle of the Cells: An Experimental Study of Interventions to Increase Payment of Court-Ordered Financial Obligations." *Criminology and Public Policy* 7(1): 9–36.

Weisburd, David, Elin Waring, and Ellen Chayet. 1995. "Specific Deterrence in a Sample of Offenders Convicted of White-Collar Crimes." *Criminology* 33(4):587–607.

Weisburd, David, Elin Waring, with Ellen F. Chayet. 2001. *White-Collar Crime and Criminal Careers.* Cambridge: Cambridge University Press.

Wheeler, Gerald R., and Rodney V. Hissong. 1988. "A Survival Time Analysis of Criminal Sanctions for Misdemeanor Offenders: A Case for Alternatives to Incarceration." *Evaluation Review* 12(5):510–37.

Whitman, James Q. 2003. *Harsh Justice: Criminal Punishment and the Widening Divide between America and Europe.* New York: Oxford University Press.

Wiebush, Richard G. 1993. "Juvenile Intensive Supervision: The Impact of Felony Offenders Diverted from Institutional Placement." *Crime and Delinquency* 39(1):68–89.

Wimer, Christopher, Robert J. Sampson, and John H. Laub. 2008. "Estimating Time-Varying Causes and Outcomes, with Application to Incarceration and Crime." In *Applied Data Analytic Techniques for Turning Points Research*, edited by Patricia Cohen. London: Routledge.

Wood, Peter B., and David C. May. 2003. "Racial Differences in Perceptions of Severity of Sanctions: A Comparison of Prison with Alternatives." *Justice Quarterly* 20(3):605–31.

Wooldredge, John D. 1988. "Differentiating the Effects of Juvenile Court Sentences on Eliminating Recidivism." *Journal of Research in Crime and Delinquency* 25(3):264–300.

Wright, Dionne T., and G. Larry Mays. 1998. "Correctional Boot Camps, Attitudes, and Recidivism: The Oklahoma Experience." *Journal of Offender Rehabilitation* 28(1/2):71–87.

Zanutto, Elaine, Bo Lu, and Robert Hornik. 2005. "Using Propensity Score Subclassification for Multiple Treatment Doses to Evaluate a National Antidrug Media Campaign." *Journal of Educational and Behavioral Statistics* 30(1): 59–73.

Zimbardo, Philip. 2007. *The Lucifer Effect: Understanding How Good People Turn Evil*. New York: Random House.

Zimring, Franklin E., and Gordon J. Hawkins. 1973. *Deterrence: The Legal Threat in Crime Control*. Chicago: University of Chicago Press.

———. 1991. *The Scale of Imprisonment*. Chicago: University of Chicago Press.

Richard S. Frase

What Explains Persistent Racial Disproportionality in Minnesota's Prison and Jail Populations?

ABSTRACT

Racial disparity in prison and jail populations, measured by the ratio of black to white per capita incarceration rates, varies substantially from state to state. To understand these variations, researchers must examine disparity at earlier stages of the criminal process and also racial differences in socioeconomic status that help explain disparity in cases entering the system. Researchers must adjust disparity ratios to correct for limitations in available data and in studies of prior incarceration rates. Minnesota has one of the highest black/white incarceration ratios. Disparities at the earliest measurable stages of Minnesota's criminal process—arrest and felony conviction—are as great as the disparity in total custody (prison plus jail) populations. Disparities are substantially greater in prison sentences imposed and prison populations than at arrest and conviction. The primary reason is the heavy weight sentencing guidelines give to offenders' prior conviction records. Highly disparate arrest rates appear to reflect unusually high rates of socioeconomic disparity between black and white residents.

Studies comparing incarceration rates by race have found wide variations among American states. For example, in 2005 the ratio of black to white per capita incarceration rates ranged from a high of 13.6 : 1

Richard S. Frase is Benjamin N. Berger Professor of Criminal Law, University of Minnesota Law School. He is grateful for helpful comments on earlier drafts received from Alfred Blumstein, Anthony Doob, Barry Feld, Marc Mauer, Myron Orfield, Joan Petersilia, Kevin Reitz, Michael Tonry, Robert Weidner, and Franklin Zimring and for outstanding research assistance by Kathleen Starr (University of Minnesota JD 2008, MPH 2009). A preliminary version of this paper was presented at the 2006 annual meeting of the American Society of Criminology.

in Iowa to a low of 1.9 : 1 in Hawaii (Mauer and King 2007, table 6). What accounts for these substantial variations? What are the policy implications?

This essay examines the nature and sources of racial disproportionality in Minnesota prison and jail populations. Minnesota is a state blessed with extensive statewide sentencing data. It is also a state with high racial disproportionality in its inmate populations. Studies of state prison populations in the 1980s and early 1990s found that Minnesota's black per capita incarceration rates were about 20 times higher than white rates—the highest ratio reported for any state. Minnesota has done better in more recent studies, but its ratio of black to white incarceration rates is still in the top quartile.

Disparate inmate populations are, of course, part of a larger problem of racial and ethnic disparity throughout the criminal justice system (Tonry 1995; Sampson and Lauritsen 1997; Cole 1999; Walker, Spohn, and DeLone 2007; Tonry and Melewski 2008). Numerous studies have shown that blacks and members of other minorities are disproportionately represented not only among inmate populations and on death rows (Snell 2006) but at virtually all the earlier stages of criminal processing. Disparity has been documented in victim surveys reporting race of the perpetrator (BJS 2007a); in pedestrian and traffic stops, searches, and arrests (Meehan and Ponder 2002; Institute and Council 2003; Engel and Calnon 2004; Leinfelt 2006); in bail and pretrial release decision making (Patterson and Lynch 1991; Minnesota Task Force 1993; Office of Justice Systems Analysis 1995); in prosecutorial screening decisions (Crutchfield et al. 1995); in the use of prison and jail sentences (Crutchfield et al. 1995; Spohn 2000; Spohn and Holleran 2000; Harrington and Spohn 2007); and in probation and parole revocations (Steen and Opsal 2007; Wisconsin Office of Justice Assistance 2008). It has been suggested that disparity is cumulative, steadily increasing at each successive stage of criminal processing (Sentencing Project 2008). But is this true in all jurisdictions? And in any given jurisdiction, do some stages of the process or some legal and extralegal decision criteria contribute much more heavily to disparity or certain forms of disparity?

In a pioneering study, Alfred Blumstein (1982) estimated that 80 percent of the black/white disproportionality in U.S. prisons in 1974 and in 1979 was accounted for by racial differences in arrest rates, and similar findings were reported in later studies (Langan 1985; Blumstein

1993; Sorensen, Hope, and Stemen 2003; Garland, Spohn, and Wodahl 2008 [summarizing these and other studies using Blumstein's method]; see also Bridges and Crutchfield [1988] examining correlations between states' black and white imprisonment rates and various social and demographic measures). But Blumstein recognized the limitations of such aggregate measures and called for further research in individual jurisdictions, tracking cases longitudinally through the various stages of the criminal process.

This essay seeks to provide some of that state-level analysis, examining several of the stages between arrest and prison and using more detailed offense and offender data than were available in the earlier studies. It provides what appears to be the first systemwide study in any American jurisdiction of racial disparities at multiple stages of the criminal process and of the socioeconomic differences that precede and help to explain racial disparities in cases entering the system.

Some of the data needed to examine these problems in Minnesota are not currently available, and the data that exist are often not kept in a consistent or complete form. However, the available data do tell us a lot about where the worst racial disparities are likely to be found and where more consistent and complete data are most needed. For reasons explained in more detail below, I examine only black versus white disparities. Even with that limitation, however, the topic is broad and very complex; the goal of this exploratory effort is to present an overview, identifying basic research concepts and problems, and suggesting tentative conclusions and specific topics worthy of more detailed study in Minnesota and other states with high rates of racial disproportionality in custody populations. The principal findings are as follows.

Racial disproportionality in Minnesota's prisons has fallen substantially in recent years, although it remains well above the national average. The state's falling black/white ratio was due primarily to higher growth in prison commitment rates for whites combined with substantial growth in the state's black population due to a large influx of recent African immigrants that was not matched by corresponding increases in numbers of black criminal defendants and inmates. Another cause of declining black/white ratios is the use of improved measures: the most recent studies have counted jail as well as prison inmates and have excluded Hispanics from race categories; these changes further lowered Minnesota's black/white ratio and the national ranking of its

TABLE 1

Minnesota and U.S. Black/White Ratios for Poverty Rates and Selected Stages of the Criminal Process (the Black Rate as a Multiple of the White Rate)

	Minnesota	All States
2000 family poverty rates (percent of families below poverty)	6.2	3.4
2002 arrest rates per 100,000 residents (Part I crimes plus drug crime)	9.1	3.2
2002–4 felony conviction rates per 100,000 residents (all crimes; population bases lagged 1 year)	8.8*	4.0[†]
2002–4 custody sentence rates per 100,000 residents (prison or jail sentence imposed, all crimes; population bases lagged 1 year)	9.0*	4.3[†]
June 2005 incarceration rates per 100,000 (inmates in prisons and jails, all crimes; population bases lagged 3 years [July 2002])	9.9[‡]	5.7[‡]

SOURCES.—MSGC (2003, 2004, 2005); BJS (2004, 2006, 2007c); USCB (2007a, 2007d, 2007e, 2007f); BCA (2008); FBI (2008a, tables 29, 43).

NOTE.—Except as indicated, Hispanics are included in the black and white race categories.

* The 3-year average was used for greater comparability to U.S. data (next note) and because conviction and sentencing data vary more by year than arrest and inmate data. Hispanics are allocated to race categories on the basis of data from the closest year (2005) with data reported both with and without Hispanics. Population base is the average of July 2001, 2002, and 2003.

[†] Equals the average of ratios for 2002 (population base: July 2001) and 2004 (population base: July 2003); U.S. sentencing data for 2003 are not available.

[‡] Hispanics are excluded from the black and white race categories (data including Hispanics are not available). If Hispanics were included, these black/white ratios would both probably be somewhat lower.

ratio. However, Minnesota's ratio and ranking in recent studies may have been lowered artificially (i.e., understated) because, as in all prior studies, the population bases used to compute black and white per capita incarceration rates were not time-lagged to adjust for recent dramatic increases in Minnesota's black population. Inmate populations must be compared to resident populations at the time inmates committed their crimes, not when they are in prison.

As shown in table 1, summarizing data on several key measures for which both state and national data are available, Minnesota has high rates of racial disparity not only in its prison and jail populations but also at earlier stages of the criminal process. Minnesota disparity ratios

TABLE 2

Minnesota and U.S. Black/White Ratios for Felony Convictions, Prison Sentences Imposed, and Prison Populations (Black Rate as a Multiple of the White Rate)

	Minnesota	All States
2002–4 felony conviction rates per 100,000 residents (population bases lagged 1 year)	8.8*	4.0[†]
2002–4 prison sentences imposed per 100,000 residents (population bases lagged 1 year)	12.1*	4.6[†]
2005 year-end prison rates (inmates per 100,000 residents; population bases lagged 3.5 years [July 2002])	12.4	6.0[‡]

SOURCES.—MSGC (2003, 2004, 2005); BJS (2004, 2007c, 2008a); USCB (2007e, 2007f); Minnesota Department of Corrections (2008).

NOTE.—Except as indicated, Hispanics are included in the black and white race categories.

* The 3-year average was used for greater comparability to U.S. data (next note) and because conviction and sentencing data vary more by year than inmate data. Hispanics are allocated to race categories on the basis of data from the closest year (2005) with data reported both with and without Hispanics. Population base is the average of July 2001, 2002, and 2003.

[†] Equals the average of ratios for 2002 (population base: July 2001) and 2004 (population base: July 2003). U.S. sentencing data for 2003 are not available.

[‡] Hispanics are excluded from the black and white race categories (data including Hispanics are not available). If Hispanics were included, the black/white ratio would probably be somewhat lower.

exceed national ratios to an even greater degree at these early stages (especially at arrest) than they do for inmate populations. And unlike the national pattern of steadily increasing disparity at later stages, racial disparity in Minnesota is not much higher at the end of the process (custody sentences and combined prison-jail populations) than at arrest.

However, as shown in table 2, disparity does increase substantially in Minnesota, after the stage of conviction, when we look only at prison sentences and prison populations. The principal cause of this disparity increase is the heavy weight that Minnesota sentencing guidelines give to prior conviction record. The national data show a much smaller increase from conviction to sentencing (but a larger increase from prison sentencing to prison populations).

The socioeconomic disparity between blacks and whites in Minnesota is comparable to the state's criminal justice disparities and is much greater than socioeconomic disparity for the nation as a whole. Minnesota blacks are also much more likely to live in high-crime urban areas and much less likely to live in low-crime rural areas—not only when compared to Minnesota whites but also when compared to blacks in other states. Such disparities and urban concentrations are consistent with elevated black offense rates and may also lead to law enforcement policies that increase black arrest rates. National data suggest that variations in socioeconomic disparity and residential patterns may also help to explain surprising state and regional patterns of custodial disproportionality.

The limited available data on charging, plea bargaining, and trial outcomes suggest that these stages contribute relatively little to Minnesota's disparate prison and jail populations. Racial disproportionality is about the same at felony conviction as at arrest (whereas for all states combined, disparity increases between these two points).

The extensive available data on Minnesota sentencing outcomes reveal little racial disparity in initial sentencing decisions. However, certain sentencing laws and guideline rules have a disparate impact on prison sentence rates for blacks. Decisions to revoke probationary and postprison release also have a disparate impact (black revocation rates are higher for both types of release), but these effects are countered by the much larger proportions of whites who obtain release and thus are at risk of revocation.

All the disparity measures discussed above and in later sections of this essay are ratios of black and white per capita rates. Minnesota's very high black/white ratios are caused in part by its very low white rates on all measures. It could be argued that the "real story" is the very low white rates. Perhaps Minnesota's high black/white ratios say more about the remarkable success of its white citizens than about the deprivations of its blacks. On most dimensions, however, the high black/white ratio is caused not just by a low white rate but also by a high black rate: Minnesota whites are better off than the national average and Minnesota blacks are worse off. The one exception is incarceration rates, for which Minnesota's per capita black rate is below the national average. This reflects Minnesota sentencing policies that discourage incarceration and benefit offenders of all races. But the high black/white incarceration ratio shows that these policies are favoring whites much more than blacks. So the question remains, why?

This essay is organized as follows. Section I describes Minnesota's sentencing laws, its criminal justice system, and the social and political milieu. Section II discusses the paper's methodological approach and limitations, beginning with an overview of the various stages of the criminal process at which racial disproportionality could arise. It is important to study all these stages, not only the sentencing and post-sentencing decisions that most directly affect prison and jail populations. Section II also examines the subjects on which current data are most limited and identifies persistent problems (which may arise at multiple stages) with the available data and interpretation of those data (the Appendix further examines these problems).

Section III summarizes prior research and presents the most recent data on black and white incarceration rates in Minnesota and other states. The patterns by state and region are somewhat surprising: the states with the highest rates of disproportionality tend to be politically liberal states of the Northeast and upper Midwest, whereas most of the states with the lowest ratios are in the South.

Section IV moves back to the earliest stage of the criminal process for which we have substantial data: arrest. Various explanations for Minnesota's unusually disparate arrest rates are examined, in particular, racial differences in criminal behavior and law enforcement practices that directly or indirectly target blacks and black neighborhoods. The underlying social causes of racial disparities in offense rates, and racially disparate law enforcement policies, are then examined for Minnesota and, briefly, for other states with particularly high or particularly low racial disparity in custody populations.

In Section V, the story jumps from arrest to felony conviction. Lack of data prevents any direct examination of the steps from arrest to filing of charges and from filing to conviction, but rough comparisons, overall and by offense, can be made between adult arrest rates and felony conviction rates. Section V also reports what is known about the contributions to custodial disproportionality of Minnesota's criminal laws, its sentencing guidelines, felony sentencing decisions (in particular, departures under the guidelines), and postsentencing decisions to revoke probation or postprison release or to delay prison release.

Section VI summarizes what we already know, and most need to find out, about racial disproportionality in Minnesota criminal justice. This section also examines the policy implications of finding (or not finding) racial disparities at various stages of the criminal process in Minnesota and other states facing similar racial disproportionality problems.

I. Minnesota and Its Criminal Justice System

The most important features of Minnesota's criminal justice system, and the ones most directly relevant to the focus of this essay, are its sentencing guidelines regime and its low incarceration rate. But other important dimensions of criminal justice must also be taken into account, along with the broader social and political context.

A. Minnesota Sentencing Laws

In 1980 Minnesota became the first American jurisdiction to adopt legally binding guidelines promulgated by a permanent sentencing commission. The guidelines were intended to reduce but not eliminate sentencing and prison release discretion and the disparities, including racial disparities, associated with such discretion (Frase 2005a). Parole release discretion was abolished except for life sentences, but inmates may reduce their pronounced prison terms by up to one-third for good behavior (since 1992, inmates may lose "good time" credits not only for disciplinary infractions but also if they refuse to participate in treatment or other assigned programming). When inmates are released from prison, they serve a "supervised release term" similar to traditional parole and subject to revocation for violation of release conditions. The duration of this term equals the sentence credit for good behavior (for sex crimes and certain other offenses a longer conditional release period applies).

The guidelines (current version, MSGC [2008b]) include recommendations as to both the duration of prison terms and the "disposition"—whether the prison term should be executed (immediately carried out) or stayed (suspended). In the latter case the offender is normally placed on probation. The length of probation may be any period up to the maximum prison term that could have been imposed, or 4 years, whichever is longer. The guidelines provide some general, nonbinding policies but no specific recommendations concerning the conditions of stayed sentences; judges thus have broad discretion to select stay conditions, which may include up to 1 year of confinement in a local jail or workhouse; treatment (residential or out-patient); home detention (with or without electronic monitoring); probation (with "intensive," regular, or no supervision); fines; restitution; victim-offender mediation; and community service. Subsequent decisions to revoke the stay are likewise subject to general policy statements but no specific, binding guidelines. Further flexibility is provided by means of charging and plea bargaining discretion, neither of which is regulated by the guidelines or other law.

Recommended guidelines sentences are based primarily on two factors: the severity of the offender's most serious current offense and the extent of his or her prior convictions. The guidelines recommendations are contained in a two-dimensional grid; as of August 2006, a separate grid is provided for sex offenses. Offense severity forms the vertical axis, with 11 levels on the main grid; the defendant's criminal history score forms the horizontal axis (seven columns on both grids) and consists primarily of previous felony convictions weighted by their severity levels (e.g., 2 points for each prior conviction at level 8 or higher; $\frac{1}{2}$ point each for convictions at levels 1 and 2); limited additional points are added for prior misdemeanor convictions, juvenile delinquency adjudications, and "custody status" (whether the offender was in custody or on some form of conditional release at the time of the current offense). The most recent version of the main grid is shown in figure 1.

Offenders with low to medium criminal history scores, convicted of lower-severity offenses, receive a recommended stayed (suspended) prison term of a specified number of months. For more serious offenses or criminal history scores, the recommended sentence is an executed prison term within a specified range. The boundary between recommended stayed and executed prison terms is shown on the grid by a heavy black line (the "disposition line"). Most cases in the shaded area below the line have presumptive stayed sentences. A few cases below the disposition line, mostly involving recidivists or the use of a dangerous weapon, are subject to mandatory minimum prison terms provided in state statutes. But in many of these cases the prison term is not really "mandatory": courts may avoid the prison term if they meet the general standards for guidelines departure, described below. There are relatively few cases subject to truly mandatory penalties. It should also be noted that state statutes and the guidelines no longer make any distinction between crack and powdered cocaine. A 1991 state Supreme Court decision based on the Minnesota constitution invalidated the distinctions previously recognized, in part because of the disparate impact on nonwhite offenders of the more severe crack penalties (*State v. Russell*, 477 NW2d 886 [Minn. 1991]). In 1992 the legislature responded by raising powder penalties to equal the crack penalties (Frase 2005*a*, pp. 157, 164).

SEVERITY LEVEL OF CONVICTION OFFENSE (Common offenses listed in italics)		CRIMINAL HISTORY SCORE						
		0	1	2	3	4	5	6 or more
Murder, 2nd Degree (intentional murder; drive-by-shootings)	XI	306 261-367	326 278-391	346 295-415	366 312-439	386 329-463	406 346-480²	426 363-480²
Murder, 3rd Degree Murder, 2nd Degree (unintentional murder)	X	150 128-180	165 141-198	180 153-216	195 166-234	210 179-252	225 192-270	240 204-288
Assault, 1st Degree Controlled Substance Crime, 1st Degree	IX	86 74-103	98 84-117	110 94-132	122 104-146	134 114-160	146 125-175	158 135-189
Aggravated Robbery, 1st Degree Controlled Substance Crime, 2nd Degree	VIII	48 41-57	58 50-69	68 58-81	78 67-93	88 75-105	98 84-117	108 92-129
Felony DWI	VII	36	42	48	54 46-64	60 51-72	66 57-79	72 62-84²
Controlled Substance Crime, 3rd Degree	VI	21	27	33	39 34-46	45 39-54	51 44-61	57 49-68
Residential Burglary Simple Robbery	V	18	23	28	33 29-39	38 33-45	43 37-51	48 41-57
Nonresidential Burglary	IV	12¹	15	18	21	24 21-28	27 23-32	30 26-36
Theft Crimes (Over $5,000)	III	12¹	13	15	17	19 17-22	21 18-25	23 20-27
Theft Crimes ($5,000 or less) Check Forgery ($251-$2,500)	II	12¹	12¹	13	15	17	19	21 18-25
Sale of Simulated Controlled Substance	I	12¹	12¹	12¹	13	15	17	19 17-22

☐ Presumptive commitment to state imprisonment. First-degree murder has a mandatory life sentence and is excluded from the guidelines by law. See Guidelines Section II.E., Mandatory Sentences, for policy regarding those sentences controlled by law.

▨ Presumptive stayed sentence; at the discretion of the judge, up to a year in jail and/or other non-jail sanctions can be imposed as conditions of probation. However, certain offenses in this section of the grid always carry a presumptive commitment to state prison. See, Guidelines Sections II.C. Presumptive Sentence and II.E. Mandatory Sentences.

¹ One year and one day

FIG. 1.—Minnesota Sentencing Guidelines main grid effective August 1, 2008: presumptive sentence lengths in months.

Judges may depart from guidelines recommendations as to prison duration or prison disposition if they cite "substantial and compelling circumstances." Some of the permissible bases for departure are specified in the guidelines, but many others have been recognized in appellate case law. In extreme cases upward durational departures may go all the way to the statutory maximum prison term for the offense. (In accordance with the requirements of *Blakely v. Washington* [542 U.S, 296 (2004)], all factual findings required for an upward departure, other than those based solely on prior record, must be admitted by the defendant or found by the jury beyond a reasonable doubt; *Blakely* has thus far not had any major impact on Minnesota sentencing procedures and outcomes [Frase 2006].) The prosecution and defense each have the right to appeal the sentence on the grounds that the departure (or refusal to depart) was improper.

B. Minnesota Sentencing Practices

Compared to other states, Minnesota was a low–incarceration rate state before the guidelines were adopted and remains so today. When the guidelines-enabling statute was enacted in 1978, Minnesota's state prison incarceration rate was 49 per 100,000 state residents; Massachusetts had the same rate, and only two states had lower rates (BJS 1980, p. 4). By 2007 Minnesota's prison rate had risen to 181 per 100,000, but that rate was still the second-lowest in the country (BJS 2008a, p. 18). And although Minnesota and national imprisonment rates have grown at about the same rate over this 29-year period (both increased by about 260 percent), the Minnesota increase was fueled to a greater extent by felony caseload increases: from 1986 to 2004 (the earliest and latest years with national data), Minnesota felony convictions increased by 145 percent whereas felony convictions in all states increased only by 85 percent (BJS 1989, table 1; 2007c, p. 2; MSGC 2008c, p. 12).

Minnesota's low imprisonment rate is due in part to its frequent use of local jail sentences in lieu of prison: in 2004, 68 percent of sentenced Minnesota felons received jail terms, and 23 percent were sent to prison. For all states these proportions were in the opposite order: 30 percent of felons received a jail term, and 40 percent were sent to prison (BJS 2007c, p. 3). However, even when jail inmates are included, Minnesota's incarceration rate (300 per 100,000) was still the second-lowest of all states in 2005 (BJS 2006, p. 9).

The Minnesota guidelines seek to achieve sentencing "neutrality": sentences should avoid disparities based on race, gender, and socioeconomic status (MSGC 1980, p. 26; 2008b, sec. I[1]). Early postguidelines evaluations by the commission and outside researchers found that racial disparities had been reduced, at least when measured against guidelines definitions of conviction offense severity and prior record score (MSGC 1984; Miethe and Moore 1985; Frase 1993a, 2005a). The commission did not expect the guidelines to have a racially disproportionate impact on prison populations, since it predicted that the guidelines policy of favoring imprisonment for violent offenses would increase white imprisonment rates more than black rates (MSGC 1980, pp. 16–17). The commission also apparently did not anticipate any racially disparate impact of the guidelines policy favoring imprisonment for offenders with high criminal history scores; however, the potential for such an impact was noted in later evaluations (MSGC 1984, pp. 83–84; Miethe and Moore 1985, p. 358).

C. Other Important Aspects of Minnesota Criminal Justice

The state department of corrections runs all state prisons and also supervises some persons on probation and postprison release in counties (mostly rural, totaling about 30 percent of the state's population) that do not participate in the state-local partnership provided in the Community Corrections Act (CCA) of 1973. All counties that participate in CCA, and some that do not, supervise released persons with county staff, and local detention facilities (jails and workhouses) in all counties are run by local governments. The cost of community corrections, in both CCA and non-CCA counties, is mostly paid from local funds.

Minnesota state judges hold elected positions, but in practice most are initially appointed by the governor to fill an unexpired term and then are routinely reelected in uncontested elections without political party endorsement.[1] Judges usually retire during their terms so that their successors can likewise be appointed. Chief prosecutors in each county are also chosen in nonpartisan elections, but (unlike judges and public defenders) they have been described as "a well-organized and active political force" (Martin 1984, p. 30).

D. The Broader Political and Social Contexts

Although Minnesota has generally been a politically liberal state since the 1970s, consistently voting Democratic in presidential elections, it has become considerably more conservative in recent years (e.g., two of the three governors elected since 1990 were Republicans, and the third was an independent). At the time the guidelines were adopted the state's political culture was one in which citizens viewed government "as a means to achieve a good community through positive

---

[1] Recent court decisions have invalidated judicial ethics standards that prevented judges from expressing political views or accepting political endorsement; see, e.g., *Republican Party of Minnesota v. White*, 536 U.S. 765 (2002). But judges and many attorneys have resisted these decisions, and it remains to be seen whether the decisions will have much effect on judicial selection and retention decisions.

political action," and the legislature had a tradition of nonpartisanship with respect to criminal justice policy issues (Martin 1984, pp. 28, 61n180). A "good government" culture still seems to characterize the state, but perhaps to a lesser extent.

Almost three-quarters of Minnesota's 5 million residents live in the Minneapolis–St. Paul metropolitan area. In 1970, 98 percent of the state population was white, mostly of northern European ancestry (Martin 1984, p. 28). Since then the state has become considerably more ethnically diverse: Minnesota's black population more than quadrupled from 1980 to 2005,[2] and there have also been major increases in the state's Asian population, due primarily to an influx of Hmong refugees after the end of the Vietnam War. Despite these changes, Minnesota's population remains quite homogeneous in comparison to other U.S. states. In the 2000 Census, 89.4 percent of Minnesotans listing one race said they were non-Hispanic whites versus 70.5 percent for the nation as a whole, 3.6 percent of Minnesotans said they were non-Hispanic blacks (vs. 12.4 percent for the nation), and 2.9 percent said they were Hispanic (vs. 12.5 percent for the nation; USCB 2007e, 2007f).

The growing diversity of Minnesota's population has produced substantial changes in the state's criminal case loads: from 1981 to 2005 the proportion of non-Hispanic whites among convicted felons declined from 82 percent to 62 percent, and there were substantial increases in all nonwhite categories except American Indians: non-Hispanic blacks increased from 11 percent in 1981 to 24 percent in 2005, Hispanics from 1.6 to 5.5 percent, and Asians from 0.2 to 2.0 percent (MSGC 2008c, p. 19).

II. Assessing Causes of Disparate Inmate Populations

The first subsection below examines the kinds of disparities that may arise at each stage of the criminal process. The second briefly discusses the stages at which current data are most limited and identifies persis-

---

[2] In 1980, 53,344 Minnesotans identified themselves as black (including Hispanics; Minnesota State Planning Agency 1991, p. 3). In the 2000 Census, 179,957 respondents said they were black (including those also identifying themselves as Hispanic), and 205,531 said they were black or black plus another race; by midyear 2005 an estimated 221,724 Minnesotans were black (only), and 257,740 were black or black plus another race (USCB 2007f).

tent problems (which may arise at multiple stages) with the available data and the interpretation of those data.

A. Stages of the Criminal Process

Racial disparities in inmate populations reflect more than sentencing laws and practices; such disparity may originate at every stage of the criminal process leading up to sentencing and at several postsentencing stages (Bridges and Crutchfield 1988; Minnesota Task Force 1993). At a minimum, research must examine disparities in the following system inputs and stages, each of which may contribute to disparate prison and jail populations.

1. *Racial Differences in Criminal Behavior.*   Such differences usually reflect socioeconomic disparities, residential patterns, and other individual, family, or social factors strongly correlated with the risk of committing crime, the types and locations of crimes, and the risk of being a crime victim.

2. *Racial Differences in Reporting of Crime.*   If such differences exist, they may reflect cultural values or different levels of trust in government officials. Since most crime is intraracial (Sampson and Lauritsen 1997; BJS 2007a; FBI 2008c, table 5), any factor that leads to underreporting of crimes against nonwhite victims tends to favor, rather than disfavor, nonwhite offenders (see the "compensating biases" discussion in subsection B below and in the Appendix).

3. *Police Decisions to Investigate and Arrest.*   These decisions could result in racially disparate overenforcement (e.g., racial profiling, overemphasis on street-level enforcement) or underenforcement (if police devote less effort to enforcement of some or all crimes committed in nonwhite neighborhoods or committed against nonwhites in any location).

4. *Victim Cooperation with Police Investigation and Prosecution.*   Just as there may be differences in victim reporting to the police, there may also be racial differences in willingness or ability to cooperate with police and prosecutors in their efforts to solve crimes, apprehend offenders, and obtain convictions. A lower level of cooperation by nonwhite victims is a factor that tends to favor nonwhite offenders.

5. *Prosecutorial Screening and Initial Charging Decisions.*   Here too, there may be overenforcement, underenforcement, or both, varying by crime and by location.

6. *Postfiling Charge Revisions and Plea Bargaining.*   These discre-

tionary decisions may cause racially disparate overenforcement or underenforcement. Even in the absence of deliberate bias, such decisions may have disparate impacts due to racial variations in factors such as victim cooperation, defense effectiveness, offense severity, and offender prior record.

7. *Ability of Defendants to Mount an Effective Defense or Propose Alternative Sentencing.*   Given the strong correlation between race and class, minority offenders are likely to be indigent and have court-appointed counsel. Public defender programs are often underfunded, resulting in high caseloads, low pay, high turnover, and limited resources for investigation and sentence planning. In addition, if indigent minority offenders are more likely to be held in pretrial detention, they will face greater disadvantage in preparing for trial, negotiating a plea, and arguing for a noncustodial sentence. At trial, they may have difficulty effectively assisting in their defense or testifying because of mental or linguistic disabilities. At sentencing they may be disadvantaged by lack of private insurance or other funding for treatment, unstable family situations, lack of employment, and limited alternative sentencing resources in their communities.

8. *Criminal and Sentencing Laws.*   Criminal statutes and sentencing guidelines may have unintended disparate impacts on different racial groups. In particular, sentence-enhancement factors related to offense severity ranking and criminal history scoring often apply more frequently to nonwhite offenders.

9. *Sentencing Practices.*   Under the Minnesota sentencing guidelines, racial disproportionality in prison populations could result from decisions to depart from the recommended disposition (execution or suspension of the prison sentence) or from the recommended prison duration. Racially disparate jail populations could result from decisions imposing jail as a condition of felony probation, as a misdemeanor sentence, or as pretrial detention.

10. *Postsentencing Policies and Practices.*   Inmate populations also depend on policies and decisions determining release conditions, revocation of probation or postprison conditional release, delay of prison or jail release through denial of good-conduct credits, and, where applicable, denial of parole release. Revocation decisions affect jail as well as prison populations, since offenders may be jailed as a sanction for alleged violations of release conditions and are often held in jail awaiting revocation proceedings. There may also be inherent racial biases

in risk assessment tools used to set probation and parole conditions, determine the timing of prison release, and respond to probation and parole violations. In addition, minority offenders may be less able to argue effectively for favorable probation conditions, prison release, or postprison release conditions; less able to mount an effective defense to alleged violations of release conditions; and less able to propose alternatives to revocation of release.

B. Missing, Inconsistent, and Hard-to-Interpret Data

Very few data are available for several of the system inputs and stages summarized above. Even when data are available, they are often not reported in a form consistent with data for other stages, or the data may be distorted by the manner in which they are reported or analyzed by researchers (for more detailed discussion of these problems, see the Appendix).

Other than arrest statistics, there are very few Minnesota-specific data on racial differences in criminal behavior and on police decisions to investigate and arrest. There are almost no race-specific Minnesota data on reporting of crime to the police, victim cooperation, pretrial detention decisions, defense resources, prosecutorial charging and plea bargaining, misdemeanor sentencing practices, postsentencing decisions that affect prison and jail populations, and, at all stages of the process, the race of crime victims.

There are also several persistent problems of inconsistent data. First, all arrest and some sentencing and prison data include Hispanics in the race categories. In other sentencing and prison data, and in most jail statistics, Hispanics are excluded from all racial categories and are reported as a separate group. Most Hispanics are white, and Hispanic whites tend to have higher arrest, conviction, and incarceration rates than non-Hispanic whites. Including Hispanics in race categories thus tends to raise the white rate and lower the black/white disparity ratio, concealing the greater disparity that exists between non-Hispanic whites and other groups. In this essay, whenever possible, data from different sources are compared using the same categorization (including or excluding Hispanics in the race categories); when the sources treat Hispanics differently, one set of data is adjusted using the best available estimates of race-ethnicity relationships in those data or related data.

Second, the major data sources employ two differing temporal perspectives. Some sources (e.g., sentencing statistics) report the "flow" of cases or offenders processed during a year or other defined time period, whereas other sources (e.g., statistics on inmate populations) report "stocks" of offenders at year end or some other time.

There are also important limitations in the scope and methodology of prior racial disproportionality studies. Most focus on black versus white disparities, ignoring other racial and ethnic groups, and do not separately examine males and females. In addition, all prior state-level studies compute per capita incarceration rates by comparing mostly adult inmate populations to the total resident population including juveniles. Furthermore, when computing per capita incarceration rates by race, these studies use no time lag between inmate measures and resident population bases. The problem is that prison inmate counts (and, to a lesser extent, jail counts) reflect crimes committed several years earlier, and the size of each race's resident population may not be changing at the same rate. The volume of crimes committed by a racial group, and of the resulting criminal caseloads and inmate stocks for that group, should be assessed relative to the population of that group when the crimes were committed.

Owing to space limitations and to facilitate comparisons with prior research, I likewise disregard gender differences and focus on black/white disparities (blacks remain the largest nonwhite group in Minnesota). For the same reasons and also because of limited state population data by race and age, my racial disproportionality measures are based on total population bases including juveniles. But readers should keep in mind that the highly disparate Minnesota and U.S. black/white ratios reported here would be even higher if they were based on adult populations (and higher still if these ratios were limited to males).

In contrast to previous studies, however, I use time-lagged population bases to compute all black and white incarceration rates and black/white ratios, except when comparison is being made to the unlagged results of prior research (as in table 3). Time lagging is also used (as was done in tables 1 and 2) when computing per capita rates for other stages after the point of arrest, that is, conviction rates, guidelines prison recommendation rates, prison sentence rates, and rates of custody sentencing (prison or jail). Such time lagging is particularly important for Minnesota, where the black population has grown very much faster than the white population in recent years. Basing black and white rates and ratios on the much higher black populations of

218   Richard S. Frase

later years would substantially understate black per capita rates and the true extent of racial disparity, particularly in prison populations.

Finally, when interpreting the limited available data on racial disproportionality, one must consider the possibility of compensating biases (Blumstein 1982). Bias against black victims tends to favor black offenders (since most crime is intraracial); if this bias coexists with bias against black offenders, the two opposing biases may cancel each other out (or at least mitigate each other somewhat), thus concealing the extent of each type of bias. Several other types of compensating bias are described in the Appendix.

Limitations on the availability and comparability of data constrain the time periods that I was able to examine. The most recent national survey of racial disparities in state prison and jail populations when I ran these analyses was as of midyear 2005. Furthermore, the U.S. Census Bureau in 2000 substantially changed the way it collects population data by race (in previous years, people were not allowed to self-identify under two or more specific races). Therefore, I primarily examine racial differences in sentencing and other matters in the years from 2000 through 2005, with only occasional references to available data for earlier or later years.

III. Prison and Jail Custody Rates by Race

Published data reveal substantial racial disproportionality in Minnesota's inmate populations. Five early studies focused on state prison populations; in each year, Minnesota's ratio of per capita black and white incarceration rates was the highest of any of the states reported:[3]

- 1982—20.9 : 1 (Bridges and Crutchfield [1988], reporting on 49 states);
- 1982—21.7 : 1 (Blumstein [1988], reporting on 33 states, male inmates only);
- 1988—19.0 : 1 (Tonry [1991], reporting on 49 states);
- 1990—20.4 : 1 (Blumstein [1993], reporting on 42 states);
- 1994—22.8 : 1 (Mauer [1997], reporting on 50 states).

No researcher or agency appears to have published state-by-state

[3] Analyzing prison *admissions* instead of populations, Sorensen, Hope, and Stemen (2003, table 3) found that in 1997 the ratio of Minnesota's black and white per capita prison admission rates was 24.0 : 1, the highest ratio of the 23 states examined.

TABLE 3

Ratio of Black to White Per Capita Prison Rates in Minnesota and for All States, 1979–2007 (Black Rate as a Multiple of the White Rate)

	Minnesota	All States		Minnesota	All States
1979	. . .*	6.9	2002	14.9	. . .
1982	20.9	. . .	2003	13.1	. . .
1988	19.0	6.9	2004	12.1	. . .
1990	20.4	7.1	2005	11.3	6.1
1994	22.8	7.7	2006	11.1	. . .
2000[†]	19.1	. . .	2007	11.4	. . .
2001	17.5	6.6			

SOURCES.—1979: Blumstein (1982); 1982: Bridges and Crutchfield (1988); 1988: Tonry (1991; Minnesota), Mauer (1997; all states); 1990: Blumstein (1993); 1994: Mauer (1997); Minnesota 2000–2007: USCB (2007e, 2007f, 2008f); Minnesota Department of Corrections (2008); all states 2001: BJS (2002; combining data reported at pp. 9 and 13); all states 2005: BJS (2006; combining data reported at pp. 8 and 11).

NOTE.—Ratios equal the black prison rate (inmates per 100,000 black residents) divided by the white prison rate. Inmate and state population data are as of July 1 of each year; all population bases are unlagged to permit comparison of ratios computed by the author with results of previous studies. Minnesota inmate counts exclude short-term offenders serving a felony prison term in a local detention facility (usually because at the time of commitment to the custody of the Department of Corrections their remaining time to serve was 180 days or less). Data on such inmates are available only for 2004 and later; in those years the black/white ratios are identical with and without inclusion of these inmates.

* Data are not available.

† Except for 2000, black and white race categories include Hispanics. If Hispanics were included in 2000 data, the black/white ratio for that year would probably be somewhat lower.

black/white prison population ratios for the years since 1994, but more recent Minnesota imprisonment rates and ratios can be computed using inmate data from the Minnesota Department of Corrections and U.S. Census Bureau population estimates.[4]

As shown in table 3, the ratio of black to white per capita incarceration rates in Minnesota's prisons has declined substantially in recent

[4] Minnesota prison data for recent years consist of inmate counts at 6-month intervals (Minnesota Department of Corrections 2008). For dates before July 2001, Hispanics are reported separately and are not included in race categories; after that date totals are reported for Hispanics, but these inmates are also included in the race categories. To simplify computations and presentation, the per capita rates reported in this essay are based on census estimates for persons listing only one race (i.e., excluding those who listed two or more races); in 2005, such multirace residents constituted an estimated 1.4 percent of all Minnesotans and 1.5 percent of the U.S. population (USCB 2007e, 2007f).

years.[5] For the United States as a whole (excluding federal prisons), black/white prison ratios also declined, but by a much lesser amount, after similarly reaching a peak in the early 1990s.

The stronger downward shift in Minnesota after 2000 appears to be primarily the result of two factors: white commitments to prison rose much faster than black commitments, and the resident black population increased much more than the white population. First, the number of white offenders sentenced to prison increased by 58 percent from 2000 to 2005, whereas for blacks the increase was only 29 percent (MSGC [2006b] and similar data sets for 2001–4).[6] The increase in white prison sentences was particularly great for methamphetamine and other drug offenses and for felony drunk driving.[7] Second, the state's black population rose by 22 percent from 2000 to 2005, whereas the white population increased only by 1.6 percent (USCB [2007f], excluding Hispanics). The rapid growth in the black population ap-

[5] All the ratios in table 3 are based on per capita black and white rates using unlagged population bases, in order to permit comparison to similarly unlagged figures reported in prior studies. All the ratios in the table would probably be higher if time-lagged bases were used. For example, the 2005 black/white prison ratio using population bases 3.5 years earlier is 12.4 : 1 (vs. 11.3 : 1, unlagged). But the direction and pace of the downward state and national trends shown in table 3 would be similar if all rate bases were time-lagged.

[6] Guidelines sentencing data are available for every year since the guidelines became effective in 1980; the data sets contain demographic, processing, and sentencing data for all felons sentenced under the guidelines that year. In the remainder of this essay, when guidelines sentencing data are reported only by year, the sources are annual guidelines data sets obtained from the Minnesota Sentencing Guidelines Commission and analyzed by the author using SPSS software.

Minnesota sentencing data generally exclude Hispanics from race categories, whereas prison data almost always include them. Prison sentences have increased at a lower rate for Hispanics than for non-Hispanics since 2000, and most Hispanics are white, so the increase in prison sentences for all whites (including Hispanics) was probably a few percentage points lower than the 58 percent (non-Hispanic white) increase reported in the text.

[7] From July 2001 to July 2005 the number of methamphetamine offenders in Minnesota prisons increased by almost 400 percent, and as of midyear 2006, 85 percent of such offenders were white (Minnesota Department of Corrections 2005, 2007). For all drug types combined, white prison sentences increased by 125 percent from 2000 to 2005, whereas for blacks the increase was only 10 percent. This racial difference is probably due to meth cases, but drug type data are available only in sentencing statistics for 2005. By that year, however, new trends seemed to be emerging, and there were very few distinctive racial patterns of drug offending: within each of the major drug type categories (heroin and opium, marijuana, powder cocaine, crack cocaine, meth or other amphetamines, and hallucinogens), about two-thirds of sentenced drug offenders were white and one-quarter were black.

The state's first felony driving while intoxicated (DWI) law went into effect in August 2002, and by July 2005 this offense accounted for 6 percent of prison inmates (Minnesota Department of Corrections 2008). In 2005, 73 percent of convicted felony DWI offenders were white, whereas only 62 percent of all convicted offenders were white.

pears to be due in large part to substantial numbers of recent immigrants from Somalia and other African nations. There is reason to believe that crime rates are lower for these immigrant populations than for native-born blacks. Differences in age demographics played only a small role in the patterns noted above and in table 3. From 2000 to 2005, both white and black populations grew slightly older, in terms of both median age and the proportions aged 18 and over; the proportion of white residents aged 20–29 (an age group accounting for 35–40 percent of prison sentences for both races) increased slightly, whereas there was a small decline in the proportion of black residents in their 20s (USCB 2007b).

The earlier national surveys and recent Minnesota prison data discussed above have three major limitations: they include Hispanics in the black and white race categories, they do not include inmates held in local jails and workhouses, and they use unlagged population bases to compute per capita incarceration rates for each race. The inclusion of Hispanics tends to understate the non-Hispanic black/white incarceration ratio. Mauer (1997, p. 8) demonstrated the converse: exclusion of Hispanics from race categories will dramatically lower the white per capita incarceration rate in some states, thus raising the black/white incarceration ratio; for example, without Hispanics the white prison rate in 1994 was 32 percent lower for California and 74 percent lower for New York.

Racial disproportionality tends to be lower in jail populations, so calculating black/white incarceration ratios solely on the basis of prison data tends to overstate racial disparities in the combined (prison plus jail) custodial population. The opposing effects of including Hispanics and excluding jail inmates vary from state to state. Recent studies correcting these two problems in the prior data suggest that for Minnesota the net effect of those problems was to exaggerate the state's black/white ratio, while also exaggerating the rank order of its total incarceration ratio when compared to ratios in other states. For example, in 2001 Minnesota's black/white ratio for prisons alone (17.5 : 1, unlagged) was almost 40 percent higher than its black/white prison-plus-jail ratio (12.6 : 1); for all states, the prison-only ratio (6.6 : 1) was only 10 percent higher than the prison-plus-jail ratio (6.0 : 1). These differential effects are the result of two Minnesota characteristics: the state has a relatively low proportion of Hispanic residents, and Minnesota felons receive jail terms much more often than felons in other states.

Two recent Department of Justice reports on inmate population disparities in each state exclude Hispanics from race categories and also include jail as well as prison inmates. The first report (BJS 2002; also reported in Sentencing Project [2004]) provides data as of midyear 2001. Minnesota's black/white incarceration ratio was 12.6 : 1, the third-highest of the 50 states (for all states combined, the ratio was 6.0 : 1). The second report (BJS 2006; also reported in Mauer and King [2007]) provides data as of midyear 2005 and showed that Minnesota's black/white ratio had fallen to 9.1 : 1 (national average: 5.6 : 1). Of the 48 states reporting both prison and jail rates by race in 2005, nine states had higher black/white ratios and four states (Illinois, New Hampshire, Pennsylvania, and Utah) had approximately the same ratio as Minnesota.

However, these two latest reports did not correct a third problem found in all prior state-by-state studies of racial disparity in custodial populations: black/white incarceration rates and ratios are computed using unlagged population bases. Failure to lag the bases tends to understate black/white ratios when (as is usually the case) black resident populations are rising faster than white populations. The use of unlagged bases has a particularly distorting effect on comparisons between Minnesota and other states. Since Minnesota's black population has recently been increasing much faster than black populations in many other states, the use of unlagged bases understates Minnesota's black/white ratio more than it understates ratios in those other states, thus probably understating Minnesota's national ranking. The state's black/white ratio would have a higher ("worse") rank if appropriately lagged bases were used. A comparison between national and Minnesota ratios shows how much more the latter are affected by the timing of population bases: using a 3-year lagged base (2002 populations) increases the 2005 national black/white ratio for prison and jail inmates only from 5.6 to 5.7, but it raises Minnesota's ratio from 9.1 to 9.9.

In later sections I examine the available evidence on black/white disproportionality at earlier stages of the criminal process, beginning with arrest. Those disparities are compared with several key numbers that summarize Minnesota incarceration rate disparities in recent years.

For Minnesota prison populations, the ratio of black to white per capita incarceration rates in 2005, including Hispanics in the race categories and using population bases lagged 3.5 years, was 12.4 : 1 (table 2 above). The estimated ratio with Hispanics excluded (based on race-ethnicity relationships in cases sentenced to prison in that year) was 13.2 : 1. With a broader, multiyear measure of prison stocks (2003–7), corresponding to the multiyear measures used in later sections of this essay for arrests, convictions, and sentencing, Minnesota's black/white, lagged-base prison ratio was 12.9 : 1 including Hispanics in the race categories and an estimated 13.8 : 1 without Hispanics (table 10 below).

For prisons and jails combined, Minnesota's black/white inmate ratio in 2005, excluding Hispanics and using population bases lagged 3 years, was 9.9 : 1 (table 1); the estimated ratio with Hispanics included (based on race-ethnicity relationships in cases sentenced to prison or jail) was 9.5 (table 10 below). (Multiyear data for prisons and jails combined are not available.)

Before I conclude this survey of previous studies, it is useful to reflect on several consistent and curious findings concerning the geography of disparity.

First, in all seven of the national studies summarized above, the states with the worst black/white ratios tended to be northeastern and upper-midwestern states with liberal political traditions; many southern states had black/white ratios lower than the national average. This pattern was previously noted by Bridges and Crutchfield (1988), Tonry (1991), Blumstein (1993), Mauer (1997), and Sorensen, Hope, and Stemen (2003). In 2005, the two regions with the lowest black/white ratios for prison and jail inmates were the South (4.02 : 1) and the West (6.03 : 1), whereas the regions with the highest ratios were the Northeast (9.16 : 1) and the Midwest (6.49 : 1; BJS 2006).

Second, states and regions with very low total incarceration rates (inmates in jail or prison per capita) tend to have very high black/white ratios, and vice versa. This was also noted by Tonry (1991), Blumstein (1993), and Mauer (1997).

Third, most states with high black/white incarceration ratios have higher than average black incarceration rates (10 out of the 13 highest-ratio states in 2005) and lower than average white rates (11 out of 13 states). Conversely, states in the low-ratio quartile, most of which are in the South, tend to show the opposite pattern: all 13 of these states had higher than average white incarceration rates in 2005, and eight had lower than average black rates. (The 13 highest-ratio and 13 lowest-ratio states in 2005 are identified and further discussed in Sec. IV.)

This pattern has existed for some time, at least in the case of southern states (Bridges and Crutchfield [1988], analyzing 1982 data).

Among the high-ratio states, Minnesota, Rhode Island, and New York show a third pattern: per capita incarceration rates are lower than average for both whites and blacks (albeit especially low for whites; hence the high black/white ratios for these states). In most prior studies Minnesota's white rate was the lowest reported for any state, whereas its black prison rate was lower than the national average in all but the first (1982) study. The low incarceration rates for Minnesota blacks and whites might suggest that there is nothing particularly interesting about the state's high black/white ratio or, at least, that the more interesting question is why the white incarceration rate is so low. However, as noted previously, other disparity ratios for Minnesota (in arrests, convictions, and socioeconomic measures) tend to conform to the majority pattern for states with a high incarceration ratio: whites are better off than the national average, and blacks are worse off. As for incarceration rates, Minnesota's lower-than-average black rate results from sentencing policies designed to minimize the use of state prison sentences. Minnesota blacks benefit from those policies when compared to blacks in other states, but they do not benefit nearly as much as Minnesota whites do.

Prior researchers (Tonry 1991; Blumstein 1993; Mauer 1997) have sought to attribute these geographic variations to state sentencing policies. A (more liberal, northern) state that uses its prisons mainly for violent offenders will have higher black incarceration rates, since blacks are more likely to be arrested and convicted of violent crimes. Other (more conservative, southern) states, where prison terms are frequently given to nonviolent offenders, will have higher white incarceration rates than the first group of states and, as a result, lower black/white prison ratios. There is undoubtedly much truth in this theory, but it works less well in explaining geographic patterns of racial disproportionality in jail populations: jails are less heavily used than prisons for violent offenders, yet the same geographic variations in racial disproportionality, albeit less pronounced, also exist in jail populations. And as I discuss in the next section, both kinds of disparity—in prisons and in jails—are preceded and to a large extent seem to be caused by equal or greater racial disproportionality at the arrest stage. Clearly, sentencing decisions and state-to-state differences in sentencing policy are not the only causes of prison and jail disparities and geographic variations in disparity. In particular, it appears that the high incarceration rates for southern whites and northern blacks reflect not just sentencing policies in these states but also offense rates for both groups (Sorensen, Hope, and Stemen 2003).

Blumstein (1993, pp. 755–56) offered two additional explanations for state and regional patterns of disparity: that blacks who have remained in the South are more "compliant and socialized to local mores" and more locally rooted than those who migrated to the North and Midwest; and that these migrants tended to move from rural, low-crime to urban, high-crime areas. The latter theory was examined on a regional basis by Sorensen, Hope, and Stemen (2003). Minnesota, regional, and national data supporting this theory are presented in Section IV.

IV. Disproportionate Arrest Rates: Differences in Offending, Policing, Both?

The focus now shifts to the first stage of criminal justice processing, arrest. Ideally, one would begin by examining data on racial patterns of offending to see whether disparities exist prior to and independent of police activity and subsequent criminal justice processing, but very little race-specific data on offending are available for Minnesota. However, several indirect measures, discussed in subsection B below, suggest that substantial racial differences in offending do exist in the state and probably explain most of the disparities found at the arrest stage.

A. Black and White Per Capita Arrest Rates

Minnesota's adult arrest rates for some types of crime are even more disparate than its inmate populations. For all types of crime, arrests in Minnesota are substantially more disparate than the national average. As shown in table 4,[8] black per capita adult arrest rates for serious ("Part I") violent crimes in 2000–2004 (the period preceding the latest survey of state prison and jail disparities) were on average over 15 times higher than white rates. For murder and robbery Minnesota's black arrest rates were almost 40 times higher. Black/white arrest ratios were

---

[8] FBI national arrest data include Hispanics in white and black race categories. Estimated U.S. total adult white and black arrests are extrapolations based on the jurisdictions reporting arrestee race and age data (these jurisdictions accounted for 70–75 percent of estimated total arrests each year). Minnesota data are from the Minnesota Bureau of Criminal Apprehension (BCA 2008), which, like the FBI national data, include Hispanics in the white and black race totals for juvenile and for adult arrests.

TABLE 4

Ratio of Black to White Per Capita Adult Arrest Rates in Minnesota and the United States, by Year and by FBI Offense Groups (Black Rate as a Multiple of the White Rate)

	Murder and Robbery		Part I Violent		Part I Property		Drug Crimes		Part I Violent Plus Drug		All Part I Crimes Plus Drug	
	Minn.	U.S.	Minn.	U.S.	Minn.	U.S.	Minn.	U.S.	Minn.	U.S.	Minn.	U.S.
1990	72.0	10.5	25.6	5.4	10.1	3.6	14.6	4.6	18.3	4.9	12.9	4.2
2000–2004 (mean)	39.8	6.6	15.4	3.8	8.5	2.9	9.0	3.4	10.2	3.5	9.5	3.3

SOURCES.—USCB (1990b, 2007e, 2007f, 2008a, 2008b); FBI (2008b, tables 29, 43) and similar reports for other years; BCA (2008). Minnesota arrest data for 2003 and 2004 exclude St. Paul, so the population bases do too; see the text.

NOTE.—Part I violent crimes are murder and nonnegligent manslaughter, forcible rape, robbery, and aggravated assault. Part I property crimes are burglary, larceny-theft, auto theft, and arson.

lower for Part I property crimes and for drug crimes in these years; for all Part I crimes plus drug crimes combined, black arrest rates averaged 9.5 times higher.[9] In all these offense categories, arrest disparities were greater in 1990.[10]

Arrest data permit only rough comparisons with prison and jail data, since the latter are "stocks" and the former are "flow" measures. In addition, data on prison and jail populations exclude Hispanics from the race categories, whereas Hispanics are included in all Minnesota and U.S. arrest data. Nevertheless, it is noteworthy that the average Minnesota black/white arrest ratio for all Part I crimes plus drugs in 2000–2004 (9.5 : 1) is identical to the estimated black/white ratio for Minnesota prison and jail populations at midyear 2005 (including Hispanics, 3-year lagged base) derived in Section III (also shown in table 10). Moreover, the higher arrest disparities in 1990 are consistent with Minnesota's higher prison disparities in earlier years (20.4 : 1 in 1990 and 22.8 in 1994, falling to 11.3 : 1 by 2005; see table 3 above).

Comparison of black/white per capita arrest ratios for Minnesota with ratios for the entire United States reveals that arrest rates are much more racially disproportionate in Minnesota than they are in many other states. In 2000–2004 Minnesota's average black/white adult arrest ratio for serious (Part I) violent crime arrests was four times higher than the U.S. ratio, and for murder and robbery Minnesota's average ratio was six times higher. Drug crime and property crime arrest rates were also more disparate in Minnesota, although to a lesser extent. Minnesota's average black/white ratio in 2000–2004 was almost three times higher than the national average for serious property crimes and over two and half times higher for drug crimes.

[9] Arrests for Part II offenses other than drugs are less suitable as predictors of prison and jail populations, since custody sentence rates and durations are lower and prison and jail populations are smaller for most of these crimes. See BJS (2007c); see also Minnesota Department of Corrections (2008). As of July 1, 2007, 70 percent of prison inmates had been convicted of violent and other "person" crimes (49 percent) or drug crimes (21 percent); the remainder consisted of property crimes (13 percent), DWI (7 percent), weapons (5 percent), and other (6 percent). Post-2004 data are excluded from the multiyear averages discussed in the text because these arrests would not have affected the most recent Minnesota and U.S. black/white prison-jail ratios reported earlier.

Minnesota arrest data (BCA 2008) for 2003 and 2004 do not include St. Paul, the state's second-largest city. In computations of 2003 and 2004 black and white per capita arrest rates included in the multiyear averages shown in tables 4 and 10, state population bases for 2003 and 2004 were revised to exclude St. Paul black and white populations (USCB 2008a, 2008b).

[10] Per capita rates and ratios for 1990 are not directly comparable with those for 2000 and later years, since the 1990 Census permitted choice of only one specified racial identity.

The finding that Minnesota arrest disparities are particularly great for violent crimes is consistent with prior research examining regional patterns. Sorensen, Hope, and Stemen (2003, p. 80) reported that the ratio of black and white violent crime arrest rates in 1996 was 15.5 : 1 for the Midwest but only 5.5 : 1 for the other three regions combined (Northeast, West, and South).

Minnesota arrest disparities would probably be even higher, and the Minnesota-U.S. differences greater, if black and white arrest rates were based on adult populations (since black populations are relatively younger than white populations, especially in Minnesota). If Hispanics were excluded from white and black race categories in arrest data, this would also probably increase black/white arrest ratios, but it would tend somewhat to reduce Minnesota-U.S. differences (since Minnesota has relatively few Hispanics compared to the national average).

Minnesota's high black/white arrest ratios are the combined result of low white rates and high black rates. For example, in 2002 per capita white arrest rates for the four primary crime categories shown in table 4 were all below the national rates for whites. The Minnesota white murder and robbery rate was 66 percent below the national rate, and the rates for Part I violent, Part I property, and drugs were, respectively, 60 percent, 26 percent, and 38 percent below the national rates. Minnesota black per capita arrest rates in that year were all well above the national rates for blacks. The Minnesota black murder and robbery rate was 165 percent above the national rate, and the rates for Part I violent, Part I property, and drugs were 59 percent, 105 percent, and 66 percent above the national rates.

B. Preliminary Assessment of Minnesota's Disparate Arrest Rates

Why are arrest rates so much more racially disparate in Minnesota than for the nation as a whole? The most likely explanations probably involve one or more of the following factors: especially high black crime rates relative to white rates in Minnesota, greater willingness of Minnesota victims of black crimes to report those crimes to the police, and police overenforcement in Minnesota black communities or underenforcement in black communities elsewhere or both. Some or all of these factors could also help explain the curious geographic patterns of racial disproportionality in prison and jail populations, previously noted (that the states with the worst black/white ratios tend to be northeastern and midwestern states with liberal political traditions, whereas conservative southern states have black/white prison and jail ratios equal to or lower than the national average).

Each of the three theories summarized above merits thorough examination, beyond the scope of this exploratory analysis. A preliminary assessment reveals substantial support for the first theory (higher black crime rates) and some support for the third (disparate law enforcement policies).

1. *Racial Differences in Criminal Behavior.*   Although arrests reflect police discretion and policies as well as offense behavior, victim survey data on the perceived race of offenders suggest that black violent crime rates are higher: although blacks represented about 13 percent of the national population in 2005, they were perceived to have committed 28 percent of single-offender violent crimes and 47 percent of multi-offender violent crimes, excluding crimes in which the offender's race was unknown or not reported (BJS 2007a, tables 40, 46; see also Wilson 1987, pp. 22–26; Tonry 1995, pp. viii, 49, 63–80; American Law Institute 2007, pp. 38–39). However, very little of this research has been done in Minnesota;[11] and of course, victim surveys cannot assess racial offending patterns for crimes without face-to-face victim-offender contact and for crimes with no direct victim at all, in particular, drug crimes. Thus, for all types of crime we can assess racial offending patterns in Minnesota only indirectly. Here are four such indirect measures.

a. Black/White Socioeconomic Disparities.   Crime is highly correlated with race and poverty, especially high concentrations of race and poverty (see studies cited in American Law Institute [2007, pp. 38–39]; see also Wilson 1987, pp. 20–62; Massey and Denton 1993, pp. 132–39; Ruth and Reitz 2003, pp. 32–37; Western 2006, pp. 34–38). If such concentrations and other measures of disparity in socioeconomic status (SES) between blacks and whites are greater in Minnesota than in other

[11] Four crime victimization surveys have been conducted in Minnesota since 1993, but in each case low response rates from minorities prevented any analysis of the data by race (see, e.g., Minnesota Criminal Justice Statistics Center 2003, p. 14). However, some indirect victimization data by race can be found in Minnesota Student Surveys of sixth, ninth, and twelfth graders (Minnesota Departments 2007) conducted from 1992 through 2004; these surveys have found consistently higher black responses to questions such as whether the child felt unsafe at school or on the way to school; gangs were a problem at the school; the child or a friend was a gang member; someone had threatened, stabbed, or shot at the child; or the child had been a victim of violence on a date or a victim of physical or sexual abuse. Since most crime is intraracial, these data imply higher black offense as well as victimization rates.

states, then Minnesota would be expected to have above-average racial differences in crime rates. High relative levels of black poverty and disadvantage in Minnesota would not be surprising, given that many of the state's blacks are recent arrivals and are therefore less socially integrated.

Prior research has only occasionally examined the effects of social status variables on custody disparities. Bridges and Crutchfield (1988) modeled white and black per capita imprisonment rates, using states as the unit of analysis, and found that higher levels of prison racial disparity were associated with higher black poverty rates, higher proportions of blacks living in inner-city areas, and smaller proportions of blacks in the total population. These authors also asserted that these factors were independent of racial differences in offending, but it appears that their models could not fully control for such differences. The white and black arrest rates Bridges and Crutchfield used to control for racial differences in offending included all index (Part I) crimes or, alternatively, all index violent or all index property crimes, but none of these measures fully captures the average severity of black and white arrest charges. Moreover, no variables directly measured racial differences in drug and other non–index crime arrests or in prior conviction records. Thus, uncontrolled racial differences in offending probably increased the apparent significance of any model variables with which crime rates are strongly correlated, including poverty rate, residential location, and percent black. These three factors do seem to be linked to racially disparate custody rates, but by a much more direct route. With high degrees of black poverty and inner-city residential concentration and a small, politically weak black population, the risks are much greater that blacks will be drawn into crime and apprehended by highly targeted law enforcement measures. And these three disparity risk factors, not coincidentally, are all present in Minnesota (tables 5, 6, and 7 below).

Table 5 reports black/white "disadvantage ratios" for Minnesota and the United States on various SES measures taken from the 2000 Census (USCB 2007d).[12] (This table includes Hispanics in the race categories to facilitate comparison with similarly categorized arrest data reported in table 4.) On each one of these SES measures, the Min-

---

[12] SES disparities in more recent surveys are very similar, and in some cases worse. For example, on the percentage of families below poverty, Minnesota's 2005 black/white ratio was 6.93 : 1, almost twice the national ratio of 3.60 : 1 (USCB 2007a).

TABLE 5

Minnesota and National Black/White Socioeconomic Disadvantage
Ratios in 2000 (Black Rate as a Multiple of the White Rate)

SES Measure	Minnesota	United States
Percent age 25 and over less than high school graduate	1.94	1.69
Percent living in a different U.S. house in 1995	1.48	1.10
Percent unemployed, of population 16 and over	3.04	2.30
Percent unemployed, of labor force 16 and over	3.28	2.52
Median household income	.60*	.66*
Median family income	.53*	.62*
Per capita income	.56*	.60*
Percent of families below poverty	6.18	3.43
Percent of individuals below poverty	4.37	2.74

SOURCE.—USCB (2007*d*).
NOTE.—Black and white race categories include Hispanics, for comparison with arrest data.
* A higher number on this measure means less relative black disadvantage.

nesota black/white disadvantage ratio was worse than the national average. On some measures, Minnesota's racial disadvantage ratio was
substantially worse than average: the black family poverty rate in Minnesota was over six times higher than the white poverty rate, whereas
for the United States as a whole the black poverty rate was 3.4 times
higher. Minnesota's high racial disadvantage ratios result from the fact
that its blacks are almost always equal to or worse off than the national
average for blacks on these SES measures, whereas on every measure,
Minnesota whites are better off than the national average for whites.

    i. *The Effects of Immigration on SES and Racial Disproportionality Mea-
sures.*   One potential problem with the above comparisons is that a
high percentage of Minnesota's blacks are immigrants: in 2000, 18
percent of the state's blacks were foreign born (excluding persons born
in Puerto Rico or other U.S. island territories or born abroad of U.S.
parents), whereas the proportion for U.S. blacks was only 6 percent
(USCB 2007*d*). As of 2005, the foreign-born proportions were 23 percent for Minnesota blacks and 8 percent for U.S. blacks (Ruggles et
al. 2004). If black immigrants to Minnesota have especially low SES
measures, their inclusion along with native-born blacks could distort
comparisons with other states. On the basis of the limited available
information, however, this does not appear to be the case. In 2000 and
2005, poverty rates were only slightly higher for foreign-born Minnesota blacks than for native-born blacks, and rates of unemployment

were actually substantially *lower* for foreign-born Minnesota blacks in both years (Ruggles et al. 2004; USCB 2007*d*). Finally, an examination of SES data for 1990, when only 5 percent of Minnesota blacks were foreign-born, reveals black/white SES disparities almost as great as those found in the 2000 and 2005 data. For example, the black/white ratio (including Hispanics) for the percentage of individuals below poverty in 1990 was 4.22 : 1 versus 4.37 : 1 in 2000 (USCB 1990*a*).

Despite the high poverty rate of Minnesota's foreign-born blacks, there is reason to believe that they are less crime-prone than native-born blacks. This pattern, if true, would be consistent with research dating back to the start of the twentieth century: first-generation immigrant groups tend to be less involved with crime, although second- and third-generation groups often have higher crime rates (Tonry 1997, pp. 19–25). And if the pattern is true, it would help to explain recent declines in the state's black/white incarceration ratios: immigrants were expanding the population base denominator of the black incarceration rate but not (yet) contributing in equal measure to the inmate numerator. Data to examine this theory properly are not available; Minnesota state and local police statistics do not report the citizenship, birthplace, or national origin of persons arrested. However, population data including place of birth are available by census tract, so an indirect assessment of the "immigrant effect" can be based on comparison of crime rates in neighborhoods with higher and lower proportions of native- and foreign-born blacks. Data from Minneapolis (where many of the recent black immigrants live) show that in 20 neighborhoods with above-average proportions of black residents, the proportion of African-born persons in the neighborhood was negatively correlated with reported violent crime rates in 2000, whereas the estimated proportion of native-born blacks in the neighborhood (total blacks minus African-born persons) was positively correlated with violent crime.[13]

---

[13] The model is based on neighborhoods (described in Minneapolis [2008*c*]) for which 2000 census tract data on place of birth (USCB 2008*e*) could be matched with police-reported crime data by precinct for that year (Minneapolis 2008*a*, 2008*b*; data were hand-tabulated for one neighborhood not included in the main data source). Such matching was available for 21 neighborhoods; of these, one downtown neighborhood of condominiums, offices, stores, bars, and sports centers (Minneapolis 2008*d*) was excluded because most of the violent crime there appears to be committed by (and against) nonresidents.

In bivariate analysis, the correlations between a neighborhood's Part I violent crime rate and the percentage of the population that is native-born black was +.441 ($p > .05$);

TABLE 6

Black/White Socioeconomic Disadvantage Ratios in 2000 and 2005 (Average) for States with the Highest and Lowest Prison-Jail Black/ White Disproportionality in 2005, and for Minnesota and the Entire United States (Black Rate as a Multiple of the White Rate)

	Minnesota	13 States with Highest Custody Rate Disparities	United States	13 States with Lowest Custody Rate Disparities
Percent age 25 and over less than high school graduate	2.34	1.79	1.85	1.60
Percent living in a different U.S. house in 1995	1.90	1.54	1.22	1.20
Percent unemployed, of population 16 and over	3.54	2.69	2.44	2.31
Percent unemployed, of labor force 16 and over	3.58	2.78	2.55	2.36
Median household income	.54*	.63*	.63*	.64*
Median family income	.48*	.59*	.60*	.62*
Per capita income	.53*	.58*	.58*	.59*
Percent of families below poverty	6.75	4.60	3.77	3.27
Percent of individuals below poverty	4.69	3.50	2.95	2.64

SOURCES.—USCB (2007a, 2007d).
NOTE.—Black and white race categories exclude Hispanics, for comparison with prisoner data.
* A higher number on this measure means less relative black disadvantage.

ii. *State-to-State Variations in Socioeconomic Disparity.*   The link between SES disparities and prison-jail disparities is corroborated by comparison of black-to-white SES disadvantage ratios in the states with the highest and lowest black/white incarceration ratios. Table 6 reports these SES ratios for Minnesota, the United States, and the highest and

---

for percentage African-born, the correlation was $-.351$ ($p > .05$). The strongest factor associated with violent crime rates in these neighborhoods was the unemployment rate ($r = +.518$, $p < .05$). When these three variables are put into a single model, only unemployment rate and African-born are significant (standardized beta $= +.827$, $p < .000$, and standardized beta $= -.743$, $p < .005$, respectively). But the African- and native-born variables are strongly and negatively correlated with each other ($r = +.591$, $p < .001$), which makes it difficult to assess their independent strengths. In separate multiple regression models of each variable with unemployment, both variables were significant, or nearly so, as predictors of Part I violent crime (for percentage African-born, standardized beta $= -.660$, $p < .001$; for percentage native-born, standardized beta $= +.378$, $p < .061$); unemployment remained significant in both models (standardized beta $= +.780$, $p < .000$, and standardized beta $= +.468$, $p < .024$, respectively).

lowest quartile of states in the most recent (2005) ranking of black/ white incarceration rate ratios (Mauer and King 2007, table 6). All but one of the high-ratio states are in the Northeast and upper Midwest, whereas 10 of the 13 low-ratio states are in the South. The 13 high-ratio states (in *decreasing* order of their 2005 black/white incarceration rate ratios) are Iowa, Vermont, New Jersey, Connecticut, Wisconsin, North Dakota, South Dakota, Rhode Island, New York, New Hampshire, Pennsylvania, Utah, and Minnesota. The 13 low-ratio states (in *increasing* order of their 2005 black/white ratios) are Georgia, Mississippi, Alabama, Arkansas, Tennessee, Idaho, Alaska, Oklahoma, Florida, South Carolina, Nevada, Louisiana, and Texas.[14]

The theory being tested here is that states with the highest black/ white incarceration ratios will have SES racial disparities greater than the national average, whereas the states with the lowest black-white incarceration ratios will have lower-than-average SES disparities. Accordingly, table 6 places the U.S. (national-average) rates in a middle column, between the high– and low–incarceration ratio states.[15] On every measure, the low-ratio states have black/white SES disparity ratios equal to or lower than the national average (because whites in these states are more disadvantaged than U.S. whites generally, because blacks in these states have a disadvantage equal to or less than that of U.S. blacks generally, or both). The SES-incarceration ratio link is less consistent for the high-ratio states. As predicted, blacks are relatively more transient (living in a different house) in these states and have higher unemployment and poverty rates. On some other SES measures (education and income levels) black/white disparities in these states are

[14] Washington, DC, is excluded from the high-ratio group because it is a city, not a state, and because the DC data cover only short-term prisoners (see BJS 2006, p. 11 n. c). Hawaii is excluded from the low-ratio group because that state has a unique racial composition (very few blacks and a very high proportion of Asians). Sorensen, Hope, and Stemen (2003, p. 76 n. 7) excluded Hawaii for similar reasons.

The 2005 SES data incorporated in table 6 are based on surveys, and some high- and low-ratio states had too few blacks to estimate black rates. Six high-ratio states reported 2005 black SES data: Connecticut, Minnesota, New Jersey, New York, Pennsylvania, and Wisconsin. Eleven low-ratio states (all but Alaska and Idaho) reported 2005 black SES data.

[15] Table 6 excludes Hispanics since the most recent state-by-state incarceration rate ratio data also exclude Hispanics from the race categories. Prison and jail populations reflect crimes committed and social disadvantages several years earlier, so this table uses the average of 2000 and 2005 SES measures, which yields a time lag of approximately 2.5 years between the dates of the SES averages and the 2005 incarceration rate data used to compute high- and low-ratio states. The 2000 and 2005 ratios show similar patterns, but most of the 2005 ratios are higher.

equal to or lower than those for the United States as a whole. Finally, it should be noted that Minnesota's black/white SES disadvantage ratios are the worst on every measure when compared to other high-ratio states, national rates, and the low-ratio states.

b. Location, Location, Location (of Residence).   Another reason why Minnesota blacks may have higher crime rates than blacks in other states, and much higher crime rates than Minnesota whites, has to do with where people of each race live. Minnesota's black population is concentrated in high-crime, urban neighborhoods, whereas in other states, particularly in the South, many blacks live in rural areas with lower crime rates. And Minnesota whites, like whites in most other states, tend to live in low-crime suburban and rural areas.

Victimization studies report crime in three locations—urban, suburban, and rural—with violent and property crime rates declining from the first to the third category (BJS 2007a, table 54). FBI "crimes-known" data are also reported for three locations—metropolitan statistical areas (MSAs), cities outside such areas, and "nonmetropolitan counties"—with the third category having the lowest rates for almost all crimes and each of the other two categories having the highest rates for certain types of crime. In 2005 MSAs had the highest rates for murder, robbery, assault, and motor vehicle theft. Cities outside any MSA had the highest rates for rape, larceny, and burglary (FBI 2008c, table 2).

Comparison of residential patterns by race with crime rates is seemingly complicated by the different geographic categories employed in the crime measures just described. Closer inspection reveals that the victim surveys and FBI crime reports both use versions of census-defined categories. Census Bureau population data are categorized, inter alia, by whether the location is within an MSA or not, with each of these two categories further subdivided: MSAs include "central city" and other areas; non-MSAs include urban and rural areas. The correspondence between victim survey, FBI, and Census of Population categories is shown in table 7. The table also shows, for Minnesota, the entire United States, and the southern region, the proportions of blacks and whites living in each crime rate area.

Sixty-three percent of Minnesota blacks live in the highest-crime area category used in victimization data (urban/central city area); this proportion is higher than for U.S. blacks (53 percent) and southern blacks (42 percent) and far higher than the proportions for Minnesota,

TABLE 7
Location of Residence in 2000, by Race and by Crime Data Categories: Percentage of Each Race Living in Each Geographic Area

	Minnesota		United States		South	
	Blacks	Whites	Blacks	Whites	Blacks	Whites
Total population	172,181	4,398,014	34,614,894	211,347,851	18,944,758	72,771,931
Victim survey categories:						
Urban (in MA, central city)	63.0%	15.4%	53.3%	24.2%	42.3%	22.9%
Suburban (in MA, not central city)	32.4%	53.3%	33.3%	53.6%	35.2%	51.0%
Rural (not in MA)	4.2%	31.4%	13.8%	22.2%	22.6%	26.1%
FBI (Uniform Crime Reports) categories:						
MSA (in MA, total)	96.6%	68.7%	86.2%	77.8%	77.4%	73.9%
Non-MSA city (not in MA, urban)	3.1%	11.5%	7.1%	8.6%	11.1%	8.8%
Nonmetro county (not in MA, rural)	1.1%	19.9%	6.6%	13.6%	11.5%	17.4%

SOURCE.—USCB (2007c).
NOTE.—MA = metropolitan area; MSA = metropolitan statistical area.

U.S., and southern whites (15, 24, and 23 percent, respectively). Conversely, almost no Minnesota blacks live in the lowest-crime areas; only 4 percent of blacks live in a rural/nonmetropolitan area, and 1 percent live in a nonmetro county, whereas substantial proportions of whites and non-Minnesota blacks (especially in the South) live in such areas.

The finding that Minnesota has particularly high racial disparity in location of residence is consistent with prior research examining regional patterns. Sorensen, Hope, and Stemen (2003, pp. 80–81) reported that the Midwest region had the greatest difference between the proportions of black and white residents living in urban areas (which they defined as areas having a population greater than 50,000 and a population density greater than 1,000 persons per square mile).

Bridges and Crutchfield (1988) found a significant relationship, independent of crime rates, between concentrations of blacks in inner-city areas and racially disparate prison populations. But as noted above, given the limited controls in these models for racial differences in offense rates and prior records, at least part of that relationship may have been due to the more direct connection between urban segregation and black crime rates. Bridges and Crutchfield also proposed a new segregation measure: percentage of blacks living in central city areas compared to the percentage of whites living there. By that measure, Minnesota's central city segregation ratio in 2000 was 4.1 : 1, the national ratio was 2.2 : 1, and for the southern region the ratio was 1.8 : 1.

Unfortunately for Minnesotans of all races, concentrations of race and poverty (and, thus, of crime) appear to be increasing. Minneapolis schools have recently become much more segregated by class and race: poverty enrollments rose from 43 to 66 percent between 1990 and 2000, and by 2003 almost half of reporting schools had nonwhite enrollments exceeding 80 percent (Orfield and Wallace 2007). Statewide, the proportion of Minnesota's black children attending schools that were 95–100 percent minority increased from zero in the 1993–94 school year to 12 percent in 2005–6; only five states had higher increases in this time period (*Minneapolis Star Tribune* 2007).[16]

---

[16] According to *Minneapolis Star Tribune* (2006), data gathered in 2002–3 showed that only 44 percent of Minnesota black students graduated from high school in 4 years, compared to 83 percent of the state's white students and a national average for black students of 52 percent. According to *Minneapolis Star Tribune* (2008a), in 2006–7 a black Minnesota student was about six times more likely than a white student to be suspended from school.

c. Racial Disproportionality in Murder Rates.   In addition to low SES and residence in high crime areas, murder rates provide a third measure that is disturbing in itself and that bears on the likelihood of high Minnesota black/white disparities in violent crime offending. In 2004 and 2005, a black Minnesotan's odds of being murdered were about 28 times higher than a white Minnesotan's (BJS [2007*b*], reporting number of homicides and percentage of homicide victims by race, for each state; these data, combined with census population data by race [USCB 2007*f*], yield estimated victimization rates per 100,000 population of each race).

For the nation as a whole in these two years, this ratio was about 6 : 1 (BJS 2007*d*). Given the predominantly intraracial nature of homicide (93 percent of U.S. black homicide victims in 2005 were killed by another black, excluding the 2 percent with assailant race unknown; FBI 2008*c*, table 5), high racial disparity in victimization rates implies highly disparate offense rates. And although murders are relatively infrequent for any race, this crime has a substantial impact on prison populations because of the long prison terms typically imposed. Moreover, the high rates of crime reporting, police clearance, and prosecution make murder a useful proxy for other violent crimes, which are not as reliably compared across jurisdictions (Zimring and Hawkins 1997, p. 41).

d. Racial Differences in Drug Use and Sale.   As shown in table 4, Minnesota's racial disproportionality in drug arrests is much lower than for violent crimes and is not as high relative to national black/white ratios (Minnesota's ratio for drug arrests is about two and a half times the national ratio, whereas its ratio for Part I violent crimes is four times greater). Nevertheless, it is important to assess the causes of drug crime arrest disparities. Drug offenders represent a substantial segment of Minnesota's state prison population (about one-fifth as of January 2008, down from one-fourth in 2004–5; Minnesota Department of Corrections 2008). Moreover, drug arrests are often more a reflection of law enforcement policies than of offense behavior: drug crime has few civilian witnesses and direct victims, so arrests are almost always the result of police decisions to target certain areas or suspects.

Since victimization data on the perceived race of offenders are unavailable for drug crimes, studies comparing drug arrest rates by race with estimated offense rates often estimate the latter by means of self-reported data on drug use. Such data have often been interpreted as showing that whites and blacks are about equal in their overall tendencies to use illegal drugs (Tonry 1995, pp. 108–10; Reiman 1998, p. 109; Cole 1999, p. 144; Mauer 1999, p. 147; Western 2006, p. 47). Data from the 2005 National Survey on Drug Use and Health tend to confirm that assessment (U.S. Department of Health and Human Services 2007b).

A number of studies have found, however, that drug use and abuse are positively correlated with neighborhood disadvantage and other social and psychological stressors that disproportionately afflict blacks (Boardman et al. 2001; Thomas 2007 [reviewing prior studies]; Williams and Latkin 2007). And although the reach of the 2005 National Survey is quite broad, sampling by residence to include children not in school and including homeless shelters, the survey did not count homeless persons who do not use shelters, and it also excluded persons in prisons, jails, and other institutional housing (U.S. Department of Health and Human Services 2006, p. 1). These excluded and underrepresented groups are likely to be disproportionately black and to be relatively high users of drugs. Furthermore, research suggests that blacks are more likely to underreport substance abuse (Kim, Fendrich, and Wisler [2000, pp. 429–30], also citing consistent prior studies). And although drug users tend to purchase from someone of their own race (Riley 1997), it remains possible that drug use patterns are not a reliable measure of drug trafficking[17] and, in particular, are not indicative of the kinds of public acts of sale, purchase, or possession that more readily allow the police to discover the violation and make an arrest. As Michael Tonry has observed, it is much easier for the police to make drug arrests in poor urban neighborhoods than in more affluent areas (1995, p. 106).

Although national data on drug use and abuse suggest some racial differences, they are probably not great enough to explain the substantial racial differences in U.S. arrest rates. Nationwide emergency room data indicate that blacks have higher rates of admissions for illegal-drug overdoses,[18] which suggests that blacks are using more dan-

[17] In 2005, almost one-fifth of drug arrests, nationwide and in the Midwest region, were for trafficking rather than possession (FBI 2008c). In 2004, 56 percent of felony drug convictions were for trafficking (BJS 2007c, p. 2), and presumably some additional cases of actual trafficking were plea-bargained down to possession.

[18] See U.S. Department of Health and Human Services (2007a, p. 23), showing that 32 percent of U.S. ER visits in 2005 for illicit drugs were made by non-Hispanic blacks, 54 percent by non-Hispanic whites, and 13 percent by Hispanics (excluding cases of unknown race and ethnicity, which were 13 percent of total visits). This source does not

gerous drugs, using them more heavily, or using them under more dangerous circumstances. The 2005 National Survey on Drug Use and Health also included data on self-reported sale of drugs and on the location and circumstances of drug purchases. Non-Hispanic blacks were twice as likely as non-Hispanic whites to report selling drugs six or more times within the last 12 months. Data on the location of drug purchases (reported only for marijuana) show that blacks often reported buying their drugs outdoors or in public buildings, whereas whites were much more likely to say they bought in a home, apartment, or dorm (U.S. Department of Health and Human Services 2007*b*; Tonry and Melewski 2008). In addition, whites often said they bought marijuana from a friend or relative; blacks were much more likely to say they bought from "someone I had just met or didn't know very well"—someone who is probably more likely to be an undercover police officer or informant. Another study (Riley 1997) found that arrested crack users were disproportionately black and were more likely to buy outdoors and from a number of suppliers.

Finally, several National Survey questions illustrate the high-crime nature of areas frequented by blacks and provide a measure of their greater exposure to being drawn into drug crime and undercover police enforcement. Blacks were more likely to report being "approached by someone selling illegal drugs in the past 30 days." For all drug types measured, blacks were more likely to say that it would be "fairly easy" or "very easy" for them to obtain the drug. The differences were small for LSD and marijuana, but for cocaine, crack, and heroin, blacks were much more likely to say the drugs would be fairly easy or very easy to obtain.

All the data summarized above are at the national level, and it is possible that racial patterns in Minnesota are different. But the limited data on Minnesota suggest higher drug use by most nonwhite race and ethnic groups.[19] And to the extent that higher rates of serious drug use

---

report ER visit rates per 100,000 population of each race, but non-Hispanic blacks are clearly disproportionately represented, since they were less than 13 percent of the total U.S. population in 2005. The disproportion was particularly high for cocaine, with blacks accounting for almost one-half of ER visits.

[19] See Council on Crime and Justice (2002, table 3), reporting that, while black and white self-reported past-year drug use was about the same in 1996–97 for cocaine, hallucinogens, stimulants, and sedatives, black rates were substantially higher for marijuana and "any drug." Drug use data from the Minnesota Student Surveys (Minnesota Departments 2007) show few consistent racial patterns, but there are very high nonresponse rates on all these questions.

and drug dealing reflect the stresses, frustrations, and temptations associated with socioeconomic deprivation and lack of opportunity (Boardman et al. 2001; Thomas 2007; Williams and Latkin 2007), Minnesota's higher-than-average socioeconomic racial disparities make it reasonable to assume that black/white disparities in drug use and drug dealing are greater in Minnesota than for the nation as a whole.

But is black drug use and trafficking conduct the most important factor behind the racial disproportionality in drug crime arrest rates shown in table 4? Or are these disparities primarily produced by law enforcement decisions to focus drug enforcement efforts on black suspects and black inner-city neighborhoods? The latter hypothesis is addressed below.

2. *Racial Differences in Crime Reporting.*   Racial differences in arrest rates across jurisdictions could also be caused in part by racial and geographic differences in crime reporting by victims. Perhaps Minnesota victims of crimes committed by blacks are particularly likely to report crime and urge the police to take action. Alternatively or in addition, perhaps victims of black crimes in other states are less likely to report and urge the police to make an arrest.

Unfortunately, there are no race-specific data by state or even by region on these matters. The available national data on crime reporting rates by race and by urban-suburban-rural area are not consistent with this theory: blacks and persons living in rural areas are actually slightly more likely to say they reported the crime to the police (BJS 2003, tables 2, 3). Of course, these national figures could very well conceal major local and regional racial variations in crime reporting by victims.

3. *Law Enforcement Policies or Biases.*   A third possible explanation for much higher black/white arrest disparities in Minnesota might be found in police practices. Perhaps Minnesota police overenforce the law in black neighborhoods and against black offenders, or police in other states engage in underenforcement.

Much attention has been given in recent years to instances of apparent racial profiling. A major study in Minnesota found that, in nearly every police jurisdiction examined, black and other nonwhite drivers were stopped at greater rates than whites (relative to the numbers of driving age persons of each race in that jurisdiction). Blacks were also searched in a higher percentage of stops, but the "hit rate" was lower. Blacks were less often found to be carrying weapons, drugs, or other contraband (Institute and Council 2003). In addition, other police practices used in Minnesota such as "Codefor," "Compstat," and similar "hot-spot" policing, while seemingly race neutral, are likely greatly to increase black arrest rates (Council on Crime and Justice 2007c, pp. 6–7). This occurs because blacks represent a high proportion of residents in the high-crime areas targeted by these policies. It is also possible that in some states, black arrest rates are artificially suppressed by police decisions not fully to enforce the law in black neighborhoods—a form of bias against black victims (Tonry 1995, p. 68; Natapoff 2006).

It is difficult to assess these patterns of possible police over- and underenforcement, even in a single jurisdiction, and to relate those patterns to racial disproportionality at later stages. Increased law enforcement is appropriate in high-crime areas, but how much of an increase is too much? It seems likely that the highly disproportionate traffic stops and searches in Minnesota are excessive relative to legitimate law enforcement needs; even if black suspects more often present proper grounds to stop and to search, the lower hit rate in searches of blacks suggests that police are exaggerating those grounds (hit rates should be approximately equal if police are stopping and searching the optimum numbers of each race).[20] But a search that yields no contraband is, for that reason, less likely to result in arrest, and fruitless searches do not, in themselves, directly contribute to racial disproportionality in arrests, convictions, and inmate populations. Of course arrests are often made without a successful search, or any search at all (e.g., if a records check reveals an open arrest warrant). Moreover, the arrests examined in the Minnesota traffic stops study were very racially disproportionate: the percentage of stops resulting in arrest was over twice as high for blacks as for whites (Institute and Council 2003, pp. 10, 15). But the Minnesota study, which was based on 65 jurisdictions representing over half the state population in 2002, produced a total of only about 8,620 arrests—less than 4 percent of the 220,850 arrests reported by Minnesota police in that year (BCA 2008). It is unknown how representative racial patterns in these traffic stop arrests were of all arrests in all jurisdictions.

Drug enforcement is an area in which law enforcement policy decisions can very easily produce racial disparities unjustified by differences in offense rates. Drug arrests are often made in disadvantaged,

---

[20] But see Harcourt (2007, pp. 112–25), arguing that a policy of maintaining equal hit rates across racial groups is not optimal in the long term.

inner-city neighborhoods in which many of the buyers, and most of the sellers, are nonwhite (Johnson et al. 1990; Tonry 1995, p. 106; Hagedorn 1998; Western 2006, p. 37). It would be much more difficult, expensive, and politically sensitive to attempt serious drug enforcement in predominantly white and middle-class communities. However, political and operational convenience is not a sufficient justification for policies with such a dramatic potential for a racially disparate impact. It might be argued, in support of the current policies of highly selective and racially targeted drug enforcement, that drug possession and trafficking in public places, especially in disadvantaged neighborhoods, cause more social harm than the same acts done in private. But current policies have not stopped the drug trade in these neighborhoods.

Comparison of over- and underenforcement levels across state boundaries raises further difficulties. Perhaps a preliminary assessment could be made by examining data on which jurisdictions have implemented hot-spot policing programs. Another possible indirect measure might be the racial composition of police forces (on the theory that departments with a high proportion of nonwhite officers, relative to the size of the nonwhite population or the size of the police force, are more likely to attempt serious and sustained law enforcement in nonwhite neighborhoods and less likely to make discriminatory case-level policing decisions). Comparison of police staffing levels (officers per capita) might provide a third indirect measure of enforcement levels across jurisdictions.

4. *Summary.*   Much more study is needed both on bias in law enforcement and on the underlying causes of crimes by whites and blacks. These are critical problems in Minnesota. There is evidence of racial profiling in Minnesota traffic stops and a strong possibility of bias in drug enforcement policies. There is also reason to think that the criminogenic factors that cause racial disparities in criminal behavior are quite concentrated and are growing worse. Future demographic shifts may further aggravate social and criminal justice disparities in Minnesota. The number of whites in the high crime ages of 18–30 is expected to decline, whereas the numbers of blacks and other minorities in this age bracket will continue to increase (Council on Crime and Justice 2007a, pp. 47–48). And if a "first-generation-immigrant" effect has recently caused black per capita arrest and inmate rates to decline, this pattern may disappear or even be reversed in the next generation. Indeed, there are indications that this change is already happening in

Minneapolis, where African-immigrant communities have recently experienced a substantial increase in murders and other violent crimes (*Minneapolis Star Tribune* 2008*b*).

V. Racial Disproportionality in Conviction Rates, Sentencing, and Postsentencing Decisions

Currently available data do not permit us to examine in detail the steps from arrest to the filing of charges and from filing to conviction. Subsection A below presents the data available, by race, on conviction rates per capita and on the relationship between arrest and conviction, by offense. Subections B–D summarize what we know about how Minnesota sentencing laws and guidelines, and their application, contribute to racially disparate custody-sentence rates and prison and jail populations. Subsection E briefly examines the limited available data on postsentencing decisions. Subsection F summarizes the racial disproportionality data from subsections A–E, combines them with arrest data from Section IV, and compares disproportionality ratios at multiple stages of the criminal process (table 10).

A. Felony Conviction Rates per Capita, by Race

The substantial racial disproportionality seen in Minnesota arrest rates is still present when we examine rates and ratios based on felony convictions (offense-specific data on misdemeanor convictions are not available). When guidelines commission conviction data for 2001–5 are pooled (MSGC [2006*a*, table 4] and similar tables in published data reports for earlier years), the ratio of black to white per capita felony conviction rates (using population bases lagged 1 year)[21] was 9.3 : 1. This figure is approximately the same as or lower than most of the arrest ratios reported in Section IV and table 4 above. For the broadest arrest measure—all Part I crimes plus drugs—the 2000–2004 Minnesota black/white arrest ratio was 9.5 : 1. However, arrest data include Hispanics in the race categories, whereas conviction data exclude them. If Hispanics were likewise included in computing black/white conviction ratios, the 5-year average conviction ratio would be somewhat

---

[21] A 1-year time lag in the conviction rate population base (and also the 1-year lag between arrest and conviction data) provides the best fit with guidelines commission data: in recent years, the average delay between date of offense and date of sentencing has been 10–11 months.

lower, probably around 8.9 : 1 (based on 2005 commission data, which separately categorized offenders by race and by Hispanic ethnicity). (These figures and other key findings on disproportionality ratios at various stages of the criminal process are summarized in table 10 and subsec. F below.)

In short, it appears that racial disproportionality declines somewhat between the stages of arrest and felony conviction, at least if Part I plus drug arrests are a suitable proxy for all felony arrests (arrest statistics do not distinguish between felony- and misdemeanor-level arrests, and several important arrest data categories [Part I property crimes, drug crimes] include a substantial number of misdemeanor arrests). Offense-specific comparisons, discussed below, support the conclusion that racial disproportionality in Minnesota declines between arrest and conviction, unlike the national pattern of increasing disparity, shown in table 1.

As was also shown in table 1, Minnesota's black/white conviction ratios are much higher than the U.S. average. The estimated Minnesota black/white felony conviction ratio of 8.8 : 1 for 2002–4 (including Hispanics; rate bases lagged 1 year) is more than twice the national ratio of 4.0 : 1.[22]

More precise comparison of disparities at the arrest and conviction stages cannot be done without collecting race-specific data on how arrests are initially charged by prosecutors, and how these charges change between filing and conviction. However, we can gain a rough idea of how charges change from arrest to conviction (while also clarifying the arrest vs. conviction ratio comparisons above) by comparing adult arrest rates from the BCA (2008) with felony conviction data from the guidelines commission (e.g., MSGC 2004), by race and offense (recognizing, of course, that BCA and commission offense categories are not identical). These comparisons are based on the following MSGC conviction-offense categories, all of which have fairly direct counterparts in BCA data, and most of which (all but drug crimes) involve behavior usually charged only at the felony level: murder and

---

[22] See BJS (2004, table 5; 2007c, table 2.1). Each source reports the percentages of blacks and whites (including Hispanics) among estimated total felony convictions in 2002 and 2004, respectively. National per capita conviction rates equal these percentages multiplied by total convictions and divided by the estimated U.S. population of each race (USCB 2007e) on July 1 of the same year for unlagged bases and July 1 of the prior year for lagged bases. The ratios of black and white lagged-base conviction rates are 3.9 : 1 for 2002 and 4.1 : 1 for 2004.

TABLE 8

Estimated White and Black Arrest-to-Conviction Retention
Rates in Minnesota, by Offense: 2000–2003 Felony
Convictions as a Percentage of 1999–2002 Adult Arrests

Offense	Retention Rate by Race*	
	Whites (%)	Blacks (%)
Murder and manslaughter	81	76
Criminal sexual conduct	36	31
Robbery	44	32
Felony assault	22	18
Subtotal (Part I violent crimes)	30	25
Burglary	49	39
Drug crimes	17	22
Total for all crimes above	23	24

Sources.—MSGC (2004) (and similar guidelines data files on convictions
in 2000, 2001, and 2002); BCA (2008). Retention rates for later years cannot
be computed because of problems in matching arrest and conviction data; see
the text.

* Arrest data include Hispanics in the race categories. Conviction data race
categories in the source exclude Hispanics; Hispanic convictions have been
allocated to the white and black categories according to data on known ethnicity
from 2005 (the earliest year for which separate race and ethnicity data are
reported).

first-degree manslaughter; criminal sexual conduct, first through fourth
degree; robbery (simple and aggravated); assault, first through third
degree; burglary, first through third degree; and controlled substance
(drug) crimes, first through fifth degree plus "other drug" crimes. The
corresponding BCA arrest categories are murder and nonnegligent
manslaughter, rape plus "other sex offenses" (most of which are probably statutory rape), robbery, aggravated assault, burglary, and "narcotics."

The results of these comparisons are shown in table 8. Arrest data
for 1999–2002 are compared with conviction data for 2000–2003 (1
year later than the arrest data). (The comparison ends with 2002 arrest
data because Minnesota data for 2003 and 2004 do not include arrests
in St. Paul, the state's second-largest city, and it is not possible to
identify and exclude St. Paul convictions in guidelines conviction data.)
As shown in the table, black arrest-to-conviction "retention" rates
(convictions as a percentage of adult arrests) are somewhat lower than
white retention rates for violent crimes and for burglary but are higher
for drug crimes. However, the latter offense category is the only one

shown in the table for which arrest data include misdemeanor crimes (mainly possession of small amounts of marijuana).[23] A lower white retention rate could be due to more frequent white drug arrests involving misdemeanor charges. Alternatively, the lower white retention rate could be due to prosecutorial charging policies if whites are favored in some way or if more lenient charging policies are applied to all offenders in (some) jurisdictions with higher proportions of white drug offenders (a third possibility, overcharging of whites at the arrest stage, seems less likely).

As for the lower black retention rates for burglary and the four violent crimes listed in table 8, this could result from overcharging of blacks at the arrest stage, the inability or unwillingness of prosecutors to obtain felony convictions against black offenders, or charging policies that are race neutral but have racially disparate impacts (e.g., if more lenient charging policies are applied in jurisdictions with higher proportions of black offenders).

Again, these comparisons are very approximate, given the unknowable differences in the categorization of crimes in arrest and conviction data. But the lower black retention rates are consistent with earlier studies in the state's largest county (Hennepin), finding that blacks had higher rates of postarrest dismissal (Minnesota Task Force 1993, pp. 11–12). Clearly, arrest and charging practices are an important area for further, in-depth research.

B. Recommended Guidelines Sentences by Race

Guidelines recommendations as to prison commitment and prison duration have a major impact on the racial composition of prisons (and, to a lesser extent, jails). Guidelines policy emphasizes the use of prison beds for serious crimes (especially crimes of violence and sexual abuse) and for offenders convicted of less serious crimes but with substantial prior-conviction records (MSGC 2008*b*). These priorities have a disproportionately severe impact on people of color, especially blacks. In 2005, 39 percent of black offenders had recommended executed prison sentences under the guidelines, versus 25 percent for whites (and 31 percent for Hispanics, 33 percent for Asians, and 35 percent for Native Americans). Similar racial disproportionality in prison commitment

---

[23] Minn. Stat. sec. 152.027, subdiv. 3: possession of more than 1.4 grams and no more than 42.5 grams of marijuana in a motor vehicle; classified as a misdemeanor; subdiv. 4: possession of no more than 42.5 grams of marijuana, a petty misdemeanor.

recommendations is found in other years; when these data are converted into per capita rates (again using population bases lagged 1 year), the average black/white ratio of recommended executed prison sentences in 2001–5 is 13.6 : 1. Thus, racial disproportionality increases substantially when we move from conviction measures (with an average lagged ratio of 9.3 : 1 in these years) to measures that focus on offenders recommended for prison commitment (both ratios are based on rates excluding Hispanics).

The two principal factors determining these guidelines recommendations are the conviction offense severity level and the offender's prior conviction record (criminal history score). Of these, racial differences are much greater for criminal history. For example, in 2005 the average offense severity scores for blacks and whites were 3.92 and 3.78, respectively, but black and white average criminal history scores were 2.20 and 1.48. The difference in black and white criminal history scores was apparently due to actual prior convictions, not multiple current offenses (even though the latter are counted as criminal history when offenders are sentenced concurrently on multiple counts). There were few differences between blacks and whites in the average number of counts reported on guidelines sentencing worksheets.

Differences between black and white offense severity and criminal history scores were similar in earlier years, but in some years (e.g., 2003) the white average severity score was higher. Racial differences are generally greater at the highest severity levels, but the differences go in both directions, depending on the year. In 2001, 2004, and 2005, a higher percentage of blacks were convicted at a severity level for which an executed prison sentence is recommended even for offenders with no criminal history (level 7 and higher in 2001–2; level 8 and higher in 2003–5), but in 2002 and 2003 a higher proportion of whites were convicted at these high levels.

In most years, black criminal history scores are higher within all major offense types (violent, property, drug, other), but the disparities tend to be highest for drug offenders. In general, blacks were not more likely than whites to have a juvenile history point or points.[24] They were more likely, however, to have a custody status point (committing

[24] For both blacks and whites in 2005, 5 percent of offenders received a juvenile point or points. But among offenders legally eligible (aged 24 or less on the date of the offense), blacks were slightly more likely to receive points (15 percent of blacks vs. 13 percent of whites).

the current offense while under supervision or in custody for an earlier offense: 41 percent vs. 34 percent for whites), a misdemeanor point (11 percent vs. 8 percent), and a higher prior-felony contribution to their criminal history scores (mean of 2.01 points vs. 1.29 for whites) (criminal history prior-felony "points" are weighted according to their guidelines severity level).

In addition to having higher average offense severity and criminal history scores, blacks are also more likely to be found to have used or possessed a dangerous weapon or be otherwise subject to a mandatory prison term. In 2005, for example, 7 percent of black offenders and 4 percent of white offenders fell below the disposition line but nevertheless had a recommended prison term because of a mandatory minimum statute.

Several differences between black and white offenders thus contribute to the higher proportion of blacks with recommended prison terms, but criminal history is the most important factor. An example, using 2005 data, illustrates the relative contribution of racial differences in offense severity, criminal history, and eligibility for a mandatory prison term. These three presumptive-commit factors correspond to three groups of offenders: (1) high-severity offenders (in 2005, those convicted at offense severity level 8 or higher) for whom prison is recommended even at zero criminal history; (2) high–criminal history offenders (those convicted at lower severity levels who, because of their criminal history score, are in a grid cell above the disposition line); and (3) offenders below the disposition line who nevertheless have a recommended prison term because of a mandatory minimum statute. The relative contribution of differences in offense severity, criminal history, and mandatory minimum statutes can be estimated by comparing the number of black offenders who fall into each of these three groups with the lower number that would be there using the proportion of whites who fall into each group (e.g., white percentage at severity level 8 or higher multiplied by the number of blacks sentenced that year). The results for each group are as follows: (1) high offense severity: 65 additional black offenders recommended for prison; (2) high criminal history: 349 additional black offenders; (3) mandatory minimum statute: 115 additional black offenders, for a total of 529 additional black offenders recommended for prison. Thus, high criminal history accounts for about two-thirds of the black/white difference in recommended-prison rates, high severity for 12 percent, and mandatory minimum statutes for 22 percent (and some of these mandatories are based on repeat offending).

Other researchers have noted the disparate racial impact of criminal history in sentencing guidelines systems (Tonry 1995, pp. 168–69; 1996, p. 57). Indeed, it appears that in most states—with or without guidelines—black offenders have more serious prior conviction records. For example, among felony defendants prosecuted in 2002 in a sample of the 75 largest counties, blacks were 40 percent more likely than whites to have a prior felony conviction, 79 percent more likely to have a prior violent-felony conviction, and 89 percent more likely to have previously served a prison term (BJS 2008b). The racially disparate effect of criminal history on sentencing severity probably accounts for much of the unexplained increase in racial disproportionality that previous studies found when comparing arrest data with prison inmate stocks (Blumstein 1982, 1993; Langan 1985).

C. Guidelines Departure Decisions

There are two kinds of departures from recommended guidelines sentences: durational departures from the length of the recommended prison term and dispositional departures from the recommendation as to execution or suspension ("stay") of the prison term. Only dispositional departures appear to involve potential racial disproportionality.

1. *Durational Departures.* In 2005 and many prior years, blacks had higher rates of both upward and downward durational departure, and this was true on both stayed and executed prison terms. Since most stayed prison terms are not revoked, the remaining analysis here focuses on executed prison terms. In such cases, downward departures are more common than upward departures (the former are from two to five times more frequent, depending on the year), so it seems likely that the combined effect of upward and downward departures is an overall (net) mitigation of the recommended term, and one that favors blacks more than whites. This is borne out by computing the difference (positive or negative) between the recommended prison term and the actual prison term for all offenders given an executed prison sentence; in 2005 the average net change was -4.3 months for black offenders and -3.0 months for whites.

Given these results, I do not further analyze durational departure decisions. Statistical analysis of durational departures is problematic in any case because such departures are mostly based on aggravating and mitigating offense details that are not captured in annual guidelines data sets. Such details have been included only in special samples collected in the early 1980s. Those samples revealed that cases of blacks and other nonwhite offenders more often had aggravating factors justifying an upward durational departure (MSGC 1984, pp. 66–67).

2. *Dispositional Departures.*   Upward dispositional departures are infrequent; 5–6 percent of offenders with a recommended stay are given an executed prison term, and many of these are agreed to by the defendant, usually because he or she is already in prison or is going to prison on other charges (MSGC 2006*a*, p. 29). Moreover, in recent years upward dispositional departure rates for blacks have been equal to or lower than those for whites.

Downward dispositional departures (a stayed sentence instead of the recommended prison term) are another matter. In most years the departure rate (as a percentage of offenders with recommended prison terms) has been lower for blacks than for whites—in some years, substantially lower. For example, in 2004 the downward dispositional departure rate was 39 percent for whites and 31 percent for blacks.

Over the past 15 years I have constructed a series of multivariate models examining the effect of race and other factors on downward dispositional departure decisions in years in which the apparent (bivariate) black versus white disproportionality was particularly great. In logistic regression models of 1987 and 1989 cases (Frase 1993*a*) and of 2000 and 2001 cases (Frase 2005*a*), race was not a statistically significant predictor of a prison sentence.[25] As shown in table 9, the same was true in 2005: after other legal and extralegal factors were taken into account, race was not a significant predictor of an executed prison sentence for presumptive (recommended) prison-commit white and black defendants (moreover, the nonsignificant effect of race was negative; blacks were *less* likely to receive a prison sentence, after control-

[25] But see Minnesota Task Force (1993, pp. 53–56, app. D), which finds statistically significant race effects in three of eight models of sentences imposed from 1986 to 1990 (combined). The four crimes analyzed were criminal sexual conduct, aggravated robbery (bodily harm or use of a dangerous weapon), second-degree assault (dangerous weapon), and other crimes involving a dangerous weapon. For offenders with no criminal history, black downward departure rates were significantly lower than white rates for one of these crimes (assault); for offenders with some criminal history, blacks rates were significantly lower in two offense categories (robbery and sex crimes). However, the four "some history" models lump together minor and very serious criminal histories, and none of the eight models examined the other independent variables included in the author's research, summarized in the text.

TABLE 9

Logistic Regression for Presumptive-Commit White and Black Defendants Sentenced in 2005
Dependent Variable: PRISON; 0 = No, 1 = Executed Prison Term

Independent Variable	Direction of Effect	Significance Level	Odds Ratio
Attempt crime	+	.0005	2.552
Offense severity	+	.0005	1.574
Custody status point	+	.0005	1.618
Other criminal history	+	.0005	2.593
Male offender	+	.0005	1.570
Black offender	−	.205	.905
Convicted by trial	+	.0005	4.227
Dangerous weapon in cell above the disposition line	+	.015	1.424
Dangerous weapon in cell below the disposition line	−	.0005	.542
DWI crime	−	.0005	.470
Constant	−	.0005	.174

Source.—MSGC (2006*b*).

Note.—Independent variables are defined and coded as follows (see the text): Attempt crime (0 = no, 1 = conviction offense involved an attempt rather than a completed offense). Offense severity: natural log transformation of guidelines severity level (original scoring: 1 = low, 11 = high). Custody status point (0 = no, 1 = defendant's criminal history score included a custody status point). Other criminal history: natural log transformation of criminal history score (without custody status; 0 = low score). Male offender (0 = female, 1 = male). Black offender (0 = white, 1 = African American). Convicted by trial (0 = defendant pled guilty; 1 = defendant pled not guilty and was found guilty at trial). Dangerous weapon in cell above the disposition line (0 = no, 1 = defendant found to have used/possessed weapon). Dangerous weapon in cell below the disposition line (0 = no, 1 = defendant found to have used/possessed weapon). DWI crime (0 = no, 1 = defendant convicted of felony drunk driving). "Direction of effect" indicates whether that variable is positively or negatively correlated with the dependent variable. "Significance level" measures the statistical significance of the findings with respect to that variable. For example, the figure .015 reported for "dangerous weapon in cell above the disposition line" means that the probability is 1.5 percent that the positive relationship (direction of effect) reported for that variable is due to chance. "Odds" ratio measures the strength of the relationship between that independent variable and the dependent variable; the value of the odds ratio shows the effect that a one-unit increase in the former has on the latter, after controlling for other variables in the model. For example, the figure 4.227 reported for "convicted by trial" means that the odds of receiving a prison sentence are 4.227 times (322.7 percent) higher if the offender is convicted at trial (coded as 1) than if the offender pleads guilty (coded as 0).

ling for other sentencing factors).[26] However, race does appear to have been a significant factor in some judicial districts in some years.[27] And without more detailed data and more elaborate statistical analysis we cannot rule out the possibility of compensating biases, for example, if some blacks benefit from generally more lenient sentencing in urban courts or from bias against black victims, whereas other blacks (those with white victims or in other parts of the state) receive harsher treatment.

These models assume that there is no bias built in to rules and decisions that determine the presumptive sentence itself. There is certainly room for debate about whether criminal history should receive so much weight under the guidelines, given the disparate impact this factor has on black (and other nonwhite) offenders. Further research is also needed on current and prior law enforcement, charging, and plea bargaining decisions that affect an offender's conviction offense, criminal history score, and other guidelines rules. And although Minnesota no longer punishes crack cocaine offenses more severely than powder, there may be other questionable sentencing laws and guide-

---

[26] Multiple-regression models assume that each of the independent variables is normally distributed around its mean, but distributions of guidelines severity ranks and criminal history scores are strongly skewed to the low end. Natural logarithmic transformations are applied to these variables to reduce their skew and make the data more consistent with model assumptions.

The curious finding that defendants convicted of attempt are more likely to receive the recommended executed prison term might be explained in several ways: these cases may reflect more serious potential harms; attempt requires proof of specific intent, whereas many other crimes do not; or some of these cases may have been completed crimes that were plea-bargained down to attempt (after which the court saw little need for further mitigation).

The model described in the text and table 9 includes two illegitimate variables in addition to race: method of conviction (plea vs. trial) and defendant gender. But when one or both of these variables are deleted, the effect and significance levels of the other variables change very little (and offender race, still negative in sign, has an even lower effect and significance level).

[27] For example, in a 2004 model (results not shown here) of seven of the state's 10 judicial districts, race was highly significant ($p < .0005$). However, the race effect was less than for many other independent variables in the model: being black rather than white increased the odds of receiving a prison term by 62 percent, whereas pleading guilty increased the odds by 425 percent, and for three other variables the odds increases were over 100 percent. This seven-district model excluded Hennepin County and two other districts lacking bivariate racial disproportionality in 2004 (i.e., there was no difference in the downward departure rates for blacks and whites in those districts). Those three districts accounted for 44 percent of the state's presumptive-commit white and black defendants in 2004. The model used the same 10 independent variables as the 2005 model whose results are shown in table 9; all nine of the other independent variables were also significant at $p < .0005$ except weapon above ($p < .002$).

lines rules that have a strong disparate impact on blacks and other minorities.

For blacks and whites, in every year, downward dispositional departures greatly outnumber upward departures, so the net effect of these departures, for both races, is that the number of prison sentences imposed is lower than the number of recommended prison sentences. Moreover, this net reduction in the number of prison commitments favors blacks: in 2001–5, the net decrease in the number of prison sentences represented 5.4 percent of white convictions, compared with a net decrease of 8.4 percent for black convictions. There are two reasons for this seeming anomaly: the higher downward dispositional departure rate for whites applies to a much lower proportion of all white offenders (since fewer whites have recommended prison sentences), so the number of downward departures as a percentage of all convicted offenders is lower for whites than it is for blacks; upward dispositional departure rates are the same or higher for whites, and these rates apply to a relatively high proportion of all white offenders, so the number of upward departures, as a percentage of all convicted offenders, is higher for whites.

D. Executed Prison and Jail Sentences

The cumulative effects of racial differences in conviction rates per capita, in guidelines prison recommendations and in guidelines departure decisions, can be seen in the ratio of black and white per capita rates of executed prison sentences. In the 5-year period 2001–5, the average ratio of black and white prison sentence rates per capita (again, using population bases lagged 1 year) was 13.3 : 1 (MSGC [2006a, table 26] and similar tables in the annual data reports for earlier years; USCB 2007f). This ratio is slightly lower than the black/white ratio for recommended executed prison sentences in these years (13.6 : 1) because of the net effects of upward and downward dispositional departures that favor blacks. But both of these ratios are significantly higher than the 9.3 : 1 black/white ratio for felony convictions. Again, the principal source of the increase in racial disproportionality from conviction to sentencing appears to be racial differences in average criminal history scores, combined with the heavy weight these scores have in determining which offenders are recommended to receive executed prison terms.

Minnesota's substantial increase in disparity between conviction and prison sentencing is greater than the average for the nation as a whole. As shown in table 2, the national estimates, based on felony convictions in 2002 and 2004, show black/white disparity ratios increasing by 15 percent (from 4.0 : 1 for conviction rates to 4.6 : 1 for prison sentence rates). In the same 3-year period, the increase in Minnesota was 38 percent (rising from 8.8 : 1 to 12.1 : 1). From averaged 5-year ratios derived from the 2001–5 data reported above (but adjusted to include estimates of white and black Hispanic offenders, since the U.S. data include Hispanics), Minnesota's black/white ratios increased by 40 percent (from 8.9 : 1 for conviction rates to 12.5 : 1 for prison sentence rates).

There are no substantial racial differences in the duration of executed prison terms. Although blacks have slightly longer average terms in most years (46.8 months in 2005 vs. 43.4 months for whites), the reverse is true within guidelines grid cells (i.e., controlling for conviction offense severity and criminal history score). In 2005, for example, in the 67 grid cells containing both whites and blacks with executed terms, the average white prison term was higher in 45 cells, the average black term was higher in 19 cells, and in three cells average black and white durations were about equal. These patterns occur because the net mitigating effect of upward and downward durational departures favors black defendants more than whites.

Except for a small number of cases, jail sentences are not regulated under the guidelines. Courts have discretion to impose a jail term of up to 1 year as a condition of felony probation. The average jail term imposed is about 3.5 months. Fewer blacks receive jail sentences: 63.3 percent of black offenders sentenced in 2001–5 compared to 69.6 percent of whites. The ratio of black and white jail sentence rates per capita in the same time period was "only" 8.5 : 1 (vs. 13.3 : 1 for prison sentences; both ratios use 1-year lagged population bases). However, since an offender can receive only a prison or a jail sentence, but not both, the higher jail sentence rate for whites is largely the result of the lower white prison sentence rate: 20.4 percent in 2001–5 versus 29.1 percent for blacks.

When the prison and jail sentence data for 2001–5 are combined, the proportion of blacks receiving a custody sentence was slightly higher: 92.3 percent versus 90.0 percent for whites. The ratio of (lagged) black and white custody sentence rates per capita in that 5-year period was 9.6 : 1. And although the average duration of custody terms is about the same (slightly longer average prison terms for blacks and slightly longer average jail terms for whites), the average duration of custody sentences (prison or jail) imposed on blacks is substantially longer since a higher proportion of them are sentenced to prison. For example, in 2005 the average custody sentence duration for blacks was 15.7 months, but only 11.0 months for whites.

E. Postsentencing Decisions

Decisions to revoke probation or postprison conditional release, to delay prison or jail release, or to jail released offenders pending revocation hearings all have impacts on the racial composition of inmate populations. The impact of revocation proceedings needs to be studied by examining "flow" data on convicted offenders received in jails and prisons, by race and offense; but no such data are currently available for jails, and only limited published data are available for prisons. There are also no published data on decisions that delay prison or jail release by denying good-conduct credits. However, a preliminary assessment of potential postsentencing disparities can be made by combining commission data on prison-sentenced offenders with two later measures: flow data on offenders admitted to prison and data on prison stocks. Both of these measures reflect the effects of revocations to prison, and prison stocks also reflect decisions to delay release (in Minnesota, these decisions almost always involve denial of good-conduct credits, since very few offenders are subject to parole release discretion).

1. *Admissions to Prison.*   Prison admissions data are available from the National Corrections Reporting Program [NCRP] (BJS 2007e), but data for the most recent year (2003) appear to be incomplete,[28] so the analysis below is based on data for 2000, 2001, and 2002. Using these data, combined with data from the guidelines commission, we can estimate the numbers of offenders of each race whose probation or postprison release was revoked during that 3-year period.

The NCRP reports three categories of prison admissions (excluding transfers): "court commitment," "mandatory parole release—new sentence," and "mandatory parole release—no new sentence." The first

---

[28] In the NCRP data for 2003, there are over 700 fewer admissions to Minnesota prisons than are shown in summary data available from the Minnesota Department of Corrections (2008), whereas for other recent years the NCRP and department totals are very similar.

category is composed of direct sentences to prison (including life sentences, which were not included in guidelines sentencing data prior to 2006) as well as revocations of probation. The second and third categories involve admissions of offenders who were sent back to prison after being placed on postprison supervised release (their prior release was "mandatory" in the sense that, under the guidelines, a prisoner must be released when his or her maximum term, reduced by earned good time credits, has been served). Cases in the third category are analogous to parole revocations for so-called technical violations (some of these offenders could have been prosecuted for new crimes but were not). Cases in the second category involve new convictions and are also included in guidelines sentencing data. Adding the first and second NCRP categories thus yields the total number of direct prison sentences plus probation revocations. If, for each race, we subtract from this total the number of direct prison sentences shown in guidelines sentencing data (plus the life sentences shown in the NCRP data), the difference is the number of probation revocations. For 2000–2002 combined, 1,146 probation revocations were of non-Hispanic whites and 683 were of non-Hispanic blacks.

These estimated probation revocation totals indicate that there were 1.68 white revocations for every black revocation. This ratio is higher ("whiter") than the totals for executed prison sentences in these years (1.54 white prison sentences for every black prison sentence); thus probation revocations have a tendency to lower the black/white ratio among prison inmates. However, the higher proportion of whites among revocations results in part from the fact that a much higher proportion of whites receive probationary sentences (a consequence of the higher rates of prison sentences for blacks, noted earlier). Actual revocation rates by race cannot be computed because of the lack of suitable statewide data on the number of felony offenders under supervision, but the rate can be estimated using as a base the number of probation sentences imposed for each race. A 1-year time lag is used (i.e., probation sentences in 1999–2001) since probation is rarely immediately revoked; on this basis, the estimated probation revocation rates in these years were 7.0 percent for whites and 10.3 percent for blacks.

The third category of NCRP data (mandatory parole release—no new sentence) represents offenders whose parole or other postprison release was revoked without a new conviction because of a violation of release conditions. From pooled data for 2000–2002, there were 1,566 revocations of non-Hispanic whites and 1,586 revocations of non-Hispanic blacks. Given that the number of whites in Minnesota prisons is considerably greater than the number of blacks, it is immediately apparent that the black postprison revocation rate is much higher than the white rate. Offenders released from prison in preceding years provide the best available base for computing revocation rates. The most appropriate time lag appears to be either 1 or 2 years,[29] and both time lags yield the same estimated postprison revocation rates: 32 percent for non-Hispanic whites and 41 percent for non-Hispanic blacks.

Thus, it appears that black revocation rates are higher for both probationers and those on postprison release. At least some of this difference may be due to black offenders having higher criminal history scores or more serious current conviction offenses. But it would not be surprising to find biased or unexplained, racially disparate revocation decisions, given that these decisions are very weakly regulated under Minnesota's guidelines and related statutes and are probably based heavily on individualized assessments of offender risk. Further research is needed on these decisions to clarify the nature of and justification for disparity in revocation rates.

The much larger numbers and proportions of white offenders on probation mean that, despite higher black revocation rates, the probation revocation process brings relatively more whites to prison (compared with direct commitments at the time of initial sentencing), thus tending to reduce racial disproportionality in prison populations. But postprison revocation has the opposite effect because of the higher rate of black revocations combined with the large numbers of blacks among prisoners and prison releasees.

2. *Prison Stocks.*   The combined impact of the offsetting revocation effects as well as the effects, if any, of racial differences in the award of good-conduct credits can be roughly assessed by comparing executed prison sentences with prison stocks. A time lag of several years must be applied, since inmates were often sentenced in a prior year. Indeed, the date of initial sentencing can be many years earlier in the case of offenders who enter prison upon revocation (representing over

[29] The average executed prison term is about 48 months, yielding an average postprison supervised release term of 16 months if all good-conduct credits are earned (most probably are; see MSGC 1984, p. 101); however, some offenders are subject to longer supervised release terms (Frase 2005*a*, p. 139).

40 percent of prison admissions each year; Frase 2005*a*); such offenders either were placed on probation and later revoked or were sent to prison, released after serving at least two-thirds of their sentence, and then revoked and reimprisoned.

A 2.5-year time lag is used between sentencing and prison population data;[30] the comparison is between initial executed prison sentences in 2001–5 and prison stocks at year end in 2003–7. To permit comparisons to data in earlier parts of this essay, black and white sentencing and inmate data are again expressed in terms of the ratio of black and white per capita rates. The same population bases (2000–2004) are used for both sentencing and imprisonment rates, since these are assumed to be the same inmates at different times. Prison sentencing rate bases are thus lagged 1 year, and prison stock rate bases are lagged 3.5 years. Prison sentence data are further adjusted to include estimated numbers of Hispanic inmates (since prison stock data include them).

The results are as follows: the average estimated black/white prison sentence ratio for 2001–5 is 12.5 : 1, and the average black/white prison stocks ratio for year end 2003–7 is 12.9 : 1. Thus, it appears that the opposing effects of probation and postprison revocation processes, combined with the effects of decisions delaying prison release by denying good-conduct credit, are adding a modest increment of disparity to what was present at the time of initial sentencing. However, if revocation rates were not higher for blacks, such disproportionality should have *declined* as a result of the higher numbers of white offenders given probationary sentences and thereby placed at risk of revocation.

F. Summary: Comparing Disproportionality Measures from Arrest through Prison and Jail Stocks

Table 10 summarizes the data presented in subsections A–E above and in Section IV. Because of limits on availability and compatibility of data, the table separates the arrest-to-conviction stage from later stages and reports black/white ratios with and without Hispanics included in the race categories (cols. 1 and 2). Various data-year and

---

[30] The average expected prison term prior to initial release is about 33 months (assuming that most offenders earn nearly all of their one-third good-conduct credit; MSGC 1984, p. 101). Many offenders further reduce the actual duration of their imprisonment by receiving credit for time they spent in pretrial detention; in addition, revoked offenders usually have less than 3 years to serve in prison. However, some revoked offenders do not arrive in prison until months or years after their initial sentencing.

TABLE 10

Minnesota Black/White Per Capita Ratios by Stage of Processing and Ethnicity, 2000–2007 (Black Rate as a Multiple of the White Rate)

	Including Hispanics (1)	Excluding Hispanics (2)
A. Arrest to conviction:		
1. 2000–2004 adult Part I violent arrests	15.4	NA
2. 2000–2004 Part I + drug arrests	9.5	NA
3. 2001–5 felony convictions*[†]	8.9[†]	9.3
B. Sentencing and inmate populations:		
4. 2001–5 recommended prison terms*	12.8[†]	13.6
5. 2001–5 prison sentences imposed*	12.5[†]	13.3
6. 2003–7 year-end prison stocks	12.9	13.8[‡]
7. 2001–5 prison* + jail sentences imposed	9.1[†]	9.6
8. Midyear 2005 prison + jail stocks	9.5[§]	9.9

SOURCES.—BJS (2006); MSGC (2006a) and similar reports for other years; USCB (2007e, 2007f, 2008a, 2008b, 2008f); BCA (2008); FBI (2008b, tables 29, 43) and similar reports for other years.

NOTE.—Ratios are based on per capita rates for each race. Except for arrest rates, population bases are lagged, using the resident population of that race 1 or more years earlier; conviction and sentencing rate bases are lagged 1 year; prison stock rate bases are lagged 3.5 years; bases for prison + jail stock rates are lagged 3 years.

* Includes offenders with mandatory life sentences.

[†] These figures are estimates based on comparisons of ratios with and without Hispanics in 2005, the earliest year for which separate race and ethnicity data are reported.

[‡] Estimate is based on comparison of 2005 prison sentence ratios with and without Hispanics.

[§] Estimate is based on comparison of 2005 custody sentence ratios with and without Hispanics.

population-base time lags are employed to provide more meaningful comparisons between ratios at different points in the criminal process.

The data and estimates in part A of the table suggest that black/white racial disproportionality does not change very much as cases move from the arrest to the conviction stage. The black/white ratio for convictions in line 3, column 1 (8.9 : 1), is slightly lower than the ratio for the broader of the two arrest measures (9.5 : 1). The lower black offense-specific retention rates reported earlier (table 8) lend support to the conclusion that, at least for burglary and serious violent offenses, racial disproportionality declines somewhat between the arrest and conviction stages.

However, a comparison of lines 3 and 5 of the table shows that disparity increases between conviction and the imposition of a prison sentence, primarily because of the much higher proportion of blacks who have recommended prison sentences under the guidelines (line 4); the black/white ratio for these recommendations is 12.8 : 1 (13.6 : 1, excluding Hispanics). The most important reason for the higher recommended prison rate for blacks is criminal history; this factor has a major effect on guidelines prison sentence recommendations, and blacks have much higher average criminal history scores.

Since there are limited usable data on prison admissions by race, the next ratios shown in table 10 are for prison inmate stocks (line 6); disparity appears to have increased slightly in comparison to the stage at which prison sentences are imposed (line 5). Prison admissions data available for some of these years (2000–2002) imply higher black rates for revocation of probation and postprison release. However, these higher revocation rates appear to have little net impact on black/white ratios in prison stocks because the effect of higher black revocation rates is counteracted by the much larger number of whites on probation (i.e., at risk of revocation).

As shown in the last two lines of table 10, black/white custodial disparity is considerably lower when jail inmates are included, reflecting the higher proportion of whites receiving felony jail sentences (which, in turn, reflects the lower proportion of whites receiving prison sentences). Again, there is a slight increase in disparity when prison and jail stock ratios (line 8) are compared to the stage at which these sentences are imposed (line 7). This increase is roughly comparable to the increased disparity observed when we compare ratios based on prison stocks and prison sentences (lines 5 and 6).

One explanation for rising disparity in both sets of measures could be the difference between flow measures (sentences imposed) and stock measures (inmate populations). The average duration of black custody sentences is higher since a lower proportion of black offenders receive jail terms. This causes black offenders to accumulate in custody (prison) stocks. Other factors may also be at work. Jail populations include not only sentenced felons but also pretrial detainees and offenders serving misdemeanor sentences. Further research is needed to determine whether these competing jail uses have especially racially disparate impacts on jail populations (an earlier study suggests that they do; see Minnesota Task Force 1993, pp. 46, 57).

Another possible cause of racial disproportionality in jail populations might be higher black rates of revocation of probation and postprison release leading to pre- or posthearing jail commitment. Given the relatively short custody terms available to sanction release violations, it is likely that a large number of these offenders are detained and sanctioned in jail rather than being sent to state prison. It would not be surprising to find that blacks have higher rates of revocation to jail, given higher black criminal history scores and higher rates of black disadvantage and crime. Research should examine whether such revocations are in fact more frequent for blacks and, if so, whether this reflects higher rates of serious noncompliance with release conditions, valid risk assessments, or the effects of conscious or unconscious bias.

VI. Conclusion

Discussions of racial disproportionality in criminal justice sometimes seem to reveal two opposing states of denial. One view denies the possibility of conscious or even unconscious racial bias, supposing that racial disproportions in criminal justice solely reflect racial differences in criminal behavior. The opposing view denies behavioral differences, supposing that the observed disproportions solely reflect bias (see Bridges and Crutchfield [1988, p. 700], describing "normative" [behavior] and "stratification" [bias] theories of disparity). Thoughtful observers such as Alfred Blumstein (1982, pp. 1280–81; 1993, p. 759), William Julius Wilson (1987, pp. 22–26), Michael Tonry (1995, pp. 63–80), and Kevin Reitz (2003, pp. 89–106) have recognized that both of these extreme positions are wrong. The analysis in this essay supports that view: the high degree of racial disproportionality in Minnesota's prison and jail populations appears to reflect racial differences in criminal behavior, the disparate impact of seemingly race-neutral sentencing policies, and, possibly, racial stereotyping or disparate impact in policing decisions and in decisions to revoke probation or postprison release.

Prison disproportionality largely reflects racial differences in presumptive sentences; presumptive sentences, in turn, largely (but not entirely) reflect racial differences already present at arrest, which in turn reflect, in large part, racial differences in offending. The latter differences represent both individual and societal failures. These differences appear to be much greater in Minnesota than in the nation as a whole, reflecting above-average differences in socioeconomic status of the state's black and white citizens and the particularly high concentration of its black residents in high-crime urban areas. These status and residential differences, and the crimes they foster, are the legacy of historic, deliberate racial bias, combined with a willful blindness that allows the modern products of that bias to continue and in some ways grow worse. In particular, city, county, and metro-level policies regarding schools, housing, transportation, and other public services and subsidies have often worsened, and rarely tried to ameliorate, criminogenic concentrations of race and poverty (Orfield 1997, 2002; Orfield and Luce 2009).

These are not just failings of society at large. The criminal justice system's response to crime in poor, nonwhite areas magnifies and perpetuates racial differences in socioeconomic status and criminal behavior. Poverty and lack of opportunity are associated with higher crime rates; crime leads to arrest, a criminal record, and usually a jail or prison sentence; past crimes lengthen those sentences; offenders released from prison or jail confront family and neighborhood dysfunction, increased risks of unemployment, and other crime-producing disadvantages; this makes them likelier to commit new crimes, and the cycle repeats itself (Council on Crime and Justice 2007c).

Social disadvantage, crime, and criminal law enforcement thus reinforce each other: disadvantage promotes crime; crime worsens the condition of already-disadvantaged victims; already-disadvantaged offenders and their families are further burdened by criminal penalties and the collateral consequences of conviction. Mass incarceration also substantially burdens the already-disadvantaged communities from which most of these offenders come and to which they will return (see, e.g., Clear 2008). As Bruce Western (2006, p. 196) has succinctly stated, "Mass incarceration is . . . a key component in a system of inequality—a social structure in which social inequalities are self-sustaining and those at the bottom have few prospects for upward mobility."

At least some of the substantial racial disproportionality in Minnesota arrest rates may reflect the disparate impacts of law enforcement decisions, in particular, decisions to target black citizens or black neighborhoods where reported crime rates are higher and drug offenses are concentrated and are easy to detect. For all crime categories, the real differences that exist in black and white offense rates are accentuated by the strongly disparate impact of sentencing guidelines policies giving heavy weight to the offender's criminal history score. What remains of unregulated sentencing discretion under the guidelines shows relatively little evidence of bias or racially disparate impact. However, black/white disparity may be further increased by decisions to revoke probation and postprison supervised release.

Further research is urgently needed on these revocation decisions and on policing policies that may exaggerate racial differences in offending. In addition, current data do not allow us to examine the possible effects of various "compensating biases" that may conceal disparities that occur at various stages of case processing and, in aggregate comparisons, tend to cancel each other out. These possibilities can be assessed only by means of a detailed, in-depth sample of cases, tracing the effects of law enforcement policies, charging, plea bargaining, pretrial detention, and other factors that shape the flow of cases entering and moving through the criminal justice system.

At the same time, research is also needed on the social roots of crime in Minnesota—the specific individual, family, neighborhood, school, and societal causes of Minnesota's stark socioeconomic disparities between whites and blacks.

There is reason to hope that much-needed data on many of these issues will soon become available in Minnesota. The Minnesota Sentencing Guidelines Commission, in partnership with the Institute on Race and Poverty at the University of Minnesota, is planning to conduct an in-depth, two-pronged assessment of racial disparity, tracing a sample of cases forward through the criminal justice system and backward into the communities from which the offenders came (MSGC 2008a, p. 6).

There are several important policy implications of this essay and of a more detailed assessment of these problems. Where racial stereotyping or other illegitimate disparities exist, they must be addressed and corrected. Seemingly race-neutral drug enforcement policies must be changed if they are found to produce disproportionately high black arrest rates relative to actual rates of black drug use and trafficking. As suggested in a recent report (King 2008, p. 31), noncriminal referral to hospitals, shelters, and treatment facilities, in lieu of arrest and criminal justice processing, would often provide a faster and more effective response to the needs of low-level drug offenders, many of whom are chemically dependent. Such a major change does not lack historical precedent: in the past four decades there has been a massive diversion of public drunks from arrest to noncriminal detoxification centers (see, e.g., Aaronson, Dienes, and Musheno 1978). Between 1970 and 2005, arrests for public drunkenness fell from 22.5 percent of all arrests to 3.9 percent (FBI 1971, p. 119; 2008*c*, table 29).

My analyses suggest that seemingly legitimate sentencing factors such as criminal history scoring can have strongly disparate impacts on nonwhite defendants. Sentencing guidelines systems like Minnesota's have a substantial capacity to identify and address such disparate impacts. These systems specify a limited number of legally relevant sentencing factors, and their permanent sentencing commissions collect and analyze detailed statistical data on cases that have been sentenced.

But it is not enough to recognize a disparate impact after it has occurred; the identification of such impacts and reexamination of underlying policies should occur before the policies are implemented. Sentencing guidelines systems like Minnesota's can more easily do this because such guidelines make sentences predictable, and sentencing commissions are already using that greater predictability to model their systems and project future resource needs. These commissions can and should adapt their resource-impact projection models so that they also show the predicted racial and ethnic impact of current and proposed sentencing policies. Regular use of such demographic impact projections is one of the most important recommendations in recent proposals to revise the sentencing and corrections provisions of the Model Penal Code (Reitz 2003, pp. 104–6; American Law Institute 2007, sec. 6A.07[3]). Several states, including Minnesota, have recently begun to make such projections (Mauer 2009).

Once past or projected future disparate impacts of certain sentencing factors are identified and quantified, policy makers must reexamine the assumptions and purposes underlying those factors. Even if a sentencing factor such as criminal history is legitimate, and indeed necessary for the protection of potential victims (most of whom are themselves disadvantaged nonwhites), policy makers must explore more creative ways to handle these problems so as to minimize the damage caused by conviction and incarceration. Criminal history scoring, and perhaps other guidelines rules that limit judicial flexibility in the use of intermediate sanctions, will probably have to be changed if Minnesotans want to reduce the racially disparate impact of the state's sentencing laws on prison and jail populations.

Michael Tonry (1995, chaps. 4–7) proposed that sentencing guidelines should explicitly allow judges to mitigate sentences on the basis of the reduced culpability and social vulnerability of disadvantaged offenders, particularly when such offenders have managed to overcome the odds and maintain stable employment and family ties. He also cited data suggesting that reduced sentencing severity would not necessarily lead to higher crime rates. Tonry has also proposed increased treatment and other services for disadvantaged offenders (pp. 201–7) and more frequent and creative use of community-based sanctions (Morris and Tonry 1990). In the past such sanctions have mostly been used for low-risk offenders, who are disproportionately white. But if we are serious about reducing the harm that criminal law enforcement and sentencing cause to vulnerable nonwhite offenders (and their families and communities), courts must be willing to extend (and even prioritize) the use of intermediate sanctions to disadvantaged offenders, even though these offenders often pose higher risks of recidivism if they are released.

To the extent that research reveals few illegitimate disparities or unacceptable disparate impacts, at least at some stages of the criminal and sentencing processes, such findings will give Minnesotans a sound basis to appreciate and retain what is good about their state's laws and practices. Minnesota and its guidelines have sometimes been blamed for the state's strongly disparate inmate populations. This exploratory essay suggests that such criticisms are only partially correct. It appears that most of the disparity is already present at arrest and that the principal contribution of the guidelines to racial disproportionality is to be found in one particular aspect of their design—the heavy weight given to prior record. That problematic design feature would be easy to change without discarding or radically changing the guidelines—a sentencing system that has served the state well. Overall, the guidelines have helped to reduce racial and other disparities (Frase 1993b). The fiscal-impact projections made possible by the guidelines permit policy makers to manage and prioritize the use of limited and expensive state prison resources (Frase 2005a, 2005b). And although Minnesota's prison and jail populations have increased steadily under the guidelines, these populations have grown no faster than national inmate populations, despite higher Minnesota growth rates in felony convictions. Given racial differences in offending, a relatively low incarceration rate will probably always tend to yield relatively high racial disproportionality. But if the solution to that problem were simply to lock up more nonviolent offenders, the result would also be to increase the absolute number of minority persons incarcerated (Zimring 2005).

To the extent that racial disproportionality at arrest reflects differences in criminal behavior, we must address the causes of those behavioral differences. One by-product of my analyses is documentation of shockingly high socioeconomic disparity between blacks and whites in Minnesota. Serious and sustained efforts must be made to reduce these and other racial/ethnic disparities, not only because reduction of hardship and of increased risk of criminal victimization and punishment is the right and decent thing to do, but also because such disparities greatly increase public expense for criminal justice and many other government programs. If the state fails to address these disparities, black citizens will continue to be disproportionately victimized, arrested, and incarcerated, and all the state's citizens will continue to incur substantial human, social, and financial costs—costs that will continue to grow, given current trends and demographic forecasts (Council on Crime and Justice 2007*a*).

At present, the state as a whole, and particularly the Twin Cities metropolitan area, where most blacks live, remains one of the most affluent in the nation. A recent survey (Bureau of Labor Statistics 2007) found that the Twin Cities was the third richest in pretax income per consumer unit of 24 major metropolitan areas surveyed. Poverty in the midst of affluence must be very frustrating to the state's most disadvantaged, predominantly nonwhite citizens, and these frustrations may contribute to further despair and criminal conduct—most of it directed at other disadvantaged nonwhites. But the good news here is that, if they choose, the state and the metro area have the resources to address some of the worst racial socioeconomic disparities and lessen their future costs.

Stark racial disparities in custodial populations are a constant reminder of society's failure to deliver on its ideals of equality. Prison and jail disparities are also extremely costly, especially in the long run. They represent a key link in the constantly repeating cycle of disadvantage, crime, incarceration, release to continued or worsened disadvantage, and repeated crime. Minnesotans must find ways to break the cycle. And so must other states with high racial disproportionality in their inmate populations.

APPENDIX
Problems of Missing, Inconsistent, and Hard-to-Interpret
Data

Very few data currently are available on many critical dimensions of race and criminal justice in Minnesota, and the available data are often reported or analyzed inconsistently, raising difficult issues of interpretation.

A. Missing Data

There are few Minnesota-specific data for many stages of the criminal process. Data on criminal behavior, crime reporting, and law enforcement are particularly sparse, which greatly limits our ability to specify to what extent racial differences in arrest rates reflect behavior, as opposed to disparate law enforcement decisions. The principal published sources include a racial-profiling study based on traffic stops in 65 jurisdictions in 2002 (Institute and Council 2003), various papers published by the Council on Crime and Justice (2007*b*) as part of its Racial Disparity Initiative, and crime victimization and drug use surveys conducted in Minnesota in the 1990s (cited and discussed in several of the Council on Crime and Justice reports; see also Minnesota Criminal Justice Statistics Center 2003; Minnesota Departments 2007).[31]

We also lack detailed data on victim cooperation, charging, plea bargaining, and defense effectiveness. Such variations could cause disparity to rise or fall between the stage of arrest and the next stage (felony conviction) for which race-specific Minnesota data are available.

The data on felony sentencing collected and published by the Minnesota Sentencing Guidelines Commission are among the most complete in any state. But there are very few Minnesota or even national data on misdemeanor sentencing, nor are there data at the state level on the proportions of jail inmates in pretrial detention or other temporary holding, serving sentences (directly or following revocation) for felonies, and serving sentences for misdemeanors (Minnesota jail data are not broken down by race, offense, or conviction status). However, the limited available Minnesota data suggest that blacks are more likely to be held in pretrial detention and more likely to receive jail sentences in misdemeanor cases (Minnesota Task Force 1993, pp. 46, 57).

There are no detailed, race-specific data on postsentencing decisions, especially revocation of probation and postprison release, and denial of good-conducts credits.

At all stages of criminal processing we lack data on the race of crime victims (Minnesota Task Force 1993, p. 10). Research in other jurisdictions has shown that this factor can have major effects on sentencing outcomes

---

[31] This is an SPSS-formatted file, provided to the author by the sponsoring agencies. The file contains same-school data from the 1992, 1995, 1998, 2001, and 2004 Minnesota Student Survey; selected findings from these surveys are reported in Minnesota Departments (2005).

(Sentencing Project 2005), and it may also affect victim reporting and co-operation and police and prosecution decisions. Minnesota surveys in the early 1990s found that substantial numbers of judges and defense attorneys believed that charges were less likely to be filed, and plea offers were more generous, when the crime victim was nonwhite (Minnesota Task Force 1993, pp. 18, 28).

B. Inconsistent Data

Much of the data we have at various stages in the process are reported in ways that make it difficult to compare with data from other stages. The treatment of offender ethnicity is a particularly difficult subject. Persons of Hispanic (or Latino) ethnicity are sometimes put in a separate nonoverlapping category (i.e., they are excluded from racial categories), whereas in other data Hispanics are included within racial categories even if their total is also reported separately. Most Hispanics in Minnesota are white: in 2005, 77 percent of sentenced Hispanics (excluding those of "unknown" race) were identified as white; if one also excludes Hispanics whose race was identified as "other" (neither white, black, American Indian, nor Asian), 96 percent of sentenced Hispanics were white. Hispanic whites tend to have higher arrest and incarceration rates than non-Hispanic whites, so inclusion of Hispanics in racial categories tends to raise white arrest, conviction, and incarceration rates (while having little effect on black rates), thus concealing the greater disparities that exist between non-Hispanic whites and blacks. Minnesota has few Hispanics compared to the United States as a whole, so inclusion of Hispanics in race categories has a much greater tendency to understate U.S. black/white ratios than Minnesota ratios.

The scope and treatment of racial categories in prior research are also problematic. Many studies have focused only on black versus white incarceration rates, even though substantial racial disproportionality also exists for other nonwhite groups, especially Hispanics and Native Americans. (However, blacks remain the largest nonwhite group in Minnesota; for that reason, and because of space limitations, my analyses likewise focused on black/white disparities.)

Comparisons of racial differences in per capita arrest, conviction, and incarceration rates are further complicated by a change in the way U.S. Census Bureau population data are collected. The 2000 Census and subsequent population estimates allow persons to list more than one specified race, whereas the prior census data used to compute per capita custody rates in earlier studies and arrest, court, and correctional data permitted only one racial identity. The use of multiracial census data as a base would distort most per capita estimates, since inmate, arrest, and court data in the numerator are not multiracial and the same person could be counted in more than one population base (denominator). These census changes also complicate comparisons to earlier per capita data. Accordingly, I generally avoid comparisons between years before and after 2000, and the population data used to compute per capita rates for 2000 and later years include only persons listing one race ("black alone" and "white alone").

Prior research also has usually not separately examined males and females. Male incarceration rates are much higher than female rates, and black/white inmate disparities are also greater for males than for females. In 2005, for example, the black/white ratio of per capita prison sentence rates in Minnesota was 12.2 : 1 for males but only 5.8 : 1 for females. However, because of the limited availability of Minnesota arrest and inmate data broken down by both race and gender and space limitations, I do not separately analyze racial disparities for males and females.

Another problem with the population bases used to compute per capita rates in prior state-level studies is that the base equals the total resident population of each race, including juveniles, even though very few juveniles are eligible to be confined in state prisons and local jails. The reason for this disconnect appears to be that the U.S. Census Bureau does not regularly publish state population estimates broken down by both race and age; thus, state-level adult population estimates for each race must be hand-calculated, combining published age-race breakdowns for males and females. Moreover, the surveys on which the published data are based are less representative than general population estimate surveys, excluding residents in low-population areas and (until 2006) also excluding all inmates and other institutionalized persons (USCB 2008d). Use of a total population base understates adult incarceration rates (relative to adult populations) and also understates black/white inmate disparities (black populations are younger, so the inclusion of juveniles in population denominators lowers black incarceration rates more than white rates). The degree of understatement is greater in states such as Minnesota, where the relative youthfulness of the black population is above the national average. (The median age of non-Hispanic blacks in 2000 was 25 in Minnesota and 30 for the United States as a whole; the median ages of Minnesota and U.S. non-Hispanic whites were 37 and 38, respectively [USCB 2007b].) Nevertheless, I use total population bases to compute adult arrest, conviction, sentencing, and incarceration rates and black/white ratios. This was done to facilitate comparisons to prior research and government data and because of the need for hand tabulation of state-level adult population estimates by race and the less representative samples on which such estimates are based. Since both U.S. and Minnesota populations have grown slightly older in recent decades, black/white ratios for later years are somewhat less understated. (It should also be noted that census data tend to undercount blacks [Tonry 1995, p. 31], thus introducing a countervailing bias: the underestimated black population base results in a higher black per capita rate, thus tending to overstate the black/white ratio.)

Available state-level data on adult populations of each race (USCB 2008c) suggest that Minnesota's black/white ratio rises more than that of many other states when rates are based on estimated adult rather than total populations. For example, Minnesota's 2005 black/white prison plus jail incarceration ratio rises from 9.14 : 1 (total population base) to 11.35 : 1 (adult population base), an increase of 24 percent; for all states, the black/white ratio rises from 5.56 : 1 to 6.18 : 1, an increase of only 11 percent. However, the rank order of state incarceration ratios does not change substantially when estimated adult populations are used as a base, and the states in the high- and low-ratio quartiles (see table 6) are almost identical.

Another problem with the black/white incarceration ratios reported in prior research is the failure to use any time lag between inmate counts and resident population bases. Per capita incarceration rates assume that, in the absence of disparity, inmate stocks should be proportional to the resident populations of each race. But jail and prison stocks reflect crimes committed several years earlier, so inmate stocks should be compared with white and black populations in those earlier years. If black populations are rising faster than white populations, comparing inmate stocks to populations in the same year tends to understate black incarceration rates more than white rates and thus tends to understate black/white ratios. This is a particular problem for research on Minnesota, since the state's black population has risen much faster than the white population in recent years and also much faster than the U.S. black population. Accordingly, I employ time-lagged population bases when computing per capita rates and black/white ratios for comparison with earlier stages of the criminal process (e.g., comparing prison stocks ratios with conviction ratios).

Finally, when comparing disproportionality at different stages of the criminal process, one must keep in mind that arrest and sentencing data are based on a "flow" of cases (analogous to the quantity of fluid flowing through a pipe in a given time period), whereas inmate population figures represent "stock" data (analogous to the quantity of fluid stored in a tank at any moment in time). Since offenders with longer sentences tend to accumulate in custodial populations, such offenders would be expected to make up a higher proportion of stocks than they do of flows, and such differences may distort race-specific comparisons, especially if offenders in some racial groups consistently receive longer sentences.

C. Problems of Interpretation

The limitations noted above make it difficult to interpret what data we have. In addition to problems of comparability, there is a problem of possible opposing or compensating biases that tend to cancel each other out, thus concealing the true nature and extent of each form of bias (Blumstein 1982, pp. 1263, 1269, 1279–80). Here are four examples.

Given the intraracial nature of many crimes (people tend to commit crimes close to where they live and tend to live with people of their own race), if there is any systematic underreporting of crime by black victims, this would tend to favor black offenders, causing them to be underrepresented among arrests and thus masking the full extent of racial disparities in arrest decisions and at all later stages of the process (i.e., the overrepresentation of blacks among arrestees, in criminal court data, and in prisons and jails would be even greater if black victims reported more crimes). Even for crimes known to the police, a pro–black offender bias would exist if black victims are less able or willing to cooperate effectively with police and prosecutors.

Similarly, any form of official bias against black crime victims or police underenforcement in black neighborhoods also causes a bias that tends to favor black offenders. Such an anti–black victim bias may then mask the full extent of other biases that disfavor black offenders, or the two biases could even cancel each other out.

Another factor that may favor or disfavor nonwhite offenders is the overall level of sentencing severity or leniency in the jurisdictions in which these offenders live. Most Minnesota blacks live in urban jurisdictions (see table 7). To the extent that sentencing is less severe in those courts than it is in many suburban and rural jurisdictions, the overall severity of black sentences will be lowered, but this may conceal other biases against blacks, especially those who live in nonurban areas. In 2004 and 2005 (the two most recent years for which sentencing data are examined in this essay), Minnesota's nonmetropolitan courts as a group had higher rates of upward dispositional departure for presumptive stays than metro courts and lower rates of downward departure for presumptive prison commits. But all such cross-jurisdictional comparisons are uncertain, given possible charging differences in these counties. Moreover, analysis of such geographic variations requires complex, hierarchical modeling of data that includes contextual (county or judicial district) and well as case-level variables (Weidner, Frase, and Schultz 2005, pp. 409–11). Even with such models, however, geographic variations are difficult to interpret when data are limited (as they are at present in Minnesota) to the conviction offense, which may not be comparable across jurisdictions because of major differences in charging and plea-bargaining practices (see, e.g., MSGC [1984, pp. 71–86], finding numerous county-to-county variations in charging and plea-bargaining practices; Feld [1991, pp. 172–78], reporting data suggesting major differences between Minnesota urban, suburban, and rural counties in prepetition screening of juvenile cases).

If one finds comparable proportions of black and white offenders at earlier and later stages of the criminal process, this does not necessarily mean that there is no bias in the intervening stages. Instead, seemingly constant black/white proportions might be due to the opposing effects of earlier and later biases. For example, suppose that overarrest of blacks (resulting in large numbers of weak or unfounded arrests) is followed by especially strict charging or sentencing of black offenders. Such an overarrest pattern would be likely to cause a high percentage of cases against blacks to be dismissed after arrest (lowering the black/white ratio at that point), but if the remaining cases against blacks are treated harshly in charging, plea bargaining, or sentencing, the black/white ratio at the conviction, sentencing, and custody stages may go back up, perhaps to the same high level originally seen at the point of arrest.

REFERENCES

Aaronson, David E., C. Thomas Dienes, and Michael C. Musheno. 1978. "Changing the Public Drunkenness Laws: The Impact of Decriminalization." *Law and Society Review* 12:405–36.

American Law Institute. 2007. *Model Penal Code: Sentencing*. Tentative draft no. 1 (April 9). Philadelphia: American Law Institute.

BCA (Minnesota Bureau of Criminal Apprehension). 2008. *Minnesota Uniform Crime Reports* (1997–2007). http://www.dps.state.mn.us/bca/CJIS/Documents/Page-15-02.html.

BJS (Bureau of Justice Statistics). 1980. *Prisoners in State and Federal Institutions on December 31, 1978*. Washington, DC: U.S. Department of Justice.

———. 1989. *Felony Sentences in State Courts, 1986*. Washington, DC: U.S. Department of Justice.

———. 2002. *Prison and Jail Inmates at Mid-year 2001*. Washington, DC: U.S. Department of Justice.

———. 2003. *Reporting Crime to the Police, 1992–2000*. Washington, DC: U.S. Department of Justice.

———. 2004. *Felony Sentences in State Courts, 2002*. Washington, DC: U.S. Department of Justice.

———. 2006. *Prison and Jail Inmates at Mid-year 2005*. Washington, DC: U.S. Department of Justice.

———. 2007*a*. *Criminal Victimization in the United States, 2005, Statistical Tables*. http://www.ojp.usdoj.gov/bjs/abstract/cvusst.htm.

———. 2007*b*. *Data Online*. http://bjsdata.ojp.usdoj.gov/dataonline/Search/Homicide/State/RunHomStatebyState.cfm.

———. 2007*c*. *Felony Sentences in State Courts, 2004*. Additional data available at http://www.ojp.usdoj.gov/bjs/abstract/scscf04st.htm.

———. 2007*d*. *Homicide Trends in the U.S.* http://www.ojp.usdoj.gov/bjs/homicide/tables/vracetab.htm.

———. 2007*e*. National Corrections Reporting Program (NCRP). Ann Arbor, MI: Inter-University Consortium for Political and Social Research. http://www.icpsr.umich.edu/.

———. 2008*a*. *Prisoners in 2007*. Washington, DC: U.S. Department of Justice.

———. 2008*b*. *State Court Processing Statistics, 1990–2002: Felony Defendants in Large Urban Counties*. http://www.icpsr.umich.edu/cgi-bin/bob/newark?study=2038.

Blumstein, Alfred. 1982. "On the Racial Disproportionality of United States Prison Populations." *Journal of Criminal Law and Criminology* 73:1259–81.

———. 1988. "Prison Populations: A System Out of Control?" In *Crime and Justice: A Review of Research*, vol. 10, edited by Michael Tonry and Norval Morris. Chicago: University of Chicago Press.

———. 1993. "Racial Disproportionality of U.S. Prison Populations Revisited." *University of Colorado Law Review* 64:743–60.

Boardman, Jason D., Brian Karl Finch, Christopher G. Ellison, David R. Williams, and James S. Jackson. 2001. "Neighborhood Disadvantage, Stress, and

Drug Use among Adults." *Journal of Health and Social Behavior* 42(June): 151–65.

Bridges, George, and Robert Crutchfield. 1988. "Social Standing and Racial Disparities in Imprisonment." *Social Forces* 66:699–724.

Bureau of Labor Statistics. 2007. *Consumer Expenditure Survey, 2004–2005.* Washington, DC: Bureau of Labor Statistics. http://www.bls.gov/cex/.

Clear, Todd R. 2008. "The Effects of High Imprisonment Rates on Communities." In *Crime and Justice: A Review of Research*, vol. 37, edited by Michael Tonry. Chicago: University of Chicago Press.

Cole, David. 1999. *No Equal Justice.* New York: New Press.

Council on Crime and Justice. 2002. *Defining the Disparity—Taking a Closer Look: Do Drug Use Patterns Explain Racial/Ethnic Disparities in Drug Arrests in Minnesota?* http://www.crimeandjustice.org/researchReports/Do%20Drug%20Use%20Patterns%20Explain%20Racial%20Diparities%20in%20Drug%20Arrests%20in%20%20Minnesota.pdf.

———. 2007*a*. *Justice Where Art Thou? A Framework for the Future.* Minneapolis: Council on Crime and Justice.

———. 2007*b*. *Racial Disparity Initiative.* Reports. http://www.racialdisparity.org/reports_main.php.

———. 2007*c*. *Reducing Racial Disparity While Enhancing Public Safety: Key Findings and Recommendations.* http://www.racialdisparity.org/files/Final%20Report-Reducing%20Disparity%20%20Enhancing%20Safety.pdf.

Crutchfield, Robert D., Joseph G. Weis, Rodney L. Engen, and Randy R. Gainey. 1995. *Racial and Ethnic Disparities in the Prosecution of Felony Cases in King County: Final Report.* Olympia, WA: Administrator for the Courts.

Engel, Robin Shepard, and Jennifer M. Calnon. 2004. "Examining the Influence of Drivers' Characteristics during Traffic Stops with the Police: Results from a National Survey." *Justice Quarterly* 21(1):49–90.

FBI (Federal Bureau of Investigation). 1971. *Uniform Crime Reports, 1970.* Washington, DC: U.S. Department of Justice.

———. 2008*a*. *Uniform Crime Reports 2002.* http://www.fbi.gov/ucr/02cius.htm.

———. 2008*b*. *Uniform Crime Reports 2004.* http://www.fbi.gov/ucr/cius_04/.

———. 2008*c*. *Uniform Crime Reports 2005.* http://www.fbi.gov/ucr/05cius.

Feld, Barry C. 1991. "Justice by Geography: Urban, Suburban, and Rural Variations in Juvenile Justice Administration." *Journal of Criminal Law and Criminology* 82:156–210.

Frase, Richard S. 1993*a*. "Implementing Commission-Based Sentencing Guidelines: The Lessons of the First Ten Years in Minnesota." *Cornell Journal of Law and Public Policy* 2:279–337.

———. 1993*b*. "The Uncertain Future of Sentencing Guidelines." *Law and Inequality: A Journal of Theory and Practice* 12:1–42.

———. 2005*a*. "Sentencing Guidelines in Minnesota, 1978–2003." In *Crime and Justice: A Review of Research*, vol. 32, edited by Michael Tonry. Chicago: University of Chicago Press.

————. 2005*b*. "State Sentencing Guidelines: Diversity, Consensus, and Unresolved Policy Issues." *Columbia Law Review* 105:1190–1232.

————. 2006. "*Blakely* in Minnesota, Two Years Out: Guidelines Sentencing Is Alive and Well." *Ohio State Journal of Criminal Law* 4:73–94.

Garland, Brett E., Cassia Spohn, and Eric J. Wodahl. 2008. "Racial Disproportionality in the American Prison Population: Using the Blumstein Method to Address the Critical Race and Justice Issue of the 21st Century." *Justice Policy Journal* 5(2). http://www.cjcj.org/files/racial_disproportionality .pdf.

Hagedorn, John M. 1998. *The Business of Drug Dealing in Milwaukee*. Thiensville: Wisconsin Policy Research Institute.

Harcourt, Bernard E. 2007. *Against Prediction: Profiling, Policing, and Punishing in an Actuarial Age*. Chicago: University of Chicago Press.

Harrington, Michael P., and Cassia Spohn. 2007. "Defining Sentence Type: Further Evidence against Use of the Total Incarceration Variable." *Journal of Research in Crime and Delinquency* 44(1):36–63.

Institute and Council (Institute on Race and Poverty, and Council on Crime and Justice). 2003. *Minnesota Statewide Racial Profiling Report: All Participating Jurisdictions. Report to the Minnesota Legislature Sept. 22, 2003*. http://www .irpumn.org/uls/resources/projects/aggregate%20report%2092303.pdf.

Johnson, Bruce, Terry Williams, Kojo A. Dei, and Harry Sanabria. 1990. "Drug Abuse in the Inner City: Impact on Hard Drug Users and the Community." In *Drugs and Crime*, edited by Michael Tonry and James Q. Wilson. Vol. 13 of *Crime and Justice: A Review of Research*, edited by Michael Tonry. Chicago: University of Chicago Press.

Kim, Julia Y. S., Michael Fendrich, and Joseph Wisler. 2000. "The Validity of Juvenile Arrestees' Drug Use Reporting: A Gender Comparison." *Journal of Research in Crime and Delinquency* 37:419–32.

King, Ryan S. 2008. *Disparity by Geography: The War on Drugs in America's Cities*. Washington, DC: Sentencing Project.

Langan, Patrick A. 1985. "Racism on Trial: New Evidence to Explain the Racial Composition of Prisons in the United States." *Journal of Criminal Law and Criminology* 76:666–83.

Leinfelt, Fredrik H. 2006. "Racial Influences on the Likelihood of Police Searches and Search Hits: A Longitudinal Analysis from an American Midwestern City." *Police Journal* 79(3):238–57.

Martin, Susan. 1984. "Interests and Politics in Sentencing Reform: The Development of Sentencing Guidelines in Minnesota and Pennsylvania." *Villanova Law Review* 29:21–113.

Massey, Douglas S., and Nancy A. Denton. 1993. *American Apartheid: Segregation and the Making of the Underclass*. Cambridge, MA: Harvard University Press.

Mauer, Marc. 1997. *Intended and Unintended Consequences: State Racial Disparities in Imprisonment*. Washington, DC: Sentencing Project.

————. 1999. *Race to Incarcerate*. New York: New Press.

————. 2009. "Racial Impact Statements: Changing Policies to Address

Disparities." http://sentencingproject.org/Admin/Documents/publications/rd_abaarticle.pdf.

Mauer, Marc, and Ryan King. 2007. *Uneven Justice: State Rates of Incarceration by Race and Ethnicity.* http://www.sentencingproject.org/PublicationDetails .aspx?PublicationID=593.

Meehan, Albert J., and Michael C. Ponder. 2002. "Race and Place: The Ecology of Racial Profiling African American Motorists." *Justice Quarterly* 19(3): 399–430.

Miethe, Terrence, and Charles Moore. 1985. "Socio-economic Disparities under Determinate Sentencing Systems: A Comparison of Pre- and Post-guideline Practices in Minnesota." *Criminology* 23:337–63.

Minneapolis, City of. 2008*a*. Minneapolis Police Department, Monthly Crime Statistics. http://www.ci.minneapolis.mn.us/police/crime-statistics/codefor/statistics.asp?year=2002.

———. 2008*b*. Minneapolis Police Department, 2000 CODEFOR Crimes by Neighborhood. http://www.ci.minneapolis.mn.us/police/crime-statistics/codefor/2000/2000-12-31-Year_End_Neighborhood_Reports.pdf.

———. 2008*c*. *Neighborhood Profiles.* http://www.ci.minneapolis.mn.us/neighborhoods/.

———. 2008*d*. *Neighborhood Profiles, Downtown West.* http://www.ci .minneapolis.mn.us/neighborhoods/downtownwest_profile_home.asp.

Minneapolis Star Tribune. 2006. "Graduation Rates Tell of Two Minnesotas." June 21.

———. 2007. "State's Schools Rank Second in Racial Change." August 31.

———. 2008*a*. "Minneapolis Focuses on Somali Killings." November 19. http://www.startribune.com/local/34717034.html?elr=KArksUUUU).

———. 2008*b*. "The Suspension Gap." May 18.

Minnesota Criminal Justice Statistics Center. 2003. *Safe at Home: The 2002 Minnesota Crime Survey.* http://www.ojp.state.mn.us/cj/publications/crime surveys/2002_Safe_at_Home.pdf.

Minnesota Department of Corrections. 2005. *The Methamphetamine Epidemic: Impact on the Minnesota Department of Corrections.* http://www.corr.state.mn .us/publications/documents/methimpact_002.pdf.

———. 2007. *Backgrounder: Drug Offenders in Prison, March 2007.* St. Paul: Minnesota Department of Corrections.

———. 2008. *Adult Inmate Profile.* Period reports from July 1, 1998 through January 1, 2008. http://www.corr.state.mn.us/aboutdoc/stats/Default.htm.

Minnesota Departments (Minnesota Departments of Education, Health, Human Services, and Public Safety). 2005. *Minnesota Student Survey 1992–2004 Trends.* St. Paul: Minnesota Departments.

———. 2007. *Trend Data File.* St. Paul: Minnesota Departments.

Minnesota State Planning Agency. 1991. *Population Notes: Minnesota Minority Populations Grow Rapidly between 1980 and 1990.* St. Paul: Minnesota State Planning Agency.

Minnesota Task Force (Minnesota Supreme Court Task Force on Racial Bias in the Judicial System). 1993. *Final Report*. St. Paul: Minnesota Supreme Court.

Morris, Norval, and Michael Tonry. 1990. *Between Prison and Probation: Intermediate Punishments in a Rational Sentencing System*. New York: Oxford University Press.

MSGC (Minnesota Sentencing Guidelines Commission). 1980. "Report to the Legislature, January 1, 1980." St. Paul: Minnesota Sentencing Guidelines Commission.

———. 1984. *The Impact of the Minnesota Sentencing Guidelines: Three Year Evaluation*. St. Paul: Minnesota Sentencing Guidelines Commission.

———. 2003. *2002 Monitoring Data*. St. Paul: Minnesota Sentencing Guidelines Commission.

———. 2004. *2003 Monitoring Data*. St. Paul: Minnesota Sentencing Guidelines Commission.

———. 2005. *2004 Monitoring Data*. St. Paul: Minnesota Sentencing Guidelines Commission.

———. 2006a. *Sentencing Practices: Annual Summary Statistics for Felony Offenders Sentenced in 2005*. St. Paul: Minnesota Sentencing Guidelines Commission.

———. 2006b. *2005 Monitoring Data*. St. Paul: Minnesota Sentencing Guidelines Commission.

———. 2008a. *Annual Report to the Legislature, January 15, 2008*. St. Paul: Minnesota Sentencing Guidelines Commission.

———. 2008b. *Minnesota Sentencing Guidelines and Commentary, Revised August 1, 2008*. St. Paul: Minnesota Sentencing Guidelines Commission.

———. 2008c. *Sentencing Practices: Annual Summary Statistics for Felony Offenders Sentenced in 2007*. St. Paul: Minnesota Sentencing Guidelines Commission.

Natapoff, Alexandra. 2006. "Underenforcement." *Fordham Law Review* 75: 1715–76.

Office of Justice Systems Analysis. 1995. *Disparities in Processing Felony Arrests in New York State: 1990–1992*. Albany: Office of Justice Systems Analysis, New York State Division of Criminal Justice Services.

Orfield, Myron. 1997. *Metropolitics: A Regional Agenda for Community and Stability*. Washington, DC: Brookings Institution Press.

———. 2002 *American Metropolitics: The New Suburban Reality*. Washington, DC: Brookings Institution Press.

Orfield, Myron, and Thomas Luce. 2009. *Region: Planning the Future of the Twin Cities*. Minneapolis: University of Minnesota Press.

Orfield, Myron, and Nicholas Wallace. 2007. "Expanding Educational Opportunity through School and Housing Choice." http://www.irpumn.org/uls/resources/projects/Expanding_Educ_Opportunity_Schl_Hsng_Choice.pdf.

Patterson, E. Britt, and Michael J. Lynch. 1991. "Bias in Formal Bail Proceedings." In *Race and Criminal Justice*, edited by M. J. Lynch and E. B. Patterson. New York: Harrow and Heston.

Reiman, Jeffrey. 1998. *The Rich Get Richer and the Poor Get Prison*. Boston: Allyn and Bacon.

Reitz, Kevin R. 2003. *Model Penal Code Sentencing, Report (April 11, 2003)*. Philadelphia: American Law Institute.

Riley, K. Jack. 1997. *Crack, Powder Cocaine, and Heroin: Drug Purchase and Use Patterns in Six U.S. Cities*. Washington, DC: U.S. Department of Justice, National Institute of Justice.

Ruggles, Steven, Matthew Sobek, Trent Alexander, Catherine A. Fitch, Ronald Goeken, Patricia Kelly Hall, Miriam King, and Chad Ronnander. 2004. *Integrated Public Use Microdata Series: Version 3.0*. Minneapolis: Minnesota Population Center [producer and distributor]. http://usa.pums.org/usa/.

Ruth, Henry, and Kevin R. Reitz. 2003. *The Challenge of Crime: Rethinking Our Response*. Cambridge, MA.: Harvard University Press.

Sampson, Robert J., and Janet L. Lauritsen. 1997. "Racial and Ethnic Disparities in Crime and Criminal Justice in the United States." In *Ethnicity, Crime, and Immigration: Comparative and Cross-National Perspectives*, edited by Michael Tonry. Vol. 21 of *Crime and Justice: A Review of Research*, edited by Michael Tonry. Chicago: University of Chicago Press.

Sentencing Project. 2004. *State Rates of Incarceration by Race*. Washington, DC: Sentencing Project.

———. 2005. *Racial Disparity in Sentencing: A Review of the Literature*. http://www.sentencingproject.org/Admin/Documents/publications/rd_sentencing_review.pdf.

———. 2008. *Reducing Racial Disparity in the Criminal Justice System: A Manual for Practitioners and Policymakers*. http://www.sentencingproject.org/PublicationDetails.aspx?PublicationID=626.

Snell, Tracy L. 2006. "Bulletin: Capital Punishment, 2005." Washington, DC: U.S. Department of Justice, Bureau of Justice Statistics.

Sorensen, Jon, Robert Hope, and Don Stemen. 2003. "Racial Disproportionality in State Prison Admissions: Can Regional Variation Be Explained by Differential Arrest Rates?" *Journal of Criminal Justice* 31:73–84.

Spohn, Cassia. 2000. "Thirty Years of Sentencing Reform: The Quest for a Racially Neutral Sentencing Process." In *Criminal Justice 2000*, vol. 3, edited by the U.S. National Institute of Justice. Washington, DC: U.S. Department of Justice, National Institute of Justice.

Spohn, Cassia, and David Holleran. 2000. "The Imprisonment Penalty Paid by Young, Unemployed Black and Hispanic Male Offenders." *Criminology* 38(1):281–306.

Steen, Sara, and Tara Opsal. 2007. "Punishment on the Installment Plan: Individual-Level Predictors of Parole Revocation in Four States." *Prison Journal* 87(3):344–66.

Thomas, Yonette F. 2007. "The Social Epidemiology of Drug Abuse." *American Journal of Preventative Medicine* 32(6S):S141–S144.

Tonry, Michael. 1991. "Black, White Incarceration Rates." *Overcrowded Times* 2(3):6–7.

————. 1995. *Malign Neglect: Race, Crime, and Punishment in America*. New York: Oxford University Press.

————. 1996. *Sentencing Matters*. New York: Oxford University Press.

————. 1997. "Ethnicity, Crime, and Immigration." In *Ethnicity, Crime, and Immigration: Comparative and Cross-National Perspectives*, edited by Michael Tonry. Vol. 21 of *Crime and Justice: A Review of Research*, edited by Michael Tonry. Chicago: University of Chicago Press.

Tonry, Michael, and Matthew Melewski. 2008. "The Malign Effects of Drug and Crime Control Policies on Black Americans." In *Crime and Justice: A Review of Research*, vol. 37, edited by Michael Tonry. Chicago: University of Chicago Press.

USCB (U.S. Census Bureau). 1990*a*. *1990 Census of Population and Housing, Summary Tape File 3; Matrices P058, P071, P082, P115A, P119*. http://factfinder.census.gov.

————. 1990*b*. *Census 1990, Summary File 1*. http://factfinder.census.gov.

————. 2007*a*. *American Community Survey, 2005, S0201*. http://factfinder.census.gov.

————. 2007*b*. *Census 2000, Fact Sheet for Race, Ethnic or Ancestry Group*. http://factfinder.census.gov.

————. 2007*c*. *Census 2000, Summary File 1*. http://factfinder.census.gov.

————. 2007*d*. *Census 2000, Summary File 4*. http://factfinder.census.gov.

————. 2007*e*. *National Population Estimates—Characteristics*. http://www.census.gov/popest/national/asrh/NC-EST2006/NC-EST2006-03.xls.

————. 2007*f*. *State Population Estimates—Characteristics—Minnesota*. http://www.census.gov/popest/states/asrh/tables/SC-EST2006-03-27.xls.

————. 2008*a*. *American Community Survey, 2003 Summary Tables*. http://www.census.gov.

————. 2008*b*. *American Community Survey, 2004 Summary Tables*. http://www.census.gov.

————. 2008*c*. *American Community Survey, 2005 Detailed Tables B01001A, B01001B*. http://factfinder.census.gov.

————. 2008*d*. *American Community Survey: A New Approach for Timely Information*. http://factfinder.census.gov/jsp/saff/SAFFInfo.jsp?_pageId = sp1_acs.

————. 2008*e*. *Census 2000 Summary File 3*. http://www.census.gov.

————. 2008*f*. *Estimates of the Population by Race and Hispanic Origin for the United States and States: July 1, 2007*. http://www.census.gov/popest/states/asrh/tables/SC-EST2007-04.xls.

U.S Department of Health and Human Services. 2006. *2005 National Survey on Drug Use and Health, Sample Design Report*. http://www.oas.samhsa.gov/nsduh/2k5MRB/2k5Sample/2k5sampleDesign.pdf.

————. 2007*a*. *Drug Abuse Warning Network, 2005: National Estimates of Drug-Related Emergency Department Visits*. http://dawninfo.samhsa.gov/pubs/edpubs/default.asp.

————. 2007*b*. *National Survey on Drug Use and Health*. http://www.oas.samhsa.gov/nhsda.htm.

Walker, Samuel, Cassia Spohn, and Miriam DeLone. 2007. *The Color of Justice: Race, Ethnicity, and Crime in America*. 4th ed. Belmont, CA: Wadsworth.

Weidner, Robert R., Richard S. Frase, and Jennifer S. Schultz. 2005. "The Impact of Contextual Factors on the Decision to Imprison in Large Urban Jurisdictions: A Multi-Level Analysis." *Crime and Delinquency* 51:400–424.

Western, Bruce. 2006. *Punishment and Inequality in America*. New York: Sage.

Williams, Chyvette T., and Carl A. Latkin. 2007. "Neighborhood Socioeconomic Status, Personal Network Attributes, and Use of Heroin and Cocaine." *American Journal of Preventative Medicine* 32(6S):S203–S210.

Wilson, William Julius. 1987. *The Truly Disadvantaged: The Inner City, the Underclass, and Public Policy*. Chicago: University of Chicago Press.

Wisconsin Office of Justice Assistance. 2008. *Commission on Reducing Racial Disparities in the Wisconsin Justice System Final Report*. Madison: Wisconsin Office of Justice Assistance.

Zimring, Franklin E. 2005. "Minimizing Harm from Minority Disproportion in American Juvenile Justice." In *Our Children, Their Children: Confronting Racial and Ethnic Differences in American Juvenile Justice*, edited by Darnell F. Hawkins and Kimberly Kempf-Leonard. Chicago: University of Chicago Press.

Zimring, Franklin E., and Gordon Hawkins. 1997. *Crime Is Not the Problem: Lethal Violence in America*. New York: Oxford University Press.

David P. Farrington and Maria M. Ttofi

Reducing School Bullying: Evidence-Based Implications for Policy

ABSTRACT

School bullying is an important social problem with serious short-term and long-term implications for physical and mental health. Bullies tend to be aggressive and delinquent, whereas victims tend to be anxious and depressed. School-based antibullying programs are effective in reducing bullying and being bullied. On average, bullying was reduced by 20–23 percent in experimental schools compared with control schools. The most important program components associated with a decrease in bullying are parent training, improved playground supervision, disciplinary methods, school conferences, videos, information for parents, classroom rules, and classroom management. The most important program elements associated with a decrease in being bullied are videos, disciplinary methods, work with peers, parent training, and cooperative group work. New antibullying programs should be designed, tested, and accredited on the basis of the most effective intervention components.

School bullying is regarded as an important social problem in many countries. Students who are bullied tend to have mental health problems such as anxiety and depression at the time and later in life (Olweus 1993c). Students who bully tend to be aggressive and delinquent at the time and later on (Farrington 1993). Not surprisingly, therefore, many attempts have been made to reduce school bullying. The main aim of

David P. Farrington is professor of psychological criminology at the Institute of Criminology, University of Cambridge, where Maria M. Ttofi is a Leverhulme Early Career Fellow. They are grateful to Peter Smith for helpful comments on earlier drafts. Parts of this essay are based on a report prepared for the Swedish National Council for Crime Prevention entitled *Effectiveness of Programmes to Reduce School Bullying*. It provides more technical details.

281

this essay is to review the highest-quality evaluations of antibullying programs and assess their effectiveness.

Given the serious short-term and long-term effects of bullying on children's physical and mental health, it is understandable why school bullying has increasingly become a topic of both public concern and research efforts. Research on school bullying has expanded worldwide, with a variety of intervention programs being implemented, and with some countries legally requiring schools to have an antibullying policy. Despite the marked increase in antibullying research, however, much still needs to be learned about how to design and implement effective intervention programs, especially taking into account the varying results of intervention research in different countries. In what ways, and why, is one antibullying program more effective than another? What intervention elements can predict the success of a program in reducing school bullying? These questions have inspired our research.

The definition of school bullying includes several key elements: physical, verbal, or psychological attack or intimidation that is intended to cause fear, distress, or harm to the victim; an imbalance of power (psychological or physical), with a more powerful child (or children) oppressing less powerful ones; and repeated incidents between the same children over a prolonged period (Farrington 1993; Olweus 1993b). School bullying can occur in school or on the way to or from school. It is not bullying when two persons of the same strength (physical, psychological, or verbal) victimize each other.

The prevalence of bullying depends on the time period inquired about and on the frequency criterion used (e.g., once or twice, sometimes, weekly, or more often). Nevertheless, bullying is surprisingly common. Pernille Due and her colleagues (2005) carried out the largest study of the prevalence of being bullied (sometimes or more often during this school term) among nationally representative samples of 11–15-year-olds in 28 industrialized Western countries (surveying over 4,000 students per country on average). Overall, 18 percent of boys and 15 percent of girls were bullied according to this criterion. In the United States, 16 percent of boys and 11 percent of girls were bullied.

This essay presents a systematic and meta-analytic review of the effectiveness of antibullying programs. Systematic reviews use rigorous methods for locating, appraising, and synthesizing evidence from prior evaluation studies in order to minimize bias in drawing conclusions. Meta-analyses summarize effect sizes of interventions and investigate factors that correlate with effect size. These two methods were used in order to draw the best possible conclusions about what works in preventing school bullying, for whom, and under what circumstances.

Undoubtedly the most influential pioneer of research on school bullying is Dan Olweus of Norway. He developed and applied a "whole-school" approach to bullying prevention in 1983. The key elements include the whole school taking responsibility for bullying and giving it a high priority; increasing awareness of bullying by teachers, students, and parents; publicizing explicit school policies designed to reduce bullying; and discussing bullying as part of the curriculum. Other elements include encouraging peer disapproval of bullying, encouraging bystanders to help victims, encouraging victims and bystanders to report bullying to teachers, and improving monitoring and supervision of students, especially in the playground.

In this essay, we focus on the 30 highest-quality evaluations of antibullying programs. These have been implemented in many different countries. Of these, seven used the now well-developed Olweus Bullying Prevention Program (OBPP). Seven others reported explicitly that their program was inspired by the work of Dan Olweus. Nine others implemented whole-school programs, usually including many intervention components and large-scale evaluations, but did not explicitly indicate that their program was inspired by Olweus. The remaining seven used more limited or focused programs and typically were evaluated in small-scale studies.

Overall, we conclude that school-based antibullying programs are effective in reducing bullying and victimization. The results indicated that bullying and victimization were reduced by 20–23 percent in experimental schools compared with control schools.

The most important program elements associated with a decrease in bullying are disciplinary methods, parent training, improved playground supervision, information for parents, school conferences, classroom rules, classroom management, teacher training, and videos. In addition, the total number of elements, and the duration and intensity of the program for children and teachers, are significantly associated with a decrease in bullying. Programs inspired by the work of Olweus worked best.

The most important program elements associated with a decrease in being bullied are videos, disciplinary methods, work with peers, parent training, and cooperative group work. In addition, the duration and intensity of the program for children and teachers are significantly associated with a decrease in victimization. The programs worked better with older children, in Norway specifically and in Europe more generally, and they were less effective in the United States. Older programs, those in which the outcome measure was two times per month or more, and those with other experimental-control and age-cohort designs, also yielded better results.

The main policy implication of our review is that new antibullying programs should be designed and tested on the basis of our results. These could be grounded in the successful Olweus program but should be modified in light of the key program elements found to be most effective. We recommend that such programs should be accredited by an international organization.

This essay is organized as follows. In Section I, we specify our objectives and describe previous efforts to summarize the effectiveness of antibullying programs. In Section II we describe the OBPP as used in Norway and in South Carolina, one other program inspired by Olweus's work, two other whole-school programs, and two more limited programs. We then describe our methods in Section III, specifying our criteria for including or excluding studies and the searches we carried out to locate relevant evaluations. The results are presented in Section IV. A total number of 593 reports were found concerning interventions to prevent school bullying, but only 59 of these (describing evaluations of 30 different programs) met our criteria for inclusion in the review. The number of reports concerned with antibullying programs has increased considerably over time.

Our conclusions are presented in Section V. In Section VI we systematically code key elements of each program and relate these elements (and other features of evaluations such as the average age of the students and the sample size) to our measures of effect size. Finally, in Section VII, we summarize the main findings, focus on the implications for policy and practice, and propose future directions for research.

I. Background

Many school-based interventions have been devised and implemented in an attempt to reduce bullying. These have targeted bullies, victims, peers, teachers, or the school in general. Many programs seem to have been based on commonsense ideas about what might reduce bullying rather than on empirically validated theories of why children bully, why children become victims, or why bullying occurs.

The first large-scale program was implemented nationally in Norway in 1983, following three well-publicized suicides of Norwegian boys that were attributed to bullying. A more intensive version of the national program was evaluated in Bergen by Dan Olweus (1991). This evaluation showed a dramatic decrease in being bullied of roughly half after the program. Since then many other large-scale antibullying programs, some inspired by Olweus and some based on other principles, have been implemented and evaluated in many countries. Anna Baldry and David Farrington (2007) reviewed 16 major evaluations in 11 different countries and concluded that eight of them produced desirable results, two produced mixed results, four found small or negligible effects, and two produced undesirable results. Most programs were rather complex, and the effectiveness of the different components of programs was not clear.

A. Objectives

Our main objective is to assess the effectiveness of school-based antibullying programs in reducing bullying. We sought to locate and summarize all the major evaluations of programs in developed countries. Bullying has been studied in (at least) Australia, Austria, Belgium, Canada, Cyprus, Denmark, England and Wales, Finland, France, Germany, Greece, Iceland, Ireland, Israel, Italy, Luxembourg, Japan, Malta, New Zealand, Northern Ireland, Norway, Portugal, Scotland, Spain, Sweden, Switzerland, the Netherlands, and the United States (Smith et al. 1999). We sought to include evaluations in all these countries.

Bullying is a type of aggressive behavior. However, it should not be equated with aggression or violence; not all aggression or violence involves bullying, and not all bullying involves aggression or violence. For example, bullying includes being called nasty names; being rejected, ostracized, or excluded from activities; having rumors spread about one; having belongings taken away; teasing; and threatening (Baldry and Farrington 1999). We were interested in programs specifically intended to prevent or reduce school bullying, not programs intended to prevent or reduce school aggression or violence.

Special methods are needed to study bullying in different countries because of the problem of capturing the term "bullying" in different languages. Peter Smith and his colleagues (2002) reviewed the meaning of bullying in 14 different countries in an attempt to examine how the use of global terms (such as "bullying") can affect the measured prevalence of bullying. They give a nice example of how even similar terms within the same language (e.g., bullying, teasing, harassment, abuse) can have different connotations and contexts and may be understood differently by persons answering questionnaires. An alternative to using global terms such as bullying in surveys is to ask for information about particular acts, such as "hit him/her on the face" or "excluded him/her from games" (Smith et al. 2002, p. 1131), and this is what researchers often do (Kalliotis 2000, p. 49; Pateraki and Houndoumadi 2001, p. 174).

B. Previous Reviews

American research has generally been targeted toward school violence or peer victimization rather than toward bullying. There are a number of existing reviews of school violence programs and school-based interventions for aggressive behavior (e.g., Howard, Flora, and Griffin 1999; Wilson, Lipsey, and Derzon 2003; Mytton et al. 2006; Wilson and Lipsey 2007). We have consulted these, but we must emphasize that our research aims to review programs explicitly designed to reduce bullying and that explicitly measured bullying (not school violence).

The most informative single source of reports of antibullying programs is a book edited by Peter Smith and his colleagues (Smith, Pepler, and Rigby 2004a). It contains descriptions of 13 programs implemented in 11 different countries. Some reviews also contain summaries of major antibullying programs (e.g., Rigby 2002; Smith, Ananiadou, and Cowie 2003; Ortega 2006). The most relevant existing reviews are by David Smith and his colleagues (2004), who summarized effect sizes in 14 whole-school antibullying programs, and by Rachel Vreeman and Aaron Carroll (2007), who reviewed 26 school-based programs. These two prior reviews are of high quality. However, neither carried out a full meta-analysis measuring weighted mean effect sizes and correlations between study features and effect sizes. David Smith and his colleagues (2004) reviewed 14 evaluations up to 2002, six of which were uncontrolled. Vreeman and Carroll (2007) reviewed 26 evaluations up to 2004, restricted to studies published in the English language.

A more recent meta-analytic review was published by Christopher

Ferguson and his colleagues (2007). However, this included searches in only one database, for articles published only between the years 1995 and 2006. It included outcome variables that measured "some element of bullying behavior or aggression toward peers, including direct aggressive behavior toward children in a school setting" (p. 407). It was thus not focused specifically on bullying behavior. A more focused meta-analytic review was completed by Kenneth Merrell and his colleagues (2008). However, this included searches in only two databases for studies published only in English, and it presented a wide range of outcome measures; there were only eight studies in which the outcome was self-reported bullying and only 10 studies in which the outcome was self-reported victimization.

Interestingly, both the Ferguson and Merrell reviews concluded that antibullying programs had little effect on school bullying. After completing our more extensive review, we believe that their conclusions are incorrect. In the present report, we go way beyond these previous reviews by doing much more extensive searches for evaluations such as hand-searching all volumes of 35 journals from 1983 through the end of April 2008, searching for international evaluations in 18 electronic databases and in languages other than English, carrying out much more extensive meta-analyses (including correlating effect sizes with study features and research design), and focusing only on programs that are specifically designed to reduce bullying and not aggressive behavior (i.e., where the outcome variables specifically measure bullying).

II. Descriptions of Programs

As mentioned, 30 different programs were included in our review. The included programs can be categorized into the Olweus Bullying Prevention Program (seven), those inspired by the work of Olweus (seven), other whole-school programs (nine), and more limited or focused programs (seven). In this section, we describe the OBPP in Norway and in South Carolina, one program inspired by the work of Olweus (the Dutch antibullying program), two other whole-school programs (Kiva and Kia Kaha), and two more limited programs (the Greek antibullying program and Youth Matters). These programs, implemented in six different countries, should give the reader a good idea of the characteristics of the more successful antibullying programs that we examined.

For all programs we have attempted to contact the evaluators of the program. By mid-July 2008, we had received positive feedback from evaluators of 24 of the 30 programs.

A. Olweus Bullying Prevention Program (OBPP)

The OBPP, as implemented in Norway, was a multilevel program aiming at targeting the individual, the school, the classroom, and the community. Apart from marked mass-media publicity, the program started with a 1-day school conference during which the problem of bullying was discussed among school staff, students, and parents. This signaled the formal commencement of the intervention. Two different types of materials were produced: a handbook or manual for teachers (entitled *Olweus' Core Program against Bullying and Antisocial Behavior*) and a folder with information for parents and families. The intervention also included a compact disc program that was used for assessing and analyzing the data obtained at the pretest period, so that school-specific interventions could then be implemented; a video on bullying; the Revised Olweus Bully/Victim Questionnaire; and the book *Bullying at School: What We Know and What We Can Do* (Olweus 1993b).

The antibullying measures mainly targeted three different levels of intervention: the school, the classroom, and the individual. At the school level, the intervention included

- meetings among teachers to discuss ways of improving peer relations and staff discussion groups,
- parent/teacher meetings to discuss the issue of bullying,
- increased supervision during recess and lunchtime,
- improvement of playground facilities so that children have better places to play during recess time,
- a questionnaire survey, and
- the formation of a coordinating group.

At the classroom level the intervention included

- information for students about the issue of bullying and active student involvement in devising class rules against bullying,
- classroom activities for students including role-playing situations that could help students learn how to deal better with bullying,
- class rules against bullying,
- class meetings with students, and
- meetings with the parents of the class.

At the individual level the intervention included

- serious talks with bullies and their parents and enforcement of nonhostile, nonphysical sanctions;
- serious talks with victims, providing support and providing assertiveness skills training to help them learn how to deal successfully with bullying, and talks with the parents of victims;
- talks with children not involved to make them become effective helpers; and
- development of individual intervention plans.

An interesting feature of the OBPP is that it offered guided information about what schools should do during both the intervention and the maintenance periods. "The Olweus program demands significant commitment from the school during the 'introductory period' which covers a period of about 18 months. Later the methodology acquired by the staff and the routines decided by the school may be maintained using less resources. . . . Yet, even for the maintenance period, the program offers a point by point description of what the school should do to continue its work against bullying in accordance with Olweus methodology" (Olweus 2004*b*, p. 1). At the school level, training was offered to the whole school staff, with additional training provided to the coordinators and key personnel. These were responsible for coordinating the overall antibullying initiative in their school. The program also included cooperation among experts and teachers (e.g., psychologists) who worked with children involved in bullying.

B. South Carolina Program

This program implemented the OBPP in South Carolina schools. It was a comprehensive school-based antibullying program essentially inspired by the Norwegian model (Melton et al. 1998, pp. 72, 74) and aimed to target bullying at school, classroom, individual, and community levels.

In accordance with the OBPP, the South Carolina program included a schoolwide intervention. In each school, coordinating committees planned and guided the school's antibullying initiative throughout the various phases of the project. The committees consisted of school psychologists or counselors and representative teachers, students, and parents. In each school, a survey was conducted prior to the implementation of the program; it aimed to assess the nature and extent of bullying problems in the school. The survey results were presented during a school conference day that aimed to increase students' awareness about this problem. There were schoolwide events to launch the program. Another element at the school level included teacher surveillance in order to crack down on "hot spots" of bullying.

At the classroom level, core elements included the formulation of clear antibullying rules, the use of consistent sanctions for violating the rules, the use of consistent praise of prosocial behavior by teachers, and the scheduling of regular classroom meetings or discussions during which teachers and peers talked about issues related to bullying in their school. Teachers had a wide variety of materials that they could use in the classroom such as videos and classroom materials, a teachers' guide, and program newsletters that they could consult (*Bully-Free Times*).

At the individual level, interventions included discussions with bullies and their parents and the development of safety plans for chronic victims of bullying. Informational newsletters for parents were provided. At the community level, an effort was made to involve community members in the antibullying initiative by making the program known among a wide range of residents in the local community; engaging community members in the school's antibullying activities; and engaging community members, students, and school personnel in antibullying efforts within the community (e.g., by introducing program elements into summer church school classes).

Other elements included the involvement of school-based mental health professionals to assist the development of individual interventions with children frequently involved in bullying as perpetrators or victims, the development of American versions of several materials used in the OBPP, and the development of additional materials for teachers and other school staff such as teachers' guidebooks and teachers' newsletters.

C. Dutch Antibullying Program

The antibullying initiative in the Netherlands was inspired by the Olweus program (Fekkes, Pijpers, and Verloove-Vanhorick 2006, p. 639). The program was specifically designed to tackle bullying behavior by involving teachers, parents, and students. It offered a 2-day training session for teachers in order to inform them about bullying behavior and to instruct them about how to deal with bullying incidents in schools. During the intervention period, teachers had access to the training staff for additional advice. Intervention schools were supported by an external organization named KPC, which specialized in training school staff and in assisting schools in setting up new curricula and guidelines. The core intervention program included antibullying training for teachers, a bullying survey, antibullying rules and a written antibullying school policy, increased intensity of surveillance, and information meetings for parents.

During the intervention, there was careful dissemination of the antibullying program to intervention schools. The researchers provided information about the number of intervention and control schools that have used the above-mentioned elements of intervention. Finally, intervention schools were supplied with the book *Bullying in Schools: How to Deal with It* and with a Bullying Test, a computerized questionnaire that children could complete anonymously in the classroom.

D. KiVa

The name of this project, implemented in Finland, is an acronym for *Kiusaamista Vastaan*, which means "against bullying." The word *kiva* in Finnish means "nice," which is another reason why the acronym was chosen. Regarding the overall perspective of the program, the KiVa project included a universal and an indicated intervention. The universal intervention concerned efforts made to influence group norms and the indicated intervention concerned the way in which specific cases were handled in schools through individual and group discussions between the teacher and the students involved (Salmivalli, Karna, and Poskiparta, forthcoming).

The KiVa program included a large variety of concrete materials for students, teachers, and parents. It also used the Internet and virtual learning environments (e.g., computer games against bullying), aiming in this way to enhance students' attitudes against bullying. Students received their own personal user identification, which they could use as a password before the completion of each Web-based questionnaire on bullying. KiVa included 20-hour student lessons, which were carried out by student teachers. The lessons involved discussions, group work, short films about bullying, and role-playing exercises. After each lesson, a class rule was adopted, based on the central theme of the lesson.

A unique feature was the use of an antibullying computer game. The game involved five levels, and the teacher always activated the next level after the relevant lesson was completed. Students were able to begin using the game after the third lesson; the second level was played after the fifth lesson, and so on until the end of the school year. Each level included three components that were named "I know," "I can," and "I do." In the first component, students were informed about basic facts on bullying. In the second component, the "I can" component, students moved around in the virtual school and faced different challenging bullying incidents. Finally, the third component was used to encourage students to make use of their knowledge and skills in real-life situations.

Another important element was teacher training. Teachers were also provided with vests that they could use during playtime while supervising the school yard. This simple technique aimed to enhance teachers' visibility in the schoolyard and to signal that bullying was taken seriously. All teachers carrying out the KiVa program could seek advice from a Web-based discussion forum, where they could share experiences and ideas about bullying with other colleagues.

Within the school framework, the program facilitated the use of a peer support group for victims of bullying. The classroom teacher was expected to arrange a group with two to four classmates—those who were prosocial and had high status in the class—who were expected to provide support to victimized students, thus sustaining healthy peer relationships. The KiVa program incorporated both punitive and no-blame approaches when dealing with perpetrators of bullying. Half of the school teams were instructed to use more punitive approaches (e.g., "what you have done is wrong and it has to stop right now"), and the rest were instructed to use no-blame approaches in their discussions with children (e.g., "your classmate is also having a hard time, and this is why he behaves like that; what could we do to help him?"). There was also cooperative group work among experts when dealing with children involved in bullying.

Finally, the KiVa program involved parents. A parents' guide was sent to the home that provided information about bullying and advice on how parents could be involved to reduce this problem. Information nights for parents were also organized and provided.

E. Kia Kaha

Kia Kaha, in New Zealand, was designed as an antibullying program, but it also met the requirements of two essential areas within the curriculum framework: social sciences and health/physical well-being (Raskauskas 2007, p. 10). The program involved a whole-school approach to bullying and victimization. In the Maori language the word *kia kaha* means "to stand strong," which is why this name was used "to represent the need for the whole-school community to stand strong to prevent bullying" (p. 9). The program covered issues such as peer relationships, identifying and dealing with bullying, making personal choices, developing feelings of self-worth, respecting differences, and working cooperatively to build a safe classroom environment.

The Kia Kaha curriculum used several resources, including a teachers' guide with an overview of the program, instructions on how to plan and implement the lessons, a video, and information to be sent home to parents. The video included five bullying situations that provided the basis for discussing what was happening and what could be done. Students were taught to take steps to defuse bullying situations: stop, think, consider options, act, and follow up. The student and teacher components were delivered through the regular classroom curriculum.

Police education officers (PEOs) are trained as educators and involved in youth education in New Zealand. PEOs visited schools and introduced the programs offered by the police, including Kia Kaha. They introduced the whole-school approach and tried to convince principals to use it in their schools. They also trained the teachers in the program, hosted parent nights, and taught up to four lessons of the curriculum.

F. Greek Antibullying Program

The Greek antibullying initiative was a 4-week intervention program that aimed to minimize both bullying and victimization. The program was implemented in schools in central Greece. The conceptual framework was based on a theoretical model proposed by Salmivalli in 1999 (Andreou, Didaskalou, and Vlachou 2007, p. 696), according to which changing an individual's behavior (e.g., the bully's behavior) entailed motivating not only the particular person but also the rest of the group members (the participant roles approach).

The program was embedded within the wider curriculum of the fourth-, fifth-, and sixth-grade classrooms and consisted of eight instructional hours, each hour corresponding to one curricular activity. The curricular activities were presented to students by their classroom teachers, who received training beforehand. The teacher training consisted of five 4-hour meetings and aimed to increase awareness of the bullying problem and its seriousness as well as to raise teachers' self-efficacy in implementing the program (Andreou, Didaskalou, and Vlachou 2007, p. 697).

The Greek antibullying curriculum was divided into three parts in accordance with the three main theoretical axes proposed by Salmivalli, namely, awareness-raising, self-reflection, and commitment to new behaviors (Andreou, Didaskalou, and Vlachou 2007, pp. 697–98).

In line with the first axis (awareness-raising), small-group and whole-class discussions were conducted (over three instructional hours) that aimed to increase students' awareness of the bullying problem. Corresponding materials included a real snapshot from the playground, a story entitled "A New Friend," and students' own drawings. In line with the second axis (self-reflection), two instructional hours involving classroom discussions were conducted. These discussions placed emphasis on the participant roles that students took in the bullying process. Corresponding materials involved each student's completion of open-ended sentences. Through this activity students were intended to reflect on critical issues concerning the causes, benefits, feelings, and consequences of adopting different roles. In line with the third axis (commitment to new behaviors), three instructional hours of small-group and whole-class discussions were conducted on different ways of approaching or solving the peer-conflict situation and the formulation of class rules. Corresponding materials involved an open-ended comic strip for group completion to find a solution to the bullying situation presented in the relevant story.

G. Youth Matters

The Youth Matters program, in Denver, Colorado, used "a curricular and a modified systemic approach to bullying prevention" (Jenson and Dieterich 2007, p. 287). The aim was to strengthen peer and school norms against antisocial behaviors by addressing critical issues (issue modules) such as the difference between teasing and bullying, building empathy, risks and norms surrounding aggression, and so on. The curriculum also aimed to promote skills (skill modules; structured skills training sessions) that students could use in order to stay safe at school, cope with bullying, enhance their social skills, and improve their peer relationships. To address systemic issues associated with bullying, curriculum modules terminated with the development of classroom or

schoolwide projects, which placed emphasis on the negative consequences of bullying for students.

The curriculum consisted of 10-session modules. Each module included a 30–40-page story, the content of which was directly linked to
the structured skills training sessions. With regard to the implementation of the program, all curriculum materials were "language sensitive": translated into Spanish for use in the three Spanish-speaking
classrooms included in the evaluation. Youth Matters curriculum modules were offered to fourth and fifth graders. According to Jenson and
Dieterich (2007, p. 287), grades 4 and 5 were selected "based on an
appropriate fit between developmental ability and curricula."

The Youth Matters program was based on a theoretically grounded
curriculum. The curriculum was based on theoretical constructs derived from the Social Development Model. The latter integrated perspectives from three theories (i.e., social control theory, social learning
theory, and differential association theory) and proposed that four factors inhibit the development of antisocial development in children.
These were bonding or attachment to family, schools, and positive
peers; belief in the shared values or norms of the above-mentioned
social units; external constraints or consistent standards against antisocial behavior; and social, cognitive, and emotional skills that can be
seen as protective tools for children to solve problems and perform
adequately in social situations. The Youth Matters curriculum addressed each of these four core areas.

III. Methods

A systematic review aims to locate and synthesize research that bears
on a particular question comprehensively, using organized, transparent,
and replicable procedures at each step in the process (Littell, Corcoran,
and Pillai 2008). It includes explicit criteria for inclusion or exclusion
of studies in a highly structured way that aims to minimize bias in the
conclusions. It allows "decisions to be made on a transparent and potentially defendable basis, as it draws on all relevant scientifically sound
research, rather than on single studies" (Petticrew and Roberts 2006,
p. 11). Systematic reviews allow for a more objective appraisal of the
evidence than traditional narrative reviews and may thus contribute to
resolving uncertainty when original research, reviews, and editorials
disagree (Egger, Smith, and O'Rourke 2001, p. 23). Given their great

potential to inform policy and practice, the marked increase in systematic reviews in both health and social sciences should come as no surprise.

Our systematic review was carried out under the aegis of the Campbell Collaboration (see http://www.campbellcollaboration.org), which publishes systematic reviews of the effectiveness of criminological, social, and educational interventions. However, the review we completed for the Swedish National Council for Crime Prevention (Ttofi, Farrington, and Baldry 2008), on which this essay is based, was more restricted than our final Campbell review will be when it is completed. In particular, this essay focuses only on the larger evaluations and on those with outcome measures of self-reported bullying and victimization.

A. Measuring the Effects of a Program

How can the effects of an antibullying program on bullying and victimization be established? The highest-quality studies are those that maximize statistical conclusion validity, internal validity, construct validity, external validity, and descriptive validity (Farrington 2003).

Statistical conclusion validity is concerned with the effect size (and its associated confidence interval) measuring the effect of the intervention. Internal validity is concerned with whether it really was the intervention that had an effect. Construct validity refers to whether the intervention really was an antibullying program and whether the outcome really was a measure of bullying. External validity refers to the generalizability of the results and can be best established in a systematic review. Descriptive validity refers to the adequacy of the presentation of key features of the evaluation in a research report.

Internal validity is the most important. The main threats to internal validity are well known (Campbell and Stanley 1966; Cook and Campbell 1979; Shadish, Cook, and Campbell 2002):

- *Selection:* The effect reflects preexisting differences between experimental and control conditions.
- *Aging/maturation:* The effect reflects a continuation of preexisting trends, for example, in normal human development.
- *History:* The effect is caused by some event occurring during the same time period as the intervention.
- *Testing:* The pretest measurement causes a change in the posttest measure.

- *Instrumentation:* The effect is caused by a change in the method of measuring the outcome.
- *Regression to the mean:* Where an intervention is implemented on units with unusually high scores (e.g., classes with high bullying rates), natural fluctuation will cause a decrease in these scores on the posttest, which may be mistakenly interpreted as an effect of the intervention.
- *Differential attrition:* The effect is caused by differential loss of children from experimental compared to control conditions.
- *Causal order:* It is unclear whether the intervention preceded the outcome.

In addition, there may be interactive effects of threats. For example, a selection-aging effect may occur if the experimental and control conditions have different preexisting trends that continue, or a selection-history effect may occur if the experimental and control conditions experience different historical events (e.g., where they are located in different settings). Also, it is important to eliminate the problem of seasonal variations in bullying by measuring it at the same time of the year before and after an intervention.

In maximizing internal validity, it is essential to compare the intervention condition with some kind of control condition, in order to estimate what would have happened in the absence of the intervention. If children are merely measured before and after receiving the intervention, it is impossible to disentangle the impact of the program from aging, history, testing, regression, and attrition effects. In particular, the prevalence of bullying decreases steadily with age from 7 to 15 (Olweus 1991). Therefore, if experimental children are tested before and 1 year after the intervention, their bullying will have decreased because of aging effects alone.

According to Tom Cook and Donald Campbell (1979), the minimum design that is interpretable requires experimental and control conditions. The best way of eliminating selection, aging, history, testing, and regression effects is to assign children randomly to experimental and control conditions. Provided that a sufficiently large number of children are randomly assigned (e.g., at least 100), those in the experimental condition will be similar to those in the control condition (before the intervention) on all measured and unmeasured variables that might influence bullying.

In research on antibullying programs, schools or school classes, not children, in most cases are randomly assigned to receive the program. No experimental study of bullying has yet randomly assigned enough classes (e.g., at least 100) to achieve the benefits of randomization in eliminating threats to internal validity. Therefore, it is not clear that randomized experiments on antibullying programs are methodologically superior to quasi-experimental evaluations with before and after measures of bullying in experimental and control conditions. It is clear that these two designs are potentially the best methodologically. The main threat to internal validity in them is differential attrition from experimental and control conditions. In addition, if the experimental classes are worse than the control classes to start with, regression to the mean could be a problem.

Comparisons of experimental and control classes with no prior measures of bullying are clearly inferior to comparisons with prior measures. Where there are no prior measures of bullying, it is important to include some pretest measures that might establish the comparability of experimental and control children. Otherwise, this design is vulnerable to selection and regression effects in particular.

The age-cohort design, in which children of a certain age X in year 1 before the intervention are compared with (different) children of the same age X in the same school in year 2 after the intervention, was pioneered by Dan Olweus (1991). It largely eliminates problems of selection, aging, regression, and differential attrition, but it is vulnerable to history and testing effects. Overall, the experimental-control comparisons and age-cohort designs might be regarded by some researchers as methodologically inferior to the randomized experiments and experimental-control/before-after designs, but all designs have advantages and problems. These are the four best designs that have been used to evaluate the effects of antibullying programs, and we will give credence to them all in providing useful information about the effectiveness of these programs.

B. Criteria for Inclusion or Exclusion

In line with our coding book, we use seven criteria for inclusion of studies: First, the study described an evaluation of a program designed specifically to reduce school (kindergarten to high school) bullying. Studies of aggression or violence were excluded. For example, a study by Tom Woods and colleagues (2007) was excluded because the researchers did not indicate that they were studying bullying specifically.

Some other reports were also excluded because they focused on the impact of a specific antibullying program on some other outcome measures such as educational attainment (e.g., Fonagy et al. 2005), knowledge about and attitudes toward bullying (e.g., Meraviglia et al. 2003), or children's safety awareness with regard to different types of potentially unsafe situations, including being bullied (e.g., Warden et al. 1997).

Second, bullying was defined as including physical, verbal, or psychological attack or intimidation that is intended to cause fear, distress, or harm to the victim; and an imbalance of power, with the more powerful child (or children) oppressing less powerful ones. Many definitions also require repeated incidents between the same children over a prolonged period, but we did not require that, because many studies of bullying do not measure or report this element of the definition.

Third, bullying was measured using self-report questionnaires. We set this restriction so that all included evaluations are comparable. A meta-analysis requires comparable effect size data. Most evaluations use self-report questionnaires, but some employ other measures such as peer ratings, teacher ratings, observational data, or school records.

Fourth, the effectiveness of the program was measured by comparing students who received it (the experimental condition) with students who did not receive it (the control condition). We required that there must have been some control of extraneous variables in the evaluation (establishing the equivalence of conditions) by randomization, pretest measures of bullying, or the choice of some kind of comparable control condition. Because of low internal validity, we excluded uncontrolled studies that had only before and after measures of bullying in experimental schools or classes. However, we included studies that controlled for age. For example, in the Olweus (1991) evaluation, all students received the antibullying program, but Olweus compared students of age X after the program with different students of the same age X in the same schools before the program. We included this kind of age-cohort design because arguably the experimental and control students were comparable. We compared results obtained in the four types of included research designs, namely, randomized experiments, before-after/experimental-control comparisons, other experimental-control comparisons, and age-cohort designs.

Fifth, published and unpublished reports of research conducted in developed countries between 1983 and April 2008 are included. We believe that no worthwhile evaluation research on antibullying programs was conducted before the pioneering research of Dan Olweus, which was carried out in 1983.

Sixth, it was possible to measure the effect size. The main measures of effect size are the odds ratio, based on numbers of bullies/nonbullies (or victims/nonvictims), and the standardized mean difference, based on mean scores on bullying and victimization. These measures are mathematically related. We used the odds ratio. Where the required information was not presented in reports, we tried to obtain it by contacting the authors directly. Some studies that included a randomized or nonrandomized experimental design (e.g., Twemlow, Fonagy, and Sacco 2005; Heydenberk, Heydenberk, and Tzenova 2006; Wiefferink et al. 2006) were not included in this analysis because they did not provide enough data to allow us to calculate an effect size. Some other controlled studies were included (e.g., Salmivalli, Karna, and Poskiparta, forthcoming),[1] even though their final results have not yet been published. In this case, we use the available evaluation data with the possibility that the final evaluation results might be different.

Seventh, the minimum initial sample size (total in experimental and control conditions) was 200. We set this minimum for the following reasons. Larger studies are usually better funded and of higher methodological quality. Moreover, we are very concerned about the frequently found negative correlations between sample size and effect size (e.g., Farrington and Welsh 2003; Jolliffe and Farrington 2007). We suspect that these correlations reflect publication bias. Smaller studies that yield statistically significant results may be published, whereas those that do not may be left in the file drawer. In contrast, larger studies (often funded by an official agency) are likely to be published irrespective of their results. Excluding smaller studies reduces problems of publication bias and therefore yields a more accurate estimate of the true effect size. In addition, larger studies are more likely to have higher external validity or generalizability. Finally, attrition (e.g., between the pretest and posttest) is less problematic in larger studies. A study with 100 children that suffers 30 percent attrition will end up with only 35 boys and 35 girls; these are very small samples (with associated large confidence intervals) for estimating the prevalence of bullying and victimization. In contrast, a study with 300 children that

---

[1] Personal communication from Christina Salmivalli via email (June 18, 2008).

suffers 30 percent attrition will end up with 105 boys and 105 girls; these are much more adequate samples.

C. Searching Strategies

We started by searching for the names of established researchers in the area of bullying prevention (e.g., Australia [Ken Rigby], Canada [Debra Repler], England [Peter K. Smith], Spain [Rosario Ortega], and Norway [Dan Olweus]). This searching strategy was used in different databases in order initially to obtain as many evaluations of known research programs in different journals as possible.

We then searched by using several keywords in different databases. In total, we carried out the same searching strategies in 18 electronic databases. In all databases, the same keywords were used with different combinations. More specifically: "bully/bullies/anti-bullying/bully-victims" AND "school" AND "intervention/program/outcome/evaluation/effect/prevention/tackling." We did not include "violence" or "aggression" as keywords along with "bully/bullies/anti-bullying/bully-victims" because we knew that this would identify many studies that are not relevant for our purposes.

We hand-searched all volumes of 35 journals—either online or in print—from 1983 through the end of April 2008. For some journals, a hard copy was not available. In this case, we tried to obtain an online version of the journal. In the Swedish report (Ttofi, Farrington, and Baldry 2008), the interested reader can see the list of databases (table 1, p. 16) and the names and exact volumes of journals (table 2, p. 17) that we searched.

We sought information from key researchers on bullying and from international colleagues in the Campbell Collaboration. In March 2008, we had a meeting with key educational users of the information in Copenhagen, organized by the Nordic Campbell Centre. When we identified a report in a language other than English (e.g., Martin, Martinez, and Tirado 2005; Sprober, Schlottke, and Hautzinger 2006), we asked colleagues to provide us with a brief translation of key features that were needed for our coding schedule. We believe that, with the cooperation of colleagues in the Campbell Collaboration, we were able to include relevant research from many different developed countries.

A stipulation was made that the title or abstract of each paper had to include one of the essential keywords that we searched. However, some book chapters, mainly from edited books on bullying prevention,

TABLE 1

Categorization of Reports Based on Their Relevance to the
Present Review

Relevance	Description
Minor relevance	Recommendations for integration of survey results into anti-bullying policies and/or talk generally about the necessity for bullying interventions
Weak relevance	Talking more specifically about antibullying programs (description of more than one antibullying program) and/or reviews of antibullying programs and/or placing emphasis on suggestions/recommendations for reducing bullying
Medium relevance	Description of a specific antibullying program
Strong relevance	Evaluation of an antibullying program, but not included because it has no experimental vs. control comparison or no outcome data on bullying
Included in the Campbell review	Evaluation of an antibullying program that has an experimental and control condition (N may be < 200; teacher and peer nominations may also be included as outcome measures)
Included in the present review	Evaluation of an antibullying program that has an experimental and control condition ($N > 200$, self-reported bullying as outcome measure)

were included even though their titles and abstracts (if provided) did
not include any of our keywords if their content concerned antibullying
programs.

IV. Results of Searches

A total number of 593 reports concerned with interventions to prevent
school bullying are encompassed in our systematic review. All studies
were categorized on the basis of a relevance scale that we constructed
(table 1).

Table 2 shows the percentage of studies within each category. The
vast majority of reports (40.8 percent) were of weak relevance, making
general suggestions about reducing bullying or, more rarely, reviewing
antibullying programs. With regard to the reports we were not able to
obtain, most were master's or PhD theses (11 theses, three unpublished
manuscripts, and two conference papers). The cost of ordering these
theses through the service of interlibrary loans was so time-consuming
or expensive as to make this option problematic. It is possible that some
of these reports would be eligible for inclusion in our meta-analysis.

TABLE 2

Percentage of Studies within Each Category

Category	Count (N)	Percentage
Not obtained	16	2.7
Minor relevance	87	14.7
Weak relevance	242	40.8
Medium relevance	94	15.9
Strong relevance	78	13.2
Campbell review	17	2.9
Present review	59	9.9

For instance, we understand, on the basis of the review by Vreeman and Carroll (2007), that the thesis of Kaiser-Ulrey (2003) might be eligible for inclusion in the Campbell review but not in the present review.[2] Only 76 reports (12.8 percent) were included in the present review or in our more comprehensive Campbell review.

The number of reports concerned with antibullying programs has increased markedly over time (Ttofi, Farrington, and Baldry 2008, fig. 2). The total time period was divided into 5-year chunks as follows: 1983–87, 1988–92, 1993–97, 1998–2002, and 2003–8. The most obvious increase of interest in implementing and evaluating bullying prevention programs occurred in the latest period. In the last 5 years or so (2003 up to April 2008), the number of studies in each category doubled compared with the previous 5-year period. It is encouraging that studies with a large sample size and comparing experimental versus control conditions were most prevalent in the latest time period.

Of the 76 reports eligible for inclusion in our comprehensive Campbell review, 17 were excluded from the present review for the following reasons:[3]

- Five measured bullying/victimization using peer nominations.
- Three measured bullying/victimization using teacher nominations.
- Ten measured bullying/victimization using self-reports but had a sample size less than 200. Consequently, 59 reports were included in the present review, some of which describe the same program (see table 3). There were evaluations of 30 different programs.

---

[2] This is the meaning of "included in the Campbell review" in table 1; all categories are mutually exclusive.

[3] More than one of the reasons could apply.

TABLE 3

30 Included Evaluations of Antibullying Programs

Randomized experiments:
 1. Bulli and Pupe [Baldry 2001; Baldry and Farrington 2004], Rome, Italy
 2. Friendly Schools [Cross et al. 2004; Pintabona 2006], Perth, Australia
 3. S.S.GRIN [De Rosier 2004; De Rosier and Marcus 2005], North Carolina
 4. Dutch antibullying program [Fekkes et al. 2006], Netherlands
 5. Steps to Respect [Frey, Edstrom, and Hirschstein 2005; Frey et al. 2005; Hirschstein et al. 2007], Seattle
 6. Antibullying Intervention in Australian Secondary Schools [Hunt 2007], Sydney, Australia
 7. Youth Matters [Jenson et al. 2005a, 2005b, 2006a, 2006b; Jenson and Dieterich 2007], Colorado
 8. Expect Respect [Rosenbluth et al. 2004; Whitaker et al. 2004], Texas
 9. Kiva [Salmivalli et al., forthcoming], Finland
Before-after, experimental-control comparisons:
 1. Greek antibullying program [Andreou et al. 2007], Thessaly, Greece
 2. Seattle trial of the Olweus Program [Bauer et al. 2007], Seattle
 3. Progetto Pontassieve [Ciucci and Smorti 1998], Italy
 4. South Carolina Program; implementation of OBPP [Melton et al. 1998], South Carolina
 5. "Bullyproofing Your School" program [Menard et al. 2008], Colorado
 6. New Bergen Project against Bullying (Bergen 2) [1997–98], Bergen, Norway
 7. Toronto antibullying program [Pepler et al. 2004], Toronto, Canada
 8. Ecological antibullying program [Rahey and Craig 2002], Canada
 9. Short intensive intervention in Czechoslovakia [Rican et al. 1996], Czechoslovakia
 10. Flemish antibullying program [Stevens, De Bourdeaudhuij, and Van Oost 2000; Stevens, Van Oost, and De Bourdeaudhuij 2000; Stevens et al. 2001, 2004], Belgium
 11. Sheffield antibullying program [Whitney et al. 1994; P. K. Smith 1997; Smith et al. 2004b], Sheffield, U.K.
Other experimental-control comparisons:
 1. Transtheoretical-based tailored antibullying program [Evers et al. 2007], United States
 2. Norwegian antibullying program [Galloway and Roland 2004], Norway
 3. SAVE [Ortega and Del Rey 1999; Ortega et al. 2004], Seville, Spain
 4. Kia Kaha [Raskauskas 2007], New Zealand
Age-cohort designs:
 1. Respect [Ertesvag and Vaaland 2007], Stavanger, Norway
Olweus Bullying Prevention Program [OBPP]:
 2. First Bergen Project against Bullying (Bergen 1) [1983–85], Bergen, Norway
 3. First Oslo Project against Bullying (Oslo 1) [November 1999–November 2000], Oslo
 4. New National Initiative against Bullying in Norway (New National) [2001–7], Norway
 5. Five-year follow-up in Oslo (Oslo 2) [2001–6], Oslo
   [Olweus 1991, 1992, 1993a, 1993b, 1994a, 1994b, 1994c, 1995, 1996a, 1996b, 1996c, 1997a, 1997b, 1997c, 2004a, 2004c, 2005, 2006; Olweus and Alsaker 1991]
 6. Finnish antibullying program [Salmivalli et al. 2004, 2005], Finland

The 59 reports were divided into four categories of research design: randomized experiments, before and after quasi-experimental designs, other quasi-experimental designs, and age-cohort designs. Table 3 lists the 59 reports included in the present systematic review. It was quite possible for different reports from a particular project to be placed in different categories, depending on the content of the report. For example, the report on the Sheffield program by Irene Whitney and her colleagues (1994) was included in the present review because information was provided about bullying before and after in experimental and control conditions (schools). A later report on the same project, however, by Mike Eslea and Peter Smith (1998) was placed in the "strong relevance" category because it presented before and after information about bullying in only four experimental schools. As another example, whereas the report by Stevens, Van Oost, and De Bourdeaudhuij (2001) was included in the present review because it contained outcome data on a specific project (the Flemish program), the report by Stevens, De Bourdeaudhuij, and Van Oost (2001) was placed in the "weak relevance" category because it reviewed several antibullying programs and did not present outcome data on one specific program.

Appendix table A1 summarizes the components of the programs, participants, and research designs of the 30 evaluations we reviewed. More detailed descriptions of all these programs can be found in the Swedish report (Ttofi, Farrington, and Baldry 2008). The category of each program (A = OBPP, B = inspired by Olweus, C = other whole-school programs, and D = more limited programs) is also indicated in the first column of table A1.

V. Analysis of Included Evaluations

A major advantage of systematic and meta-analytic reviews is that they provide detailed descriptions of the methods and analyses in a way that facilitates repetition and verification of the conclusions by other researchers. In the systematic review prepared for the Swedish National Council for Crime Prevention, we presented detailed information for each evaluation on the prevalence or mean level of bullying and victimization (being bullied) before and after the intervention. The information presented in the relevant table (Ttofi, Farrington, and Baldry 2008, table 6, p. 51) was based on published reports and on personal communications with the evaluators of each program. In this essay, we summarize our analysis of effect sizes for bullying and victimization in each program.

A. Analysis of Effect Sizes

The main measure of effect size that we used was the odds ratio (OR). Where other effect sizes were calculated, they were converted into the OR. The OR is calculated as shown below:

	Nonbullies	Bullies
Experimental	a	b
Control	c	d

a, b, c, and d are numbers of students and OR $= (a \times d)/(b \times c)$. An OR greater than one indicates a desirable effect of the antibullying program, and an OR less than one indicates an undesirable effect. The chance value of the OR is one, indicating no effect. Examples of the meaning of specific OR values are given later.

Table 4 shows the analysis of effect sizes for bullying and victimization. In the technical appendix we prepared for the Swedish National Council for Crime Prevention Report (Ttofi, Farrington, and Baldry 2008), the interested reader can find more detailed technical information about how all the ORs were calculated.[4]

Only one of the nine randomized experiments (Salmivalli, Karna, and Poskiparta, forthcoming) found a significant effect of the program on bullying, although one other evaluation (Hunt 2007) reported a near-significant effect. Overall, the nine randomized experiments yielded a weighted mean OR of 1.07, indicating a very small and non-significant effect of these programs on bullying. In contrast, five of the nine evaluations with before-after/experimental-control designs found a significant effect, and one other (Olweus/Bergen 2) reported a near-significant result. Overall, these nine studies yielded a large weighted mean OR of 1.60 ($p < .0001$).

Two of the four other experimental-control comparisons found significant effects on bullying, and the weighted mean OR for all four studies was 1.43. All six age-cohort designs yielded significant effects, with a weighted mean OR of 1.56. Over all 28 studies, the weighted mean OR was 1.41, indicating a substantial effect of these programs

[4] The results obtained in the Flemish antibullying program (Stevens, De Bourdeaudhuij, and Van Oost 2000) were excluded. Bullying and victimization were each measured using eight items, each measured on a 5-point scale (from "it has not happened" to "several times a week"). It might be expected, therefore, that scores might range from 8 to 40. And yet, the mean scores in the crucial table (Stevens, Van Oost, and De Bourdeaudhuij 2004, table 8.1) were all between 0.99 and 1.16, with the vast majority between 1.00 and 1.10. The reason was that only logarithms of scores were reported. We requested the raw data from Veerle Stevens, but she informed us (e-mail, October 3, 2008) that she no longer had access to the data. Since all the means were so close to 1.0 (making the test of the effects of the program very insensitive) and since we did not know the number of students on which each mean was based, we excluded this program from our analyses.

on bullying. To give a concrete example, if there were 20 bullies and 80 nonbullies in the experimental condition and 26 bullies and 74 nonbullies in the control condition, the OR would be 1.41. Hence, OR = 1.41 can correspond to 30 percent more bullies in the control condition (or, conversely, 23 percent fewer bullies in the experimental condition).

In the analysis of effect sizes for victimization (being bullied), only two of the randomized experiments found significant effects of the program on victimization, and the weighted mean OR of 1.18 was not significant. Three of the 10 studies with before-after/experimental-control designs yielded significant results, and the weighted mean OR (1.10) was just statistically significant.

All four studies with other experimental-control designs found significant results, with a weighted mean OR of 1.70. Five of the six age-cohort designs yielded significant results, and the other one (Ertesvag and Vaaland 2007) was nearly significant. The weighted mean OR was 1.57. Over all 29 studies, the weighted mean OR was 1.33, indicating a significant effect of these programs on victimization. To give a concrete example, if there were 20 victims and 80 nonvictims in the experimental condition and 25 victims and 75 nonvictims in the control condition, then OR = 1.33. Hence, this value of the OR corresponds to about 25 percent more victims in the control condition (or, conversely, to about 20 percent fewer victims in the experimental condition).

We conclude that the following 12 antibullying programs were clearly effective in reducing bullying and victimization: Melton et al. (1998); Salmivalli, Kaukianen, and Voeten (2005); Andreou, Didaskalou, and Vlachou (2007); Ertesvag and Vaaland (2007); Evers et al. (2007); Raskauskas (2007); Salmivalli, Karna, and Poskiparta (forthcoming); Olweus/Bergen 1; Olweus/Bergen 2; Olweus/New National; Olweus/Oslo 1; and Olweus/Oslo 2. The following 10 programs were probably effective, as judged by their effect sizes or by their significance in relation to either bullying or victimization or by other results presented by the authors: Whitney et al. (1994); Rican, Ondrova, and Svatos (1996); Baldry and Farrington (2004); Galloway and Roland (2004); Ortega, Del Rey, and Mora-Mercan (2004); Pepler et al. (2004); Fekkes, Pijpers, and Verloove-Vanhorick (2006); Hunt (2007); Jenson and Dieterich (2007); and Menard et al. (2008). The remaining seven programs had little effect on bullying or victimization: Ciucci and Smorti (1998); Rahey and Craig (2002); Cross et al. (2004); De Rosier

TABLE 4
Effect Sizes for Bullying and Victimization

	Bullying		Victimization	
Project	OR	Significance	OR	Significance
Randomized experiments:				
Bulli and Pupe; Baldry and Farrington (2004)	1.14	NS	1.69	NS
Friendly Schools; Cross et al. (2004)	.77	NS	1.07	NS
S.S.GRIN; De Rosier (2004)	.87	NS	1.04	NS
Dutch antibullying program; Fekkes et al. (2006)	1.12	NS	1.25	NS
Steps to Respect; Frey et al. (2005)	1.04	NS	1.09	NS
Antibullying Intervention in Australia; Hunt (2007)	1.46	.097	1.26	NS
Youth Matters; Jenson and Dieterich (2007)	1.17	NS	1.63	NS
Expect Respect; Rosenbluth et al. (2004)	.99	NS	.70	.032
KiVa; Salmivalli et al. (forthcoming)	1.47	.038	1.66	.0001
Weighted mean	1.07	NS	1.18	NS
Before-after, experimental-control:				
Greek antibullying program; Andreou et al. (2007)	1.75	.004	1.48	.047
Seattle Trial of the Olweus Program; Bauer et al. (2007)	. . .	. . .	1.01	NS
Progetto Pontassieve; Ciucci and Smorti (1998)	1.20	NS	1.21	NS
South Carolina Program; Melton et al. (1998)	1.52	.0001	1.06	NS
Bullyproofing Your School; Menard et al. (2008)	1.64	.0001	1.22	.032
New Bergen Project against Bullying; OBPP (1997–98)	1.79	.057	1.43	.026
Toronto antibullying program; Pepler et al. (2004)	1.69	.002	.94	NS
Ecological Antibullying Program; Rahey-Craig (2002)	1.19	NS	.79	NS
Intervention in Czechoslovakia; Rican et al. (1996)	2.52	NS	2.43	NS
Sheffield antibullying program; Whitney et al. (1994)	2.12	.013	1.26	NS
Weighted mean	1.60	.0001	1.10	.041
Other experimental-control:				
Transtheoretical-based Program; Evers et al. (2007)	2.15	.001	2.33	.0001
Norwegian Program; Galloway and Roland (2004)	1.20	NS	1.59	.001
SAVE; Ortega et al. (2004)	1.63	NS	2.12	.016
Kia Kaha; Raskauskas (2007)	1.20	.035	1.35	.0004
Weighted mean	1.43	.011	1.70	.0001

TABLE 4 *(Continued)*

Project	Bullying		Victimization	
	OR	Significance	OR	Significance
Age-cohort designs:				
Respect; Ertesvag and Vaaland (2007)	1.34	.0008	1.18	.060
First Bergen Project against Bullying (1983–85)	1.69	.0006	2.89	.0001
First Oslo Project against Bullying (1999–2000)	2.14	.012	1.81	.002
New National Initiative in Norway (2001–7)	1.78	.0001	1.59	.0001
Five-year follow-up in Oslo (2001–6)	1.75	.0001	1.48	.0001
Finnish antibullying program; Salmivalli et al. (2004)	1.31	.010	1.30	.014
Weighted mean	1.56	.0001	1.57	.0001
Weighted mean (total)	1.41	.0001	1.33	.0001

NOTE.—OR = odds ratio; the weighted mean OR is calculated using the random effects model.

(2004); Rosenbluth et al. (2004); Frey et al. (2005); and Bauer, Lozano, and Rivara (2007). In fact, there were some indications that the Rosenbluth et al. (2004) program had harmful effects. Why were some programs effective and others ineffective? We address this question below.

B. Effect Size versus Research Design and Categories of Programs

Table 4 shows that the weighted mean OR effect size measure varied across the four types of research design. In order to test whether this variation is statistically significant, it was necessary to calculate the heterogeneity between groups, or QB, which has a chi-squared distribution (Lipsey and Wilson 2001, pp. 135–38). For bullying, $QB = 29.08$ (3 df, $p < .0001$). For victimization, $QB = 41.85$ (3 df, $p < .0001$). Therefore, we can conclude that effect sizes varied significantly across research designs. Weisburd, Lum, and Petrosino (2001) also found lower effect sizes in randomized experiments than in other designs.

Randomized experiments and before-after/experimental-control designs might be regarded by some researchers as methodologically superior to the other experimental-control and age-cohort designs. However, all designs have advantages and problems. For example, randomized experiments (if a sufficiently large number of units are randomly assigned) can minimize many threats to internal validity. However, experiments on bullying usually randomly assign only a small number of schools (Ttofi, Farrington, and Baldry 2008, table 9, p. 63) and are vulnerable to differential attrition. The age-cohort design, by contrast, largely eliminates problems of differential attrition (as well as selection, aging, and regression effects) but is potentially vulnerable to history and testing effects. However, Olweus (2005) argued convincingly that these were unlikely, especially since the effects of programs have been investigated in many different time periods. We believe that these are the four best designs that have been used to evaluate the effects of antibullying programs, and we give credence to results obtained in all of them.

A similar analysis was carried out to investigate whether the effect sizes varied significantly according to our categories of programs (the OBPP, programs inspired by Olweus, other whole-school programs, and more limited programs). Effect sizes for bullying varied significantly over the four categories (QB = 19.11, 3 df, p = .0003). Effect sizes were greatest for the OBPP (OR = 1.71) and similar for the other three categories of programs (ORs 1.36, 1.30, and 1.32, respectively; all significant at the p = .05 level). Effect sizes for victimization also varied significantly over the four categories (QB = 23.26, 3 df, $p < .0001$). They were highest for the OBPP (OR = 1.45) and for the more limited programs (OR = 1.52). The OR was also significant for other whole-school programs (OR = 1.19), but not for programs inspired by Olweus (OR = 1.10).

ORs for bullying and victimization were correlated (r = .58, $p <$ .0001). However, results can be different for the two measures because one bully can have several victims and one victim can have several bullies. Therefore, a decrease in the prevalence of bullies could be different from a corresponding decrease in the prevalence of victims. It was striking that the more limited programs tended to have more effect on victims than on bullies. This was especially true of the programs examined by Baldry and Farrington (2004), Galloway and Roland (2004), and Jenson and Dieterich (2007).

VI. Coding of Study Features

In most cases, the antibullying programs overlap in many of their intervention components. An attempt was made to code as many program elements as possible (see table 5) and to correlate them with effect sizes for bullying and victimization in order to investigate why some programs were more effective than others. By mid-July 2008, we received positive feedback from evaluators of 24 of the 30 programs regarding the way we had coded the program components. Tables 5 and 6 are unique, and this kind of information has seldom been presented in systematic reviews. These tables show key elements of each program (i.e., intervention components) and key features of each evaluation (e.g., sample size, research design, average age, etc.). In order to avoid bias, the coding was completed in the absence of knowledge about effect sizes.[5]

A. Key Features of the Evaluation

We have already discussed one feature of the evaluation, namely, the research design. In order to investigate the relationship between evaluation features and effect size in a comparable way, all features were dichotomized (in order to produce roughly equal groups as much as possible). For example, research design was dichotomized into randomized experiments plus before-after/experimental-control designs (20 studies) versus other experimental-control designs plus age-cohort designs (10 studies). Other features of the evaluation that were investigated were as follows:

- sample size (experimental plus control conditions), dichotomized into 1,500 children or more (16) versus 1,499 children or less (14);
- publication date, dichotomized into 2004 or later (19) versus 2003 or earlier (11);
- average age of the children, dichotomized into 10 or less (14) versus 11 or more (16);
- location in the United States (8) versus other places (22);
- location in other places (23) versus Norway (7);
- location in other places (13) versus Europe (17);
- outcome measure, dichotomized into others (23) versus a dichotomous measure of two or more times per month (7); this latter measure was associated with larger effect sizes than mean scores or simple prevalences.

---

[5] The coding of elements of antibullying programs was pioneered by J. David Smith and his colleagues (2004, table 3, p. 553), who coded 14 elements of 14 whole-school programs. Our coding system is more extensive, and we have coded 30 programs and attempted to verify the coding with all the researchers.

TABLE 5

Key Elements of the Intervention

Study	Element																			
	1	2	3	4	5	6	7	8	9	10	11	12	13	14	15	16	17	18	19	20
Randomized experiments:																				
Baldry and Farrington 2004	X	X	✓	✓	X	X	X	X	X	✓	X	X	X	X	X	X	X	X	✓	X
Cross et al. 2004	✓	X	X	✓	✓	✓	✓	✓	✓	X	✓	X	X	✓	X	X	✓	X	✓	X
De Rosier 2004	X	X	X	✓	X	X	X	X	X	X	X	X	X	X	X	X	X	X	X	✓
Fekkes et al. 2006	✓	✓	✓	✓	X	✓	X	X	X	✓	✓	✓	✓	X	X	X	✓	X	X	X
Frey et al. 2005	✓	✓	X	✓	✓	X	X	✓	X	✓	✓	X	X	X	X	X	X	X	✓	X
Hunt 2007	✓	X	✓	✓	X	X	X	X	X	✓	X	X	X	X	X	X	X	X	X	X
Jenson and Dieterich 2007	X	X	✓	✓	X	X	X	X	X	✓	X	X	X	X	X	X	X	X	X	X
Rosenbluth et al. 2004	✓	X	X	✓	✓	✓	X	✓	✓	✓	✓	X	X	✓	X	X	✓	EP	X	X
Salmivalli et al. 2007	✓	✓	X	✓	✓	✓	✓	✓	✓	✓	✓	X	✓	✓	X	X	✓	IN	✓	✓
Before-after experimental-control comparisons:																				
Andreou et al. 2007	X	✓	X	✓	✓	X	X	X	X	✓	X	✓	X	X	X	X	✓	X	X	X
Bauer et al. 2007	✓	✓	✓	✓	✓	X	✓	✓	X	✓	✓	✓	X	X	X	X	✓	X	X	X
Ciucci and Smorti 1998	X	X	✓	X	X	✓	✓	X	✓	✓	X	X	X	X	X	X	✓	X	X	X
Melton et al. 1998	✓	✓	✓	✓	✓	✓	✓	X	✓	✓	✓	✓	✓	X	X	X	✓	X	✓	X
Menard et al. 2008	✓	X	X	✓	✓	✓	X	X	X	✓	✓	X	X	X	X	X	✓	CP	X	X
OBPP, Bergen 2 (1997–98)	✓	✓	✓	✓	✓	✓	✓	✓	X	✓	✓	✓	✓	X	X	✓	✓	MP	✓	X

312

Pepler et al. 2004
Rahey and Craig 2002
Rican et al. 1996
Stevens et al. 2000
Whitney et al. 1994

Other experimental-control comparisons:
Evers et al. 2007
Galloway and Roland 2004
Ortega et al. 2004
Raskauskas 2007

Age-cohort designs:
Ertesvag and Vaaland 2007
Bergen 1 (1983–85)
Oslo 1 (1999–2000)
New National (2001–7)
Oslo 2 (2001–6)
Salmivalli et al. 2004

NOTE.—1 = whole-school antibullying policy; 2 = classroom rules; 3 = school conferences providing information about bullying to students; 4 = curriculum materials; 5 = classroom management; 6 = cooperative group work among experts (e.g., among teachers, counselors, and interns); 7 = work with bullies; 8 = work with victims; 9 = work with peers (e.g., peer mediation, peer mentoring, peer group pressure as bystanders); 10 = information for teachers; 11 = information for parents; 12 = increased playground supervision; 13 = disciplinary methods; 14 = nonpunitive methods (e.g., Pikas or no-blame approach); 15 = restorative justice approaches; 16 = school tribunals/school bully courts; 17 = teacher training; 18 = parent training; 19 = videos; 20 = virtual reality environments/computer games; EP = educational presentations to parents; MP = meetings with parents; CP = consultation for parents; IN = information nights.

313

TABLE 6
Key Features of the Evaluation

Study						Feature						
	NC	TO	DC	IC	DT	IT	OM	SS	PD	AA	IL	MD
Baldry and Farrington 2004	A	D	E	G	X	X	M	O	R	T	V	Y
Cross et al. 2004	B	D	F	G	I	K	M	P	R	S	W2	Y
De Rosier 2004	A	D	E	G	X	X	M	O	R	S	W1	Y
Fekkes et al. 2006	A	C	F	H	I	■	M	P	R	S	V	Y
Frey et al. 2005	A	D	E	G	■	K	M	O	R	S	W1	Y
Hunt 2007	A	D	E	G	X	X	M	O	R	T	W2	Y
Jenson and Dieterich 2007	A	D	F	H	X	X	M	O	R	S	W1	Y
Rosenbluth et al. 2004	B	C	E	G	I	L	M	P	R	T	W1	Y
Salmivalli et al. 2007	B	D	F	H	J	L	N	P	R	S	V	Y
Andreou et al. 2007	A	D	E	G	J	L	M	O	R	S	V	Y
Bauer et al. 2007	B	C	E	G	J	K	M	P	R	T	W1	Y
Ciucci and Smorti 1998	A	D	F	■	■	■	M	O	Q	S	V	Y
Melton et al. 1998	B	C	F	H	■	■	M	P	Q	T	W1	Y
Menard et al. 2008	A	D	F	G	L	L	M	P	R	T	W1	Y
Bergen 2 (1997–98)	B	C	E	H	J	L	N	P	R	T	U	Y
Pepler et al. 2004	B	C	F	■	J	K	M	O	R	S	W2	Y

Study	NC	TO	DC	IC	DT	IT	OM	SS	PD	AA	IL	MD
Rahey and Craig 2002	B	D	E	G	I	■	M	O	Q	S	W2	Y
Rican et al. 1996	A	C	E	■	X	X	M	O	Q	S	V	Y
Stevens et al. 2000	B	C	E	G	■	L	M	O	Q	T	V	Y
Whitney et al. 1994	B	C	F	■	X	X	M	P	Q	S	V	Y
Evers et al. 2007	A	D	■	G	X	X	M	O	R	T	W1	Z
Galloway and Roland 2004	A	D	F	■	J	L	M	O	R	S	U	Z
Ortega et al. 2004	B	D	F	H	J	L	N	O	R	T	V	Z
Raskauskas 2007	A	D	E	G	X	X	M	P	R	S	W2	Z
Ertesvag and Vaaland 2007	B	D	F	■	J	L	M	P	R	T	U	Z
Bergen 1 (1983–85)	B	C	F	H	J	L	N	P	Q	T	U	Z
Oslo 1 (1999–2000)	B	C	F	H	J	L	N	P	R	T	U	Z
New National (2001–7)	B	C	F	H	J	L	N	P	R	T	U	Z
Oslo 2 (2001–6)	B	C	F	H	J	L	N	P	R	T	U	Z
Salmivalli et al. 2004	A	C	F	■	J	L	M	P	R	T	V	Z

NOTE.—NC = number of intervention components (A = 10 or less, B = 11 or more); TO = theoretical orientation (C = based/inspired by Olweus, D = different from Olweus); DC = duration of intervention for children (E = 240 days or less, F = 270 days or more); IC = intensity of intervention for children (G = 19 hours or less, H = 20 hours or more); DT = duration of intervention for teachers (I = 3-day meetings or less, J = 4-day meetings or more); IT = intensity of intervention for teachers (K = 14 hours or less, L = 15 hours or more); OM = outcome measure (M = means, prevalence, other measures; N = 2 or more measures; N = 2 or more times per month); SS = sample size (O = 1,499 or less, P = 1,500 or more); PD = publication date (Q = 2003 or before, R = 2004 or later); AA = average age (S = 10 or less, T = 11 or more); IL = location of intervention (U = in Norway, V = elsewhere in Europe, W1 = in the United States, W2 = other than Europe and the United States); MD = methodological design (Y = randomized experiment or before after experimental-control comparison, Z = other experimental-control comparison or an age-cohort design); X = not an intervention element; ■ = missing value.

B. Key Elements of the Program

Each antibullying program included a variety of intervention elements. Table 5 presents the elements of the intervention in different programs. As mentioned, our coding is based on feedback from evaluators. For instance, even though the Seattle controlled trial of OBPP (Bauer, Lozano, and Rivara 2007) included an antibullying video, this antibullying method was involved in only two out of seven intervention schools, so we did not code this element as included in this program. For similar reasons, for Youth Matters (Jenson and Dieterich 2007) we did not code the use of antibullying videos, even though the formal description of the program included this method. The elements were as follows.

Element 1 (whole-school antibullying policy) involves the presence of a formal antibullying policy on behalf of the school. In many schools, as indicated by researchers, such a policy was already in effect. It was not possible for us to know whether, for each program, the same antibullying policy was incorporated in the intervention schools.

Element 2 (classroom rules) refers to the use of rules against bullying that students were expected to follow. In many programs, these rules were the result of cooperative group work between the teachers and the students, usually after some extent of exposure of the students to the philosophy or messages of the antibullying program. In many cases the rules were written on a notice that was displayed in a distinctive place in the classroom.

Element 3 (school conferences) refers to the organization of school assemblies during which children were informed about bullying. In many programs, these conferences were organized after collection of the pretest data and aimed to inform students about the extent of bullying behavior in their school. This was perceived as an initial way to sensitize students about bullying and as a means of announcing the formal beginning of the intervention program in the school.

Element 4 (curriculum materials) refers to the use of materials about bullying during classroom lessons. Some programs were curriculum-based, whereas in others teachers incorporated antibullying materials into the regular curriculum.

Element 5 (classroom management) refers to an emphasis on classroom management techniques in detecting and dealing with bullying behavior.

Element 6 (cooperative group work) refers to the cooperation among different professionals (usually among teachers and some other professional groups) in working with bullies and victims of bullying.

Elements 7 and 8 (work with bullies and victims, respectively) concern individualized work (not offered at the classroom level) with children involved in bullying as victims or perpetrators. In most programs, this service was offered by professionals, such as interns or psychologists, who collaborated with teachers in the school.

Element 9 (work with peers) refers to the formal engagement of peers in tackling bullying. This could involve the use of several strategies such as peer mediation (students working as mediators in the interactions among students involved in bullying) and peer mentoring, which was usually offered by older students. The philosophy of many antibullying programs also placed emphasis on the engagement of bystanders in bullying situations in such a way that disapproval of bullying behavior was expressed adequately while support was offered to victims.

Elements 10 and 11 (information for teachers and parents, respectively): Many programs offered information for teachers and parents, but it was not possible for us to assess the quality of the information provided. For instance, many programs reported the presence of a manual that teachers could consult in the implementation of the intervention, but the extent to which this manual was structured is difficult for us to assess. The same can be said about the information provided to parents. It was clear to us that programs differed a lot in the quality of this information. In some programs parents were provided with newsletters regarding the antibullying initiative in their school, whereas in others parents were provided with guides on how to help their child deal with bullying as well as information about the antibullying initiative implemented in their school. However, the overall information that we had regarding this element of the intervention did not allow us to differentiate among different levels of its implementation across programs.

Element 12 (improved playground supervision): Some antibullying programs aimed to identify "hot spots" or "hot times" of bullying (mostly during playtime or lunchtime) and provided improved playground supervision of children.

Element 13 (disciplinary methods): Some programs emphasized punitive methods in dealing with bullying situations. One program (KiVa; Salmivalli, Karna, and Poskiparta, forthcoming) used both punitive and nonpunitive methods. In half of the 78 intervention schools, teachers were encouraged to use strong disciplinary methods; in the rest of the intervention schools, teachers were encouraged to deal with bullying situations in a nonpunitive way.

Elements 14 and 15 (nonpunitive methods): Some programs included restorative justice approaches (element 15) and other nonpunitive methods such as the Pikas method and the no-blame approach (element 14) in dealing with children involved in bullying.

Element 16 (school tribunals and bully courts) was not used to any great extent in any of the present studies. Bully courts were offered as an optional element within the Sheffield program, but no school actually established one.

Element 17 (teacher training): This was coded as present or absent. We also coded both the duration (number of meetings among experts and teachers) and the intensity (number of hours) of this training (see below). Again, we sent e-mails to the evaluators of the different programs and asked for their advice. Some researchers were responsive and offered us adequate information on both the duration and the intensity of teacher training to the extent that we could be confident about our accuracy in coding these elements. For other programs, however, we could not code one or both of these features of teacher training.

Element 18 (parent training): For all programs this refers to the organization on behalf of the school of "information nights/educational presentations" for parents or "teacher-parent meetings" during which parents were given information about the antibullying initiative in the school.

Elements 19 and 20 (videos and virtual reality computer games, respectively): Some programs utilized technology in their antibullying materials such as the use of antibullying videos or virtual reality computer games to raise students' awareness regarding bullying.

We also coded other features of the intervention programs:

- the number of elements included out of 20, dichotomized into 10 or less (14 programs) versus 11 or more (16 programs); Olweus (2005) reported a dose-response relationship between the number of components implemented in a school and the effect on bullying;
- the extent to which the program was not (16) or was (14) inspired by the work of Olweus;

TABLE 7

Significant Relationships with Bullying

	Cat (N) OR	Cat (N) OR	QB*	Significance
Program elements:				
Disciplinary methods	No (18) 1.30	Yes (10) 1.66	18.27	.0001
Parent training	No (17) 1.28	Yes (11) 1.59	15.55	.0001
Intensity for children	19− (11) 1.28	20+ (10) 1.65	14.85	.0001
Playground supervision	No (18) 1.29	Yes (10) 1.60	14.31	.0002
Duration for children	240− (10) 1.18	270+ (17) 1.51	14.13	.0002
Duration for teachers	3− (13) 1.20	4+ (12) 1.55	14.10	.0002
Inspired by Olweus	No (16) 1.31	Yes (12) 1.60	12.77	.0004
Intensity for teachers	14− (11) 1.23	15+ (13) 1.54	12.21	.0005
Total elements	10− (14) 1.31	11+ (14) 1.54	8.32	.004
Information for parents	No (9) 1.24	Yes (19) 1.48	6.03	.014
School conferences	No (12) 1.33	Yes (16) 1.52	5.80	.016
Classroom rules	No (7) 1.22	Yes (21) 1.46	4.55	.033
Classroom management	No (7) 1.23	Yes (21) 1.46	4.10	.043
Teacher training	No (8) 1.28	Yes (20) 1.47	3.53	.060
Videos	No (14) 1.35	Yes (14) 1.50	3.17	.075
Design features:				
Age of children	10− (14) 1.21	11+ (14) 1.57	20.09	.0001
Publication year	04+ (18) 1.31	03− (10) 1.69	18.75	.0001
Outcome measure	Other (21) 1.33	2+M (7) 1.74	18.51	.0001
In Norway	Rest (21) 1.34	Nor (7) 1.58	7.76	.005
In Europe	Rest (12) 1.32	EU (16) 1.53	6.47	.011
Sample size	1,500+ (15) 1.31	1,499− (13) 1.47	2.89	.089

NOTE.—Cat = category of variable; OR = weighted mean odds ratio; QB = heterogeneity between groups. Duration is in days; intensity is in hours; outcome measure 2+M: two times per month or more (vs. other measures).

* QB is distributed as chi-squared with 1 df.

- the duration of the program for children, dichotomized into 240 days or less (12) versus 270 days or more (17);
- the intensity of the program for children, dichotomized into 19 hours or less (12) versus 20 hours or more (11);
- the duration of the program for teachers, dichotomized into 3 days or less (13) versus 4 days or more (13);
- the intensity of the program for teachers, dichotomized into 14 hours or less (13) versus 15 hours or more (13).

C. Effect Size versus Study Features

There have been few other attempts to relate effect size to program elements (see, e.g., Kaminski et al. 2008). Table 7 shows the program elements and design features that were significantly (or nearly significantly in three cases) related to effect sizes for bullying.[6] Because of small numbers, five of the 20 program elements could not be investigated (curriculum materials, information for teachers, restorative justice approaches, school tribunals/bully courts, and virtual reality computer games). As explained before, the significance test is based on the heterogeneity between groups, QB. The weighted mean OR effect sizes are also given for the different categories. For example, for the 10 programs that included disciplinary methods, the weighted mean OR for bullying was 1.66; for the other 18 programs, the weighted mean OR was 1.30 (QB = 18.27, 1 df, $p < .0001$).

The most important program elements that were associated with a decrease in bullying were disciplinary methods, parent training, improved playground supervision, information for parents, school conferences, classroom rules, classroom management, teacher training, and videos. In addition, the total number of elements, and the duration and intensity of the program for children and teachers, were significantly associated with a decrease in bullying. Also, programs inspired by the work of Olweus worked best. Regarding the design features, the programs worked better with older children, in smaller-scale studies, in Norway specifically, and in Europe more generally. Older programs, and those in which the outcome measure was two times per month or more, also worked better. No program element was significantly associated with an increase in bullying.

Table 8 shows the program elements and design features that were significantly (or, in one case, nearly significantly) related to effect sizes for victimization (being bullied). The most important program elements that were associated with a decrease in victimization were videos, disciplinary methods, work with peers, parent training, cooperative group work, and an antibullying policy (weakly related). In addition, the duration and intensity of the program for children and teachers were significantly associated with a decrease in victimization. Regarding the design features, the programs worked better in Norway specifically and in Europe more generally, and they were less effective in the United States. Older programs, those in which the outcome measure was two times per month or more, and those with other experimental-control and age-cohort designs also worked better. No program element was significantly associated with an increase in victimization.

---

[6] Tables 7 and 8 have been updated to take account of information received after the Swedish report was completed.

TABLE 8
Significant Relationships with Victimization

	Cat (N) OR	Cat (N) OR	QB*	Significance
Program elements:				
Videos	No (14) 1.15	Yes (15) 1.47	25.69	.0001
Disciplinary methods	No (19) 1.21	Yes (10) 1.50	21.64	.0001
Duration for children	240− (11) 1.13	270+ (17) 1.42	18.09	.0001
Intensity for teachers	14− (12) 1.18	15+ (13) 1.47	17.02	.0001
Work with peers	No (20) 1.11	Yes (9) 1.41	15.43	.0001
Parent training	No (19) 1.23	Yes (10) 1.47	15.24	.0001
Intensity for children	19− (11) 1.22	20+ (11) 1.46	10.77	.001
Cooperative group work	No (14) 1.22	Yes (15) 1.42	9.51	.002
Duration for teachers	3− (13) 1.23	4+ (13) 1.44	7.27	.007
Antibullying policy	No (8) 1.34	Yes (21) 1.53	2.79	.095
Design features:				
Outcome measure	Other (22) 1.18	2+M (7) 1.64	49.19	.0001
In Europe	Rest (13) 1.13	EU (16) 1.52	40.90	.0001
Design	12 (19) 1.13	34 (10) 1.53	40.73	.0001
In Norway	Rest (22) 1.20	Nor (7) 1.55	30.77	.0001
Not in United States	US (8) 1.10	Rest (21) 1.45	27.26	.0001
Publication year	04+ (19) 1.23	03− (10) 1.52	21.04	.0001

NOTE.—Cat = category of variable; OR = weighted mean odds ratio; QB = heterogeneity between groups; design: 12 = randomized experiments + before-after/experimental-control vs. 34 = other experimental-control + age-cohort designs; duration in days; intensity in hours; outcome measure 2+M: two times per month or more (vs. other measures).

* QB is distributed as chi-squared with 1 df.

Our finding that antibullying programs work better with older children might be considered surprising in light of the arguments of Peter Smith (forthcoming). We therefore investigated this result further by dividing the age range of children into 7–9 (eight programs), 10 (six programs), 11–12 (eight programs), and 13–14 (eight programs). The OR effect size varied significantly with age for both bullying (QB = 20.79, 3 df, $p < .0001$) and victimization (QB = 11.75, 3 df, $p = .008$).

Effect sizes for bullying were higher at the older ages 11–12 (OR = 1.59) and 13–14 (OR = 1.52) than at 7–9 (OR = 1.17) or 10 (OR = 1.23). Effect sizes for victimization were higher at the medium ages 10 (OR = 1.39) and 11–12 (OR = 1.44) than at ages 7–9 (OR = 1.14) or 13–14 (OR = 1.27). All these ORs were significant at $p = .05$. We conclude that these programs work best for ages 11–12 and worst for ages 7–9. However, where possible, it would be interesting to investigate how results vary with age within a particular program. This might provide a more controlled test of the relationship between age and effect size.

Variables that might help to explain differential treatment effects in meta-analysis (e.g., elements of the intervention, study features, etc.) cannot be assumed to be statistically independent. Researchers should try to disentangle the relationships among them and identify those that truly have significant independent relationships with effect sizes (Lipsey 2003, p. 78). Multivariate techniques can be used to solve this problem in meta-analysis (Hedges 1982). Weighted regression analyses (Lipsey and Wilson 2001, pp. 138–40) were carried out to investigate which elements of the programs and which features of the evaluations were independently related to bullying and victimization effect sizes.

These analyses were severely limited by the small number of studies. Nevertheless, they showed that the most important elements of the program that were related to a decrease in bullying were disciplinary methods and parent training. The most important elements of the program that were related to a decrease in victimization were videos and the intensity of the program for teachers. When the design features were added, the most important factors that were related to a decrease in bullying were the age of the children and disciplinary methods. The most important factors that were related to a decrease in victimization were the outcome measure (two or more times per month vs. other measures) and the design (other experimental-control comparisons and age-cohort designs vs. other designs).

VII. Conclusions

We have shown that school-based antibullying programs are often effective, with an average reduction in bullying of 20–23 percent. Particular program elements were associated with a decrease in bullying and victimization. No program element was significantly associated with an increase in bullying or victimization. Our results give a very positive message with clear implications for policy.

A. Policy Implications

In developing new policies and practices, policy makers and practitioners should draw on high-quality evidence-based programs that have been proved to be effective. New antibullying initiatives should be inspired by existing successful programs (such as the OBPP) but should be modified in light of the key program elements that we have found to be most effective. It should be borne in mind, however, that we have merely identified the program elements that are most highly correlated with effectiveness. This does not prove that they cause effectiveness, but this is the best evidence we have at present.

A system of accrediting effective antibullying programs should be developed. In England and Wales in 1996, a system of accrediting effective programs in prison and probation was established (McGuire 2001). For a program to be accredited, it had to meet explicit criteria based on knowledge about what worked to reduce offending. Only accredited programs can be used in England and Wales, and similar systems have been developed in other countries including Scotland and Canada. A similar system should be developed for accrediting antibullying programs in schools to ensure that programs contain elements that have been proved to be effective in high-quality evaluations. This accreditation system could perhaps be organized by an international body such as the International Observatory on Violence in Schools.

New antibullying programs should be established using high-quality standards of implementation in a way that ensures that the program is more likely to have an impact. The quality of a program is undoubtedly important, but so is the way it is implemented. Implementation procedures should be transparent in order to enable researchers to know whether effects are related to key features of the intervention or key features of the evaluation. It is regrettable, for instance, that only one of the 30 evaluations included in the present review (Fekkes, Pijpers, and Verloove-Vanhorick 2006) provided key information about the percentage of intervention and control schools that implemented each intervention component.

The intensity and duration of a program are directly linked to its effectiveness. Olweus (2005) also found a "dose-response" relationship between the number of components of a program that were implemented in a school and its effect on bullying. For example, even though teacher training was only marginally significantly related to the reduction of bullying, both the duration (number of meetings of teachers and experts) and intensity (number of hours) of teacher training were. Similarly, the intensity (number of hours) and duration (number of days) of the program for children were significantly related to a reduction of bullying and victimization. What these findings show is that programs need to be intensive and long-lasting. It could be that a considerable time period is needed in order to build up an appropriate school ethos.

New antibullying initiatives should also pay attention to enhancing playground supervision. It is plausible that this is effective since a lot of bullying occurs during recess time. Improving the school playground environment (e.g., through reorganization or identification of hot spots) may also be a promising and low-cost intervention component.

Disciplinary methods (i.e., firm methods for tackling bullying) were an intervention component that was significantly related to both bullying and victimization. Disciplinary methods also were related to bullying effect sizes independently of all other variables. To some extent, this may be attributable to the big effects of the Olweus program, which included a range of firm sanctions including serious talks with bullies, sending them to the principal, making them stay close to the teacher during recess time, and depriving them of privileges.

The results of the KiVa project promise to provide useful answers in the future about the effectiveness of disciplinary methods.[7] An interesting element of the KiVa program is that it incorporated both punitive and nonpunitive approaches to deal with perpetrators of bullying. Half of the school teams, chosen at random, were instructed to use more punitive approaches (e.g., "what you have done is wrong, and it has to stop right now") and the other half of the school teams were instructed to use no-blame approaches in their discussions with children (e.g., "your classmate is also having a hard time, and this is why he behaves like that; what could we do to help him?"). A very preliminary observation from unpublished data is that disciplinary methods (the punitive approach) seem to work better for younger children (grade 4), whereas nonpunitive approaches seem to work better for older children (grade 6); for grade 5 children there seemed to be little difference. The current results are very important in that they also suggest the necessity of developing more age-specific programs.

Contrary to the arguments of Peter Smith (forthcoming), the results of our review show that programs have a bigger impact on bullying for older children (age 11 or older). This is an age range when bullying is decreasing anyway. Smith argued that programs were less effective in secondary schools because peer influence was more important and

[7] Personal communication from Christina Salmivalli, January 31, 2009.

because secondary schools were larger and students did not spend most of their time with one teacher who could be very influential. We speculate that programs may be more effective in reducing bullying by older children because of their superior cognitive abilities, lower impulsiveness, and greater likelihood of making rational decisions. Many programs are based on social learning ideas of encouraging and rewarding prosocial behavior and discouraging and punishing bullying. These programs are likely to work better, for example, in building empathy and perspective-taking skills with older students.

Perhaps surprisingly, establishing a whole-school antibullying policy was not significantly related to effect sizes for either bullying or victimization. Nor was individual work with bullies or victims. More efforts should be made to implement effective programs with individual bullies and victims, perhaps based on child skills training programs (Losel and Beelman 2003).

New antibullying initiatives should go beyond the scope of the school and target wider systemic factors such as the family. Bullied children often do not communicate their problem to anyone, and parents and teachers often do not talk to bullies about their conduct (e.g., Fekkes, Pijpers, and Verloove-Vanhorick 2005). Parent training was significantly related to a decrease in both bullying and victimization. More important, on the basis of the results of the weighted regression analyses, parent training was related to bullying effect sizes independently of other program components. Efforts, therefore, should be made to sensitize parents about the issue of school bullying through educational presentations and teacher-parent meetings.

Future evaluations of antibullying programs should be designed in light of our results. Attention should be paid not only to the quality of the program but also to the way it is implemented. Different features of the evaluation were significantly related to a decrease in bullying and victimization. In particular, the way bullying was measured and the age of the children were important. Programs should be targeted to children aged 11 or older rather than to younger children. The outcome measure of bullying or victimization should be two times per month or more. Programs implemented in Norway and Europe seem to work best, and this could be related to the long tradition of European—and especially Scandinavian—countries in bullying research. Other factors are that Scandinavian schools are of high quality, with small classes and well-trained teachers, and there is a Scandinavian tradition of state intervention in matters of social welfare (J. D. Smith et al. 2004, p. 557).

Cost-benefit analyses of antibullying programs should be carried out to investigate how much money is saved for the money expended (Welsh, Farrington, and Sherman 2001). Saving money is a powerful argument to convince policy makers and practitioners to implement intervention programs (Farrington 2009). There never has been a cost-benefit analysis of an antibullying program.

Finally, antibullying programs should be based more on theories about bullying and victimization. Most past programs have been based on general social learning ideas. Future programs should be based on newer theories such as defiance theory and restorative justice approaches (Ttofi and Farrington 2008a, 2008b). For example, poor social relationships at school can be repaired through restorative justice approaches that involve bringing together all children (bullies, victims, and other children) "in a participatory process that addresses wrongdoing while offering respect to the parties involved" (Morrison 2007, p. 198). Defiance theory is useful because it places emphasis on improving bonding to the sanctioner, shame management, and legitimate, respectful sanctioning of antisocial behavior.

B. Implications for Future Research

There are many implications of our review for future research. Several questions have been raised that should be addressed. For example:

- Why are there different effects of program elements and design features on bullying and victimization?
- Why do results vary in different countries?
- Why do results vary by research design?
- Why do programs work better with older children?
- Why are larger and more recent studies less effective than smaller-scale and older studies?
- Why do results vary with the outcome measure of bullying or victimization?

Future evaluations should have before and after measures of bullying and victimization in experimental and control schools. Bullying and victimization should be carefully defined and measured. Since it is difficult to assign a large number of schools randomly, it may be best to place schools in matched pairs and randomly assign one member of each pair to the experimental condition and one member to the control condition. It seems unsatisfactory to randomly assign school classes because of the danger of contamination of control children by experimental children. Only children who are tested both before and after the intervention should be analyzed in order to minimize problems of differential attrition. Research is needed on the best methods of measuring bullying, on what time periods to inquire about, and on seasonal variations.

It is important to develop methodological quality standards for evaluation research that can be used by systematic reviewers, scholars, policy makers, the mass media, and the general public in assessing the validity of conclusions about the effectiveness of interventions in reducing crime (Farrington 2003, p. 66). Such quality standards could include guidelines to program evaluators with regard to what elements of the intervention should be included in published reports, perhaps under the aegis of the Campbell Collaboration Crime and Justice Group (Farrington and Petrosino 2001; Farrington and Weisburd 2007). If such guidelines had been in existence, they would have been very helpful to our effort to code fully the elements of the intervention in all studies.

With positive responses from 24 out of 30 evaluators of antibullying programs, we were fairly successful. However, because of time limitations and lack of information, we were unable to investigate varying results of the intervention programs according to subgroups of students—defined, for example, by gender, ethnicity, participant roles in bullying, developmental needs, or capacities of children. Other researchers have also indicated the lack of specific intervention work based on the above factors (Smith and Ananiadou 2003; Pepler, Smith, and Rigby 2004). Several of the above features were not mentioned in reports, making it difficult for us to code them. For the 20 program elements that we did code, only one study (Fekkes, Pijpers, and Verloove-Vanhorick 2006) provided the percentage of intervention and control schools that actually implemented these elements. More information about implementation is needed.

Future systematic reviewers could attempt to detect the impact of antibullying programs on different subgroups of students. Future reports should provide key information about features of evaluations, according to a checklist that should be developed (inspired perhaps by the CONSORT Statement for medical research: Altman et al. 2001;

Moher, Schulz, and Altman 2001). Information about key elements of programs, and about the implementation of programs, should be provided. Where bullying and victimization are measured on 5-point scales, the full 5 × 2 table should be presented, so that the Area under the ROC Curve can be used as a measure of effectiveness (Farrington, Jolliffe, and Johnstone 2008). This would avoid the problem of results varying according to the particular cutoff points that were chosen.

Research is needed to develop and test better theories of bullying and victimization, for example, using vignettes with children to ask about what factors promote or prevent bullying. The advantages and disadvantages and validity of different outcome measures (e.g., self-reports, peer ratings, teacher ratings, systematic observation) should be studied. The short-term and long-term effects of antibullying programs should be investigated in prospective longitudinal studies. Effects on different types of bullying, and effects on different types of children, teachers, schools, and contexts, should be investigated.

Results obtained so far in evaluations of antibullying programs are encouraging. The time is ripe to mount a new program of international collaborative research on the effectiveness of these programs.

TABLE A1

Key Features of Evaluations

Program [Category]	Components of the Program	Participants	Research Design
Randomized experiments:			
Bulli and Pupe; Baldry and Farrington (2004) [D]	Kit of three videos and a booklet divided into three parts; used in active methods such as role-playing, group discussions, and focus groups	239 students aged 10–16 in 13 schools: • 131 in the experimental group • 106 in the control group • experimental and control students from the same schools but from 10 different classes; classes randomly assigned	Intervention and control groups, random assignment, pretest, and posttest measures
Friendly Schools; Cross et al. (2004) [C]	Targeting three levels: (a) the whole-school community (whole-school planning and strategy manual), (b) students' families (home activities linked to classroom-learning activities; 16 skills-based newsletter items), (c) grades 4–5 students along with their teachers (classroom curriculum)	2,068 students (aged 9–10 from 29 schools) of which • 1,046 intervention students • 922 control students • 15 intervention schools • 14 control schools	Pretest and posttest data from intervention and control schools; 3-year randomized controlled trial
S.S.GRIN; De Rosier (2004); De Rosier and Marcus (2005) [D]	Program for children experiencing peer dislike, bullying, or social anxiety; highly structured manualized intervention combining social learning and cognitive-behavioral techniques	1,079 students: • 50.8% boys • 49.2% girls • mean age 8.6 years, of which • 415 eligible to participate in S.S.GRIN (664 children as nonidentified)	Pretest, posttest, experimental, and control groups; 18 children in each school (11 public elementary schools, North Carolina) randomly assigned to the treatment group and the remainder of the list assigned to the no-treatment control group
Dutch antibullying program; Fekkes et al. (2006) [B]	An antibullying school program including antibullying training for teachers, a whole-school antibullying policy, and an antibullying curriculum	3,816 students aged 9–12 years (50% of the sample girls)	2-year follow-up randomized intervention group control-group design; schools randomly assigned

TABLE A1 (*Continued*)

Program [Category]	Components of the Program	Participants	Research Design
Steps to Respect; Frey et al. (2005) [C]	Training manual for staff (staff training) including a core instructional session for all school staff and two in-depth training sessions for counselors, administrators, and teachers; classroom curriculum (10 semi-scripted skill lessons); parent engagement (take-home letters etc.)	A random subsample ($N = 544$) of a longitudinal study ($N = 1,023$) observed and their behavior being coded	Pretest, posttest, experimental, and control groups; schools randomly assigned
Antibullying Intervention in Australian Secondary Schools; Hunt (2007) [C]	Information at parent and teacher meetings about the nature of bullying in schools; school staff conducted a 2-hour classroom-based discussion of bullying using activities from an antibullying workbook	444 students at time 1 (155 intervention students and 289 control students) and of those 318 at time 2	Pretest, posttest, experimental, and control groups; schools randomly assigned to intervention or wait-list condition
Youth Matters; Jenson and Dieterich (2007) [D]	Youth Matters Prevention Curriculum; series of instructional modules; 10-session module during each of the 4 semesters of 2 academic years	Fourth graders from 28 schools: 456 control students and 670 experimental students	Group-randomized trial; fourth-grade classrooms from 28 schools randomly assigned
Expect Respect; Rosenbluth et al. (2004) [B]	Five program components including classroom curriculum, staff training, policy development, parent education, support services for individual students	Fifth graders from elementary schools (929 students in the intervention group and 834 in the comparison group)	Pretest, posttest, intervention, and control groups; pair of schools matched and randomly allocated to experimental or control conditions
KiVa; Salmivalli et al. (2007) [C]	Universal/whole-school intervention; indicated intervention/work with individual students; comprehensive program with manuals for teachers, information for parents; increased supervision; Internet–virtual learning environments; Web-based discussions forum for teachers; peer support for bullies and victims of bullying	All Finnish comprehensive schools invited to volunteer; of the 300 schools that were willing to participate, a representative sample of 78 schools was chosen; program still running, no final results yet	An age-cohort design and a random-ized experiment "nested" in the same program; results only for the latter available

330

Before-after, experimental-control comparisons:

Greek antibullying program; Andreou et al. (2007) [D]	Set of curricular activities to create classroom opportunities for (a) awareness raising, (b) self-reflection and, (c) problem-solving situations relevant to bullying	454 pupils: • 206 control: 123 boys and 83 girls • 248 experimental: 126 boys and 122 girls Sample size by grade: 145 fourth graders, 162 fifth graders, and 147 sixth graders	An experimental pretest, posttest design with a control group; classes assigned to the experimental and control groups on the basis of teachers' willingness to be involved in the intervention
Seattle trial of the Olweus program; Bauer et al. (2007) [A]	OBPP components targeting school-, classroom-, individual-, and community-level interventions	4,959 intervention students of which • 2,522 females • 1,672 sixth graders • 1,629 seventh graders • 1,588 eighth graders 1,559 control students of which • 782 females • 570 sixth graders • 515 seventh graders • 449 eighth graders	A nonrandomized controlled trial with 10 public middle schools (seven intervention implementing the OBPP and three control)
Progetto Pontassieve; Ciucci and Smorti (1998) [D]	Three levels: school (first 2 years) to promote an antibullying policy; class- and individual-level (third year) quality circles and role-playing to promote cooperative and problem-solving skills	167 students participated in the treatment group; 140 students are part of the control group; all children are from one secondary school	Experimental pretest, posttest control-group design
South Carolina program; implementation of OBPP; Melton et al. (1998) [A]	Schoolwide, classroom, individual, and community interventions based on the OBPP	Fourth- through eighth-grade students from six nonmetropolitan school districts; districts organized into matched pairs: group A schools implemented the project for 2 years; group B schools served as a comparison group for the first year of the project and received the intervention the second year: baseline: 6,389 students (grades 4–6); time 1: 6,263 students (grades 5–7); time 2: 4,928 students (grades 6–8)	Before-after, experimental-control comparison with three measurements: baseline (March 1995), time 1 (March 1996), and time 2 (May 1997)

TABLE A1 (*Continued*)

Program [Category]	Components of the Program	Participants	Research Design
Bullyproofing Your School program; Menard et al. (2008) [C]	Comprehensive, school-based intervention; classroom curriculum (seven core sessions and two optional)	All students in each of the third-through fifth-grade classrooms in seven elementary schools (3,497 students) and all students in sixth-through eighth-grade classrooms in three middle schools (1,627)	Multiple nonequivalent control group pretest, posttest design with ex ante selection of treatment and comparison groups; matched treatment and comparison groups at baseline
New Bergen Project against Bullying; OBPP (1997–98) [A]	School-level (e.g., staff discussion groups, bullying prevention coordinating committee), classroom-level (e.g., classroom rules), individual-level (e.g., supervision of students), and community-level components	Approximately 2,400 students in grades 5, 6, and 7 (OBPP had been in place for only 6 months when the second measurement took place)	An experimental pretest, posttest design with a control group; 11 intervention and 11 comparison schools
Toronto antibullying program; Pepler et al. (2004) [B]	Systemic school-based program; three similar elements of intervention across the three schools: staff training, codes of behavior, and improved playground intervention	Pupils from three schools (aged 5–11); two classes from each grades 1–6 (12 classes in all) from each school were randomly selected to participate; 319 children from school A and 300 children from school B the first year of the program; 325, 240, and 303 children from schools A, B, and C accordingly during the second year; 306, 163, and 289 children from schools A, B, and C accordingly in the second year of the program	Quasi-experimental with two waiting-list controls; in year 1, school A started the program and school B served as a waiting-list control; in year 2, school A continued the program, school B started the program, and school C served as a waiting-list control; in year 3, schools A and B continued the program, and school C began the antibullying program
Ecological antibullying program; Rahey and Craig (2002) [C]	12-week program based on the Bullyproofing Your School Program; psycho-educational program within the classroom; a peer mediation program; groups for children referred for involvement in bullying/victimization	Students from one intervention (114 boys and 126 girls) and one comparison school (123 boys and 128 girls); children in grades 1–8	An experimental pretest, posttest design with a control group (one experimental school and one control school)

Short intensive intervention in Czechoslovakia; Rican et al. (1996) [B]	Program inspired by the OBPP; components of the OBPP: e.g., Olweus videocassette used along with other methods (e.g., "class charter")	Eight fourth-grade elementary school classes used (half in each condition): • 100 students in experimental condition • 98 students in control condition	Pretest, posttest experimental-control comparison
Flemish antibullying program; Stevens et al. (2000) [B]	Training sessions for teachers; manual with video; three modules; booster sessions	1,104 students aged 10–16 from 18 schools: • 151 primary and 284 secondary students in treatment with support • 149 primary and 277 secondary students in treatment without support • 92 primary and 151 secondary students in the control group	Experimental pretest/posttest comparison including a control group (two experimental groups—treatment with support and treatment without support—and one control group)
Sheffield antibullying program; Whitney et al. 1994 [B]	Whole-school approach, curriculum classroom strategies, the Heartstone Odyssey, quality circles, "Only Playing Miss" theatrical play, peer counseling, bully courts, changes to playgrounds and lunch breaks	27 schools in total in this second survey, 8,309 students aged 8–16 from 16 primary and seven secondary (intervention) schools; four control schools; one primary (99 pupils) and three secondary (1,742 pupils)	Pretest and posttest 18 months later; 3-year follow-up in four intervention schools
Other experimental-control comparisons:			
Transtheoretical-based tailored antibullying program; Evers et al. (2007) [D]	The Build Respect, Stop Bullying Program was offered, a multicomponent intervention package	12 middle schools and 13 high schools in the United States (1,237 middle and 1,215 high school students): • 483 middle and 309 high school students in control group • 488 middle and 375 high school students in treatment 1 • 266 middle and 531 high school students in treatment 2	3 × 2 experimental design crossing three experimental groups with two treatment groups; pretest and posttest measures; schools matched on key variables (type of community, region of country, and percentage of students eligible for free lunches)

TABLE A1 (*Continued*)

Program [Category]	Components of the Program	Participants	Research Design
Norwegian antibullying program; Galloway and Roland (2004) [D]	Professional development program for teachers; 4 in-service days over a 9-month period; 15 2-hour peer supervision sessions; handouts for teachers	Nine intervention schools and six control groups: • comparison sample 1 • experimental sample 1 • experimental sample 2 • comparison sample 2 300–350 pupils in each sample apart from comparison sample 2 (151 students)	Longitudinal design with two experimental and two comparison samples of first graders—primary schools only in a 2-year period (1992–94)
SAVE; Ortega et al. (2004) [C]	Educational intervention model; democratic management of interpersonal relationships; cooperative group work; education of feelings and values; direct intervention with high-risk students	In the five intervention schools: 731 intervention pupils at pretest and 901 intervention students at posttest; in the four control schools: 440 control pupils	Five intervention schools (three primary, two secondary) had pretest and posttest measures, compared to four control schools with only posttest measures; follow-up after 4 years
Kia Kaha; Raskauskas (2007) [C]	Whole-school approach	49 schools, excluding four schools that intended to implement the program (31 intervention schools that implemented Kia Kaha for a 3-year period with 22 control schools all together)	Comparison of intervention schools with matched-comparison groups
Age-cohort designs: Respect; Ertesvag and Vaaland (2007) [C]	Teachers and school management staff participate in series of seminars; a 2-day seminar for the school management personnel and school representatives was also run in advance of the implementation period	• Pupils from three primary and one secondary school in Norway • Pupils in grades 5–6 (aged 11–13) at the primary schools and grades 8–10 (aged 14–16 years) at the secondary school • Number of pupils completing the survey at times 1–4 was 745, 769, 798, and 792, respectively	Age-longitudinal design with adjacent or consecutive cohorts with four measurement points (age-cohort)

Program	Intervention components	Sample	Design
First Bergen Project against Bullying; OBPP (1983–85) [A]	School-level (e.g., staff discussion groups; bullying prevention coordinating committee), classroom-level (e.g., classroom rules), individual-level (e.g., supervision of students), and community-level components	Students from 112 grade 4–7 classes in 42 primary and junior high schools; each of the four age cohorts consisted of 600–700 subjects with a roughly equal distribution of boys and girls	Extended selection cohorts design with three measurements: May 1983, May 1984, and May 1985 (age-cohort)
First Oslo Project against Bullying; OBPP (1999–2000) [A]	School-level (e.g., staff discussion groups; bullying prevention coordinating committee), classroom-level (e.g., classroom rules), individual-level (e.g., supervision of students), and community-level components	Approximately 900 students (at both time points) in grades 5–7	Extended selection cohorts design with two measurements: 1999 and 2000 (age-cohort)
New National Initiative against Bullying in Norway; OBPP (2001–7) [A]	School-level (e.g., staff discussion groups; bullying prevention coordinating committee), classroom-level (e.g., classroom rules), individual-level (e.g., supervision of students), and community-level components	Students in grades 4–7 from only three (out of five) different cohorts of schools are provided	Extended selection cohorts design; data provided for three measurements: October 2001, October 2002, and October 2003 (age-cohort)
5-year follow-up in Oslo; OBPP (2001–6) [A]	School-level (e.g., staff discussion groups; bullying prevention coordinating committee), classroom-level (e.g., classroom rules), individual-level (e.g., supervision of students), and community-level components	Data for assessments for the 14 out of 19 Oslo schools from the first cohort are provided; students in grades 4–7 followed from 2001 until 2005; students in grades 8–10 followed from 2001 until 2003	Extended selection cohorts design; data provided for five measurements for students in grades 4–7; data provided for three measurements for students in grades 8–10 (age-cohort)
Finnish antibullying program; Salmivalli et al. (2004, 2005) [B]	Intervention training for teachers, class-level interventions, school-level interventions (whole-school antibullying policy), individual-level interventions	Eight schools from Helsinki and eight schools from four towns near Turku; 1,220 students aged 9–12 in 16 schools (600 girls)	Age-longitudinal design with adjacent cohorts (age-cohort)

NOTE.—Categories of programs: A = Olweus program, B = inspired by Olweus, C = other whole-school programs, and D = more limited programs. All dates in the tables specify the year of publication of the report (not the year the evaluation took place), with the exception of the Olweus evaluations; for those, the period the evaluation took place is shown. Not all published evaluations of a specific program are presented in this table, only the most relevant ones.

335

REFERENCES

Altman, Douglas G., Kenneth F. Schulz, David Moher, Mattias Egger, Frank Davidoff, Diana Elbourne, Peter C. Gotzsche, and Thomas Lang. 2001. "The Revised CONSORT Statement for Reporting Randomized Trials: Explanation and Elaboration." *Annals of Internal Medicine* 8:663–94.

*Andreou, Elenia, Eleni Didaskalou, and Anastasia Vlachou. 2007. "Evaluating the Effectiveness of a Curriculum-Based Anti-bullying Intervention Program in Greek Primary Schools." *Educational Psychology* 27:693–711.

*Baldry, Anna C. 2001. "Bullying in Schools: Correlates and Intervention Strategies." PhD thesis, Cambridge University.

Baldry, Anna C., and David P. Farrington. 1999. "Types of Bullying among Italian School Children." *Journal of Adolescence* 22:423–26.

*———. 2004. "Evaluation of an Intervention Program for the Reduction of Bullying and Victimization in Schools." *Aggressive Behavior* 30:1–15.

———. 2007. "Effectiveness of Programs to Prevent School Bullying." *Victims and Offenders* 2:183–204.

*Bauer, Nerissa S., Paula Lozano, and Frederick P. Rivara. 2007. "The Effectiveness of the Olweus Bullying Prevention Program in Public Middle Schools: A Controlled Trial." *Journal of Adolescent Health* 40:266–74.

Campbell, Donald T., and Julian C. Stanley. 1966. *Experimental and Quasi-Experimental Designs for Research*. Chicago: Rand McNally.

*Ciucci, Enrica, and Andrea Smorti. 1998. "Il fenomeno delle pretonenze nella scuola: Problemi e prospettive di intervento" [The phenomenon of bullying in school: Problems and prospects for intervention]. *Psichiatria dell'Infanzia e dell'Adolescenza* 65:147–57.

Cook, Thomas D., and Donald T. Campbell. 1979. *Quasi-Experimentation: Design and Analysis Issues for Field Settings*. Chicago: Rand McNally.

*Cross, Donna, Margaret Hall, Greg Hamilton, Yolanda Pintabona, and Erin Erceg. 2004. "Australia: The Friendly Schools Project." In *Bullying in Schools: How Successful Can Interventions Be?* edited by Peter K. Smith, Debra Pepler, and Ken Rigby. Cambridge: Cambridge University Press.

*DeRosier, Melissa E. 2004. "Building Relationships and Combating Bullying: Effectiveness of a School-Based Social Skills Group Intervention." *Journal of Clinical Child and Adolescent Psychology* 33:196–201.

*DeRosier, Melissa E., and Sarah R. Marcus. 2005. "Building Friendships and Combating Bullying: Effectiveness of S.S.GRIN at One-Year Follow-up." *Journal of Clinical Child and Adolescent Psychology* 34:140–50.

Due, Pernille, Bjorn E. Holstein, John Lynch, Finn Diderichsen, Saoirse N. Gabhain, Peter Scheidt, Candace Currie, and the Health Behaviour in School-Aged Children Bullying Working Group. 2005. "Bullying and Symptoms among School-Aged Children: International Comparative Cross Sectional Study in 28 Countries." *European Journal of Public Health* 15:128–32.

Egger, Matthias, George D. Smith, and Keith O'Rourke. 2001. "Rationale, Potentials and Promise of Systematic Reviews." In *Systematic Reviews in*

---

* Asterisks indicate studies that have been included in the meta-analysis.

Health Care: Meta-Analysis in Context, edited by Matthias Egger, George D. Smith, and Douglas G. Altman. London: BMJ Books.

*Ertesvag, Sigrun K., and Grete S. Vaaland. 2007. "Prevention and Reduction of Behavioural Problems in School: An Evaluation of the Respect Program." *Educational Psychology* 27:713–36.

Eslea, Mike, and Peter K. Smith. 1998. "The Long-Term Effectiveness of Anti-bullying Work in Primary Schools." *Educational Research* 40:203–18.

*Evers, Kerry E., James O. Prochaska, Deborah F. Van Marter, Janet L. Johnson, and Janice M. Prochaska. 2007. "Transtheoretical-Based Bullying Prevention Effectiveness Trials in Middle Schools and High Schools." *Educational Research* 49:397–414.

Farrington, David P. 1993. "Understanding and Preventing Bullying." In *Crime and Justice: A Review of Research*, vol. 17, edited by Michael Tonry. Chicago: University of Chicago Press.

———. 2003. "Methodological Quality Standards for Evaluation Research." *Annals of the American Academy of Political and Social Sciences* 587:49–68.

———. 2009. "Conduct Disorder, Aggression, and Delinquency." In *Handbook of Adolescent Psychology*, vol. 1, *Individual Bases of Adolescent Development*, 3rd ed., edited by Richard M. Lerner and Laurence Steinberg. Hoboken, NJ: Wiley.

Farrington, David P., Darrick Jolliffe, and Lorraine Johnstone. 2008. "Assessing Violence Risk: A Framework for Practice." Edinburgh: Risk Management Authority Scotland.

Farrington, David P., and Anthony Petrosino. 2001. "The Campbell Collaboration Crime and Justice Group." *Annals of the American Academy of Political and Social Science* 578:35–49.

Farrington, David P., and David Weisburd. 2007. "The Campbell Collaboration Crime and Justice Group." *Criminologist* 32(1):1–5.

Farrington, David P., and Brandon C. Welsh. 2003. "Family-Based Prevention of Offending: A Meta-Analysis." *Australian and New Zealand Journal of Criminology* 36:127–51.

Fekkes, Minne, Frans I. M. Pijpers, and Pauline S. Verloove-Vanhorick. 2005. "Bullying: Who Does What, When and Where? Involvement of Children, Teachers and Parents in Bullying Behavior." *Health Education Research* 20:81–91.

*———. 2006. "Effects of Antibullying School Program on Bullying and Health Complaints." *Archives of Pediatrics and Adolescent Medicine* 160:638–44.

Ferguson, Christopher J., Claudia S. Miguel, John C. J. Kilburn, and Patricia Sanchez. 2007. "The Effectiveness of School-Based Anti-bullying Programs: A Meta-Analytic Review." *Criminal Justice Review* 32:401–14.

Fonagy, Peter, Stuart W. Twemlow, Eric Vernberg, Frank C. Sacco, and Todd D. Little. 2005. "Creating a Peaceful School Learning Environment: The Impact of an Anti-bullying Program on Educational Attainment in Elementary Schools." *Medical Science Monitor* 11:317–25.

*Frey, Karin S., Miriam K. Hirschstein, Jennie L. Snell, Leihua van Schoiack

Edstrom, Elizabeth P. MacKenzie, and Carole J. Broderick. 2005. "Reducing Playground Bullying and Supporting Beliefs: An Experimental Trial of the Steps to Respect Program." *Developmental Psychology* 41:479–91.

*Frey, Karin S., Leihua van Schoiack Edstrom, and Miriam K. Hirschstein. 2005. "The Steps to Respect Program Uses a Multi-level Approach to Reduce Playground Bullying and Destructive Playground Behaviors." In *Proceedings of Persistently Safe Schools*, edited by D. L. White, M. K. Faber, and B. C. Glenn. Washington, DC: Hamilton Fish Institute, George Washington University.

*Galloway, David, and Erling Roland. 2004. "Is the Direct Approach to Reducing Bullying Always the Best?" In *Bullying in Schools: How Successful Can Interventions Be?* edited by Peter K. Smith, Debra Pepler, and Ken Rigby. Cambridge: Cambridge University Press.

Hedges, Larry V. 1982. "Fitting Continuous Models to Effect Size Data." *Journal of Educational and Behavioral Statistics* 7:245–70.

Heydenberk, Roberta A., Warren R. Heydenberk, and Vera Tzenova. 2006. "Conflict Resolution and Bully Prevention: Skills for School Success." *Conflict Resolution Quarterly* 24:55–69.

*Hirschstein, Miriam K., Leihua van Schoiack Edstrom, Karin S. Frey, Jennie L. Snell, and Elizabeth P. Mackenzie. 2007. "Walking the Talk in Bullying Prevention: Teacher Implementation Variables Related to Initial Impact of Steps to Respect Program." *School Psychology Review* 36:3–21.

Howard, Kim A., June Flora, and Marle Griffin. 1999. "Violence-Prevention Programs in Schools: State of Science and Implications for Future Research." *Applied and Preventive Psychology* 8:197–215.

*Hunt, Caroline. 2007. "The Effect of an Education Program on Attitudes and Beliefs about Bullying and Bullying Behaviour in Junior Secondary School Students." *Child and Adolescent Mental Health* 12:21–26.

*Jenson, Jeffrey M., and William A. Dieterich. 2007. "Effects of a Skills-Based Prevention Program on Bullying and Bully Victimization among Elementary School Children." *Prevention Science* 8:285–96.

*Jenson, Jeffrey M., William A. Dieterich, Anne Powell, and S. Stoker. 2006*a*. "Effects of a Skills-Based Intervention on Aggression and Bully Victimization among Elementary School Children." Paper presented at the annual meeting of the Society for Prevention Research, San Antonio, May 31–June 2.

*———. 2006*b*. "Effects of the Youth Matters Prevention Curriculum on Bullying and Other Aggressive Behaviors in Elementary School Students." Paper presented at the annual meeting of the Society for Social Work and Research, San Antonio, January 12–15.

*Jenson, Jeffrey M., William A. Dieterich, and Jennifer R. Rinner. 2005*a*. "Effects of a Skills-Based Prevention Program on Bullying and Bully Victimization among Elementary School Children." Paper presented at the annual meeting of the American Society of Criminology, Toronto, November 15–19.

*———. 2005*b*. "The Prevention of Bullying and Other Aggressive Behaviors

in Elementary School Students: Effects of the Youth Matters Curriculum." Paper presented at the annual meeting of the Society for Prevention Research, Washington, DC, May 25–27.

Jolliffe, Darrick, and David P. Farrington. 2007. "A Rapid Evidence Assessment of the Impact of Mentoring on Reoffending." Online Report no. 11/07. London: Home Office. http://www.homeoffice.gov.uk/rds/pdfs07/rdsolr 1107.pdf.

Kaiser-Ulrey, Cheryl. 2003. "Bullying in Middle Schools: A Study of B.E.S.T.—Bullying Eliminated from Schools Together—an Anti-bullying Program for Seventh Grade Students." PhD thesis, Florida State University, College of Education.

Kalliotis, Panayiotis. 2000. "Bullying as a Special Case of Aggression: Procedures for Cross-Cultural Assessment." *School Psychology International* 21: 47–64.

Kaminski, Jennifer W., Linda A. Valle, Jill H. Filene, and Cynthia L. Boyle. 2008. "A Meta-Analytic Review of Components Associated with Parent Training Program Effectiveness." *Journal of Abnormal Child Psychology* 36: 567–89.

Lipsey, Mark W. 2003. "Those Confounded Moderators in Meta-Analysis: Good, Bad, and Ugly." *Annals of the American Academy of Political and Social Science* 587:69–81.

Lipsey, Mark W., and David B. Wilson. 2001. *Practical Meta-Analysis.* Thousand Oaks, CA: Sage.

Littell, Julian H., Jacqueline Corcoran, and Vijayan Pillai. 2008. *Systematic Reviews and Meta-Analysis.* Oxford: Oxford University Press.

Losel, Friedrich, and Andreas Beelman. 2003. "Effects of Child Skills Training in Preventing Antisocial Behavior: A Systematic Review of Randomized Evaluations." *Annals of the American Academy of Political and Social Science* 587:84–109.

Martin, Francisco D. F., Maria Del C. P. Martinez, and Jost L. A. Tirado. 2005. "Diseño, aplicación y evaluación de un programa piloto para la prevención del maltrato entre compañeros" [Design, implementation, and evaluation of a bullying prevention pilot program]. *Revista Mexicana de Psicologia* 22:375–84.

McGuire, James. 2001. "What Works in Correctional Intervention? Evidence and Practical Implications." In *Offender Rehabilitation in Practice: Implementing and Evaluating Effective Programs,* edited by Gary A. Bernfeld, David P. Farrington, and Alan W. Leschield. Chichester, UK: Wiley.

*Melton, Gary B., Susan P. Limber, Vicki Flerx, Maury Nation, Wayne Osgood, Jeff Chambers, Scott Henggeler, Phillippe Cunningham, and Dan Olweus. 1998. "Violence among Rural Youth." Washington, DC: Office of Juvenile Justice and Delinquency Prevention.

*Menard, Scott, Jennifer Grotpeter, Daniella Gianola, and Maura O'Neal. 2008. "Evaluation of Bullyproofing Your School." Final report to the U.S. Department of Justice, National Criminal Justice Reference Service. http://www.ncjrs.gov/pdffiles1/nij/grants/221078.pdf.

Meraviglia, Martha G., Heather Becker, Barri Rosenbluth, Ellen Sanchez, and
Trina Robertson. 2003. "The Expect Respect Project: Creating a Positive
Elementary School Climate." *Journal of Interpersonal Violence* 18:1347–60.

Merrell, Kenneth W., Barbara A. Gueldner, Scott W. Ross, and Duane M.
Isava. 2008. "How Effective Are School Bullying Intervention Programs? A
Meta-Analysis of Intervention Research." *School Psychology Quarterly* 23:
26–42.

Moher, David, Kenneth F. Schulz, and Douglas G. Altman. 2001. "The CON-
SORT Statement: Revised Recommendations for Improving the Quality of
Reports of Parallel Group Randomized Trials." *Journal of the American Med-
ical Association* 285:1987–91.

Morrison, Brenda. 2007. *Restoring Safe School Communities: A Whole School Response to Bullying, Violence and Alienation.* Sydney: Federation Press.

Mytton, Julie A., Carolyn DiGuiseppi, David Gough, Rod S. Taylor, and Stuart
Logan. 2006. "School-Based Secondary Prevention Programs for Preventing
Violence." *Cochrane Database of Systematic Reviews* 3:CD004606.

*Olweus, Dan. 1991. "Bully/Victim Problems among School Children: Basic
Facts and Effects of a School-Based Intervention Program." In *The Devel-
opment and Treatment of Childhood Aggression*, edited by Debra J. Pepler and
Kenneth H. Rubin. Hillsdale, NJ: Erlbaum.

*———. 1992. "Bullying among School Children: Intervention and Preven-
tion." In *Aggression and Violence throughout the Lifespan*, edited by Ray D.
Peters, Robert J. McMahon, and Vernon L. Quinsey. London: Sage.

*———. 1993a. "Bully/Victim Problems among Schoolchildren: Long-Term
Consequences and an Effective Intervention Program." In *Mental Disorder
and Crime*, edited by Sheilagh Hodgins. Thousand Oaks, CA: Sage.

———. 1993b. *Bullying at School: What We Know and What We Can Do.* Oxford:
Blackwell.

———. 1993c. "Victimization by Peers: Antecedents and Long-Term Outcomes." In *Social Withdrawal, Inhibition and Shyness in Childhood*, edited by
Kenneth H. Rubin and Jens B. Asendorpf. Hillsdale, NJ: Erlbaum.

*———. 1994a. "Bullying at School: Basic Facts and an Effective Intervention
Programme." *Promotion and Education* 1:27–31.

*———. 1994b. "Bullying at School: Basic Facts and Effects of a School Based
Intervention Program." *Journal of Child Psychology and Psychiatry* 35:1171–90.

*———. 1994c. "Bullying at School: Long-Term Outcome for the Victims and
an Effective School-Based Intervention Program." In *Aggressive Behavior:
Current Perspectives*, edited by L. Rowell Huesmann. New York: Plenum.

*———. 1995. "Peer Abuse or Bullying at School: Basic Facts and a School-
Based Intervention Programme." *Prospects* 25:133–39.

*———. 1996a. "Bully/Victim Problems at School: Facts and Effective Inter-
vention." *Reclaiming Children and Youth: Journal of Emotional and Behavioral
Problems* 5:15–22.

*———. 1996b. "Bullying at School: Knowledge Base and Effective Interven-
tion." *Annals of the New York Academy of Sciences* 784:265–76.

*———. 1996c. "Bullying or Peer Abuse in School: Intervention and Preven-

tion." In *Psychology, Law and Criminal Justice: International Developments in Research and Practice*, edited by Graham Davies, Sally Lloyd-Bostock, Mary McMurran, and Clare Wilson. Berlin: de Gruyter.

*————. 1997a. "Bully/Victim Problems in School: Facts and Intervention." *European Journal of Psychology of Education* 12:495–510.

*————. 1997b. "Bully/Victim Problems in School: Knowledge Base and an Effective Intervention Project." *Irish Journal of Psychology* 18:170–90.

*————. 1997c. "Tackling Peer Victimization with a School-Based Intervention Program." In *Cultural Variation in Conflict Resolution: Alternatives to Violence*, edited by Douglas P. Fry and Kaj Bjorkqvist. Mahwah, NJ: Erlbaum.

*————. 2004a. "Bullying at School: Prevalence Estimation, a Useful Evaluation Design, and a New National Initiative in Norway." *Association for Child Psychology and Psychiatry Occasional Papers* 23:5–17.

————. 2004b. *Continuation of the Olweus Programme against Bullying and Antisocial Behaviour*. Bergen, Norway: University of Bergen, Department of Psychology.

*————. 2004c. "The Olweus Bullying Prevention Programme: Design and Implementation Issues and a New National Initiative in Norway." In *Bullying in Schools: How Successful Can Interventions Be?* edited by Peter K. Smith, Debra Pepler, and Ken Rigby. Cambridge: Cambridge University Press.

*————. 2005. "A Useful Evaluation Design, and Effects of the Olweus Bullying Prevention Program." *Psychology, Crime and Law* 11:389–402.

*————. 2006. "Bullying in Schools: Facts and Intervention." In *Acoso y violencia en la escuela*, edited by Angela Serrano. Valencia, Spain: Queen Sofia Center for the Study of Violence.

*Olweus, Dan, and Francoise D. Alsaker. 1991. "Assessing Change in a Cohort-Longitudinal Study with Hierarchical Data." In *Problems and Methods in Longitudinal Research*, edited by David Magnusson, Lars R. Bergman, Georg Rudinger, and Bertil Torestad. Cambridge: Cambridge University Press.

Ortega, Rosario. 2006. "Prevention Programs for Pupils." In *Acoso y violencia en la escuela*, edited by Angela Serrano. Valencia, Spain: Queen Sofia Center for the Study of Violence.

*Ortega, Rosario, and Rosario Del Rey. 1999. "The Use of Peer Support in the S.A.V.E. Project." Paper presented at the Ninth European Conference on Developmental Psychology, Spetses, Greece, September 1–5.

*Ortega, Rosario, Rosario Del Rey, and Joaquin A. Mora-Mercan. 2004. "SAVE Model: An Anti-bullying Intervention in Spain." In *Bullying in Schools: How Successful Can Interventions Be?* edited by Peter K. Smith, Debra Pepler, and Ken Rigby. Cambridge: Cambridge University Press.

Pateraki, Lena, and Anastasia Houndoumadi. 2001. "Bullying among Primary School Children in Athens, Greece." *Educational Psychology* 21:167–75.

*Pepler, Debra J., Wendy M. Craig, Paul O'Connell, Rona Atlas, and Alice Charach. 2004. "Making a Difference in Bullying: Evaluation of a Systemic School-Based Program in Canada." In *Bullying in Schools: How Successful Can*

Interventions Be? edited by Peter K. Smith, Debra Pepler, and Ken Rigby. Cambridge: Cambridge University Press.

Pepler, Debra, Peter K. Smith, and Ken Rigby. 2004. "Looking Back and Looking Forward: Implications for Making Interventions Work Effectively." In *Bullying in Schools: How Successful Can Interventions Be?* edited by Peter K. Smith, Debra Pepler, and Ken Rigby. Cambridge: Cambridge University Press.

Petticrew, Mark, and Helen Roberts. 2006. *Systematic Reviews in the Social Sciences: A Practical Guide.* Malden, MA: Blackwell.

*Pintabona, Yolanda C. 2006. "Frequently Bullied Students: Outcomes of a Universal School-Based Bullying Preventive Intervention on Peer Victimization and Psychological Health." PhD thesis, Curtin University of Technology, Bentley, Western Australia.

*Rahey, Leila, and Wendy M. Craig. 2002. "Evaluation of an Ecological Program to Reduce Bullying in Schools." *Canadian Journal of Counselling* 36: 281–95.

*Raskauskas, Juliana. 2007. "Evaluation of the Kia Kaha Anti-bullying Programme for Students in Years 5–8." Final Report to the New Zealand Police. Wellington: New Zealand Police.

*Rican, Pavel, Katerina Ondrova, and Jiri Svatos. 1996. "The Effect of a Short, Intensive Intervention upon Bullying in Four Classes in a Czech Town." *Annals of the New York Academy of Sciences* 794:399–400.

Rigby, Ken. 2002. "A Meta-Evaluation of Methods and Approaches to Reducing Bullying in Preschools and Early Primary School in Australia." Canberra: Attorney General's Department, Crime Prevention Branch.

*Rosenbluth, Barri, Daniel J. Whitaker, Ellen Sanchez, and Linda A. Valle. 2004. "The Expect Respect Project: Preventing Bullying and Sexual Harassment in US Elementary Schools." In *Bullying in Schools: How Successful Can Interventions Be?* edited by Peter K. Smith, Debra Pepler, and Ken Rigby. Cambridge: Cambridge University Press.

*Salmivalli, Christina, Atti Karna, and Elisa Poskiparta. Forthcoming. "From Peer Putdowns to Peer Support: A Theoretical Model and How It Translated into a National Anti-bullying Program." In *The International Handbook of School Bullying*, edited by Shane R. Jimerson, Susan M. Swearer, and Dorothy L. Espelage. Mahwah, NJ: Erlbaum.

*Salmivalli, Christina, Ari Kaukiainen, and Marinus Voeten. 2005. "Anti-bullying Intervention: Implementation and Outcome." *British Journal of Educational Psychology* 75:465–87.

*Salmivalli, Christina, Ari Kaukiainen, Marinus Voeten, and Mirva Sinisammal. 2004. "Targeting the Group as a Whole: The Finnish Anti-bullying Intervention." In *Bullying in Schools: How Successful Can Interventions Be?* edited by Peter K. Smith, Debra Pepler, and Ken Rigby. Cambridge: Cambridge University Press.

Shadish, William R., Thomas D. Cook, and Donald T. Campbell. 2002. *Experimental and Quasi-Experimental Designs for Generalized Causal Inference.* Boston: Houghton-Mifflin.

Smith, J. David, Barry H. Schneider, Peter K. Smith, and Katerina Ananiadou. 2004. "The Effectiveness of Whole-School Anti-bullying Programs: A Synthesis of Evaluation Research." *School Psychology Review* 33:547–60.

*Smith, Peter K. 1997. "Bullying in Schools: The UK Experience and the Sheffield Anti-bullying Project." *Irish Journal of School Psychology* 18:191–201.

———. Forthcoming. "Bullying in Primary and Secondary Schools: Psychological and Organizational Comparisons." In *The International Handbook of School Bullying*, edited by Shane R. Jimerson, Susan M. Swearer, and Dorothy L. Espelage. Mahwah, NJ: Erlbaum.

Smith, Peter K., and Katerina Ananiadou. 2003. "The Nature of School Bullying and the Effectiveness of School-Based Interventions." *Journal of Applied Psychoanalytic Studies* 5:189–209.

Smith, Peter K., Katerina Ananiadou, and Helen Cowie. 2003. "Interventions to Reduce School Bullying." *Canadian Journal of Psychiatry* 48:591–99.

Smith, Peter K., Helen Cowie, Ragnar F. Olafsson, and Andy P. D. Liefooghe. 2002. "Definitions of Bullying: A Comparison of Terms Used, and Age and Gender Differences, in a 14-Country International Comparison." *Child Development* 73:1119–33.

Smith, Peter K., Yohji Morita, Josine Junger-Tas, Dan Olweus, Richard Catalano, and Philip T. Slee, eds. 1999. *The Nature of School Bullying: A Cross-National Perspective*. London: Routledge.

Smith, Peter K., Debra Pepler, and Ken Rigby, eds. 2004a. *Bullying in Schools: How Successful Can Interventions Be?* Cambridge: Cambridge University Press.

*———. 2004b. "England: The Sheffield Project." In *Bullying in Schools: How Successful Can Interventions Be?* edited by Peter K. Smith, Debra Pepler, and Ken Rigby. Cambridge: Cambridge University Press.

Spröber, Nina, Peter F. Schlottke, and Martin Hautzinger. 2006. "Pro-ACT + E: Ein Programm zur Prävention von 'Bullying' an Schulen und zur Förderung der positiven Entwicklung von Schülern: Evaluation eines schulbasierten, universalen, primarpraventiven Programms fur weiterführenden Schulen unter Einbeziehung von Lehrern, Schulen und Eltern" [ProACT +E: A program to prevent bullying in schools and to increase the positive development of students: Evaluation of a school-based, universal, primary preventative program for secondary schools that includes teachers, students, and parents]. *Zeitschrift fur Klinische Psychologie und Psychotherapie: Forschung und Praxis* 35:140–50.

*Stevens, Veerle, Ilse De Bourdeaudhuij, and Paulette Van Oost. 2000. "Bullying in Flemish Schools: An Evaluation of Anti-bullying Intervention in Primary and Secondary Schools." *British Journal of Educational Psychology* 70:195–210.

———. 2001. "Anti-bullying Interventions at School: Aspects of Programme Adaptation and Critical Issues for Further Programme Development." *Health Promotion International* 16:155–67.

*Stevens, Veerle, Paulette Van Oost, and Ilse De Bourdeaudhuij. 2000. "The Effects of an Anti-bullying Intervention Programme on Peers' Attitudes and Behaviour." *Journal of Adolescence* 23:21–34.

*———. 2001. "Implementation Process of the Flemish Anti-bullying Intervention and Relation with Program Effectiveness." *Journal of School Psychology* 39:303–17.

*———. 2004. "Interventions against Bullying in Flemish Schools." In *Bullying in Schools: How Successful Can Interventions Be?* edited by Peter K. Smith, Debra Pepler, and Ken Rigby. Cambridge: Cambridge University Press.

Ttofi, Maria M., and David P. Farrington. 2008*a*. "Bullying: Short-Term and Long-Term Effects, and the Importance of Defiance Theory in Explanation and Prevention." *Victims and Offenders* 3:289–312.

———. 2008*b*. "Reintegrative Shaming Theory, Moral Emotions and Bullying." *Aggressive Behavior* 34:352–68.

Ttofi, Maria M., David P. Farrington, and Anna C. Baldry. 2008. *Effectiveness of Programmes to Reduce School Bullying*. Stockholm: Swedish National Council for Crime Prevention.

Twemlow, Stuart W., Peter Fonagy, and Frank C. Sacco. 2005. "A Developmental Approach to Mentalizing Communities: II. The Peaceful Schools Experiment." *Bulletin of the Menninger Clinic* 69:282–304.

Vreeman, Rachel C., and Aaron E. Carroll. 2007. "A Systematic Review of School-Based Interventions to Prevent Bullying." *Archives of Pediatrics and Adolescent Medicine* 161:78–88.

Warden, David, Ellen Moran, John Gillies, Gillian Mayes, and Lindsey Macleod. 1997. "An Evaluation of a Children's Safety Training Programme." *Educational Psychology* 17:433–48.

Weisburd, David, Cynthia M. Lum, and Anthony Petrosino. 2001. "Does Research Design Affect Study Outcomes in Criminal Justice?" *Annals of the American Academy of Political and Social Science* 578:50–70.

Welsh, Brandon C., David P. Farrington, and Lawrence W. Sherman, eds. 2001. *Costs and Benefits of Preventing Crime*. Boulder, CO: Westview.

*Whitaker, Daniel J., Barri Rosenbluth, Linda A. Valle, and Ellen Sachez. 2004. "Expect Respect: A School-Based Intervention to Promote Awareness and Effective Responses to Bullying and Sexual Harassment." In *Bullying in American Schools: A Social-Ecological Perspective on Prevention and Intervention*, edited by Dorothy L. Espelage and Suzan M. Swearer. Mahwah, NJ: Erlbaum.

*Whitney, Irene, Ian Rivers, Peter K. Smith, and Sonia Sharp. 1994. "The Sheffield Project: Methodology and Findings." In *School Bullying: Insights and Perspectives*, edited by Peter K. Smith and Sonia Sharp. London: Routledge.

Wiefferink, Carin, H. Hoekstra, J. T. Beek, and A. Van Dorst. 2006. "Effects of an Anti-bullying Programme in Elementary Schools in the Netherlands." *European Journal of Public Health* 16:76.

Wilson, Sandra J., and Mark W. Lipsey. 2007. "School-Based Interventions for Aggressive and Disruptive Behavior: Update of a Meta-Analysis." *American Journal of Preventive Medicine* 33:S130–S143.

Wilson, Sandra J., Mark W. Lipsey, and James H. Derzon. 2003. "The Effects of School-Based Intervention Programs on Aggressive Behavior: A Meta-Analysis." *Journal of Consulting and Clinical Psychology* 71:136–49.

Woods, Tom, Kim Coyle, Wendy Hoglund, and Bonnie Leadbeater. 2007. "Changing the Contexts of Peer Victimization: The Effects of a Primary Prevention Program on School and Classroom Levels of Victimization." In *Bullying, Victimization, and Peer Harassment: A Handbook of Prevention and Intervention*, edited by Joseph E. Zins, Maurice J. Elias, and Charles A. Maher. New York: Haworth.

Julian V. Roberts

Listening to the Crime Victim: Evaluating Victim Input at Sentencing and Parole

ABSTRACT

Crime victims play an increasingly important role in the criminal process. One manifestation of this is the proliferation in the use of victim impact statements at sentencing and parole hearings. Across the common-law world victims are allowed to submit an impact statement to a sentencing court or parole board. Many U.S. states go further and encourage (or allow) victims to recommend a specific sentence to the court or to express their views on the release of the offender on parole. Research into the use of impact evidence at sentencing suggests that victims can benefit from the experience, and most who submit impact statements affirm that they would do so again. However, few victims participate in impact statement regimes, which tend to be poorly administered. There is no systematic evidence that impact statements make sentencing harsher, and research suggests that victim impact evidence is perceived by judges to be beneficial to the sentencing process. There is less justification for allowing victim input at parole, as victims seldom possess information relevant to the parole decision. Victim input at corrections is an example of what has been termed "punitive victim rights" and is inconsistent with sound correctional principles or principles of fundamental justice.

Over the past 30 years crime victims have acquired participatory rights at all stages of the criminal process. All 50 American states now provide a wide range of statutory rights for victims, and most have amended

Julian V. Roberts is professor of criminology in the Faculty of Law, University of Oxford. I would like to thank the following individuals for comments on an earlier draft of this essay or for providing information: Michael Tonry, Michael O'Connell, Kent Roach, Edna Erez, Fiona Leverick, and Susan MacDonald.

their constitutions to protect these rights. Much of the impetus for these reforms came from the 1982 final report of the President's Task Force on Victims of Crime.[1]

More recently, victims' rights in the United States have been enhanced by the federal Crime Victims' Rights Act. In addition to the right to "reasonable, accurate and timely notice of any public court proceeding, or any parole proceeding, involving the crime or any release or escape of the accused" (18 U.S.C. § 3771 [2]), a crime victim also has the right to "be reasonably heard at any public proceeding in the district court involving release, plea, sentencing, or any parole proceeding" (18 U.S.C. § 3771 [3]; see Cassell 2009). Similar statutes conferring rights upon victims and obligations upon criminal justice officials to ensure that those rights are respected exist around the common-law world.[2] In *Payne v. Tennessee* (111 S. Ct. 2597 [1991]), the U.S. Supreme Court affirmed the admissibility of impact evidence at a capital sentencing hearing.

Criminal justice agencies are often required to provide detailed information about case developments to victims. Few criminal justice scholars contest the provision of information about the case—court dates, remands, sentencing hearings, and the like. But behind the question of information lies the issue of input. Why would victims wish to be kept informed of developments unless they also sought to be consulted or to offer input into decisions taken? Why ask for notice of an impending parole hearing unless you also wish to submit material to the parole board or to oppose the release of the offender?

The focus of this essay is upon victim input into the determination and subsequent administration of legal punishments. Despite the diversity of sentencing arrangements across the common-law world, one feature is present everywhere: all jurisdictions now permit crime victims to provide impact evidence at sentencing, and most allow input into parole hearings.[3] The right to submit impact evidence at sentenc-

---

[1] See Tobolowsky (1999) for a review of developments since the publication of this landmark report.

[2] See Shapland (2009) for a discussion of victims and criminal justice in civil law systems.

[3] In some jurisdictions victim input extends beyond the punishment of convicted offenders. For example, victims in Canada are allowed input into decisions pertaining to the treatment of accused found not criminally responsible on account of mental disorder. Boards reviewing the treatment of these individuals are required to consider victim impact statements in making their dispositions. Victim impact statements arising from a criminal offense may also find their way into noncriminal proceedings—such as custody disputes between parents or professional discipline hearings.

ing is, as Dubber observes, "the most controversial of procedural victims' rights" (2002, p. 336). Allowing victims to submit evidence about the effect of the crime creates a potential threat to the liberty interests of the defendant, and the increasingly intrusive presence of the victim also represents a significant challenge to the adversarial model of justice. As the justice system expands the rights of victims and imposes more obligations upon criminal justice officials to inform or consult victims about key decisions, the bipartite (state-offender) character of adversarial proceedings expands to reflect the interests of victims.

Impact evidence is usually placed before a sentencing court or a parole board in the form of a victim impact statement, which is completed by a crime victim, sometimes with the assistance of victim services personnel. The earliest statutory victim impact regimes in the United States have been in place for well over a generation now. The first victim impact statement was deposed in a criminal proceeding in California in 1976 as part of a presentence report, and the concept was placed on a statutory footing in that state 6 years later (Alexander and Lord 1994). All states provide victims with the right to be heard at sentencing, and most allow for input at parole hearings (Office for Victims of Crime 1999). Victims in 16 states also have a right to be heard at pardon, commutation, or clemency proceedings.

Other common-law jurisdictions soon followed the U.S. example. Victim statements at sentencing were introduced in New Zealand in 1987 (Wallace 1989), while South Australia was the first jurisdiction in that country to enact legislation permitting victim input into sentencing. Impact statements were introduced on an ad hoc basis in 1985 and received statutory recognition in 1988. The government of South Australia has introduced legislation to expand the scope of its victim impact legislation.[4] Canada introduced impact statements the next year (1989; see Roberts 2003). Victim statements for use at sentencing emerged in England and Wales in 1996 (Hoyle and Zedner 2007). Finally, victims of crimes prosecuted at the International Criminal Court in The Hague also have the right to submit a statement docu-

---

[4] If passed, the legislation will give victims an absolute right to read their impact statements in court, and offenders will be obliged to be present when the impact statement is read or to be linked by closed-circuit television to the court in order that they listen to the statement if one is read into the record. As well, two new forms of impact statement will be created—a neighborhood statement and a social impact statement (personal communication with Michael O'Connell, e-mail December 10, 2008).

menting the injury, loss, or harm that they have sustained (International Criminal Court 2008).

Kent Roach (1999, pp. 29–37) has usefully distinguished between punitive and nonpunitive victims' rights. Punitive rights favor the use of criminal sanctions and are aligned in opposition to due process claims of defendants. In contrast, nonpunitive rights emphasize the right to be heard and to express views in a way that is not directed toward promoting a punishment-based model of justice. Whether victim impact statements constitute a punitive or nonpunitive reform depends upon the nature of the input and the purpose served by the specific victim input regime. These elements will in turn influence victims' submissions and ultimately the effect, if any, on sentencing practices. Impact schemes are either dispositive—allowing victims to determine or influence the outcome—or nondispositive in nature (Edwards 2004). Under nondispositive regimes the crime victim describes the effect of the crime but does not recommend a specific sentence. It seems reasonable to conclude that the U.S. regimes where victims are encouraged to recommend a sentence or a parole decision are examples of a punitive victim input regime, as they place the victim squarely in opposition to the interests of the offender.

In contrast, if victims are directed to address the impact of the crime and opinions about the appropriate sentence are explicitly proscribed, it is harder to construe victim input schemes as simply contributing to a more punitive sentencing environment. Allowing the court and the offender to hear a direct account of the impact of the crime is surely not an unreasonable step to take; the imposition of a sentence is determined, after all, at a public hearing, where the individuals primarily affected by the crime should be able to express themselves. A crime is a public wrong but one also committed against a private individual. Allowing victim allocution is objectionable only if this expression disturbs fundamental principles of sentencing (including fairness), impairs the liberty interests of the defendant, or affects the decorum of courtroom proceedings.[5]

Since their inception, victim impact statements have generated considerable scholarly commentary and, at times, heated debate. For read-

---

[5] One of the practical objections to allowing victims to deliver their statements orally is that they occasionally wander off the topic and denigrate the offender or make allegations of other, unproven misconduct. This underscores the need to ensure that victims receive adequate direction regarding the purpose and nature of victim impact statements.

ings advocating or accepting the use of impact statements, see Erez (1990, 1999, 2004) and Spencer (2004). In contrast, Ashworth (1993), Hinton (1995), and Sanders (2004) oppose the use of such statements or regard victim statements as contributing little to the sentencing process. Between these opposing perspectives can be found a via media, represented by scholars who support the use of victim impact statements to help determine harm and culpability but who vigorously oppose regimes that solicit sentence recommendations from the victim (e.g., Hall 1991, p. 266).

This essay cannot explore in depth the complex normative issues arising from the use of victim impact evidence; these have already spawned a large number of articles and exchanges. At the heart of the debate lie the principal questions of whether victims actually benefit from submitting impact statements and whether allowing victim input constitutes a threat to due process and the adversarial model of justice. Here I examine the empirical research relating to victim impact statements at sentencing and parole. The research record regarding the effect of allowing victim impact statements in this way is now extensive, with the result that many of the claims of both advocates and critics may be reviewed in light of the accumulated empirical evidence. Scholars have been divided on the benefits of victim input, but few writers have adopted an evidence-based approach to the question of whether the practice of allowing victim impact statements does more harm than good. As Williams notes, "the research evidence is confusing because so much of it is passionately argued" (2005, p. 105).

The research on victim input at sentencing and parole suffers from certain deficiencies. First, many scholars have adopted a rather parochial approach to determining the propriety or utility of victim input. Their conclusions have been founded upon studies or sometimes one study conducted in a single jurisdiction.[6] To date, no systematic cross-jurisdictional review has been conducted.[7] Second, little consideration has been given to determining the criteria of success; many claims have been made by victim input advocates. Third, scholars have failed to distinguish the concept of victim impact from the practice of victim

---

[6] For example, Sanders et al. (2001) draw very robust conclusions about the disutility of victim impact statements—encapsulated in their eye-catching and often quoted title, "Victim Impact Statements: Don't Work, Can't Work"—yet their conclusions are based upon one study from a single jurisdiction.

[7] For a summary of earlier research, see Erez (1999); a thorough discussion of findings from U.S. research is provided by Tobolowsky (1999).

input schemes. Determining whether victim impact evidence carries benefits for the victim, the offender, or the sentencing court requires a more comprehensive approach, which recognizes that victim input regimes vary widely in terms of their scope and manner of implementation.

The debate over victim participation in criminal justice often takes sentencing and parole to constitute two stages of a relatively seamless criminal justice system; according to this view, victim impact evidence is as relevant to a parole board as it is to a sentencing court. This approach overlooks important differences between the decision taken at sentencing or parole. For this reason, in this essay I discuss the two stages of criminal justice separately. A reasonable argument can, I believe, be made to justify the introduction of victim impact evidence at sentencing. Allowing this kind of evidence can carry benefits for victims without impairing defendants' interests. Moreover, there has long been widespread support for the position that the harm caused by a crime is something that judges can legitimately consider at sentencing, and victim impact statements represent a means to that end. The case for victim participation seems harder to make at parole, where the legitimate considerations appear to be the prisoner's risk of reoffending and evidence germane to his or her prospects of leading a law-abiding life on release from prison. On these matters, few victims will have much to contribute.

In the pages that follow I explore the accumulated empirical evidence concerning the utility and effects of victim impact statements at sentencing and then at parole. Section I of the essay reviews the purposes of victim impact evidence and describes some representative statutory regimes across the common-law world. Section II evaluates the effects of impact statements upon crime victims. Section III discusses the effects that impact statement regimes have had upon courts and the reactions of legal practitioners. Section IV explores the role of the victim at parole, where victim input is a more recent phenomenon than at sentencing, at least in jurisdictions outside the United States. In Section V, I draw some conclusions about the utility of victim statements as a source of legally relevant information at sentencing and parole and lay out a short research agenda for the future.

This essay is restricted to the input of individual crime victims, although in some cases of drunk driving and federal cases involving drug offenses, neighborhood or community impact statements are deposed.

Community impact statements are sometimes submitted in cases involving hate-motivated violence to establish the generalized harm of this form of offending, and they have recently been proposed in a more general context in South Australia in the Statutes Amendment (Victims of Crime) Bill 2008. Finally, no discussion is provided about the use of victim impact statements in capital sentencing hearings, as the role of victim statements in death penalty proceedings raises a separate set of issues about a sanction found in only one common-law jurisdiction.

I. Purpose of Impact Statements and Representative Regimes

Any attempt to evaluate the utility of victim impact regimes must begin by identifying the purposes served by allowing victim input into sentencing. Victim impact schemes are generally vague and evasive in this respect, often assuming a purpose that they should be articulating for the benefit of victims and the justice professionals who administer the schemes. This nebulousness is reflected in the specific statutory provisions. It might be argued that statutes provide general directions to sentencers and that the interpretation of these provisions is left to courts. But appellate courts across the common-law world have been reluctant to engage with victim impact statement legislation, and there is little appellate jurisprudence on the issue. One reason for this lack of appellate scrutiny is that unless a trial court imposes a particularly severe sentence and cites the impact evidence of the victim, the court of appeal is unlikely to be asked for a review.[8] In jurisdictions such as the state of Minnesota, which use presumptive sentencing guidelines, the influence of the statement will be constrained by guideline ranges; "upward departures" (on the grounds of heightened victim impact) from the prescribed ranges will be rare. However, most common-law jurisdictions do not employ formal sentencing guidelines of this nature.

Much of the debate about victim impact statements has focused on whether they "work," although few writers have offered a definition of success. The following might be offered as one such definition. Victim impact statements are successful to the extent that they achieve some

---

[8] Courts of first instance in some jurisdictions have evolved their own guidelines with respect to the content of impact statements (for a discussion of case law in New Zealand, see Sankoff and Wansborough [2007, p. 477]; in Canada, see Policy Centre for Victim Issues [2008]).

benefit for the victim, the offender, or the sentencer, without interfering with consensual principles of sentencing. In practical terms, these benefits may include promoting victim satisfaction with sentencing and criminal justice; enhancing the transformative potential of a criminal sanction on the offender; increasing the accuracy of judicial determination of crime seriousness and the likelihood that, where appropriate, restitution will be ordered; and increasing criminal justice professionals' awareness of the true effects of criminal victimization. Whether these objectives have been achieved, or are achievable, is the subject of this essay. But I return later to make the point that a fair test of the extent to which these objectives have been achieved assumes that existing victim input regimes have been appropriately conceived and implemented. There is ample evidence that this assumption is unfounded.

A. Victim Impact Evidence and the Objectives of Sentencing

Most common-law jurisdictions have placed a number of sentencing objectives on a statutory footing (Roberts and Baker 2007). This occurred in Canada in 1996, New Zealand in 2002, and England and Wales in 2003. Sentencing guidelines manuals across the United States identify a number of objectives that the guidelines are presumably created to promote, including deterrence, incapacitation, rehabilitation, and retribution. How does victim impact evidence relate to the traditional sentencing goals? In the absence of some link, the relevance of victim impact is questionable. Hearing about the impact of the crime—either indirectly through trial testimony and prosecutorial submissions at sentencing or directly from the victim herself—is unlikely to promote the utilitarian goals of deterrence or incapacitation. However, the rehabilitation of offenders may be facilitated by arousing feelings of remorse or sympathy for the victim, although this remains a hypothesis requiring substantiation. In this respect victim impact statements may be of use in promoting the objective of rehabilitation (see discussion in Henderson [1985]; Talbert [1988]; Black [1994]).

Victim impact statements have a role to play within a retributive account of sentencing. Retributive sentencing seeks to impose a sentence the severity of which is commensurate with the seriousness of the offense and the offender's level of culpability (von Hirsch 1993). In determining the harm inflicted or threatened, a court requires evidence of the impact on the victim; seriousness levels cannot be determined a priori, beyond a crude ranking of offenses in terms of their relative seriousness. It is with respect to this determination that the claim of the victim to provide input becomes more plausible. Desert-based theories are essentially communicative theories of sentencing. A message of disapprobation is conveyed to the offender, and the severity of the sentence reflects the measure of legal censure. But the communication is not restricted to a single message conveyed by a legal authority to an offender; communication exists (or has the potential to exist) in other directions as well. The message of censure treats the offender as a person capable of moral decisions, and there is an expectation (even if in practice unfulfilled) that the offender will respond, by acknowledging the harm caused, accepting responsibility for the offense, and ultimately desisting from future offending.

The sentence also carries a judicial communication for the victim of the crime. The imposition of a sanction constitutes official recognition that this individual has been wronged and not simply suffered adventitious loss or harm. By permitting a victim to present a statement of impact in open court, the sentencing process introduces another possible communication: between the victim and the offender. The victim's statement thus can play a central role within communicative sentencing (e.g., Duff 2001, p. 177). The communicative function is in part designed to induce remorse in the offender. The offender may well be more likely to feel and subsequently express remorse during a sentencing hearing in which the victim, rather than a prosecutor, addresses the impact of the crime. Messages of blame carry more weight when conveyed by people whom we know. In addition, for many crimes of violence, a relationship between the victim and offender will have predated the commission of the crime.

Restorative justice has emerged as the principal alternative to retributive or utilitarian models of criminal justice. The primary goal of a restorative approach to crime is to achieve reconciliation and restoration: reconciliation of victim and offender, and restoration of the offender to the community. Such a goal may be unrealistic in many cases of serious criminal violence, yet it is a laudable aim nonetheless and cannot be achieved without acceptance of responsibility by the offender (accompanied by a genuine expression of remorse). First, however, the offender must understand the nature and extent of the harm inflicted upon an individual victim and the community to which both offender and victim belong. Duff and Marshall note the importance of confronting the offender with "an authentic account of the wrong [that he has committed]" (2004, p. 47). The authenticity is established by hearing the voice of the individual victim. In a similar fashion, Whiteley argues that the criminal justice system has "to a great extent insulated wrongdoers from the human impact of their crimes" (1998, p. 49). Allowing the victim to speak at sentencing may strip away this insulation to ensure that the offender is as fully aware as other community members of the consequences of his actions.

Many victims express a desire to communicate with the offender, to say things that they may not have had the chance to express until that point. Some victims hope to arouse a sense of remorse in the offender—which may generate a subsequent apology. The impact statement thus offers a vehicle for communication from the victim to the offender and from the judge to the victim and the offender. In fact, the impact statement is a communication directed at two audiences: the sentencing judge and the offender. To date, almost all the emphasis in the scholarly literature has been upon the former. Encouraging these forms of communication need not transform the sentencing hearing into a tripartite proceeding, nor should it undermine the central assumption of the adversarial system that a crime is committed against the state and not a private party.

The importance of the message to the offender should not be underestimated. Hearing from the victim involves a different communicative dynamic from learning about the impact of the crime through the sentencing submissions of the prosecutor. The adversarial system creates an antagonistic dynamic between the accused or offender and the prosecutor that may well undermine the effectiveness of the communication. Hearing from the victim may thus serve as a salutary reminder to the offender of the consequences of his actions.[9] This should not entail humiliating the offender or result in any public debasement. Nor is it a message of intimidation associated with a deterrent sentence. Rather, it is a message of sensitization; an appeal from one individual to another: the victim sensitizes the offender to the effects of his or her conduct on other people.

If the victim impact statement is meant to be a communication from the victim to the court and the offender, this may need to be brought

---

[9] There is considerable anecdotal support for this conclusion, often from offenders. For example, in one Canadian case the court observed that "the accused has said that although he knew he had caused [the victims] harm, he did not realize how much until he read the [impact] statements" (R. v. E. G. K. [2001] S.J. no. 390 [Sask. CA]).

more clearly to the attention of victims by the information provided by criminal justice professionals. At present, victim information materials exclusively address the victim's message for the court. In Michigan, for example, one impact statement form notes that "the report *may* be made available to the defense attorney and the defendant" (Washtenaw County Prosecutor's Office 2008, p. 4; emphasis added). Offenders in Ohio are not always permitted to read the victim's statement. Similarly some Canadian victim impact statement forms merely warn the victim that "The accused *may see it too*" (Northwest Territories 2008; emphasis added). This kind of language is inconsistent with contemporary disclosure requirements and diminishes the communicative function of the victim impact statement by representing it solely in terms of a source of information for the court. Judges in Canada and some other jurisdictions are obliged to inquire of the prosecution whether the victim has been apprised of the right to submit a victim impact statement. Perhaps courts should also inquire whether the offender has actually read the statement. If this inquiry is directed to the offender at the sentencing hearing—and particularly in the presence of the victim—it may create an opportunity for the offender to respond to the victim with an acceptance of responsibility and the possible expression of remorse.

B. Representative Victim Input Regimes at Sentencing

Statutory frameworks for the consideration of victim impact statements tend to be very general in nature, simply directing courts to "consider" any victim impact statement that has been submitted to the court. For example, section 722 of the Criminal Code of Canada states the following: "For the purposes of determining the sentence to be imposed on an offender or whether the offender should be discharged pursuant to section 730 in respect of any offense, the court shall consider any statement that may have been prepared in accordance with subsection (2) of a victim of the offense describing the harm done to, or loss suffered by, the victim arising from the commission of the offense." In England and Wales, section 5 of the Criminal Justice Act 1993 states that "in determining the sentence to be imposed on a person for an offense [of violence or sexual violence] a court shall take into account, and may, where necessary, receive evidence or submissions concerning any effect (whether long-term or otherwise) of the offense on the person in respect of whom the offense was committed."

A practice direction regarding the use of victim statements issued by the Lord Chancellor's Department in England and Wales is equally laconic and unhelpful to courts, simply noting that "The Victim Personal Statement and any evidence in support should be considered and taken into account by the court prior to passing sentence" and "The court must pass what it judges to be the appropriate sentence having regard to the circumstances of the offense . . . taking into account, so far as it considers it appropriate, the consequences to the victim" (Lord Chancellor's Department 2001). Finally, section 8 of the Sentencing Act 2002 in New Zealand states that "in sentencing or otherwise dealing with an offender the court— . . . (f) must take into account any information provided to the court concerning the effect of the offending on the victim."

Victim impact statement provisions never specify the purpose of allowing this evidence or the kind of the impact information to be placed before the court. Nor do they provide any practical guidance with respect to the way in which a court should take the contents of the statement into account. The vague nature of these provisions reflects, in all probability, the ambivalence and lack of conceptual clarity surrounding victim impact statements, a deficiency of victim input regimes noted by a number of scholars (e.g., Hinton 1996, p. 320). It is hard to avoid the conclusion that legislatures have created victim input regimes and then transferred to courts the responsibility of clarifying the role of the statement at a sentencing hearing. Ambiguous or nonspecific provisions of this kind, while by no means exceptional in legislative drafting, do little to promote a clear and consensual understanding of the purpose of impact statements. They are also likely to confuse victims and criminal justice professionals alike. If the provisions specified the reason for soliciting victim input, provided some precision with respect to the utility of this information to a sentencing court, and directed courts to ignore victim sentence recommendations, the consideration of impact evidence by courts would be more uniform. In addition, the problem of arousing unrealizable victim expectations would be far less likely to arise.[10]

The central dichotomy in the literature is whether the victim should be allowed to recommend a specific sentence. One Australian state and many U.S. jurisdictions allow or encourage victims to express their

---

[10] For a proposal for a more detailed statutory provision in South Africa, see Terblanche (2008).

views with respect to the sentence that should be imposed. Section 106B(5A) of the Sentencing Act 1995 in the Australian Northern Territory provides that victim impact statements "may contain a statement as to the victim's wishes in respect of the order that the court may make in relation to the offense." Similarly, in Michigan, MCL 780.763(3)(d) stipulates that victim impact statements may include "the Victim's recommendation for an appropriate sentence." A typical impact statement form used in that state asks victims to "please write your thoughts on sentencing the offender" (Washtenaw County Prosecutor's Office 2008; in fact, the form allows more space in response to this direction than the issue of "Victim's Physical Injury"). Similarly, in Kentucky, victims are asked, "What is your recommendation for an appropriate sentence of [*sic*] the offender?" (Office of the Attorney General [Kentucky] 2008).[11] Finally, in Minnesota, victims are directed to provide a statement of the sentencing outcome that they "would like," with "their reasons, including support for, or opposition to, treatment or community service programs" (Minnesota Office of Justice Programs 2004).

Despite their popularity across the United States, victim impact statement programs that permit sentence recommendations are opposed by most scholars (e.g., Guastello 2005, pp. 1336–37). Victim input regimes that encourage or permit sentencing recommendations are likely to exacerbate victim suffering and undermine principled sentencing. Victim services generally do not provide victims with information about sentencing trends. Most crime victims will be no more familiar with sentencing practices than other members of the public and will assume that courts have more discretion and greater powers to punish than is in fact the case. Few members of the public are aware that sentencing guidelines or judicial precedent constrains the sentencing decisions of courts. People tend to assume that unprincipled leniency—rather than conformity to guidelines or precedents—accounts for the sentences imposed in court (see Roberts and Hough [2005, chap. 4] for discussion).

In addition, when victims express a view on sentencing, they do so

---

[11] Some U.S. jurisdictions use impact statement forms that even solicit sentence recommendations from young children. One such form asks, "If you were the judge, what would you do to [the offender]?" The options include send to jail, pay some money, go to a doctor, nothing, stay away from kids, and "Put your own idea here!!" (Office of the Attorney General [Kentucky] 2008). It is unclear how a 10-year-old's sentence recommendations will help to inform the sentencing process.

from the one-dimensional perspective of the offense, based solely on their perception of the crime's seriousness, and will overlook the issue of the offender's level of culpability. Yet the other actors in a sentencing hearing—the judge, the prosecution, defense counsel, and the proba- tion officer—express an opinion on sentencing that incorporates con- sideration of the offender as an individual. In short, the sentencing process considers the actor as well as the act. Recommendations on sentence that fail to adopt this more rounded approach will be un- helpful to the court. For example, a victim may be opposed to an intensive probation order or an electronically monitored home con- finement sanction because these options seem inappropriate in light of the seriousness of the offense. The other participants in the sentencing hearing may be aware of offender characteristics—an absence of pre- vious convictions, the presence of a family, or a steady employment history, which may make a tough community sanction particularly ap- propriate, and custody particularly inappropriate, for this particular of- fender.

In light of their lack of knowledge about sentencing, victims are likely to recommend a sentence that is disproportionate to the per- ceived seriousness of the crime, or outside the tariff or guideline range for the offense, or inconsistent with the statutory objectives of sen- tencing. Any lift in the victim's sense of importance or influence over events is likely to be short-lived, and disappointment will ensue when the court imposes a significantly less punitive sanction. One of the most robust findings in the victim impact literature is that victims who ex- pect their statement to have a direct influence on sentencing react with disappointment and anger once it becomes clear that their sentencing "submission" will not be followed (e.g., Erez and Tontodonato 1992, p. 403; Hinton 1995, p. 86). This reaction underscores the importance of ensuring that victims who elect to submit a statement have a clear and realistic idea of the role of their statement at sentencing.

On the other hand, if the court accedes to the victim's recommen- dations on sentencing, the state, which initiated and has conducted the prosecution of the case to the point of sentencing, will lose control of the ultimate outcome; the interests of a nonparty (the crime victim) will trump those of one of the official parties to the proceedings, namely, the state. In short, a public prosecution will have become pri- vate. The consequences will inevitably be a loss of fairness for offenders as well as more unpredictable, unprincipled sentencing.

In some countries the content of the impact statement is limited by statute. For example, the Sentencing Act of Western Australia stipulates that the statement is "not to address the way in which or the extent to which the offender ought to be sentenced." Elsewhere, the content is regulated by the instructions provided to the victim, which neither encourage nor proscribe sentence recommendations. In contrast, victim input regimes in some jurisdictions such as South Australia provide detailed guidance to crime victims with respect to all aspects of the form, including the issues that should be addressed and the areas or subjects that the victim should avoid discussing in the statement (e.g., Government of South Australia 2007). Finally, victims in some jurisdictions are allowed considerable latitude regarding the content of their statement. One form used in Washington State tells victims "You can be as creative as you wish, so long as it is reasonably easy to present to the judge" (Grant County Prosecutor's Office 2008). The guidelines provided to victims are an example of poor implementation of the concept of victim input.

II. Effects on Victims

Early writings on the role of victim input at sentencing promoted the concept as a general panacea for the problems confronting victims passing through the criminal process. Writing a quarter century ago, Davis, Fisher, and Paykin asserted that "Victim impact statements are clearly an idea whose time has come. . . . These statements provide reassurance that [victims'] voice will be heard [and] ensure the judges are aware of the human cost of a crime" (1985, p. 19). Experience has suggested that incorporating the voice of the victim is not as straightforward as this quote suggests.

A. Participation Rates

Scholars may have underestimated the complexities of the relationship between crime victims, the nature of the adversarial system of justice, and the administrative difficulties associated with victim impact schemes. The most recent research has confirmed some of the limits on the application and utility of the victim impact statements. Indeed, if there is one finding on which critics and advocates can agree, it is that impact statements are likely to prove beneficial in only a minority of crimes against the person and an even smaller percentage of the total victim population. The reason for this is the low participation rate.

The explanations for the low participation rates are found in the reactions of crime victims, many of whom wish to minimize their engagement with the criminal justice system. Nonparticipation should not be interpreted as a failure of the impact statement scheme as much as evidence that impact statements are relevant to only a minority of crime victims. Moreover, although significant minorities fail to report crimes to the police out of a lack of confidence or apprehension about poor treatment, nonparticipation in victim input schemes usually reflects the victim's perception that the seriousness of the crime did not warrant this level of engagement with the criminal process. For example, Leverick, Chalmers, and Duff found that the most frequent reason for not submitting a statement was "simply that the crime was not perceived as serious" (2007, p. 84).

Direct comparisons between participation rates uncovered in different studies are inappropriate because victim impact statement regimes vary widely with respect to the offenses included, and rates will vary according to the profile of victims included in the victim impact statement program. However, several clear trends emerge. First, even for input schemes targeting victims of the more serious offenses, only a minority of victims participate. An early review of participation rates based on interviews with probation personnel in 1985 suggested participation rates in over half of all felony actions (McLeod 1987, table 1). However, most research reported since then has revealed significantly lower rates.

Rates of statement submission or participation have ranged from 15 percent in the most recent and systematic study to date (conducted in Scotland; see Leverick, Chalmers, and Duff 2007) to 42 percent of a sample of domestic violence victims (Tapley 2005, p. 51). Hoyle et al. (1998) reported a response rate of 30 percent in a more diverse sample of victims in England and Wales. A recent survey of over 10,000 victims in England and Wales found that only approximately one-third of victims recalled being given the opportunity to submit a statement, and of these only half availed themselves of the opportunity to complete one (Moore and Blakeborough 2008, p. 22). Other participation rates include 23 percent in Canada (Giliberti 1990, p. 12), 16 percent in Victoria (Mitchell 1996, table 2), and 14 percent in New Zealand (Church 1995, table B1). Hall (1991) found approximately one-quarter of a sample of victims across five states submitted an impact statement. These low participation rates are confirmed by the results of surveys and interviews involving practitioners: a sample of Canadian judges reported seeing victim impact statements in approximately one sentencing hearing in 10 (Roberts and Edgar 2006, p. 1; see also Texas Department of Criminal Justice 1997, p. v). It is also clear that, not surprisingly, victims of more serious crimes are more likely to submit a statement, a finding that emerges from all empirical studies to date (e.g., Ranish and Shichor 1985, p. 53).

B. Victims' Reasons for Submitting an Impact Statement

One of the most basic issues explored by researchers concerns the motivations of crime victims. Why do victims elect to submit an impact statement? What do they hope to achieve by completing the statement and in some cases delivering it orally at a sentencing hearing? A number of studies have asked victims questions such as these. Erez (2004) notes that the original purpose of an impact statement scheme was to permit the victim to express feelings about the crime and not necessarily to influence the sentencing outcome. Although it was overlooked in favor of an instrumental analysis, the expressive function of victim impact statements is now attracting more interest from scholars (e.g., Roberts and Erez 2004; Szmania and Gracyalny 2006). Research can shed important light on the purpose of a victim impact statement from the perspective of the crime victim. This research also helps to resolve the question of whether victim impact statements fall into the punitive or nonpunitive categories proposed by Roach (1999).

The results suggest that no single objective is uppermost in victims' minds. As with punishment in general (see Orth 2002), multiple goals for participating at sentencing exist. Victim impact statements serve different purposes for different people and, for some, several objectives. Differences in the specific questions posed to victims make it hard to make comparisons across studies. In addition, since victims' opinions on this issue are generally solicited after they have been given information about the program in their jurisdiction, their views may in part reflect the "official" objectives described in materials provided to them or what they have been told by victim services personnel. Nevertheless, victims' responses across studies do reveal some consistent trends.

First, there is more support for the expressive rather than the utilitarian function. Thus, Leverick, Chalmers, and Duff (2007, table 6.14) found that the most frequently cited reason for making a statement was expressive rather than instrumental. Indeed, this study of victims in Scotland provides strong support for the expressive function of victim input, as fully half the participants who had submitted a statement acknowledged that they did not know whether, or to what degree, the court had considered their statement, yet they were still intending to submit a statement in the future in the event of further victimization. The responses of victims who declined to submit a statement make the same point: only 6 percent said that this was because they believed it would not make a difference to the sentence (see Chalmers, Duff, and Leverick 2007; Leverick, Chalmers, and Duff 2007, p. 48). Miller notes that "all victims explained that they had been primarily motivated by belief in the expressive purpose of the VIS" (2008, p. 33).

A survey of victims in South Australia found that communicating with the offender was the most frequent reason offered by victims for completing a victim impact statement (Justice Strategy Unit 2000, table 11). Similarly, over half (60 percent) of the victims interviewed by Hoyle et al. (1998, p. 26) cited expressive reasons for submitting a statement. Erez, Roeger, and Morgan found that only 5 percent of their victims sought to influence the sentence imposed on the offender—suggesting expressive and communicative motives were more important (1997, p. 49). Results from the Canadian research suggest that victims were divided between wishing to communicate a message to the offender and wanting to perform a "civic duty" and to ensure that "justice was done" (Department of Justice Canada 1990, p. 14). Miller reports that all the participants in her qualitative study of sexual assault victims "explained that they had been primarily motivated in the expressive purpose of the VIS, namely the use of the victim VIS to communicate to offenders and to judges" (2008, p. 33). Similarly, the most frequently cited reasons for submitting a statement among victims in Canadian research were to help the court understand the effect of the crime and to make the offender understand the effect of the crime. One of these two reasons was cited by over 90 percent of the sample (Prairie Research Associates 2005c, table 28). Research with victims in Australia demonstrated that although victims wanted to affect the sentence imposed, they did compose an impact statement in order to enhance the severity of the sentence (Justice Strategy Unit 2000). Finally, further support for the expressive purpose of impact evidence comes from two contexts in which victims participate in the clear absence of any possibility of affecting outcomes. The first of these involves victim impact panels.

The concept underlying these sessions is simple: panels composed of victims and offenders meet to exchange views and describe experiences. Unlike the encounter that takes place in a sentencing court, no relationship exists between the two. The individualized and instrumental elements of victim input are absent, but participating crime victims still have the opportunity to express themselves. Since they are not participating in an adversarial proceeding involving their offender, there is a disinterested aspect to their participation in these panels. The findings from these panels lend further support to the debate about expressive versus instrumental motives. Although only some studies have focused on the victim participants, the results have been generally positive. Fulkerson (2001, p. 364) found that 80 percent of participating victims responded positively to the impact panel session, and 85 percent of the victims stated that they would recommend the use of such panels in the criminal justice system. These findings further underscore the strong desire on the part of many victims to express a view and to communicate with offenders even in the clear absence of any likelihood of influencing the nature or level of legal punishment imposed.

The second example comes from a nonadversarial justice context, namely, the proceedings of the Truth and Reconciliation Commission of South Africa. Despite the clear absence of any ability to influence punishment of the alleged perpetrators, the commission received 21,290 statements from victims, almost all of whom were found to have been victims of a gross violation of human rights (Truth and Reconciliation Commission of South Africa 2002, p. 1).

C. Levels of Victim Satisfaction

Advocates and critics of victim impact regimes hold very different views of the effect of impact statements on satisfaction levels of participating victims. Advocates claim that the experience of submitting an impact statement will increase the victim's level of satisfaction with the sentencing process. This claim is founded upon the literature on procedural justice. Research by Tyler (2006) and others has demonstrated that participants in judicial proceedings place a high value on being able to express themselves. People report feeling more fairly treated if they have the opportunity to express their views—even if they are aware that these views will have no impact on the nature of the decision taken (Tyler 2006, p. 127). This research—conducted in other domains of the criminal justice system—nevertheless captures the expressive function to which Erez and others have drawn attention.

Critics claim to the contrary that victims are unlikely to benefit from submitting a statement. They argue that since victims generally wish to control the outcome of the sentencing decision, disappointment is inevitable, and this will lower, not increase, satisfaction levels. Although a number of researchers have explored the effect of victim input upon victim satisfaction, the research is, as Walklate observes, "patchy and relatively unsystematic" (2002, p. 153). Few of these studies employ a strong research design. For example, a number of studies simply compare the expressed satisfaction levels of victims who did or did not submit a statement, without controlling for the influence of other case or participant characteristics. This limitation considered, the overall pattern of findings is more positive than negative.

Table 1 summarizes the findings relating to victim reactions from all available studies to date, including both quantitative and qualitative approaches. The principal finding is noted along with any important qualifications. One of the critics of impact schemes has concluded that "VIS are probably more popular with people who have never used them than with those who have" (Sanders 2004, p. 106). The studies summarized in table 1 suggest a different conclusion.

The research has used different methodologies, variable and at times small samples of crime victims; yet, with the exception of the early studies conducted 20 years ago (see table 1), victims who submit statements report being satisfied that they had done so. The most recent analysis of victim reactions confirms the positive response of victims to the experience of submitting a statement. Leverick, Chalmers, and Duff (2007, p. 45) found that almost two-thirds of the sample of Scottish victims who submitted a statement held the view that it was the right thing to do, and almost two-thirds responded affirmatively when asked whether making the statement had made them feel better. The early studies—which found little change in satisfaction—may be explained by the fact that the statement was written by someone other than the victim (Davis and Smith 1994*a*), and many victims failed to notice that they had actually submitted a statement (see below).

TABLE 1

Victim Reactions and Impact Statements: Summary of Research Outcomes (1988–2007)

Jurisdiction and Year of Research	Citation	No. Participants	Principal Dependent Variable	Principal Outcome	Qualifications of Study
1. Ohio (data from 1985–88)	Erez and Tontodonato (1992)	77	Rating of the justice system	No significant relationship between whether victim filed a statement and rating of system. "Victims who had completed a VIS and were disappointed as to its effects reported lower satisfaction [with the system] than those whose hopes were not unrealized" (p. 403)	"Half of those who believed they had not filled out a VIS in fact had done so" (p. 400)
2. New York (1988)	Davis and Smith (1994b)	104	Satisfaction with how the case was handled	"The results do not support the idea that victim impact statements are an effective means to promote victim satisfaction with the justice system" (p. 10)	"About half of the victims [who provided a statement] did not remember it" (p. 9)

TABLE 1 (*Continued*)

Jurisdiction and Year of Research	Citation	No. Participants	Principal Dependent Variable	Principal Outcome	Qualifications of Study
3. Canada (1989)	Giliberti (1990)	469	Level of satisfaction with criminal justice system	"Participants reported a high level of satisfaction with VIS programs" (p. 17); percentage satisfied ranged from 68% to 83% across different sites	
4. United States (1992)	Sobieski (1997)	307	Level of satisfaction with criminal justice system	"In cases where victims were given the opportunity to submit an impact statement 56% were satisfied . . . when victims were not afforded the opportunity victim satisfaction dropped to a low of 14%" (p. 1)	Data based on responses to a victims' rights publication
5. South Australia (1996)	Erez, Roeger, and Morgan (1997)	152	Satisfaction with criminal justice system	"The differences between the mean ratings [on satisfaction scale] were not statistically significant" (p. 51)	"Almost half [of] victims did not remember whether they had [submitted a statement]" (p. 55)
6. England and Wales (1997)	Hoyle et al. (1998)	148	Were victims happy that they had submitted a statement?	In exit interviews, 57% responded "right decision"; 20% "wrong decision"; 20% "don't know/neutral/other" (p. 32)	Slightly more positive response in entry to program interview
7. Canada (2000)	Meredith and Paquette (2001)	38	Attitude to victim impact statement program	Victims "generally very positive in their views of their experience with VIS" (p. 13); 79% would submit statement again	Uncertainty expressed about whether statement was actually used

8. Canada (2002)	Prairie Research Associates (2005c)	65	Whether victims were glad that they had submitted a statement	"Over four-fifths of victims who completed a statement said that they were pleased they had done so" (p. 55); only 6% dissatisfied	Less than half of the victims who submitted a statement thought that the court had considered the statement
9. England and Wales (2003)	Graham et al. (2004)	28	Satisfaction with impact statement scheme	"Respondents positive about participation in VIS scheme; no participant felt that VIS not a valuable outcome" (pp. 20, 30)	Considerable uncertainty among victims about the way the statement had been used; very little understanding and awareness of scheme
10. Scotland (2005)	Leverick, Chalmers, and Duff (2007)	88	Whether respondent believed making a statement was the right decision	"The vast majority . . . considered that making a statement was the right decision" (p. 42; table 6.16)	Over half of victims did not know whether their statement was considered
11. Canada (2006)	Miller (2008)	28	Whether victim would advise other victims to submit a statement	"Victims were "steadfast in their support for the VIS" (p. 51)	

D. Intention to Submit a Victim Impact Statement in the Future

Victim satisfaction is a vague concept that is susceptible to multiple interpretations, and victims' responses can be affected by many events occurring during the course of the prosecution of a case. A clearer measure of victim reaction to the concept, one with obvious "face validity," involves asking victims if they would submit another statement in the event of subsequent victimization. Several researchers have put this question to crime victims, and the outcome is very consistent: most victims state that they would submit a statement in the future.

Meredith and Paquette (2001) found that four-fifths of their Canadian victims said that they would submit again. In England and Wales, the Home Office study found that fully three-quarters of the participating victims said that they would submit another statement if they were victimized again (Hoyle et al. 1998, p. 33). The most recent study by Leverick, Chalmers, and Duff found that two-thirds of victims in Scotland who had submitted a statement reported that they "definitely would" submit a statement again in the event of further victimization— an undeniably positive outcome. A further 21 percent of victims said that they "probably" would submit again, while only 5 percent responded that they definitely would not (Leverick, Chalmers, and Duff 2007, table 6.24). More tellingly perhaps, victims who had not submitted a statement were significantly more likely to state that they would submit a statement in the future: over half (57 percent) stated that they would submit a statement if they were victimized again, compared to only one-third who predicted that they would not submit in the future (Leverick, Chalmers, and Duff 2007, table 6.28).[12] Taken together, over three-quarters of the victims in the Scottish study reported an intention to submit an impact statement in the event of further victimization. Finally, Miller reports the reactions of a small number of victims of sexual aggression; her qualitative study found that victims were "steadfast in their support for the victim impact statement" (2008, p. 51).[13] Victims clearly see sufficient merit in victim impact statement schemes to want to repeat the experience.

---

[12] It is also worth noting that a quarter of the victims who had not submitted a statement stated that they would have submitted one had they been allowed to change their minds about the decision to submit a statement (Leverick, Chalmers, and Duff 2007, table 6.26).

[13] These victims had all submitted a statement. In this sense the study further underscores the point that victims who actually submit a statement are generally supportive of the concept, although others who have made a decision not to participate may have a different attitude.

E. Placing Victim Satisfaction Findings in Context

Research findings on victim satisfaction also need to be evaluated with some recognition of the ways in which input schemes are administered. Whether impact statements promote, weaken, or have no effect on victim satisfaction will depend upon victims' expectations of the purpose served by these statements and the use to which they will be put. Indeed, regardless of their view on the utility of impact statements, scholars agree that raising unrealistic expectations may result in lower, not higher, levels of victim satisfaction. Empirical support for this interaction between expectation and satisfaction emerges from Erez and Tontodonato (1992, p. 403), who demonstrated that victims who submitted an impact statement expecting the statement to have a perceptible impact on the sentence imposed reported lower levels of satisfaction.

Victim impact statement regimes that do not solicit views on sentencing and do not affect sentencing are, from the perspective of the public, counterintuitive. Telling a victim that it is important to complete a statement, and that the statement is unlikely to change the sentence, conveys a confusing message, since there will be an initial reaction to ascribe an instrumental purpose to the statement. It is surely akin to telling graduate school applicants to submit reference letters while simultaneously telling them that these letters will not influence their chances of admission to graduate school. The less obvious, communicative purposes of submitting an impact statement are harder to explain. The consequence—borne out by research in a number of jurisdictions—is that most victims have unrealistic expectations of the role of an impact statement at sentencing and that the misunderstanding primarily involves an expectation that submitting a statement will result in a harsher sentence or a sentence closer to the victim's position on sentencing. This expectation of impact constitutes a major impediment to promoting the expressive and communicative purposes of introducing victim impact evidence.

Victims' expectations in this regard reflect more basic misunderstandings about the structure of the adversarial system of justice. To take but one example, a representative survey of the Canadian public found that four out of five respondents believed that the role of the prosecutor is to represent the crime victim (Roberts 2001, p. 10). In view of this, it is unlikely that most people have an accurate idea of the true role of an impact statement program and may well be understandably confused about the purpose and function of an impact statement. The criminal justice professionals who assist victims in completing these forms face an uphill battle in educating victims; this task is not helped by the conceptual confusion that surrounds the use of the victim impact statement at sentencing.

Finally, the data on victim satisfaction must be considered within the context of victim impact schemes, most of which appear to have been operationalized poorly. Evidence for this comes from victims themselves. For example, many victims across different studies report being confused about the purpose of the statement, not knowing whether they were obliged to complete the form, whether the form had actually been used by the prosecution or the court, and, in some studies, not even knowing whether they had in fact submitted an impact statement. Thus, in the research reported by Erez, Roeger, and Morgan (1994) and Davis and Smith (1994b, p. 9), almost half of the victims did not remember whether they had submitted a statement (see also Erez and Tontodonato 1992, p. 400; Davis and Smith 1994b, p. 9; Meredith and Paquette 2001, p. 8; Graham et al. 2004; Tapley 2005, p. 51).

It is therefore hardly surprising that no statistically significant differences emerged in satisfaction ratings between participants and nonparticipants. These findings demonstrate the inability of many victim input programs to engage the victim even to the extent that they recall having submitted a statement. As with the problem of extraneous material, however, it is possible to remedy. As a result of poor implementation of the concept of victim input, tests of the utility of impact statements are to a degree biased toward generating a negative outcome.

III. Effects of Impact Statements on Courts and Practitioners

Located within an adversarial model of justice, victim input schemes represent a paradox. If the statement changes the sentence that would otherwise have been imposed, the scheme undermines the rule of law: offenders should not receive different penalties depending upon the reactions of their victims. If impact statements change the outcome of the hearing, this would undermine the two-party structure of adversarial justice. What does the research say about the impact of victim input on sentencing patterns?

A. Impact on Sentencing Practices

Determining whether the introduction of victim impact regimes creates a drift toward more punitive sentencing or whether on an individual level the presence of a statement renders certain dispositions such as prison or compensation more likely is methodologically challenging. Nevertheless, enough tests of the hypothesis have been conducted to draw the conclusion that aggregate sentencing practices appear unaffected by the introduction of victim impact statement regimes. This is another of the few conclusions on which advocates and critics agree. Thus, Morgan and Sanders write that "Our principal conclusion, however, is that [victim statements] seldom influence sentencing decisions in any direction" (1999, p. 18).

A number of jurisdictions have introduced impact statements at different times over the past 2 decades, and they may serve as natural "time-series" experiments to evaluate the impact of this legal reform. For example, Erez and Roeger (1995, pp. 367–69) conducted a careful time-series analysis of sentencing patterns in South Australia and found no increase in custody rates or sentence lengths following the introduction of victim impact statements. The same pattern has emerged from Canadian research focusing on the introduction of impact statements at selected locations across the country. For example, Muir examined the impact on sentencing outcomes in the 1990s and summarizes the results in the following way: "It must be concluded from this [analysis] that the availability of victim impact statements did not have any important or noticeable impact on sentences handed down by the courts" (Muir 1990, p. 95). A similar pattern of findings emerged from other sites in this research program (e.g., Sloan Associates 1990).

The point can also be made by looking at aggregate, national sentencing patterns in Canada. Victim impact statements were introduced in 1988 when courts were simply permitted to consider them at sentencing. In 1996 the statutory provisions were amended to make consideration of impact statements mandatory, while in 1999 further amendments raised still further the profile of impact statements at sentencing (Roberts 2003). The reforms included codifying a statutory obligation on courts to inquire of the prosecution whether the victim had been apprised of his or her right to submit a statement, and victims were accorded the right to deliver their statements orally at the sentencing hearing. In addition, research conducted in that country has demonstrated an increase in the volume of cases in which an impact statement is submitted, as well as increasingly positive attitudes toward victim input on the part of the judiciary (Roberts and Edgar 2006). Despite these developments, no increase in sentence lengths or the proportion of custodial sentences has been observed over this period (Webster and Doob 2007, fig. 7).

Another methodological approach to determining the effect of victim input involves comparing sentencing outcomes in cases in which impact statements were present or absent. Drawing causal inferences here is problematic, as a large sample and a multivariate analysis controlling for all potentially relevant variables are necessary, and these research requirements are almost never fulfilled. For example, cases in which a statement was submitted are likely to be the more serious ones that would naturally result in a harsher sentence. Nevertheless, here too the evidence suggests that the presence of a statement has little impact on case outcome (e.g., Villemoare and Neto 1987, p. 5; Walsh 1992, p. 301; Davis and Smith 1994a, p. 41; Douglas, Laster, and Inglis 1994, p. 108; Erez and Roeger 1995, pp. 372–73). The Walsh "non-finding" of a relationship between victim input and sentence outcome is particularly interesting because the study concerned cases of sexual aggression where the seriousness and emotional nature of victim reaction might be expected to have an impact on sentencers. The one study that showed an effect of impact statements on the probability (but not length) of custody involves felony cases sentenced in Ohio between 1985 and 1988 (Erez and Tontodonato 1990). It is unclear why the effect emerged in this study, and it has not been replicated since.

A final source of information about the impact of victim impact statements is legal professionals.[14] Here too, the evidence is consistent: judges in a number of jurisdictions hold the view that impact statements have little influence upon sentencing outcomes (e.g., Erez and Roeger 1995, p. 374; Morgan and Sanders 1999; Schuster 2006, p. 6). Finally, Erez and Rogers (1999, p. 223) report consensus among legal professionals in South Australia that victim input at sentencing had not affected sentencing severity. Fears that the introduction of victim im-

---

[14] I do not review studies using students as simulated jurors to determine whether victim impact evidence affects sentencing decisions. These studies lack external validity, have produced conflicting results regarding the effect of victim impact evidence, and usually deal with capital cases that are not the subject of this review (see Fosterlee et al. [2004] for an example of this research tradition).

pact statements would result in harsher sentencing appear to have been groundless.

1. *Explaining the Lack of Effect on Sentencing Practices.* There are several explanations for the lack of effect of victim impact statements on sentencing patterns. First, as noted, these statements appear in a small percentage of all cases appearing for sentencing, insufficient to affect the overall severity of sentencing patterns. Second, research on the reaction of criminal justice professionals—at least in the earlier years—suggested that they resisted introducing the statements (Davis and Smith 1994*a*, p. 467). Third, as Elias (1993, p. 95) and others have suggested, the increasing adoption of mandatory and presumptive sentencing has restricted the influence of victim impact statements at sentencing. The resulting lack of discretion at sentencing explains why an early prototype of a victim input scheme in the late 1970s (the Victim Involvement Project) had little impact on case outcomes (see Davis, Kunreuther, and Connick 1984, p. 500).

However, the most likely reason why victim impact statements have little effect upon sentencing outcomes is that criminal justice professionals are able to protect the sentencing process from the influence of "extralegal" material. Prosecutors often exercise editorial control over the statements, and this usually means excising material designed to enhance the severity of the statement, including allegations of unprosecuted misconduct by the defendant or appeals for a specific (and punitive) sanction. Judges too, trained to ignore evidence with no probative value, appear unaffected by any appeals for severity from the crime victim. This conclusion is supported by surveys and interviews with prosecutors, defense counsel, and judges (e.g., Leverick, Chalmers, and Duff 2007). Other factors also militate against victim impact statements having the kind of effect on sentencing outcomes that can be detected by an aggregate analysis. Most sentencing hearings take place following a guilty plea rather than as a result of a trial resulting in a conviction. The plea is itself often the result of negotiations between counsel, and these discussions may well have resulted in agreement to place a joint submission before the court. The case is most likely to proceed expeditiously to a sentencing hearing, and the prosecution will not always or often have the time or the resources to contact the victim.

2. *Mitigating Sentence Severity as a Result of Victim Impact Statements.* Although victim impact statements have the potential to influence sen-

tencing in two directions, critics focus on the possibility that sentencing practices will be harsher if an impact statement is submitted. However, it is also possible that the statement may contain information that will result in the imposition of a more lenient sentence, either because the information reveals a crime that is atypical in some respect or, more controversially, because the victim expresses a desire that the offender be spared a particular penalty, usually imprisonment. Leverick, Chalmers, and Duff (2007, p. 77) found that some victims used their statement to indicate an absence of impact or to encourage the prosecution to discontinue prosecuting the case.

There is some evidence that victim input favorable to the offender can affect sentencing patterns. For example, in the Walsh (1992, p. 304) study, some sex offenders who received terms of probation would have been sent to prison had it not been for the probation recommendations emanating from victim input. Victim recommendations for imprisonment did not result in the incarceration of the offender. However, if they favored probation, this was a more likely outcome than it would have been in the absence of victim input.[15] In practice, then, an asymmetry appears to exist: judges do not enhance the severity of the sentence because the victim expresses a desire to see the offender receive a harsher penalty but sometimes impose a shorter period of custody or an alternative disposition to custody if incarcerating the offender would create undue hardship for the victim of the crime. Indeed, there is a principled justification for this asymmetry: the court is unwilling to allow retributive motives to exacerbate the victim's suffering (see discussion in Ashworth [2005]).

Acceding to the victim's wishes in even this limited respect represents a significant concession on the part of the adversarial model of justice. A more lenient sentence may result from a prosecution submission. Indeed, the charge may be withdrawn or stayed, but this decision falls within the exercise of prosecutorial discretion: the state has decided to exercise clemency or otherwise accord some leniency toward the offender. There is an argument, therefore, that the state should retain its power and excise from the statement any such appeal by the victim—unless the victim's view is consistent with that of the state.

---

[15] Case law in some jurisdictions also supports the proposition that, in exceptional circumstances, the views of the victim with respect to disposition may mitigate the punishment that otherwise would be imposed (e.g., R. v. Gabriel [1999], 26 C.R. [5th] 364, 137 C.C.C. [3d] 1, [Ont. Sup. Ct.]).

The appeal for leniency in this model should first pass the test of prosecutorial scrutiny. However, few prosecutors will overrule victims in this respect if there is a strong argument that the imposition of a "deserved" sentence will create significant additional hardship for the crime victim. In this context, then, victim interests would take precedence over proportionality considerations, an example, perhaps, of the loosening of retributive constraints upon contemporary sentencing. One reason for this is that the victim and the offender are in agreement, and research suggests that curbing the influence of retributivism in such cases is supported by the community, although this support is unlikely to extend to the most serious offenses.[16]

B. Content of Victim Impact Statements: Probative, Prejudicial, or Redundant?

A recurrent criticism of impact statements is that they contain irrelevant information or material prejudicial to the defendant or that has already emerged at trial (e.g., Abramovsky 1992, p. 33; Paciocco 1999, p. 372). Is there research evidence to support these criticisms? In light of the ambiguous or misleading directions provided to crime victims, it would not be surprising if prejudicial information made its way into the statements or the testimony at hearings in jurisdictions in which oral delivery is permitted. Considerable variability emerges with respect to the frequency of victim sentence recommendations in jurisdictions that prohibit such material. Independent of any benefits to victims accruing from the expression of their views in a public forum, do impact statements carry any probative information—or rather any legally relevant material that might not emerge at trial or from sentencing submissions from the prosecution? Further to this, do impact statements ever or often contain information prejudicial to the defendant?

There are two principal sources of data relevant to these questions: content analyses of victim impact statements and surveys or interviews with prosecutors and judges. The results suggest that the instructions provided to victims are important in determining the nature of the input provided by victims. This is a good example of a weakness of

[16] For example, when a public survey asked whether a victim's appeal for leniency should be considered in the case of culpable driving causing death, most respondents were opposed to considering this as grounds for the imposition of a more lenient response from the court (see Hough et al. 2008).

impact regimes, albeit one that can be corrected by a more thoughtful and comprehensive package of information for the victim prior to the completion of the form.

In Canada, almost half of the prosecutors and approximately one-third of defense counsel interviewed for research by the Department of Justice identified the presence of inappropriate material as a problem with the victim impact statements that they had encountered (Prairie Research Associates 2005*a*, table 16). For this reason prosecutors in that jurisdiction review the statement before it is submitted as evidence and occasionally edit out extraneous or inappropriate material such as appeals for severity. Unsurprisingly, this exercise of editorial control sometimes creates conflict with crime victims, who usually expect to be allowed to tell their story directly, not in an abridged format. Leverick, Chalmers, and Duff, in contrast, found that in Scotland, in only 3 percent of victim impact statements had the victim disregarded the instructions and expressed an opinion about the sentence that should be imposed (2007, p. 88).

A number of studies have examined the content of victim statements at sentencing with a view to determining whether they add anything to other sources of information, and the results suggest that they do. The large multisite study conducted in Canada in the 1990s found that victim impact statements contained useful sentencing-related material unavailable from other sources such as police records (Department of Justice Canada 1990, pp. 24–25). In England, Hoyle et al. found that in the majority of cases the victim impact statement added something to the victim's evidential statement (1998, p. 28).

Legal professionals also find victim impact statements to be a unique source of legally relevant information. For example, in Ontario approximately half the sample of judges responded that impact statements were useful for the purposes of sentencing in all or most of the cases in which they were submitted (Roberts and Edgar 2006, table 15). Respondents noted that statements were particularly useful for crimes of violence; property offenses where the extent of loss was unclear; or cases in which the harm to the victim was unusual, exceptional, or "not clearly manifest to an objective observer" (Roberts and Edgar 2006, p. 15). Judges also agreed that victim statements contained information unavailable from other sources (such as prosecutorial submissions; p. 15). This positive reaction on the part of the judiciary was shared by prosecutors: two-thirds of Crown counsel held the view that statements were useful to the courts "in most cases" (see also Cole 2003; D'Avignon 2001).

C. Reactions of Criminal Justice Professionals to Victim Input at Sentencing

Reviewing the literature on victim impact statements over the past 30 years suggests that, at the outset, practitioners were hostile, skeptical, or indifferent to the concept of victim input. However, over time, their attitudes appear to have become more positive.

The attitudes and behavior of criminal justice professionals with respect to the issue of victim input are important. First, if these individuals are antagonistic toward the concept of victim involvement, victim input provisions will prove less than effective. The history of criminal justice is replete with examples of reforms that have been impeded or undermined by skeptical or antagonistic professionals. Unlike some legislative initiatives, there would appear to be ample scope for professionals to vitiate the effectiveness of victim input regimes, if they so desired. After all, the statutory provisions regulating the use of impact statements allow considerable judicial discretion. A prosecution appeal on the grounds that the court had failed to consider a victim impact statement is highly unlikely to result in appellate intervention. Phrases such as "may have regard to any impact statement submitted on behalf of the victim" permit courts to ignore provisions that they deem inappropriate.

Professional resistance to victim input has emerged in several jurisdictions. Erez and Laster (1999) refer to techniques of neutralization—professional strategies that permit legal practitioners to distance themselves from the crime and its victims. These techniques also have the effect of emasculating reforms designed to promote the voice of the victim at various stages of the criminal process. Legal professionals may be resistant to reforms perceived to undermine the adversarial system of justice or that may appear to impede the efficient processing of cases.[17] In their research conducted in South Australia, Erez and Laster (1999) provide examples of this professional resistance to reform in this area. Earlier research in the field of victim impact would appear

[17] One of the objections to the use of victim impact statements is that they delay sentencing or prolong sentencing hearings on occasions when the victim decides to read the statement aloud in court. If the offender is not held in custody at the time of sentencing, courts will sometimes defer the hearing in order to allow the prosecution time to contact the crime victim.

to confirm a significant degree of professional opposition. Erez cites evidence from Australia and the United States that this was the case (1999, pp. 234–35; Erez and Rogers 1999). Where overt opposition was not observed, these earlier studies of professionals revealed indifference to the concept of victim impact (Henley, Davis, and Smith 1994, pp. 88–89).[18]

The second reason for exploring attitudes is that while justice professionals may have a vested interest in preserving the status quo and of protecting their discretion, groups such as appointed judges are less likely to be affected by the politics of the victims' rights movement. There are many explanations for the rise (or return) of the victim in criminal justice during the last decades of the twentieth century. However, penal politics has undoubtedly played an important role, particularly in Britain and the United States. For example, the statutory reform in California that created a right for victims to present an impact statement at sentencing arose as a result of a populist plebiscite in that state that resulted in Proposition 8, the so-called Victims' Bill of Rights. As Stevens notes, "a pragmatic politician would commit electoral suicide by opposing *any* victims' rights" (2000, p. 15). Representative polls of the public in the United States, Canada, and Britain have repeatedly revealed strong public support for allowing victim input into all stages of the criminal process. Polls in states as diverse as Colorado and Alabama found over four-fifths of the public endorsed the concept of victim input at sentencing and parole (see Roberts and Hough 2005, pp. 133–34). In Canada, the same percentage supported the introduction of victim impact statements at sentencing (Department of Justice Canada 1998).

The United Kingdom provides a more recent example of the confluence of victims' rights and penal populism. The Labour government in power in from 1997 to the present (2009) introduced and has heavily promoted a policy of "re-balancing the justice system" in favor of the victim. The government argued that the criminal justice system had become tilted in favor of the accused or offender and that creating additional victim rights was one way of redressing the balance. In a speech delivered in 2008, the Minister of Justice noted that "since 1997

[18] One example of judicial resistance to victim impact provisions can be found in Canada, where sec. 722.1(1) of the Criminal Code requires courts to inquire of the prosecution whether the victim has been notified of his or her right to submit a statement. In practice, such inquiries are almost never made.

we have continued to reform the system to get the balance right between the rights of the accused and the rights of the victim" (Straw 2008, p. 2). A number of scholars have plausibly argued that this pro-victims movement is more about politics than victims (e.g., Tonry 2004, pp. 25–28). Criminal justice professionals are better placed to make a judgment as to whether a particular victim right is appropriate or consistent with principles of fundamental justice and are more likely than politicians to be sensitive to any threat to the due process rights of defendants.

The most recent surveys of criminal justice professionals reveal a positive picture from the perspective of victim input. Leverick, Chalmers, and Duff conducted interviews with a range of legal professionals in Scotland and concluded that "there were very few objections to the victim impact statement scheme among criminal justice professionals" (2007, p. 90). Judges, in particular, report finding victim impact statements to be a useful way of learning about the seriousness of the crime. Morgan and Sanders note that the small number of sentencers they interviewed were "broadly in favour of a [victim impact statement] system" (1999, p. 22). Equally positive reactions are recorded by Miller (2008, p. 23) in her research upon justice personnel in Canada. Even defense counsel, who might be expected to hold negative views of victim impact statements, appear untroubled by the introduction of impact statements, as long as they have the right to cross-examine the victim on the contents of the statement (e.g., Prairie Research Associates 2005a, p. 18).

Positive reactions on the part of professionals to victim impact statements at sentencing were also noted in earlier Canadian research (Department of Justice Canada 1990, p. 27) and in research conducted in Minnesota (Schuster and Propen 2007, p. 7); South Australia, where the researcher found "widespread support for impact statements" (O'Connell 2009, p. 10); Manitoba, where 84 percent of respondents responded that impact statements were of assistance at sentencing (D'Avignon 2001, p. 24); and nationally across the United States, where juvenile court judges were significantly more likely to agree than disagree with the statement that "victims should have input into sanctioning and dispositional decisions of the court" (Bazemore and Leip 2000, table 1). These findings would suggest that another criticism of impact statements, that "few . . . judges or magistrates were willing to take any notice of a [victim statement]" (Sanders and Young 2007, p. 666), is refuted by the findings from empirical research.

IV. Victims and Parole

If we accept that victim input has a principled place in the sentencing process, it surely follows that victims should also be allowed to express themselves at parole hearings. Or does it? A generation ago, victim participation in criminal justice in most common-law jurisdictions ended with the imposition of sentence. Correctional authorities assumed the responsibility for offenders sentenced to custody, and victims were neither consulted nor even informed about conditional release decisions. It was perhaps inevitable that claims for victim input into the criminal process would carry beyond the imposition of sentence, and, as with sentencing, the United States was the first jurisdiction to allow victim input into the parole process. By 1987, victims were entitled or authorized to submit statements to parole authorities in 38 states (McLeod 1989). A recent correctional survey noted that input from victims is allowed in 94 percent of releasing authorities, making the victim the most frequent participant, with in-person input permissible in 87 percent of jurisdictions (Kinnevy and Caplan 2008, table 14).

A number of other jurisdictions, including England and Wales, Canada, and New Zealand, have recently enhanced the role of the victim with respect to the domain of corrections and, in particular, parole. Today, victim input provisions at parole are almost as common as at sentencing. Usually this means allowing victims to submit an impact statement and to attend and participate in parole hearings.[19] Although victim input into parole has become routine across many jurisdictions, as Tobolowsky observed a decade ago, "it has been the subject of limited judicial interpretation and empirical research" (1999, p. 92). Regrettably, little has changed since. Once again, it is important first to understand the reasons for allowing victim input at this point in the criminal justice system. When victim input moves from sentencing to

---

[19] In some jurisdictions victim input is not automatic but may be solicited. Parole committees exist across the island of Jamaica to advise the parole board about possible releases. Victims are consulted by these committees, which then include victims' views in their recommendations to the board (Ministry of Justice [Jamaica] 2006, pp. 9–10).

parole, the justification for the practice becomes more obscure and the threats to due process more apparent.

A. *Justifying the Dissemination of Information Relating to Prisoners*

First, it is important to make a distinction between providing information about case-related developments and allowing input into parole decision making. If victims have a legitimate interest in knowing the sentence that will be imposed, they should be informed about the administration of the sentence, including the date of the offender's release from prison on parole. Victims have a legitimate interest beyond that of other members of society. This is particularly true in jurisdictions such as New Zealand and Canada, where the existence of discretionary release on parole has a large influence upon the duration of time that the offender spends in custody. In Canada, for example, most prisoners become eligible for day parole after having served one-sixth of the sentence and full parole at the one-third point. Informing the victim that the sentence imposed was, say, 9 years' imprisonment tells them little about the critical question of how much time will be spent in custody. The offender could be released after 18 months (on day parole), or he may have to serve every day of 9 years before leaving prison at the expiry of the court's warrant.

Victims now receive very detailed information about the administration of a sentence of imprisonment. All correctional systems provide, upon application, information to the crime victim about developments relating to the offender. Usually the individual requesting the information has to register as an official victim to receive this information. In some countries, a considerable level of detail is provided to the victim. For example, victims in New Zealand can request a list of any correctional programs that the prisoner may have attended since admission to custody, the prisoner's security classification at any given time, as well as any convictions that he may have acquired since beginning the sentence (New Zealand Parole Board 2007, p. 6).

Similarly, in Western Australia, the Victims of Crime Rights and Services Act 2006 states that if a victim makes an application, correctional authorities are obliged to provide a range of information, including any institutional transfers, the offender's security level (and any changes in this level), any courses or programs undertaken by the prisoner, and whether he has received any approved leaves from prison. This almost unrestricted dissemination of information raises difficult questions about the privacy interests of the prisoners, which are compromised by the provision of information about their participation in institutional programs, parole applications, institutional transfers, or residential address upon release. An unresolved question in many jurisdictions is whether the privacy interests of a prisoner can legitimately be "trumped" by a demand for information on behalf of the crime victim.

B. From Information to Input and Influence

Providing information about significant developments during the sentence is one thing; allowing input into the releasing decision is quite another. From the inception of victim input, scholars have expressed reservations about the propriety of allowing victims to participate in parole hearings. For example, Ranish and Shichor concluded that "it seems clear that the victim's participation in the [parole] hearing is designed to put pressure on the board" (1985, p. 55; see also May 1989, p. 72).

There is a clear threat to the integrity of the parole decision if the victim's expression of opinion regarding release is placed before parole board members. Unlike the sentencing phase, there is no expressive function being served—the victim has already had the chance (and may well have taken the opportunity) to express a message to the court and the offender. Restorative justice advocates may advance an optimistic account of a parole hearing involving the victim. According to this view, the offender may benefit from understanding the longer-term impact of the crime upon his victim, while by visiting the correctional facility the victim may accept that the offender has paid a price for his offending. This mutual awareness may lead to the possibility of reconciliation. There does not seem to be much evidence to support this view, however, if only because victim input is usually provided in the absence of the prisoner. Restorative justice programs that take place in prison adopt a quite different approach to reconciling victims and offenders (Robert and Peters 2003). It has also been argued that the submission of an impact statement at parole may achieve therapeutic outcomes for both the victim and the offender (Verdun-Jones and Tijerino 2005, p. 17), although there is no research evidence to support this hypothesis.

Allowing victims to influence the decision to release the offender also creates a clear anomaly in jurisdictions in which input at sentencing is restricted to a statement about the impact of the crime. Having been silenced with respect to the question of whether the offender should be incarcerated, the victim is now allowed to express a view on the question of whether he should be released from custody. A victim's right denied at one stage of the criminal process is inexplicably accorded at a later stage. Moreover, if victims have a right to express an opinion on whether the prisoner is released, should they not be allowed input into the decision of whether he is recalled to prison in the event of an alleged breach of conditions? Exactly where does the state draw the line with respect to the administration of a sentence of imprisonment?

The right to provide input into the releasing decision may therefore be an example of Roach's category of punitive victim rights. At sentencing, the level of harm inflicted is an important determinant of the sentence ultimately imposed. An analysis of harm is necessary to determine the seriousness of the crime—one of the primary components of a proportional sanction. The victim is clearly an important source of information, whether this material is placed before the court directly or emerges through testimony at trial or through prosecutorial submissions at sentencing. A sentencing process that determined crime seriousness, say, by reference to preestablished categories of offense severity, would fail to capture proportionality with much accuracy. Important distinctions between, for example, cases of robbery that involved different levels of harm would be lost. Similarly, victim impact evidence may be a fruitful source of information about the offender's level of culpability for the offense; important culpability-related circumstances, such as racial motivation, are established by reference to the victim's testimony or impact statement, in both cases subject to cross-examination.

1. *From Retribution to Risk and Back Again.*   At parole, the decision-making context changes, however. When the offender applies for release on parole, sometimes years after the sentencing hearing, the decision, the factors determining the decision, and the objectives of the process are very different. Although parole serves a number of purposes including controlling the prison population, the guiding criteria in any individual parole application are clear. The decision to grant parole usually depends upon the response of parole authorities to two principal questions: does the prisoner represent a significant risk to the community, and will his release on conditions promote his rehabilita-

tion? For example, in England and Wales the criteria are found in the practice directions governed by section 239(6) of the Criminal Justice Act 2003: "The Parole Board shall consider primarily the risk to the public of a further offense being committed at a time when the prisoner would otherwise be in prison." Shute argues that the act "refocuses parole entirely on risk and risk assessment" (2007, p. 22; see also Hood and Shute 2000). Similarly, in Canada, section 102 of the Corrections and Conditional Release Act (1995) identifies two criteria used to determine whether parole is granted: the risk of reoffending and whether the release of the offender will facilitate his or her reintegration into society.

From sentencing to parole, the justice system therefore moves from consideration of retribution into one preoccupied with risk, and only latterly the rehabilitation of the offender. In New Zealand, "the most important consideration for the Board is community safety" (New Zealand Parole Board 2007, p. 10). It is hard to see how the crime victim's input will help the parole board answer the critical questions relating to risk and rehabilitation, despite the upbeat conclusion in the *U.S. Handbook for New Parole Board Members*, which concludes that victim statements "can offer very useful information for decision-making" (Burke 2003, p. 71).[20] In rare cases the prisoner may have sent threats to the victim, or the victim may have acquired information about the offender's potential risk to the community. Such information should be placed before a releasing authority—as long as the prisoner has the opportunity to respond. However, to allow victims the right to make representations regarding the release decision, to submit another or updated impact statement anonymously, or to deny the prisoner access to the information—as is the case in some U.S. jurisdictions—clearly violates principles of procedural fairness.

2. *Legitimate Victim Input into Parole Decision Making.*   There is no doubt that victims have an interest in developments occurring after the offender is admitted to custody. A survey of victims in the United States found that they assigned high importance to being informed of the date of the earliest release from custody (Kilpatrick, Beatty, and Howley 1998, p. 4). Similarly, in Canada there has been a dramatic

---

[20] The handbook later notes that "it is not unusual for parole board members to experience some frustration that victim input statement information is not always helpful or relevant to decision-making," a statement that seems more accurate (Burke 2003, p. 73).

increase in the number of victims registering for correctional information since victims were given the right to make submissions to the National Parole Board (Brzozowski 2007, p. 7).

Victims have a legitimate interest in the decisions taken by releasing authorities, and they may have security concerns to be considered by the parole board. Victims who register to receive information about critical decisions should be informed about the release of the offender on parole. In addition, parole authorities should consider the location where the prisoner will be serving his sentence in the community, in case that location is close to the victim's residence. Victims of serious violent crimes should not have to worry about bumping into their aggressor on a routine shopping trip. This is one limited way in which victims may reasonably provide input. It would surely be inappropriate for parole authorities to release the prisoner to live in close proximity to his or her victim. In this sense the victim provides input with respect to one specific element of the release plan, not a general opinion regarding the timing of parole or the nature of conditions imposed upon the parolee. The restrictions on the prisoner's freedom of movement should be subject to some proportionality analysis—in this case between the restrictiveness of the condition and the likely level of distress caused to the victim that the mobility restriction attempts to avoid. A second source of legitimate victim input would be any information pertaining to the offender's previous history with complying with release conditions—such as bail or probation conditions. But parole authorities need to consider carefully the reliability of this material, and the offender should have the right to respond, although in practice this is not always permitted.

C. Victim Input Regimes at Parole

As with sentencing, victim input arrangements vary considerably across different jurisdictions, with an important distinction being made between those that permit victims to take a position on whether the offender should be granted parole and those that restrict the victim's input to submissions about the conditions that might be imposed in the event parole is granted. Missouri is an example of the former, more expansive regimes in which victim input is dispositive. In this state, crime victims may attend parole hearings and provide input to the parole board. Victims may also specifically request that the board deny parole to the offender in their case (Attorney General of Missouri

2008, p. 20). In contrast, in England and Wales, as a result of the Victim's Charter in that jurisdiction, releasing authorities are required to consult the victim with respect to the conditions of release but not the decision to grant or deny parole. A similar arrangement exists in Canada. There is little consistency across Australian jurisdictions regarding victim input at parole hearings (see Black [2003] for a review).

This important dichotomy aside, one commonality between sentencing and parole is the nebulousness of the input provisions. The exact way in which victim input is incorporated remains as conceptually confused at parole as at sentencing, although there seems little doubt about the importance of this input. Writing of the work of the parole board in England and Wales, the chief executive recently wrote that "We hear the voice of the prisoners, of the members and *most importantly of the victim*" (Glenn 2007, p. 233; emphasis added) and further that "We always seek to place the victim at the heart of our decisions" (Glenn 2007, p. 235). But what exactly does this phrase mean? As with input schemes at sentencing, the directions to the victim preparing an impact statement are often vague and susceptible to variable interpretations. In many respects, victim input regimes at parole encourage a subjective interpretation of relevance: victims are directed to submit information that they believe is relevant.

Some parole boards provide direction about the appropriate contents of the impact statement. For example, victims in New Jersey are encouraged to include material about the continuing effect of the crime upon their lives, the extent of any loss of earnings or ability to work, but also, critically, to provide "any other information that would help the State Parole Board to determine *the likelihood of the inmate committing a new crime*" (State of New Jersey Parole Board 2008, p. 1; emphasis added). This direction at least focuses the victim's attention on providing information of relevance to the parole decision. Generally speaking, however, victims are encouraged to adopt an expansive approach to the contents of their statement. A typical example is the Ohio Department of Rehabilitation and Correction, which provides victims with "Tips on Testimony." One of these is "to share with the Board any information you would like them to consider when making their decision" (Ohio Department of Rehabilitation and Correction 2008, p. 2).

The Virginia Parole Board guidelines state that victims of crime or their relatives or other representatives are encouraged to provide the board with such information as "they consider necessary or helpful to the board to make a decision" (Virginia Parole Board 2006, p. 10). In Georgia, victims wishing to submit an impact statement to the Board of Pardons and Paroles are told "This [the statement] allows you the opportunity to voice your opinion about the possible parole of the inmate. . . . Please explain how this crime has affected you. Include *all information and concerns* you want taken into consideration by the Parole Board" (Georgia State Board of Pardons and Paroles 2008; emphasis added). Similarly, the National Parole Board in Canada encourages crime victims to "send any new or additional information that he/she thinks is relevant for the NPB to consider" (National Parole Board of Canada 2008). Such directions can and likely will be interpreted in a wide variety of ways by crime victims.

It is not surprising that there are important parallels between the victim input regimes at sentencing and parole. In both contexts victims are asked to describe the impact of the crime upon their lives and the lives of their families. However, there are also important differences. One important difference between victim input at sentencing and parole concerns the subject matter of the impact statement. None of the impact schemes at sentencing canvass the victim's opinion of the impact that any particular sentence will have upon their lives, yet victims are often asked to express a view on whether the prisoner should be granted parole and to answer the related question of how they will feel in the event that parole is granted. Thus, in the Australian state of Tasmania, the parole board is directed to take a number of matters into account when considering a prisoner's application for parole, including "any statement provided by a victim." The directions to victims note the following three issues: how the crime has affected and continues to affect them, "how they *would feel about the prisoner being released* from prison," and what conditions they would like to see included in the parole order (Tasmania Department of Justice 2008, p. 1; emphasis added).

A similar arrangement exists in New South Wales, where prisoners serving terms of more than 3 years fall under the jurisdiction of the parole board. The Crimes (Administration of Sentences) Act 1999 stipulates the factors that this board must consider when determining whether to grant or deny parole. These factors include some predictable items such as the prisoner's institutional conduct and the availability of community support for the offender in the event of release but also "the likely effect on the victim and the victim's family of the offender being released." Victims in the state are provided with the following directions regarding their impact statement: "The submission should state how you, as the victim, feel about the impending release of the offender," and, more surprisingly, "The submission should not include any additional evidence" (New South Wales Victims of Crime Bureau and Department of Corrective Services 2001, p. 5; for an input form with similar wording, see Victoria Department of Justice [2008]). If no additional evidence is forthcoming, all the victim is offering is pure opinion—feelings, not facts.

The same consideration may arise in England and Wales. Victims in England and Wales who submit a Victim Personal Statement (VPS) to the parole board are expressly prevented from offering an opinion on whether the offender should or should not be released.[21] The reason cited for this is that the parole board's decision to release "must be based solely upon the potential risk presented by the offender" and not, presumably, the opinions of the victim (National Probation Service 2007, p. 4). Yet the VPS may consist of an updated statement of the impact of the crime as well as a statement about "the likely impact of the offender's release on the victim, or those with close emotional ties to the victim's family" (National Probation Service 2007, p. 4). This kind of language can only confuse victims. Are they supposed to provide an opinion about the likelihood that the offender will target them again or to describe the impact that knowing he is under supervision in the community will have upon them?

The Ontario Parole Board directions to crime victims state that the decision to grant or deny parole is based on "an assessment of risk," specifically "whether the offender is likely to commit another offense if released on parole; and whether parole will contribute to the protection of society by facilitating reintegration as a law abiding citizen" (Ontario Parole and Earned Release Board 2008). So far so good; as noted earlier, these are the conventional parole criteria used in correctional systems around the world. But what specifically are victims asked to provide as input? The directions continue: "The Board is interested in knowing about the physical, financial and emotional impact of the

---

[21] This policy may soon change in the direction of the dispositive input regimes in the United States. As part of its policy of "rebalancing" the criminal justice system, the current Labour government has argued that there is a case for taking into account victims' views regarding the release of the prisoner.

offense on the victim, the ongoing impact, and any conditions the victim would like the Board to impose if the offender is granted release" (Ontario Parole and Earned Release Board 2008). Many victims undoubtedly continue to suffer the consequences of serious crime months and even years afterward, but how exactly does their suffering inform a decision to release the offender based upon principles of risk management and offender reintegration? These directions appear to be a veiled direction to board members to consider the seriousness of the offense—as manifested by recent impact statements—as a criterion to determine parole, although this is not part of the board's mandate. This is an example of punitive victim rights trumping sound correctional practices. Indeed, interviews with parole board members reported by Polowek indicated concern that the presence of the victim undermined the ability of the board to conduct an adequate risk assessment (2005, p. 129).

In New South Wales, victim input at parole goes far beyond describing the impact of the crime. It engages the victim, if he or she so desires, in correctional decisions taken throughout the prisoner's correctional career. For example, prisoners with the lowest security classification may be considered for unsupervised external release for educational, professional, or personal reasons. When a recommendation is made to release such a prisoner, the releasing authority is obliged to notify any victim who has registered on the victims' register. The victim may, in turn, serve notice of intention to make a submission (presumably) contesting the release proposal. The releasing authority is then obliged to consider the consequences to the victim and the victim's family of releasing the prisoner.

At parole, the role of the victim has therefore evolved from speaking about the impact of the crime to reflecting on the impact of a condition of the sentence imposed for the crime, a very different matter. The adjudicating authority has moved from considering the consequences of the crime to the impact of its own decisions on third parties. The determination of release conditions placed upon prisoners granted parole should reflect any statutory conditions as well as bespoke restrictions and requirements designed to minimize the risk of reoffending and promote rehabilitation and reintegration; they should not be constructed to offer solace to the crime victim. Even when the mandate of the releasing authority directs parole boards to consider risk and not retribution, research suggests both will enter the equation. Thus, in Canada, when members of the National Parole Board were asked how they consider victim input, "measuring the impact of the crime" was one of the ways cited (Prairie Research Associates 2005*b*, p. 12).

Finally, what about the impact of the crime—the issue on which the victim gives evidence at sentencing and now at parole? There are surely questions about whether even this material should be placed before the releasing authority. The impact of the crime on the victim prior to conviction has been reflected in the sentence imposed and need not be repeated. Parole boards, after all, will usually have a copy of any victim impact statement at sentencing. What about crime impacts occurring— or continuing—after sentencing? Many victims of serious violent crimes do continue to suffer physically and mentally long after the offender leaves the court to begin serving his sentence in prison (e.g., Shapland 1984).

This much is clear. What is unclear is why the protracted suffering of the crime victim should be a consideration for the releasing authority charged with evaluating the risk of reoffending and offender rehabilitation. Taking either the pre- or postsentencing suffering into account in determining whether the offender should be granted parole reflects a logic that either the court underestimated the seriousness of the crime (and imposed an inappropriately lenient sentence) or the court was not in a position to anticipate the longer-term consequences, an error that can now be rectified by the releasing authority. In the past, releasing authorities have been accused of using their authority to "second guess" the decisions of courts.

If this logic is correct, the role of the victim at parole would perhaps be better framed as "victim input" rather than victim impact. This approach suggests a two-stage structure of victim participation: victim impact evidence is submitted at sentencing and then victim input at parole, with the latter including the areas identified here, such as safety concerns and submissions regarding the offender's likely progress toward rehabilitation if granted parole.

D. Due Process Concerns Arising from Victim Input at Parole Hearings

Aside from the substantive questions of whether and to what degree a parole board should consider victim impact evidence, a number of important procedural issues arise. If victims are allowed to depose and parole boards are required to consider impact evidence, careful attention needs to be paid to ensure procedural fairness. At sentencing, due process concerns arising from the use of victim impact statements are addressed by disclosure requirements, by swearing the witness with respect to the evidence, and by allowing cross-examination of the victim's testimony. Defense counsel are often reluctant to cross-examine victims on the contents of their impact statements for fear of antagonizing the court (e.g., Morgan and Sanders 1999); however, the option of cross-examination remains for counsel to exercise. Indeed, a survey of victims in South Australia found that almost half the respondents had been cross-examined on the content of their statements (Justice Strategy Unit 2000, table 15). McLeod (1987) reported a generation ago that disclosure of an impact statement to the defendant was the norm in almost all U.S. jurisdictions (p. 168). These procedural safeguards are absent at the stage of parole.

Parole hearings are generally held in custodial settings, and victim input is not subject to the procedural safeguards of a criminal proceeding. Some jurisdictions take extraordinary steps to protect the victim's evidence from any kind of adversarial scrutiny. Crime victims in New Jersey, for example, may present testimony to the state parole board during a confidential hearing, or they may submit written comments regarding the possible release of the prisoner. Neither the testimony nor the comments are shared with the parole applicant. In Virginia, one of the questions posed and answered for crime victims in the information package is "Will the offender know that I sent in my views?" The official response ("absolutely not") makes the point clearly (Virginia Department of Corrections 2008). Similarly, in New Jersey "the inmate is not informed as to whether any victim chose to provide spoken or written testimony" (State of New Jersey Parole Board 2008). A prisoner will not know whether a victim has submitted a statement, the contents of any statement, or have any inkling of the weight that the board members may have ascribed to such a statement.

Across the United States, disclosure to the inmate of any victim impact statement has historically been the exception rather than the norm (McLeod 1989, p. 43; Bernat, Parsonage, and Helfgott 1994, table 2). Even in England and Wales, where reports and submissions to the parole board are all potentially disclosable to the prisoner, victims may request that certain information remain confidential. The probation service circular that deals with victim statements at parole notes that "information from victims is frequently withheld from the prisoner" (National Probation Service 2007, p. 15). If the information is deemed nondisclosable, the prisoner will be informed of the existence of such information but will be left guessing as to its specific contents; he or she will not be aware of what it is or who has submitted it (National Probation Service 2007, p. 15). In Florida, victims may attend a release hearing. Any representations on behalf of the prisoner will be made first at the hearing, followed by the victim's statement. Since the commission does not allow rebuttal of any testimony, not only will victims have the last word but there is no opportunity for the offender's representative to respond to the victim's submissions. The offender is denied attendance at the hearing (Florida Parole Commission 2008).

In contrast, Utah is an example of a state that takes disclosure requirements more seriously. As a result of a number of Utah Supreme Court decisions, the parole board in that state is required to provide the offender with copies of all documents reviewed by the board when considering parole, except where confidentiality is "absolutely required," and this includes the victim impact statement. In addition, if confidentiality is deemed necessary, the board provides a summary of the original document (State of Utah Board of Pardons and Parole 2008). The threat to the liberty interests of restricting access to the victim's submissions is demonstrated by research. Smith, Watkins, and Morgan (1997) found that the prisoner's chances of being granted parole diminished significantly if the victim attended the hearing in his absence (p. 69).

Victims' rights advocates might respond that parole is not an absolute right but a privilege for which prisoners must apply. But whether it is a right or a privilege, there is little doubt that the liberty interests of the offender are affected, and therefore the decision to grant or deny parole should be taken with careful regard to procedural fairness. The need for confidentiality should be evaluated, but absent evidence of a threat to the victim's security, the statement should be disclosed to the offender.

Victims are often allowed to bring supporters to the parole hearing. In Arkansas, crime victims are allowed to bring "as many people as they would like" to the parole hearing and, with prior approval of the board, are also allowed to bring members of the press or news media (Arkansas Board of Parole 2008). Crime victims in New Zealand may bring a lawyer and up to three support people (New Zealand Parole Board 2007, p. 8). How can the presence of a band of victims' supporters or news reporters promote rational decision making by parole board members? The presence of the news media simply creates pressure upon the members of the parole board and impairs the prisoner's chances of obtaining parole. And as is the case in other states, the victim and his or her group of followers are placing arguments before the board in the absence of the prisoner, who remains not just unable to respond but unable even to know the nature of the submissions by victims.

Such arrangements may strengthen the voice of the victim, but they also undermine the integrity of the parole process. Research by Smith, Watkins, and Morgan (1997, p. 71) found that the number of victims participating was inversely related to the probability of the prisoner being granted parole. Similarly, a survey of releasing authorities across the United States found that the number of victims was a more important factor affecting release decisions than the offender's institutional behavior (Kinnevy and Caplan 2008, table 18). In fact, input from the victim was cited more often as a consideration than input from law enforcement officials (94 percent of respondents compared to 81 percent; see Kinnevy and Caplan 2008, table 14).

E. Social Distance and Punitiveness

There are reasons, aside from those related to procedural fairness, why victims' views on whether parole is granted should be heard—if they are to be heard at all—in the presence of the individual whose liberty is at stake, or at least after victims have received information about the grounds advanced by the prisoner for requesting parole. First, there is a natural human tendency for people to be more punitive as the distance between the subject and the object increases and to change their minds about punishment when given more information about an offender. Research has demonstrated that people are more punitive when asked to sentence general categories of offenders or when they are provided with few details about the offender (e.g., Roberts 2002; for a review, see Roberts and Hough [2005]). As social distance between the respondent and the individual increases, it becomes easier to respond punitively. With respect to victim sentence recommendations, victims who make sentence recommendations for the offender in their case are more punitive when the offender is absent (e.g., McDonald 1982).[22]

---

[22] In this early study in which victims made sentence recommendations to the prose-

Second, victims enter the parole equation with an image of the offender that is frozen in time, when the crime occurred. For victims of the most serious crimes, several years will have passed since they last had any contact with the offender. For example, survivors of homicide victims in Canada are allowed to submit impact statements at hearings relating to parole eligibility dates for the offender convicted in their case. These hearings take place more than 15 years after the original sentencing took place. As a result of the passage of time—and his experiences in custody—the prisoner may have undergone a significant change in terms of his risk of reoffending, his moral development, or his intention to desist from offending.

Third, few victims will have any familiarity with the correctional process, issues such as risk-needs assessment, or the benefits of conditional release on parole. At the very least, victims should have an opportunity to weigh these matters before deposing their impact evidence and any recommendation regarding the decision to grant or deny parole. Releasing authorities should provide victims who intend to make a submission with clear and comprehensive information about the purpose and nature of parole. Victims in New Zealand considering submitting an impact statement to the parole board are allowed to request information about the prisoner's record while in prison, but this is a selective way of disseminating information.

F. Effect of Victim Input on Parole Outcomes

Paradoxically, although it appears harder to justify victim input at the stage of parole, the limited research on impact statements at parole suggests that, unlike sentencing, victim input at parole does influence the outcome of hearings. It is surprising, in light of the prevalence of victim participation in conditional release decisions around the world, that few empirical studies have tested the effect of victim input on parole outcomes. One such study was reported by Parsonage, Bernat, and Helfgott, who found a significant association between the presence of victim statements and a negative parole decision in hearings in Pennsylvania (1992, p. 194). These researchers compared parole outcomes in cases in which victim input was present or absent. Parole was refused in 43 percent of the victim testimony group even though the

cutor, approximately half requested the maximum possible legal sentence. Victims recommending sentence in the presence of the defendant were significantly less punitive (McDonald 1982, pp. 400–401).

state parole guidelines recommendation was refusal in only 7 percent of these cases. Smith, Watkins, and Morgan (1997) found the same pattern of results in parole hearings in Alabama: victim participation was a highly significant predictor of parole outcome.

The most recent test of the effect of victim input was reported by Morgan and Smith (2005), who conducted a careful analysis of parole files in Alabama. These researchers examined the independent and interactive effects of variables related to the parole decision and found that victim participation was a highly significant predictor of parole decision making: when the victim submitted impact evidence, the prisoner was less likely to be granted parole. This finding existed independently of the influence of other factors related to the parole decision. This relationship alone raises questions about the fairness of the parole decision-making process. But an important nonfinding of the study suggests that parole boards may have lost sight of one of their primary objectives. Morgan and Smith found that neither the prisoner's institutional conduct nor the number and nature of rehabilitation-related programs taken predicted the ultimate parole decision. Were parole boards losing sight of the issue of rehabilitation?

Polowek conducted interviews with parole board members and found that almost all participants in the research believed that victim input had an impact on decisions taken (2005, p. 189). A recent survey of releasing authorities found that 40 percent of participants acknowledged that victim input was "very influential" in their decisions to grant or deny release on parole (Kinnevy and Caplan 2008, p. 18). Finally, prisoners appear to believe that the presence of the victim influences outcomes. Polowek found that almost a third of parole board interviewees believed that prisoners postponed or waived a hearing because of the likely presence of the victim (2005, p. 127).

G. Explaining the Impact of Victims at Parole

It would not be surprising if victim input has a greater effect at parole than at sentencing. First, in many jurisdictions, parole boards have more discretionary power than sentencing courts. In England and Wales, courts follow sentencing guidelines issued by the Sentencing Guidelines Council—no such guidelines regulate the parole board. Second, crime victims have multiple motives for submitting an impact statement at sentencing, namely, to communicate to the offender, to receive official recognition of their suffering, to obtain compensation, and to influence the sentence imposed. Few of these motivations remain at this late stage of the criminal process.

The principal reason for victims to make a submission to a parole board or to attend a hearing must be to oppose the application for parole. Some parole boards appear to acknowledge as much in their instructions to victims. Thus, victims in South Carolina are told, "If you plan to attend a parole hearing to oppose parole" (South Carolina Department of Probation, Parole and Pardon Services 2008, p. 1). The only study to interview victims attending parole hearings used a small sample but found that they wished to oppose release (Gaudreault 2003, p. 5). If only a minority of crime victims submit an impact statement at sentencing, a much smaller number will subsequently express a desire to have input into the parole decision. Those victims who do wish to participate are likely to be those who suffered the most significant degree of harm and who are most likely to oppose any perceived leniency, such as temporary absences or release on parole. They are also likely to prove the most influential victims, as research has suggested.

The third reason why victim input may have a greater influence at parole rather than sentencing concerns the nature of the decision maker. In most common-law jurisdictions, sentencing is determined by professional judges, usually with years of practice as legal practitioners. The judiciary is trained to disregard material that has prejudicial rather than probative value—such as an emotional impact statement or an eloquent and moving plea for a harsher sentence. Parole board members are seldom legally trained and are often political appointees. They may be less able (or less willing) to set aside emotional appeals from the victim that have no probative value in terms of offender risk or rehabilitation.

Awareness of community views may also play a role. I have already noted the strong public support for victims' rights generally and, in particular, victim impact statements at sentencing. This is likely to place further pressure on parole boards to accede to the wishes of the crime victim. In his analysis of parole board decisions in Nebraska, Proctor (1999) found that parole decisions reflected the presence of individuals or letters opposing parole as well as institutional recommendations to release or deny parole. Public representations were better predictors of release than program participation, offense severity, or prior incarcerations (1999, table 3).

Finally, in addition to being potentially more susceptible to victim input, some board members may believe their role on the board is to ensure that the victim's voice is heard. Indeed, members of parole boards are sometimes appointed for this very purpose. Thus, in New South Wales, one member of the parole board must be a person who has "an appreciation of the interests of victims of crime" (Booth and Carrington 2007, p. 401). In England and Wales, the appointment process to the parole board now includes "a specific competence to ensure that all prospective members demonstrate a strong understanding of victim issues" (Parole Board for England and Wales 2007, p. 26). Individuals with a professional background of this nature are likely to be particularly responsive to victim input. The presence of a victim's rights representative creates a clear conflict of interest (see Ellis [2007] for discussion in the New Zealand context).

To conclude, Herman and Wasserman assert that victims' "parole-related rights are highly relevant to the re-entry process" (2001, p. 434) and further that "victims' voices and participation should be welcomed" (p. 442). Many prisoners may well disagree with this upbeat conclusion.

V. Conclusions

Victim input at sentencing and at parole raise different issues. The purposes of the two decisions are different, as are the arguments that can be offered in support of a role for victims. It is difficult to devise principled arguments for why a victim's views should be invited about the sentence to be imposed or whether a prisoner should be released on parole. The evidence suggests that victim input has greater influence in parole hearings than in sentencing, even though the procedural safeguards are typically much less extensive.

A. Sentencing

It is hard to conceive of a contemporary justice system that would exclude victims from some degree of participation in the sentencing process. Nor is it possible to imagine how the adversarial model would survive if victims are given a determinative role regarding the nature of the sentence imposed. Between these two extremes, however, it is possible to find a place for the crime victim.

Ultimately, the research literature and commentary on victim statements boils down to a single question: Is the sentencing process better off for allowing victim impact evidence? I would respond affirmatively, while acknowledging the variable degree of success of current input regimes as well as the significant potential for victim impact schemes to backfire and exacerbate victim frustration with criminal justice. The populist rush to exploit public and victim dissatisfaction with the criminal justice system has led to a proliferation of ill-conceived and poorly administered victim impact regimes. These regimes are often confusing and misleading for both victims and criminal justice practitioners. Empirical research on the effects of these regimes has, predictably, generated mixed findings or positive effects of a modest magnitude. This in turn has fueled skepticism about victim input and obscured sight of the possibility that a carefully constructed victim input initiative may be of benefit to the sentencing process without doing harm to fundamental sentencing principles or the legitimate interests of defendants. The most recent research reveals a positive picture with respect to a number of important issues, including victim satisfaction, which is why this essay concludes that victim impact statements can work and do work for a minority of victims passing through a well-administered regime. In order to contribute to a principled sentencing regime, however, victim input schemes need to stress the expressive and communicative functions of impact statements.

As Walklate rightly observes, "there has been very little research that has reliably evaluated schemes that have been implemented in different ways" (2007, p. 118). Victim impact regimes at sentencing reveal clear evidence of policy transfer from jurisdiction to jurisdiction. Input schemes around the common-law world reveal some consistency with respect to victim services and victim rights. However, the field would clearly benefit from a "best-practices" analysis that would identify the elements of a successful scheme to incorporate victim input into the sentencing process. For example, none of the victim input materials reviewed for this essay provided any explanation or justification for excluding victim sentencing recommendations. Since most victims would intuitively expect to make a recommendation, one of the primary objectives of impact evidence information should be to explain why, in an adversarial model of justice, this is inappropriate.

What would an ideal victim impact statement scheme look like? First, victims need to have a better understanding of why they are being given the opportunity to depose impact evidence. The materials provided to victims, and the information supplied by victim support personnel and other criminal justice professionals, need to be systematic and comprehensive—far more so than appears to be the case in almost all jurisdictions at the present. Second, in a system with resource limitations, victim impact schemes should focus on victims of serious personal injury offenses, where the consequences of the crime and the danger of subsequent disenchantment with sentencing are greatest. Third, most jurisdictions provide victims with a form on which to document the impact of the crime accompanied by information on how to complete the form. Yet, many of these forms raise more questions than they resolve. The form should clearly delineate the kind of information that should be included and that should be omitted. Indeed, in light of the prevalence of forms to capture the victim's impact evidence, far more attention should be paid to their construction. Few studies have explored the issue, but there is scope for improving the forms provided to crime victims as well as the information that accompanies them and the procedures regulating the introduction of this information (see Alexander and Lord 1994; Roberts and Edgar 2003, pp. 30–32; Australian Law Reform Commission 2006, pp. 400–401).

Fourth, if communication is central to the enterprise of victim participation, it is important to expose the offender to the impact statement. The purpose is not to denigrate or demean the offender but rather to awaken a conscience that on recent evidence at least was insufficiently alert to the consequences of offending. Fifth, sentencers need training on the appropriate use of victim impact evidence, to ensure that this information is used in a systematic fashion. Although judicial education programs exist in all jurisdictions, few ever include training on victim-related issues. Research has clearly shown that judicial acknowledgment of the victim's suffering can be most beneficial. As Graham et al. have noted, there is a "clear need for further training of front line staff administering the [victim impact statement] scheme" (2004, p. iv).

B. Parole

In contrast to sentencing, the arguments for allowing victim input at parole hearings and generally in the correctional process are less compelling. There seems no principled justification for allowing victims to intrude into the releasing decision—unless they have specific security concerns or hold information about the offender's risk of reoffending. This information should then be subject to some external or objective scrutiny. Allowing victims to express an opinion about the decision to grant or deny parole or to describe the adverse effect that the release of the prisoner would have upon their lives violates sound correctional principles and undermines the prisoner's right to a fair hearing.[23] If parole boards are to consider the ongoing suffering of the victim or the victim's likely reaction to the prisoner's release, their mandates should reflect this consideration.

In short, allowing the victim input into the parole process, and not simply information about any security concerns, smacks more of penal populism than a rational attempt to enhance the treatment of crime victims. Victims should be encouraged to submit any information relevant to the criteria for release and should be clearly apprised of the different mandates of a sentencing court and parole hearing. If this does not occur, the disappointment felt by some victims at sentencing will occur at parole, as victims expect the board to deny parole. A good example of how to proceed can be found in South Australia, where Correctional Services Victim Assistance personnel spend much time explaining to victims that the parole board is concerned with risk and rehabilitation and is not able to "re-sentence" the offender to reflect the victim's suffering (personal communication with Michael O'Connell, e-mail December 10, 2008).

C. Research Priorities

With respect to victim impact at sentencing, the research priorities include the following:

- How should a victim impact statement form be constructed to maximize the benefit to the sentencing process and to minimize the likelihood of prejudicial or extraneous material?
- How are offenders affected by hearing about the impact of the crime from the victim in open court?
- To what extent does providing information to the crime victim about the purpose of victim input attenuate any subsequent dissatisfaction with the sentence ultimately imposed?

[23] O'Hara has recently proposed giving victims control over the last 10 percent of the custodial sentence, arguing that this will "serve the interests of victims, convicts and society" (2006, p. 134). It is hard to see how; victims who wish to oppose release are unlikely to be satisfied with their "tithe," while prisoners are unlikely to see the benefit of remaining in prison for an additional period simply because the victim opposes their release. The proposal also fails to resolve the conflict between victim wishes and correctional principles. Moriarty (2005) acknowledges the potential for unfairness in allowing victims to participate in parole hearings but argues that "having all victims testify at parole hearings will have a positive effect on victims, offenders, and society" (p. 390).

Although the picture is becoming clearer with respect to the benefits and drawbacks of victim input at sentencing, we still know very little about the benefits to victims of submitting impact evidence or the effects on prisoners or parole boards. The research questions include the following (see Black [2003] for further research proposals):

- Are victims motivated by instrumental or expressive concerns when they make submissions to parole boards?
- How much or how often do victims benefit from deposing impact evidence at parole hearings?
- How often do victim impact statements or oral evidence at parole contain information germane to the criteria for granting release on parole?
- Are parole boards influenced by emotional arguments against releasing the prisoner?
- How do prisoners react to the concept of victim input into the decision to release from custody?
- Do parole applicants ever benefit from hearing from the crime victim?
- Is there a restorative potential to the process of allowing victims to participate in parole hearings?

D. Coda

Victims clearly have a role to play at sentencing, but their input should be carefully defined and circumscribed. The Rome statute of the International Criminal Court provides a useful framework for regulating victim input into the determination of sentence and release on parole. Article 68(3) affords crime victims the right to have "their views and concerns to be presented and considered at stages of the proceedings determined to be appropriate by the Court." However, the provision continues with the following critical words: "in a manner which is not prejudicial to or inconsistent with the rights of the accused." In most jurisdictions, victim input into sentencing is consistent with this standard; the same cannot be said for victim participation at parole.

REFERENCES

Abramovsky, Abraham. 1992. "Victim Impact Statements: Adversely Impacting upon Judicial Fairness." *St. John's Journal of Legal Commentary* 8:21–33.

Alexander, Ellen, and Janice Lord. 1994. *Impact Statements*. Arlington, VA: National Victim Center.

Arkansas Board of Parole. 2008. *What Crime Victims Need to Know about the Parole Process*. Little Rock: Arkansas Board of Parole.

Ashworth, Andrew. 1993. "Victim Impact Statements and Sentencing." *Criminal Law Review* (July):498–509.

———. 2005. *Sentencing and Criminal Justice*. 4th ed. Cambridge: Cambridge University Press.

Attorney General of Missouri. 2008. *Crime Victims' Rights*. Jefferson City: Attorney General of Missouri.

Australian Law Reform Commission. 2006. *Same Crime, Same Time: Sentencing of Federal Offenders*. Report 103. Sydney: Australian Law Reform Commission.

Bazemore, Gordon, and Leslie Leip. 2000. "Victim Participation in the New Juvenile Court: Tracking Judicial Attitudes towards Restorative Justice Reforms." *Justice System Journal* 21:199–226.

Bernat, Francis, William Parsonage, and Jacqueline Helfgott. 1994. "Victim Impact Laws and the Parole Process in the United States: Balancing Victim and Inmate Rights and Interests." *International Review of Victimology* 3:121–40.

Black, Matt. 2003. "Victim Submissions to Parole Boards: The Agenda for Research." *Trends and Issues in Criminal Justice*, no. 251. Canberra: Australian Institute of Criminology.

Black, Robert. 1994. "Forgotten Penological Purposes: A Critique of Victim Participation in Sentencing." *American Journal of Jurisprudence* 39:225–40.

Booth, Tracey, and Kerry Carrington. 2007. "A Comparative Analysis of the Victim Policies across the Anglo-Speaking World." In *Handbook of Victims and Victimology*, edited by Sandra Walklate. Cullompton, UK: Willan.

Brzozowski, Jodi-Anne. 2007. "Victim Services in Canada, 2005/2006." *Juristat* 27:1–13.

Burke, Peggy, ed. 2003. *A Handbook for New Parole Board Members*. Association of Paroling Authorities. Available at http://www.apaintl.org/en/aw_publications.html.

Cassell, Paul. 2009. "Treating Crime Victims Fairly: Integrating Victims into the Federal Rules of Criminal Procedure." *Utah Law Review* (forthcoming).

Chalmers, James, Peter Duff, and Fiona Leverick. 2007. "Victim Impact Statements: Can Work, Do Work (or Those Who Bother to Make Them)." *Criminal Law Review* (May):360–79.

Church, Alison. 1995. *Victims' Court Assistance: An Evaluation of the Pilot Scheme*. Wellington: New Zealand Department of Justice.

Cole, Michael. 2003. *Losing One's Voice: The Victim Impact Statement at Sentencing*. Ottawa: Department of Criminology, University of Ottawa.

D'Avignon, Julie. 2001. *Victim Impact Statements: A Judicial Perspective*. Winnipeg: University of Manitoba.

Davis, Robert, Pamela Fisher, and Alice Paykin. 1985. "Victim Impact Statements: The Experiences of State Probation Officers." *Journal of Probation and Parole* 16:18–20.

Davis, Robert, Frances Kunreuther, and Elizabeth Connick. 1984. "Expanding the Victim's Role in the Criminal Court Dispositional Process: The Results of an Experiment." *Journal of Criminal Law and Criminology* 75:491–505.

Davis, Robert, and Barbara Smith. 1994*a*. "The Effects of Victim Impact Statements on Sentencing Decisions: A Test in an Urban Setting." *Justice Quarterly* 11:453–512.

———. 1994*b*. "Victim Impact Statements and Victim Satisfaction: An Unfulfilled Promise?" *Journal of Criminal Justice* 22:1–12.

Department of Justice Canada. 1990. *Victim Impact Statements in Canada: A Summary of Findings*. Vol. 7. Ottawa: Department of Justice Canada.

———. 1998. *An Analysis of Public Attitudes toward Justice Related Issues*. Ottawa: Department of Justice Canada, Research and Development Directorate.

Douglas, Roger, Kathy Laster, and Nicole Inglis. 1994. "Victims of Efficiency: Tracking Victim Information through the System in Victoria." *International Review of Victimology* 3:95–110.

Dubber, Marcus. 2002. *Victims in the War on Crime: The Use and Abuse of Victims' Rights*. New York: New York University Press.

Duff, R. Antony. 2001. *Punishment, Communication, and Community*. New York: Oxford University Press.

Duff, R. Antony, and Sandra Marshall. 2004. "Communicative Punishment and the Role of the Victim." *Criminal Justice Ethics* 23:39–50.

Edwards, Ian. 2004. "An Ambiguous Participant: The Crime Victim and Criminal Justice Decision-Making." *British Journal of Criminology* 44:967–82.

Elias, Robert. 1993. *Victims Still: The Political Manipulation of Crime Victims*. London: Sage.

Ellis, Tom. 2007. "The New Zealand Parole Board, Its Independence and Some Domestic and International Legal Challenges." In *Who to Release? Parole, Fairness and Criminal Justice*, edited by Nicola Padfield. Cullompton, UK: Willan.

Erez, Edna. 1990. "Victim Participation in Sentencing: Rhetoric and Reality." *Journal of Criminal Justice* 18:19–31.

———. 1999. "Who's Afraid of the Big Bad Victim? Victim Impact Statements as Victim Empowerment and Enhancement of Justice." *Criminal Law Review* (July):545–56.

———. 2004. "Victim Voice, Impact Statements and Sentencing: Integrating Restorative Justice and Therapeutic Jurisprudence Principles in Adversarial Proceedings." *Criminal Law Bulletin* (September–October):483–500.

Erez, Edna, and Kathy Laster. 1999. "Neutralizing Victim Reform: Legal Professionals' Perspectives on Victims and Impact Statements." *Crime and Delinquency* 45:530–53.

Erez, Edna, and Leigh Roeger. 1995. "The Effect of Victim Impact Statements on Sentencing Patterns and Outcomes: The Australian Experience." *Journal of Criminal Justice* 23:363–75.

406   Julian V. Roberts

Erez, Edna, Leigh Roeger, and Frank Morgan. 1994. *Victim Impact Statements in South Australia: An Evaluation*. Adelaide: Office of Crime Statistics, South Australian Attorney-General's Department.

———. 1997. "Victim Harm, Impact Statements and Victim Satisfaction with Justice: An Australian Experience." *International Review of Criminology* 5:37–60.

Erez, Edna, and Linda Rogers. 1999. "Victim Impact Statements and Sentencing: Outcomes and Processes." *British Journal of Criminology* 39:216–39.

Erez, Edna, and Pamela Tontodonato. 1990. "The Effect of Victim Participation in Sentencing on Sentence Outcome." *Criminology* 28:451–74.

———. 1992. "Victim Participation in Sentencing and Satisfaction with Justice." *Justice Quarterly* 9:393–417.

Florida Parole Commission. 2008. *Victims' Rights*. Available at http://fpc.fl.us/Victims.htm.

Fosterlee, Lynne, G. Fox, R. Forsterlee, and R. Ho. 2004. "The Effects of a Victim Impact Statement and Gender on Juror Information Processing in a Criminal Trial: Does the Punishment Fit the Crime?" *Australian Psychologist* 39:57–67.

Fulkerson, Andrew. 2001. "The Use of Victim Impact Panels in Domestic Violence Cases: A Restorative Justice Approach." *Contemporary Justice Review* 4:355–68.

Gaudreault, Arlene. 2003. *Victims of Crime: A Look at Their Experiences with Canada's Correctional System*. Montreal: University of Montreal, School of Criminology.

Georgia State Board of Pardons and Paroles. 2008. *Victim Impact Statement*. Available at http://oldweb.pap.state.ga.us/victim.nsf/fVIS2?openform.

Giliberti, Carolina. 1990. *Victim Impact Statements in Canada*. Vol. 7, *A Summary of the Findings*. Ottawa: Department of Justice Canada, Research Development and Directorate.

Glenn, Christine. 2007. "Pulling Together the Threads: Public Confidence and Perceptions of Fairness." In *Who to Release? Parole, Fairness and Criminal Justice*, edited by Nicola Padfield. Cullompton, UK: Willan.

Government of South Australia. 2007. *Victims of Crime Booklet*. Available at http://www.justice.sa.gov.au/publications.

Graham, Jenny, Kandy Woodfield, Mike Tibble, and Sarah Kitchen. 2004. *Testaments of Harm: A Qualitative Evaluation of the Victim Personal Statements Scheme*. London: Home Office.

Grant County Prosecutor's Office. 2008. *Victim Impact Statement*. Ephrata, WA: Grant County Prosecutor's Office.

Guastello, Catherine. 2005. "Victim Impact Statements: Institutionalized Revenge." *Arizona State Law Journal* 37:1321–40.

Hall, Donald. 1991. "Victims' Voices in Criminal Court: The Need for Restraint." *American Criminal Law Review* 28:233–66.

Henderson, Lynne. 1985. "The Wrongs of Victims' Rights." *Stanford Law Review* 37:937–1021.

Henley, Madeline, Robert Davis, and Barbara Smith. 1994. "The Reactions of

Prosecutors and Judges to Victim Impact Statements." *International Review of Victimology* 3:83–93.

Herman, Susan, and Cressida Wasserman. 2001. "A Role for Victims in Offender Re-entry." *Crime and Delinquency* 47:428–45.

Hinton, Martin. 1995. "Expectations Dashed: Victim Impact Statements and the Common Law Approach to Sentencing in South Australia." *University of Tasmania Law Review* 14:81–99.

———. 1996. "Guarding against Victim-Authored Victim Impact Statements." *Criminal Law Journal* 20:310–20.

Hood, Roger, and Stephen Shute. 2000. *The Parole System at Work: A Study of Risk-Based Decision-Making*. London: Home Office.

Hough, Mike, Julian Roberts, Jessica Jacobson, Alan Bredee, and Nick Moon. 2008. *Attitudes to the Sentencing of Offenders Convicted of Offences Involving Death by Driving*. London: Sentencing Advisory Panel.

Hoyle, Carolyn, Ed Cape, Rod Morgan, and Andrew Sanders. 1998. *Evaluation of the "One Stop Shop" and Victim Statement Pilot Projects*. London: Home Office, Research Development and Statistics Directorate.

Hoyle, Carolyn, and Lucia Zedner. 2007. "Victims, Victimization, and Criminal Justice." In *The Oxford Handbook of Criminology*, edited by Mike Maguire, Rod Morgan, and Robert Reiner. 4th ed. Oxford: Oxford University Press.

International Criminal Court. 2008. *Victims before the International Criminal Court: A Guide for the Participation of Victims in the Proceedings of the Court*. The Hague: International Criminal Court.

Justice Strategy Unit. 2000. *Victims of Crime Review*. Report 2, *Survey of Victims of Crime*. Available at http://www.voc.sa.gov.au/Publications/Reports/victims ofcrimesurvey.

Kilpatrick, Dean, David Beatty, and Susan Howley. 1998. *The Rights of Crime Victims—Does Legal Protection Make a Difference?* Research in Brief. Washington, DC: National Institute of Justice.

Kinnevy, Susan, and Joel Caplan. 2008. *Findings from the APAI International Survey of Releasing Authorities*. Philadelphia: Center for Research on Youth and Policy.

Leverick, Fiona, James Chalmers, and Peter Duff. 2007. *An Evaluation of the Pilot Victim Statement Schemes in Scotland*. Edinburgh: Scottish Executive Social Research. Available at http://www.scotland.gov.uk/publications.

Lord Chancellor's Department. 2001. *Practice Direction on Victim Personal Statements*. October 16, 2001. Available at http://www.gnn.gov.uk.

May, Mark. 1989. "Victims' Rights and the Parole Hearing." *Journal of Contemporary Law* 15:71–80.

McDonald, William. 1982. "The Victim's Role in the American Administration of Criminal Justice: Some Developments and Findings." In *The Victim in International Perspective*, edited by H. J. Schneider. New York: de Gruyter.

McLeod, Maureen. 1987. "An Examination of the Victim's Role at Sentencing: Results of a Survey of Probation Administrators." *Judicature* 71:162–68.

———. 1989. "Getting Free: Victim Participation in Parole Board Decisions." *Criminal Justice* 4:13–15, 41–43.

Meredith, Colin, and Chantal Paquette. 2001. *Report on Victim Impact Statement Focus Groups*. Victims of Crime and Research Series. Ottawa: Department of Justice Canada.

Miller, Karen. 2008. *Empowering Victims: The Use of the Victim Impact Statement in the Case of Sexual Assault in Nova Scotia; The Perspective of Victims and Victim Services Staff*. Toronto: Centre of Criminology, University of Toronto.

Ministry of Justice (Jamaica). 2006. *Victims' Charter*. Kingston, Jamaica: Ministry of Justice.

Minnesota Office of Justice Programs. 2004. *Victim Impact Statements*. St. Paul: Minnesota Office of Justice Programs.

Mitchell, Diane. 1996. "Victim Impact Statements: A Brief Examination of Their Implementation in Victoria." *Current Issues in Criminal Justice* 8: 163–74.

Moore, Louise, and Laura Blakeborough. 2008. *Early Findings from WAVES: Information and Service Provision*. London: Ministry of Justice.

Morgan, Kathryn, and Brent Smith. 2005. "Victims, Punishment, and Parole: The Effect of Victim Participation on Parole Hearings." *Crime and Public Policy* 4:333–60.

Morgan, Rod, and Andrew Sanders. 1999. *The Uses of Victim Statements*. London: Home Office, Research Development and Statistics Directorate.

Moriarty, Laura. 2005. "Victim Participation at Parole Hearings: Balancing Victim, Offender, and Public Interest." *Crime and Public Policy* 4:385–90.

Muir, Judith. 1990. *Victim Impact Statements in Canada*. Vol. 2, *Evaluation of the Calgary Project*. Working document WD1990-4a. Ottawa: Department of Justice Canada.

National Parole Board of Canada. 2008. *Facts: Victims; Providing Information*. Available at http://www.npb-cnlc.gc.ca/infocntr/factsh/provide.htm.

National Probation Service. 2007. *Victim Representation at Parole Board Hearings: Probation Circular*. London: National Offender Management Service.

New South Wales Victims of Crime Bureau and Department of Corrective Services. 2001. *Submissions*. Sydney: New South Wales.

New Zealand Parole Board. 2007. *Information for Victims*. Wellington: New Zealand Parole Board.

Northwest Territories. 2008. *Victim Impact Statement*. Available at http://www.justice.nt.ca/pdf/victimservices/victim_statement.

O'Connell, Michael. 2009. "Victims in the Sentencing Process: South Australia's Judges and Magistrates Give Their Verdict." *International Perspectives in Victimology* (forthcoming).

Office for Victims of Crime. 1999. *Promising Practices and Strategies for Victim Services in Corrections*. Washington, DC: U.S. Department of Justice, Office for Victims of Crime.

Office of the Attorney General (Kentucky). 2008. *Victim Impact Statement*. Available at http://ag.ky.gov/criminal/victims/publications.htm.

O'Hara, Erin. 2006. "Victims and Prison Release: A Modest Proposal." *Federal Sentencing Reporter* 19:130–35.

Ohio Department of Rehabilitation and Correction. 2008. *Full Board Hearings.* Columbus: Ohio Department of Rehabilitation and Correction.

Ontario Parole and Earned Release Board. 2008. *Release Information.* Available at http://www.operb.gov.on.ca/english/victim/victim.html.

Orth, Uli. 2002. "Secondary Victimization of Crime Victims by Criminal Proceedings." *Social Justice Research* 15:313–26.

Paciocco, David. 1999. *Getting Away with Murder: The Canadian Criminal Justice System.* Toronto: Irwin.

Parole Board for England and Wales. 2007. *Forty Years: Annual Report and Accounts, 2006–2007.* London: H.M. Stationery Office.

Parsonage, William, Frances Bernat, and Jacqueline Helfgott. 1992. "Victim Impact Testimony and Pennsylvania's Parole Decision-Making Process: A Pilot Study." *Criminal Justice Policy Review* 6:187–206.

Policy Centre for Victim Issues. 2008. *Victim Impact Statements—Case Law Review.* Ottawa: Department of Justice Canada, Policy Centre for Victim Issues.

Polowek, Kim. 2005. "Victim Participatory Rights in Parole: Their Role and the Dynamics of Victim Influence as Seen by Board Members." Doctoral dissertation, School of Criminology, Simon Fraser University.

Prairie Research Associates. 2005*a*. *Multi-Site Survey of Victims of Crime and Criminal Justice Professionals across Canada: Summary of Defence Counsel Respondents.* Ottawa: Department of Justice, Policy Centre for Victim Issues.

———. 2005*b*. *Multi-Site Survey of Victims of Crime and Criminal Justice Professionals across Canada: Summary of Probation Officer, Corrections, and Parole Board Respondents.* Ottawa: Policy Centre for Victim Issues, Department of Justice Canada.

———. 2005*c*. *Multi-Site Survey of Victims of Crime and Criminal Justice Professionals across Canada: Summary of Victims of Crime Respondents.* Ottawa: Department of Justice, Policy Centre for Victim Issues.

President's Task Force on Victims of Crime. 1982. *Final Report.* Washington, DC: U.S. Government Printing Office.

Proctor, John. 1999. "The 'New Parole': An Analysis of Parole Board Decision Making as a Function of Eligibility." *Journal of Crime and Criminal Justice* 22:193–217.

Ranish, Donald, and David Shichor. 1985. "The Victim's Role in the Penal Process: Recent Developments in California." *Federal Probation* 49:50–57.

Roach, Kent. 1999. *Due Process and Victims' Rights: The New Law and Politics of Criminal Justice.* Toronto: University of Toronto Press.

Robert, Luc, and Tony Peters. 2003. "How Restorative Justice Is Able to Transcend the Prison Walls: A Discussion of the 'Restorative Detention' Project." In *Restorative Justice in Context: International Practice and Directions,* edited by Elmar Weitekamp and Hans Kerner. Cullompton, UK: Willan.

Roberts, Julian. 2001. *Public Perceptions of the Prosecution Function: An International Perspective.* Ottawa: Department of Criminology, University of Ottawa.

———. 2002. "Determining Parole Eligibility Dates for Life Prisoners: Lessons from Jury Hearings in Canada." *Punishment and Society* 4:103–14.

———. 2003. "Victim Impact Statements and the Sentencing Process: Enhancing Communication in the Courtroom." *Criminal Law Quarterly* 47: 365–96.

Roberts, Julian, and Estella Baker. 2007. "Sentencing in Common Law Jurisdictions." In *International Handbook of Penology and Criminal Justice*, edited by Shlomo Shoham, Ori Beck, and Martin Kett. New York: Routledge.

Roberts, Julian, and Allen Edgar. 2003. *Improving the Use of Victim Impact Statements at Sentencing: Exploring the Reform Options*. Ottawa: Department of Justice Canada.

———. 2006. *Victim Impact Statements at Sentencing: Judicial Experiences and Perceptions*. Ottawa: Policy Centre for Victim Issues, Department of Justice Canada.

Roberts, Julian, and Edna Erez. 2004. "Communication in Sentencing: Exploring the Expressive and the Impact Model of Victim Impact Statements." *International Review of Victimology* 10:223–44.

Roberts, Julian, and Mike Hough. 2005. *Understanding Public Attitudes to Criminal Justice*. Maidenhead, UK: Open University Press.

Sanders, Andrew. 2004. "Involving Victims in Sentencing: A Conflict with Defendants' Rights?" In *Reconcilable Rights? Analysing the Tension between Victims and Defendants*, edited by Ed Cape. London: Legal Action Group.

Sanders, Andrew, Carolyn Hoyle, Rod Morgan, and Ed Cape. 2001. "Victim Impact Statements: Don't Work, Can't Work." *Criminal Law Review* (June): 47–58.

Sanders, Andrew, and Richard Young. 2007. *Criminal Justice*. 3rd ed. Oxford: Oxford University Press.

Sankoff, Peter, and Lisa Wansborough. 2007. "Is Three Really a Crowd? Thoughts about Victim Impact Statements and New Zealand's Revamped Sentencing Regime." *New Zealand Law Journal* 7:459–94.

Schuster, Mary Lay. 2006. Victim Impact Statements—Do They Make a Difference? *Watch Post* 14, no. 3.

Schuster, Mary Lay, and Amy Propen. 2007. *2006 WATCH Victim Impact Study*. Minneapolis: University of Minnesota, Department of Rhetoric.

Shapland, Joanna. 1984. "Victims, the Criminal Justice System and Compensation." *British Journal of Criminology* 24:131–49.

———. 2009. "Victims and Criminal Justice in Europe." In *The International Handbook of Victimology*, edited by Paul Knepper and Shlomo Shoham. London: Francis & Taylor (forthcoming).

Shute, Stephen. 2007. "Parole and Risk Assessment." In *Who to Release? Parole, Fairness, and Criminal Justice*, edited by Nicola Padfield. Cullompton, UK: Willan.

Sloan Associates. 1990. *Victim Impact Statements in Canada*. Vol. 4, *Evaluation of the Winnipeg Project*. Research Report WD 1990-6a. Ottawa: Department of Justice Canada.

Smith, Brent, Erin Watkins, and Kathryn Morgan. 1997. "The Effect of Victim Participation on Parole Decisions: Results from a Southeastern State." *Criminal Justice Policy Review* 8:7–74.

Sobieski, Regina. 1997. *Victim Impact Statements: Do They Increase Victim Satisfaction?* Available at http://www.ovc.gov./publications/infores/impact/impact .htm.

South Carolina Department of Probation, Parole and Pardon Services. 2008. *Victim Services.* Available at http://www.dppps.sc.gov/victim_services_parole .html.

Spencer, John. 2004. "Criminal Procedure: The Rights of the Victim versus the Rights of the Defendant." In *Reconcilable Rights? Analysing the Tension between Victims and Defendants,* edited by Ed Cape. London: Legal Action Group.

State of New Jersey Parole Board. 2008. *Victim Services.* Available at http:// www.state.nj.us/parole/victim.html.

State of Utah Board of Pardons and Parole. 2008. *Victim Information.* Available at http://bop.utah.gov/victims.html.

Stevens, Mark. 2000. "Victim Impact Statements Considered at Sentencing: Constitutional Concerns." *California Criminal Law Review* 2:1–13.

Straw, Jack. 2008. "Victims." Speech delivered at Royal Society of Arts, London, October 27.

Szmania, Susan, and Monica Gracyalny. 2006. "Addressing the Court, the Offender, and the Community: A Communication Analysis of Victim Impact Statements in a Non-capital Sentencing Hearing." *International Review of Victimology* 13:231–49.

Talbert, Philip. 1988. "The Relevance of Victim Statements to the Criminal Sentencing Decision." *University of California Law Review* 36:199–232.

Tapley, Jacki. 2005. "Political Rhetoric and the Reality of Victims' Experiences." *Prison Service Journal* 158:45–52.

Tasmania Department of Justice. 2008. *Having Your Say.* Available at http:// www.tas.gov.au/victims/victimsregister/parole/having_your_say.

Terblanche, Stephan. 2008. *Research on the Sentencing Framework Bill.* Report no. 4. Newlands: Open Society of South Africa.

Texas Department of Criminal Justice. 1997. *It's Your Turn: A Victims' and Survivors' Handbook to Victim Impact Information.* Dallas: Texas Department of Criminal Justice, Victim Services Division.

Tobolowsky, Peggy. 1999. "Victim Participation in the Criminal Justice Process: Fifteen Years after the President's Task Force on Victims of Crime." *Journal of Criminal and Civil Confinement* 25:21–92.

Tonry, Michael. 2004. *Punishment and Politics.* Cullompton, UK: Willan.

Truth and Reconciliation Commission of South Africa. 2002. *Truth and Reconciliation Commission of South Africa.* Vol. 7. Capetown: Truth and Reconciliation Commission of South Africa.

Tyler, Tom. 2006. *Why People Obey the Law.* Princeton, NJ: Princeton University Press.

Verdun-Jones, Simon, and Adamira Tijerino. 2005. *Victim Participation in Disposition Hearings Involving Accused Persons Who Have Been Found Not Criminally Responsible on Account of Mental Disorder.* Ottawa: Department of Justice Canada.

Victoria Department of Justice. 2008. *Written Submission to the Adult Parole Board*. Available at http://www.justice.vic.gov.au/wps/wcm/connect.

Villemoare, Edwin, and Virginia Neto. 1987. *Victim Appearances at Sentencing Hearings under California's Victims' Bill of Rights*. Washington, DC: National Institute of Justice.

Virginia Department of Corrections (Victim Services). 2008. *Victim Input Program*. Available at http://www.vadoc.state.va.us/victim/input-program.shtm.

Virginia Parole Board. 2006. *Policy Manual*. Available at http://www.vadoc.state .va.us.

von Hirsch, Andrew. 1993. *Censure and Sanctions*. Oxford: Clarendon.

Walklate, Sandra. 2002. "Victim Impact Statements." In *Reparation and Victim Focused Social Work*, edited by Brian Williams. London: Kingsley.

———. 2007. *Imagining the Victim of the Crime*. Maidenhead, UK: Open University Press.

Wallace, S. 1989. *Victim Impact Statements: A Monograph*. Wellington: New Zealand Department of Justice.

Walsh, Anthony. 1992. "Placebo Justice: Victim Recommendations and Offender Sentences in Sexual Assault Cases." In *Towards a Critical Criminology*, edited by Ezzat Fattah. New York: St. Martin's.

Washtenaw County Prosecutor's Office. 2008. *Victim Impact Statement*. Ann Arbor, MI: Washtenaw County Prosecutor's Office, Victim/Witness Services.

Webster, Cheryl, and Anthony Doob. 2007. "Punitive Trends and Stable Imprisonment Rates in Canada." In *Crime, Punishment, and Politics in Comparative Perspective*, edited by Michael Tonry. Vol. 36 of *Crime and Justice: A Review of Research*, edited by Michael Tonry. Chicago: University of Chicago Press.

Whiteley, Diane. 1998. "The Victim and the Justification of Punishment." *Criminal Justice Ethics* 17:42–54.

Williams, Brian. 2005. *Victims of Crime and Community Justice*. London: Jessica Kingsley.

Gary LaFree and Laura Dugan

Research on Terrorism and Countering Terrorism

ABSTRACT

Social and behavioral research on terrorism has expanded dramatically. However, theoretical work that incorporates terrorism and collection of valid data on it has lagged behind theoretical work on other criminological subjects. Theorizing has been dominated by deterrence perspectives. Threats of severe consequence for terrorist acts in general show little promise, but there is evidence that increasing the certainty of consequences works in some situations. Research on terrorism will be improved if it moves beyond deterrence to include concepts drawn from legitimacy, strain, and situational perspectives. Limitations of traditional criminology data sources for studying terrorism have encouraged the development of open-source-event databases. The most comprehensive, created by combining the Global Terrorism Database with RAND-MIPT data, documents more than 77,000 terrorist incidents from 1970 to 2006. Attacks peaked in the early 1990s and then declined substantially until 9/11. They have since substantially increased. The regional concentration of terrorism has moved from Western Europe in the 1970s, to Latin America in the 1980s, to the Middle East and Persian Gulf in the twenty-first century. Despite the enormous resources devoted to countering terrorism, surprisingly little empirical information is available on which strategies are most effective.

Support for this research was provided by the Department of Homeland Security (DHS) through the National Consortium for the Study of Terrorism and Responses to Terrorism (START), grant N00140510629, and from the National Institute of Justice (NIJ), grant 2005-IJ-CX-0002. Any opinions, findings, and conclusions or recommendations in this document are those of the authors and do not necessarily reflect views of the DHS or NIJ. Some of the materials in this essay are revisions to a final report for the NIJ grant, coauthored with Kim Cragin and Anna Kasupski. We thank David Cook, James Hendrickson, Erin Miller, and Amber Stoesser for their assistance. We would also like to thank our colleagues in the START Consortium for their help and support.

Although social science research on terrorism has expanded dramatically, especially since the 1970s,[1] the number of studies based on systematic empirical analysis is surprisingly limited. In an encyclopedic review of political terrorism, Schmid and Jongman (1988) identify more than 6,000 published works but note that "there are probably few areas in the social science literature in which so much is written on the basis of so little research" (p. 179). More recently, Lum, Kennedy, and Sherley (2006) reviewed more than 20,000 articles on terrorism published between 1971 and 2004 and found only seven that met their criteria of being moderately rigorous evaluation studies.

To be fair to researchers and policy makers, terrorism represents a type of behavior that is difficult to define and measure. Compared to collecting data on other types of criminal violence, collecting valid terrorism data raises unique challenges. Moreover, while criminology and law and social science scholars have been making important contributions to the research literature on terrorism and responses to terrorism for many years (e.g., Smith 1994; Hamm 1997), and several decades ago scholars such as Kittrie (1978) and Turk (1982, 1984) included terrorism in their research on political crime, much of this early work was isolated, scattered, and done without federal research funding. It took the Murrah Federal Building bombing in Oklahoma City in 1995 and the September 11, 2001, attacks in New York City, Washington, DC, and Pennsylvania before major funding to support social science research on terrorism in the United States became available.

After these events, funding through the National Memorial Institute for the Prevention of Terrorism; terrorism research solicitations by the National Science Foundation, the National Institute of Justice, and the Bureau of Justice Administration; and the creation of the Department of Homeland Security's Centers of Excellence program all strengthened support for social scientific studies of terrorism and responses to terrorism. The newly announced Minerva program, funded by the Department of Defense, promises to increase further levels of support (Glod 2008). Moreover, spurred by brutal attacks such as the Madrid bombings of March 11, 2004, and the London bombings of July 7, 2005, funding of social science research on terrorism and responses to terrorism has also expanded greatly in Europe (Eder and Senn 2008).

---

[1] For reviews, see Schmid and Jongman (1988), Mickolus (1991), Prunkun (1995), Mickolus and Simmons (1997), Babkina (1998), and Hoffman (1998).

These developments are encouraging rapid growth of social and behavioral science research on terrorism and responses to terrorism.

This essay is divided into two major parts. In the first, we concentrate on the criminology-related literature on terrorism. While a comprehensive review of this rapidly expanding literature is beyond the scope of this essay, we focus instead on two more limited tasks. In Section I, we consider the problem of defining and measuring terrorism and how it raises challenges that are somewhat different from what criminologists face in collecting data on more common crimes. In Section II, we consider criminological theories of terrorism and the research literature that tests these theories. This section begins with rational choice perspectives, which have thus far been applied most frequently by criminologists to the study of terrorism. We then consider how other theoretical perspectives—legitimacy, anomie and strain, and situational—could also provide useful theoretical insights.

In the second half of this essay, we introduce original empirical data that allow us to describe some of the salient characteristics of worldwide terrorism since 1970. Where relevant, we also consider the theoretical implications of the results. Over the past 4 decades there has been a growing interest in collecting open-source-event data on terrorist attacks.

In Section III, we briefly describe these developments and consider some of the strengths and weaknesses of event data on terrorism. We follow up in Section IV with a description of a newly available database on terrorist attacks from 1970 to 2006 based on a joint project between the National Consortium for the Study of Terrorism and Responses to Terrorism (START) and the RAND Corporation (Dugan et al. 2008). For this project we synthesized transnational and domestic data on terrorism from 1970 to 1997 from the Global Terrorism Database (GTD; see LaFree and Dugan 2007) with transnational data from the RAND Terrorism Chronology (Jenkins and Johnson 1975) for the same years, and transnational and domestic incident data from 1998 to 2006 from the RAND-MIPT database (MIPT 2002). The resulting longitudinal data set contains over 77,000 cases and is, to our knowledge, the most comprehensive open-source-event database on terrorist attacks assembled to date.

We devote Section V to a descriptive analysis of these newly available data. We focus especially on trends in terrorism over time for the world as a whole and for regions of the world. We examine differences

over time and by region for total attacks and fatalities, and terrorist
targets, tactics, and weapons. We also examine the terrorist groups that
have been responsible for the greatest number of attacks and fatalities
and the countries that have sustained the most attacks and fatalities.
Finally, in Section VI, we conclude with a brief discussion of promising
directions for further research, especially with regard to using event
data to study both the etiology of terrorism and methods for countering it.

Our goal is to provide a theoretical and empirical introduction to
the criminological study of terrorism. Traditional sources for main-
stream criminology—official data and victimization and self-report surveys—have been of limited value in the study of terrorism. This helps
explain why research on terrorism has been uniquely dependent on
open-source-event databases. Theorizing about terrorism has thus far
been dominated by rational choice perspectives. A growing literature
examines attempts to deter terrorists by increasing the probability of
their apprehension or the severity of their punishment. The findings
from this research are similar to the findings on deterrence in criminology: approaches based on severity alone show little promise, while
there is evidence that approaches based on increasing certainty work
in some but not all situations. It would be very beneficial for future
research on terrorism to expand beyond traditional deterrence perspectives to include theories that incorporate legitimacy, strain, and
situational variables. This strategy is supported by some recent research
suggesting that strategies aimed at decreasing the benefits of terrorism
through improving the legitimacy of government, solving widespread
grievances that produce strain, or attending to situational features that
increase the costs of terrorism might be more effective than strategies
based only on increasing punishment. In general, despite the enormous
resources devoted to countering terrorism, we have surprisingly little
empirical information about which strategies are most effective. One
conclusion seems certain: the divergent reactions by terrorists across
differing contexts strongly suggest that selecting an appropriate counterterrorism strategy is not a task that should be taken lightly.

Open-source-event databases on terrorism have received a good deal
of attention and have grown more comprehensive and systematic over
time. We report on the most extensive to date—formed by merging
the GTD with the RAND-MIPT database. While event databases have
serious limitations compared to more traditional criminology data, they

also have important advantages. In particular, because of the unique interest that terrorist groups have in media attention, open-source information may be uniquely useful in the study of terrorism. And compared to most criminology data, terrorism event data are not limited to highly industrialized countries.

Examination of global trends shows that attacks peaked in the early 1990s and then declined substantially in the years leading up to 9/11. Following 9/11 they have again substantially increased. Attacks in the 1970s were most frequent in the Western European region, attacks in the 1980s in the Latin American region, and attacks in the first decade of the twenty-first century in the Middle East and Persian Gulf region. In general, terrorism in Western Europe has been characterized by fewer deaths per attack while terrorism in the Middle East/Persian Gulf has been characterized by a much higher proportion of fatalities to attacks. Terrorism in Latin America is intermediate with regard to the ratio of attacks to fatalities but closer to the Middle East/Persian Gulf than to Western Europe. Most terrorist attacks are rather mundane—based on commonly available, unsophisticated weapons, no fatalities, and low levels of planning.

Future research would benefit from a more complete understanding of the operational aspects of terrorist behavior, including variation in the decisions of terrorists to target or kill, by which tactic, and using what types of weapons. Much more research is needed that integrates sociocultural studies of the influence of ideology on strategy and tactics with theoretical insights gained from formal decision analysis, research on social movements and collective violence, and organizational and social psychology. In addition, there is a dearth of social science research on how specific antiterrorism and counterterrorism efforts affect the behavior of terrorists.

I. Defining and Measuring Terrorism

Compared to most types of criminal violence, terrorism poses special conceptual and methodological challenges. To begin with, the term "terrorism" yields varying definitions, often loaded with political and emotional implications. As Palestine Liberation Organization (PLO) Chairman Arafat famously noted in a 1974 speech before the United Nations, "One man's terrorist is another man's freedom fighter." This is not a trivial issue. For example, the U.S. State Department maintains a list of Foreign Terrorist Organizations (FTOs; U.S. State Department 2007) that designates FTO status according to, among other things, its threat to U.S. interests. Yet, others perceive some of the FTOs as revolutionaries fighting for just causes. For example, Hamas is listed as an FTO despite its status among many Palestinians as a legitimate political party that recently won a major democratically held election. Indeed, many of the groups that are most prominent in the GTD-RAND merged database (including Shining Path, Basque Fatherland and Freedom [ETA], Farabundo Marti National Liberation Front [FMLN], Irish Republican Army [IRA], Revolutionary Armed Forces of Colombia [FARC], National Liberation Army of Columbia [ELN], and Kurdish Workers Party [PKK]) often define themselves as freedom fighters. This fundamental characteristic of terrorism no doubt explains why international organizations such as the United Nations have not succeeded in adopting a universally accepted definition (European Commission 2008, pp. 3–4). Defining terrorism is no less complex for researchers. In their influential review of terrorism research, Schmid and Jongman (1988, p. 5) found 109 different research definitions of terrorism. Indeed, the first chapter of many influential books on terrorism (e.g., Schmid and Jongman 1988; Hoffman 1998; Smelser 2007) is devoted to exploring and defending competing definitions.

Beyond the challenge of arriving at a defensible definition are considerable challenges in collecting valid data. In criminology, data on illegal violence come traditionally from three sources, corresponding to the major social roles connected to criminal events: "official" data collected by legal agents, especially the police; "victimization" data collected from the general population of victims and nonvictims; and "self-report" data collected from offenders (LaFree and Dugan 2004, pp. 53–74). In the United States, the most widely used form of official crime data has long been the Federal Bureau of Investigation's Uniform Crime Report. Major official sources of data on international crime include the International Criminal Police Organization (Interpol), the United Nations crime surveys, and, for homicides only, the World Health Organization (LaFree 1999, pp. 124–48).

Since 1973, the major source of victimization data in the United States has been the National Crime Victimization Survey. For international data, the International Crime Victimization Survey has collected several waves of data from samples of individuals in several dozen nations around the world (Mayhew and Van Dijk 1997; Van Dijk, van Kesteren, and Smit 2008), and many other victimization surveys have now been completed for individual countries or groups of countries (for a review, see Groves and Cork [2008]). Compared to the collection of victimization data in the United States, the collection of self-report survey data has been more sporadic. Nevertheless, several major large-scale national self-report surveys now exist (Elliott, Huizinga, and Menard 1989). Similarly, several waves of an international self-reported crime study have been undertaken (Junger-Tas, Terlouw, and Klein 1994) and have produced a variety of empirical analyses (Farrington et al. 1996; for a review, see Junger-Tas and Marshall [1997]). In general, data concerning terrorist events from these three sources either are entirely lacking or face important additional limitations.

Although government departments in some countries do collect official data on terrorism (e.g., the U.S. National Counter Terrorism Center), these data face at least two major difficulties. First, as mentioned above, terrorism data collected by government entities are suspicious either because they are influenced by political considerations or because many fear that they might be so influenced. And second, while huge amounts of detailed official data on common crimes are routinely produced by the various branches of the criminal justice system in most nations, this is rarely the case for terrorism. For example, most suspected terrorists in the United States are not legally processed for their acts of terrorism but rather for other related offenses. It is true that this situation continues to evolve. For example, in the United States in 1995, chapter 113B of the Federal Criminal Code and Rules added "terrorism" as a separate offense, and the Antiterrorism and Effective Death Penalty Act was signed into law in 1996. Among other things, the 1996 act attempts to cut fund-raising by those affiliated with terrorist organizations, enhances the security measures employed by the aviation industry, and expands the reach of U.S. law enforcement over selected crimes committed abroad. Similarly, the U.S. Patriot Act, passed in 2001, strengthens criminal laws against terrorism by adding to the criminal code terrorist attacks against mass transportation systems, domestic terrorism, harboring or concealing terrorists, or providing material support to terrorists (115 Stat. 374, Public Law 107-56—October 26, 2001). Nevertheless, it still remains the case that most of those persons who are officially designated as terrorists in the annual reports produced by the FBI either are not prosecuted at all (e.g., the likely outcome for many of those detained at the U.S.'s Guantanamo Detention Facility) or are prosecuted under traditional criminal statutes. So, there is no easy way to gather official data on those arrested, prosecuted, or convicted of terrorist activities unless you do as Smith and his colleagues have done (Smith and Orvis 1993, pp. 661–81; Smith et al. 2002) and assemble the data on a case-by-case basis. And of course the ability to use official data to study terrorism in most other nations is even more limited. In particular, much terrorism data are collected by intelligence agencies that operate partially or entirely outside the realm of domestic criminal justice systems.

Victimization data, which have played an increasingly important role in the study of common crime in the United States and elsewhere, are almost entirely irrelevant to the study of terrorist activities. Several features of terrorism make it highly unlikely that victimization surveys will ever have widespread applicability. To begin with, despite the attention it gets in the global media, terrorism is much rarer than violent crime. This means that even with extremely large sample sizes, few individuals in most countries will have been victimized by terrorists. Moreover, because one of the hallmarks of terrorism is that victims are often chosen at random, victims of terrorist events are unlikely to know their perpetrator, making it difficult to produce details about the offender. And finally, in many cases, victims of terrorism are killed by their attackers—a problem in criminology limited to the study of homicides.

Self-report data on terrorists have been more important than victimization data, but they too face serious limitations. Most active terrorists are unwilling to participate in interviews. And even if they are willing to participate, getting access to known terrorists for research purposes raises obvious challenges. As Merari (1991, p. 88) has put it, "The clandestine nature of terrorist organizations and the ways and means by which intelligence can be obtained will rarely enable data collection which meets commonly accepted academic standards." Still, we can learn a good deal from direct contact with terrorists or former terrorists. Examples include recent work by Horgan (2005), based on interviews with terrorists, and McCauley (2003), based on examining notebooks and letters left behind by the 9/11 suicide bombers. Increasingly, the Internet provides access to the motives and strategies of individuals and groups that employ terrorism. There may also be useful information on the self-reported strategies of terrorists available through analysis of blogs, Web sites, and chat rooms (Weimann 2006).

II. Criminological Theories of Terrorism

While Schmid and Jongman's (1988, p. 61) strong critique of theory development with regard to terrorism may still be warranted to some extent, there has been considerable progress in the 20 years following their assessment. In particular, a rapidly expanding literature applies rational choice perspectives to understand both terrorist behavior and governmental strategies for countering terrorism. In this section, we review rational choice perspectives and then consider several related theoretical perspectives that could usefully broaden future research.

A. Rational Choice Perspectives

The belief that credible threats of apprehension and punishment deter crime is as old as criminal law itself and has broad appeal to both policy makers and the public. As elaborated by social reformers such as Bentham and Beccaria, or jurists such as Blackstone, Romilly, or Feuerbach, rational actor perspectives assume that crime can be deterred by increasing the costs of crime or increasing the rewards of noncrime (Gibbs 1975; Ross and LaFree 1986; Paternoster 1987). In particular, Bentham's principle of utility proposed that individuals act in view of their own self-interest and that the effective use of punishment serves to deter individuals from specific actions (including crime) that serve their self-interest.

Rational choice models have been applied to a wide variety of criminal behavior, including drunk driving (Nagin and Paternoster 1993), burglary (Wright and Decker 1994), robbery (Wright and Decker 1997), shoplifting (Piquero and Tibbetts 1996), income tax evasion (Klepper and Nagin 1989), drug selling (Jacobs 1996), and white-collar crimes (Paternoster and Simpson 1996; Simpson, Paternoster, and Piquero 1998). Rational choice models would seem to be especially appropriate for understanding terrorist violence, given that many terrorist attacks are carefully planned and appear to include at least some consideration for risks and rewards. Indeed, rational choice assumptions have dominated counterterrorist policies in most countries since the origins of modern terrorism in the late 1960s (Frey and Luechinger 2002; Collins 2004; Braithwaite 2005).

Many contemporary rational choice models of crime (Becker 1968; Carroll 1978; Landes 1978) express utilitarian philosophy in mathematical terms, with individuals maximizing satisfaction by choosing one of a finite set of alternatives, each with its particular costs and benefits (Cornish and Clarke 1986; Clarke and Felson 1993, p. 5). Thus, in an econometric analysis of international terrorist incidents, Enders and Sandler (1993) argue that terrorists may be viewed as "rational actors who attempt to maximize a *shared goal*, subject to a resource constraint" (p. 830). They claim that this shared goal may be conceptualized in economic terms as utility or expected utility derived from the consumption of basic commodities, produced from terrorist and counterterrorist activities. For example, a particular terrorist group may gain utility from political instability, which is a basic commodity derived from various terrorist tactics or modes of attack (e.g., bombings, assassinations). Political instability results either if the government appears ineffective in curbing these acts or if the government overreacts and appears repressive and brutal.

According to the rational choice perspective, benefits to offenders can be both internal (e.g., monetary gain) and external (e.g., achieving political recognition). Further, as prospective terrorists witness the success of others who use terrorist methods, they may be more likely to use terrorism to achieve their own goals (Pape 2003; Dugan, LaFree, and Piquero 2005). Piquero and Pogarsky (2002) and others (Stafford and Warr 1993; Paternoster and Piquero 1995; Piquero and Paternoster 1998) have found that this vicarious experience with punishment avoidance is an important determinant of both the perception of sanctions and criminal behavior. The rational choice perspective posits that offenders evaluate the costs associated with their offending decisions. Such costs include the probability of apprehension as well as the severity of punishment experiences. Thus, members of terrorist organizations might make tactical decisions that reduce their likelihood of apprehension, such as exploding bombs rather than implementing armed attacks, which requires direct contact between the terrorists and their targets.

Empirical research assessing rational choice perspectives on terrorism has emphasized tests of policies aimed at increasing either the probability of apprehension or the severity of punishment.

1. *Attempts to Deter by Increasing the Probability of Apprehension.* Consistent with the rational choice perspective is a series of policy

responses, commonly referred to as target hardening, that is designed to prevent terrorists from successfully completing their operation. Examples of target hardening include installing metal detectors in airports, increasing the security of vulnerable targets such as shopping malls and seaports, and fortifying the security of attractive targets such as embassies or other government buildings. While target hardening is commonly used, there have been few empirical evaluations of this strategy.

An exception is Enders and Sandler (1993), who conducted evaluations of target-hardening strategies by estimating their impact on different attack modes perpetrated by transnational terrorists. They used ITERATE data (Mickolus 1982) from 1968 to 1988 to estimate the effects on transnational attacks of six counterterrorism strategies, two of which were directed at increasing the chances of apprehension: the installation of metal detectors and the fortification of embassies. After noting that by impeding access to airports and embassies the relative cost of hijacking a plane or infiltrating an embassy has increased compared to other forms of hostage taking, Enders and Sandler test for substitution effects into other modes of hostage taking. While they found significant deterrent effects due to these strategies, they also found increases in other kinds of hostage-based attacks and assassinations.

Using data from the Federal Aviation Administration from 1931 to 1985, Dugan, LaFree, and Piquero (2005) found that the 1973 installation of metal detectors decreased the risk of continued airline hijackings. However, their findings were specific to nonterrorist-related attacks. Models run exclusively on terrorist-motivated hijackings provided there is no evidence of deterrence. Furthermore, findings for an earlier target-hardening strategy to tighten screening at U.S. airports provided no evidence of deterrence of hijacking motivated by terrorism or other goals.

2. Attempts to Deter by Increasing the Severity of Punishment. A more common approach to deterring terrorism is to respond aggressively in order to demonstrate that terrorism is intolerable and perpetrators will be punished severely. President Ronald Reagan typified this approach in an antiterrorist speech made in 1983: "Let terrorists beware that when the rules are violated, our policy will be one of swift and effective retribution" (Donohue 2001, p. 15). U.S. presidents before and since Reagan have often claimed that they will not tolerate any terrorist violence perpetrated against U.S. citizens, which has encouraged policy makers to design counterterrorism strategies that immediately punish perpetrators of military strikes or targeted assassinations. According to Donohue (2001), as a liberal democracy, the United States must appear to respond immediately to attacks against its citizens. However, others (Frey and Luechinger 2002; Bueno de Mesquita and Dickson 2007; Siqueira and Sandler 2007) claim that by aggressively countering terrorism, the United States and other countries may also be undermining their legitimacy and increasing popular support for those who use terrorist methods.

Despite the critical importance of responding effectively to terrorism but also preserving national legitimacy, very few empirical evaluations have examined the effects of government responses to terrorism (Lum, Kennedy, and Sherley 2006). Based on our review below, we conclude that efforts to counter terrorism through severe punishment have produced mixed outcomes, suggesting that we need to be more attentive to the context of terrorist threats before responding to them.

Enders and Sandler (1993) estimated the impact of three components of President Reagan's "get tough" policy that were enacted in the 1980s. The first two components were signed into law by Reagan in 1984 and included harsher penalties for those who took U.S. hostages or who used any weapons against U.S. aircraft. The third intervention occurred when the United States bombed Libya in April of 1986 in retaliation for its involvement in the terrorist bombing of a discotheque in West Berlin earlier that month. The authors found no significant impact of the 1984 Reagan law on subsequent terrorist attacks. However, they did find increases in a number of different types of terrorist attacks after the Libyan raid. These increases appear to have been temporary.

More recent research by LaFree, Dugan, and Korte (2009) found evidence of a backlash effect when evaluating six counterterrorism interventions against republican terrorist organizations in Northern Ireland—all aimed toward strengthening the severity of punishment for terrorism. Three of the interventions—internment, criminalization, and targeted assassinations in Gibraltar—led to increases rather than declines in subsequent terrorist attacks. The only evidence of deterrence was found after Operation Motorman, which was a massive and well-advertised military deployment of over 30,000 British troops aimed at eliminating "no go" areas in Londonderry and Belfast.

Metelsky (2006) examined changes in trends of abortion-related violence after the passage of the 1994 Freedom of Access to Abortion Clinic Entrances Act (FACE), which was a response to the increased threat to the safety of abortion providers and the women who sought their services. The act increased the penalties for any persons who prevent or attempt to prevent a person from receiving reproductive health services. Using the GTD data, Metelsky showed that there was a decrease in tactics that were directly in violation of the FACE act, such as murders, bombings, arsons, butyric acid attacks, invasions, and blockades. Conversely, acts that fell outside the purview of FACE, such as hate mail and picketing, increased substantially after its passage. However, this conclusion was not supported in a recent study by Pridemore and Freilich (2007), who found neither deterrence nor backlash effects in an analysis of the impact of state-level legislation aimed at protecting abortion clinics, staff, and patients.

Other research that has conducted qualitative evaluations of the consequences of the United States' 1998 attempt to repress terrorist attacks in Afghanistan found that the efforts seemed to have increased rather than reduced subsequent levels of violence and support for terrorism. After the military strikes, Osama bin Laden's popularity increased throughout the region, intensifying public animosity toward the United States (Malvesti 2002). Also, the bombings created substantial collateral damage, prompting accusations that the United States placed little value on Afghan lives, thereby undermining the legitimacy of the U.S. strikes (Roberts 2002). Eppright (1997) also found a substantial increase in support for the terrorist organization Hezbollah after Israel's 1996 invasion of Lebanon—despite a significant drop in Hezbollah's rocket attacks in Israel (see also Greener-Barcham 2002).

Finally, in Dugan, LaFree, and Piquero's (2005) assessment of policies on aerial hijacking, the researchers found that when Cuba applied criminal sanctions against aerial hijackings, hijacking attempts to Cuba dropped substantially. However, few of these hijackings were terrorism. When the researchers limited the analysis to terrorist hijackings, they found no evidence that any of the policy initiatives of the 1970s were effective.

3. *Conclusions about Rational Choice Perspectives.* When examining the sensitivity of individual actors to the severity of punishment, researchers distinguish between specific (or special) deterrence, which

occurs when offenders already punished for breaking the law decide not to repeat their behavior because they fear punishment, and general deterrence, which occurs when members of the public decide not to break the law because they fear punishment. Expectations about specific deterrence in particular are called into question by terrorist tactics that require individuals to give their own lives, such as suicide bombings. It seems unreasonable to expect suicide terrorists to be deterred by threats of sanctions when they have already demonstrated willingness to sacrifice their lives for an organization. Nevertheless, according to research by Roberts (2007), most terrorists do value their own lives, and only a small percentage desire to participate in suicide operations.

In general, we find no conclusive evidence that terrorists are consistently deterred by harsh sanctions alone. This is unsurprising because much research on suicide bombers as well as terrorists using other methods shows that terrorists are often wholly willing to suffer extreme consequences to advance the goals of the organizations and movements to which they give their allegiance (Pedahzur 2005). In fact, in her examination of why terrorist groups desist, only two of the eight reasons that Cronin (2006) gives for a terrorist group's decline are directly related to deterrence through harsher sanctions.[2] Military intervention or repression has in some cases contributed to a group's decline, as was the case of the Shining Path in Peru and the Kurdistan Workers' Party in Turkey (Cronin 2006).

However, Cronin cautions that in other cases it appears that repression increased violence, as with the Chechen rebels in Russia and the Irish Republican Army (IRA) in Northern Ireland. Also, long-term repressive measures may compromise civil liberties and human rights, which can undermine governmental legitimacy (Cronin 2006). In an analysis of British efforts to stop IRA violence, LaFree, Dugan, and Korte (2009) found that while targeted assassinations, military curfews, and harsher criminal justice policies (internment, criminalization) either were ineffective or were associated with increased attacks, there was evidence that a military surge (Operation Motorman) was effective. In short, much evidence suggests that relying on severe sanctioning alone to counter terrorism is unlikely to be successful.

Deterrence strategies that increase sanction certainty, such as target

[2] Other reasons that terrorist groups might end include unsuccessful generational transition, achievement of the cause, transition to a legitimate political process, and transition out of terrorism to another form of violence such as crime or insurgency (Cronin 2006).

hardening, have been shown to deter airline hijacking (Dugan, LaFree, and Piquero 2005). Even in the case of suicide operations, where individuals are willingly sacrificing their own lives, there is some evidence that rational choice considerations are relevant. Anthony (2003) shows suicide terrorists sometimes delay their attack until success is more certain, reducing the chances that they are imprisoned rather than killed (see also Roberts 2007). Yet, even strategies based on increasing sanction certainty should be implemented with caution. Enders and Sandler (1993) found that the deterrence gained from installing metal detectors in airports and fortifying U.S. embassies is counterbalanced by an increase in other kinds of hostage-based attacks and assassinations, suggesting that the terrorists simply substituted tactics to avoid hard targets.

Although rational choice perspectives have been valuable for the study of terrorism, there is ample evidence that other theoretical perspectives could be equally, if not more, important. Particularly promising are alternatives based on legitimacy, anomie or strain, and situational perspectives. We consider each of these perspectives in the sections that follow.

B. Legitimacy

Weber (1948, 1968) defined legitimate power (or authority) as the probability that commands from a given source will be obeyed, adding that a basic criterion of legitimate power was voluntary submission. Instead of compliance based on power, force, or the fear of these things, Weber argued that legitimate authorities are obeyed because people feel they ought to be. More recently, a number of researchers have argued that individuals are more likely to obey laws when those laws, and the legal authorities executing them, are perceived to be legitimate (Tyler 1990; Sherman 1993). Studies have found support for these theories, linking high levels of perceived legitimacy to a range of desistance-related measures, including lower official crime rates (LaFree 1998), lower self-reported law breaking (Tyler 1990, 2003), lower reoffending rates (Paternoster et al. 1997), greater cooperation with and support for authorities (Sunshine and Tyler 2003; Tyler and Wakslak 2004), greater voluntary acceptance of police (Mastrofski, Snipes, and Supina 1996; Tyler and Huo 2002) and court (Tyler 1984) decisions, and less tolerance for crime in general (Stille 1996; Sampson and Bartusch 1998; for a review, see LaFree and Miller [forthcoming]).

While rational choice perspectives emphasize individual motivation to stop offending, legitimacy perspectives also recognize the importance of significant others in reducing deviance. Granovetter (1985) uses the term "embeddedness" to describe the social relations that link individuals to institutions and thereby regulate their behavior. Most individuals are embedded in a complex web of social connections that either makes them think long and hard before committing crime or simply provides enough surveillance to make crime more difficult. For most people, the first hurdles to crime are informal: the potential embarrassment they will face when their misdeeds become known to their families—spouse, children, parents, and other relatives. Beyond the family, there is the shame associated with those with whom they work or attend school, members of religious organizations or military companies, civic or fraternal organizations to which they belong, and so on. Legitimacy perspectives stress that crime is prevented when individuals are embedded in social networks that channel their behavior into noncriminal paths.

Perceived legitimacy should be especially important in explaining terrorism, because terrorists, unlike common criminals, actively seek public recognition. Jenkins (1975, p. 4) famously declared that "terrorism is theatre" and explained how terrorist attacks are often carefully choreographed to attract the attention of the electronic media and the international press. Terrorist and counterterrorist strategies can be conceptualized as a battle over legitimacy. Crenshaw (1983) argues that those who use terrorism generally deny the legitimacy of the target that they are opposing. For the state to succeed against terrorists, it must defend its legitimacy while delegitimizing terrorist challenges. As Crenshaw writes, "The power of terrorism is through political legitimacy, winning acceptance in the eyes of a significant population and discrediting the government's legitimacy" (1983, p. 25). Similar reasoning prompted Kydd and Walter to argue that the problem of responding to terrorism "is not a problem of applying force per se, but one of acquiring intelligence and affecting beliefs" (2006, p. 79).

Because of the dominance of rational choice explanations of terrorism and reactions to terrorism, most research to date has focused on whether counterterrorist policies significantly reduce violence. However, legitimacy perspectives provide strong theoretical reasons to expect counterterrorist policies sometimes to increase violence. Support for the argument that the imposition of punishment on a particular individual or group may increase future levels of violence is found in research on terrorism, and more generally in research from criminology and psychology. Researchers (Crenshaw 1983; Higson-Smith 2002) have long argued that terrorists frequently rely on the response of governments to mobilize the sympathies of would-be supporters. To the extent that government-based counterterrorist strategies outrage participants or energize a base of potential supporters, such strategies may increase the likelihood of further terrorist strikes. Sharp (1973) refers to this phenomenon as "jujitsu politics," and McCauley (2006) points out that because of this principle, responses to terrorism can be more dangerous than terrorism itself. Betts (2002, p. 28) argues that the contest between terrorists and counterterrorists is in effect tripartite, not only involving insurgents and counterinsurgents but gaining the support of those in the middle (see also Karstedt 2003). According to Betts, "the yet-unmobilized Muslim elites and masses of the Third World—those who were not already actively committed either to supporting Islamist radicalism or to combating it—are the target population in the middle" (2002, p. 28). There is some evidence that an understanding of these principles motivated bin Laden to support the attacks against the United States in 2001. Bin Laden appears to have understood that the administration of George W. Bush was hawkish in its foreign policy and in its attitude toward the use of military power, and in a November 2004 videotape, bin Laden bragged that al-Qaeda found it "easy for us to provoke the administration" (Kydd and Walter 2006, p. 71).

More generally, there is an extensive psychological literature supporting the conclusion that under the right circumstances, punishment may elicit increases in proscribed behavior. Thus, in their formulation of reactance theory, Brehm and Brehm argue that when an individual or group is threatened with some new form of social control, it is immediately motivated to act to eliminate this control and restore its original freedom (1981, p. 4). Relatedly, much psychological literature suggests that threats from out-groups generally increase the cohesion of in-groups and also the pressure on in-group deviants to conform and to support in-group leaders (LeVine and Campbell 1972; Duckitt and Fisher 2003).

The criminology literature also provides some support for legitimacy models. Thus, Sherman (1993) has argued that whether punishment results in deterrence will depend on whether offenders experience sanctioning as legitimate, the social bonds between the sanctioning agent and the individuals or groups being sanctioned, and the extent to which offenders can deny their shame by seeking support from others in the community. Support for the conclusion that punishment is more likely to be seen as legitimate by the punished when the punishment is perceived to be procedurally fair is supplied in several survey-based studies by Tyler (2003; for a review, see Tyler [2006]).

It is important to note that the perceived legitimacy of government actions is likely to be far more salient to the large number of potential supporters of terrorism than to the handful of individuals already actively involved in terrorism—a group that may be particularly unresponsive to government actions of any type. In other words, legitimacy perspectives predict that government responses to terrorist violence not only may embolden those already participating in terrorist attacks but also may encourage others to join terrorist organizations, to support those organizations, or to simply look the other way when they witness the activities of supporters. For example, based on face-to-face interviews in Egypt, Morocco, and Singapore, Franke and LaFree (2008) found that respondents who attributed greater legitimacy to the United States were less tolerant of terrorist attacks against the United States.

C. Anomie and Strain Perspectives

The dominance of rational choice perspectives in the study of terrorism has meant that research and policy have generally emphasized the possibility that increased punishment aimed at terrorists will reduce violence rather than examined whether rewards for nonterrorist behavior might also reduce violence. When we explicitly build the impact of rewards into rational choice conceptualizations, there are clear connections to anomie and strain theories. The core idea of strain perspectives is that if individuals or groups are treated unfairly, or they perceive themselves to be treated unfairly, they are more likely to resort to criminal violence, including terrorism. The idea that terrorism and other forms of political violence are directly related to strains caused by strongly held grievances has been one of the most common explanations to date and can be traced to a diverse set of theoretical concepts including relative deprivation (Gurr 1970; Feierabend, Feierabend, and Gurr 1972), social disorganization (Davies 1962; Smelser 1962), breakdown (Tilly, Tilly, and Tilly 1975; Useem 1985), tension (Lodhi and

Tilly 1973), and anomie (Merton 1938; Rosenfeld 2004). For convenience, we consider all of these distinct yet closely related concepts as grievances, defined by Gurr and Moore as "widely shared dissatisfaction among group members about their cultural, political and/or economic standing vis a vis dominant groups" (1997, p. 1081).

Merton (1938) identifies anomie as a cultural condition of frustration, in which values regarding goals and how to achieve them conflict with limitations on the means of achievement. Agnew's (1985, 1992) strain theory expands on Merton's work to identify both causes of strain and important coping and response mechanisms. He identifies strain broadly as any stimulus that is painful, aversive, or blocks the achievement of goals, including perceptions of injustice (cf. Berkowitz's [1989] reformulation of the frustration-aggression hypothesis to a pain-aggression hypothesis). Agnew (1992) also points out that strain is cumulative and varies with respect to magnitude, duration, recency, and clustering. Like Merton, Agnew regards crime as one of many potential coping mechanisms in response to strain. Furthermore, an individual's capacity to cope with adverse situations through legitimate means varies, depending on the degree of social support, social control, and resources such as problem-solving skills, self-esteem, and intelligence. Empirical evaluations of Agnew's strain theory have yielded support for many but not all of these components (Agnew and White 1992; Paternoster and Mazerolle 1994; Brezina 1996; Mazerolle 1998; Piquero and Sealock 2000).

The emphasis that the strain perspective places on grievances and mechanisms for coping with grievances strongly reflects the importance of alternative strategies for achieving change found in the terrorism literature (Ross and Gurr 1989; Crenshaw 1991; U.S. Institute of Peace 1999; Cronin 2006). In particular, research from terrorism consistently emphasizes the importance of public support for the use of violence as a means to an end. Given the availability of effective, legitimate alternatives for political expression, such as viable social movements or political parties, it is more likely that an organization's constituency will abandon terrorist tactics in favor of alternatives (Crenshaw 1991). For example, Ross and Gurr (1989) identify the electoral success of the *Parti Québécois* (PQ)—a legitimate, nonviolent political party—as one of the leading reasons that the *Front de Libération du Québec* (FLQ) experienced a decline in political strength. Similarly, the U.S. Institute of Peace (1999) report identifies the initiation of political negotiations as a way of increasing public support for a peaceful solution and diminishing public support for terrorism in the cases of the IRA and the PLO. Note also that this emphasis on the perceived fairness of political institutions links the strain perspective to the legitimacy perspective discussed above.

Although applying strain perspectives to the study of terrorism seems promising, thus far few studies have explicitly taken this approach. However, many of the subjects in Sageman's (2008) study of terrorist Islamic groups seemed to be experiencing strains of the type identified here. For example, Sageman finds that 60 percent of his subjects joined a terrorist organization while living in a country in which they did not grow up, and another 20 percent were second- or third-generation offspring of Muslim immigrants to Western countries. To the extent that these individuals were not well assimilated into their adopted countries, it is easy to imagine them experiencing a good deal of strain. And such strain is likely magnified when these individuals are in large part concentrated in diaspora communities with other similarly situated immigrants and children of immigrants. Work by Young and Dugan (2009) finds that terrorism is more common in countries where the policy process incorporates more opportunity to veto unpopular policies. In other words, when legitimate avenues to shift policy are cumbersome, terrorism is more prevalent. This suggests that those seeking change may be more frustrated by vetoed policy and are more willing to seek illegitimate, and possibly violent, means to promote change.

When rational choice models are expanded to include increasing benefits of nonterrorist behavior as well as increasing costs of terrorist behavior, they can also be linked directly to research that examines the impact of grievances on terrorist behavior. In empirical research on terrorism and other forms of civil violence, grievances have typically been measured indirectly by reference to variables assumed to cause grievances, especially economic inequality, unequal distribution of land, political discrimination, rapidly expanding educational opportunities, low caloric intake, rapid urbanization, high inflation rates, and unequal economic growth (Russett 1964; Feierabend and Feierabend 1966; Gurr 1968; Nagel 1976; Muller 1985). Early research in this area must be judged inconclusive, with some researchers (e.g., Nagel 1976; Muller 1985) finding strong connections between indirect measures of grievances and political violence, and other researchers (e.g., Tilly 1978; Hardy 1979; Weede 1981) finding either weak or no connections.

Recent research on connections between grievances and political violence has grown increasingly sophisticated, with more comprehensive measures of grievances and also analytic strategies that allow for the possibility that grievances interact with other variables to foster political violence. Thus, Gurr and Moore (1997, p. 1084) argue that grievances are a function of economic and political discrimination, demographic distress, lost political autonomy, and past repression. By economic and political discrimination, they mean the systematic and selective limitation of peoples' access to economic opportunities or political positions based on their ascriptive characteristics. Gurr (1993, pp. 42–48) argues that active discrimination may be the result of deliberate state policies or of pervasive social practice by dominant groups, while residual discrimination is the result of such policies and practices in the past. By demographic stress, Gurr and Moore (1997, p. 1084) refer to conditions of deprivation. For example, ethnopolitical groups with high demographic stress will have relatively high birth rates and poor public health conditions and will face pressures (e.g., forced development or resettlement) on traditional lands or resources. The historical loss of political autonomy is relevant because leaders of ethnonational and indigenous rights movements invoke it widely and with considerable effect. In their analysis of ethnopolitical rebellions in the 1980s, Gurr and Moore (1997) find evidence that rebellion is produced by grievances, although most of the effect is indirect through the impact of grievances on mobilization.

More recently, these ideas have been subsumed by the term "root causes" of terrorism, which Newman defines as the assertion that there is "some form of causal relationship between underlying social, economic, political and demographic conditions and terrorist activity" (2006, p. 749). The root causes proposition is that grievances and underlying conditions help to explain where, how, and why terrorism occurs. While this perspective is beginning to generate more empirical research (O'Neill 2002), the results are so far inconclusive. Thus, Krueger and Maleckova (2003) conclude that there is very little support for a causal connection between poverty (measured at the individual level) and participation in terrorism. By contrast, Ranstorp (2003, p. 11) argues that poverty not only may provide grounds for grievances but also may enable terrorist behavior through its links to poor or weak government and failed states. In a review, Newman concludes that "root causes tend to be most relevant in helping to understand terrorism associated with ideological, ethno-nationalist, and Islamist groups in developing countries" and that "root causes are a fruitful focus in counterterrorist policy" (2006, p. 770).

D. Situational Perspectives

The importance of situational explanations of crime was recognized by Sutherland (1947) in his distinction between "mechanistic" and "historical" explanations, although Sutherland never included situational considerations in his influential differential association theory. More recently, opportunity theorists (e.g., Hindelang, Gottfredson, and Garofalo 1978; Cohen and Felson 1979; Cook 1986) have formulated a situational model according to which crime results from "the convergence in space and time of . . . (1) motivated offenders, (2) suitable targets, and (3) the absence of capable guardians against a violation" (Cohen and Felson 1979, p. 589). Similarly, symbolic interaction theory has been applied to violent crime situations (e.g., Athens 1980; Felson 1987), and researchers have examined various situational aspects of offender behavior, including the "journey to crime" (Harries 1980; Rhodes and Conly 1981) and offense planning (Petersilia, Greenwood, and Lavin 1978; Feeney 1986; Erez 1987).

Situational theorists argue that individual patterns of everyday activity are strongly linked to the likelihood of involvement (as either victims or offenders) in illegal activity. In other words, the distribution of how and where individuals spend time, whether at home, at a place of employment, or at leisure activities, affects whether they will be suitable victims, encounter likely offenders, or lack capable guardians. If any one of these ingredients is missing, the crime may not occur. A target that is more exposed (visible, accessible), that is not well guarded, that is proximal in distance to the offender, and that is more attractive or desirable is more likely to be victimized. In addition, there are properties that define the specific crime itself, such as the ease of committing a burglary without a weapon (Cohen, Kluegel, and Land 1981). Fundamentally, this theory asserts that all humans have routine activities or patterns of conduct that they engage in as they live, work, and play. Crimes feed off the routine activities of legal actions. Thus, a pickpocketing will be more likely than an assault to occur against a stranger, during the day, and in an indoor location (LaFree and Birk-beck 1991).

LaFree and Birkbeck argue that "situational analysis involves the search for regularities in relationships between behavior and situations" (1991, p. 75). These regularities ought to occur in some situations more than others, and if they do, then it is possible to predict which situations will occur based on these characteristics. LaFree and Birkbeck test these ideas in a cross-national analysis of instrumental (robbery, pickpocketing/snatching) and expressive crime (assault). The situational characteristics they examined included personal features of the target (age, gender, relationship to offender), the degree of monitoring over the victim, and the type of domain (private versus public places). Their results showed that instrumental crimes were more situationally clustered than expressive crimes and that these characteristics could be used to predict crime types based on situational characteristics. For example, pickpocketings in the United States were far less likely than assaults to involve outside or nighttime locations, lone victims, or young (less than 40 years old) victims.

Situational perspectives may also provide a useful avenue for understanding terrorist behavior. Situational perspectives suggest paying greater attention to the circumstances that bring motivated offenders in close contact with suitable targets and in the absence of guardians. For example, Clarke and Newman (2006, p. 117) point out that the tools terrorists need almost always include cars and trucks, credit cards and cash, and cell phones. They provide three general approaches for tightening up controls on these tools: modify them to make them more difficult to use for terrorist purposes, tighten up their supply to make them more difficult to get, and track their distribution so authorities can tell who has acquired them (p. 121). The practice of modifying tools to make them more difficult to use for criminal purposes has a long history, beginning as far back as the end of the seventeenth century with the introduction of milled edges for silver coins to prevent them from being shaved to collect enough silver for additional coins (Clarke and Newman 2005). To make access to stolen cars more difficult, many are now equipped with built-in electronic immobilizers that make them harder to steal. Clark and Newman (2006, p. 123) point out that terrorist and criminal money laundering would be much more difficult if governments produced no bills in denominations larger than the equivalent of US$20—$1 million in $20 bills weighs

about 115 pounds and fills two suitcases! Similarly, transponders routinely fitted to all vehicles, together with monitoring points on high-
ways, could make it much more difficult for terrorists as well as ordinary criminals to obtain and use stolen vehicles.

We should also remain open to the possibility that broader situational forces may produce rapid rises and declines in terrorist attacks.
The choice of American embassies in Kenya and Tanzania, where security was relatively lax, for the truck bombings of August 1998 suggests that terrorists sometimes do take into account the suitability of
their targets and may be deterred by target hardening (U.S. Institute
of Peace 1999; Hamm 2007). Recent research on the attack patterns
of 53 foreign terrorist groups (LaFree, Yang, and Crenshaw, forthcoming) confirms that at the aggregate level, target choices of terrorist
groups are strongly situational: they are far more likely to strike domestic
than transnational targets. Similarly, terrorists frequently take advantage
of readily available weapons. Thus, a report by Burgoon and Varadan
(2006) claims that the rapid rise of the use of improvised explosive devices (IEDs) by terrorists and insurgents in contemporary Iraq after 2003
can be explained in large part by the situational fact that the overthrow
of the Hussein government left a vast amount of the raw materials for
constructing IEDs scattered throughout the country.

Unlike rational choice perspectives, situational perspectives do not
rely on solving crime by changing the motivation of offenders or their
bonds with others. For example, Clarke and Newman argue that we
should not waste much time on changing "the hearts and minds of
terrorists" because the motivation for terrorism results in complex
long-term social, cultural, and psychological forces that are difficult or
impossible to alter (2006, pp. 11–12). Instead, they argue that it is
easier to reduce opportunities for terrorism, and therefore we should
focus on the situational features of society that make terrorism easier.
This means, among other things, concentrating on the most vulnerable
targets, designing antiterrorist strategies that are unique to distinct
forms of terrorism, and accepting that the threat of terrorism will never
completely disappear.

Clarke and Newman (2006) apply situational crime prevention concepts explicitly to terrorism, arguing that when thinking about terrorism, it is critical to focus on very specific forms of terrorism rather
than thinking about terrorism in general. They claim that the opportunities for committing different forms of terrorism—aircraft hijacking,

suicide bombing, assassination, hostage taking, chemical attacks—are likely to differ from each other, and hence, successful preventive interventions must also differ (pp. 11–12). The authors claim that even a specific form of terrorism—like suicide bombing—may require very different preventative actions in different political and social contexts. By systematically analyzing the specific situational opportunities that terrorists exploit, the authors suggest that governments can direct their efforts toward developing more effective means to block those opportunities.

E. Conclusions about Terrorism Theories

The mixed findings for rational choice models that emphasize punishment strongly suggest that we should be cautious before implementing counterterrorism strategies that attempt to stop terrorism only by raising its costs. Others have suggested instead that strategies aimed at decreasing the benefits of terrorism through improving the legitimacy of government, solving widespread grievances that produce strain, or attending to situational features that increase the costs of terrorism might be more effective (Frey and Luechinger 2002; Frey 2004; Braithwaite 2005). While largely untested, these strategies include negotiating with groups, diffusing media attention, providing social services and other support to target populations, and developing situational policies that reduce the risk of terrorism. Historical evidence suggests that conciliatory policies, such as those in Italy in the early 1980s (Chenoweth 2007) and more recent negotiations in Northern Ireland (O'Leary 2005), have at times been effective in ending terrorism. But despite some successes, there is also evidence that similar agreements have failed in other contexts (e.g., Zirakzadeh 2002).

The research described above demonstrates very different outcomes in responses to government efforts to reduce terrorist violence. In some cases, terrorists have been strengthened after harsh efforts by the government to punish perpetrators. During the height of the violence in Northern Ireland, one IRA member was quoted as saying that "the British security forces are the best recruitin' officer we have" (Geraghty 2000, p. 36). Yet, in other cases, such as when the U.S. government imposed harsher sanctions against those convicted of abortion-related violence, the level of violence appears to have decreased—suggesting some value in government deterrence efforts. The British government's use of military surge in the early 1970s appears to have been

effective, but more recently, conciliatory strategies such as bigovern-
mentalism, consociation, and federalizing institutions have also shown
promise (O'Leary 2005). In short, the divergent reactions by terrorists
across differing contexts strongly suggest that selecting an appropriate
counterterrorism strategy is not a task that should be taken lightly.
Casual generalizations from one context to another could increase both
human and material costs.

III. The Promise of Open-Source Databases on Terrorism

The challenges in collecting valid data on terrorism through traditional
outlets such as official records or victimization and self-report survey
data have encouraged researchers to seek alternative sources for data.
In particular, there has been a growing interest in unclassified, open-
source research on terrorism. One of the most notable advances in this
area has been the construction of large and comprehensive data sets
tracing terrorist attacks over time. LaFree and Dugan (2007) describe
eight of these event databases, with varying coverage going back as far
as 1968. Analyses based on these open-source-event databases have
provided important insights into a wide range of terrorism-related empirical questions, including trends in terrorism over time (Enders and
Sandler 2006; LaFree and Dugan, forthcoming), the deterrent impact
of new antiterrorism policies (Dugan, LaFree, and Piquero 2005;
LaFree, Dugan, and Korte 2009), and the economic impact of terrorist
attacks (Enders and Sandler 2006; Greenbaum, Dugan, and LaFree
2007). However, these data sources have faced at least three serious
limitations. First, efforts to collect data on terrorism by government
agencies are limited by the fact that either they are influenced by political considerations or they face the perception that they are influenced by political considerations. While this has also long been a problem with official crime data in general (e.g., Geis 1972; Skogan 1984),
the political nature of terrorism makes it an especially difficult problem
with this specific form of criminality.

Second, many of the organizations that have assembled data on terrorism in the past have been unable to maintain consistent data collection strategies over time. For example, the data collected by the
Pinkerton Global Intelligence Service (PGIS), which we rely on ex-
tensively in this report, ended data collection in 1997. More recently,

the MIPT database, which was collected by RAND after 1998, stopped reporting terrorism data in March 2008.

The final and most important limitation of past databases is that although instances of domestic terrorism greatly outnumber transnational terrorist attacks, until recently most cases of domestic terrorism were not included in existing long-term publicly available databases. In general, transnational terrorist attacks are those involving a national or a group of nationals from one country crossing international borders and attacking targets in another country. Domestic attacks are those involving a national or a group of nationals attacking targets in their home country.[3] Part of the reason for excluding domestic attacks is bureaucratic. Many governmental agencies, including the U.S. State Department, have had a long history of concentrating on transnational terrorist attacks (Pluchinsky 2006). But beyond the tradition of dividing bureaucratic responsibility for terrorism according to transnational-domestic distinctions was the practical challenge of collecting global data on a very large number of incidents: sources that have compared domestic and transnational terrorist attacks (Schmid 2004; Asal and Rethemeyer 2007; LaFree and Dugan 2007; Neumayer and Plumper 2008) have concluded that the former outnumber the latter by as much as seven to one.

The gravity of excluding domestic attacks can be felt when we consider that two of the most noteworthy terrorist events of the 1990s, the March 1995 nerve gas attack on the Tokyo subway and the April 1995 bombing of the federal office building in Oklahoma City, would remain unrecorded because both lack any known foreign involvement.

The data presented in this essay do not face any of these three limitations: they were collected by two nongovernmental organizations; we imposed a similar, consistent format on the data through the merger process; and the resulting database includes both transnational and domestic attacks.

We present data on terrorist attacks from 1970 to 2006 based on a joint project between START and the RAND Corporation (Dugan et al. 2008), in which we synthesized transnational and domestic data from 1970 to 1997 from the GTD (see LaFree and Dugan 2007) with

[3] Further complexity is added when the country of the attack and the nationality of the target are different. For example, attacks by Nigerian nationals against the Nigerian embassy in the United States have generally been treated as transnational by most open-source databases, even though they involve nationals from one country attacking nationals from the same country.

transnational data from the RAND Terrorism Chronology (Jenkins and Johnson 1975) for the same years, and transnational and domestic incident data from 1998 to 2006 from the RAND-MIPT database (MIPT 2002). The resulting longitudinal data set contains 77,163 cases and is, to our knowledge, the most comprehensive open-source database on terrorist attacks assembled to date.

Despite the challenges outlined above, collecting information on terrorist events has one considerable advantage: terrorists, unlike most common criminals, actively seek public recognition. The media are so central to contemporary terrorist groups that some researchers have argued that the birth of modern terrorism should be directly linked to the launch by the United States of the first television satellite in 1968 (Hoffman 1998, pp. 136–37). This invention meant that news could be transmitted for the first time from local studios back to network headquarters almost instantaneously. That terrorists are seeking to attract attention through the media means that media coverage can tell us far more about terrorism than other types of crime. Thus, while no responsible researcher would seriously argue that we can accurately track burglary or car theft rates by studying electronic and print media, it is much more defensible to claim that we can track terrorist attacks in this way. It is hard to imagine that it is any longer possible for an aerial hijacking or politically motivated assassination—even in remote parts of the world—to elude the scrutiny of the global media.

Event databases on terrorism also have another important advantage. One of the most serious limitations of cross-national crime research is that it has been focused overwhelmingly on a small number of highly industrialized Western-style democracies (Butchart and Engstrom 2002; Stamatel 2006). In a review of cross-national research on homicide, LaFree (1999) found that most prior research had been based on fewer than 40 of the world's countries. And of course these countries are not a random sample of the nations of the world but rather strongly overrepresent Europe and North America while almost entirely excluding Africa, the Middle East, and Asia. By contrast, the event data we present in this essay include information on every known terrorist attack from any country in the world.

Before turning to the descriptive results, in the next section we describe the merged, open-source-event database created by START and the RAND Corporation. Although these data are more extensive than earlier event databases, they also have important limitations, which we return to in the conclusions.

IV. The Merged GTD-RAND Database

The data analyzed in this essay are based on a standardized, comprehensive database on both transnational and domestic terrorist events from 1970 until 2006. To create this database, we combined data from the GTD from 1970 to 1997 with data from the RAND Terrorism Chronology from 1998 to 2006. We began the GTD in 2002 by computerizing data originally collected by the PGIS, including more than 67,000 events that occurred around the world from 1970 to 1997 (LaFree and Dugan 2007). PGIS applied a standard definition to its terrorism data collection for 37 years. From 1970 to 1997, PGIS trained researchers to identify and record terrorism incidents from wire services (including Reuters and the Foreign Broadcast Information Service [FBIS]), U.S. State Department reports, other U.S. and foreign government reporting, U.S. and foreign newspapers (including the *New York Times*, British *Financial Times*, *Christian Science Monitor*, *Washington Post*, *Washington Times*, and *Wall Street Journal*), and information provided by PGIS offices around the world.

We completed computerizing the original PGIS data in December 2005.[4] We refer to the resulting database—constructed on the original PGIS platform—as the GTD. In April 2006, the START Consortium received additional funding from the Human Factors Division of the Department of Homeland Security to extend the GTD beyond 1997. The extended GTD was not yet complete when this essay was being prepared. The new GTD data collection captures information on more than 120 variables and stores the original open-source texts upon which each case is based. The START Consortium released an updated, synthesized version of the complete GTD in June 2009 (see http://www.start.umd.edu/gtd).

In 1972, the RAND Corporation, a nonprofit policy research institution, began collecting a chronology of information on international terrorist attacks. Although there were major changes in staffing of

---

[4] Most of the 1993 data in the GTD were lost by the original collectors (LaFree and Dugan 2007). We were able to reconstruct aggregate estimates provided in a surviving report. In 2006, we re-collected the 1993 data, but the new data collection did not match the totals from the original data collection. We are still working on this problem, but it is unlikely that the original PGIS data for 1993 will ever be fully restored.

this project and resources supporting it over the years (see Dugan et al. 2008), RAND continued collecting the chronology continuously through 1997. Data collection on the chronology resumed in April 2001 under the sponsorship of the National Memorial Institute for the Prevention of Terrorism (MIPT), an institute created with funding from Congress in the wake of the Oklahoma City bombing of 1995.

One of the most important changes in the new RAND partnership with MIPT was that, starting in 1998, the chronology began including domestic terrorism cases. Because the GTD included domestic and international attacks from 1970 to 1997 and the RAND-MIPT chronology included domestic and international attacks from 1998 on, synthesizing the two databases had obvious appeal. With funding from the National Institute of Justice, a team from START led by the authors of this essay worked with a team from RAND led by Kim Cragin to develop a continuous GTD-RAND database from 1970 to the present. The procedures are described in detail in Dugan et al. (2008). Major steps included translating the original GTD data into the same format as the RAND data, adding the RAND data to the GTD data after 1998, and removing duplicate cases for the years in which there was GTD-RAND overlap: transnational cases from 1970 to 1997.

The first major challenge we encountered in merging the two databases was that they employed different definitions of terrorism. The terrorism definition used by PGIS, which we used to create the original GTD, was "the threatened or actual use of illegal force and violence by non-state actors to attain a political, economic, religious or social goal through fear, coercion or intimidation" (LaFree and Dugan 2007, p. 184).

In order to construct a synthesized version of the GTD and the RAND-MIPT data, in this essay we relied instead on the definition of terrorism that RAND adopted in 1998:[5]

> *Terrorism* is defined by the nature of the act, not by the identity of the perpetrators or the nature of the cause. Terrorism is violence, or the threat of violence, calculated to create an atmosphere of fear and alarm. These acts are designed to coerce others into ac-

---

[5] RAND's pre-1998 definition of international terrorism was: "Incidents in which terrorists go abroad to strike their targets, select victims or targets that have connections with a foreign state (e.g. diplomats, foreign businessmen, offices of foreign corporations), or create international incidents by attacking airline passengers, personnel, and equipment" (Cordes et al. 1984, p. 1).

tions they would otherwise not undertake or refrain from taking actions that they desired to take. All terrorist acts are crimes. Many would also be violations of the rules of war, if a state of war existed. This violence or threat of violence is generally directed against civilian targets. The motives of all terrorists are political, and terrorist actions are generally carried out in a way that will achieve maximum publicity. The perpetrators are members of an organized group and, unlike other criminals, they often claim credit for their acts. Finally, terrorist acts are intended to produce effects beyond the immediate physical damage they cause; having long-term psychological repercussions on a particular audience. (Hoffman and Hoffman 1998, p. 89)

Although this definition is more detailed than the original PGIS definition of terrorism, note that the basic elements of both are quite similar: threatened or actual use of illegal force, directed against civilian targets, by nonstate actors, in order to attain a political goal, through fear, coercion, or intimidation. We turn now to a descriptive analysis of the synthesized data.

V. Descriptive Analysis of the GTD-RAND Data, 1970–2006

In this section, we first provide an overview of worldwide terrorism by showing overall trends of terrorist violence over time and across global regions. We then present the 20 most active terrorist organizations and the 20 most frequently attacked countries during this period. We also describe patterns of fatalities, targeting, tactics, and weapons.

A. Patterns of Terrorist Violence

Figure 1 presents trends in global terrorism from 1970 to 2006.[6] The trend lines were strongly affected by the U.S.-led invasion of Iraq that began on March 20, 2003. The RAND-MIPT data, like the GTD data, are designed to exclude cases involving open combat between opposing armed forces, even if these are nonstate actors. But during wartime, it is often difficult to distinguish between acts of terror, other types of criminal violence, and violent acts resulting from warfare. Because of these considerations, one recent report concludes that no intentional killings of civilians in Iraq during this period should be

---

[6] The estimate for 1993 in this figure and in the other trend figures in this chapter was calculated by taking the average value for 1992 and 1994.

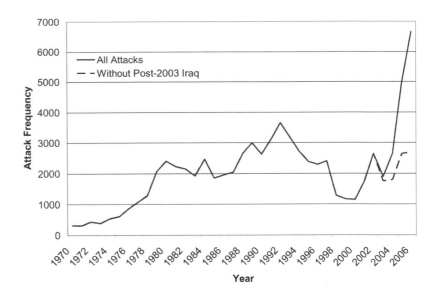

FIG. 1.—Global terrorism attacks, 1970–2006 ($n = 77,163$)

counted as terrorist attacks (Human Security Brief 2008, p. 2). While we agree that the war in Iraq makes distinguishing terrorist attacks from other types of violence difficult, we also argue that there are clearly many attacks taking place in Iraq that fit the definition of terrorism being applied here. Nevertheless, we thought it useful to distinguish terrorist attacks in Iraq from those occurring elsewhere in the post-2003 trend data presented in this essay.

According to figure 1, there are two early peaks (1980 and 1992), ending with a series peak in 2006. Through 1976, recorded terrorist attacks were relatively infrequent, with fewer than 1,000 incidents reported each year. However, from 1977 to 1979, the frequency of reported attacks nearly doubled, peaking in 1980 with 2,407 events.[7] The

[7] We recognize that the relatively small number of recorded incidents from 1970 through 1976 could be in part a consequence of the fact that PGIS data collectors simply invested fewer resources in data collection during the early years of data collection. Based on an analysis of the data, we do know that the early data are based on fewer recorded sources than the later data. Thus, for the year 1970, PGIS reported only six different sources, but by 1977 it reported 53 separate sources. However, this assessment is further complicated by the fact that PGIS data collectors frequently excluded their sources in the early years; 68 percent of the cases in 1970 and 42 percent in 1977 included no sources. Media-related information sources also increased dramatically during this period, especially media penetration of the industrializing world, which might account for at least part of the increase in rates since 1970.

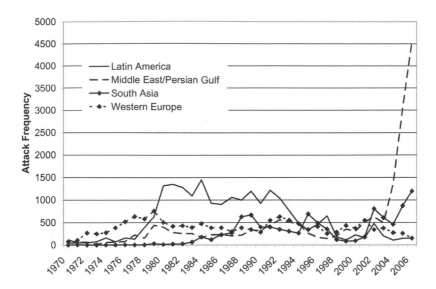

FIG. 2.—Terrorist attacks by region, 1970–2006 (high-frequency regions; $n = 63,454$)

next peak in 1992 shows 3,654 attacks worldwide. Following 1992, annual attacks decline before reaching a low point of 1,151 in 2000—the year before the 9/11 attacks. Following 9/11, terrorist attacks again increased considerably, reaching a global peak of 6,660 in 2006. Figure 1 shows that nearly one-half of all terrorist attacks in the GTD-RAND database after 2003 took place in Iraq. Without these cases, total attacks in 2006 (2,692) are about the same as they were at the prewar 2002 level (2,648).

To develop geographic comparisons for terrorist attacks, we next divided the countries of the world into nine major regions (for a list of countries in each region, see app. A).[8] Figure 2 shows the trends for the four most highly active regions, and figure 3 shows the trends for the five least active regions. Perhaps the most obvious conclusion from

[8] Note that for purposes of this analysis, we treat the country as the target. Thus, an attack on the U.S. embassy in Switzerland would be treated here as a Swiss attack. Similarly, an attack on a Swiss ambassador living in the United States would be counted as a U.S. attack. Although it is the case that the vast majority of cases in the database involve attacks where the location of the target and the nationality of the target are the same, there are some interesting variations across attacks, depending on the geographical country attacked, the nationality of the perpetrators, and the nationality of the target. We are exploring these issues in much greater detail in ongoing research.

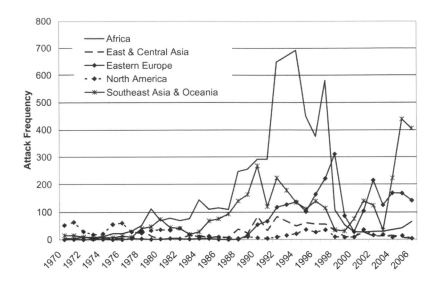

FIG. 3.—Terrorist attacks by region, 1970–2006 (low-frequency regions; n = 13,704)

figure 2 is that attacks in the highly active regions vary greatly over time. For the years 1970–79, terrorism was mostly a Western European problem. Well-known attacks include terrorist campaigns by Republicans and Loyalists in Northern Ireland, the Red Brigades in Italy, and ETA in Spain. However, after peaking in 1979 with 758 attacks, terrorism in Western Europe drops to an average of 390 attacks per year. Annual attacks in Latin America, by contrast, continue to rise after 1979 and peak in 1984 with over 1,400 incidents—driven especially by *Sendero Luminoso* in Peru and the Movement of the Revolutionary Left in Chile. After 1984, Latin America averages about 580 attacks a year but with large fluctuations. It is not until the mid-1990s that total Latin American attacks fall below total attacks for South Asia (1995) and the Middle East (1998). From 2002 to the end of the series, South Asia and the Middle East overtake Western Europe and Latin America to have the highest number of terrorist attacks per year. If we drop post-2003 Iraq from the analysis, trends for the Middle East/Persian Gulf region fall to about one-half those in South Asia, with 573 attacks in 2006.

Figure 3 also shows considerable variation over time for the five regions with lower frequencies of terrorist attacks. The frequency of

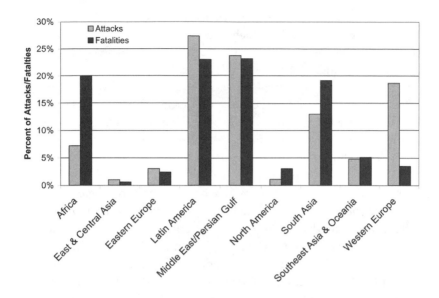

FIG. 4.—Worldwide terrorist attacks by region, 1970–2006 ($n = 74,258$)

attacks in Africa is largely driven by activity between 1984 and 1998 when there were well over 100 attacks per year. A closer examination of these attacks shows that a high proportion of attacks occurred in South Africa (28 percent) and Algeria (24 percent), two countries with very different types of terrorism that nevertheless both experienced massive terrorism campaigns during this period. The other regions in figure 3 generally show increasing trends over the entire period. Southeast Asia and Oceania have two peaks, the first in 1990 with 267 attacks and the second in 2005 with 438 attacks. The more recent surge of attacks in this region is driven especially by a large number of attacks in Thailand.

We next compare the total distribution of attacks and fatalities by region. Figure 4 shows that more than half of the terrorist attacks in the merged database (51.2 percent) occurred in Latin America (27.4 percent) and the Middle East (23.8 percent).[9] Western Europe (18.7 percent) and South Asia (13.0 percent) follow, accounting for another 30 percent of all terrorist attacks. None of the remaining regions ac-

[9] The RAND 1993 attacks are included in this and other nontrend figures, while the GTD cases are missing.

count for more than 10 percent of total attacks, and North America
and East and Central Asia each account for only 1 percent of total
attacks. When we exclude the post-2003 Iraq cases from this distribution, the Middle East/Persian Gulf region ranks third, accounting
for 16 percent of all terrorist attacks—falling behind Western Europe,
which accounts for 20 percent of all attacks. Without wartime Iraq,
Latin America accounts for nearly 30 percent of all attacks.

Figure 4 also shows substantial variation across regions in terms of
the relationship of attacks to fatalities. In particular, Africa stands out
for having a larger percentage of total attacks than fatalities while
Western Europe stands out for having a larger percentage of attacks
than fatalities. When we looked more closely at the fatality rates for
Africa, we found that four countries averaged 10 or more fatalities per
attack: Rwanda (22.6), Chad (15.4), Burundi (13.9), and Mozambique
(10.1). Much of the terrorist violence in Rwanda and Burundi was
driven by the conflict between the Tutsis and the Hutus. The Lord's
Resistance Army in Uganda also staged a series of terrorist attacks with
large numbers of fatalities during the period spanned by the data. By
contrast, groups such as the IRA and ETA operating in Western Europe staged large numbers of attacks with relatively few fatalities.

B. The Most Active Terrorist Organizations

In table 1, we present rankings of the 20 most active terrorist organizations found in the GTD-RAND data and the 20 most fatal.
Organizations that rank in both lists are highlighted in boldface.
The largest number of attacks for any terrorist group in the database
(Shining Path) is nearly 3,000 attacks, and the twentieth ranked group
(al-Fatah) is associated with nearly 250 attacks. Only five terrorist
groups in the merged database have over 1,000 attacks during the 37
years spanned by the data. The number of attacks committed by the
most active terrorist groups in the list is substantially higher than the
number committed by less active groups. Thus, number 1, Shining
Path, was responsible for more than 10 times as many attacks as number 20, al-Fatah.

Note that 11 of the terrorist organizations are in the top 20 for both
total attacks and fatalities. Several major Western European terrorist
groups had lots of attacks but proportionately fewer fatalities. Thus,
ETA and the Corsican National Liberation Front are on the top 20
list for attacks but not fatalities, and the IRA moves from number 4

TABLE 1

20 Most Active Terrorist Organizations in Terms of Attack Frequency and Fatalities, 1970–2006

Rank	Most Frequent Perpetrators		Most Fatalities	
	Organization	Frequency	Organization	Fatality Count
1	**Shining Path (SL)**	2,817	**Shining Path (SL)**	6,057
2	Basque Fatherland and Freedom (ETA)	1,378	Liberation Tigers of Tamil Eelam (**LTTE**)	4,038
3	**Farabundo Marti National Liberation Front (FMLN)**	1,249	Al Qaeda	3,460
4	**Irish Republican Army (IRA)**	1,165	Hutus	3,222
5	**Revolutionary Armed Forces of Colombia (FARC)**	1,066	Mozambique National Resistance Movement (MNR)	2,247
6	National Liberation Army of Colombia (ELN)	784	**Farabundo Marti National Liberation Front (FMLN)**	1,856
7	**Hamas (Islamic Resistance Movement)**	608	**Revolutionary Armed Forces of Colombia (FARC)**	1,791
8	**Liberation Tigers of Tamil Eelam (LTTE)**	569	Tanzim Qa'idat al-Jihad fi Bilad al-Rafidayn	1,646
9	Manuel Rodriguez Patriotic Front (FPMR)	568	**Nicaraguan Democratic Force (FDN)**	1,342
10	**Kurdish Workers' Party (PKK)**	535	National Union for the Total Independence of Angola (UNITA)	1,151
11	**New People's Army (NPA)**	472	**New People's Army (NPA)**	1,084
12	Corsican National Liberation Front (FLNC)	455	**Kurdistan Workers' Party (PKK)**	1,071
13	**Taliban**	438	Lord's Resistance Army (LRA)	1,060
14	Tupac Amaru Revolutionary Movement (MRTA)	412	Hezbollah	899
15	Communist Party of Nepal-Maoists (CPN-M)	403	**Taliban**	876
16	M-19 (Movement of April 19)	321	Tutsi	858
17	**Nicaraguan Democratic Force (FDN)**	287	Armed Islamic Group (GIA)	807
18	People's Liberation Front (JVP)	274	**Irish Republican Army (IRA)**	728
19	Movement of the Revolutionary Left (MIR) (Chile)	257	National Liberation Army of Colombia (ELN)	646
20	al-Fatah	243	**Hamas (Islamic Resistance Movement)**	630

TABLE 2

20 Top Ranking Countries in Terms of Total Terrorist Attacks and
Fatalities, 1970–2006

	Most Frequently Attacked		Most Fatalities	
Rank	Country	Frequency	Country	Fatality Count
1	Iraq	7,511	Iraq	19,415
2	Colombia	5,180	India	10,035
3	Peru	4,147	Colombia	7,608
4	India	3,907	Sri Lanka	7,086
5	El Salvador	3,163	Peru	6,769
6	Spain	3,067	El Salvador	6,698
7	Turkey	2,693	Algeria	6,338
8	Northern Ireland	2,690	Pakistan	4,742
9	Israel	2,436	Guatemala	4,325
10	Pakistan	2,212	United States	3,265
11	West Bank/Gaza	2,022	Philippines	3,169
12	Chile	1,903	Lebanon	3,077
13	France	1,876	Rwanda	2,693
14	Lebanon	1,653	Burundi	2,668
15	Guatemala	1,628	Turkey	2,414
16	Italy	1,509	Mozambique	2,344
17	Philippines	1,475	South Africa	2,293
18	Sri Lanka	1,398	Russia	2,196
19	South Africa	1,384	Nicaragua	2,170
20	Algeria	1,142	Israel	2,017

on attacks to number 18 on fatalities. However, note that while al
Qaeda is missing from the list of top 20 groups with the largest number
of attacks (with just 32 recorded attacks, al Qaeda ranked 134 among
terrorist groups), al Qaeda ranks third in terms of total fatalities. The
top two most lethal organizations, Shining Path and the Liberation
Tigers of Tamil Eelam, have also been responsible for large numbers
of attacks, ranking first and eighth.

C. Most Targeted Countries

Table 2 shows the top 20 countries in terms of total attacks and
fatalities, with countries on both lists highlighted in boldface. Iraq
ranks first in terms of total attacks. However, when we exclude Iraqi
attacks since 2003, it drops to 196 attacks and is no longer in the top
20 countries. Countries ranked second, third, fifth, twelfth, and fif-
teenth are all Latin American—a region that dominated terrorism statistics during the 1980s and early 1990s. Besides Iraq, three other Mid-

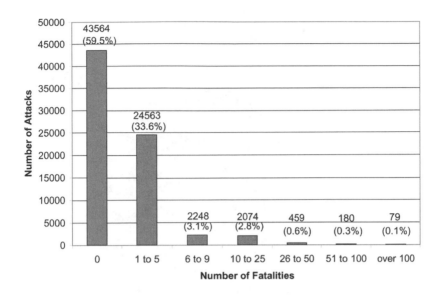

Fig. 5.—Fatalities per attack, 1970–2006 ($n = 73,167$)

dle Eastern/Persian Gulf countries are in the top 20 for total attacks: Turkey, Israel, and the West Bank/Gaza. India ranks fourth in terms of total attacks.

Table 2 shows that Iraq also ranks first in terms of fatalities. However, if we drop the post-2003 cases, Iraq again falls out of the top 20 with 681 fatalities, and India has the most fatalities (10,035). Fourteen countries were in the top 20 for both attacks and fatalities. However, six countries (Spain, Northern Ireland, West Bank/Gaza, Chile, France, and Italy) were in the top 20 for total attacks but not total fatalities, and six countries (United States, Rwanda, Burundi, Mozambique, Russia, and Nicaragua) were in the top 20 for total fatalities but not total attacks. As we have already seen, Western European countries tend to have a lower ratio of fatalities to attacks, while Middle Eastern, African, and East and Central Asian countries tend to have a higher rate of fatalities to attacks. That the United States is in the top 20 list for fatalities but not attacks is due mostly to the 9/11 attacks.

D. Fatalities per Attack

Figure 5 shows the distribution of fatalities per attack. Some may be surprised that in 59.5 percent of the events included in the database,

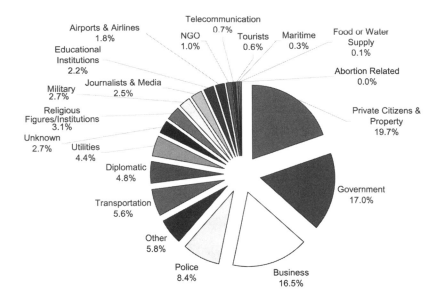

FIG. 6.—Distribution of terrorist targets globally, 1970–2006 ($n = 74,263$)

there were no fatalities. In many cases, terrorist groups target property and do not intend to cause casualties. In other cases, they plan to cause casualties but fail. Moreover, some well-known terrorist groups such as the IRA and ETA frequently provide warnings before attacks to minimize casualties. Twenty years ago these considerations led Jenkins to suggest that "terrorists want a lot of people watching, not a lot of people dead" (1985, p. 12). Of course, it is still the case that 40.5 percent of the cases in the GTD-RAND data (or more than 29,000 attacks) involved at least one fatality. The attacks that are especially worrisome are the 0.11 percent (or 79 attacks) that produced more than 100 fatalities. Jenkins has recently revisited his earlier statement and, after reviewing the stated plans of terrorist groups operating in the early twenty-first century, concluded that indeed "many of today's terrorists want a lot of people watching and a lot of people dead" (2007, p. 119).

E. Selecting Targets

Figure 6 presents the distribution of terrorist targets worldwide. There is considerable variation in terrorist targeting, with the most

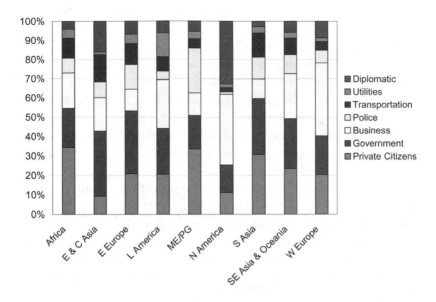

Fig. 7.—Targets of terrorism, 1970–2006 ($n = 56,761$)

common target (private citizens and property) representing less than 20 percent of the total. Together, private citizens, property, and businesses account for more than 35 percent of all terrorist attacks in the merged database. The next most common targets are police,[10] transportation, diplomats, and utilities. The remaining targets are attacked less than 4 percent of the time and include religious figures or institutions, noncombatant military, journalists and other media, and educational institutions. Important target types in the "other" category include other terrorists or criminals, professionals, and sports figures. If we exclude the post-2003 Iraqi cases from the analysis, businesses and government switch rankings, although both still account for about 17 percent of the attacks. Also, police account for only 5.3 percent of the attacks (down from 8.4 percent), and transportation and diplomats account for a slightly larger percentage of attacks (6.1 percent and 5.2 percent, respectively).

In figure 7, we present the relative frequencies of terrorist targets for each region. We limit the comparisons here to the four most com-

[10] We included attacks against the police in the merged database only if police were not acting in concert with and under the direct authority of the military apparatus.

mon targets and the three additional target types that were among the top four in at least one of the regions. According to figure 7, private citizens are the modal target for Africa, the Middle East/Persian Gulf, and South Asia. Many attacks on private citizens took place in public spaces, such as marketplaces and sidewalk cafés. The most common target in East and Central Asia, Eastern Europe, and Southeast Asia and Oceania is government. Many of these attacks were directed toward government offices or the homes or vehicles of government officials. Businesses are most commonly targeted in Latin America, North America, and Western Europe, followed closely by government in Latin America, private citizens in Western Europe, and diplomats in North America. Diplomats are targeted in North America nearly as often as businesses. Diplomats are also common targets in Eastern and Central Asia, ranking third behind government and businesses. Transportation infrastructure was among the top four targets in five of the regions, but utilities were among the top four targets only in Latin America.

Note that compared to other regions, terrorists operating in the Middle East/Persian Gulf are more likely to target private citizens and police and less likely to target government and businesses. If we remove post-2003 Iraq from the analysis, private citizens still remain the most common target for the Middle East/Persian Gulf, but businesses and government become second and third most important, and attacks on police drop to sixth most important.

Figure 8 presents trends for the top four targets over time. Here we see that private citizens, government, and businesses track each other closely until around 2001, when attacks against private citizens increased substantially, while attacks against businesses remained relatively stable at around 200 per year. Shortly after this divergence in 2004, attacks against police rise dramatically to become the most common target in 2006, with more than 2,100 attacks. However, more than 70 percent of all attacks against police after 2003 took place in Iraq.

F. Selecting Tactics and Weapons

We turn now to a discussion of the tactical choices made by terrorists. For reference, appendix B lists the definitions of tactics adopted for the GTD-RAND database. Figure 9 shows the total distribution of terrorist tactics. Perhaps the most striking result here is that half of all terrorist attacks are bombings. More than a quarter of the attacks

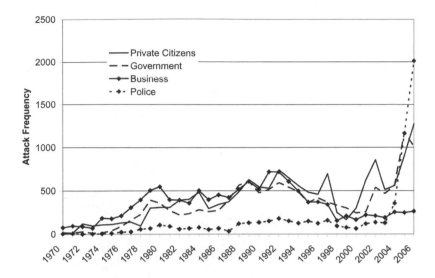

FIG. 8.—Top four terrorist targets, 1970–2006 ($n = 47,611$)

are armed attacks. Because armed attacks require weapons rather than explosives, terrorists in these cases are more likely to have direct contact with targets. The next most common tactic is assassination, followed by kidnapping, barricade/hostage situations, and arson. Figure 9 shows that hijacking and unconventional attacks (including chemical weapons) were rare, jointly accounting for only about one-half of 1 percent of all cases.

In figure 10, we present distributions of the four most common terrorist tactics by region. Perhaps the most striking comparison is between bombings and armed attacks. While, in the aggregate, bombings are about twice as common as armed attacks (see fig. 9), figure 10 shows that there is substantial regional variation in bombings. Bombings were especially common in North America and Western Europe but much less common in Africa and Southeast Asia. For these two regions, armed attacks were about as common as bombs. In both North America and Western Europe, assassinations were more common than armed attacks. Kidnappings were most common in the Middle East/ Persian Gulf, Africa, Eastern Europe, and South Asia. By contrast, kidnappings were very rare in North America and Western Europe. Assassinations are most common in South Asia, Africa, and Latin America. When we remove the post-2003 Iraqi cases, the ranking of

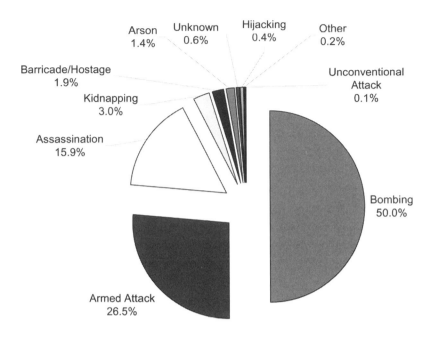

FIG. 9.—Distribution of terrorism tactics, 1970–2006 ($n = 74,262$)

tactics remains the same, but the percentages of bombings and kid-nappings drop, while the percentages of armed attacks and assassinations increase.

In figure 11, we show trends in the four major terrorist tactics over time. Bombing is the most common tactic throughout the entire period except for the years 1994–97, when it is briefly surpassed by armed attacks. Armed attacks became increasingly common over time until declining somewhat in 1998 and then dramatically increasing again in 2004, when 66 percent of the armed attacks occurred in Iraq. A look at country-level results shows that armed attacks were especially prominent in Algeria, Pakistan, and Colombia during this 4-year period, representing, respectively, 9 percent, 8 percent, and 7 percent of all armed attacks. Only 39.6 percent of the armed attacks in these countries during this period were attributed to specific groups. However, for armed attacks that were attributed to specific groups, most of those in Algeria and Pakistan were perpetrated by Islamic groups, and most of those in Colombia were perpetrated by ELN and FARC.

Kidnapping was the least common of the four tactics reviewed.

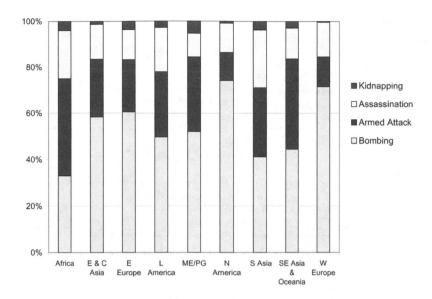

Fig. 10.—Distribution of the four most common tactics by region, 1970–2006 ($n = 74,258$).

However, rates of kidnapping increased considerably after 2001 and surpass assassinations during the last few years of the series. Assassinations increased steadily throughout the 1970s, reaching a peak in 1980 and another peak in 1992. Assassinations were the least common of the four tactics during the final year of the series. When we remove the post-2003 Iraqi cases from the analysis, the large increase in bombings and armed attacks at the end of the series increases only to levels comparable to those in the early 1990s for bombings and only to two-thirds the level of armed attacks in the late 1990s.

Figure 12 shows that explosives and firearms are the dominant weapons used by terrorists, jointly accounting for 79.5 percent of total attacks. The most common explosives used are dynamite, car bombs, grenades, and mortars. The most common firearms used are shotguns, pistols, and automatic weapons. Fire or firebombs contribute another 8 percent, and knives and sharp objects just under 5 percent. Less than 2 percent of the attacks involved remote detonated explosives, chemical, or biological agents. In short, most of the weapons used in these cases were conventional and readily available. Fortunately, sophisticated weaponry, especially chemical, biological, and nuclear weapons,

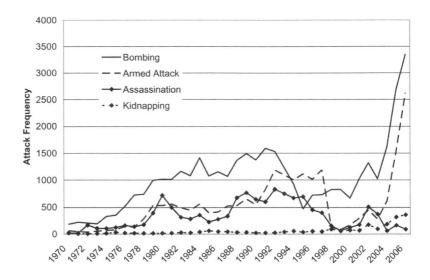

FIG. 11.—Global frequency of terrorist tactics, 1970–2006

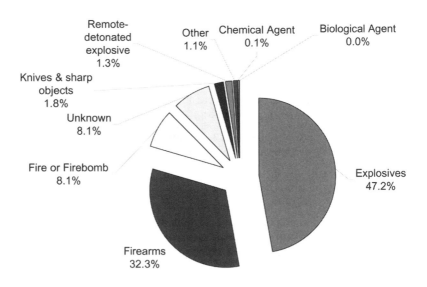

FIG. 12.—Weapons used in terrorist attacks, 1970–2006

is quite rare, accounting for less than one-tenth of 1 percent of all attacks. In 8 percent of the attacks there was not enough detail to classify weapon type. When we exclude the post-2003 Iraqi cases, the distribution remains virtually the same.

In figure 13, we examine the distribution of the five most common weapons over the nine regions of the world. According to figure 13, explosives are the modal weapon of choice for terrorists regardless of the region in which they operate. Firearms are the second most common weapon in all but three regions. Terrorists operating in Eastern and Central Asia, North America, and Western Europe are more likely to use fire or firebombs than firearms. Knives and sharp objects show up as most common for terrorists operating in Africa and Eastern and Central Asia. Finally, remote-detonated explosives are most common in Eastern Europe and Southeast Asia. When we remove the post-2003 Iraqi cases, the ordering for the Middle East remains the same, but the percentage of attacks using firearms drops by about 10 percent.

In figure 14, we examine trends in weapon use over time. Here, explosives and firearms are closely related ($r = 0.93$), with the exception of the years 1981–87, when firearms were used substantially less often than explosives. Explosives and firearms increased dramatically in the last few years of the data, in large part a consequence of the Iraqi cases. Fire and firebomb use increased slowly from the 1970s, reaching a series peak in 1995 and then falling off somewhat. Knives and sharp objects were most common in the 1990s. Remote-detonated explosives were rare until the late 1990s but in recent years increased to more than 200 attacks per year. This is likely due in large part to the advancement and proliferation of cell phone technology, as cell phones are often used as remote detonators. When we remove the post-2003 Iraqi cases from the analysis, in 2006 there are just under 1,500 attacks that use explosives, 700 attacks that use firearms, and just over 900 attacks that used a remote-detonated explosive.

VI. Conclusions and Directions for Further Research

Although criminology has had a relatively small footprint in the study of terrorism and the control of terrorism, the attention that criminologists have devoted to understanding theory and crime data suggests the potential for important contributions in the future (LaFree and Hendrickson 2007). We began this essay by considering some of the chal-

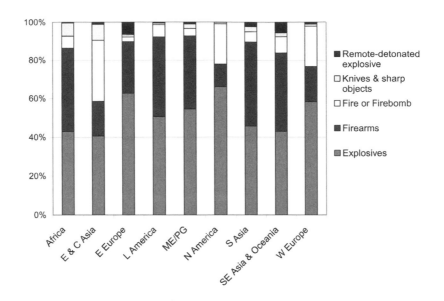

FIG. 13.—Weapon use across regions, 1970–2006

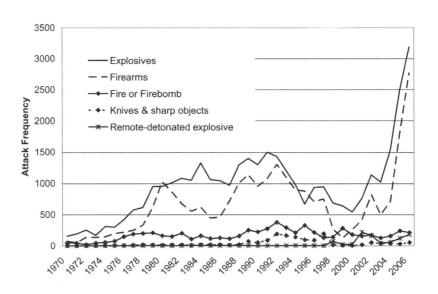

FIG. 14.—Terrorist weapon use, 1970–2006 ($n = 69,933$)

lenges in defining and measuring terrorism and considered problems with using more traditional criminological data sources to study terrorism. We then examined major criminological approaches that can be used to inform the study of terrorism. We first framed our discussion by examining rational choice perspectives and then argued for the utility of incorporating other theoretical perspectives, especially legitimacy, anomie and strain, and situational. As should be evident in our earlier discussion, rigorous empirical evaluations of any policies for countering terrorism are rare. The clear conclusion from the mixture of research findings is that counterterrorism policies based solely on retribution can do more harm than good by perpetuating ongoing violence between adversaries, ensuring continued grievances, and providing opportunities to terrorist organizations for further recruitment. Nevertheless, there may be instances where punitive policies are appropriate.

What is desperately needed in formulating policy on terrorism is more and better information about the circumstances under which different types of intervention strategies are likely to be most effective. It is tempting to hypothesize, for example, that differences between the members of the anti-abortion movement in the United States and members of the IRA in Northern Ireland can explain their differing responses to aggressive government policies. The primarily middle-class members of the anti-abortion movement are likely to have had a greater investment in avoiding severe punishment and a greater stake in conformity than the militants of Northern Ireland, most of whom were born into a struggling culture where their heroes were punished by a government perceived to be unjust. However, without more careful empirical evidence, these types of generalizations are unwarranted.

Some scholars believe that there is promise in focusing our attention on reducing the benefits of joining a terrorist movement by non-military approaches such as addressing grievances or engaging in negotiations. While there is some evidence that strategies like this might work, without systematic evaluations, strong conclusions cannot be drawn. The START Center is currently supporting several projects that will investigate the conditions under which conciliatory state responses, as opposed to more repressive responses, are most effective in responding to terrorism. Research now under way will also assess the types of organizations that are the best candidates for conciliatory policies and those that are decidedly not candidates for such interventions.

And finally, several research projects will attempt to estimate the political and strategic costs of conciliatory policies.

The scope of open-source databases on terrorist events has greatly expanded since the early 1970s. The GTD-RAND merger contributes to this development by creating the most comprehensive open-source database on terrorist events ever collected. Major strengths of this database are that it was collected by two nongovernmental organizations using a consistent coding framework throughout the merger process and that it includes both transnational and domestic attacks. However, open-source databases on terrorism generated from the print and electronic media also have important limitations. In particular, the media may report inaccuracies and falsehoods. In some cases there may be conflicting information or false, multiple, or no claims of responsibility. Government censorship and disinformation may also affect results. We noted in the presentation of the descriptive results the difficulty of accurately recording terrorism in Iraq after the 2003 invasion, but this problem may also apply to any other parts of the world that are experiencing war, insurrection, or massive civil unrest. Of all the complexities of separating terrorist violence from war-related violence, perhaps the most vexing is distinguishing between armed targets with civilian collateral damage and civilian attack with noncivilian casualties. And although the media now seemingly peer into every corner of the world, media coverage still varies across time and geographic space.

An important method for assessing the quality of event databases on terrorism is to do systematic comparisons between event data on terrorism and terrorism data drawn from other sources. Thus far, there have been very few studies of this type, owing to many of the methodological problems we discussed above in the section on defining and measuring terrorism: no universally accepted definition of terrorism, the absence of international data from official sources, and difficulties in conducting victimization or self-report surveys. Still, much more can be done. For example, it would be possible to compare GTD-RAND data to police, court, and corrections statistics on terrorism from individual countries. It would also be possible to examine media sources used in the GTD-RAND data to look for differential patterns of bias and incorrect or incomplete reporting. In addition, many primary data are collected by intelligence agents, including data from communications intercepts, surveillance, informers, defectors, interrogation of prisoners, and captured internal documents (e.g., memos, training manuals). While most of these sources are not readily accessible to researchers working in an open, unclassified environment, there are important opportunities provided by official data on terrorism that have not been adequately exploited. In particular, researchers could do more to examine court records and transcripts, government reports and hearings, and unclassified intelligence reports.

While the GTD-RAND data have obvious limitations, they also offer a wide variety of analysis opportunities. They are likely to be particularly useful for assessing the impact of specific policies or events on the future risk of terrorist activity of a particular type. Thus, we can use the database to examine the impact of specific counterterrorism policies on specific terrorist groups in specific countries over time. The data have particular promise for geospatial analysis. The data can also be merged with other databases to allow analysis of global or regional determinants of terrorist attacks or to examine the effect of global or regional terrorist attacks on other variables.

We close by offering two general areas where future research on terrorism is especially critical. First, while the operational aspects of terrorist behavior are routine subjects for intelligence and law enforcement analysts, there is quite often little empirical or theoretical grounding for their analyses. The variations in the decisions of terrorists to target or kill, by which tactic, and using what type of weapon are stark. To better understand these variations, much more research is needed that will integrate sociocultural studies of the influence of ideology on strategy and tactics with theoretical insights gained from formal decision analysis, research on social movements and collective violence, and organizational and social psychology. Such research could address the following questions:

- How do terrorists make operational planning decisions? How do time horizons, risk thresholds, perceptual biases, and other decision-making factors affect these decisions? Do these factors vary according to the structural makeup of groups, for example, small self-organizing groups versus large well-organized groups?
- How do terrorist strategies relate to criminal activities? What determines when terrorists will resort to ordinary crimes? Can some identified set of "precursor" crimes predict potential or actual terrorists?
- What accounts for the selection of tactics, such as weapon selection? When and why do groups employ or condone suicide at-

tacks? When and how do tactics change, whether through innovation or imitation?

- What influences drive the selection of particular targets for particular attacks?
- How do different terrorist groups obtain the logistical and resource support that they require to launch attacks? This could include activities ranging from the acquisition of human capital and the procurement of weapons to the movement of finances and the provision of safe havens.
- How can criminal justice processing be used to prevent, mitigate, or punish terrorist activity? What types of investigation, prosecution, and punishment are most effective against terrorism?
- What is the role of leadership in decisions to escalate targets or tactics?

Second, as this essay has shown, there is a dearth of social science research on how specific antiterrorism and counterterrorism efforts affect the behavior and activities of terrorists or potential terrorists. We need far more information on the impact of counter- and antiterrorism interventions and their expected effect on trajectories of terrorist activities. Such research could address the following questions:

- How can we measure the success of counter- and antiterrorist measures? Which metrics are most useful from both a scholarly and policy standpoint? How do we build consensus regarding the evaluation of counterterrorism measures?
- What have been the short- and long-term impacts on terrorist activity of counterterrorist initiatives taken at the local, national, and international levels? Which initiatives have fostered terrorist group deterrence and desistance and which have led to defiance and innovation by groups? Do specific initiatives have a consistent or a variable effect on different terrorist groups? To what extent do counterterrorism initiatives alienate communities?
- What factors and societal conditions have had an impact on the nature of counterterrorism approaches that governments have implemented? Do specific measures have variable impacts across countries?
- Which strategies are most effective against loosely organized networks of radicals (rather than tightly structured terrorist organizations)?

- How should captured terrorists be held: segregated in one prison or dispersed in many prisons?
- When does terrorist activity decline after loss of a leader?
- How does domestic politics within a state constrain responses to terrorism?

This effort is only the beginning. A thorough understanding of the possible policy responses to terrorism requires cooperation across disciplines. By applying only rational choice perspectives to terrorism, we can develop a limited set of policy alternatives and possible responses. By incorporating the motivations of individual actors, the organizational structure, and the situational context, we can expand our set space to better account for a broader and more realistic set of policy alternatives and possible outcomes.

TABLE A1

Countries within Regions

Region	Countries/Territories
Africa	Algeria, Angola, Benin, Botswana, Burkina Faso, Burundi, Cameroon, Central African Republic, Chad, Comoros, Congo, Djibouti, Egypt, Equatorial Guinea, Eritrea, Ethiopia, Gabon, Gambia, Ghana, Guinea, Ivory Coast, Kenya, Lesotho, Liberia, Libya, Madagascar, Malawi, Mali, Mauritania, Mauritius, Morocco, Mozambique, Namibia, Niger, Nigeria, Rwanda, Senegal, Seychelles, Sierra Leone, Somalia, South Africa, Sudan, Swaziland, Tanzania, Togo, Tunisia, Uganda, Zaire, Zambia, and Zimbabwe
East and Central Asia	China, Hong Kong, Japan, Kazakhstan, Kyrgyzstan, Macao, North Korea, South Korea, Taiwan, Tajikistan, Turkmenistan, and Uzbekistan
Eastern Europe	Albania, Armenia, Azerbaijan, Belarus, Bosnia-Herzegovina, Bulgaria, Croatia, Czech Republic, Estonia, Georgia, Hungary, Latvia, Lithuania, Macedonia, Moldova, Poland, Romania, Russia, San Marino, Serbia-Montenegro (Yugoslavia), Slovak Republic, Slovenia, and Ukraine
Latin America	Antigua and Barbuda, Argentina, Bahamas, Barbados, Belize, Bermuda, Bolivia, Brazil, Cayman Islands, Chile, Colombia, Costa Rica, Cuba, Dominica, Dominican Republic, Ecuador, El Salvador, Falkland Islands, French Guiana, Grenada, Guadeloupe, Guatemala, Guyana, Haiti, Honduras, Jamaica, Martinique, Mexico, Nicaragua, Panama, Paraguay, Peru, Puerto Rico, St. Kitts and Nevis, Suriname, Trinidad and Tobago, Uruguay, Venezuela, and the Virgin Islands (U.S.)
Middle East and Persian Gulf	Bahrain, Cyprus, Iran, Iraq, Israel, Jordan, Kuwait, Lebanon, Oman, Qatar, Saudi Arabia, Syria, Turkey, United Arab Emirates, West Bank/Gaza, and Yemen
North America	Canada and the United States
South Asia	Afghanistan, Bangladesh, Brunei, Guam, India, Nepal, New Caledonia, Pakistan, Sri Lanka, Tonga, Vanuatu, Wallis and Futuna, and Western Samoa
Southeast Asia and Oceania	Australia, Cambodia, Fiji, French Polynesia, Indonesia, Laos, Malaysia, Myanmar, New Zealand, Papua New Guinea, Philippines, Singapore, Thailand, and Vietnam
Western Europe	Andorra, Austria, Belgium, Denmark, Finland, France, Germany, Gibraltar, Greece, Iceland, Ireland, Isle of Man, Italy, Luxembourg, Malta, Netherlands, Norway, Portugal, Spain, Sweden, Switzerland, and United Kingdom

APPENDIX B

Terrorist Tactics

Armed Attack: Any assault on a person or group of people that does not principally involve a bombing or a targeted assassination.

Arson: An attack in which perpetrators intentionally set fire to a building, buildings, or pieces of property that do not belong to them.

Assassination: An attack that involves the specific, targeted killing of a high-profile or prominent figure.

Barricade/Hostage: An attack in which perpetrators take hostages and/or barricade themselves inside of an edifice.

Bombing: An attack that employs the use of a bomb or multiple bombs, including bombs detonated by remote, timer, manually, and suicide bombings.

Hijacking: Any attack that involves the forcible takeover of a vehicle, whether it includes land, sea, or air vehicles.

Kidnapping: Any abduction of a person or group of people in which ransom is not demanded.

Other: All of those attacks for which the tactic is not covered by the other categories.

Unconventional Attack: Chemical, biological, radiological, nuclear.

Unknown: Those attacks for which the tactic is unknown.

REFERENCES

Agnew, Robert. 1985. "A Revised Strain Theory of Delinquency." *Social Forces* 64:151–67.

———. 1992. "Foundation for a General Strain Theory of Crime and Delinquency." *Criminology* 30:47–87.

Agnew, Robert, and Helene R. White. 1992. "An Empirical Test of General Strain Theory." *Criminology* 30:475–500.

Anthony, Robert W. 2003. *Deterrence and the 9-11 Terrorists*. IDA Document D-2802. Alexandria, VA: Institute for Defense Analysis.

Asal, Victor, and R. Karl Rethemeyer. 2007. "Targeting and Attacking America: Ideology and Capability." Unpublished manuscript. Albany: State University of New York.

Athens, Lonnie. 1980. *Violent Criminal Acts and Actors*. London: Routledge.

Babkina, Aleksandr M. 1998. *Terrorism: An Annotated Bibliography*. Commack, NY: Nova Science.

Becker, Gary S. 1968. "Crime and Punishment: An Economic Approach." *Journal of Political Economy* 76:169–217.

Berkowitz, Leonard. 1989. "The Frustration-Aggression Hypothesis: An Examination and Reformulation." *Psychological Bulletin* 106:59–73.

Betts, Richard K. 2002. "The Soft Underbelly of American Primacy: Tactical Advantages of Terror." *Political Science Quarterly* 117:19–36.

Braithwaite, John. 2005. "Pre-empting Terrorism." *Current Issues in Criminal Justice* 17:96–114.

Brehm, Sharon S., and Jack Brehm. 1981. *Psychological Reactance: A Theory of Freedom and Control.* New York: Academic Press.

Brezina, Timothy. 1996. "Adapting to Strain: An Examination of Delinquent Coping Responses." *Criminology* 34:39–60.

Bueno de Mesquita, Ethan, and Eric S. Dickson. 2007. "The Propaganda of the Deed: Terrorism, Counterterrorism, and Mobilization." *American Journal of Political Science* 51:364–81.

Burgoon, Judee, and Vasu Varadan. 2006. "Workshop Report on Detecting and Countering IEDs and Related Threats." Grant Report no. 063142. Arlington, VA: National Science Foundation.

Butchart, Alexander, and Karin Engstrom. 2002. "Sex- and Age-Specific Relations between Economic Development, Economic Inequality and Homicide Rates in People Aged 0–24 Years: A Cross-Sectional Analysis." *Bulletin of the World Health Organization* 80(10):797–805.

Carroll, John. 1978. "A Psychological Approach to Deterrence: The Evaluation of Crime Opportunities." *Journal of Personality and Social Psychology* 36: 1512–20.

Chenoweth, Erica. 2007. "Italy and the Red Brigades: The Success of Repentance Policy in Counterterrorism." In *Countering Terrorism in the 21st Century*, edited by James Forest. Westport, CT: Praeger.

Clarke, Ronald V., and Marcus Felson, eds. 1993. *Routine Activities and Rational Choice.* New Brunswick, NJ: Transaction.

Clarke, Ronald V., and Graeme R. Newman, eds. 2005. *Designing Out Crime from Products and Systems.* Crime Prevention Studies, vol. 18. Monsey, NY: Criminal Justice Press.

———. 2006. *Outsmarting the Terrorists.* Westport, CT: Praeger Security International.

Cohen, Lawrence E., and Marcus Felson. 1979. "Social Change and Crime Rate Trends: A Routine Activity Approach." *American Sociological Review* 44: 588–608.

Cohen, Lawrence, James R. Kluegel, and Kenneth C. Land. 1981. "Social Inequality and Predatory Criminal Victimization: An Exposition and Test of a Formal Theory." *American Sociological Review* 46:505–24.

Collins, S. D. 2004. "Dissuading State Support of Terrorism: Strikes or Sanctions? An Analysis of Dissuasion Measures Employed against Libya." *Studies in Conflict and Terrorism* 27:1–18.

Cook, Philip. 1986. "The Demand and Supply of Criminal Opportunities." In *Crime and Justice: An Annual Review of Research*, vol. 7, edited by Michael Tonry and Norval Morris. Chicago: University of Chicago Press.

Cordes, Bonnie, Bruce Hoffman, Brian M. Jenkins, Konrad Kellen, Sue E. Moran, and William F. Sater. 1984. *Trends in International Terrorism, 1982 and 1983.* Santa Monica, CA: Rand.

Cornish, Derek B., and Ronald V. Clarke. 1986. *The Reasoning Criminal: Rational Choice Perspectives on Offending*. New York: Springer-Verlag.

Crenshaw, Martha. 1983. *Terrorism, Legitimacy, and Power*. Middleton, CT: Wesleyan University Press.

———. 1991. "How Terrorism Declines." *Terrorism and Political Violence* 3: 69–87.

Cronin, Audrey K. 2006. "How al-Qaida Ends." *International Security* 31:7–48.

Davies, James C. 1962. "Toward a Theory of Revolution." *American Sociological Review* 27:5–19.

Donohue, Laura K. 2001. "In the Name of National Security: U.S. Counterterrorist Measures, 1960–2000." *Terrorism and Political Violence* 13(3):15–60.

Duckitt, John, and Kirstin Fisher. 2003. "The Impact of Social Threat on Worldview and Ideological Attitudes." *Political Psychology* 24:199–222.

Dugan, Laura, Gary LaFree, Kim Cragin, and Anna Kasupski. 2008. *Building and Analyzing a Comprehensive Open-Source Data Base on Global Terrorist Events*. Final report submitted to U.S. Department of Justice, National Institute of Justice, March.

Dugan, Laura, Gary LaFree, and Alex Piquero. 2005. "Testing a Rational Choice Model of Airline Hijackings." *Criminology* 43:1031–66.

Eder, Franz, and Martin Senn, eds. 2008. *Europe and Transnational Terrorism: Assessing Threats and Countermeasures*. Baden-Baden, Germany: Nomos.

Elliott, Delbert S., David Huizinga, and Scott Menard. 1989. *Multiple Problem Youth: Delinquency, Substance Abuse, and Mental Health Problems*. New York: Springer-Verlag.

Enders, Walter, and Todd Sandler. 1993. "The Effectiveness of Antiterrorism Policies: A Vector-Autoregression-Intervention Analysis." *American Political Science Review* 87:829–44.

———. 2006. *The Political Economy of Terrorism*. Cambridge: Cambridge University Press.

Eppright, Charles T. 1997. "'Counter Terrorism' and Conventional Military Force: The Relationship between Political Effect and Utility." *Studies in Conflict and Terrorism* 20:333–44.

Erez, Edna. 1987. "Situational or Planned Crime and the Criminal Career." In *From Boy to Man, from Delinquency to Crime*, edited by M. E. Wolfgang, T. P. Thornberry, and R. M. Figlio. Chicago: University of Chicago Press.

European Commission. 2008. "Defining Terrorism." http://www.transnational terrorism.eu.

Farrington, David P., Rolf Loeber, Magda Stouthamer-Lober, Welmoet B. Van Kammen, and Laura Schmidt. 1996. "Self-Reported Delinquency and a Combined Delinquency Seriousness Scale Based on Boys, Mothers, and Teachers: Concurrent and Predictive Validity for African-Americans and Caucasians." *Criminology* 34:493–517.

Feeney, Floyd. 1986. "Robbers as Decision-Makers." In *The Reasoning Criminal: Rational Choice Perspectives on Offending*, edited by D. B. Cornish and R. V. G. Clarke. New York: Springer-Verlag.

Feierabend, Ivo K., and Rosalind L. Feierabend. 1966. "Aggressive Behaviors within Polities, 1948–1962." *Journal of Conflict Resolution* 10:249–71.

Feierabend, Ivo K., Rosalind L. Feierabend, and Ted R. Gurr. 1972. "Systemic Conditions of Political Aggression: An Application of Frustration-Aggression Theory." In their *Anger, Violence and Politics*. Englewood Cliffs, NJ: Prentice-Hall.

Felson, Marcus. 1987. "Routine Activities and Crime Prevention in the Developing Metropolis." *Criminology* 25:911–32.

Franke, Derrick, and Gary LaFree. 2008. "Does Legitimacy Matter? Support for Anti-American Violence in Three Predominantly Muslim Countries." Unpublished manuscript. College Park: University of Maryland.

Frey, Bruno S. 2004. *Dealing with Terrorism: Stick or Carrot?* Cheltenham, UK: Elgar.

Frey, Bruno S., and Simon Luechinger. 2002. "Terrorism: Deterrence May Backfire." Zurich IEER Working Paper no. 136. Zurich: Institute for Empirical Research in Economics, University of Zurich.

Geis, Gilbert. 1972. "Statistics concerning Race and Crime." In *Race, Crime and Justice*, edited by C. E. Reasons and J. L. Kuykendall. Pacific Palisades, CA: Goodyear.

Geraghty, Tony. 2000. *The Irish War*. Baltimore: Johns Hopkins University Press.

Gibbs, Jack P. 1975. *Crime, Punishment, and Deterrence*. New York: Elsevier.

Glod, Maria. 2008. "Military's Social Science Grants." *Washington Post* (August 3), p. A05.

Granovetter, Mark. 1985. "Economic Action and Social Structure: The Problem of Embeddedness." *American Journal of Sociology* 91:481–510.

Greenbaum, Robert, Laura Dugan, and Gary LaFree. 2007. "The Impact of Terrorism on Italian Employment and Business Activity." *Urban Studies* 44: 1093–1108.

Greener-Barcham, Beth K. 2002. "Before September: A History of Counterterrorism in New Zealand." *Australian Journal of Political Science* 37:509–24.

Groves, Robert M., and Daniel L. Cork. 2008. *Surveying Victims: Options for Conducting the National Crime Victimization Survey*. Washington, DC: National Academy Press.

Gurr, Ted Robert. 1968. "A Causal Model of Civil Strife." *American Political Science Review* 62:1104–24.

———. 1970. *Why Men Rebel*. Princeton, NJ: Princeton University Press.

———. 1993. "Why Minorities Rebel: A Global Analysis of Communal Mobilization and Conflict since 1945." *International Political Science Review* 14: 161–201.

Gurr, Ted R., and William H. Moore. 1997. "Ethnopolitical Rebellion: A Cross-Sectional Analysis of the 1980s with Risk Assessments for the 1990s." *American Journal of Political Science* 41:1079–1103.

Hamm, Mark S. 1997. *Apocalypse in Oklahoma: Waco and Ruby Ridge Revenged*. Boston: Northeastern University Press.

———. 2007. *Terrorism as Crime*. New York: New York University Press.

Hardy, Melissa. 1979. "Economic Growth, Distributional Inequality, and Political Conflict in Industrial Societies." *Journal of Political and Military Sociology* 5:209–27.

Harries, K. D. 1980. *Crime and the Environment*. Springfield, IL: Charles C. Thomas.

Higson-Smith, C. 2002. "A Community Psychology Perspective on Terrorism: Lessons from South Africa." In *The Psychology of Terrorism*, edited by C. Stout. Westport, CT: Praeger.

Hindelang, Michael J., Michael R. Gottfredson, and James Garofalo. 1978. *Victims of Personal Crime: An Empirical Foundation for Theory of Personal Victimization*. Cambridge, MA: Ballinger.

Hoffman, Bruce. 1998. *Recent Trends and Future Prospects of Terrorism in the United States*. Santa Monica, CA: Rand.

Hoffman, Bruce, and Donna K. Hoffman. 1998. *The Rand–St. Andrews Chronology of International Terrorist Incidents, 1995*. Santa Monica, CA: Rand. (Originally published 1995.)

Horgan, John. 2005. *The Psychology of Terrorism*. New York: Routledge.

Human Security Brief 2007. 2008. "Dying to Lose: Explaining the Decline in Global Terrorism." Human Security Report Project. Vancouver: Simon Fraser University.

Jacobs, Bruce A. 1996. "Crack Dealers and Restrictive Deterrence: Identifying Narcs." *Criminology* 34:409–31.

Jenkins, Brian M. 1975. "International Terrorism: A New Model of Conflict." In *International Terrorism and World Security*, edited by David Carlton and Carla Schaerf. London: Croom Helm.

———. 1985. "International Terrorism: The Other World War." Report no. R-3302-AF. Santa Monica, CA: Rand.

———. 2007. "The New Age of Terrorism." http://www.rand.org/pubs/reprints/2006/RAND_RP1215.pdf.

Jenkins, Brian M., and Janera Johnson. 1975. *International Terrorism: A Chronology, 1968–1974*. Santa Monica, CA: Rand.

Junger-Tas, Josine, and Ineke H. Marshall. 1997. "The Interethnic Generalizability of Social Control Theory: An Empirical Test." *Journal of Research in Crime and Delinquency* 34:79–112.

Junger-Tas, Josine, Gert-Jan Terlouw, and M. Klein, eds. 1994. *Delinquent Behavior among Young People in the Western World*. Amsterdam: Kugler

Karstedt, Susanne. 2003. "Terrorism and 'New Wars.'" In *11 September, 2001: War, Terror and Judgement*, edited by Bulent Gokay and R. B. J. Walker. London: Cass.

Kittrie, N. 1978. "A New Look at Political Crime and Terrorism." In *International Terrorism in the Contemporary World*, edited by Marius Livingston. Westport, CT: Greenwood.

Klepper, Stephen, and Daniel Nagin. 1989. "The Deterrent Effect of Perceived Certainty and Severity of Punishment Revisited." *Criminology* 27: 721–46.

Krueger, Alan B., and Jitka Maleckova. 2003. "Education, Poverty and Terrorism: Is There a Causal Connection?" *Journal of Economic Perspectives* 17: 119–44.

Kydd, A. H., and B. F. Walter. 2006. "The Strategies of Terrorism." *International Security* 31:49–80.

LaFree, Gary. 1998. *Losing Legitimacy: Street Crime and the Decline of Institutions in America*. Boulder, CO: Westview Perseus.

———. 1999. "A Summary and Review of Cross-National Comparative Studies of Homicide." In *Homicide: A Sourcebook of Social Research*, edited by M. Dwayne Smith and Margaret A. Zahn. Thousand Oaks, CA: Sage.

LaFree, Gary, and Christopher Birkbeck. 1991. "The Neglected Situation: A Cross-National Study of the Situational Characteristics of Crime." *Criminology* 29:73–98.

LaFree, Gary, and Laura Dugan. 2004. "How Does Studying Terrorism Compare to Studying Crime?" In *Terrorism and Counter-terrorism: Criminological Perspectives*, edited by Mathieu DeFlem. New York: Elsevier.

———. 2007. "Introducing the Global Terrorism Database." *Terrorism and Political Violence* 19:181–204.

———. Forthcoming. "Tracking Global Terrorism, 1970–2004." In *To Protect and to Serve: Police and Policing in an Age of Terrorism*, edited by David Weisburd, Thomas Feucht, Idit Hakimi, Lois Mock, and Simon Perry. New York: Springer.

LaFree, Gary, Laura Dugan, and Raven Korte. 2009. "Is Counter Terrorism Counterproductive? Northern Ireland 1969–1992." *Criminology* 47:501–30.

LaFree, Gary, and James Hendrickson. 2007. "Build a Criminal Justice Policy for Terrorism." *Criminology and Public Policy* 6:781–90.

LaFree, Gary, and Erin Miller. Forthcoming. "Desistance from Terrorism: What Can We Learn from Criminology?" *Dynamics of Asymmetric Conflict*.

LaFree, Gary, Sue-Ming Yang, and Martha Crenshaw. Forthcoming. "Trajectories of Terrorism: Attack Patterns of Foreign Groups That Have Targeted the United States, 1970 to 2004." *Criminology and Public Policy*.

Landes, William M. 1978. "An Economic Study of U.S. Aircraft Hijackings, 1961–1976." *Journal of Law and Economics* 21:1–31.

LeVine, Robert A., and Donald T. Campbell. 1972. *Ethnocentrism*. New York: Wiley.

Lodhi, Abdul Q., and Charles Tilly. 1973. "Urbanization, Crime and Collective Violence in Nineteenth Century France." *American Journal of Sociology* 79:296–318.

Lum, Cynthia, Leslie W. Kennedy, and Alison J. Sherley. 2006. "Are Counterterrorism Strategies Effective? The Results of the Campbell Systematic Review on Counter-terrorism Evaluation Research." *Journal of Experimental Criminology* 2:489–516.

Malvesti, Michele L. 2002. "Bombing Bin Laden: Assessing the Effectiveness of Air Strikes as a Counter-terrorism Strategy." *Fletcher Forum of World Affairs* 26:17–29.

Mastrofski, Stephen D., J. B. Snipes, and A. E. Supina. 1996. "Compliance on

Demand: The Public's Response to Specific Police Requests." *Journal of Research in Crime and Delinquency* 33:269–305.

Mayhew, Patricia, and Jan J. M. van Dijk. 1997. *Criminal Victimisation in Eleven Industrialised Countries: Key Findings from the 1996 International Crime Victims Survey.* The Hague: Ministry of Justice, WODC.

Mazerolle, Paul. 1998. "Gender, General Strain, and Delinquency: An Empirical Examination." *Justice Quarterly* 15:65–91.

McCauley, Clark. 2003. "Psychological Issues in Understanding Terrorism and the Response to Terrorism." In *The Psychology of Terrorism*, edited by C. Stout. Westport, CT: Praeger.

———. 2006. "Psychological Issues in Understanding Terrorism and the Response to Terrorism." In *Psychology of Terrorism*, edited by B. Bongar, L. M. Brown, L. E. Beutler, J. N. Breckenridge, and P. G. Zimbardo. Oxford: Oxford University Press.

Merari, Aerial. 1991. "Academic Research and Government Policy on Terrorism." *Terrorism and Political Violence* 3:88–102.

Merton, Robert. 1938. "Social Structure and Anomie." *American Sociological Review* 3:672–82.

Metelsky, Lauren. 2006. "From Violence to Protest: The Freedom of Access to Clinic Entrances Act and the Shifting Tactics of Anti-abortion Activists." Unpublished manuscript. College Park: University of Maryland.

Mickolus, E. F. 1982. *International Terrorism: Attributes of Terrorist Events, 1968–1977 (ITERATE 2).* Ann Arbor, MI: Inter-university Consortium for Political and Social Research.

———. 1991. *Terrorism, 1988–1991: A Chronology of Events and a Selectively Annotated Bibliography.* Boulder, CO: Westview.

Mickolus, E. F., and Susan L. Simmons. 1997. *Terrorism, 1992–1995: A Chronology of Events and a Selectively Annotated Bibliography.* Westport, CT: Greenwood.

MIPT (Memorial Institute for the Prevention of Terrorism). 2002. "Understanding the Terrorism Database." *MIPT Quarterly Bulletin*, first quarter.

Muller, Edward. 1985. "Income Inequality, Regime Repressiveness, and Political Violence." *American Sociological Review* 50:47–61.

Nagel, Jack. 1976. "Erratum." *World Politics* 28:315.

Nagin, Daniel S., and Raymond Paternoster. 1993. "Enduring Individual Differences and Rational Choice Theories of Crime." *Law and Society Review* 27:467–96.

Neumayer, Eric, and Thomas Plumper. 2008. "Foreign Terror on Americans." Unpublished manuscript. London: London School of Economics.

Newman, Edward. 2006. "Exploring the 'Root Causes' of Terrorism." *Studies in Conflict and Terrorism* 29:749–72.

O'Leary, Brendan. 2005. "Looking Back at the IRA." *Field Day Review* (March–April):216–46.

O'Neill, William. 2002. "Conference Report." In *Responding to Terrorism: What Role for the United Nations?* Report of a conference organized by the International Peace Academy. New York: International Peace Academy.

Pape, Robert A. 2003. "The Strategic Logic of Suicide Terrorism." *American Political Science Review* 97:343–61.

Paternoster, Raymond. 1987. "The Deterrent Effect of the Perceived Certainty and Severity of Punishment: A Review of the Evidence and Issues." *Justice Quarterly* 4:173–217.

Paternoster, Raymond, R. Brame, R. Bachman, and L. Sherman. 1997. "Do Fair Procedures Matter? The Effect of Procedural Justice on Spouse Assault." *Law and Society Review* 31:163–204.

Paternoster, Raymond, and P. Mazerolle. 1994. "General Strain Theory and Delinquency: A Replication and Extension." *Journal of Research in Crime and Delinquency* 31:235–63.

Paternoster, Raymond, and Alex Piquero. 1995. "Reconceptualizing Deterrence: An Empirical Test of Personal and Vicarious Experiences." *Journal of Research in Crime and Delinquency* 32:251–86.

Paternoster, Raymond, and S. Simpson. 1996. "Sanction Threats and Appeals to Morality: Testing a Rational Choice Model of Corporate Crime." *Law and Society Review* 30:549–84.

Pedahzur, Ami. 2005. *Suicide Terrorism*. Cambridge: Polity.

Petersilia, Joan, Peter W. Greenwood, and Monica Lavin. 1978. *Criminal Careers of Habitual Felons*. Washington, DC: U.S. Department of Justice.

Piquero, Alex R., and Raymond Paternoster. 1998. "An Application of Stafford and Warr's Reconceptualization of Deterrence to Drinking and Driving." *Journal of Research in Crime and Delinquency* 35:3–39.

Piquero, Alex R., and G. Pogarsky. 2002. "Beyond Stafford and Warr's Reconceptualization of Deterrence: Personal and Vicarious Experiences, Impulsivity, and Offending Behavior." *Journal of Research in Crime and Delinquency* 39:153–86.

Piquero, Nicole L., and M. D. Sealock. 2000. "Generalizing General Strain Theory: An Examination of an Offending Population." *Justice Quarterly* 17:449–84.

Piquero, Alex R., and Stephen G. Tibbetts. 1996. "Specifying the Direct and Indirect Effects of Low Self-Control and Situational Factors in Offenders' Decision Making: Toward a More Complete Model of Rational Offending." *Justice Quarterly* 13:481–510.

Pluchinsky, Dennis A. 2006. "The Evolution of the U.S. Government's Annual Report on Terrorism: A Personal Commentary." *Studies in Conflict and Terrorism* 29:91–98.

Pridemore, William Alex, and Joshua D. Freilich. 2007. "The Impact of State Laws Protecting Abortion Clinics and Reproductive Rights on Crimes against Abortion Providers: Deterrence, Backlash or Neither?" *Law and Human Behavior* 31:611–27.

Prunkun, Henry W. 1995. *Shadow of Death: An Analytical Bibliography on Political Violence, Terrorism, and Low-Intensity Conflict*. Lanham, MD: Scarecrow.

Ranstorp, Magnus. 2003. "Statement to the National Commission on Terrorist Attacks upon the United States, 31 March 2003." Unpublished manuscript. Stockholm: Swedish National Defence College.

Rhodes, W. M., and C. Conly. 1981. "Crime and Mobility: An Empirical Study." In *Environmental Criminology*, edited by P. J. Brantingham and P. L. Brantingham. Beverly Hills, CA: Sage.

Roberts, Adam. 2002. "Counter-terrorism, Armed Force and the Laws of War." *Survival* 44:7–32.

Roberts, Brad. 2007. *Deterrence and WMD Terrorism: Calibrating Its Potential Contributions to Risk Reduction.* IDA Paper no. P-4231. Alexandria, VA: Institute for Defense Analysis.

Rosenfeld, Richard. 2004. "Terrorism and Criminology." In *Terrorism and Counter-terrorism: Criminological Perspectives*, edited by Mathieu Deflem. Amsterdam: Elsevier.

Ross, H. Lawrence, and Gary LaFree. 1986. "Deterrence in Criminology and Social Policy." In *Behavioral and Social Science: Fifty Years of Discovery*, edited by N. J. Smelser and D. R. Gerstein. Washington, DC: National Academy Press.

Ross, J. I., and Ted R. Gurr. 1989. "Why Terrorism Subsides: A Comparative Study of Canada and the United States." *Comparative Politics* 21:405–26.

Russett, B. M. 1964. "Inequality and Instability: The Relation of Land Tenure to Politics." *World Politics* 16:442–54.

Sageman, M. 2008. *Leaderless Jihad: Terror in the Twenty-first Century.* Philadelphia: University of Pennsylvania Press.

Sampson, Robert J., and Dawn J. Bartusch. 1998. "Legal Cynicism and (Subcultural?) Tolerance of Deviance: The Neighborhood Context of Racial Differences." *Law and Society Review* 32:777–804.

Schmid, Alex P. 2004. "Statistics on Terrorism: The Challenge of Measuring Trends in Global Terrorism." *Forum on Crime and Society* 4:49–69.

Schmid, Alex P., and Albert J. Jongman. 1988. *Political Terrorism: A New Guide to Actors, Authors, Concepts, Databases, Theories and Literature.* Amsterdam: North-Holland.

Sharp, G. 1973. *The Politics of Non-violent Action.* Boston: Porter Sargent.

Sherman, Lawrence W. 1993. "Defiance, Deterrence, and Irrelevance: A Theory of the Criminal Sanction." *Journal of Research in Crime and Delinquency* 30:445–73.

Simpson, Sally, Raymond Paternoster, and Nicole L. Piquero. 1998. "Exploring the Micro-Macro Link in Corporate Crime Research." In *Research in the Sociology of Organizations: Deviance in and of Organizations*, vol. 15, edited by P. Bamberger and W. J. Sonnenstuhl. Greenwich, CT: JAI.

Siqueira, Kevin, and Todd Sandler. 2007. "Terrorist Backlash, Terrorism Mitigation, and Policy Delegation." *Journal of Public Economics* 91(9):1800–1815.

Skogan, Wesley G. 1984. "Reporting Crimes to the Police: The Status of World Research." *Journal of Research in Crime and Delinquency* 21:113–37.

Smelser, Neil J. 1962. *Theory of Collective Behavior.* New York: Free Press.

———. 2007. *The Faces of Terrorism: Social and Psychological Dimensions.* Princeton, NJ: Princeton University Press.

Smith, Brent L. 1994. *Terrorism in America: Pipe Bombs and Pipe Dreams.* Albany, NY: SUNY Press.

Smith, Brent L., Kelly R. Damphousse, Freedom Jackson, and Amy Sellers. 2002. "The Prosecution and Punishment of International Terrorists in Federal Courts: 1980–1998." *Criminology and Public Policy* 3:311–38.

Smith, Brent L., and G. P. Orvis. 1993. "America's Response to Terrorism: An Empirical Analysis of Federal Intervention Strategies during the 1980s." *Justice Quarterly* 10:661–81.

Stafford, Mark, and Michael Warr. 1993. "A Reconceptualization of General and Specific Deterrence." *Journal of Research in Crime and Delinquency* 30: 123–35.

Stamatel, Janet P. 2006. "Incorporating Socio-Historical Context into Quantitative Cross-National Criminology." *International Journal of Comparative and Applied Criminal Justice* 30:177–207.

Stille, Alexander. 1996. *Excellent Cadavers: The Mafia and the Death of the First Italian Republic.* New York: Vintage.

Sunshine, Jason, and Tom R. Tyler. 2003. "The Role of Procedural Justice and Legitimacy in Shaping Public Support for Policing." *Law and Society Review* 37:513–48.

Sutherland, Edwin H. 1947. *Principles of Criminology*, 4th ed. Chicago: Lippincott.

Tilly, Charles. 1978. *From Mobilization to Revolution.* Reading, MA: Random House.

Tilly, Charles, Louise Tilly, and Richard Tilly. 1975. *The Rebellious Century.* Cambridge, MA: Harvard University Press.

Turk, Austin T. 1982. *Political Criminality: The Defiance and Defense of Authority.* Beverly Hills, CA: Sage.

———. 1984. "Political Crime." In *Major Forms of Crime*, edited by Robert F. Meier. Beverly Hills, CA: Sage.

Tyler, Tom R. 1984. "The Role of Perceived Injustice in Defendants' Evaluations of Their Courtroom Experience." *Law and Society Review* 18:59–71.

———. 1990. *Why People Obey the Law.* New Haven, CT: Yale University Press.

———. 2003. "Process Based Regulation: Procedural Justice, Legitimacy, and the Effective Rule of Law." In *Crime and Justice: A Review of Research*, vol. 30, edited by Michael Tonry. Chicago: University of Chicago Press.

———. 2006. "Psychological Perspectives on Legitimacy and Legitimation." *Annual Review of Psychology* 57:375–400.

Tyler, Tom R., and Y. Huo. 2002. *Trust in the Law: Encouraging Public Cooperation with the Police and Courts.* New York: Sage.

Tyler, Tom R., and C. J. Wakslak. 2004. "Profiling and Police Legitimacy: Procedural Justice, Attributions of Motive and Acceptance of Police Authority." *Criminology* 18:267–74.

Useem, Bert. 1985. "Disorganization and the New Mexico Prison Riot of 1980." *American Sociological Review* 50:677–88.

U.S. Institute of Peace. 1999. "How Terrorism Ends." Special Report no. 48. Washington, DC: U.S. Institute for Peace.

U.S. State Department. 2007. "Country Reports on Terrorism 2006." http://www.terrorisminfo.mipt.org/pdf/Country-Reports-Terrorism-2006.pdf.

van Dijk, Jan J. M., John N. van Kesteren, and Paul Smit. 2008. *Criminal Victimisation in International Perspective: Key Findings from the 2004–2005 ICVS and EU ICS*. The Hague: Boom Legal.

Weber, Max. 1948. *From Max Weber: Essays in Sociology*. London: PRK.

———. 1968. *Economy and Society*, edited by G. Roth and C. Wittich. New York: Bedminster.

Weede, Erich. 1981. "Income Inequality, Average Income, and Domestic Violence." *Journal of Conflict Resolution* 25:639–53.

Weimann, Gabriel. 2006. *Terror on the Internet*. Washington, DC: U.S. Institute for Peace.

Wright, Richard T., and Scott H. Decker. 1994. *Burglars on the Job: Street Life and Residential Break-ins*. Boston: Northeastern University Press.

———. 1997. *Armed Robbers in Action: Stickups and Street Culture*. Boston: Northeastern University Press.

Young, Joe, and Laura Dugan. 2009. "Veto Players and Terror." Unpublished manuscript. Carbondale: University of Southern Illinois.

Zirakzadeh, Cyrus. 2002. "From Revolutionary Dreams to Organizational Fragmentation: Disputes over Violence within ETA and Sendero Luminoso." *Terrorism and Political Violence* 14(4):66–92.